T0201612

AUTOMATED PLANNING AND ACTING

Autonomous AI systems need complex computational techniques for planning and performing actions. Planning and acting require significant deliberation because an intelligent system must coordinate and integrate these activities in order to act effectively in the real world. This book presents a comprehensive paradigm of planning and acting using the most recent and advanced automated-planning techniques. It explains the computational deliberation capabilities that allow an actor, whether physical or virtual, to reason about its actions, choose them, organize them purposefully, and act deliberately to achieve an objective.

Useful for students, practitioners, and researchers, this book covers state-of-the-art planning techniques, acting techniques, and their integration which will allow readers to design intelligent systems that are able to act effectively in the real world.

Malik Ghallab is a Research Director at the National Center for Scientific Research, France. For most of his career he has been with LAAS-CNRS, University of Toulouse. His research activity is mainly focused on planning, acting and learning in robotics and AI. He has co-authored several books and more than two hundred scientific publications. He has been head of a French research program in Robotics, director of LAAS-CNRS and CEO for Science and Technology of INRIA. He is an ECCAI Fellow.

Dana Nau is a Professor at the University of Maryland, in the Department of Computer Science and the Institute for Systems Research. He has more than 300 refereed technical publications. Some of his best-known research contributions include the discovery of pathological game trees, the strategic planning algorithm that Bridge Baron used to win the 1997 world championship of computer bridge, applications of AI in automated manufacturing, automated planning systems such as SHOP, SHOP2, and Pyhop, and evolutionary game-theoretic studies of cultural evolution. He is an AAAI Fellow and an ACM Fellow.

Paolo Traverso is the Director of FBK ICT IRST, the Research Center at Fondazione Bruno Kessler (FBK). Paolo has worked in the advanced technology groups of companies in Chicago, London, and Milan, leading projects in safety critical systems, data and knowledge management, and service oriented applications. His research activity is mainly focused on planning and acting under uncertainty. His contributions to research in automated planning include the technique called "planning via symbolic model checking." He has published more than one hundred papers in artificial intelligence. He is an ECCAI Fellow.

AUTOMATED PLANNING AND ACTING

MALIK GHALLAB
LAAS-CNRS, University of Toulouse, France

DANA NAU
University of Maryland, U.S.A.

PAOLO TRAVERSO
FBK ICT IRST, Trento, Italy

CAMBRIDGE
UNIVERSITY PRESS

CAMBRIDGE
UNIVERSITY PRESS

One Liberty Plaza, 20th Floor, New York, NY 10006, USA

Cambridge University Press is part of the University of Cambridge.

It furthers the University's mission by disseminating knowledge in the pursuit of
education, learning, and research at the highest international levels of excellence.

www.cambridge.org
Information on this title: www.cambridge.org/9781107037274

© Malik Ghallab, Dana Nau, and Paolo Traverso 2016

First published 2016

Printed in the United States of America by Sheridan Books, Inc.

A catalog record for this publication is available from the British Library.

Library of Congress Cataloging in Publication Data
Names: Ghallab, Malik, author. | Nau, Dana S., author. | Traverso, Paolo, author.
Title: Automated planning and acting / Malik Ghallab (Le Centre national de la recherche scientifique,
France), Dana Nau (University of Maryland, U.S.A.), Paolo Traverso (ITC-IRST (Center for Scientific and
Technological Research), Italy).
Description: New York, NY : Cambridge University Press, 2016. | Includes bibliographical references and
index.
Identifiers: LCCN 2016017697| ISBN 9781107037274 (hardback ; alk. paper) | ISBN 1107037271 (hardback ;
alk. paper)
Subjects: LCSH: Production planning–Data processing.
Classification: LCC TS183.3 .G43 2016 | DDC 658.5/03–dc23
LC record available at https://lccn.loc.gov/2016017697

ISBN 978-1-107-03727-4 Hardback

To think is easy, to act is hard.
The hardest is to act in accordance with your thinking.
Elective Affinities, Johann Wolfgang von Goethe

Contents

List of Algorithms

Table of Notation

Notation	Meaning
a, A	action, set of actions
$\alpha, \mathcal{A}$	action template, set of action templates
$\text{cost}(a), \text{cost}(s, a)$	cost of a, cost of a in state s
$\text{cost}(\pi), \text{cost}(s, \pi)$	cost of π, cost of π in state s
$\text{Dom}(f), \text{Dom}(\pi)$	domain of a function or plan
$\text{eff}(a)$	effects of action a
g, S_g	goal conditions, goal states
$\gamma(s, a)$	progression, i.e., predicted result of applying a in s
$\gamma^{-1}(g, a)$	regression, i.e., conditions needed for a to produce s
$\widehat{\gamma}(s_0, \pi)$	{all states reachable from s_0 using π}, if π is a policy
$\widehat{\gamma}(s_0, \pi)$	sequence of states π produces from s_0, if π is a plan
h	heuristic function
m, M	refinement method, set of methods
$\text{head}(a)$	a's name and argument list
$\Pr(s'\|s, a)$	probability of transition to s' if a is used in s
$P, \mathcal{P}$	planning problem
π, Π	plan or policy, set of plans or policies
$\text{pre}(a)$	preconditions of action a
$\text{Range}(v)$	range of a function or variable
s, S	predicted state, set of states for the planner
ξ, Ξ	actual state, set of states for the actor
s_0, S_0	initial state, set of initial states
$\Sigma = (S, A, \gamma)$	planning domain
$\Sigma = (B, R, X, \mathcal{I}, \mathcal{A})$	state-variable representation of a planning domain:
$a.\pi, \pi.a, \pi.\pi'$	concatenation of actions and plans
$(a, b, \ldots, u)$	tuple
$\langle a, b, \ldots, u \rangle$	sequence
$s \models g, s \not\models g$	s satisfies g, s does not satisfy g

Foreword

Over ten years ago, Malik Ghallab, Dana Nau, and Paolo Traverso gave us the first – and to date only – comprehensive textbook dedicated to the field of Automated Planning, providing a much needed resource for students, researchers and practitioners. Since then, this rich field has continued to evolve rapidly. There is now a unified understanding of what once seemed disparate work on classical planning. Models and methods to deal with time, resources, continuous change, multiple agents, and uncertainty have substantially matured. Cross-fertilization with other fields such as software verification, optimization, machine learning, and robotics has become the rule rather than the exception. A phenomenal range of applications could soon be within reach – given the right future emphasis for the field.

Today, the authors are back with a new book, *Automated Planning and Acting*. As the title indicates, this is not a mere second edition of the older book. In line with the authors' analysis of where the future emphasis should lie for the field to realize its full impact, the book covers deliberative computational techniques for both planning *and acting*, that is, for deciding *which* actions to perform and also *how* to perform them. *Automated Planning and Acting* is more than a graduate textbook or a reference book. Not only do the authors outstandingly discharge their duties of educating the reader about the basics and much of the recent progress in the field, but they also propose a new framework from which the community can start to intensify research on deliberative acting and its integration with planning.

These aims are reflected in the book's content. The authors put the integration of planning and acting at the forefront by dedicating an entire chapter to a unified hierarchical model and refinement procedures that suit the needs of both planning and acting functions. Each chapter devoted to a particular class of representations also includes significant material on the integration of planning and acting using these representations. Overall, the book is more focused than its predecessor, and explores in even greater depth models and approaches motivated by the needs of planning and acting in the real world, such as handling time and uncertainty. At the same time, the authors successfully balance breadth and depth by providing an elegant, concise synthesis of a larger body of work than in their earlier text.

There is no doubt that *Automated Planning and Acting* will be the text I require my students to read when they first start, and the goto book on my shelf for my own reference. As a timely source of motivation for game-changing research on the integration of planning and acting, it will also help shape the field for the next decade.

Sylvie Thiébaux
The Australian National University

Preface

This book is about methods and techniques that a computational agent can use for deliberative planning and acting, that is, for deciding both *which* actions to perform and *how* to perform them, to achieve some objective. The study of deliberation has several scientific and engineering motivations.

Understanding deliberation is an objective for most cognitive sciences. In artificial intelligence research, this is done by modeling deliberation through computational approaches both to enable it and to allow it to be explained. Furthermore, the investigated capabilities are better understood by mapping concepts and theories into designed systems and experiments to test empirically, measure, and qualify the proposed models.

The engineering motivation for studying deliberation is to build systems that exhibit deliberation capabilities and develop technologies that address socially useful needs. A technological system needs deliberation capabilities if it must autonomously perform a set of tasks that are too diverse – or must be done in environments that are too diverse – to engineer those tasks into innate behaviors. Autonomy and diversity of tasks and environments is a critical feature in many applications, including robotics (e.g., service and personal robots; rescue and exploration robots; autonomous space stations, satellites, or vehicles), complex simulation systems (e.g., tutoring, training or entertainment), or complex infrastructure management (e.g., industrial or energy plants, transportation networks, urban facilities).

MOTIVATION AND COVERAGE

The coverage of this book derives from the view we advocated for in our previous work [231], which we now briefly summarize.

Automated planning is a rich technical field, which benefits from the work of an active and growing research community. Some areas in this field are extensively explored and correspond to a number of already mature techniques. However, there are other areas in which further investigation is critically needed if automated planning is to have a wider impact on a broader set of applications. One of the most important such areas, in our view is the *integration of planning and acting*. This book covers several different kinds of models and approaches – deterministic, hierarchical, temporal, nondeterministic and probabilistic – and for each of them, we discuss not only the techniques themselves but also how to use them in the integration of planning and acting.

The published literature on automated planning is large, and it is not feasible to cover all of it in detail in a single book. Hence our choice of what to cover was motivated by putting the integration of planning and acting at the forefront. The bulk of research on automated planning is focused on a restricted form called classical planning, an understanding of which is prerequisite introductory material, and we cover it in part of Chapter 2. But we have devoted large parts of the book to extended classes of automated planning and acting that relax the various restrictions required by classical planning.

There are several other kind of deliberation functions, such as monitoring, reasoning about one's goals, reasoning about sensing and information-gathering actions, and learning and otherwise acquiring deliberation models. Although these are not our focus, we cover them briefly in Chapter 7.

The technical material in this book is illustrated with examples inspired from concrete applications. However, most of the technical material is theoretical. Case studies and application-oriented work would certainly enrich the integration of planning and acting view developed in here. We plan to devote a forthcoming volume to automated planning and acting applications.

USING THIS BOOK

This work started as a textbook project, to update our previous textbook on automated planning [230]. Our analysis of the state of the art led us quickly to embrace the objective of covering planning and acting and their integration and, consequently, to face two obstacles:

- The first problem was how to cover a domain whose scope is not easily amenable to a sharp definition and that requires integrating conceptually heterogenous models and approaches. In contrast to our previous book, which was focused on planning, this one proved harder to converge into a reasonably united perspective.
- The second problem was how to combine a textbook approach, i.e., a coherent synthesis of the state of the art, with the development of new material. Most of this new material is presented in comprehensive detail (e.g., in Chapter 3) consistent with a textbook use. In a few parts (e.g., Section 4.5.3), this new material is in preliminary form and serves as an invitation for further research.

This book can be used as a graduate-level textbook and as an information source for scientists and professionals in the field. We assume the reader to be familiar with the basic concepts of algorithms and data structures at the level that one might get in an undergraduate-level computer science curriculum. Prior knowledge of heuristic search techniques would also be helpful, but is not strictly necessary because the appendices provide overviews of needed tools.

A complete set of lecture slides for this book and other auxiliary materials are available online.[1]

ACKNOWLEDGMENTS

We are thankful to several friends and colleagues who gave us very valuable feedback on parts of this book. Among these are Hector Geffner, Robert Goldman, Patrik Haslum, Joachim Hertzberg, Jörg Hoffmann, Felix Ingrand, Ugur Kuter, Marco Pistore, Mak Roberts, Vikas Shivashankar, Sylvie Thiébaux, and Qiang Yang.

We also wish to acknowledge the support of our respective organizations, which provided the support and facilities that helped to make this work possible: LAAS-CNRS in Toulouse, France; the University of Maryland in College Park, Maryland; and FBK, ICT-IRST in Trento, Italy. Dana Nau thanks ONR for their support of his planning work, and the students who took courses from rough drafts of this book.

Finally, we wish to acknowledge the support of our families, who remained patient during a project that consumed much more of our time and attention than we had originally anticipated.

---

[1] http://www.laas.fr/planning

CHAPTER 1

Introduction

This chapter introduces informally the concepts and technical material developed in the rest of the book. It discusses in particular the notion of *deliberation*, which is at the core of the interaction between planning and acting. Section 1.1 motivates our study of deliberation from a computational viewpoint and delineates the scope of the book. We then introduce a conceptual view of an artificial entity, called an *actor*, capable of acting deliberately on its environment, and discuss our main assumptions. Deliberation models and functions are presented next. Section 1.4 describes two application domains that will be simplified into illustrative examples of the techniques covered in rest of the book.

1.1 PURPOSE AND MOTIVATIONS

1.1.1 First Intuition

What is deliberative acting? That is the question we are studying in this book. We address it by investigating the computational reasoning principles and mechanisms supporting how to choose and perform actions.

We use the word *action* to refer to something that an agent does, such as exerting a force, a motion, a perception or a communication, in order to make a change in its environment and own state. An agent is any entity capable of interacting with its environment. An agent acting deliberately is motivated by some intended objective. It performs one or several actions that are justifiable by sound reasoning with respect to this objective.

Deliberation for acting consists of deciding which actions to undertake and how to perform them to achieve an objective. It refers to a *reasoning process*, both before and during acting, that addresses questions such as the following:

- If an agent performs an action, what will the result be?
- Which actions should an agent undertake, and how should the agent perform the chosen actions to produce a desired effect?

Such reasoning allows the agent to predict, to decide what to do and how do it, and to combine several actions that contribute jointly to the objective. The reasoning consists in using predictive models of the agent's environment and capabilities to simulate what will happen if the agent performs an action. Let us illustrate these abstract notions intuitively.

Example 1.1. Consider a bird in the following three scenes:

- To visually track a target, the bird moves its eyes, head, and body.
- To get some food that is out of reach, the bird takes a wire rod, finds a wedge to bend the wire into a hook, uses the hook to get the food.
- To reach a worm floating in a pitcher, the bird picks up a stone and drops it into the pitcher, repeats with other stones until the water has risen to a reachable level, and then picks up the worm.   □

Example 1.1 mentions actions such as moving, sensing, picking, bending and throwing. The first scene illustrates a precise coordination of motion and sensing that is called visual servoing. This set of coordinated actions is certainly purposeful: it aims at keeping the target in the field of view. But it is more *reactive* than deliberative. The other two scenes are significantly more elaborate: they demand reasoning about causal relations among interdependent actions that transform objects, and the use of these actions to achieve an objective. They illustrate our intuitive notion of acting deliberately.

The mechanisms for acting deliberately have always been of interest to philosophy.[1] They are a subject of intense research in several scientific disciplines, including biology, neuroscience, psychology, and cognitive sciences. The deliberative bird behaviors of Example 1.1 have been observed and studied from the viewpoint of how deliberative capabilities are developed, in species of corvids such as crows [597] or rooks [71, 70]. Numerous other animal species have the ability to simulate their actions and deliberate on the basis of such simulations.[2] The sophisticated human deliberation faculties are the topic of numerous research, in particular regarding their development in infants and babies, starting from the work of Piaget (as in [478, 479]) to the recent diversity of more formal psychology models (e.g., [563, 19, 461]).

We are interested here in the study of computational deliberation capabilities that allow an *artificial* agent to reason about its actions, choose them, organize them purposefully, and act deliberately to achieve an objective. We call this artificial agent an *actor*. This is to underline the acting functions on which we are focusing and to differentiate them from the broader meaning of the word "agent." We consider *physical actors* such as robots, as well as *abstract actors* that act in simulated or virtual environments, for example, through graphic animation or electronic Web transactions. For both kinds of actors, sensory-motor functions designate in a broad sense the low-level functions that implement the execution of actions.

---

[1] In particular, the branch of philosophy called *action theory*, which explores questions such as, "What is left over if I subtract the fact that my arm goes up from the fact that I raise my arm?" [610].

[2] In the interesting classification of Dennett [150], these species are called *Popperian*, in reference to the epistemologist Karl Popper.

1.1.2 Motivations

We address the issue of how an actor acts deliberately by following the approaches and methods of *artificial intelligence* (AI). Our purpose proceeds from the usual motivations of AI research, namely:

- To understand, through effective formal models, the cognitive capabilities that correspond to acting deliberately.
- To build actors that exhibit these capabilities.
- To develop technologies that address socially useful needs.

Understanding deliberation is an objective for most cognitive sciences. The specifics of AI are to model deliberation through computational approaches that allow us to explain as well as to generate the modeled capabilities. Furthermore, the investigated capabilities are better understood by mapping concepts and theories into designed systems and experiments to test empirically, measure, and qualify the proposed models. The technological motivation for endowing an artificial actor with deliberation capabilities stems from two factors:

- *autonomy* – that is, the actor performs its intended functions without being directly operated by a person and
- *diversity* in the tasks it can perform and the environments in which it can operate.

Without autonomy, a directly operated or teleoperated device does not usually need to deliberate. It simply extends the acting and sensing capabilities of a human operator who is in charge of understanding and decision making, possibly with the support of advice and planning tools, for example, as in surgical robotics and other applications of teleoperation.

An autonomous system may not need deliberation if it operates only in the fully specified environment for which it has been designed. Manufacturing robots autonomously perform tasks such as painting, welding, assembling, or servicing a warehouse without much deliberation. Similarly, a vending machine or a driverless train operates autonomously without a need for deliberation. For these and similar examples of automation, deliberation is performed by the designer. The system and its environment are engineered so that the only variations that can occur are those accounted for at the design stage in the system's predefined *functioning envelope*. Diversity in the environment is not expected. A state outside of the functioning envelope puts the system into a failure mode in which a person takes deliberate actions.

Similarly, a device designed for a unique specialized task may perform it autonomously without much deliberation, as long the variations in its environment are within its designed range. For example, a vacuum-cleaning or lawn-mowing robot does not deliberate yet can cope autonomously with its specialized tasks in a reasonable range of lawns or floors. But it may cease to function properly when it encounters a slippery floor, a steep slope, or any condition outside of the range for which it was designed.

When a designer can account, within some functioning envelope, for all the environments and tasks a system will face and when a person can be in charge of deliberating outside of this envelope, by means of teleoperation or reprogramming, then deliberation generally is not needed in the system itself. Such a system will be endowed with a library of *reactive* behaviors (e.g., as the bird's visual target tracking in Example 1.1) that cover efficiently its functioning envelope. However, when an autonomous actor has to face a diversity of tasks, environments and interactions, then achieving its purpose will require some degree of deliberation. This is the case in many robotics applications, such as service and personal robots, rescue and exploration robots, autonomous space stations and satellites, or even driverless cars. This holds also for complex simulation systems used in entertainment (e.g., video games) or educational applications (serious games). It is equally applicable to many control systems that manage complex infrastructures such as industrial or energy plants, transportation networks, and urban facilities (smart cities).

Autonomy, diversity in tasks and environments, and the need for deliberation are not binary properties that are either true or false. Rather, the higher the need for autonomy and diversity, the higher the need for deliberation. This relationship is not restricted to artificial systems. Numerous natural species (plants and some invertebrates such as sponges or worms) have been able to evolve to fit into stable ecological niches, apparently without much deliberation. Species that had to face rapid changes in their environment and to adapt to a wide range of living conditions had to develop more deliberation capabilities.

1.1.3 Focus and Scope

We address deliberation from an AI viewpoint. Our focus is on the *reasoning functions* required for acting deliberately. This focus involves two restrictions:

- We are not interested in actions that consists solely of internal computations, such as adding "2 + 3" or deducing that "Socrates is mortal." These computations are not actions that change the state of the world.[3] They can be used as part of the actor's deliberation, but we take them as granted and outside of our scope.
- We are not concerned with techniques for designing the sensing, actuation, and sensory-motor control needed for the low-level execution of actions. Sensory-motor control (e.g., the visual servoing of Example 1.1) can be essential for acting, but its study is not within our scope. We assume that actions are performed with a set of primitives, which we will call *commands*, that implement sensory-motor control. The actor performs its actions by executing commands. To deliberate, it relies on models of how these commands work.

The scope of this book is not limited to the most studied deliberation function, which is *planning* what actions to perform. Planning consists in choosing and organizing the actions that can achieve a given objective. In many situations, there is not much need for planning: the actions to perform are known. But there is a need for significant deliberation in deciding *how* to perform each action, given the context and changes in the environment. We develop the view that planning can be needed for deliberation but is seldom sufficient. We argue that acting goes beyond the execution of low-level commands.

---

[3] The borderline between computational operations and actions that change the external world is not as sharp for an abstract actor as for a physical one.

Example 1.2. Dana finishes breakfast in a hotel restaurant, and starts going back to his room. On the way, he notices that the elevator is not on his floor and decides to walk up the stairs. After a few steps he becomes aware that he doesn't have his room key, which he left on the breakfast table. He goes back to pick it up.   □

In this example, the actor does not need to plan the simple task of going to his room. He *continually* deliberates while acting: he makes opportunistic choices, simulates in advance and monitors his actions, stops when needed and decides on alternate actions.

Deliberation consists of reasoning with predictive models as well as *acquiring* these models. An actor may have to *learn* how to adapt to new situations and tasks, as much as to use the models it knows about for its decision making. Further, even if a problem can be addressed with the actor's generic models, it can be more efficient to transform the explicit computations with these models into low-level sensory-motor functions. Hence, it is natural to consider learning to act as a deliberation function. Section 7.3 offers a brief survey on learning and model acquisition for planning and acting. However, our focus is on deliberation techniques using predefined models.

1.2 CONCEPTUAL VIEW OF AN ACTOR

1.2.1 A Simple Architecture

An actor interacts with the external environment and with other actors. In a simplified architecture, depicted in Figure 1.1(a), the actor has two main components: a set of *deliberation functions* and an *execution platform*.

The actor's sensory-motor functions are part of its execution platform. They transform the actor's commands into actuations that execute its actions (e.g., the movement of a limb or a virtual character). The execution platform also transforms sensed signals into features of the world (e.g., to recognize a physical or virtual object, or to query information from the Web). The capabilities of the platform are explicitly described as models of the available commands.

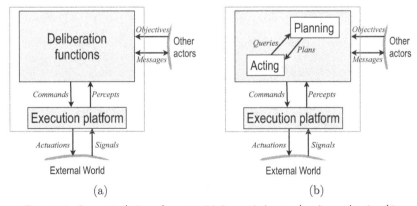

Figure 1.1. Conceptual view of an actor (a); its restriction to planning and acting (b).

Deliberation functions implement the reasoning needed to choose, organize, and perform actions that achieve the actor's objectives, to react adequately to changes in the environment, and to interact with other actors, including human operators. To choose and execute commands that ultimately achieve its objectives, the actor needs to perform a number of deliberation functions. For example, the actor must commit to intermediate goals, plan for those goals, refine each planned action into commands, react to events, monitor its activities to compare the predicted and observed changes, and decide whether recovery actions are needed. These deliberation functions are depicted in Figure 1.1(b) as two main components: planning and acting. The acting component is in charge of refining actions into commands, reacting to events, and monitoring.

1.2.2 Hierarchical and Continual Online Deliberation

The view presented in Section 1.2.1 can be a convenient first approach for describing an actor, but one must keep in mind that it is an oversimplification.

Example 1.3. To respond to a user's request, a robot has to bring an object o7 to a location room2 (see Figure 1.2). To do that, it plans a sequence of abstract actions such as "navigate to," "fetch," and "deliver." One of these refines into "move to door," "open door," "get out," and "close door." Once the robot is at the door, it refines the "open door" action appropriately for how it perceives that particular door.

The robot's deliberation can be accomplished by a collection of hierarchically organized components. In such a hierarchy, a component receives tasks from the component

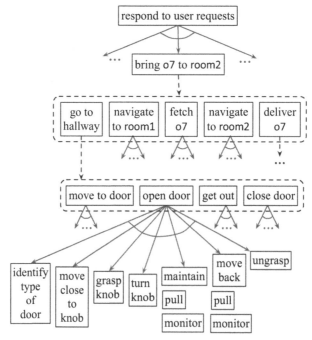

Figure 1.2. Multiple levels of abstraction in deliberative acting. Each solid arrow indicates a refinement of an abstract action into more concrete ones. Each dashed arrow maps a task into a plan of actions.

above it, and decides what activities need to be performed to carry out those tasks. Performing a task may involve refining it into lower-level steps, issuing subtasks to other components below it in the hierarchy, issuing commands to be executed by the platform, and reporting to the component that issued the task. In general, tasks in different parts of the hierarchy may involve concurrent use of different types of models and specialized reasoning functions. □

This example illustrates two important principles of deliberation: hierarchical organization and continual online processing.

- *Hierarchically organized deliberation.* Some of the actions the actor wishes to perform do not map directly into a command executable by its platform. An action may need further refinement and planning. This is done online and may require different representations, tools, and techniques from the ones that generated the task. A hierarchized deliberation process is not intended solely to reduce the search complexity of offline plan synthesis. It is needed mainly to address the heterogeneous nature of the actions about which the actor is deliberating, and the corresponding heterogeneous representations and models that such deliberations require.
- *Continual online deliberation.* Only in exceptional circumstances will the actor do all of its deliberation offline before executing any of its planned actions. Instead, the actor generally deliberates at runtime about how to carry out the tasks it is currently performing. The deliberation remains partial until the actor reaches its objective, including through flexible modification of its plans and retrials. The actor's predictive models are often limited. Its capability to acquire and maintain a broad knowledge about the current state of its environment is very restricted. The cost of minor mistakes and retrials are often lower than the cost of extensive modeling, information gathering, and thorough deliberation. Throughout the acting process, the actor refines and monitors its actions; reacts to events; and extends, updates, and repairs its plan on the basis of its perception focused on the relevant part of the environment.

Different parts of the actor's hierarchy often use different representations of the state of the actor and its environment. These representations may correspond to different amounts of detail in the description of the state and different mathematical constructs. In Figure 1.2, a graph of discrete locations may be used at the upper levels, while the lower levels may use vectors of continuous configuration variables for the robot limbs.

Finally, because complex deliberations can be compiled down by learning into low-level commands, the frontier between deliberation functions and the execution platform is not rigid; it evolves with the actor's experience.

1.2.3 Assumptions

We are not seeking knowledge representation and reasoning approaches that are effective across every kind of deliberation problem and at every level of a hierarchically organized actor. Neither are we interested in highly specialized actors tailored for a single niche, because deliberation is about facing diversity. Instead, we are proposing a few generic approaches that can be adapted to different classes of environments and, for a given actor, to different levels of its deliberation. These approaches rely on restrictive assumptions that are needed from a computational viewpoint, and that are acceptable for the class of environments and tasks in which we are interested.

Deliberation assumptions are usually about how variable, dynamic, observable, and predictable the environment is, and what the actor knows and perceives about it while acting. We can classify them into assumptions related to the dynamics of the environment, its observability, the uncertainty managed in models, and how time and concurrency are handled.

- *Dynamics* of the environment. An actor may assume to be in a static world except for its own actions, or it may take into account exogenous events and changes that are expected and/or observed. In both cases the dynamics of the world may be described using discrete, continuous or hybrid models. Of these, hybrid models are the most general. Acting necessarily involves discontinuities in the interaction with the environment,[4] and these are best modeled discretely. But a purely discrete model abstracts away continuous processes that may also need to be modeled.
- *Observability* of the environment. It is seldom the case that all the information needed for deliberation is permanently known to the actor. Some facts or parameters may be always known, others may be observable if specific sensing actions are performed, and others will remain hidden. The actor may have to act on the basis of reasonable assumptions or beliefs regarding the latter.
- *Uncertainty* in knowledge and predictions. No actor is omniscient. It may or may not be able to extend its knowledge with specific actions. It may or may not be able to reason about the uncertainty regarding the current state of the world and the predicted future (e.g., with nondeterministic or probabilistic models). Abstracting away uncertainty during a high-level deliberation can be legitimate if the actor can handle it at a lower level and correct its course of action when needed.
- *Time and concurrency.* Every action consumes time. But deliberation may or may not need to model it explicitly and reason about its flow for the purpose of meeting deadlines, synchronizing, or handling concurrent activities.

Different chapters of the book make different assumptions about time, concurrency, and uncertainty. Except for Section 7.4 on hybrid models, we'll restrict ourself to discrete approaches. This is consistent with the focus and scope discussed in Section 1.1.3, because it is primarily in sensory-motor functions and commands that continuous models are systematically needed.

1.3 DELIBERATION MODELS AND FUNCTIONS

1.3.1 Descriptive and Operational Models of Actions

An actor needs predictive models of its actions to decide *what* actions to do and *how* to do them. These two types of knowledge are expressed with, respectively, descriptive and operational models.

---

[4] Think of the phases in a walking or grasping action.

- *Descriptive models* of actions specify the actor's "know what." They describe which state or set of possible states may result from performing an action or command. They are used by the actor to reason about what actions may achieve its objectives.
- *Operational models* of actions specify the actor's "know how." They describe how to perform an action, that is, what commands to execute in the current context, and how organize them to achieve the action's intended effects. The actor relies on operational models to perform the actions that it has decided to perform.

In general, descriptive models are more abstract than operational models. Descriptive models abstract away the details, and focus on the main effects of an action; they are useful at higher levels of a deliberation hierarchy. This abstraction is needed because often it is too difficult to develop very detailed predictive models, and because detailed models require information that is unknown at planning time. Furthermore, reasoning with detailed models is computationally very complex. For example, if you plan to take a book from a bookshelf, at planning time you will not be concerned with the available space on the side or on the top of the book to insert your fingers and extract the book from the shelf. The descriptive model of the action will abstract away these details. It will focus on where the book is, whether it is within your reach, and whether you have a free hand to pick it up.

The simplifications allowed in a descriptive model are not possible in an operational model. To actually pick up the book, you will have to determine precisely where the book is located in the shelf, which positions of your hand and fingers are feasible, and which sequences of precise motions and manipulations will allow you to perform the action.

Furthermore, operational models may need to include ways to respond to *exogenous* events, that is, events that occur because of external factors beyond the actor's control. For example, someone might be standing in front of the bookshelf, the stool that you intended to use to reach the book on a high shelf might be missing, or any of a potentially huge number of other possibilities might interfere with your plan.

In principle, descriptive models can take into account the uncertainty caused by exogenous events, for example, through nondeterministic or probabilistic models (see Chapters 5 and 6), but the need to handle exogenous events is much more compelling for operational models. Indeed, exogenous events are often ignored in descriptive models because it is impractical to try to model all of the possible joint effects of actions and exogenous events, or to plan in advance for all of the contingencies. But operational models must have ways to respond to such events if they happen because they can interfere with the execution of an action. In the library example, you might need to ask someone to move out of the way, or you might have to stand on a chair instead of the missing stool.

Finally, an actor needs descriptive models of the available commands in order to use them effectively, but in general it does not need their operational models. Indeed, commands are the lower-level sensory-motor primitives embedded in the execution platform; their operational models correspond to what is implemented in these primitives. Taking this remark to the extreme, if one assumes that every known action corresponds to an executable command, then all operational models are embedded in the execution platform and can be ignored at the deliberation level. This assumption seldom holds.

1.3.2 Description of States for Deliberation

To specify both descriptive and operational models of actions, we will use representational primitives that define the state of an actor and its environment; these are called *state variables*. A state variable associates a value, which changes over time, to a relevant attribute of the world. The definition of a state with state variables needs to include enough details for the actor's deliberations, but it does not need to be, nor can it be, exhaustive.

In a hierarchically organized actor, different deliberative activities may need different amounts of detail in the state description. For example, in actions such as "grasp knob" and "turn knob" at the bottom of Figure 1.2, to choose the commands for grasping the handle and operating it, the actor needs to reason about detailed parameters such as the robot's configuration coordinates and the position and shape of the door handle. Higher up, where the actor refines "bring o7 to room2" into actions such as "go to hallway" and "navigate to room1," such details are not needed. It is more convenient there to reason about the values of more abstract variables, such as location(robot) = room1 or position(door) = closed. To establish correspondences between these abstract variables and the detailed ones, the actor could have definitions saying, for example, that location(robot) = room1 corresponds to a particular area in an Euclidean reference frame.

The precise organization of a hierarchy of data structures and state representations is a well-known area in computer science (e.g., [522]). It may take different forms in application domains such as robotics, virtual reality, or geographic information systems. Here, we'll keep this point as simple as possible and assume that at each part of an actor's deliberation hierarchy, the state representation includes not only the variables used in that part of the hierarchy (e.g., the robot's configuration coordinates at the bottom of Figure 1.2), but also the variables used higher up in the hierarchy (e.g., location(robot)).

An important issue is the distinction and correspondence between *predicted* states and *observed* states. When an actor reasons about what might happen and simulates changes of state to assess how desirable a course of action is, it uses predicted states. When it reasons about how to perform actions in some context, it relies on observed states; it may contrast its observations with its expectations. Predicted states are in general less detailed than the observed one; they are obtained as a result of one or several predictions starting from an abstraction of the current observed state. To keep the distinction clear, we'll use different notations:

- $s \in S$ is a predicted state;
- $\xi \in \Xi$ is an observed state.

Because of partial and inaccurate observations, there can be uncertainty about the *present observed* state as well as about the *future predicted* states. Furthermore, information in a dynamic environment is ephemeral. Some of the values in ξ may be out-of-date: they may refer to things that the actor previously observed but that it cannot currently observe. Thus, ξ is the state of the actor's knowledge, rather than the true state of the world. In general, the actor should be endowed with appropriate means to manage the uncertainty and temporality of the data in ξ.

Observability is an additional issue. As underlined in Section 1.2.3, some information relevant to the actor's behavior can be momentarily or permanently hidden; it has to be indirectly inferred. In the general case, the design of an actor should include the following distinctions among state variables:

- A variable is *invisible* if it is not observable but can only be estimated from observations and a priori information.
- A variable is *observable* if its value can be obtained by performing appropriate actions. At various points, it may be either *visible* if its value is known to the actor, or *hidden* if the actor must perform an observation action to get its value.

For simplicity, we'll start out by assuming that the values of all state variables are precisely known at every moment while acting. Later in the book, we'll consider more realistically that some state variables are observable but can only be observed by performing some specific actions. In Chapter 5, we deal with a specific case of partial observability: in Section 5.8.4, we transform a partially observable domain into an abstracted domain whose states are sets of states. We also examine (in Chapter 6) the case in which some state variables are permanently or momentarily observable but others remain hidden. The class of models known as partially observable models, in which every state variable is assumed to be always known or always hidden, is discussed in Section 6.8.3.

1.3.3 Planning Versus Acting

The simple architecture of Figure 1.1(b) introduces planning and acting as respectively finding what actions to perform and how to refine chosen actions into commands. Here, we further discuss these two functions, how they differ, and how they can be associated in the actor's deliberation.

The purpose of *planning* is to synthesize an organized set of actions to carry out some activity. For instance, this can be done by a lookahead procedure that combines prediction steps (Figure 1.3: when in state s, action a is predicted to produce state s') within a search through alternative sets of actions for a set that leads to a desired goal state.

Planning problems vary in the kinds of actions to be planned for, the kinds of predictive models that are needed, and the kinds of plans that are considered satisfactory.

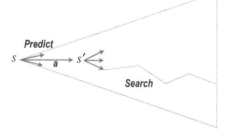

Figure 1.3. Planning as a combination of prediction steps and a search mechanism.

For some kinds of problems, *domain-specific* planning methods have been developed that are tailor-made for that kind of problem. For instance, motion planning synthesizes a geometric and kinematic trajectory for moving a mobile system (e.g., a truck, a robot, or a virtual character); perception planning synthesizes an organized set of sensing and interpretation actions to recognize an object or to build a three-dimensional model of a scene; infrastructure planning synthesizes plans to deploy and organize facilities, such as a public transportation infrastructure, to optimize their usage or to meet the needs of a community. Many other such examples can be given, such as flight navigation planning, satellite configuration planning, logistics planning, or industrial process planning.

There are, however, commonalities to many forms of planning. *Domain-independent* planning tries to grasp these commonalities at an abstract level, in which actions are generic state transformation operators over a widely applicable representation of states as relations among objects.

Domain-independent and domain-specific planning complement each other. In a hierarchically organized actor, planning takes place at multiple levels of the hierarchy. At high levels, abstract descriptions of a problem can be tackled using domain-independent planning techniques. The example shown in Figure 1.2 may require a path planner (for moving to locations), a manipulation planner (for grasping the door handle), and a domain-independent planner at the higher levels of the hierarchy.

Acting involves deciding how to perform the chosen actions (with or without the help of a planner) while reacting to the context in which the activity takes place. Each action is considered as an abstract task to be refined, given the current context, progressively into more concrete actions or commands. Whereas planning is a search over predicted states, acting requires a *continual assessment of the current state* ξ, to contrast it with a predicted state s and adapt accordingly. Consequently, acting also includes *reacting* to unexpected changes and exogenous events, which are independent from the actor's activity.

The techniques used in planning and acting can be compared as follows. Planning can be organized as an open-loop search, whereas acting needs to be a closed-loop process. Planning relies on descriptive models (know-what); acting uses mostly operational models (know-how). Domain-independent planners can be developed to take advantage of commonalities among different forms of planning problems, but this is less true for acting systems, which require more domain-specific programming.

The relationship between planning and acting is more complex than a simple linear sequence of "plan then act." Seeking a complete plan before starting to act is not always feasible, and not always needed. It is feasible when the environment is predictable and well modeled, for example, as for a manufacturing production line. It is needed when acting has a high cost or risk, and when actions are not reversible. Often in such applications, the designer has to engineer out the environment to reduce diversity as much as possible beyond what is modeled and can be predicted.

In dynamic environments where exogenous events can take place and are difficult to model and predict beforehand, plans should be expected to fail if carried out blindly until the end. Their first steps are usually more reliable than the rest and steer toward the objectives. Plan modification and replanning are normal and should be embedded

Figure 1.4. Receding horizon scheme for planning and acting.

in the design of an actor. Metaphorically, planning is useful to shed light on the road ahead, not to lay an iron rail all the way to the goal.

The interplay between acting and planning can be organized in many ways, depending on how easy it is to plan and how quickly the environment changes. A general paradigm is the *receding horizon* scheme, which is illustrated in Figure 1.4. It consists of repeating the two following steps until the actor has accomplished its goal:

  (i) Plan from the current state toward the goal, but not necessarily all the way to the goal.
 (ii) Act by refining one or a few actions of the synthesized plan into commands to be executed.

A receding horizon approach can be implemented in many ways. Options include various planning horizon, number of actions to perform at each planning stage, and what triggers replanning. Furthermore, the planning and acting procedures can be run either sequentially or in parallel with synchronization.

Suppose an actor does a depth-first refinement of the hierarchy in Figure 1.2. Depending on the actor's planning horizon, it may execute each command as soon as one is planned or wait until the planning proceeds a bit farther. Recall from Section 1.3.2 that the observed state ξ may differ from the predicted one. Furthermore, ξ may evolve even when no commands are being executed. Such situations may invalidate what is being planned, necessitating replanning.

The interplay between acting and planning is relevant even if the planner synthesizes alternative courses of action for different contingencies (see Chapters 5 and 6). Indeed, it may not be worthwhile to plan for all possible contingencies, or the planner may not know in advance what all of them are.

1.3.4 Other Deliberation Functions

We have mentioned deliberation functions other than planning and acting: perceiving, monitoring, goal reasoning, communicating, and learning. These functions (surveyed in Chapter 7) are briefly described here.

Perceiving goes beyond sensing, even with elaborate signal processing and pattern matching methods. Deliberation is needed in bottom-up processes for getting meaningful data from sensors, and in top-down activities such as focus-of-attention mechanisms, reasoning with sensor models, and planning how to do sensing and information gathering. Some of the issues include how to maintain a mapping between sensed data and deliberation symbols, where and how to use the platform sensors, or how to recognize actions and plans of other actors.

Monitoring consists of comparing observations of the environment with what the actor's deliberation has predicted. It can be used to detect and interpret discrepancies, perform diagnosis, and trigger initial recovery actions when needed. Monitoring may require planning what observation actions to perform, and what kinds of diagnosis tests to perform. There is a strong relationship between planning techniques and diagnosis techniques.

Goal reasoning is monitoring of the actor's objectives or mission, to keep the actor's commitments and goals in perspective. It includes assessing their relevance, given the observed evolutions, new opportunities, constraints or failures, using this assessment to decide whether some commitments should be abandoned, and if so, when and how to update the current goals.

Communicating and *interacting* with other actors open numerous deliberation issues such as communication planning, task sharing and delegation, mixed initiative planning, and adversarial interaction.

Learning may allow an actor to acquire, adapt, and improve through experience the models needed for deliberation and to acquire new commands to extend and improve the actor's execution platform. Conversely, techniques such as active learning may themselves require acting for the purpose of better learning.

1.4 ILLUSTRATIVE EXAMPLES

To illustrate particular representations and algorithms, we'll introduce a variety of examples inspired by two application domains: robotics and operations management. We'll use highly simplified views of these applications to include only the features that are relevant for the issue we're trying to illustrate. In this section, we provide summaries of the real-world context in which our simple examples might occur.

1.4.1 A Factotum Service Robot

We will use the word *factotum* to mean a general-purpose service robot that consists of a mobile platform equipped with several sensors (lasers, cameras, etc.) and actuators (wheels, arms, forklift) [329]. This robot operates in structured environments such as a mall, an office building, a warehouse or a harbor. It accomplishes transportation and logistics tasks autonomously, (e.g., fetching objects, putting them into boxes, assembling boxes into containers, move them around, delivering them or piling them up in storage areas).

This robot platform can execute parameterized commands, such as localize itself in the map, move along a path, detect and avoid obstacles, identify and locate items, and grasp, ungrasp and push items. It knows about a few actions using these commands, for example, map the environment (extend or update the map), goto a destination, open a door, search for or fetch an item.

These actions and commands are specified with descriptive and operational models. For example, move works if it is given waypoints in free space or an obstacle-free path that meet kinematics and localization constraints; the latter are, for example, visual landmarks required by action localize. These conditions need to be checked and monitored by the robot while performing the actions. Concurrency has to be managed. For example, goto should run in parallel with detect, avoid, and localize.

Factotum needs domain-specific planners, for example, a motion planner for move, a manipulation planner for grasp (possibly using locate, push, and move actions). Corresponding plans are more than a sequence or a partially ordered set of commands; they require closed-loop control and monitoring.

At the mission-preparation stage (the upper levels in Figure 1.2), it is legitimate to view a logistics task as an organized set of abstract subtasks for collecting, preparing, conveying, and delivering the goods. Each subtask may be further decomposed into a sequence of still abstract actions such as goto, take, and put. Domain-independent task planning techniques are needed here.

However, deliberation does not end with the mission preparation stage. A goto action can be performed in many ways depending on the environment properties: it may or may not require a planned path; it may use different localization, path following, motion control, detection, and avoidance methods (see the "goto" node in Figure 1.2). A goto after a take is possibly different from the one before because of the held object. To perform a goto action in different contexts, the robot relies on a collection of *skills* defined formally by *methods*. A method specifies a way to refine an action into commands. The same goto may start with a method (e.g., follow GPS waypoints) but may be pursued with more adapted methods when required by the environment (indoor without GPS signal) or the context. Such a change between methods may be a normal progression of the goto action or a retrial due to complications. The robot also has methods for take, put, open, close, and any other actions it may need to perform. These methods endow the robot with operational models (its know-how) and knowledge about how to choose the most adapted method with the right parameters.

The methods for performing actions may use complex control constructs with concurrent processes (loops, conditionals, semaphores, multithread and real-time locks). They can be developed from formal specifications in some representation and/or with plan synthesis techniques. Different representations may be useful to cover the methods needed by the factotum robot. Machine learning techniques can be used for improving the methods, acquiring their models, and adapting the factotum to a new trade.

In addition to acting with the right methods, the robot has to monitor its activity at every level, including possibly at the goal level. Prediction of what is needed to correctly perform and monitor foreseen activities should be made beforehand. Making the right predictions from the combined models of actions and models of the environment is a difficult problem that involves heterogeneous representations.

Finally, the robot requires extended *perception* capabilities: reasoning on what is observable and what is not, integrating knowledge-gathering actions to environment changing actions, acting to maintain sufficient knowledge for the task at hand with a consistent interpretation of self and the world.

1.4.2 A Complex Operations Manager

A *Harbor Operations Manager (HOM)* is a system that supervises and controls all the tasks performed in a harbor.[5] Examples of such tasks include unloading cars from ships, parking them in storage areas, moving them to a repair area, performing the repair,

---

[5] Example inspired from a facility developed for the port of Bremen, Germany [76, 100].

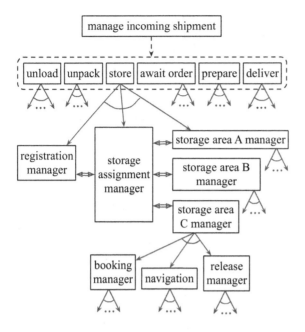

Figure 1.5. Deliberation components for a Harbor Operation Manager.

preparing the delivery of cars according to orders, and loading them onto trucks when the trucks arrive at the harbor. Some of these operations are performed by human workers, others automatically by machines such as the factotum robot of previous section. This complex environment has several features that require deliberation:

- It is *customizable*: for example, delivery procedures can be customized according to the car brand, model, or retailer-specific requirements.
- It is *variable*: procedures for unloading/loading cars depend on the car brands; storage areas have different parking procedures, for example.
- It is *dynamic*: ships, cars, trucks, and orders arrive dynamically.
- It is partially *predictable* and *controllable*: cars may be damaged and need repair, storage areas may not be available, orders have unpredictable requirements, ships and trucks have random delays, for example.

At a high level, an HOM has to carry out a simple sequence of abstract tasks: ⟨unload, unpack, store, wait-for-order, treatment, delivery⟩ (see Figure 1.5). This invariant plan is easily specified by hand. The deliberation problem in an HOM is not in the synthesis of this plan but in the dynamic refinement of its tasks in more concrete subtasks. For example, an HOM refines the abstract task store of Figure 1.5 into subtasks for registering a car to be stored, moving it, and other tasks, down to executable commands.

Moreover, the tasks to be refined and controlled are carried out by different *components*, for example, ships, gates, and storage or repair areas. Each ship has its own procedure to unload cars to a gate. A gate has its own procedure to accept cars that are unloaded to the deck. A natural design option is therefore to model the HOM in a distributed way, as a set of interacting deliberation components. The interactions between ships and gates, gates and trucks, and trucks and storage areas must be controlled with respect to the global constraints and objectives of the system. To do that, HOM must deal with uncertainty and nondeterminism due to exogenous events, and to the fact that each component may – from the point of view of the management facility – behave non-deterministically. For instance, in the task to synchronize a ship with a gate to unload cars, the ship may send a request for unloading cars to the unloading manager, and the gate may reply either that the request meets its requirements and the unloading operation can proceed according to some unloading specifications, or that the request cannot be handled. The management facility may not know a priori what the request, the unloading specifications, and reply will be.

In summary, HOM relies on a collection of interacting components, each implementing its own procedures. It refines the abstract tasks of the high-level plan into a composition of these procedures to address each new object arrival and adapt to each exogenous event. The refinement and adaptation mechanisms can be designed through an approach in which the HOM is an actor organized into a hierarchy of components, each abstract action is a task to be further refined and planned for, and where online planning and acting are performed continually to adapt and repair plans. The approach embeds one or several planners within these components, which are called at run-time, when the system has to refine an abstract action to adapt to a new context. It relies on refinement mechanisms that can be triggered at run-time whenever an abstract action in a procedure needs to be refined or an adaptation needs to be taken into account.

1.5 OUTLINE OF THE BOOK

This chapter has provided a rather abstract and broad introduction. Chapter 2 offers more concrete material regarding deliberation with deterministic models and full knowledge about a static environment. It covers the "classical planning" algorithms and heuristics, with state-space search, forward and backward, and plan-space search. It also presents how these planning techniques can be integrated online with acting.

Chapter 3 is focused on refinement methods for acting and planning. It explores how a unified representation can be used for both functions, at different levels of the deliberation hierarchy, and in different ways. It also discusses how the integration of planning and acting can be performed.

Chapter 4 is about deliberation with explicit time models using a representation with timelines and chronicles. A temporal planner, based on refinement methods, is presented together with the constraint management techniques needed for handling temporal data. Using the techniques from Chapter 3, we also discuss the integration of planning and acting with temporal models.

Uncertainty in deliberation is addressed in Chapters 5 and 6. The main planning techniques in nondeterministic search spaces are covered in Chapter 5, together with model checking and determinization approaches. In this chapter, we present online lookahead methods for the interleaving of planning and acting. We also show how nondeterministic models can be used with refinements techniques that intermix plans, actions, and goals. We discuss the integration of planning and acting with input/output automata to cover cases such as the distributed deliberation in the HOM example.

We cover probabilistic models in Chapter 6. We develop heuristic search techniques for stochastic shortest path problems. We present online approaches for planning and acting, discuss refinement methods for acting with probabilistic models, and analyze the specifics of descriptive models of actions in the probabilistic case together with several practical issues for modeling probabilistic domains.

Chapters 2 through 6 are devoted to planning and acting. Chapter 7 briefly surveys the other deliberation functions introduced in Section 1.3.4, – perceiving, monitoring, goal reasoning, interacting, and learning. It also discusses hybrid models and ontologies for planning and acting.

CHAPTER 2 Deliberation with Deterministic Models

Having considered the components of an actor and their relation to the actor's environment, we now need to develop some representational and algorithmic tools for performing the actor's deliberation functions. In this chapter, we develop a simple kind of descriptive model for use in planning, describe some planning algorithms that can use this kind of model, and discuss some ways for actors to use those algorithms.

This chapter is organized as follows. Section 2.1 develops state-variable representations of planning domains. Sections 2.2 and 2.3 describe forward-search planning algorithms, and heuristics to guide them. Sections 2.4 and 2.5 describe backward-search and plan-space planning algorithms. Section 2.6 describes some ways for an actor to use online planning. Sections 2.7 and 2.8 contain the discussion and historical remarks, and the student exercises.

2.1 STATE-VARIABLE REPRESENTATION

The descriptive models used by planning systems are often called *planning domains*. However, it is important to keep in mind that a planning domain is not an a priori definition of the actor and its environment. Rather, it is necessarily an imperfect approximation that must incorporate trade-offs among several competing criteria: accuracy, computational performance, and understandability to users.

2.1.1 State-Transition Systems

In this chapter, we use a simple planning-domain formalism that is similar to a finite-state automaton:

Definition 2.1. A *state-transition system* (also called a *classical planning domain*) is a triple $\Sigma = (S, A, \gamma)$ or 4-tuple $\Sigma = (S, A, \gamma, \text{cost})$, where

- S is a finite set of *states* in which the system may be.
- A is a finite set of *actions* that the actor may perform.

- $\gamma : S \times A \to S$ is a partial function called the *prediction function* or *state transition function*. If (s, a) is in γ's domain (i.e., $\gamma(s, a)$ is defined), then a is *applicable* in s, with $\gamma(s, a)$ being the *predicted* outcome. Otherwise a is *inapplicable* in s.
- $\text{cost} : S \times A \to [0, \infty)$ is a partial function having the same domain as γ. Although we call it the *cost function*, its meaning is arbitrary: it may represent monetary cost, time, or something else that one might want to minimize. If the cost function isn't given explicitly (i.e., if $\Sigma = (S, A, \gamma)$), then $\text{cost}(s, a) = 1$ whenever $\gamma(s, a)$ is defined. □

To avoid several of the difficulties mentioned in Chapter 1, Definition 2.1 requires a set of restrictive assumptions called the *classical planning* assumptions:

1. *Finite, static environment.* In addition to requiring the sets of states and actions to be finite, Definition 2.1 assumes that changes occur only in response to actions: if the actor does not act, then the current state remains unchanged. This excludes the possibility of actions by other actors, or exogenous events that are not due to any actor.
2. *No explicit time, no concurrency.* There is no explicit model of time (e.g., when to start performing an action, how long a state or action should last, or how to perform other actions concurrently). There is just a discrete sequence of states and actions $\langle s_0, a_1, s_1, a_2, s_2, \ldots \rangle$.[1]
3. *Determinism, no uncertainty.* Definition 2.1 assumes that we can predict with certainty what state will be produced if an action a is performed in a state s. This excludes the possibility of accidents or execution errors, as well as nondeterministic actions, such as rolling a pair of dice.

In environments that do not satisfy the preceding assumptions, classical domain models may introduce errors into the actor's deliberations but this does not necessarily mean that one should forgo classical models in favor of other kinds of models. The errors introduced by a classical model may be acceptable if they are infrequent and do not have severe consequences, and models that don't require the above assumptions may be much more complex to build and to reason with.

Let us consider the computational aspects of using a state-transition system. If S and A are small enough, it may be feasible to create a lookup table that contains $\gamma(s, a)$ and $\text{cost}(s, a)$ for every s and a, so that the outcome of each action can be retrieved directly from the table. For example, we could do this to represent an actor's possible locations and movements in the road network shown in Figure 2.1.

In cases in which Σ is too large to specify every instance of $\gamma(s, a)$ explicitly, the usual approach is to develop a *generative* representation in which there are procedures for computing $\gamma(s, a)$ given s and a. The specification of Σ may include an explicit description of one (or a few) of the states in S; other states can be computed using γ.

The following is an example of a *domain-specific* representation, that is, one designed specifically for a given planning domain. We then develop a *domain-independent* approach for representing any classical planning domain.

---

[1] This does not prohibit one from encoding some kinds of time-related information (e.g., timestamps) into the actions' preconditions and effects. However, to represent and reason about actions that have temporal durations, a more sophisticated planning-domain formalism is usually needed, such as that discussed in Chapter 4.

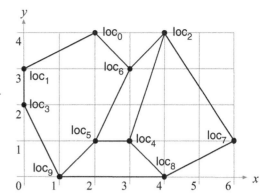

Figure 2.1. A two-dimensional network of locations connected by roads.

Example 2.2. Consider the task of using machine tools to modify the shape of a metal workpiece. Each state might include a geometric model of the workpiece (see Figure 2.2), and information about its location and orientation, the status and capabilities of each machine tool, and so forth. A descriptive model for a drilling operation might include the following:

- The operation's name and parameters (e.g., the dimensions, orientation, and machining tolerances of the hole to be drilled).
- The operation's *preconditions*, that is, conditions that are necessary for it to be used. For example, the desired hole should be perpendicular to the drilling surface, the workpiece should be mounted on the drilling machine, the drilling machine should have a drill bit of the proper size, and the drilling machine and drill bit need to be capable of satisfying the machining tolerances.
- The operation's *effects*, that is, what it will do. These might include a geometric model of the modified workpiece (see Figure 2.2(b)) and estimates of how much time the action will take and how much it will cost. □

The advantage of domain-specific representations is that one can choose whatever data structures and algorithms seem best for a given planning domain. The disadvantage is that a new representation must be developed for each new planning domain. As an alternative, we now develop a domain-independent way to represent classical planning domains.

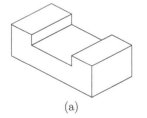

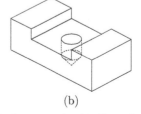

(a)   (b)

Figure 2.2. Geometric model of a workpiece, (a) before and (b) after computing the effects of a drilling action.

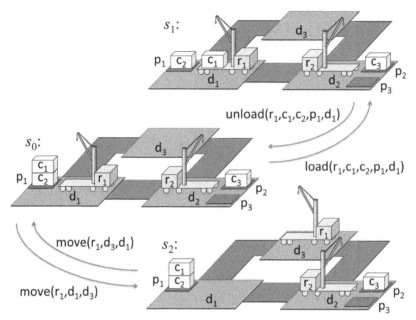

Figure 2.3. A few of the states and transitions in a simple state-transition system. Each robot can hold at most one container, and at most one robot can be at each loading dock.

2.1.2 Objects and State Variables

In a state-transition system, usually each state $s \in S$ is a description of the properties of various objects in the planner's environment. We will say that a property is *rigid* if it remains the same in every state in S, and it is *varying* if it may differ from one state to another. To represent the objects and their properties, we will use three sets B, R, and X, which we will require to be finite:

- B is a set of names for all of the objects, plus any mathematical constants that may be needed to represent properties of those objects. We will usually divide B into various subsets (robots, locations, mathematical constants, and so forth).
- To represent Σ's rigid properties, we will use a set R of *rigid relations*. Each $r \in R$ will be an n-ary (for some n) relation over B.
- To represent Σ's varying properties, we will use a set X of syntactic terms called *state variables*, such that the value of each $x \in X$ depends solely on the state s.

Which objects and properties are in B, R, and X depends on what parts of the environment the planner needs to reason about. For example, in Figure 1.2, the orientation of the robot's gripper may be essential for deliberating about a low-level task such as "open door," but irrelevant for a high-level task such as "bring o7 to room2." In a hierarchically organized actor, these tasks may be described using two state spaces, S and S' whose states describe different kinds of objects and properties.

Here are examples of B and R. We will say more about X shortly.

Example 2.3. Figure 2.3 depicts some states in a simple state-transition system. B includes two robots, three loading docks, three containers, three piles (stacks of containers), the Boolean constants T and F, and the constant nil:

$$B = Robots \cup Docks \cup Containers \cup Piles \cup Booleans \cup \{nil\};$$

$$Booleans = \{T, F\};$$

$$Robots = \{r_1, r_2\};$$

$$Docks = \{d_1, d_2, d_3\};$$

$$Containers = \{c_1, c_2, c_3\};$$

$$Piles = \{p_1, p_2, p_3\}.$$

We will define two rigid properties: each pair of loading docks is *adjacent* if there is a road between them, and each pile is *at* exactly one loading dock. To represent these properties, $R = \{adjacent, at\}$, where

$$adjacent = \{(d_1, d_2), (d_2, d_1), (d_2, d_3), (d_3, d_2), (d_3, d_1), (d_1, d_3)\};$$

$$at = \{(p_1, d_1), (p_2, d_2), (p_3, d_2)\}.$$

In the subsequent examples that build on this one, we will not need to reason about objects such as the roads and the robots' wheels, or properties such as the colors of the objects. Hence, B and R do not include them.   □

Definition 2.4. A *state variable* over B is a syntactic term

$$x = sv(b_1, \ldots, b_k), \tag{2.1}$$

where sv is a symbol called the state variable's *name*, and each b_i is a member of B. Each state variable x has a *range*,[2] $\mathrm{Range}(x) \subseteq B$, which is the set of all possible values for x.   □

Example 2.5. Continuing Example 2.3, let

$$X = \{cargo(r), loc(r), occupied(d), pile(c), pos(c), top(p)$$

$$\mid r \in Robots, d \in Docks, c \in Containers, p \in Piles\},$$

where the state variables have the following interpretations:

- Each robot r can carry at most one container at a time. We let $cargo(r) = c$ if r is carrying container c, and $cargo(r) = nil$ otherwise. Hence $\mathrm{Range}(cargo(r)) = Containers \cup \{nil\}$.
- $loc(r)$ is robot r's current location, which is one of the loading docks. Hence $\mathrm{Range}(loc(r)) = Docks$.
- Each loading dock d can be occupied by at most one robot at a time. To indicate whether d is occupied, $\mathrm{Range}(occupied(d)) = Booleans$.
- $pos(c)$ is container c's position, which can be a robot, another container, or nil if c is at the bottom of a pile. Hence $\mathrm{Range}(pos(c)) = Containers \cup Robots \cup \{nil\}$.
- If container c is in a pile p then $pile(c) = p$, and if c is not in any pile then $pile(c) = nil$. Hence $\mathrm{Range}(pile(c)) = Piles \cup \{nil\}$.

---

[2] We use *range* rather than *domain* to avoid confusion with *planning domain*.

- Each pile p is a (possibly empty) stack of containers. If the stack is empty then $\text{top}(p) = \text{nil}$, and otherwise $\text{top}(p)$ is the container at the top of the stack. Hence $\text{Range}(\text{top}(p)) = \textit{Containers} \cup \{\text{nil}\}$.   □

A *variable-assignment* function over X is a function s that maps each $x_i \in X$ into a value $z_i \in \text{Range}(x_i)$. If $X = \{x_1, \ldots, x_n\}$, then because a function is a set of ordered pairs, we have

$$s = \{(x_1, z_1), \ldots, (x_n, z_n)\}, \tag{2.2}$$

which we often will write as a set of assertions:

$$s = \{x_1 = z_1, \ x_2 = z_2, \ \ldots, \ x_n = z_n\}. \tag{2.3}$$

Because X and B are finite, so is the number of variable-assignment functions.

Definition 2.6. A *state-variable state space* is a set S of variable-assignment functions over some set of state variables X. Each variable-assignment function in S is called a *state* in S.   □

If the purpose of S is to represent some environment E, then we will want each state in s to have a sensible interpretation in E. Without getting into the formal details, an *interpretation* is a function $\mathcal{I}$ that maps B, R, and X to sets of objects, rigid properties, and variable properties in some environment E, in such a way that each $s \in S$ corresponds to a situation (roughly, a combination of the objects and properties in the image of $\mathcal{I}$) that can occur in E.[3] If a variable-assignment function does not correspond to such a situation, then should not be a state in S.[4]

Example 2.7. Continuing Example 2.5, let us define the state-variable state space S depicted in Figure 2.3. The state s_0 is the following variable-assignment function:

$$
\begin{aligned}
s_0 = \{ &\text{cargo}(r_1) = \text{nil}, \quad \text{cargo}(r_2) = \text{nil}, \\
&\text{loc}(r_1) = d_1, \quad \text{loc}(r_2) = d_2, \\
&\text{occupied}(d_1) = \text{T}, \ \text{occupied}(d_2) = \text{T}, \ \text{occupied}(d_3) = \text{F}, \\
&\text{pile}(c_1) = p_1, \quad \text{pile}(c_2) = p_1, \quad \text{pile}(c_3) = p_2, \\
&\text{pos}(c_1) = c_2, \quad \text{pos}(c_2) = \text{nil}, \quad \text{pos}(c_3) = \text{nil}, \\
&\text{top}(p_1) = c_1, \quad \text{top}(p_2) = c_3, \quad \text{top}(p_3) = \text{nil}\}.
\end{aligned}
\tag{2.4}
$$

In the same figure, the state s_1 is identical to s_0 except that $\text{cargo}(r_1) = c_1, \text{pile}(c_1) = \text{nil}$, $\text{pos}(c_1) = r_1$, and $\text{top}(p_1) = c_2$.

---

[3] The details are quite similar to the definition of an interpretation in first-order logic [535, 517]. However, in first-order logic, E is a static domain rather than a dynamic environment, hence the interpretation maps a single state into a single situation.

[4] This is ideally how an interpretation should work, but in practice it is not always feasible to define an interpretation that satisfies those requirements completely. As we said in Section 2.1, a planning domain is an imperfect approximation of the actor and its environment, not an a priori definition.

In Example 2.5, the sizes of the state variables' ranges are

$|\text{Range}(\text{cargo}(r_1))| = |\text{Range}(\text{cargo}(r_2))| = 4,$

$|\text{Range}(\text{loc}(r_1))| = |\text{Range}(\text{loc}(r_2))| = 3,$

$|\text{Range}(\text{occupied}(d_1))| = |\text{Range}(\text{occupied}(d_2))| = |\text{Range}(\text{occupied}(d_3))| = 2,$

$|\text{Range}(\text{pile}(c_1))| = |\text{Range}(\text{pile}(c_2))| = |\text{Range}(\text{pile}(c_3))| = 4,$

$|\text{Range}(\text{pos}(c_1))| = |\text{Range}(\text{pos}(c_2))| = |\text{Range}(\text{pos}(c_3))| = 6,$

$|\text{Range}(\text{top}(p_1))| = |\text{Range}(\text{top}(p_2))| = |\text{Range}(\text{top}(p_3))| = 4.$

Thus the number of possible variable-assignment functions is

$$4^2 \times 3^2 \times 2^3 \times 4^3 \times 6^3 \times 4^3 = 1{,}019{,}215{,}872.$$

However, fewer than 750 of these functions are states in S. A state-variable assignment function is a state in S iff it has an interpretation in the environment depicted in Figure 2.3.

One way to specify the members of S is to give a set of *consistency constraints* (i.e., restrictions on what combinations of variable assignments are possible) and to say that a state-variable assignment function is a state in S iff it satisfies all of the constraints. Here are some examples of consistency constraints for S. A state s cannot have both $\text{loc}(r_1) = d_1$ and $\text{loc}(r_2) = d_1$, because a loading dock can only accommodate one robot at a time; s cannot have both $\text{pos}(c_1) = c_3$ and $\text{pos}(c_2) = c_3$, because two containers cannot have the same physical location; and s cannot have both $\text{pos}(c_1) = c_2$ and $\text{pos}(c_2) = c_1$, because two containers cannot be on top of each other. Exercise 2.2 is the task of finding a complete set of consistency constraints for S.   □

The preceding example introduced the idea of using consistency constraints to determine which variable-assignment functions are states but said nothing about how to represent and enforce such constraints. Throughout most of this book, we avoid the need to represent such constraints explicitly, by writing action models in such a way that if s is a state and a is an action that is applicable in s, then $\gamma(s, a)$ is also a state. However, in Chapter 4, we will use a domain representation in which some of the constraints are represented explicitly and the planner must make sure never to use an action that would violate them.

2.1.3 Actions and Action Templates

To develop a way to write action models, we start by introducing some terminology borrowed loosely from first-order logic with equality:

Definition 2.8. A *positive literal*, or *atom* (short for *atomic formula*), is an expression having either of the following forms:

$$rel(z_1, \ldots, z_n) \qquad \text{or} \qquad sv(z_1, \ldots, z_n) = z_0,$$

where *rel* is the name of a rigid relation, *sv* is a state-variable name, and each z_i is either a variable (an ordinary mathematical variable, not a state variable) or the name of an object. A *negative literal* is an expression having either of the following forms:

$$\neg rel(z_1, \ldots, z_n) \qquad \text{or} \qquad sv(z_1, \ldots, z_n) \neq z_0.$$

A literal is *ground* if it contains no variables, and *unground* otherwise. □

In the atom $sv(z_1, \ldots, z_n) = z_0$, we will call $sv(z_1, \ldots, z_n)$ the atom's *target*. Thus in Equation 2.3, a state is a set of ground atoms such that every state variable $x \in X$ is the target of exactly one atom.

Definition 2.9. Let l be an unground literal, and Z be any subset of the variables in l. An *instance* of l is any expression l' produced by replacing each $z \in Z$ with a term z' that is either an element of $\text{Range}(z)$ or a variable with $\text{Range}(z') \subseteq \text{Range}(z)$. □

Definition 2.9 generalizes straightforwardly to any syntactic expression that contains literals. We will say that such an expression is *ground* if it contains no variables and it is *unground* otherwise. If it is unground, then an *instance* of it can be created as described in Definition 2.9.

Definition 2.10. Let R and X be sets of rigid relations and state variables over a set of objects B, and S be a state-variable state space over X. An *action template*[5] for S is a tuple $\alpha = (\text{head}(\alpha), \text{pre}(\alpha), \text{eff}(\alpha), \text{cost}(\alpha))$ or $\alpha = (\text{head}(\alpha), \text{pre}(\alpha), \text{eff}(\alpha))$, the elements of which are as follows:

- head(α) is a syntactic expression[6] of the form

$$act(z_1, z_2, \ldots, z_k),$$

  where *act* is a symbol called the *action name*, and $z_1, z_2, \ldots, z_k$ are variables called *parameters*. The parameters must include all of the variables (here we mean ordinary variables, not state variables) that appear anywhere in pre(α) and eff(α). Each parameter z_i has a range of possible values, $\text{Range}(z_i) \subseteq B$.
- pre$(\alpha) = \{p_1, \ldots, p_m\}$ is a set of *preconditions*, each of which is a literal.
- eff$(\alpha) = \{e_1, \ldots, e_n\}$ is a set of *effects*, each of which is an expression of the form

$$sv(t_1, \ldots, t_j) \leftarrow t_0, \tag{2.5}$$

  where $sv(t_1, \ldots, t_j)$ is the effect's *target*, and t_0 is the value to be assigned. No target can appear in eff(α) more than once.
- cost(α) is a number $c > 0$ denoting the cost of applying the action.[7] If it is omitted, then the default is cost$(\alpha) = 1$.

---

[5] In the artificial intelligence planning literature, these are often called *planning operators* or *action schemas*; see Section 2.7.1.

[6] The purpose of head(α) is to provide a convenient and unambiguous way to refer to actions. An upcoming example is load$(r_1, c_1, c_2, p_1, d_1)$ at the end of Example 2.12.

[7] This can be generalized to make cost(α) a numeric formula that involves α's parameters. In this case, most forward-search algorithms and many domain-specific heuristic functions will still work, but most domain-independent heuristic functions will not, nor will backward-search and plan-space search algorithms (Sections 2.4 and 2.5).

We usually will write action templates in the following format (e.g., see Example 2.12). The "cost" line may be omitted if $c = 1$.

$$act(z_1, z_2, \ldots, z_k)$$
$$\text{pre: } p_1, \ldots, p_m$$
$$\text{eff: } e_1, \ldots, e_n$$
$$\text{cost: } c \qquad \qquad \square$$

Definition 2.11. A *state-variable action* is a ground instance a of an action template α that satisfies the following requirements: all rigid-relation literals in pre(a) must be true in R, and no target can appear more than once in eff(a). If a is an action and a state s satisfies pre(a), then a is *applicable* in s, and the predicted outcome of applying it is the state

$$\gamma(s, a) = \{(x, w) \mid \text{eff}(a) \text{ contains the effect } x \leftarrow w\}$$
$$\cup \{(x, w) \in s \mid x \text{ is not the target of any effect in eff}(a)\}. \quad (2.6)$$

If a isn't applicable in s, then $\gamma(s, a)$ is undefined. $\qquad \qquad \square$

Thus if a is applicable in s, then

$$(\gamma(s, a))(x) = \begin{cases} w, & \text{if eff}(a) \text{ contains an effect } x \leftarrow w, \\ s(x), & \text{otherwise.} \end{cases} \quad (2.7)$$

Example 2.12. Continuing Example 2.5, suppose each robot r has an execution platform that can perform the following commands:

- if r is at a loading dock and is not already carrying anything, r can load a container from the top of a pile;
- if r is at a loading dock and is carrying a container, r can unload the container onto the top of a pile; and
- r can move from one loading dock to another if the other dock is unoccupied and there is a road between the two docks.

To model these commands, let $\mathcal{A}$ comprise the following action templates:

$load(r, c, c', p, d)$
   pre: $at(p, d), cargo(r) = nil, loc(r) = d, pos(c) = c', top(p) = c$
   eff: $cargo(r) = c, pile(c) \leftarrow nil, pos(c) \leftarrow r, top(p) \leftarrow c'$
$unload(r, c, c', p, d)$
   pre: $at(p, d), pos(c) = r, loc(r) = d, top(p) = c'$
   eff: $cargo(r) \leftarrow nil, pile(c) \leftarrow p, pos(c) \leftarrow c', top(p) \leftarrow c$
$move(r, d, d')$
   pre: $adjacent(d, d'), loc(r) = d, occupied(d') = F$
   eff: $loc(r) \leftarrow d', occupied(d) \leftarrow F, occupied(d') \leftarrow T$

In the action templates, the parameters have the following ranges:

$$\text{Range}(c) = \textit{Containers}; \quad \text{Range}(c') = \textit{Containers} \cup \textit{Robots} \cup \{\text{nil}\};$$
$$\text{Range}(d) = \textit{Docks}; \quad \text{Range}(d') = \textit{Docks};$$
$$\text{Range}(p) = \textit{Piles}; \quad \text{Range}(r) = \textit{Robots}.$$

Let a_1 be the state-variable action $\text{load}(r_1, c_1, c_2, p_1, d_1)$. Then

$$\text{pre}(a_1) = \{\text{at}(p_1, d_1), \text{cargo}(r_1) = \text{nil}, \text{loc}(r_1) = d_1, \text{pos}(c_1) = c_2, \text{top}(p_1) = c_1\}.$$

Let s_0 and s_1 be in Example 2.5 and Figure 2.3. Then a_1 is applicable in s_0, and $\gamma(s_0, a_1) = s_1$. □

2.1.4 Plans and Planning Problems

Definition 2.13. Let B, R, X, and S be as in Section 2.1.2. Let $\mathcal{A}$ be a set of action templates such that for every $\alpha \in \mathcal{A}$, every parameter's range is a subset of B, and let $A = \{\text{all state-variable actions that are instances of members of } \mathcal{A}\}$. Finally, let γ be as in Equation 2.6. Then $\Sigma = (S, A, \gamma, \text{cost})$ is a *state-variable planning domain*. □

Example 2.14. If B, R, X, S, $\mathcal{A}$ and γ are as in Examples 2.3, 2.5, 2.7, and 2.12, then $(S, \mathcal{A}, \gamma)$ is a state-variable planning domain. □

Just after Definition 2.6, we discussed the notion of an interpretation of a state space S. We now extend this to include planning domains. An *interpretation* $\mathcal{I}$ of a state-variable planning domain Σ in an environment E is an interpretation of S in E that satisfies the following additional requirement: under $\mathcal{I}$, each $a \in A$ corresponds to an activity in E such that whenever a is applicable in a state $s \in S$, performing that activity in a situation corresponding to s will produce a situation corresponding to $\gamma(s, a)$.[8]

Definition 2.15. A *plan* is a finite sequence of actions

$$\pi = \langle a_1, a_2, \ldots, a_n \rangle.$$

The plan's *length* is $|\pi| = n$, and its *cost* is the sum of the action costs: $\text{cost}(\pi) = \sum_{i=1}^{n} \text{cost}(a_i)$.

As a special case, $\langle \rangle$ is the *empty plan*, which contains no actions. Its length and cost are both 0. □

---

[8] Ideally one would like to put a similar requirement on the interpretation of the action's cost, but we said earlier that its interpretation is arbitrary.

Definition 2.16. Let $\pi = \langle a_1, \ldots, a_n \rangle$ and $\pi' = \langle a'_1, \ldots, a'_{n'} \rangle$ be plans and a be an action. We define the following *concatenations*:

$$\pi.a = \langle a_1, \ldots, a_n, a \rangle;$$
$$a.\pi = \langle a, a_1, \ldots, a_n \rangle;$$
$$\pi.\pi' = \langle a_1, \ldots, a_n, a'_1, \ldots, a'_{n'} \rangle;$$
$$\pi.\langle \rangle = \langle \rangle.\pi = \pi. \qquad \square$$

Definition 2.17. A plan $\pi = \langle a_1, a_2, \ldots, a_n \rangle$ is *applicable* in a state s_0 if there are states $s_1, \ldots, s_n$ such that $\gamma(s_{i-1}, a_i) = s_i$ for $i = 1, \ldots, n$. In this case, we define

$$\gamma(s_0, \pi) = s_n;$$
$$\widehat{\gamma}(s_0, \pi) = \langle s_0, \ldots, s_n \rangle.$$

As a special case, the empty plan $\langle \rangle$ is applicable in every state s, with $\gamma(s, \langle \rangle) = s$ and $\widehat{\gamma}(s, \langle \rangle) = \langle s \rangle$. $\qquad \square$

In the preceding, $\widehat{\gamma}$ is called the *closure* of γ. In addition to the predicted final state, it includes all of the predicted intermediate states.

Definition 2.18. A *state-variable planning problem* is a triple $P = (\Sigma, s_0, g)$, where Σ is a state-variable planning domain, s_0 is a state called the *initial state*, and g is a set of ground literals called the *goal*. A *solution* for P is any plan $\pi = \langle a_1, \ldots, a_n \rangle$ such that the state $\gamma(s_0, \pi)$ satisfies g.

Alternatively, one may write $P = (\Sigma, s_0, S_g)$, where S_g is a set of *goal states*. In this case, a solution for P is any plan π such that $\gamma(s_0, \pi) \in S_g$. $\qquad \square$

For a planning problem P, a solution π is *minimal* if no subsequence of π is also a solution for P, *shortest* if there is no solution π' such that $|\pi'| < |\pi|$, and *cost-optimal* (or just *optimal*, if it is clear from context) if

$$\text{cost}(\pi) = \min\{\text{cost}(\pi') \mid \pi' \text{ is a solution for } P\}.$$

Example 2.19. Let $P = (\Sigma, s_0, g)$, where Σ is the planning domain in Example 2.12 and Figure 2.3, s_0 is as in Equation 2.4, and $g = \{\text{loc}(r_1) = d_3\}$. Let

$$\pi_1 = \langle \text{move}(r_1, d_1, d_3) \rangle;$$
$$\pi_2 = \langle \text{move}(r_2, d_2, d_3), \text{move}(r_1, d_1, d_2), \text{move}(r_2, d_3, d_1), \text{move}(r_1, d_2, d_3) \rangle;$$
$$\pi_3 = \langle \text{load}(r_1, c_1, c_2, p_1, d_1), \text{unload}(r_1, c_1, c_2, p_1, d_1), \text{move}(r_1, d_1, d_3) \rangle.$$

Then π_1 is a minimal, shortest, and cost-optimal solution for P; π_2 is a minimal solution but is neither shortest nor cost-optimal; and π_3 is a solution but is neither minimal nor shortest nor cost-optimal. $\qquad \square$

Algorithm 2.1 Forward-search planning schema.

Forward-search (Σ, s_0, g)
    $s \leftarrow s_0$; $\pi \leftarrow \langle\rangle$
    loop
       if s satisfies g, then return π
       $A' \leftarrow \{a \in A \mid a$ is applicable in $s\}$
       if $A' = \varnothing$, then return failure
       nondeterministically choose $a \in A'$ (i)
       $s \leftarrow \gamma(s, a)$; $\pi \leftarrow \pi.a$

2.2 FORWARD STATE-SPACE SEARCH

Many planning algorithms work by searching forward from the initial state to try to construct a sequence of actions that reaches a goal state. Forward-search, Algorithm 2.1, is a procedural schema for a wide variety of such algorithms. In line (i), the nondeterministic choice is an abstraction that allows us to ignore the precise order in which the algorithm tries the alternative values of a (see Appendix A). We will use nondeterministic algorithms in many places in the book to discuss properties of all algorithms that search the same search space, irrespective of the order in which they visit the nodes.

Deterministic-Search, Algorithm 2.2, is a deterministic version of Forward-search. *Frontier* is a set of nodes that are candidates to be visited, and *Expanded* is a set of nodes that have already been visited. During each loop iteration, Deterministic-Search selects a node, generates its children, prunes some unpromising nodes, and updates *Frontier* to include the remaining children.

In the Deterministic-Search pseudocode, each node is written as a pair $v = (\pi, s)$, where π is a plan and $s = \gamma(s_0, \pi)$. However, in most implementations v includes other information, for example, pointers to v's parent and possibly to its children, the value

---

Algorithm 2.2 Deterministic-Search, a deterministic version of Forward-search.

Deterministic-Search(Σ, s_0, g)
    Frontier $\leftarrow \{(\langle\rangle, s_0)\}$ // $(\langle\rangle, s_0)$ is the initial node
    Expanded $\leftarrow \varnothing$
    while *Frontier* $\neq \varnothing$ do
       select a node $v = (\pi, s) \in$ *Frontier* (i)
       remove v from *Frontier* and add it to *Expanded*
       if s satisfies g then (ii)
          return π
       Children $\leftarrow \{(\pi.a, \gamma(s, a)) \mid s$ satisfies pre$(a)\}$
       prune (i.e., remove and discard) 0 or more nodes
          from *Children*, *Frontier* and *Expanded* (iii)
       Frontier $\leftarrow$ *Frontier* $\cup$ *Children* (iv)
    return failure

---

of cost(π) so that it will not need to be computed repeatedly, and the value of $h(s)$ (see Equation 2.8). The "parent" pointers make it unnecessary to store π explicitly in v; instead, v typically contains only the last action of π, and the rest of π is computed when needed by following the "parent" pointers back to s_0.

Many forward-search algorithms can be described as instances of Deterministic-Search by specifying how they select nodes in line (*i*) and prune nodes in line (*iii*). Presently we will discuss several such algorithms; but first, here are some basic terminology and concepts.

The *initial* or *starting* node is $(\langle \rangle, s_0)$, that is, the empty plan and the initial state. The *children* of a node v include all nodes $(\pi.a, \gamma(s, a))$ such that a is applicable in s. The *successors* or *descendants* of v include all of v's children and, recursively, all of the children's successors. The *ancestors* of v include all nodes v' such that v is a successor of v'. A *path* in the search space is any sequence of nodes $\langle v_0, v_1, \ldots, v_n \rangle$ such that each v_i is a child of v_{i-1}. The *height* of the search space is the length of the longest acyclic path that starts at the initial node. The *depth* of a node v is the length of the path from the initial node to v. The *maximum branching factor* is the maximum number of children of any node. To *expand* a node v means to generate all of its children.

Most forward-search planning algorithms attempt to find a solution without exploring the entire search space, which can be exponentially large.[9] To make informed guesses about which parts of the search space are more likely to lead to solutions, node selection (line (*i*) of Deterministic-Search) often involves a *heuristic function $h : S \to$* R that returns an estimate of the minimum cost of getting from s to a goal state:

$$h(s) \approx h^*(s) = \min\{\text{cost}(\pi) \mid \gamma(s, \pi) \text{ satisfies } g\}. \tag{2.8}$$

For information on how to compute such an h, see Section 2.3.

If $0 \leq h(s) \leq h^*(s)$ for every $s \in S$, then h is said to be *admissible*. Notice that if h is admissible, then $h(s) = 0$ whenever s is a goal node.

Given a node $v = (\pi, s)$, some forward-search algorithms will use h to compute an estimate $f(v)$ of the minimum cost of any solution plan that begins with π:

$$f(v) = \text{cost}(\pi) + h(s) \approx \min\{\text{cost}(\pi.\pi') \mid \gamma(s_0, \pi.\pi') \text{ satisfies } g\}. \tag{2.9}$$

If h is admissible, then $f(v)$ is a lower bound on the cost of every solution that begins with π.

In many forward-search algorithms, the pruning step (line (*iii*) of Deterministic-Search) often includes a *cycle-checking* step:

remove from *Children* every node (π, s) that has an ancestor
(π', s') such that $s' = s$.

In classical planning problems (and any other planning problems where the state space is finite), cycle-checking guarantees that the search will always terminate.

---

[9] The worst-case computational complexity is EXPSPACE-equivalent (see Section 2.7), although the complexity of a specific planning domain usually is much less.

2.2.1 Breadth-First Search

Breadth-first search can be written as an instance of Deterministic-Search in which the selection and pruning are done as follows:

- *Node selection.* Select a node $(\pi, s) \in Children$ that minimizes the length of π. As a tie-breaking rule if there are several such nodes, choose one that minimizes $h(s)$.
- *Pruning.* Remove from *Children* and *Frontier* every node (π, s) such that *Expanded* contains a node (π', s). This keeps the algorithm from expanding s more than once.

In classical planning problems, breadth-first search will always terminate and will return a solution if one exists. The solution will be shortest but not necessarily cost-optimal.

Because breadth-first search keeps only one path to each node, its worst-case memory requirement is $O(|S|)$, where $|S|$ is the number of nodes in the search space. Its worst-case running time is $O(b|S|)$, where b is the maximum branching factor.

2.2.2 Depth-First Search

Although *depth-first search* (DFS) is usually written as a recursive algorithm, it can also be written as an instance of Deterministic-Search in which the node selection and pruning are done as follows:

- *Node selection.* Select a node $(\pi, s) \in Children$ that maximizes the length of π. As a tie-breaking rule if there are several such nodes, choose one that minimizes $h(s)$.
- *Pruning.* First do cycle-checking. Then, to eliminate nodes that the algorithm is done with, remove v from *Expanded* if it has no children in *Frontier* $\cup$ *Expanded*, and do the same with each of v's ancestors until no more nodes are removed. This *garbage-collection* step corresponds to what happens when a recursive version of depth-first search returns from a recursive call.

In classical planning problems, depth-first search will always terminate and will return a solution if one exists, but the solution will not necessarily be shortest or cost-optimal. Because the garbage-collection step removes all nodes except for those along the current path, the worst-case memory requirement is only $O(bl)$, where b is the maximum branching factor and l is the height of the state space. However, the worst-case running time is $O(b^l)$, which can be much worse than $O(|S|)$ if there are many paths to each state in S.

2.2.3 Hill Climbing

A *hill climbing* (or *greedy*) search is a depth-first search with no backtracking:

- *Node selection.* Select a node $(\pi, s) \in Children$ that minimizes $h(s)$.
- *Pruning.* First, do cycle-checking. Then assign *Frontier* $\leftarrow \varnothing$, so that line (*iv*) of Algorithm 2.2 will be the same as assigning *Frontier* $\leftarrow$ *Children*.

The search follows a single path, and prunes all nodes not on that path. It is guaranteed to terminate on classical planning problems, but it is not guaranteed to return an optimal solution or even a solution at all. Its worst-case running time is $O(bl)$, and its worst-case memory requirement is $O(l)$, where l is the height of the search space and b is the maximum branching factor.

2.2.4 Uniform-Cost Search

Like breadth-first search, *uniform-cost* (or *least-cost first*) search does not use a heuristic function. Unlike breadth-first search, it does node selection using the accumulated cost of each node:

- *Node selection.* Select a node $(\pi, s) \in$ *Children* that minimizes cost(π).
- *Pruning.* Remove from *Children* and *Frontier* every node (π, s) such that *Expanded* contains a node (π', s). In classical planning problems (and any other problems in which all costs are nonnegative), it can be proved that cost$(\pi') \leq$ cost(π), so this step ensures that the algorithm only keeps the least costly path to each node.

In classical planning problems, the search is guaranteed to terminate and to return an optimal solution. Like breadth-first search, its worst-case running time and memory requirement are $O(b|S|)$ and $O(|S|)$, respectively.

2.2.5 A*

A* is similar to uniform-cost search, but uses a heuristic function:

- *Node selection.* Select a node $v \in$ *Children* that minimizes $f(v)$ (defined in Equation 2.9).
- *Pruning.* For each node $(\pi, s) \in$ *Children*, if A* has more than one plan that goes to s, then keep only the least costly one. More specifically, let

$$V_s = \{(\pi', s') \in Children \cup Frontier \cup Expanded \mid s' = s\};$$

and if V_s contains any nodes other than (π, s) itself, let (π', s) be the one for which cost(π') is smallest (if there is a tie, choose the oldest such node). For every node $v \in V_s$ other than (π', s), remove v and all of its descendants from *Children*, *Frontier*, and *Expanded*.

Here are some of A*'s properties:

- *Termination, completeness, and optimality.* On any classical planning problem, A* will terminate and return a solution if one exists; and if h is admissible, then this solution will be optimal.
- *Epsilon-optimality.* If h is ϵ-*admissible* (i.e., if there is an $\epsilon > 0$ such that $0 \leq h(s) \leq h^*(s) + \epsilon$ for every $s \in S$), then the solution returned by A* will be within ϵ of optimal [491].
- *Monotonicity.* If $h(s) \leq$ cost$(\gamma(s, a)) + h(\gamma(s, a))$ for every state s and applicable action a, then h is said to be *monotone* or *consistent*. In this case, $f(v) \leq f(v')$ for every child v' of a node v, from which it can be shown that A* will never prune any nodes from *Expanded*, and will expand no state more than once.

- *Informedness.* Let h_1 and h_2 be admissible heuristic functions such that h_2 *dominates* h_1, i.e., $0 \leq h_1(s) \leq h_2(s) \leq h^*(s)$ for every $s \in S$.[10] Then A* will never expand more nodes with h_2 than with h_1,[11] and in most cases, it will expand fewer nodes with h_2 than with h_1.

A*'s primary drawback is its space requirement: it needs to store every state that it visits. Like uniform-cost search, A*'s worst-case running time and memory requirement are $O(b|S|)$ and $O(|S|)$. However, with a good heuristic function, A*'s running time and memory requirement are usually much smaller.

2.2.6 Depth-First Branch and Bound

Depth-first branch and bound (DFBB) is a modified version of depth-first search that uses a different termination test than the one in line (*ii*) of Algorithm 2.2. Instead of returning the first solution it finds, DFBB keeps searching until *Frontier* is empty. DFBB maintains two variables π^* and c^*, which are the least costly solution that has been found so far, and the cost of that solution. Each time DFBB finds a solution (line (*ii*) of Deterministic-Search), it does not return the solution but instead updates the values of π^* and c^*. When *Frontier* is empty, if DFBB has found at least one solution then it returns π^*, and otherwise it returns failure. Node selection and pruning are the same as in depth-first search, but an additional pruning step occurs during node expansion: if the selected node v has $f(v) \geq c^*$, DFBB discards v rather than expanding it. If the first solution found by DFBB has a low cost, this can prune large parts of the search space.

DFBB has the same termination, completeness, and optimality properties as A*. Because the only nodes stored by DFBB are the ones in the current path, its space requirement is usually much lower than A*'s. However, because it does not keep track of which states it has visited, it may regenerate each state many times if there are multiple paths to the state; hence its running time may be much worse than A*'s. In the worst case, its running time and memory requirement are $O(b^l)$ and $O(bl)$, the same as for DFS.

2.2.7 Greedy Best-First Search

For classical planning problems where nonoptimal solutions are acceptable, the search algorithm that is used most frequently is *Greedy Best-First Search* (GBFS). It works as follows:

- *Node selection.* Select a node $(\pi, s) \in$ *Children* that minimizes $h(s)$.
- *Pruning.* Same as in A*.

Like hill climbing, GBFS continues to expand nodes along its current path as long as that path looks promising. But like A*, GBFS stores every state that it visits. Hence it can easily switch to a different path if the current path dead-ends or ceases to look promising (see Exercise 2.4).

---

[10] Dominance has often been described by saying that "h_2 is *more informed* than h_1," but that phrase is somewhat awkward because h_2 always dominates itself.

[11] Here, we assume that A* always uses the same tie-breaking rule during node selection if two nodes have the same f-value.

Like A*, GBFS's worst-case running time and memory requirement are $O(b|S|)$ and $O(|S|)$. Unlike A*, GBFS is not guaranteed to return optimal solutions; but in most cases, it will explore far fewer paths than A* and find solutions much more quickly.

2.2.8 Iterative Deepening

There are several search algorithms that do forward-search but are not instances of Deterministic-Search. Several of these are *iterative-deepening* algorithms, which gradually increase the depth of their search until they find a solution. The best known of these is iterative deepening search (IDS), which works as follows:

> for $k = 1$ to ∞,
> > do a depth-first search, backtracking at every node of depth k
> > if the search found a solution, then return it
> > if the search generated no nodes of depth k, then return failure

On classical planning problems, IDS has the same termination, completeness, and optimality properties as breadth-first search. Its primary advantage over breadth-first search is that its worst-case memory requirement is only $O(bd)$, where d is the depth of the solution returned if there is one, or the height of the search space otherwise. If the number of nodes at each depth k grows exponentially with k, then IDS's worst-case running time is $O(b^d)$, which can be substantially worse than breadth-first search if there are many paths to each state.

A closely related algorithm, IDA*, uses a cost bound rather than a depth bound:

> $c \leftarrow 0$
> loop
> > do a depth-first search, backtracking whenever $f(v) > c$
> > if the search found a solution, then return it
> > if the search did not generate an $f(v) > c$, then return failure
> > $c \leftarrow$ the smallest $f(v) > c$ where backtracking occurred

On classical planning problems, IDA*'s termination, completeness, and optimality properties are the same as those of A*. IDA*'s worst-case memory requirement is $O(bl)$, where l is the height of the search space. If the number of nodes grows exponentially with c (which usually is true in classical planning problems but less likely to be true in nonclassical ones), then IDA*'s worst-case running time is $O(b^d)$, where d is the depth of the solution returned if there is one or the height of the search space otherwise. However, this is substantially worse than A* if there are many paths to each state.

2.2.9 Choosing a Forward-Search Algorithm

It is difficult to give any hard-and-fast rules for choosing among the forward-search algorithms presented here, but here are some rough guidelines.

If a nonoptimal solution is acceptable, often the best choice is to develop a planning algorithm based on GBFS (e.g., [510, 613]). There are no guarantees as to GBFS's performance; but with a good heuristic function, it usually works quite well.

If one needs a solution that is optimal (or within ϵ of optimal) and has a good heuristic function that is admissible (or ϵ-admissible), then an A*-like algorithm is a good choice if the state space is small enough that every node can be held in main memory. If the state space is too large to hold in main memory, then an algorithm such as DFBB or IDA* may be worth trying, but there may be problems with excessive running time.

For integration of planning into acting, an important question is how to turn any of these algorithms into online algorithms. This is discussed further in Section 2.6.

2.3 HEURISTIC FUNCTIONS

Recall from Equation 2.8 that a heuristic function is a function h that returns an estimate $h(s)$ of the minimum cost $h^*(s)$ of getting from the state s to a goal state and that h is admissible if $0 \leq h(s) \leq h^*(s)$ for every state s (from which it follows that $h(s) = 0$ whenever s is a goal node).

The simplest possible heuristic function is $h_0(s) = 0$ for every state s. It is admissible and trivial to compute but provides no useful information. We usually will want a heuristic function that provides a better estimate of $h^*(s)$ (e.g., see the discussion of dominance at the end of Section 2.2.5). If a heuristic function can be computed in a polynomial amount of time and can provide an exponential reduction in the number of nodes examined by the planning algorithm, this makes the computational effort worthwhile.

The best-known way of producing heuristic functions is *relaxation*. Given a planning domain $\Sigma = (S, A, \gamma)$ and planning problem $P = (\Sigma, s_0, g)$, relaxing them means weakening some of the constraints that restrict what the states, actions, and plans are; restrict when an action or plan is applicable and what goals it achieves; and increase the costs of actions and plans. This produces a *relaxed* domain $\Sigma' = (S', A', \gamma')$ and problem $P' = (\Sigma', s'_0, g')$ having the following property: for every solution π for P, P' has a solution π' such that $\text{cost}'(\pi') \leq \text{cost}(\pi)$.

Given an algorithm for solving planning problems in Σ', we can use it to create a heuristic function for P that works as follows: given a state $s \in S$, solve (Σ', s, g') and return the cost of the solution. If the algorithm always finds optimal solutions, then the heuristic function will be admissible.

Just as domain representations can be either domain-specific or domain-independent, so can heuristic functions. Here is an example of the former:

Example 2.20. Let us represent the planning domain in Figure 2.1 as follows. The objects include a set of locations and a few numbers:

$$B = \textit{Locations} \cup \textit{Numbers};$$

$$\textit{Locations} = \{\text{loc}_1, \ldots, \text{loc}_9\};$$

$$\textit{Numbers} = \{1, \ldots, 9\}.$$

There is a rigid relation adjacent that includes every pair of locations that have a road between them, and rigid relations x and y that give each location's x and y coordinates:

$$\text{adjacent} = \{(\text{loc}_0, \text{loc}_1), (\text{loc}_0, \text{loc}_6), (\text{loc}_1, \text{loc}_0), (\text{loc}_1, \text{loc}_3), \ldots\};$$

$$\text{x} = \{(\text{loc}_0, 2), (\text{loc}_1, 0), (\text{loc}_2, 4), \ldots\};$$

$$\text{y} = \{(\text{loc}_0, 4), (\text{loc}_1, 3), (\text{loc}_2, 4), \ldots\}.$$

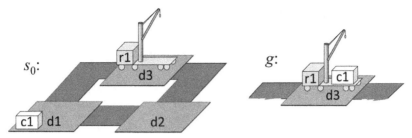

Figure 2.4. Initial state and goal for Example 2.21.

There is one state variable loc with $\mathrm{Range}(\mathrm{loc}) = Locations$, and 10 states:

$$s_i = \{\mathrm{loc} = \mathrm{loc}_i\}, \quad i = 0, \ldots, 9.$$

There is one action template:

$$
\begin{aligned}
&\mathrm{move}(l, m) \\
&\quad \mathrm{pre}\colon \mathrm{adjacent}(l, m), \mathrm{loc} = l \\
&\quad \mathrm{eff}\colon \mathrm{loc} \leftarrow m \\
&\quad \mathrm{cost}\colon \mathrm{distance}(l, m)
\end{aligned}
$$

where $\mathrm{Range}(l) = \mathrm{Range}(m) = Locations$, and $\mathrm{distance}(l, m)$ is the Euclidean distance between l and m:

$$\mathrm{distance}(l, m) = \sqrt{(\mathrm{x}(l) - \mathrm{x}(m))^2 + (\mathrm{y}(l) - \mathrm{y}(m))^2}.$$

Consider the planning problem (Σ, s_0, s_8). One possible heuristic function is the Euclidean distance from loc to the goal location,

$$h(s) = \mathrm{distance}(s(\mathrm{loc}), \mathrm{loc}_8),$$

which is the length of an optimal solution for a relaxed problem in which the actor is not constrained to follow roads. This is a lower bound on the length of every route that follows roads to get to loc_8, so h is admissible. □

It is possible to define a variety of *domain-independent* heuristic functions that can be used in any state-variable planning domain. In the following subsections, we describe several such heuristic functions and illustrate each of them in the following example.

Example 2.21. Figure 2.4 shows a planning problem $P = (\Sigma, s_0, g)$ in a planning domain $\Sigma = (B, R, X, \mathcal{A})$ that is a simplified version of the one in Figure 2.3. B includes one robot, one container, three docks, no piles, and the constant nil:

$$B = Robots \cup Docks \cup Containers \cup \{\mathrm{nil}\};$$

$$Robots = \{\mathrm{r}_1\};$$

$$Docks = \{\mathrm{d}_1, \mathrm{d}_2, \mathrm{d}_3\};$$

$$Containers = \{\mathrm{c}_1\}.$$

There are no rigid relations, that is, $R = \varnothing$. There are two state variables, $X = \{\text{cargo}(r1), \text{loc}(c1)\}$, with

$$\text{Range}(\text{cargo}(r1)) = \{c1, \text{nil}\};$$

$$\text{Range}(\text{loc}(c1)) = \{d1, d2, d3, r1\}.$$

$\mathcal{A}$ contains three action templates:

> load(r, c, l)
>> pre: cargo(r) = nil, loc(c) = l, loc(r) = l
>> eff: cargo(r) ← c, loc(c) ← r
> cost: 1

> unload(r, c, l)   move(r, d, e)
>> pre: cargo(r) = c, loc(r) = l pre: loc(r) = d
>> eff: cargo(r) ← nil, loc(c) ← l eff: loc(r) ← e
> cost: 1   cost: 1

The action templates' parameters have the following ranges:

$$\text{Range}(c) = \textit{Containers}; \quad \text{Range}(d) = \text{Range}(e) = \textit{Docks};$$
$$\text{Range}(l) = \textit{Locations}; \quad \text{Range}(r) = \textit{Robots}.$$

P's initial state and goal are

$$s_0 = \{\text{loc}(r1) = d3, \text{cargo}(r1) = \text{nil}, \text{loc}(c1) = d1\};$$

$$g = \{\text{loc}(r1) = d3, \text{loc}(c1) = r1\}.$$

Suppose we are running GBFS (see Section 2.2.7) on P. In s_0, there are two applicable actions: $a_1 = \text{move}(r1, d3, d1)$ and $a_2 = \text{move}(r1, d3, d2)$. Let

$$s_1 = \gamma(s_0, a_1) = \{\text{loc}(r1) = d1, \text{cargo}(r1) = \text{nil}, \text{loc}(c1) = d1\}; \qquad (2.10)$$

$$s_2 = \gamma(s_0, a_2) = \{\text{loc}(r1) = d2, \text{cargo}(r1) = \text{nil}, \text{loc}(c1) = d1\}. \qquad (2.11)$$

In line (i) of Algorithm 2.2, GBFS chooses between a_1 and a_2 by evaluating $h(s_1)$ and $h(s_2)$. The following subsections describe several possibilities for what h might be. □

2.3.1 Max-Cost and Additive Cost Heuristics

The *max-cost* of a set of literals $g = \{g_1, \ldots, g_k\}$ is defined recursively as the largest max-cost of each g_i individually, where each g_i's max-cost is the minimum, over all actions that can produce g_i, of the action's cost plus the max-cost of its preconditions. Here are the equations:

$$\Delta^{\max}(s, g) = \max_{g_i \in g} \Delta^{\max}(s, g_i);$$

$$\Delta^{\max}(s, g_i) = \begin{cases} 0, & \text{if } g_i \in s, \\ \min\{\Delta^{\max}(s, a) \mid a \in A \text{ and } g_i \in \text{eff}(a)\}, & \text{otherwise}; \end{cases}$$

$$\Delta^{\max}(s, a) = \text{cost}(a) + \Delta^{\max}(s, \text{pre}(a)).$$

In a planning problem $P = (\Sigma, s_0, g)$, the *max-cost heuristic* is

$$h^{\max}(s) = \Delta^{\max}(s, g).$$

As shown in the following example, the computation of $h^{\max}$ can be visualized as an And/Or search going backward from g.

At the beginning of Section 2.3, we said that most heuristics are derived by relaxation. One way to describe $h^{\max}$ is that it is the cost of an optimal solution to a relaxed problem in which a goal (i.e., a set of literals such as g or the preconditions of an action) can be reached by achieving just one of the goal's literals, namely, the one that is the most expensive to achieve.

Example 2.22. In Example 2.21, suppose GBFS's heuristic function is $h^{\max}$. Figure 2.5 shows the computation of $h^{\max}(s_1) = 1$ and $h^{\max}(s_2) = 2$. Because $h^{\max}(s_1) < h^{\max}(s_2)$, GBFS will choose s_1.   □

Although $h^{\max}$ is admissible, it is not very informative. A closely related heuristic, the *additive cost* heuristic, is not admissible but generally works better in practice. It is similar to $h^{\max}$ but adds the costs of each set of literals rather than taking their maximum. It is defined as

$$h^{\mathrm{add}}(s) = \Delta^{\mathrm{add}}(s, g),$$

where

$$\Delta^{\mathrm{add}}(s, g) = \sum_{g_i \in g} \Delta^{\mathrm{add}}(s, g_i);$$

$$\Delta^{\mathrm{add}}(s, g_i) = \begin{cases} 0, & \text{if } g_i \in s, \\ \min\{\Delta^{\mathrm{add}}(s, a) \mid a \in A \text{ and } g_i \in \mathrm{eff}(a)\}, & \text{otherwise;} \end{cases}$$

$$\Delta^{\mathrm{add}}(s, a) = \mathrm{cost}(a) + \Delta^{\mathrm{add}}(s, \mathrm{pre}(a)).$$

As shown in the following example, the computation of h^{add} can be visualized as an And/Or search nearly identical to the one for $h^{\max}$.

Example 2.23. In Example 2.21, suppose GBFS's heuristic function is h^{add}. Figure 2.6 shows the computation of $h^{\mathrm{add}}(s_1) = 2$ and $h^{\mathrm{add}}(s_2) = 3$. Because $h^{\mathrm{add}}(s_1) < h^{\mathrm{add}}(s_2)$, GBFS will choose s_1.

To see that h^{add} is not admissible, notice that if a single action a could achieve both loc(r1)=d3 and loc(c1)=r1, then $h^{\mathrm{add}}(g)$ would be higher than $h^*(g)$, because h^{add} would count a's cost twice.   □

Both $h^{\max}$ and h^{add} have the same time complexity. Their running time is nontrivial, but it is polynomial in $|A| + \sum_{x \in X} |\mathrm{Range}(x)|$, the total number of actions and ground atoms in the planning domain.

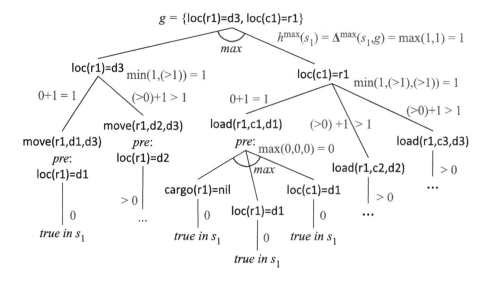

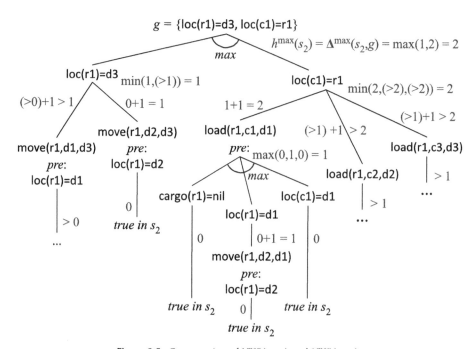

Figure 2.5. Computation of $h^{\max}(s_1, g)$ and $h^{\max}(s_2, g)$.

2.3.2 Delete-Relaxation Heuristics

Several heuristic functions are based on the notion of *delete-relaxation*, a problem relaxation in which applying an action never removes old atoms from a state, but simply adds new ones.[12]

---

[12] The h^{add} and $h^{\max}$ heuristics can also be explained in terms of delete-relaxation; see Section 2.7.9.

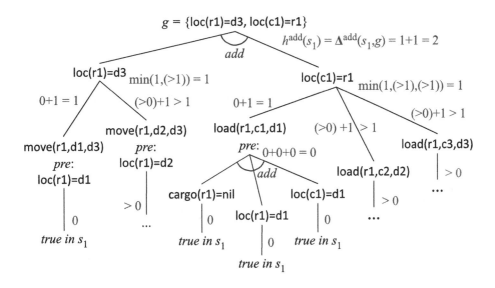

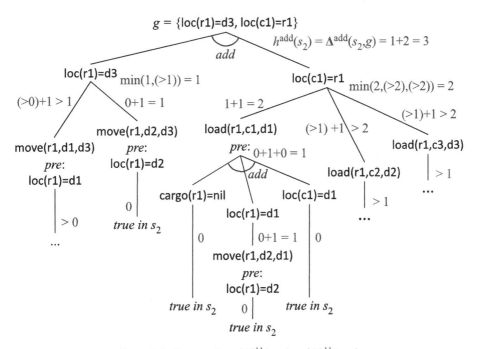

Figure 2.6. Computation of $h^{\text{add}}(s_1, g)$ and $h^{\text{add}}(s_2, g)$.

If a state s includes an atom $x = v$ and an applicable action a has an effect $x \leftarrow w$, then the delete-relaxed result of applying a will be a "state" $\gamma^+(s, a)$ that includes both $x = v$ and $x = w$. We will make the following definitions:

- A *relaxed state* (or *r-state*, for short) is any set $\hat{s}$ of ground atoms such that every state variable $x \in X$ is the target of at least one atom in $\hat{s}$. It follows that every state is also an r-state.

- A relaxed state $\hat{s}$ *r-satisfies* a set of literals g if S contains a subset $s \subseteq \hat{s}$ that satisfies g.
- An action a is *r-applicable* in an r-state $\hat{s}$ if $\hat{s}$ r-satisfies pre(a). In this case, the predicted r-state is

$$\gamma^+(\hat{s}, a) = \hat{s} \cup \gamma(s, a). \tag{2.12}$$

- By extension, a plan $\pi = \langle a_1, \dots, a_n \rangle$ is r-applicable in an r-state $\hat{s}_0$ if there are r-states $\hat{s}_1, \dots, \hat{s}_n$ such that

$$\hat{s}_1 = \gamma^+(\hat{s}_0, a_1), \ \hat{s}_2 = \gamma^+(\hat{s}_1, a_2), \ \dots, \ \hat{s}_n = \gamma^+(\hat{s}_{n-1}, a_n).$$

In this case, $\gamma^+(\hat{s}_0, \pi) = \hat{s}_n$.

- A plan π is a *relaxed solution* for a planning problem $P = (\Sigma, s_0, g)$ if $\gamma^+(s_0, \pi)$ r-satisfies g. Thus the cost of the optimal relaxed solution is

$$\Delta^+(s, g) = \min\{\text{cost}(\pi) \mid \gamma^+(s, \pi) \text{ r-satisfies } g\}.$$

For a planning problem $P = (\Sigma, s_0, g)$, the *optimal relaxed solution* heuristic is

$$h^+(s) = \Delta^+(s, g).$$

Example 2.24. Let P be the planning problem in Example 2.21. Let $\hat{s}_1 = \gamma^+(s_0, \text{move}(\text{r1}, \text{d3}, \text{d1}))$ and $\hat{s}_2 = \gamma^+(\hat{s}_1, \text{load}(\text{r1}, \text{c1}, \text{d1}))$. Then

$$\hat{s}_1 = \{\text{loc}(\text{r1}) = \text{d1}, \text{loc}(\text{r1}) = \text{d3}, \text{cargo}(\text{r1}) = \text{nil}, \text{loc}(\text{c1}) = \text{d1}\};$$

$$\hat{s}_2 = \{\text{loc}(\text{r1}) = \text{d1}, \text{loc}(\text{r1}) = \text{d3}, \text{cargo}(\text{r1}) = \text{nil}, \text{cargo}(\text{r1}) = \text{c1},$$

$$\text{loc}(\text{c1}) = \text{d1}, \text{loc}(\text{c1}) = \text{r1}\}.$$

The r-state $\hat{s}_2$ r-satisfies g, so the plan $\pi = \langle \text{move}(\text{r1}, \text{d3}, \text{d1}), \text{load}(\text{r1}, \text{c1}, \text{d1}) \rangle$ is a relaxed solution for P. No shorter plan is a relaxed solution for P, so $h^+(s) = \Delta^+(s_0, g)$. □

Because every ordinary solution for P is also a relaxed solution for P, it follows that $h^+(s) \leq h^*(s)$ for every s. Thus h^+ is admissible, so h^+ can be used with algorithms such as A* to find an optimal solution for P. On the other hand, h^+ is expensive to compute: the problem of finding an optimal relaxed solution for a planning problem P is NP-hard [68].[13]

We now describe an approximation to h^+ that is easier to compute. It is based on the fact that if A is a set of actions that are all r-applicable in a relaxed state $\hat{s}$, then they will produce the same predicted r-state regardless of the order in which they are applied. This r-state is

$$\gamma^+(\hat{s}, A) = \hat{s} \cup \bigcup_{a \in A} \text{eff}(a). \tag{2.13}$$

H^{FF}, Algorithm 2.3, starts at an initial r-state $\hat{s}_0 = s$ and uses Equation 2.13 to generate a sequence of successively larger r-states and sets of applicable actions,

$$\hat{s}_0, A_1, \hat{s}_1, A_2, \hat{s}_2 \dots,$$

---

[13] If we restrict P to be ground (see Section 2.7.1), then the problem is NP-complete.

Algorithm 2.3 H^{FF}, an algorithm to compute the Fast-Forward heuristic.

$H^{FF}(\Sigma, s, g)$
  $\hat{s}_0 = s; \ A_0 = \varnothing$
  for $k = 1$ by 1 until a subset of $\hat{s}_k$ r-satisfies g do   (*i*)
    $A_k \leftarrow \{$all actions that are r-applicable in $\hat{s}_{k-1}\}$
    $\hat{s}_k \leftarrow \gamma^+(\hat{s}_{k-1}, A_k)$
    if $\hat{s}_k = \hat{s}_{k-1}$ then   // (Σ, s, g) has no solution   (*ii*)
      return ∞
  $\hat{g}_k \leftarrow g$
  for $i = k$ down to 1 do   (*iii*)
    arbitrarily choose a minimal set of actions
      $\hat{a}_i \subseteq A_i$ such that $\gamma^+(\hat{s}_i, \hat{a}_i)$ satisfies $\hat{g}_i$
    $\hat{g}_{i-1} \leftarrow (\hat{g}_i - \text{eff}(\hat{a}_i)) \cup \text{pre}(\hat{a}_i)$
  $\hat{\pi} \leftarrow \langle \hat{a}_1, \hat{a}_2, \ldots, \hat{a}_k \rangle$ (*iv*)
  return $\sum\{\text{cost}(a) \mid a$ is an action in $\hat{\pi}\}$

---

until it generates an r-state that r-satisfies g. From this sequence, H^{FF} extracts a relaxed solution and returns its cost. Line (*ii*) whether the sequence has converged to an r-state that does not r-satisfy g, in which case the planning problem is unsolvable.

The *Fast-Forward* heuristic, $h^{FF}(s)$, is defined to be the value returned by H^{FF}.[14] The definition of h^{FF} is ambiguous, because the returned value may vary depending on H^{FF}'s choices of $\hat{a}_k, \hat{a}_{k-1}, \ldots, \hat{a}_1$ in the loop (*iii*). Furthermore, because there is no guarantee that these choices are the optimal ones, h^{FF} is not admissible.

As with $h^{\max}$ and h^{add}, the running time for H^{FF} is polynomial in $|A| + \sum_{x \in X} |\text{Range}(x)|$, the number of actions and ground atoms in the planning domain.

Example 2.25. In Example 2.21, suppose GBFS's heuristic function is h^{FF}, as computed by H^{FF}.

To compute $h^{FF}(s_1)$, H^{FF} begins with $\hat{s}_0 = s_1$, and computes A_1 and $\hat{s}_1$ in the loop at line (*i*). Figure 2.7 illustrates the computation: the lines to the left of each action show which atoms in $\hat{s}_0$ satisfy its preconditions, and the lines to the right of each action show which atoms in $\hat{s}_1$ are its effects. For the loop at line (*iii*), H^{FF} begins with $\hat{g}_1 = g$ and computes $\hat{a}_1$ and $\hat{g}_0$; these sets are shown in boldface in Figure 2.7. In line (*iv*), the relaxed solution is

$$\hat{\pi} = \langle \hat{a}_1 \rangle = \langle \{\text{move}(r_1, d_1, d_3), \text{load}(r_1, c_1, d_1)\} \rangle.$$

Thus H^{FF} returns $h^{FF}(s_1) = \text{cost}(\hat{\pi}) = 2$.

Figure 2.8 is a similar illustration of H^{FF}'s computation of $h^{FF}(s_2)$. For the loop at line (*i*), H^{FF} begins with $\hat{s}_0 = s_2$ and computes the sets $A_1, \hat{s}_1, A_2$, and $\hat{s}_2$. For the loop at line (*iii*), H^{FF} begins with $\hat{g}_2 = g$ and computes $\hat{a}_2, \hat{g}_1, \hat{a}_1$, and $\hat{g}_0$, which are shown in

---

[14] The name comes from the FF planner in which this heuristic was introduced; see Section 2.7.9.

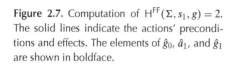
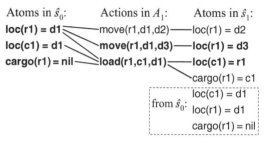

Figure 2.7. Computation of $H^{FF}(\Sigma, s_1, g) = 2$. The solid lines indicate the actions' preconditions and effects. The elements of $\hat{g}_0$, $\hat{a}_1$, and $\hat{g}_1$ are shown in boldface.

boldface in Figure 2.8. In line (iv), the relaxed solution is

$$\hat{\pi} = \langle \hat{a}_1, \hat{a}_2 \rangle = \langle \{move(r_1, d_2, d_1)\}\}, \{\langle move(r_1, d_1, d_3), load(r_1, c_1, d_1)\}\rangle,$$

so H^{FF} returns $h^{FF}(s_2) = \text{cost}(\hat{\pi}) = 3$.

Thus $h^{FF}(s_1) < h^{FF}(s_2)$, so GBFS will choose to expand s_1 next. □

The graph structures in Figures 2.7 and 2.8 are called *relaxed planning graphs*.

2.3.3 Landmark Heuristics

Let $P = (\Sigma, s_0, g)$ be a planning problem, and let $\phi = \phi_1 \vee \ldots \vee \phi_m$ be a disjunction of atoms. Then ϕ is a *disjunctive landmark* for P if every solution plan produces an intermediate state (i.e., a state other than s_0 and g) in which ϕ is true.

The problem of deciding whether an arbitrary ϕ is a disjunctive landmark is PSPACE-complete [281]. However, that is a worst-case result; many disjunctive landmarks can often be efficiently discovered by reasoning about relaxed planning graphs [281, 509].

One way to to do this is as follows. Let s be the current state, and g be the goal; but instead of requiring g to be a set of atoms, let it be a set $g = \{\phi_1, \ldots, \phi_k\}$ such that each ϕ_i is a disjunction of one or more atoms. For each ϕ_i, let $R_i = \{$every action whose effects include at least one of the atoms in $\phi_i\}$. Let from R_i every action a for which we can show (using a relaxed-planning-graph computation) that a's preconditions cannot be achieved without R_i, and let $N_i = \{a_1, a_2, \ldots, a_k\}$ be the remaining set

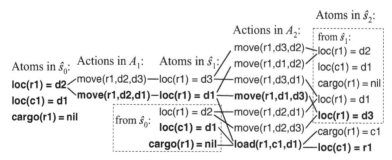

Figure 2.8. Computation of $H^{FF}(\Sigma, s_2, g) = 3$. The solid lines indicate the actions' preconditions and effects. The atoms and actions in each $\hat{g}_i$ and $\hat{a}_i$ are shown in boldface.

of actions. If we pick a precondition p_j of each a_j in N, then $\phi' = p_1 \vee \ldots \vee p_k$ is a disjunctive landmark. To avoid a combinatorial explosion, we will not want to compute every such ϕ'; instead we will only compute landmarks consisting of no more than four atoms (the number 4 being more-or-less arbitrary). The computation can be done by calling RPG-landmark(s, ϕ_i) once for each ϕ_i, as follows:

RPG-landmark(s, ϕ) takes two arguments: a state s, and a disjunction ϕ of one or more atoms such that ϕ is false in s (i.e., s contains none of the atoms in ϕ). It performs the following steps:

1. Let *Relevant* = {every action whose effects include at least one member of ϕ}. Then achieving ϕ will require at least one of the actions in *Relevant*. If some action $a \in$ *Relevant* has all of its preconditions satisfied in s, then $\langle a \rangle$ is a solution, and the only landmark is ϕ itself, so return ϕ.

2. Starting with s and using only the actions in $A \setminus$ *Relevant* (i.e., the actions that *cannot* achieve ϕ), construct a sequence of r-states and r-actions $\hat{s}_0, A_1, \hat{s}_1, A_2, \hat{s}_2, \ldots$ as in the H^{FF} algorithm. But instead of stopping when H^{FF} does, keep going until an r-state $\hat{s}_k$ is reached such that $\hat{s}_k = \hat{s}_{k-1}$. Then $\hat{s}_k$ includes every atom that can be produced without using the actions in *Relevant*.

3. Let *Necessary* = {all actions in *Relevant* that are applicable in $\hat{s}_k$}. Then achieving ϕ will require at least one of the actions in *Necessary*. If *Necessary* = $\varnothing$ then ϕ cannot be achieved, so return failure.

4. Consider every disjunction of atoms $\phi' = p_1 \vee \ldots \vee p_m$ having the following properties: $m \leq 4$ (as we noted earlier, this is an arbitrary limit to avoid a combinatorial explosion), every p_i in φ' is a precondition of at least one action in *Necessary*, every action in *Necessary* has exactly one of $p_1, \ldots, p_m$ as a precondition, and no p_i is in s_0. Then none of the actions in *Necessary* will be applicable until ϕ' is true, so ϕ' is a disjunctive landmark.

5. For every landmark ϕ' found in the previous step, recursively call RPG-landmark(s, ϕ') to find additional landmarks.[15] These landmarks *precede* ϕ', that is, they must be achieved before ϕ'. Return every ϕ' and all of the landmarks found in the recursive calls.

The *simple landmark heuristic* is

$h^{sl}(s)$ = the total number of landmarks found by the preceding algorithm.

Although the algorithm is more complicated than the H^{FF} algorithm, its running time is still polynomial.

Better landmark heuristics can be devised by doing additional computations to discover additional landmarks and by reasoning about the order in which to achieve the landmarks. We discuss this further in Section 2.7.9.

Example 2.26. As before, consider the planning problem in Example 2.21.

To compute $h^{sl}(s_1)$, we count the number of landmarks between s_1 and g. If we start in s_1, then every solution plan must include a state in which cargo(r1) = c1. We will skip

---

[15] In implementations, this usually is done only if every atom in ϕ' has the same type, for example, $\phi' =$ loc(r1) = d1 $\vee$ loc(r2) = d1.

Algorithm 2.4 Backward-search planning schema. During each loop iteration, π is a plan that achieves g from any state that satisfies g.

Backward-search(Σ, s_0, g_0)
   $\pi \leftarrow \langle\rangle$; $g \leftarrow g_0$ (i)
   loop
      if s_0 satisfies g then return π
      $A' \leftarrow \{a \in A \mid a$ is relevant for $g\}$
      if $A' = \varnothing$ then return failure
      nondeterministically choose $a \in A'$
      $g \leftarrow \gamma^{-1}(g, a)$ (ii)
      $\pi \leftarrow a.\pi$ (iii)

---

the computational details, but this is the only landmark that the landmark computation will find for s_1. Thus $h^{\text{sl}}(s_1) = 1$.

If we start in state s_2, then the landmark computation will find two landmarks: cargo(s1) = c1 as before, and loc(r1) = d1 (which was not a landmark for s_1 because it was already true in s_1). Thus $h^{\text{sl}}(s_2) = 2$.   □

2.4 BACKWARD SEARCH

Backward-search, Algorithm 2.4, does a state-space search backward from the goal. As with Forward-search, it is a nondeterministic algorithm that has many possible deterministic versions. The variables in the algorithm are as follows: π is the current partial solution, g' is a set of literals representing all states from which π can achieve g, *Solved* is a set of literals representing all states from which a suffix of π can achieve g, and A' is the set of all actions that are *relevant* for g', as defined next.

Informally, we will consider an action a to be relevant for achieving a goal g if a does not make any of the conditions in g false and makes at least one of them true. More formally:

Definition 2.27. Let $g = \{x_1 = c_1, \ldots, x_k = c_k\}$, where each x_i is a state variable and each c_i is a constant. An action a is *relevant* for g if the following conditions hold:

- For at least one $i \in \{1, \ldots, k\}$, eff$_a$ contains $x_i \leftarrow c_i$.
- For $i = 1, \ldots, k$, eff$_a$ contains no assignment statement $x_i \leftarrow c'_i$ such that $c'_i \neq c_i$.
- For each x_i that is not affected by a, pre(a) does not contain the precondition $x_i \neq c_i$, nor any precondition $x_i = c'_i$ such that $c'_i \neq c_i$.   □

In line (ii) of Backward-search, $\gamma^{-1}(g, a)$ is called the *regression* of g through a. It is a set of conditions that is satisfied by every state s such that $\gamma(s, a)$ satisfies g. It includes all of the literals in pre(a), and all literals in g that a does not achieve:

$$\gamma^{-1}(g, a) = \text{pre}(a) \cup \{(x_i, c_i) \in g \mid a \text{ does not affect } x_i\} \qquad (2.14)$$

We can incorporate loop-checking into Backward-search by inserting the following line after line (*i*):

> *Solved* ← {*g*}

and adding these two lines after line (*iii*):

> if *g* ∈ *Solved* then return failure
> *Solved* ← *Solved* ∪ {*g*}

We can make the loop-checking more powerful by replacing the preceding two lines with the following *subsumption test*:

> if *g* ∈ *Solved* then return failure
> if ∃*g'* ∈ *Solved* s.t. *g'* ⊆ *g* then return failure

Here, *Solved* represents the set of all states that are "already solved," that is, states from which π or one of π's suffixes will achieve g_0; and g' represents the set of all states from which the plan $a.\pi$ will achieve g_0. If every state that $a.\pi$ can solve is already solved, then it is useless to prepend a to π. For any solution that we can find this way, another branch of the search space will contain a shorter solution that omits a.

Example 2.28. Suppose we augment Backward-search to incorporate loop checking and call it on the planning problem in Example 2.21. The first time through the loop,

$$g = \{\text{cargo}(r1) = c1, \text{loc}(r1) = d3\},$$

and there are three relevant actions: move(r1, d1, d3), move(r1, d2, d3), and load(r1, c1, d3). Suppose Backward-search's nondeterministic choice is move(r1, d1, d3). Then in lines 7–10,

$$g \leftarrow \gamma^{-1}(g, \text{move}(r1, d1, d3)) = \{\text{loc}(r1) = d1, \text{cargo}(r1) = c1\};$$

$$\pi \leftarrow \langle \text{move}(r1, d1, d3) \rangle;$$

$$Solved \leftarrow \{\{\text{cargo}(r1) = c1, \text{loc}(r1) = d3\}, \{\text{loc}(r1) = d1, \text{cargo}(r1) = c1\}\}.$$

In its second loop iteration, Backward-search chooses nondeterministically among three relevant actions in line 6: move(r1, d2, d1), move(r1, d3, d1), and load(r1, c1, d1). Let us consider two of these choices.

If Backward-search chooses move(r1, d3, d1), then in lines 7–9,

$$g \leftarrow \gamma^{-1}(g, \text{move}(r1, d3, d1)) = \{\text{loc}(r1) = d3, \text{cargo}(r1) = c1\};$$

$$\pi \leftarrow \langle \text{move}(r1, d3, d1), \text{move}(r1, d1, d3) \rangle;$$

$$g \in Solved, \text{ so Backward-search returns failure.}$$

If Backward-search instead chooses $\mathsf{load}(r1, c1, d1)$, then in lines 7–10,

$$g \leftarrow \gamma^{-1}(g, \mathsf{load}(r1, c1, d1)) = \{\mathsf{loc}(r1) = d1, \mathsf{cargo}(r1) = \mathsf{nil}\};$$

$$\pi \leftarrow \langle \mathsf{load}(r1, c1, d1), \mathsf{move}(r1, d1, d3) \rangle;$$

$$\textit{Solved} \leftarrow \{\{\mathsf{cargo}(r1) = c1, \mathsf{loc}(r1) = d3\}, \{\mathsf{loc}(r1) = d1, \mathsf{cargo}(r1) = c1\},$$

$$\{\mathsf{loc}(r1) = d1, \mathsf{cargo}(r1) = \mathsf{nil}\}\}.$$

Consequently, one of the possibilities in Backward-search's third loop iteration is to set

$$\pi \leftarrow \langle \mathsf{move}(r1, d1, d3), \mathsf{load}(r1, c1, d1), \mathsf{move}(r1, d1, d3) \rangle.$$

If Backward-search does this, then it will return π at the start of the fourth loop iteration.   □

To choose among actions in A, Backward-search can use many of the same heuristic functions described in Section 2.3, but with the following modification: rather than using them to estimate the cost of getting from the current state to the goal, what should be estimated is the cost of getting from s_0 to $\gamma^{-1}(g, a)$.

2.5 PLAN-SPACE SEARCH

Another approach to plan generation is to formulate planning as a constraint satisfaction problem and use constraint-satisfaction techniques to produce solutions that are more flexible than linear sequences of ground actions. For example, plans can be produced in which the actions are partially ordered, along with a guarantee that every total ordering that is compatible with this partial ordering will be a solution plan.

Such flexibility allows some of the ordering decisions to be postponed until the plan is being executed, at which time the actor may have a better idea about which ordering will work best. Furthermore, the techniques are a first step toward planning concurrent execution of actions, a topic that we will develop further in Chapter 4.

2.5.1 Definitions and Algorithm

The PSP algorithm, which we will describe shortly, solves a planning problem by making repeated modifications to a "partial plan" in which the actions are partially ordered and partially instantiated, as defined here.

A *partially instantiated* action is any instance of an action template. It may be either ground or unground.

Informally, a partially ordered plan is a plan in which the actions are partially ordered. However, some additional complication is needed to make it possible (as it is in ordinary plans) for actions to occur more than once. The mathematical definition is as follows:

Definition 2.29. A *partially ordered plan* is a triple $\pi = (V, E, act)$ in which V and E are the nodes and edges of an acyclic digraph, and each node $v \in V$ contains an action

$act(v)$.[16] The edges in E represent ordering constraints on the nodes in V, and we define $v \prec v'$ if $v \neq v'$ and (V, E) contains a path from v to v'. A *total ordering* of π is any (ordinary) plan $\pi' = \langle act(v_1), \ldots, act(v_n) \rangle$ such that $v_1 \prec v_2 \prec \ldots \prec v_n$ and $\{v_1, \ldots, v_n\} = V$.

A *partially ordered solution* for a planning problem P is a partially ordered plan π such that every total ordering of π is a solution for P. □

Definition 2.30. A *partial plan* is a 4-tuple $\pi = (V, E, act, C)$, where (V, E, act) is the same as in Definition 2.29 except that each action $act(v)$ may be partially instantiated, and C is a set of constraints. Each constraint in C is either an inequality constraint or a causal link:

- An *inequality constraint* is an expression of the form $y \neq z$, where y and z may each be either a variable or a constant.
- A *causal link* is an expression $v_1 \xrightarrow{x=b} v_2$, where v_1 and v_2 are two nodes such that $v_1 \prec v_2$, $x = b$ is a precondition of $act(v_2)$, and $x \leftarrow b$ is an effect of $act(v_1)$. □

The purpose of a causal link is to designate $act(v_1)$ as the (partially instantiated) action that establishes $act(v_2)$'s precondition $x = b$. Consequently, for every node such that $v_1 \prec v_3 \prec v_2$, we will say that v_3 *violates* the causal link if x is the target of one of $act(v_3)$'s effects, even if the effect is $x \leftarrow b$.[17]

A partial plan $\pi = (V, E, act, C)$ is *inconsistent* if (V, E) contains a cycle, C contains a self-contradictory inequality constraint (e.g., $y \neq y$) or a violated causal link, or an action $act(v)$ has an illegal argument. Otherwise π is *consistent*.

Definition 2.31. If $\pi = (V, E, act, C)$ is a consistent partial plan, then a *refinement* of π is any sequence ρ of the following modifications to π:

- *Add an edge* (v, v') *to* E. This produces a partial plan (V, E', act, C) in which $v \prec v'$.
- *Instantiate a variable* x. This means replacing all occurrences of x with an object $b \in \text{Range}(x)$ or a variable y with $\text{Range}(y) \subseteq \text{Range}(x)$. This produces a partial plan (V, E, act', C'), where C' and act' are the instances of C and act produced by replacing x.
- *Add a constraint* c. This produces a partial plan $(V, E, act, C \cup \{c\})$.
- *Add a new node* v containing a partially instantiated action a. This produces a partial plan $\pi' = (V', E, act', C)$, where $V' = V \cup \{v\}$ and $act' = act \cup \{(v, a)\}$.

A refinement ρ is *feasible* for π if it produces a consistent partial plan. □

2.5.2 Planning Algorithm

The PSP algorithm is Algorithm 2.5. Its arguments include a state-variable planning domain $\Sigma = (B, R, X, \mathcal{A})$ and a partial plan $\pi = (V, E, act, C)$ that represents a planning problem $P = (\Sigma, s_0, g)$. The initial value of π is as follows, where v_0 and v_g are

---

[16] For readers familiar with partially ordered multisets [233], we essentially are defining a partially ordered plan to be a pomset in which $act(.)$ is the labeling function.

[17] The reason for calling this a violation even if the effect is $x \leftarrow b$ is to ensure that PSP (Algorithm 2.5) performs a *systematic* search [411, 336], that is, it does not generate the same partial plan several times in different parts of the search space.

Algorithm 2.5 PSP, plan-space planning.

$PSP(\Sigma, \pi)$
  loop
    if $Flaws(\pi) = \varnothing$ then return π
    arbitrarily select $f \in Flaws(\pi)$ (i)
    $R \leftarrow \{$all feasible resolvers for $f\}$
    if $R = \varnothing$ then return failure
    nondeterministically choose $\rho \in R$ (ii)
    $\pi \leftarrow \rho(\pi)$
  return π

---

nodes containing two *dummy actions* that PSP uses to represent the initial state and goal:

- $V = \{v_0, v_g\}$ and $E = \{(v_0, v_g)\}$,
- $act(v_0)$ is a dummy action a_0 that has $pre(a_0) = \varnothing$ and $eff(a_0) = s_0$.
- $act(v_g)$ is a dummy action a_g that has $pre(a_g) = g$ and $eff(a_g) = \varnothing$.
- $C = \varnothing$, that is, there are not (yet) any constraints.

The reason for calling a_0 and a_g "dummy actions" is that they look syntactically like actions but are not instances of action templates in $\mathcal{A}$. Their sole purpose is to represent s_0 and g in a way that is easy for PSP to work with.

PSP repeatedly makes feasible refinements to π in an effort to produce a partially ordered solution for P. PSP does this by finding *flaws* (things that prevent π from being a solution to P) and for each flaw applying a *resolver* (a refinement that removes the flaw).

In PSP, $Flaws(\pi)$ is the set of all flaws in π. There are two kinds of flaws: open goals and threats. These and their resolvers are described next.

Open goals. If a node $v \in V$ has a precondition $p \in pre(act(v))$ for which there is no causal link, then p is an *open goal*. There are two kinds of resolvers for this flaw:

- *Establish p using an action in π.* Let v' be any node of π such that $v \nprec v'$. If $act(v)$ has an effect e that can be *unified* with p (i.e., made syntactically identical to p by instantiating variables), then the following refinement is a resolver for p: instantiate variables if necessary to unify p and e; add a causal link $v' \overset{e'}{\dashrightarrow} v$ (where e' is the unified expression); and add (v', v) to E unless $v' \prec v$ already.
- *Establish p by adding a new action.* Let a' be a *standardization* of an action template $a \in \mathcal{A}$ (i.e., a' is a partially instantiated action produced by renaming the variables in a to prevent name conflicts with the variables already in π). If $eff(a')$ has an effect e that can be unified with p, then the following refinement is a resolver for p: add a new node v' to V; add (v', a') to act; instantiate variables if necessary to unify p and e; add a causal link $v' \overset{e'}{\dashrightarrow} v$; make $v_0 \prec v'$ by adding (v_0, v') to E; and add (v', v) to E.

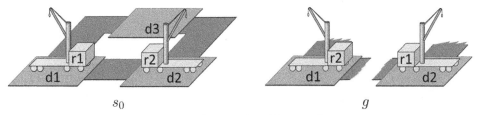

Figure 2.9. Initial state and goal for Example 2.32.

Threats. Let $v_1 \xrightarrow{x=b} v_2$ be any causal link in π, and $v_3 \in V$ be any node such that $v_2 \not\prec v_3$ and $v_3 \not\prec v_1$ (hence it is possible for v_3 to come between v_1 and v_2). Suppose $act(v_3)$ has an effect $y \leftarrow w$ that is *unifiable* with x, that is, π has an *instance* (here we extend Definition 2.9 to plans) in which both x and y are the same state variable). Then v_3 is a *threat* to the causal link. There are three kinds of resolvers for such a threat:

- Make $v_3 \prec v_1$, by adding (v_3, v_1) to E.
- Make $v_2 \prec v_3$, by adding (v_2, v_3) to E.
- Prevent x and y from unifying, by adding to C an inequality constraint on their parameters.

Example 2.32. Figure 2.9 shows the initial state and goal for a simple planning problem in which there are two robots and three loading docks, that is, $B = Robots \cup Docks$, where $Robots = \{r1, r2\}$ and $Docks = \{d1, d2, d3\}$. There are no rigid relations. There is one action template,

$$\begin{aligned} &\text{move}(r, d, d') \\ &\quad \text{pre: } \text{loc}(r) = d, \text{occupied}(d') = F \\ &\quad \text{eff: } \text{loc}(r) \leftarrow d', \end{aligned}$$

where $r \in Robots$ and $d, d' \in Docks$. The initial state and the goal (see Figure 2.9) are

$$s_0 = \{\text{loc}(r1) = d1, \text{loc}(r2) = d2, \text{occupied}(d1) = T,$$
$$\text{occupied}(d2) = T, \text{occupied}(d3) = F\};$$
$$g = \{\text{loc}(r1) = d2, \text{loc}(r2) = d1\}.$$

Figure 2.10 shows the initial partial plan, and Figures 2.11 through 2.14 show successive snapshots of one of PSP's nondeterministic execution traces. Each action's preconditions are written above the action, and the effects are written below the action. Solid arrows represent edges in E, dashed arrows represent causal links, and dot-dashed arrows represent threats. The captions describe the refinements and how they affect the plan. □

2.5.3 Search Heuristics

Several of the choices that PSP must make during its search are very similar to the choices that a backtracking search algorithm makes to solve constraint-satisfaction

Figure 2.10. The initial partial plan contains dummy actions a_0 and a_g that represent s_0 and g. There are two flaws: a_g's two preconditions are open goals.

problems (CSPs); for example, see [517]. Consequently, some of the heuristics for guiding CSP algorithms can be translated into analogous heuristics for guiding PSP. For example:

- Flaw selection (line (i) of PSP) is not a nondeterministic choice, because all of the flaws must eventually be resolved, but the order in which PSP selects the flaws can affect the size of the search space generated by PSP's nondeterministic choices in line (ii). Flaw selection is analogous to variable ordering in CSPs, and the Minimum Remaining Values heuristic for CSPs (choose the variable with the fewest remaining values) is analogous to a PSP heuristic called Fewest Alternatives First: select the flaw with the fewest resolvers.
- Resolver selection (line (ii) of PSP) is analogous to value ordering in CSPs. The Least Constraining Value heuristic for CSPs (choose the value that rules out the fewest values for the other variables) translates into the following PSP heuristic: choose the resolver that rules out the fewest resolvers for the other flaws.

  The preceding heuristic ignores an important difference between plan-space planning and CSPs. Ordinarily, the number of variables in a CSP is fixed in advance, hence the search tree is finite and all solutions are at exactly the same depth. If one of PSP's resolvers introduces a new action that has n new preconditions to achieve, this is like introducing n new variables (and a number of new constraints) into a CSP, which could make the CSP much harder to solve.

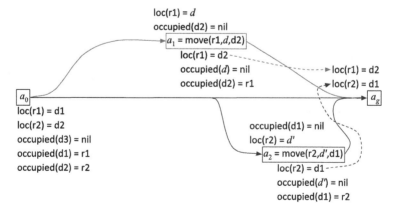

Figure 2.11. Resolving a_g's open-goal flaws. For one of them, PSP adds a_1 and a causal link. For the other, PSP adds a_2 and another causal link.

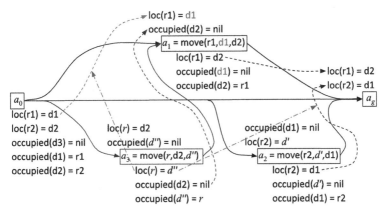

Figure 2.12. Resolving a_1's open-goal flaws. For one of them, PSP substitutes d1 for d (which also resolves a_1's free-variable flaw) and adds a causal link from a_0. For the other, PSP adds a_3 and a causal link. The new action a_3 causes two threats (shown as red dashed-dotted lines).

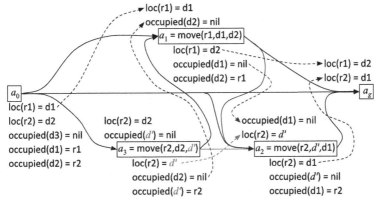

Figure 2.13. Resolving a_2's open-goal flaws. For one of them, PSP substitutes r2 for r and d' for d'' and adds a causal link from a_3. For the other, PSP adds a causal link from a_1. As a side effect, these changes resolve the two threats.

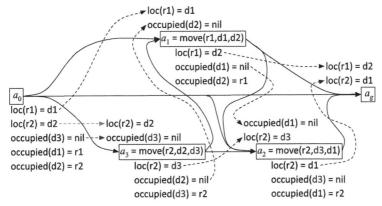

Figure 2.14. Resolving a_3's open-goal flaws. For one of them, PSP adds a causal link. For the other, PSP substitutes d3 for d' and adds a causal link. The resulting partially ordered plan contains no flaws and hence solves the planning problem.

$go(r, l, l')$
  pre: $adjacent(l, l')$, $loc(r) = l$ $take(r, l, o)$
  eff: $loc(r) \leftarrow l'$ pre: $loc(r) = l$, $pos(o) = l$,
                                                            $cargo(r) = nil$
$navigate(r, l, l')$ eff: $pos(o) \leftarrow r$, $cargo(r) \leftarrow o$
  pre: $\neg adjacent(l, l')$, $loc(r) = l$
  eff: $loc(r) \leftarrow l'$

Figure 2.15. Action templates for Example 2.33.

One way of adapting this heuristic to PSP is by first looking for resolvers that do not introduce open goals, and if there are several such resolvers, *then* to choose the one that rules out the fewest resolvers for the other flaws.

Although the preceding heuristics can help speed PSP's search, implementations of PSP tend to run much more slowly than the fastest state-space planners. Generally the latter are GBFS algorithms that are guided by heuristics like the ones in Section 2.3, and there are several impediments to developing an analogous version of PSP. Because plan spaces have no explicit states, the heuristics in Section 2.3 are not directly applicable, nor is it clear how to develop similar plan-space heuristics. Even if such heuristics were available, a depth-first implementation of PSP would be problematic because plan spaces generally are infinite. Consequently, for solving problems like the ones in the International Planning Competitions [291], most automated-planning researchers have abandoned PSP in favor of forward-search algorithms.

On the other hand, some important algorithms for temporal planning (see Chapter 4) are extensions of PSP and are useful for maintaining flexibility of execution in unpredictable environments. An understanding of PSP is useful to provide the necessary background for understanding those algorithms.

2.6 INCORPORATING PLANNING INTO AN ACTOR

We now consider what is needed for actors to utilize the planning algorithms in this chapter. Because it is quite unlikely that the environment will satisfy all of the assumptions in Section 2.1.1, a planning domain will almost never be a fully accurate model of the actor's environment. Hence if a planning algorithm predicts that a plan π will achieve a goal g, this does not ensure that π will achieve g when the actor performs the actions in π.

Example 2.33. To illustrate some of the things that can go wrong, suppose a robot, rbt, is trying to accomplish the task "bring o7 to loc2" near the top of Figure 1.2. To create an abstract plan for this task, suppose rbt calls a planner on a planning problem $P = (\Sigma, s_0, g)$ in which Σ contains the action templates shown in Figure 2.15, and

$$s_0 = \{loc(rbt) = loc3, pos(o7) = loc1, cargo(rbt) = nil\},$$

$$g = \{pos(o7) = loc2\}.$$

The planner will return a solution plan $\pi = \langle a_1, a_2, a_3, a_4, a_5 \rangle$ in which the actions are slightly more detailed versions of the ones near the top of Figure 1.2:

$$a_1 = \text{go(rbt,loc3,hall)}, \quad a_2 = \text{navigate(rbt,hall,loc1)},$$

$$a_3 = \text{take(rbt,loc1,o7)}, \quad a_4 = \text{navigate(rbt,loc1,loc2)},$$

$$a_5 = \text{put(rbt,loc2,o7)}.$$

When rbt tries to perform π, several kinds of problems may occur:

1. *Execution failures.* Suppose rbt's refinement of a_1 involves opening a door, as in Figure 1.2. Then a_1 will succeed if the lower-level actions work correctly or if there is a fixable problem (e.g., rbt's gripper may slip on the doorknob, but rbt may be able to reposition its gripper and continue). However, if there is a problem that rbt cannot fix (e.g., the door is locked or broken), then a_1 will fail, and rbt will need to revise π (e.g., by taking an alternate route to loc1).
2. *Unexpected events.* Suppose that once rbt finishes a_1 and reaches the hallway, someone puts an object o6 onto rbt. Then a_2 is still applicable, but a_3 is not, because rbt can only hold one object at a time. Depending on what o6 is and why it was put there, some possible courses of action might be to remove o6 and then go to loc1, to take o6 to loc1 and remove it there, or to take o6 somewhere else before going to loc1.
3. *Incorrect information.* Suppose that when rbt tries to perform a_2, a navigation error causes it to go to a different location, loc4. To recover, it will need to navigate from loc4 to loc1.
4. *Partial information.* Suppose loc1 is where o7 is normally stored, but rbt cannot observe whether o7 is there except by going there. Because state-variable representations assume that the current state is always fully known, a planner that uses this formalism cannot create a conditional plan such as

    look for o7 in loc1; and if it's not there then look for it in loc4.

    As a work-around, if rbt thinks o7 is likely to be at loc1, then it could include $\text{pos(o7)} = \text{loc1}$ in s_0 when calling the planner. If rbt reaches loc1 and o7 is not there, then rbt could call the planner with another guess for o7's location; and so forth.
    Alternatively, we might want to give rbt a planner that can create conditional plans or policies (see Chapters 5 and 6). But even then, situations can arise in which the planner did not plan for all of the possible contingencies because it did not know they were possible. Thus rbt may still need work-arounds such as that just described. □

Consequently, actors need ways to change their plans when problems are detected. The following section describes some ways to do that.

2.6.1 Repeated Planning and Replanning

Algorithms 2.6 through 2.8 illustrate some ways for an actor to use a planner. In each of them, (Σ, s, g) is a planning problem, and Lookahead is an *online* planning algorithm, that is, a planning algorithm that incorporates modifications (which we discuss in Section 2.6.2) to facilitate interaction between planning and acting. An important consequence of these modifications is that the plan returned by Lookahead is not guaranteed

---

Algorithm 2.6 Run-Lookahead replans before every action.

Run-Lookahead(Σ, g)
    while ($s \leftarrow$ abstraction of observed state ξ) $\not\models g$ do
        $\pi \leftarrow$ Lookahead(Σ, s, g)
        if $\pi = $ failure then return failure
        $a \leftarrow$ pop-first-action(π); perform(a)

---

to solve (Σ, s, g). Ideally we might like it to be at least a *partial* solution, that is, a plan that can be extended to produce a solution—but even that cannot be guaranteed.

Recall from Section 1.3.2 that the planner's initial state s is an abstraction that may differ from the actor's current state ξ. It may omit parts of ξ that are irrelevant for planning and may include hypothesized values of state variables that the actor cannot currently observe, or it may be a hypothetical future state. Similarly, the goal g in Algorithms 2.6–2.8 is for planning purposes and may sometimes differ from what the actor ultimately wants to achieve. For example, it may be a subgoal (see Section 2.6.2).

In each algorithm, pop-first-action removes and returns the first action in π; and perform calls the actor's acting component—which may execute the action if it is a command to the execution platform or else refine it into lower-level actions and commands.

Here are some comparisons among the procedures:

- Run-Lookahead is a simple version of the receding-horizon approach in Figure 1.4. Each time it calls Lookahead, it performs only the first action of the plan that Lookahead returned. This is useful, for example, in unpredictable or dynamic environments in which some of the states are likely to be different from what the planner predicted.

  The biggest disadvantage of Run-Lookahead is that repeatedly waiting for Lookahead may be impractical if Lookahead has a large running time, and may be unnecessary if the action models are known to give very accurate predictions.

- Run-Lazy-Lookahead executes each plan π as far as possible, calling Lookahead again only when π ends or a plan simulator says that π will no longer work properly. This can be useful in environments where it is computationally expensive to call Lookahead and the actions in π are likely to produce the predicted outcomes.

  Simulate is the plan simulator, which may use the planner's prediction function γ or may do a more detailed computation (e.g., a physics-based simulation) that would be too time-consuming for the planner to use. Simulate should return failure if its simulation indicates that π will not work properly – for example, if it finds that an action in π will

---

Algorithm 2.7 Run-Lazy-Lookahead replans only when necessary.

Run-Lazy-Lookahead(Σ, g)
    $s \leftarrow$ abstraction of observed state ξ
    while $s \not\models g$ do
        $\pi \leftarrow$ Lookahead(Σ, s, g)
        if $\pi = $ failure then return failure
        while $\pi \neq \langle\rangle$ and $s \not\models g$ and Simulate(Σ, s, g, π) $\neq$ failure do
            $a \leftarrow$ pop-first-action(π); perform(a)
            $s \leftarrow$ abstraction of observed state ξ

Algorithm 2.8 Run-Concurrent-Lookahead does acting and replanning concurrently.

Run-Concurrent-Lookahead(Σ, g)

$\quad \pi \leftarrow \langle \rangle; \quad s \leftarrow$ abstraction of observed state ξ

$\quad$ thread 1:   // threads 1 and 2 run concurrently

$\quad\quad$ loop

$\quad\quad\quad \pi \leftarrow$ Lookahead(Σ, s, g)

$\quad$ thread 2:

$\quad\quad$ loop

$\quad\quad\quad$ if $s \models g$ then return success

$\quad\quad\quad$ else if $\pi =$ failure then return failure

$\quad\quad\quad$ else if $\pi \neq \langle \rangle$ and Simulate$(\Sigma, s, g, \pi) \neq$ failure then

$\quad\quad\quad\quad a \leftarrow$ pop-first-action(π); perform(a)

$\quad\quad\quad\quad s \leftarrow$ abstraction of observed state ξ

---

have an unsatisfied precondition or if π is supposed to achieve g and the simulation indicates that it will not do so.

The biggest disadvantage of Run-Lazy-Lookahead is that sometimes it can be difficult to predict that replanning is needed without actually doing the replanning to find out. In such cases, Run-Lazy-Lookahead may fail to detect problems until it is too late to fix them easily. For example, in Example 2.33, suppose rbt uses Run-Lazy-Lookahead, and Lookahead returns the partial solution $\langle a_1, a_2 \rangle$. In problem 2 of the example, rbt will take o6 to loc1 without considering whether to leave o6 in the hallway or take it elsewhere.

- Run-Concurrent-Lookahead is a receding-horizon procedure in which the acting and planning processes run concurrently. Each time an action is performed, the action comes from the most recent plan that Lookahead has provided. This avoids Run-Lookahead's problem with waiting for Lookahead to return. Like Run-Lazy-Lookahead, it risks continuing with an old plan in situations where it might be better to wait for a new one, but the risk is lower because the plan is updated more frequently.

The foregoing procedures are not the only possibilities. For example, there are variants of Run-Lazy-Lookahead that maintain information [196] about which actions in π establish the preconditions of other actions in π. This information can be used to detect situations where an action can be removed from π because it is no longer needed, or where a specific part of π needs to be revised.

2.6.2 Online Planning

Most of the planning algorithms earlier in this chapter were designed to run off-line. We now discuss how to adapt them for use with the acting procedures in Section 2.6.1, which need to interact with planners that run online. The biggest issue is that the planning algorithms were designed to find plans that (according to the planner's domain model) are complete (and in some cases, optimal) solutions to the planning problem. In online planning, the actor may need to start acting before such a plan can be found.

Most of the planning algorithms presented earlier – especially the ones that use forward search – can be modified to end their search early and return the best "partial solution" that they have found, and we now discuss several techniques for how to do that.

The term *partial solution* is somewhat misleading because there is no guarantee that the plan will actually lead to a goal. But neither can we guarantee that an actor will reach the goal if it uses a purported "complete solution plan." As we discussed in Section 2.6.1, acting procedures may need to deal with a variety of problems that were not in the planner's domain model.

Subgoaling. In each of the algorithms in the previous section, the goal g' given to the planner does not have to be the actor's ultimate goal g; instead it may be a subgoal. If g' is a subgoal, then once it has been achieved, the actor may formulate its next subgoal and ask the planner to solve it.

How to formulate these subgoals is somewhat problematic, but one can imagine several possible techniques. The elements of a compound goal $g = \{g_1, \ldots, g_k\}$ could be used as subgoals, if one can decide on a reasonable order in which to try to achieve them. Another possibility may be to compute an ordered set of landmarks and choose the earliest one as a subgoal.

In practical applications, g' usually is selected in a domain-specific manner. For example, subgoaling with short-term objectives such as "get to shelter" is used to plan actions for the computerized opponents in *Killzone 2*, a "first-person shooter" video game [585, 113]. The acting algorithm is similar to Run-Concurrent-Lookahead, and the planner is similar to the SeRPE algorithm that we discuss in Chapter 3. The actor runs the planner several times per second, and the planner generates plans that are typically about four or five actions long. The main purpose of the planner is to generate credible humanlike actions for the computerized opponents, and it would not work well to do more elaborate planning because the current state changes quickly as the game progresses.

Limited-horizon planning. Recall that in the receding-horizon technique, the interaction between the actor and planner is as depicted in Figure 1.4. Each time the actor calls Lookahead, the planner starts at the current state and searches until it either reaches a goal or exceeds some kind of limit, and then it returns the best solution or partial solution it has found. Several of the algorithms in this section can easily be modified to do that. Following are some examples.

We can modify A* (Section 2.2.5) to return if the least costly node in *Frontier* has a cost that exceeds a limit $c_{\max}$, by putting the following step immediately after line (i) of Algorithm 2.2:

$$\text{if } \cost(\pi) + h(s) > c_{\max}, \text{ then return } \pi$$

Here is a modified version of IDS (Section 2.2.8) that uses a depth limit, $k_{\max}$:

> for $k = 1$ to $k_{\max}$:
>   do a depth-first search, backtracking at every node of depth
> k, and keeping track of which node $v = (\pi, s)$ at depth k
>   has the lowest value $f(v)$
>   if the search finds a solution, then return it
>   return π

Both A* and IDS can also be modified to use a time limit, by having them throw an exception when time runs out. When the exception is thrown, IDS would return the plan π mentioned in the preceding pseudocode, and A* would return the plan found in the node $v = (\pi, s) \in$ *Frontier* that minimizes $f(v)$.

Sampling. In a *sampling* search, the planner uses a modified version of hill-climbing (see Section 2.2.3) in which the node selection is randomized. The choice can be purely random, or it can be weighted toward the actions in *Actions* that produce the best values for $h(\gamma(s, a))$, using techniques similar to the ones that we describe later in Section 6.4.4. The modified algorithm could do this several times to generate multiple solutions and either return the one that looks best or return the n best solutions so that the actor can evaluate them further. Such a technique is used in the UCT algorithm (Algorithm 6.20) in Chapter 6.

2.7 DISCUSSION AND HISTORICAL REMARKS

2.7.1 Classical Domain Models

Classical representations. Problem representations based on state variables have long been used in control-system design [244, 528, 161] and operations research [559, 4, 285], but their use in automated-planning research came much later [29, 31, 215]. Instead, most automated-planning research has used representation and reasoning techniques derived from mathematical logic. This began with the early work on GPS [451] and the situation calculus [413] and continued with the STRIPS planning system [197] and the widely used *classical*[18] representations [460, 472, 384, 230, 517].

In a classical representation, all atoms have the same syntax as our rigid relations. Each state s is represented as the set of all atoms that are true in s, hence any atom not in this set is false in s. Each *planning operator* (the classical counterpart of an action template) has preconditions and effects that are literals.

Example 2.34. Here is a classical representation of s_0 in Equation 2.4:

$$s_0 = \{\text{loc}(r_1, d_1), \quad \text{loc}(r_2, d_2),$$
$$\text{occupied}(d_1), \text{occupied}(d_2),$$
$$\text{pile}(c_1, p_1), \quad \text{pile}(c_2, p_1), \quad \text{pile}(c_3, p_2),$$
$$\text{pos}(c_1, c_2), \quad \text{pos}(c_2, \text{nil}), \quad \text{pos}(c_3, \text{nil}),$$
$$\text{top}(p_1, c_1), \quad \text{top}(p_2, c_3), \quad \text{top}(p_3, \text{nil})\}.$$

Here is a classical planning operator corresponding to the load action template in Example 2.12:

$$\text{load}(r, c, c', p, d)$$
$$\text{pre: } \text{at}(p, d), \neg\text{cargo}(r), \text{loc}(r, d), \text{pos}(c, c'), \text{top}(p, c)$$
$$\text{eff: } \text{cargo}(r), \neg\text{pile}(c, p), \text{pile}(c, \text{nil}), \neg\text{pos}(c, c'), \text{pos}(c, r),$$
$$\neg\text{top}(p, c), \text{top}(p, c') \qquad\qquad \square$$

---

[18] These are also called *STRIPS* representations but are somewhat simpler than the representation used in the STRIPS planner [197].

The well-known PDDL planning language ([204, 216]) is based on a classical representation but incorporates a large number of extensions.

Classical planning domains can be translated to state-variable planning domains, and vice versa, with at most a linear increase in size:

- Translating a classical planning operator into an action template involves converting each logical atom $p(t_1, \ldots, t_n)$ into a Boolean-valued state variable $x_p(t_1, \ldots, t_n)$. This can be done by replacing each negative literal $\neg p(t_1, \ldots, t_n)$ with $x_p(t_1, \ldots, t_n) = \mathsf{F}$, and each positive literal $p(t_1, \ldots, t_n)$ with $x_p(t_1, \ldots, t_n) = \mathsf{T}$. This produces an action template that has the same numbers of parameters, preconditions, and effects as the classical operator.

- Translating an action template α into a classical planning operator involves converting each state-variable $x(t_1, \ldots, t_n)$ into a set of logical atoms

$$\{p_x(t_1, \ldots, t_n, v) \mid v \in \text{Range}(x(t_1, \ldots, t_n)\}.$$

The conversion can be done as follows. For each expression $x(t_1, \ldots, t_n) = v$ or $x(t_1, \ldots, t_n) \neq v$ in α's preconditions, replace it with $p_x(t_1, \ldots, t_n, v)$ or $\neg p_x(t_1, \ldots, t_n, v)$, respectively. For each expression $x(t_1, \ldots, t_n) \leftarrow v'$ in α's effects, replace it with $p_x(t_1, \ldots, t_n, v')$, and also do the following. If α's preconditions include $p_x(t_1, \ldots, t_n, v)$ for some v, then add to α a new effect $\neg p_x(t_1, \ldots, t_n, v)$. Otherwise, add to α a new parameter u, a new precondition $p_x(t_1, \ldots, t_n, u)$, and a new effect $\neg p_x(t_1, \ldots, x_n, u)$.

Note that the planning operator may have twice as many effects and parameters as the action template. The reason is that each state variable $x(t_1, \ldots, t_n)$ has only one value at a time, so the planning operator must ensure that $p_x(t_1, \ldots, t_n, v)$ is true for only one v at a time. In the state-variable representation, this happens automatically; but in the classical representation, asserting a new value requires explicitly deleting the old one.

The classical and state-variable representation schemes are EXPSPACE-equivalent [182, 230]. In both of them, the time needed to solve a classical planning problem may be exponential in the size of the problem description. We emphasize, however, that this is a *worst-case* result; most classical planning problems are considerably easier.

Ground representations. A classical representation is *ground* if it contains no unground atoms. With this restriction, the planning operators have no parameters; hence each planning operator represents just a single action. Ground classical representations usually are called *propositional* representations [105] because the ground atoms can be rewritten as propositional variables.

Every classical representation can be translated into an equivalent propositional representation by replacing each planning operator with all of its ground instances (i.e., all of the actions that it represents), but this incurs a combinatorial explosion in the size of the representation. For the load operator in Example 2.34, if r, c, p, and d are the numbers of robots, containers, piles, and locations, then the the number of load actions represented by the operator is rc^2pd.

More generally, if a planning operator has p parameters and each parameter has v possible values, then there are v^p ground instances. Each of them must be written explicitly, so the ground classical representation is larger by a multiplicative factor of v^p.

A *ground state-variable representation* is one in which all of the state variables are ground. Each ground state variable can be rewritten as a state variable that has no arguments (like an ordinary mathematical variable) [31, 267, 510]. Every state-variable representation can be translated into an equivalent ground state-variable representation, with a combinatorial explosion like the one in the classical-to-propositional conversion. If an action template has p parameters and each parameter has v possible values, then the ground representation is larger by a factor of v^p.

The propositional and ground state-variable representation schemes are both PSPACE-equivalent [104, 30]. They can represent exactly the same set of planning problems as classical and state-variable representations; but as we just discussed, they may require exponentially more space to do so. This lowers the complexity class because computational complexity is expressed as a function of the size of the input.

In a previous work [230, Section 2.5.4], we claimed that propositional and ground state-variable representations could each be converted into the other with at most a linear increase in size, but that claim was only partially correct. Propositional actions can be converted to state-variable actions with at most a linear increase in size, using a procedure similar to the one we used to convert planning operators to action templates. For converting in the reverse direction, the worst-case size increase is polynomial but superlinear.[19]

The literature contains several examples of cases in which the problem representation and the computation of heuristic functions can be done more easily with state variables than with propositions [268, 510]. Helmert [267, Section 1.3] advances a number of arguments for considering ground state-variable representations superior to propositional representations.

2.7.2 Generalized Domain Models

The state-variable representation in Section 2.1 can be generalized to let states be arbitrary data structures, and an action template's preconditions, effects, and cost be arbitrary computable functions operating on those data structures. Analogous generalizations can be made to the classical representation by allowing a predicate's arguments to be functional terms whose values are calculated procedurally rather than inferred logically (see Fox and Long [204]). Such generalizations can make the domain models applicable to a much larger variety of application domains.

With the preceding modifications, the forward-search algorithms in Section 2.2 will still work correctly [460, 357, 287], but they will not be able to use the domain-independent heuristic functions in Section 2.3, because those heuristics work by

---

[19] We believe it is a multiplicative factor between $\lg v$ and v, where v is the maximum size of any state variable's range. The lower bound follows from the observation that if there are n state variables, then representing the states may require $n \lg v$ propositions, with commensurate increases in the size of the planning operators. The upper bound follows from the existence of a conversion procedure that replaces each action's effect $x(c_1, \ldots, c_n) \leftarrow d$ with the following set of literals:

$$\{p_x(c_1, \ldots, c_n, d)\} \cup \{\neg x(c_1, \ldots, c_n, d') \mid d' \in \text{Range}(x(c_1, \ldots, c_n)) \setminus \{d\}\}.$$

manipulating the syntactic elements of state-variable and classical representations. Instead, domain-specific heuristic functions will be needed.

One way to generalize the action model while still allowing the use of domain-independent heuristics is to write each action as a combination of two parts – a "classical" part that uses a classical or state-variable representation and a "nonclassical" part that uses some other kind of representation – and write separate algorithms to reason about the classical and nonclassical parts. Ivankovic et al. [295] coordinate the two parts in a manner somewhat like planning with abstraction (see Section 2.7.6). Gregory et al. [246] use a "planning modulo theories" approach that builds on recent work on SAT modulo theories [456, 41].

The action models in Section 2.1.3 can also be generalized in several other ways, for example, to explicitly model the actions' time requirements or to model uncertainty about the possible outcomes. Such generalizations are discussed in Chapters 4, 5, and 6.

2.7.3 Heuristic Search Algorithms

Heuristic functions that estimated the distance to the goal were first developed in the mid-1960s [450, 387, 160], and the A* algorithm was developed a few years later by Hart et al. [255, 256]. A huge amount of subsequent work has been done on A* and other heuristic search algorithms. Nilsson [460] and Russell and Norvig [517][20] give tutorial introductions to some of these algorithms, and Pearl [467] provides a comprehensive analysis of a large number of algorithms and techniques. Our definition of problem relaxation in Section 2.3 is based on Pearl's.

Branch-and-bound algorithms have been widely used in combinatorial optimization problems [373, 33, 425, 508]. DFBB (Section 2.2.6) is the best-known version, but most forward-search algorithms (including, e.g., A*) can be formulated as special cases of branch-and-bound [290, 356, 447].

Although some related ideas were explored much earlier by Pohl [491], the first version of GBFS that we know of is the algorithm that Russell and Norvig [517] called "greedy search." We believe the name "greedy best-first search" was coined by Bonet and Geffner [82].

Computer programs for games such as chess and checkers typically use an acting procedure similar to Run-Lookahead (Algorithm 2.8). In these programs, the Lookahead subroutine is similar to the time-limited version of depth-first iterative deepening in Section 2.6.2, except that the depth-first search is the well-known alpha-beta algorithm [338, 460, 517].

The IDA* algorithm in Section 2.2.8 is attributable to Korf [351]. Iterative-deepening algorithms are a special case of *node-regeneration* algorithms that retract nodes to save space and regenerate them later if they need to examine them again. There are several other search algorithms (e.g., the RBFS algorithm [353]) that do

---

[20] The version of A* in Russell and Norvig [517] does not guarantee optimality unless h is monotone (see Section 2.2.5) because of a subtle flaw in its pruning rule.

node regeneration in one way or another. Zhang [625] provides a survey of such algorithms.

2.7.4 Planning Graphs

A *planning graph* is similar to H^{FF}'s relaxed planning graphs (see Figures 2.7 and 2.8), but it also includes various *mutex* (i.e., mutual exclusion) conditions: for example, two actions are mutex if they change the same state variable to different values. Rather than including all r-applicable actions, each A_k only includes the ones whose preconditions are not mutex in $\hat{s}_k$. Weld [598] gives a good tutorial account of this.

Planning graphs were first used in Blum and Furst's GraphPlan algorithm [74]. Graphplan does an iterative-deepening search to generate successively larger r-states. For each r-state $\hat{s}_k$ such that the atoms of g are non-mutex in $\hat{s}_k$, GraphPlan uses a backward-search backtracking algorithm to look for a relaxed solution π such that the actions in each $\hat{a}_i$ are non-mutex. Such a π is often called a *parallel plan* or *layered plan*, and it is a partially ordered solution (although not necessarily an optimal one).

It can be proven that if a planning problem P has a solution, then a sufficiently large planning graph will contain a solution to P. Hence Graphplan is complete. Furthermore, because GraphPlan's backward search is restricted to the planning graph, it usually can solve classical planning problems much faster than planners based on Backward-search or PSP [598].

GraphPlan inspired a large amount of follow-up research on planning-graph techniques. These can be classified roughly as follows. Some of them extend planning graphs in various nonclassical directions, such as conformant planning [548], sensing [600], temporal planning [549, 221, 395], resources [340, 341, 556], probabilities [73], soft constraints [422], and distributed planning [296].

Others modify the planning-graph techniques to obtain improved performance on classical-planning problems. Kautz and Selman's BlackBox planner [323] translates a planning graph into a satisfiability problem and searches for a solution using a satisfiability solver. Long and Fox's STAN [393] uses a combination of efficient planning-graph implementation and domain analysis. Gerevini and Serina's LPG [225] does a stochastic local search on a network of the actions in the planning graph.

2.7.5 Converting Planning Problems into Other Problems

Earlier we mentioned BlackBox's technique of translating a planning graph into a satisfiability problem. Blackbox can also be configured so that it instead will translate the planning problem itself into a satisfiability problem [321]. The basic idea is, for $n = 1, 2 \ldots$, to take the problem of finding a plan of length n, rewrite it as a satisfiability formula f_n, and try to solve f_n. If the planning problem is solvable, then f_n will be solvable for sufficiently large n.

Some related approaches involve translating the planning graph into a constraint-satisfaction problem [45] and translating a network-flow representation of the planning problem into an integer programming problem [571, 572]. Nareyek et al. [443] give an overview of such techniques.

2.7.6 Planning with Abstraction

Planning with abstraction refers not to the kind of abstraction described in Chapter 1, but instead to a relaxation process in which an *abstract* planning problem $P' = (\Sigma', s_0', g')$ is formed from a classical planning problem $P = (\Sigma, s_0, g)$ by removing some of the atoms (and any literals that contain those atoms) from P [519, 335, 333, 616, 235]. If a planner finds a solution $\pi' = \langle a_1', \ldots, a_n' \rangle$ for P', then π' can be used to constrain the search for a solution to P. The idea is to look for solutions $\pi_0, \pi_1, \ldots, \pi_n$, respectively, for the following sequence of planning problems, in which each a_i is the action whose abstraction is a_i':

$$P_0 = (\Sigma, s_0, \text{pre}(a_1));$$

$$P_1 = (\Sigma, s_1, \text{pre}(a_2)), \text{ where } s_1 = \gamma(s_0, \pi_0);$$

$$\ldots;$$

$$P_{n-1} = (\Sigma, s_{n-1}, \text{pre}(a_n)), \text{ where } s_{n-1} = \gamma(s_{n-2}, \pi_{n-2});$$

$$P_n = (\Sigma, s_n, g), \text{ where } s_n = \gamma(s_{n-1}, \pi_{n-1}).$$

If a condition called the *downward refinement property* [616, 402, 403] is satisfied, then $\pi_1, \ldots, \pi_n$ will exist and their concatenation will be a solution for P.

Planning with abstraction typically is done at multiple levels. To constrain the search for a solution to P', one can first create and solve an abstraction P'' of P'; to constrain the search for a solution to P'', one can first create and solve an abstraction P''' of P''; and so forth.

An important characteristic of this approach is that in an abstraction of a planning problem P, each state or action represents an equivalence class of states or actions in P. Earlier, these equivalence classes were induced by the removal of atoms, but there are other ways to create equivalence classes with analogous properties and use them for planning with abstraction [402, 403].

There are many cases in which it is not possible to satisfy the downward refinement property mentioned earlier, whence planning with abstraction is not guaranteed to work. However, abstracted planning problems can also be used to provide heuristic functions to guide the search for a solution to the unabstracted problem (see *abstraction heuristics* in Section 2.7.9).

2.7.7 HTN Planning

In some planning domains, we may want the planner to use a set of recipes or "standard operating procedures" for accomplishing some task. For example, if we want to move container c_1 from dock d_1 to dock d_2, then we might want to specify that the proper way to accomplish this task is as follows:

Have a robot r go to d_1, pick up c_1, and then go to d_2.

Such recipes can be written as *HTN methods*; see Section 3.5.2 for details.

The expressive power of HTN methods can be useful for developing practical applications [603, 444, 382], and a good set of methods can enable an HTN planner to perform well on benchmark problems [394]. A drawback of this approach is that it requires the domain author to write and debug a potentially complex set of domain-specific recipes [308]. However, research is being done on techniques for aiding this process (see Section 7.3.3).

2.7.8 Temporal Logic

Search-control rules written in temporal logic [28, 367] can be used to describe constraints that must be satisfied by the sequence of states that a plan will generate. As an example, we discuss *linear temporal logic* (LTL) [178, 106], a modal logic that extends first-order logic [535] and can be used to reason about the sequences of states that a state-transition system might go through.

LTL formulas may include four modal operators X, F, G, and U (for "neXt," "Future," "Globally," and "Until"). These operators refer to properties of an infinite sequence of states $M_i = \langle s_i, s_{i+1}, \ldots \rangle$. Here are the possible forms an LTL formula ϕ might have, and the conditions under which M_i satisfies ϕ:

- If ϕ is a statement in first-order logic, then $M_i \models \phi$ if $s_i \models \phi$.
- If ϕ has the form X ψ where ψ is an LTL formula, then $M_i \models \phi$ if $M_{i+1} \models \psi$.
- If ϕ has the form F ψ where ψ is an LTL formula, then $M_i \models \phi$ if there is a $j \geq i$ such that $M_j \models \psi$.
- If ϕ has the form G ψ where ψ is an LTL formula, then $M_i \models \phi$ if for every $j \geq i$, $M_j \models \psi$.
- If ϕ has the form ψ_1 U ψ_2 where ψ_1 and ψ_2 are LTL formulas, then $M_i \models \phi$ if there is a $k \geq i$ such that $M_k \models \psi_2$ and $M_j \models \psi_1$ for $i \leq j < k$.

As in the HTN example earlier, suppose we want a robot r to move container c_1 from dock d_1 to dock d_2. Then we might want to specify the following restriction on r's behavior:

r should not leave d_1 without first picking up c_1, and r should not put c_1 down until it reaches d_1.

If we represent states and actions using the classical representation in Example 2.34, we can write that restriction as the following LTL formula:

$$G[\text{at}(r, d_1) \Rightarrow (\text{at}(r, d_1) \cup \text{pos}(c_1, r))]$$

$$\wedge G[\text{pos}(c_1, r) \Rightarrow (\text{pos}(c_1, r) \cup \text{at}(r, d_2))]$$

Such a formula can be used as a search-control rule in a forward-search algorithm similar to the ones in Section 2.2, with modifications to make the algorithm backtrack whenever the current plan π produces a sequence of states such that $\widehat{\gamma}(s_0, \pi)$ does not satisfy the formula.

One domain-independent planner that works this way is TLPlan [28, 367]. Another that uses a different kind of temporal logic is TALplanner [156, 155]. In addition, LTL has become popular for motion planning in robotics [69, 611, 314].

The benefits and drawbacks of this approach are similar to the ones that we stated earlier for HTN planning. On one hand, a good set of control rules can enable an temporal-logic planner to perform well [394], and the expressive power of the control rules can be important in practical applications [157]. On the other hand, the domain author must write and debug a potentially complex set domain-specific information [308], but research is being done on techniques to aid this process (see Section 7.3.3).

2.7.9 Domain-Independent Planning Heuristics

For many years, it was tacitly assumed that good heuristic functions were necessarily domain-specific. This notion was disproven when the domain-independent h^{add} and h^{max} heuristics in Section 2.3.1 were developed by Bonet and Geffner [82] for use in their HSP planning system. HSP's excellent performance in the 1998 planning competition [416] sparked a large amount of subsequent research on domain-independent planning heuristics. Most of them can be classified roughly as delete-relaxation heuristics, landmark heuristics, critical-path heuristics, and abstraction heuristics [269]. We discuss each of these classes next.

Delete-Relaxation Heuristics

Delete-relaxation and the h^+ and h^{FF} heuristics (see Section 2.3.2) were pioneered primarily by Hoffmann [276, 280], and the name of the h^{FF} heuristic comes from its use in the FF planning system [278]. Delete-relaxation can also be used to describe the h^{add} and h^{max} heuristics in Section 2.3.1; h^{max} is the optimal parallel solution (see Section 2.7.4) for the delete-relaxed problem [270, 68].

Helmert's [266, 267] *causal graph* heuristic involves analyzing the planning domain's causal structure using a directed graph whose nodes are all of the state variables in the planning domain, and whose edges represent dependencies among the state variables. Although it is not immediately obvious that this is a delete-relaxation heuristic, a delete-relaxation heuristic h^{cea} has been developed that includes both the causal graph heuristic and h^{add} as special cases [270].

Landmark Heuristics

The early work on landmarks by Porteous, Sebastia, and Hoffmann [493] has been hugely influential, inspiring a large amount of additional work on the subject. The landmark heuristic that we described in Section 2.3.3 is a relatively simple one, and there are many ways to improve it.

The problem of determining whether a fact is a landmark is PSPACE-complete, and so is the problem of deciding whether one landmark must precede another. Consequently, research on landmark generation has focused on the development of polynomial-time criteria that are sufficient (but not necessary) to guarantee that a fact is a landmark or that one landmark must proceed another. Some of the better-known approaches involve relaxed planning graphs [281], domain transition graphs [509, 510], and hitting sets [90].

Other work on landmarks includes, for example, using them to find optimal solutions to planning problems [316], improving the efficiency of planning by splitting planning problems into subproblems [584], and the development of landmark heuristics for use in temporal planning [317].

Critical-Path Heuristics

There is a set $\{h^m \mid m = 1, 2, \ldots\}$ of heuristic functions based loosely on the notion of critical paths (an important concept in project scheduling). They approximate the cost of achieving a goal g by the cost of achieving the most costly subset of size m [261, 259]. More specifically, for $m = 1, 2, \ldots$, let

$$\Delta_m(s, g) = \begin{cases} 0 & \text{if } s \models g, \\ \min_{a \in Rel(g)} \text{cost}(a) + \Delta_m(s, \gamma^{-1}(g, a)) & \text{if } |g| \leq m, \\ \max_{g' \subseteq g \text{ and } |g'| \leq m} \Delta_m(s, g') & \text{otherwise,} \end{cases}$$

where $Rel(g)$ is the set of all actions that are relevant for g (see Definition 2.27). Then $h^m(s) = \Delta_m(s, g)$. It is easy to show that $h^1 = h^{\max}$.

For each m, the heuristic h^m is admissible; and if we hold m fixed then h^m can be computed in polynomial time in $|A| + \sum_{x \in X} |\text{Range}(x)|$, the number of actions and ground atoms in the planning domain. However, the computational complexity is exponential in m.

Abstraction Heuristics

An *abstraction* of a planning domain Σ is a γ-preserving homomorphism from Σ onto a smaller planning domain Σ'. For each planning problem $P = (\Sigma, s_0, g)$, this defines a corresponding abstraction $P' = (\Sigma', s_0', g')$; and if we let c^* denote the cost of an optimal solution to a planning problem, then it follows that $c^*(P') \leq c^*(P)$. If Σ' is simple enough that we can compute $c^*(P')$ for every planning problem P' in Σ', then the function $h(s) = c^*(\Sigma', s', g')$ is an admissible heuristic for P.

The best-known such abstraction is *pattern database* abstraction, an idea that was originally developed by Culberson and Schaeffer [132] and first used in domain-independent classical planning by Edelkamp [167]. The *pattern* is a subset X' of the state variables in Σ, and the mapping from Σ to Σ' is accomplished by removing all literals with variables that are not in X'. The pattern database is a table (constructed by brute force) that gives $c^*(P')$ for every planning problem P' in Σ'.

One problem is deciding which state variables include in X'; algorithms have been developed to do this automatically [260, 272]. A bigger problem is that the size of the pattern database and the cost of computing each entry, both grow exponentially with the size of X'. This problem can be alleviated [168, 34] using symbolic representation techniques that we discuss in Section 5.4, but it still is generally necessary to keep X' small [273]. Because the database provides no information pertaining to variables not in X', this limits the informedness of h.

An awareness of this limitation has led to research on other kinds of criteria for aggregating sets of states in Σ into individual state in Σ', including merge-and-shrink abstraction [271, 273] and structural-pattern abstraction [319], as well as ways to improve the heuristic's informedness by composing several different abstractions [318].

2.7.10 Plan-Space Planning

The two earliest plan-space planners were NOAH [519] and NONLIN [561], both of which combined plan-space search with HTN task refinement (see Section 3.5.2). Initially plan-space planning was known as *nonlinear* planning, reflecting some debate over whether "linear" planning referred to the structure of the planner's current set of actions (a sequence instead of a partial order) or to its search strategy that addresses one goal after the previous one has been completely solved.

Korf [352] introduced distinctions among problems with fully independent goals, *serializable* goals (where there is an ordering for solving the goals without violating the previously solved ones), and arbitrarily interacting goals.[21] This goal dependence hierarchy was further refined by Barrett and Weld [40], who introduced a planner-dependent notion of *trivially* and *laboriously serializable* goals. According to their analysis, plan-space planners can more often lead to trivially serializable goals that are easily solved.

In a linear sequence of actions, it is trivial to check whether some condition is true or not in some current state. But in a partially ordered and partially instantiated set of actions, it is less easy to verify whether a proposition is true before or after the execution of an action in a partially ordered and partially instantiated set of actions. The so-called *modal truth criterion* (MTC) [114] provided a necessary and sufficient condition for the truth of a proposition at some point in a partial plan π and showed that if π contains actions with conditional effects, then the evaluation of the MTC is NP-hard. This complexity result led to a belief that plan-space planning with extended representation is impractical, which is incorrect because planning does not require a necessary and sufficient truth condition. It only has to enforce a sufficient truth condition, which basically corresponds in PSP to the identification and resolution of flaws, performed in polynomial time. A detailed analysis of the MTC in planning appears in [311].

The SNLP algorithm [411] introduced the concept of a *systematic* search in which a plan-space planner generates each partial plan at most once [306, 336]. We use this concept in Definition 2.30 (see the paragraph after the definition).

The UCPOP planner [472, 38, 599] extended SNLP to handle some extensions to the classical domain representation, including conditional effects and universally quantified effects [469, 470] Several other extensions have also been studied, such as, incomplete information and sensing actions [474, 184, 238] and some kinds of extended goals [601].

Other work related to planning performance has included studies of search control and pruning [223], commitment strategies [423, 424, 622], state space versus plan space [579], and domain features [337].

Kambhampati et al. [312, 310] provide a general formalization that takes into account most of the above issues.

---

[21] For example, Exercise 2.10 in the next section uses a nonserializable planning problem known as the Sussman anomaly [593].

2.7.11 Online Planning

The automated planning literature started very early to address the problems of integrating a planner in the acting loop of an agent. Concomitant to the seminal paper on STRIPS [197], Fikes [196] proposed a program called Planex for monitoring the execution of a plan and revising planning when needed. Numerous contributions followed (e.g., [18, 252, 539, 580, 492, 442, 97]). Problems involving integration of classical planning algorithms (as discussed in this chapter) into the control architecture of specific systems, such as spacecraft, robots, or Web services, have been extensively studied. However, the dominant focus of many contributions has been the integration of planning and *execution* (rather than acting), under an assumption that the plans generated by the planning algorithms were directly executable – an assumption that is often unrealistic. In the next chapter, we return to the integration of planning and acting, with refinement of actions into commands, and ways to react to events.

The receding-horizon technique has been widely used in control theory, specifically in model-predictive control. The survey by Garcia et al. [211] traces its implementation back to the early sixties. The general idea is to use a predictive model to anticipate over a given horizon the response of a system to some control and to select the control such that the response has some desired characteristics. Optimal control seeks a response that optimizes a criterion. The use of these techniques together with task planning has been explored by Dean and Wellman [146].

Subgoaling has been used in the design of several problem-solving and search algorithms (e.g., [371, 352]). In planning, issues such as serializable goals and abstraction hierarchies with interesting properties have been extensively studied (e.g., [39, 334, 616]). Sampling techniques have been developed and are widely used for handling stochastic models of uncertainty and nondeterminism, about which more is said in Chapter 6.

2.8 EXERCISES

2.1. Let $P_1 = (\Sigma, s_0, g_1)$ and $P_2 = (\Sigma, s_0, g_2)$ be two state-variable planning problems with the same planning domain and initial state. Let $\pi_1 = \langle a_1, \ldots, a_n \rangle$ and $\pi_2 = \langle b_1, \ldots, b_n \rangle$ be solutions for P_1 and P_2, respectively. Let $\pi = \langle a_1, b_1, \ldots, a_n, b_n \rangle$.

  (a) If π is applicable in s_0, then is it a solution for P_1? For P_2? Why or why not?

  (b) E_1 be the set of all state variables that are targets of the assignment statements in $\text{eff}(a_1), \ldots, \text{eff}(a_n)$, and E_2 be the set of all state variables that are targets of the assignment statements in $\text{eff}(b_1), \ldots, \text{eff}(b_n)$. If $E_1 \cap E_2 = \varnothing$, then is π applicable in s_0? Why or why not?

  (c) Let P_1 be the set of all state variables that occur in $\text{pre}(a_1), \ldots, \text{pre}(a_n)$, and P_2 be the set of all state variables that occur in the preconditions of $\text{pre}(b_1), \ldots, \text{pre}(b_n)$. If $P_1 \cap P_2 = \varnothing$ and $E_1 \cap E_2 = \varnothing$, then is π applicable in s_0? Is it a solution for P_1? For P_2? Why or why not?

2.2. Let S be the state-variable state space discussed in Example 2.7. Give a set of restrictions such that s is a state of S if and only if it satisfies those restrictions.

2.3. Give a state-variable planning problem P_1 and a solution π_1 for P_1 such that π_1 is minimal but not shortest. Give a state-variable planning problem P_2 and a solution π_2 for P_2 such that π_2 is acyclic but not minimal.

2.4. Under what conditions will GBFS switch to a different path if its current path is not a dead end?

2.5. Let P be any solvable state-variable planning problem.
  (a) Prove that there will always be an execution trace of Forward-search that returns a shortest solution for P.
  (b) Prove that there will always be an execution trace of Backward-search that returns a shortest solution for P.

2.6. What might be an effective way to use h^{add}, h^{max}, h^{FF}, and h^{sl} with Backward-search?

2.7. Figure 2.16 shows a planning problem involving two robots whose actions are controlled by a single actor.
  (a) If we run Forward-search on this problem, how many iterations will the shortest execution traces have, and what plans will they return? For one of them, give the sequence of states and actions chosen in the execution trace.
  (b) If we run Backward-search on this problem, how many iterations will the shortest execution traces have, and what plans will they return? For one of them, give the sequence of goals and actions chosen in the execution trace.
  (c) Compute the values of $h^{add}(s_0)$ and $h^{max}(s_0)$.
  (d) In the H^{FF} algorithm, suppose that instead of exiting the loop at the first value of k such that $\hat{s}_k$ r-satisfies g, we instead keep iterating the loop. At what value of k will $|\hat{s}_k|$ reach its maximum? At what value of k will $|A_k|$ reach its maximum?
  (e) Compute the value of $h^{FF}(s_0)$.
  (f) Compute the value of $h^{sl}(s_0)$.

take(r, l, c)
    pre: $\mathsf{loc}(r) = l$, $\mathsf{pos}(c) = l$,
        $\mathsf{cargo}(r) = \mathsf{nil}$
    eff: $\mathsf{cargo}(r) = c$, $\mathsf{pos}(c) \leftarrow r$

put(r, l, c)
    pre: $\mathsf{loc}(r) = l$, $\mathsf{pos}(c) = r$
    eff: $\mathsf{cargo}(r) \leftarrow \mathsf{nil}$, $\mathsf{pos}(c) \leftarrow l$

move(r, l, m)
    pre: $\mathsf{loc}(r) = l$
    eff: $\mathsf{loc}(r) \leftarrow m$

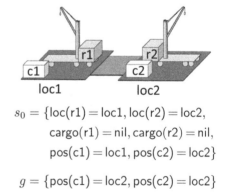

$s_0 = \{\mathsf{loc}(\mathsf{r1}) = \mathsf{loc1}, \mathsf{loc}(\mathsf{r2}) = \mathsf{loc2},$
$\qquad \mathsf{cargo}(\mathsf{r1}) = \mathsf{nil}, \mathsf{cargo}(\mathsf{r2}) = \mathsf{nil},$
$\qquad \mathsf{pos}(\mathsf{c1}) = \mathsf{loc1}, \mathsf{pos}(\mathsf{c2}) = \mathsf{loc2}\}$

$g = \{\mathsf{pos}(\mathsf{c1}) = \mathsf{loc2}, \mathsf{pos}(\mathsf{c2}) = \mathsf{loc2}\}$

(a) action templates   (b) initial state and goal

Figure 2.16. Planning problem for Exercise 2.7. In the action templates, r is a robot, l and m are locations, and c is a container. In this problem, unlike some of our previous examples, both robots may have the same location.

2.8. Here is a state-variable version of the problem of swapping the values of two variables. The set of objects is $B = Variables \cup Numbers$, where $Variables = \{foo, bar, baz\}$, and $Numbers = \{0, 1, 2, 3, 4, 5\}$. There is one action template:

$$\text{assign}(x_1, x_2, n)$$
$$\text{pre: value}(x_2) = n$$
$$\text{eff: value}(x_1) \leftarrow n$$

where $\text{Range}(x_1) = \text{Range}(x_2) = Variables$, and $\text{Range}(n) = Numbers$. The initial state and goal are

$$s_0 = \{\text{value(foo)} = 1, \text{value(bar)} = 5, \text{value(baz)} = 0\};$$

$$g = \{\text{value(foo)} = 5, \text{value(bar)} = 1\}.$$

At s_0, suppose GBFS is trying to choose between the actions $a_1 = \text{assign(baz,foo,1)}$ and $a_2 = \text{assign(foo,bar,5)}$. Let $s_1 = \gamma(s_0, a_1)$ and $s_2 = \gamma(s_0, a_2)$. Compute each pair of heuristic values below, and state whether or not they will produce the best choice.
- **(a)** $h^{\text{add}}(s_1)$ and $h^{\text{add}}(s_2)$.
- **(b)** $h^{\text{max}}(s_1)$ and $h^{\text{max}}(s_2)$.
- **(c)** $h^{\text{FF}}(s_1)$ and $h^{\text{FF}}(s_2)$.
- **(d)** $h^{\text{sl}}(s_1)$ and $h^{\text{sl}}(s_2)$.

2.9. Figure 2.17 shows a partial plan for the variable-swapping problem in Exercise 2.8.
- **(a)** How many threats are there? What are they? What are their resolvers?
- **(b)** Can PSP generate this plan? If so, describe an execution trace that will produce it. If no, explain why not.
- **(c)** In PSP's search space, how many immediate successors does this partial plan have?
- **(d)** How many solution plans can PSP produce from this partial plan?
- **(e)** How many of the preceding solution plans are minimal?
- **(f)** Trace the operation of PSP if we start it with the plan in Figure 2.17. Follow whichever of PSP's execution traces finds the shortest plan.

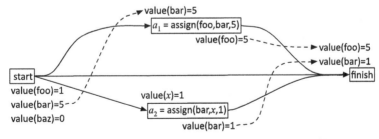

Figure 2.17. Partial plan for swapping the values of two variables.

2.10. *Blocks world* is a well-known classical planning domain in which some children's blocks, *Blocks* = {a, b, c, ...}, are arranged in stacks of varying size on an infinitely large table, table. To move the blocks, there is a robot hand, hand, that can hold at most one block at a time.

pickup(x)
    pre: loc(x) = table, top(x) = nil,
        holding = nil
    eff: loc(x) ← hand, holding ← x

putdown(x)
    pre: holding = x
    eff: loc(x) ← table, holding ← nil

unstack(x, y)
    pre: loc(x) = y, top(x) = nil,
        holding = nil
    eff: loc(x) ← hand, top(y) ← nil,
        holding ← x

stack(x, y)
    pre: holding = x, top(y) = nil
    eff: loc(x) ← y, top(y) ← x,
        holding ← nil

$\text{Range}(x) = \text{Range}(y) = Blocks$

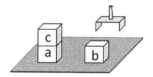

$Objects = Blocks \cup \{\text{hand}, \text{table}, \text{nil}\}$
$Blocks = \{\text{a}, \text{b}, \text{c}\}$

$s_0 = \{\text{top(a)} = \text{c}, \text{top(b)} = \text{nil},$
    $\text{top(c)} = \text{nil}, \text{holding} = \text{nil},$
    $\text{loc(a)} = \text{table}, \text{loc(b)} = \text{table},$
    $\text{loc(c)} = \text{a}\}$

$g = \{\text{loc(a)} = \text{b}, \text{loc(b)} = \text{c}\}$

(a) action templates   (b) objects, initial state, and goal

Figure 2.18. Blocks world planning domain, and a planning problem.

Figure 2.18(a) gives the action templates. For each block x, loc(x) is x's location, which may be table, hand, or another block; and top(x) is the block (if any) that is on x, with top(x) = nil if nothing is on x. Finally, holding tells what block the robot hand is holding, with holding = nil if the hand is empty.

(a) Why are there four action templates rather than just two?

(b) Is the holding state variable really needed? Why or why not?

(c) In the planning problem in Figure 2.18(b), how many states satisfy g?

(d) Give necessary and sufficient conditions for a set of atoms to be a state.

(e) Is every blocks world planning problem solvable? Why or why not?

2.11. Repeat Exercise 2.8 on the planning problem in Figure 2.18(b), with $s_1 = \gamma(s_0, \text{unstack(c,a)})$ and $s_2 = \gamma(s_0, \text{pickup(b)})$.

2.12. Repeat Exercise 2.9 using the planning problem in Figure 2.18(b) and the partial plan shown in Figure 2.19.

2.13. Let π be a partially ordered solution for a planning problem $P = (\Sigma, s_0, g)$.

(a) Write a simple modification of Run-Lazy-Lookahead to execute π.

(b) Suppose your procedure is executing π, and let π' be the part of π that it has not yet executed. Suppose an unanticipated event invalidates some of the total orderings of π' (i.e., not all of them will still achieve g). Write an algorithm to choose a total ordering of π' that still achieves g, if one exists.

2.14. If $\pi = \langle a_1, \ldots, a_n \rangle$ is a solution for a planning problem P, other orderings of the actions in π may also be solutions for P.

(a) Write an algorithm to turn π into a partially ordered solution.

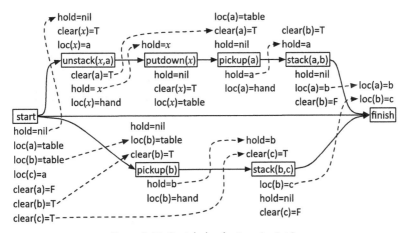

Figure 2.19. Partial plan for Exercise 2.12.

(b) Are there cases in which your algorithm will find a partially ordered solution that PSP will miss? Are there cases in which PSP will find a partially ordered solution that your algorithm will miss? Explain.

2.15. Let P be a planning problem in which the action templates and initial state are as shown in Figure 2.16, and the goal is $g = \{\text{loc}(\text{c1}) = \text{loc2}\}$. In the Run-Lazy-Lookahead algorithm, suppose the call to Lookahead(P) returns the following solution plan:

$$\pi = \{\text{take(r1,loc1,c1), move(r1,loc1,loc2), put(r1,loc2,c1)}\}.$$

(a) Suppose that after the actor has performed take(r1,loc1,c1) and move(r1,loc1,loc2), monitoring reveals that c1 fell off of the robot and is still back at loc1. Tell what will happen, step by step. Assume that Lookahead(P) will always return the best solution for P.

(b) Repeat part (a) using Run-Lookahead.

(c) Suppose that after the actor has performed take(r1,loc1,c1), monitoring reveals that r1's wheels have stopped working, hence r1 cannot move from loc1. What should the actor do to recover? How would you modify Run-Lazy-Lookahead, Run-Lookahead, and Run-Concurrent-Lookahead to accomplish this?

CHAPTER 3

Deliberation with Refinement Methods

Chapter 2 concentrated mostly on planning with descriptive action models. Although it described some ways for an actor to receive guidance from such a planner, it did not describe the operational models that an actor might need to perform the planned actions. In the current chapter, we present a formalism for operational models and describe how to use these models for deliberative acting.

Section 3.1 describes a formalism for operational models based on *refinement methods*. A method specifies how to accomplish a *task* (an abstract activity of some kind) by refining it into other activities that are less abstract. These activities may include other tasks that will need further refinement and commands that can be sent to the execution platform. Section 3.2 describes an acting procedure, RAE, that uses a collection of refinement methods to generate and traverse a refinement tree similar to the one in Figure 1.2. It recursively refines abstract activities into less abstract activities, ultimately producing commands to the execution platform.

If we modify the refinement methods by replacing the commands with descriptive models, the modified methods can also be used for planning. The basic idea is to augment the acting procedure with predictive lookahead of the possible outcome of commands that can be chosen. Section 3.3 describes a planner, SeRPE, that does this. Section 3.4 describes how to integrate such a planner into acting procedures.

Although the formalism in this chapter removes many of the simplifying assumptions that we made in Chapter 2, it still incorporates some assumptions that do not always hold in practical applications. Section 3.5 discusses these and also includes historical remarks.

3.1 OPERATIONAL MODELS

In this section, we present a formalism for operational models of actions and describe how to use these models for deliberative acting. This formalism weakens or removes several of the simplifying assumptions that we made in Section 2.1.1:

- *Dynamic environment.* The environment is not necessarily static. Our operational models deal with exogenous events, that is, events due to other causes than the actor's actions.

- *Imperfect information.* In Section 2.1.1, we assumed that the actor had perfect information about its environment. In reality, it is rare for an actor to be able to know the current value of every state variable and to maintain this knowledge while the world evolves. Operational models often need to deal with what the actor knows or does not know and how to acquire necessary information.

  A convenient notation for handling partial knowledge is to extend the range of every state variable to include a special symbol, unknown, which is the default value of any state variable that has not been set or updated to another value.

- *Overlapping actions.* Actions take time to complete, and multiple actions may proceed simultaneously. To manage an agenda of overlapping activities, the formalism in this chapter includes cases in which actions may proceed simultaneously. However, we will not introduce a formal model of time durations until Chapter 4. For now, facts are not time stamped but simply refer to the current state of the world.[1]

- *Nondeterminism.* An action may have multiple possible outcomes, because of accidents, interfering exogenous events, or sensing and information acquisition. The actor has to systematically observe which outcomes actually occur to respond accordingly. Our operational models provide a way to deal with such observations. However, we will not introduce a formal model of nondeterministic actions and the ability to reason about them until Chapter 5 and Chapter 6.

- *Hierarchy.* Actors are often organized hierarchically, and our operational models provide a way to represent and organize a hierarchical actor's deliberations. However, the formalism still incorporates some simplifying assumptions that do not always hold in practical applications. For example, a hierarchical actor may use different state and action spaces in different parts of the hierarchy (rather than the same ones throughout, as assumed in Section 3.1), and there are several ways in which it may traverse the hierarchy (e.g., in layers, or as a collection of components), rather than using depth-first recursion as described in Section 3.2 and Section 3.3. For further discussion of these issues, see Section 3.5.

- *Discrete and Continuous Variables.* Actors may need to deal with both discrete and continuous variables. The operational model introduced in this chapter allows for state variables whose range can be finite or nonfinite, discrete or continuous. In Section 7.4, we discuss how to reason about hybrid models that allow for both discrete and continuous variables.

3.1.1 Basic Ingredients

We will use a state variable representation similar to the one in Definition 2.6, but with some generalizations. One of them is that if $x \in X$ is a state variable, then Range(x) can be finite or nonfinite, discrete or continuous. State variables ranging over multidimensional domains, such as vectors, matrices and other data structures, are also permitted. For example, we could let coordinates(r1) $\in R^3$ be the current coordinates (in some reference frame) of a robot r1.

Recall from Chapters 1 and 2 that ξ is the actor's currently observed state. A *fact* is any ground atom $x=v$ in ξ. For example, if ξ contains position(door3)=open and

---

[1] This does not preclude the author of a domain model from including a time stamp as an ordinary state variable; other limited capabilities for handling temporal conditions are briefly discussed in Section 3.2.4.

coordinates(r1)=(3.5, 7.61, 1.58), then door3 is currently open, and r1 is at the coordinates (3.5, 7.61, 1.58) in some reference frame.

One way we used state variables in Chapter 2 was to test their values (e.g., in an action's preconditions). We do the same in this chapter, but the tests will be more general. A *simple* test has the form $(x \circ v)$, where $\circ \in \{=, \neq, <, >\}$. A *compound* test is a negation, conjunction, or disjunction of simple and compound tests. Tests are evaluated with respect to the current state ξ. In tests, the symbol unknown is not treated in any special way; it is just one of the state variable's possible values.

As in Chapter 2, a state variable also can be the target of an assignment statement, but here the assignments are more general. An assignment is a statement of the form $x \leftarrow expr$, where *expr* may be any ground value in Range(x), or any expression that returns a ground value in Range(x) without having side effects on the current state. When the assignment is executed, it will update the value of the state variable x to the value that *expr* has in the current state ξ.

Three additional ingredients are needed in this representation:

- *Tasks*: a task is a label naming an activity to be performed. It is of the form task-name(*args*), where task-name designates the task considered and the task arguments *args* is an ordered list of objects and values. A task is refined into subtasks and commands. The actor has to perform external tasks, which are specified by the user or a planner, as well as internal tasks that result from the refinement of other tasks.
- *Events*: an event designates an occurrence detected by the execution platform; it is in the form event-name(*args*). Events are, for example, the activation of an emergency signal or the arrival of a transportation vehicle; they correspond to exogenous changes in the environment to which the actor may have to react.
- *Commands*: a command is the name of a primitive function that can be executed by the execution platform. It is in the form command-name(*args*). When a command is triggered, there is a state variable in ξ, denoted status(*command*) $\in \{$running, done, failed$\}$; it is updated by the platform to express that the execution of that *command* is going on, has terminated or failed.

Example 3.1. Consider a simple domain where a single robot is servicing a harbor navigating in a topological map, searching for a particular container. The objects are *Robots* = {r1}, *Containers* = {c1, c2, ...}, and *Locations* = {loc1, loc2, ...}. The following state variables are kept up-to-date by the robot's execution platform:

- loc(r) $\in$ *Locations* is the current location of robot r.
- load(r) $\in$ *Containers* $\cup$ {nil} indicates whether robot r is carrying a container, and if so then which one.
- pos(c) $\in$ *Locations* $\cup$ *Robots* $\cup$ {unknown} gives a container's position at a location, on a robot, or unknown.
- view(l) $\in$ {T, F} indicates whether the robot has perceived the content of location l. When view(l)=T then for every container c in l, pos(c) $= l$ is a fact in ξ.

The robot's execution platform can execute the following commands:

- move-to(r, l): robot r goes to location l
- take(r, o, l): r takes object o at location l

- put(r, o, l): r puts o in l
- perceive(r, l): r perceives which objects are in a location l

These commands are applicable under some conditions, for example, move-to requires the destination l to be reachable from the current location, and take and put require r to be in l. Upon the completion of a command, the platform updates the corresponding state variables. For example, when perceive(r, l) terminates, view(l)=T and pos(c) $= l$ for every container c in l.   □

3.1.2 Refinement Methods

A refinement method is either a triple (*task, precondition, body*) or a triple (*event, precondition, body*). The first field in a method, either a task or an event, is its *role*; it tells what the method is about. When the *precondition* holds in the current state, the method can be used to address the task or event in its role by running a program given in the method's *body*. This program refines the task or event into a sequence of subtasks, commands, and assignments.

As for actions, refinement methods are specified as parametrized method templates that have one of the following forms:

$$method\text{-}name(arg_1, \ldots, arg_k) \qquad method\text{-}name(arg_1, \ldots, arg_k)$$
$$\text{task: } task\text{-}identifier \qquad\qquad \text{event: } event\text{-}identifier$$
$$\text{pre: } test \qquad\qquad\qquad \text{pre: } test$$
$$\text{body: } program \qquad\qquad\quad \text{body: } program$$

where

- *method-name* is a unique symbol designating the method;
- $arg_1, \ldots, arg_k$ are variables appearing in the method; an applicable instance of a method binds these variables to objects and values;
- *task-identifier* gives the task to which the method is applicable; similarly for an event;
- *test* specifies conditions under which the method may be used;
- *program* is a sequences of steps with the usual control constructs (if-then-else, while, loop, etc.).[2] A step in this sequence is either an assignment, a command to the execution platform or a task that needs further refinement. Assignments and commands are as defined in previous section.

An instance of a method template is given by the substitution of its variables $arg_1, \ldots, arg_k$ by constants. A method whose role matches a current task or event and whose precondition is satisfied by the current values of the state variables in ξ has an applicable current instance. A method may have several applicable instances for the current state, tasks, and events. An applicable instance of a method, if executed, addresses a task or an event by refining it into subtasks, commands, and updates in ξ, as specified in its body.

---

[2] We use informal pseudocode descriptions of the bodies of methods.

3.1.3 Illustrations

Let us illustrate the refinement method representation with a few examples.

Example 3.2. Consider the task for the robot in Example 3.1 to pick up a particular container c. The robot may know the location of c (i.e., this information may be in ξ), in which case the robot goes to that location to take c. Otherwise, the robot will have to look at the locations it can reach until it finds what it is looking for. This is expressed through two tasks, fetch and search, and the following refinement methods:

> m-fetch(r, c)
>   task: fetch(r, c)
>   pre:
>   body: if $pos(c)$ = unknown then search(r, c)
>   else if $loc(r) = pos(c)$ then take$(r, c, pos(c))$
>   else do
>   move-to$(r, pos(c))$
>   take$(r, c, pos(c))$

m-fetch refines the task fetch into a task search when the position of c is unknown; otherwise, it triggers the appropriate take and, if needed, move-to commands to pick up c.

> m-search(r, c)
>   task: search(r, c)
>   pre: $pos(c)$ = unknown
>   body: if $\exists l \in Locations$ such that view$(l) = F$ then do
>   move-to(l)
>   perceive(l)
>   if $pos(c) = l$ then take(r, c, l)
>   else search(r, c)
>   else fail

The method performs a search by going to a location l, the content of which is not yet known, perceiving l; if c is there, the robot takes it; otherwise, the method recursively searches in other locations. If all locations have been perceived, the search task fails.   □

The above example illustrates two *task* refinement methods. Let us provide the robot with a method for reacting to an event.

Example 3.3. Suppose that a robot in the domain of Example 3.1 may have to react to an emergency call by stopping its current activity and going to the location from where the emergency originates. Let us represent this with an event emergency(l, i) where l is the emergency origin location and $i \in N$ is an identification number of this event. We also need an additional state variable: emergency-handling$(r) \in \{T, F\}$ indicates whether the robot r is engaged in handling an emergency.

$$
\begin{aligned}
&\text{m-emergency}(r, l, i) \\
&\quad \text{event: emergency}(l, i) \\
&\qquad \text{pre: emergency-handling}(r) = F \\
&\qquad \text{body: emergency-handling}(r) \leftarrow T \\
&\qquad\qquad \text{if load}(r) \neq \text{nil then put}(r, \text{load}(r)) \\
&\qquad\qquad \text{move-to}(l) \\
&\qquad\qquad \text{address-emergency}(l, i)
\end{aligned}
$$

This method is applicable if robot r is not already engaged in handling an emergency. In that case, the method sets its emergency-handling state variable; it unloads whatever the robot is loaded with, if any; it triggers the command to go the emergency location, then it sets a task for addressing this emergency. Other methods are supposed to switch back emergency-handling(r) when r has finished with the task address-emergency. □

The previous simple examples introduced the representation. Let us now illustrate how refinement methods can be used to handle the more complex tasks discussed in Figure 1.2, such as opening a door. To keep the example readable, we consider a one-arm robot and assume that the door is unlocked (Exercises 3.9 and 3.10 cover other cases).

Example 3.4. Let us endow the robot with methods for opening doors. In addition to the four state variables loc, load, pos, view introduced previously, we need to characterize the opening status of the door and the position of the robot with respect to it. The two following state variables fill that need:

- reachable$(r, o) \in \{T, F\}$: indicates that robot r is within reach of object o, here o is the door handle;
- door-status$(d) \in \{closed, cracked, open, unknown\}$: gives the opening status of door d, a cracked door is unlatched.

Furthermore, the following rigid relations will be used:

- adjacent(l, d): means that location l is adjacent to door d;
- toward-side(l, d): location l is on the "toward" side of door d (i.e., where the door hinges are);
- away-side(l, d): location l is on the "away" side of door d;
- handle(d, o): o is the handle of door d;
- type$(d, rotates)$ or type$(d, slide)$: door d rotates or slides;
- side$(d, left)$ or side$(d, right)$: door d turns or slides to left or to the right respectively with respect to the "toward" side of the door.

The commands needed to open a door are as follows:

- move-close(r, o): robot r moves to a position where reachable$(r, o) = T$;
- move-by(r, λ): r performs a motion of magnitude and direction given by vector λ;
- grasp(r, o): robot r grasps object o;

- ungrasp(r, o): r ungrasps o;
- turn(r, o, α): r turns a grasped object o by angle $\alpha \in [-\pi, +\pi]$;
- pull(r, λ): r pulls its arm by vector λ;
- push(r, λ): r pushes its arm by λ;
- monitor-status(r, d): r focuses its perception to keep door-status updated;
- end-monitor-status(r, d): terminates the monitoring command.

We assume that commands that take absolute parameters stop when an obstacle is detected, for example, turn(r, o, α) stops when the turning reaches a limit for the rotation of o, similarly for move-by.

> m-opendoor(r, d, l, o)
>   task: opendoor(r, d)
>   pre: loc(r) = l $\wedge$ adjacent(l, d) $\wedge$ handle(d, o)
>   body: while $\neg$reachable(r, o) do
>   move-close(r, o)
>   monitor-status(r, d)
>   if door-status(d)=closed then unlatch(r, d)
>   throw-wide(r, d)
>   end-monitor-status(r, d)

m-opendoor is a method for the opendoor task. It moves the robot close to the door handle, unlatches the door if it is closed, then pulls it open while monitoring its status. It has two subtasks: unlatch and throw-wide.

> m1-unlatch(r, d, l, o)
>   task: unlatch(r, d)
>   pre: loc(r, l)$\wedge$ toward-side(l, d)$\wedge$ side(d, left)$\wedge$ type(d, rotate)
> $\wedge$ handle(d, o)
>   body: grasp(r, o)
>   turn(r, o, alpha1)
>   pull(r, val1)
>   if door-status(d)=cracked then ungrasp(r, o)
>   else fail
> m1-throw-wide(r, d, l, o)
>   task: throw-wide(r, d)
>   pre: loc(r, l)$\wedge$ toward-side(l, d)$\wedge$ side(d,left)$\wedge$ type(d, rotate)
> $\wedge$ handle(d, o)$\wedge$ door-status(d)=cracked
>   body: grasp(r, o)
>   pull(r, val1)
>   move-by(r, val2)

The preceding two methods are for doors that open by rotating on a hinge, to the left and toward the robot. Other methods are needed for doors that rotate to the right, doors that rotate away from the robot, and sliding doors (see Exercise 3.7).

The method m1-unlatch grasps the door handle, turns then pulls the handle before ungrasping. The method m1-throw-wide grasps the handle, pulls, then moves backward. Here alpha1 is a positive angle corresponding to the maximum amplitude of the rotation of a door handle (e.g., about 1.5 rad), val1 is a small vector toward the robot (an amplitude of about 0.1 meter), and val2 is a larger vector backward (of about 1 meter). More elaborate methods may, for example, survey the grasping status of whatever the robot is grasping, or turn the handle in the opposite direction before ungrasping it (see Exercise 3.8). □

3.1.4 Updates of the Current State

Recall that ξ is the actual state of the world, not a predicted state. For example, position(door3) gets the value open not when the robot decides to open it but when it actually perceives it to be open. This state variable is said to be *observable*. This does not mean that it is always known; it only means that there are states in which it can be observed. In Examples 3.2 and 3.4, all state variables are observable. The value of some of them can be at some point unknown, for example, pos(c) for containers at location l where view(l)=F. Observable state variables are updated by the execution platform when adequate sensing is performed.

Some state variables represent the deliberation state of the actor. In Example 3.3, the state variable emergency-handling corresponds to a deliberation decision. It is said to be a *computable* state variable. Another illustration of computable state variables is, for example, stable($o,pose$)=T, meaning that object o in some particular *pose* is stable, as a result of some geometric and dynamic computation. Computable state variables are updated by methods when the corresponding decision or computation is performed.

Further, there are state variables that refer to observable properties of the environment that change independently of the actor's activity. For example, when in room1 the robot detects that a person is there. But outside of room1, the robot cannot trust such a fact indefinitely. At some point, it has to consider that the location of that person is unknown unless it can sense it again.

The general problem of maintaining the current state of the world requires complex handling of uncertainty, time, and nonmonotonic reasoning. For example, there is a difference between knowing nothing about the whereabouts of a person and having seen her some time ago in room1. This knowledge erodes with time.

To keep things simple, we assume in this chapter that updates in ξ for observed and computed state variables are timely and exact. Every state variable has a value, possibly unknown. Known values correctly reflect the current state of the actor and its environments.

3.2 A REFINEMENT ACTING ENGINE

Refinement methods provide operational models for how to accomplish a task or react to an event. This section defines a Refinement Acting Engine (RAE), which provides the techniques needed for acting with this representation. RAE is inspired from

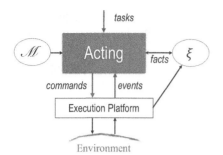

Figure 3.1. A simple architecture for a refinement acting engine.

a programming language and open source software, called OpenPRS, widely used in robotics.[3] RAE is capable of trying alternative methods in nondeterministic choices. Planning techniques for performing informed choices are discussed in the following section.

After a global view, we describe three procedures that implement a simple version of RAE (Section 3.2.2). Some of the possible extensions of that engine are then discussed (Section 3.2.4).

3.2.1 Global View

RAE uses a library of methods $\mathcal{M}$ to address new tasks the actor has to perform and new events it has to react to. The input to RAE consists of (i) a set of *facts* reflecting the current state of the world ξ, (ii) a set of *tasks* to be performed and (iii) a set of *events* corresponding to exogenous occurrences to which the actor may have to react. These three sets change continually. Tasks come from task definition sources, for example, a planner or a user. Events come from the execution platform, for example, through a sensing and event recognition system. Facts come either from the execution platform, as updates of the perceived state of the world, or from RAE, as updates of its own reasoning state.

RAE outputs commands to the execution platform. It gets the platform feedback about the perceived state of the world as updates in its input through new facts and events. Figure 3.1 schematically depicts a simple architecture for RAE that can be viewed as part of a more complete architecture, as in Figure 1.1(a).

Tasks given by the planner or the user, and events sent from the platform, are called *external* (to distinguish them from tasks in refinement methods). They appear in the *input stream* of the engine. RAE repeatedly reads its input stream and addresses an external task or event as soon as it arrives. At some point, there can be several external tasks and events being processed *concurrently*.

To each external task or event τ that RAE reads in its stream, it associates a LIFO stack that keeps track of how the refinement of τ is progressing. There can be several such stacks being concurrently processed. The refinement of τ is done according to a method in $\mathcal{M}$, which may, at some point, lead to a subtask τ' that will be put on top of

---

[3] We depart from the OpenPRS system (https://git.openrobots.org/projects/openprs/wiki) by using a state variable representation and an abstract syntax and by dropping a few nonessential programming facilities.

the stack of τ. This is pursued recursively. A refinement at any level by a method may fail, but other methods may be applicable and are tried.

For each external task or event that RAE is currently processing, it maintains a *refinement stack* that is analogous to the execution stack of a computer program. A refinement stack contains the following items:

- all pending subtasks in which an external task or event is being refined,
- the method currently tried for each pending subtask,
- the current execution step of each method, and
- previous methods tried for each subtask that failed.

A refinement stack is organized as a LIFO list of tuples: $stack=\langle tuple_1,\ldots,tuple_k\rangle$. Each tuple is of the form $(\tau, m, i, tried)$ where τ is a task or an event, m is an instance of a method in $\mathcal{M}$ addressing τ, i is a pointer to the current step in the body of m, and *tried* is a set of instances of methods already tried for τ that failed to accomplish it. The top tuple of a refinement stack corresponds to the active method.

Progressing in a refinement stack means advancing sequentially by *one* step in the body of the topmost method in the stack. The external task or event that initiates a refinement stack remains under progress, at the bottom of the stack, as long as this stack is not empty.

While RAE is advancing on a refinement stack, other external tasks and events may appear in its input stream. RAE will create refinement stacks for them too and will process all of its refinement stacks concurrently. At this stage, RAE does not consider the possible dependencies among concurrent stacks (extensions are discussed in Section 3.2.4). In particular, it does not perform any ordering or synchronization between them. The management of possible conflicts between concurrent stacks has to be taken care of in the specification of the methods.

3.2.2 Main Algorithms

To describe RAE in more detail, we will use the following notation:

- $\mathcal{M}$ is the library of methods.
- Instances($\mathcal{M}, \tau, \xi$) is the set of instances of methods in $\mathcal{M}$ whose preconditions hold in ξ and whose role matches the task or event τ.
- m is an instance of a method in $\mathcal{M}$.
- $m[i]$ is the step in the body of m pointed at by pointer i; moving from $m[i]$ to the next step is done according to control statements in the body of m, which are not counted as steps.
- type($m[i]$) is either a command, an assignment or a task; if type($m[i]$) =command then status($m[i]$) $\in$ {running, failure, done} is a state variable in ξ updated by the platform; its value informs RAE about the execution status of that command.
- *Agenda* is the set of refinement stacks concurrently under progress,
- a *stack* $\in$ *Agenda* is a LIFO list of tuples of the form $(\tau, m, i, tried)$ where τ is an event, task, subtask, or goal; m is an instance of a method that matches τ; i is a pointer to the current step in the body of m initialized to nil (no step has been executed); and *tried* is a set of instances of methods already tried for τ that failed to accomplish it.

Algorithm 3.1 Main procedure of the Refinement Acting Engine (RAE).

Rae($\mathcal{M}$)
  Agenda ← ∅
  loop
    until the input stream of external tasks and events is empty do
      read τ in the input stream
      Candidates ← Instances($\mathcal{M}, \tau, \xi$)
      if *Candidates* = ∅ then output("failed to address" τ)
      else do
        arbitrarily choose $m \in$ *Candidates*
        Agenda ← *Agenda* ∪ {⟨(τ, m, nil, ∅)⟩}
    for each *stack* ∈ *Agenda* do
    Progress(*stack*)
    if *stack* = ∅ then *Agenda* ← *Agenda* \ {*stack*}

RAE relies on three procedures named Rae, Progress, and Retry. Rae is the main loop of the engine (Algorithm 3.1). It repeats two steps forever: *(i)* update of *Agenda* with respect to new external tasks and events that are read in the input stream and *(ii)* progress by one step in the topmost method of each stack in *Agenda*.

To progress a refinement stack, Progress (Algorithm 3.2) focuses on the tuple ($\tau, m, i, tried$) at the top of the stack. If the method m has already started ($i \neq$ nil) and the current step $m[i]$ is a command, then the running status of this command is checked. If the command is still running, then this stack has to wait. If the command failed, then alternative methods will be tried. The execution of the next step of the top-most method takes place only when the command is done. If i is the last step in the body of method m, the current tuple is removed from the stack: method m has successfully addressed τ. The following task in the stack will be resumed at the next Rae iteration. If i is not the last step, the engine proceeds to the next step in the body of m.

nextstep(m, i) increments pointer i taking into account control statements, if any. These control statements are conditioned on tests deterministically computed for the current ξ. The next step $m[i]$ is either a state variable assignment, which is performed in ξ, a command whose execution is triggered in the platform, or a task τ'. In the latter case, instances of methods applicable to τ' for current ξ are computed, one of which is chosen to address τ'. The corresponding tuple is added on top of the stack. If there is no applicable method to τ, then the current method m failed to accomplish τ, other methods are tried.

The method m chosen by RAE to address τ may fail. If that happens, RAE uses the Retry procedure to try other methods for τ (Algorithm 3.3). Retry adds m to the set of method instances that have been tried for τ and failed. If there are any method instances for τ that are *not* in that set and are applicable in the current state ξ, then Retry chooses one of them; the refinement of τ will proceed with that method. Otherwise, RAE cannot accomplish τ. If the stack is empty, then τ is an external task or event. Otherwise, Retry calls itself recursively on the topmost stack element, which is the one that generated τ as a subgoal.

Algorithm 3.2 RAE: progressing a refinement stack.

Progress(*stack*)
  $(\tau, m, i, tried) \leftarrow$ top(*stack*)
  if $i \neq$ nil and $m[i]$ is a command then do
    case status($m[i]$)
      running: return
      failure: Retry(*stack*); return
      done: continue
  if i is the last step of m then
      pop(*stack*)   // remove *stack*'s top element
  else do
    $i \leftarrow$ nextstep(m, i)
    case type($m[i]$)
      assignment: update ξ according to $m[i]$; return
      command: trigger command $m[i]$; return
      task: continue
    $\tau' \leftarrow m[i]$
    Candidates $\leftarrow$ Instances($\mathcal{M}, \tau', \xi$)
    if *Candidates* $= \varnothing$ then Retry(*stack*)
    else do
      arbitrarily choose $m' \in$ *Candidates*
      stack $\leftarrow$ push($(\tau', m', $ nil$, \varnothing), stack$)

Although Retry implements a mechanism similar to backtracking, it is not backtracking in the usual sense. It does not go back to a previous computational node to pick up another option among the candidates that *were* applicable when that node was first reached. It finds another method among those that are *now* applicable for the *current* state of the world ξ. This is essential because RAE interact with a dynamic world.

Algorithm 3.3 RAE: trying alternative methods for a task.

Retry(*stack*)
  $(\tau, m, i, tried) \leftarrow$ pop(*stack*)
  tried $\leftarrow$ *tried* $\cup \{m\}$
  Candidates $\leftarrow$ Instances($\mathcal{M}, \tau, \xi$)\ *tried*
  if *Candidates* $\neq \varnothing$ then do
    arbitrarily choose $m' \in$ *Candidates*
      stack $\leftarrow$ push($(\tau, m', $ nil$, tried), stack$)
  else do
    if *stack* $\neq \varnothing$ then Retry(*stack*)
    else do
      output("failed to accomplish" τ)
      Agenda $\leftarrow$ *Agenda**stack*

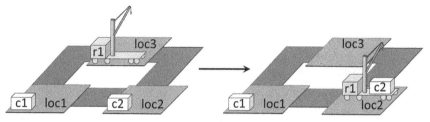

Figure 3.2. A simple environment.

It cannot rely on the set of Instances($\mathcal{M}, \tau, \xi$) computed earlier, because some of these may no longer be applicable, while new methods may be applicable.

Note that the same method instance that failed at some point may succeed later on. However, RAE does not attempt to retry method instances that it has already tried. In general, this would require a complex analysis of the conditions responsible for the failed method to be sure that these conditions no longer hold.

Example 3.5. Let us illustrate how RAE works, using the two methods given in Example 3.2 and the problem depicted in Figure 3.2. The robot r1 is at location loc3, which has been observed. Container c1 is in loc1 and container c2 in loc2, but neither location has been observed, hence the positions of c1 and c2 are unknown. The task fetch(r1,c2) is given to RAE.

Figure 3.3 shows the tree of RAE methods called for fetch(r1,c2). Initially, method m-fetch(r1,c2) is applicable. That method refines fetch(r1,c2) into search(r1,c2). Method m-search finds a location, say loc1, that has not been seen yet. It triggers the commands move-to(loc1) then perceive(loc1); because c2 is not in loc1, the method recursively refines into another search task. At this point, only loc2 remains unseen. The

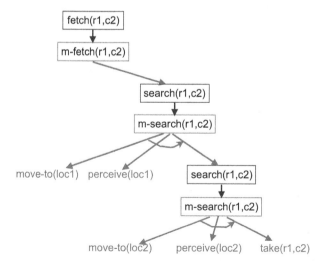

Figure 3.3. Refinement tree of tasks, methods, and commands for the task fetch(r1,c2).

second instance of m-search triggers the commands move-to(loc2), perceive(loc2), then take(r1,c2). This terminates successfully the three methods in the stack.   □

Example 3.6. To illustrate the concurrent progressing of several stacks, let us take a simple abstract example. A task τ_1 is addressed with a method m_1 which refines it successively into subtasks τ_{11} then τ_{12}. At this point RAE has just one stack $Agenda = \{\langle(\tau_{11}, m_{11}, i', \varnothing), (\tau_1, m_1, i, \varnothing)\rangle\}$. Note that τ_{12} is not in the stack until τ_{11} finishes.

A task τ_2 appears in the input stream of RAE. A new stack $\langle(\tau_2, m_2, \text{nil}, \varnothing)\rangle$ is created: $Agenda = \{\langle(\tau_{11}, m_{11}, i', \varnothing), (\tau_1, m_1, i, \varnothing)\rangle, \langle(\tau_2, m_2, \text{nil}, \varnothing)\rangle\}$.

The next iteration of Rae progresses with one step in m_{11} and one step in m_2. The latter refines τ_2 into τ_{21} then τ_{22}. This gives $Agenda = \{\langle(\tau_{11}, m_{11}, i', \varnothing), (\tau_1, m_1, i, \varnothing)\rangle, \langle(\tau_{21}, m_{21}, j', \varnothing), (\tau_2, m_2, j, \varnothing)\rangle\}$.

The following iterations progress one step at a time in m_{11} and m_{21} until one of these methods finishes, refines into some other subtasks (to be pushed in its stack), or fails (leading to try other methods for the task).   □

Note that dependencies between activities corresponding to concurrent stacks are not handled by this simple version of RAE (see Section 3.2.4).

3.2.3 Goals in RAE

Goals, like tasks, refer to an actor's objectives. The objective for a task is to perform some activity. The objective for a goal is to reach a state ξ where some condition g holds (see Definition 2.18). In some cases, an actor's objectives are more easily expressed through goals than through tasks.

Refinement methods are convenient for expressing and performing tasks. We can easily extend the refinement method approach of RAE to handle goals in a restricted way.[4] Our previous definition of a method as a triple (*role, precondition, body*) still holds. The *role* is now either a task, an event or a goal. A goal g is specified syntactically by the construct achieve(g).

The body of a refinement method for any type of role is, as before, a sequence of steps with control statements; each step is a command, an assignment, or a refinement into a subtask or a subgoal. As we explain shortly, a few modifications to RAE are sufficient to enable it to use such methods. However, there is an important limitation.

Unlike the planning algorithms in Chapter 2, RAE does not search for arbitrary sequences of commands that can achieve a goal g. Instead, just as it would do for a task, RAE will choose opportunistically among the methods in $\mathcal{M}$ whose roles match g. If $\mathcal{M}$ does not contain such a method, then g will not be reachable by RAE. The same actor, with exactly the same set of commands and execution platform, might be able to reach the goal g if $\mathcal{M}$ contained a richer collection of methods. This limitation can be overcome, but it requires using a planner, as we discuss in Sections 3.3 and 3.4.2.

---

[4] See Section 5.7 for a more general handling of goals.

Example 3.7. Consider the task fetch of Example 3.2. Instead of refining it with another task, we may choose to refine it with a goal of making the position of the container c known. The methods in Example 3.1 can be rewritten as follows:

```
m-fetch(r, c)
   task: fetch(r, c)
   pre:
   body: achieve(pos(c) ≠ unknown)
         move-to(pos(c))
         take(r, c)
     m-find-where(r, c)
        goal: achieve(pos(c) ≠ unknown)
        pre:
        body: while there is a location l such that view(l)=F do
                move-to(l)
                perceive(l)
```

The last method tests its goal condition and succeeds as soon as g is met with respect to current ξ. The position of c may become known by some other means than the perceive command, for example, if some other actor shares this information with the robot. These two methods are simpler than those in Example 3.2.   □

Because achieve(g) has the semantics and limitations of tasks, it is processed by RAE as a task. One may ask what is the advantage of introducing goals in RAE? The main advantage is to allow for *monitoring* of the condition g with respect to the observed environment expressed in ξ. For a method m whose role is achieve(g), RAE can check before starting the body of m whether g holds in current state ξ. It also performs this test at every progression step in the body of m and when m finishes. If the test succeeds, then the goal is achieved, and the method stops. If the test fails when the progression finishes, then the method has failed, and the Retry process is performed.

In the previous example, nothing needs to be done if pos(c) is known initially; if not, the m-find-where method stops if that position becomes known at some point of the while loop.

The monitoring test is easily implemented by making three modifications to the Progress procedure, Algorithm 3.2:

- If the previous step $m[i]$ is a command that returns failure: a Retry is performed only when g does not hold in current ξ.
- If i is the last step of m: if g is met in current ξ, then the top tuple is removed from the stack (success case); if not a Retry on current stack is performed.
- After i is updated with nextstep(m, i): if g is met in current ξ, then the top tuple is removed from current stack without pursuing further the refinement.

Note that if the previous step is a command that is still running, we postpone the test until it finishes (no progress for the method in that case).

The monitoring capability allowed with goals is quite convenient. It can be generalized to tasks by adding an extra field in methods: (*role, precondition, expected-results, body*). The *expected-results* field is a condition to be tested in the same way as a goal.

3.2.4 Additional Features for RAE

As illustrated in previous examples, the behavior of the RAE is quite simple. Additional features are needed to extend its capabilities and simplify the specification of methods. For example, it can be desirable to *suspend, resume*, or *stop* a task depending on specific conditions or to refine a task into *concurrent* subtasks. Furthermore, the choice of a method instance among the set of candidates in Rae, Progress, and Retry needs to be well informed (steps expressed as "arbitrarily choose $m \in Candidates$"). Let us discuss informally a few possible extensions of this simple version of RAE.

Controlling the progress of tasks. The need for controlling the progress of tasks can be illustrated in Example 3.3. The method m-emergency is not supposed to be running in parallel with other previously started tasks. The state variable emergency-handling, when set to true, should suspend other currently running tasks.

A simple extension for controlling the progress of a task is to generalize the condition field in methods: the designer should be able to express not only preconditions, as seen earlier, but also conditions under which the engine is required to stop, suspend, or resume the progress of a task. The needed modifications in the RAE procedures are the following:

- The precondition of a method is checked only once to define the applicable Instances(M, τ, ξ); the stop and suspend conditions of a method m, if any, have to be tested at each call of Progress for a *stack* where m appears.
- This test has to be performed not only for the method m on top of the *stack*, but also for the methods beneath it: stopping or suspending a task means stopping or suspending the subtasks in which it is currently being refined, that is, those that are above it in the stack.
- When a task is stopped the corresponding stack is removed from the agenda; when a task is suspended, the corresponding stack remains pending with no further progress, but its resume condition is tested at each iteration of RAE to eventually pursue its progression.

Some commands may be running when a stop or suspend condition is set on: the engine has to trigger corresponding orders to the execution platform to stop or suspend these commands when this is feasible.

It can be convenient to express control statements with respect to relative or absolute time. Let us assume that the value of the current time is maintained in ξ as a state variable, called *now*. Alarms, watchdog timers, periodic commands, and other temporal statements can be expressed in the body of methods, for example by conditioning the progress of a task (suspend, resume, stop) with respect to values of *now*. Because the main loop of RAE progresses by just one step in the top-most methods of pending stacks, it is possible to implement a real-time control of tasks at an intermediate level of reactivity (see Section 3.5).

Refining into concurrent subtasks. In the simple version of RAE, a task is refined into sequential subtasks. It can be desirable to allow for concurrent subtasks in a refinement step. For example, a robot may have to tour a location exhaustively while concurrently performing appropriate sensing actions to correctly accomplish a perceive action.

To specify a concurrent refinement, a step in the body of a method can be expressed with a "concurrent" operator as follows:

{concurrent: $\langle v_{1,1}, \ldots, v_{1,n} \rangle \langle v_{2,1}, \ldots, v_{2,m} \rangle \ldots \langle v_{k,1}, \ldots, v_{k,l} \rangle$}

where each $\langle v_{i,1}, \ldots, v_{i,j} \rangle$ is a sequence of steps as seen in the body of methods so far.

The refinement of a concurrent step splits into k parallel branches that share the current instance of that method. The corresponding stack is split into k substacks. There is an important difference with what we saw earlier for the concurrent progression of several stacks. The latter correspond to independent tasks that may succeed or fail independently of each others. Here, all the k substacks in which a concurrent refinement splits have to succeed before considering that concurrent refinement step as being successful.

Choosing methods and stack ordering. Two types of choices have been left open in RAE:

- which method among applicable ones to choose for addressing a task and
- in which order to progress the stacks in the current agenda.

Because all stacks have to be progressed at each iteration, the second open choice is not as critical as the first. One may envision general heuristics such as reacting to events first and then addressing new tasks, before progressing on the old ones. Application specific heuristics should allow refinement of this ordering choice.

The choice of the appropriate method for addressing a task when several are applicable should be based on an estimate of how effective a method will be in the current context for that task. Domain-specific heuristics can be convenient for making informed choices. Ideally, however, one needs predictive models and a lookahead capability to be able to compare alternative courses of actions but RAE uses operational models without predictive capability: the refinement methods defined so far are solely reactive.[5] Let us first extend them for the purpose of planning in the next section, then we'll come back to this issue of informed choices in RAE with look-ahead mechanisms in Section 3.4.

3.3 REFINEMENT PLANNING

One way to help RAE make choices is to do *refinement planning*, that is, to explore RAE's search space in order to predict the outcomes of different possible courses of action. This section describes two refinement-planning algorithms, SeRPE and IRT, that can be used for that purpose. In both of them, the basic idea is to do predictive simulations of RAE's task refinement process.

The planner's initial state s_0 will be RAE's current state ξ, and the planner will use methods like the ones that RAE uses; but instead of using commands to an execution platform, the planner will use descriptive models – action templates as in Chapter 2 – to

---

[5] This does not prevent from embedding in these methods planning capabilities for performing specific tasks or steps, as illustrated in Exercises 3.1, 3.2, and 3.3.

predict the effects of the commands. At points where RAE would choose a method m to use for some task or goal τ, the planner will use search techniques like the ones in Chapter 2 to explore several of the possible choices for m to predict for each m whether it will succeed in accomplishing τ.

As written, SeRPE and IRT require the classical planning assumptions discussed in Section 2.1.1. Consequently, they cannot reason about how RAE might handle situations in which actions have outcomes that are not known in advance. For example, Example 3.2 involved searching for a container using a command called perceive. We know in advance that if the actor performs the perceive action, the values of some state variables will *become* known, but we do not know what those values will be. Hence we cannot write a classical action template for perceive.

3.3.1 Sequential Refinement Planning

Algorithm 3.4 is SeRPE (Sequential Refinement Planning Engine), a refinement planning algorithm for situations in which there are no concurrent tasks. In other words, these are situations in which RAE has only one refinement stack and none of the refinement methods contain the "concurrent" operator defined in Section 3.2.4. In Section 3.3.2, we discuss another planning algorithm, IRT, that loosens this restriction.

SeRPE generates plans by simulating RAE's task refinement process. It chooses task-refinement methods nondeterministically, but an implementation of SeRPE would make the choice using a search mechanism like the ones in Section 2.2. SeRPE's arguments are a set $\mathcal{M}$ of refinement methods, a set $\mathcal{A}$ of action templates that are models of RAE's commands, the state s in which SeRPE's planning should begin, and τ, a task to accomplish.

SeRPE nondeterministically chooses a method instance m that is both relevant for τ and applicable in s, and calls Progress-to-finish to simulate RAE's execution of body(m). RAE would call Progress once for each step in the execution of body(m); each of these calls is simulated by an iteration of Progress-to-finish's loop. In this loop, if $m[i]$ is a command to perform, Progress-to-finish uses a descriptive model of the command to predict what the command will do. If $m[i]$ is a task to accomplish, Progress-to-finish calls SeRPE recursively: here, SeRPE's recursion stack corresponds to RAE's refinement stack for τ. If the execution trace completes successfully, Progress-to-finish returns a plan that it predicts will accomplish τ. If the execution trace fails, then SeRPE returns failure.

Lines (*ii*) and (*iii*) are SeRPE's way of simulating the goal monitoring described in Section 3.2.3.

In line (*ii*), SeRPE returns early if τ is a goal and s satisfies τ (denoted by $s \models \tau$). In line (*iii*), SeRPE fails if τ is a goal and m does not produce a state that satisfies τ.

In line (*i*), SeRPE returns failure because there are no methods for τ. If τ is a goal rather than a task, then a possible fallback might be to search for any plan whose outcome satisfies τ, regardless of whether there are any refinement methods to produce that plan. To modify SeRPE to do this, we can replace line (*i*) with this:

if *Candidates* $= \varnothing$ then
    if τ is a goal achieve(g) then return find-plan(Σ, s, g)
    else return failure

Algorithm 3.4 SeRPE, the Sequential Refinement Planning Engine.

SeRPE($\mathcal{M}, \mathcal{A}, s, \tau$)
  Candidates ← Instances($\mathcal{M}, \tau, s$)
  if *Candidates* = ∅ then return failure   (*i*)
  nondeterministically choose $m \in$ *Candidates*
  return Progress-to-finish($\mathcal{M}, \mathcal{A}, s, \tau, m$)

Progress-to-finish($\mathcal{M}, \mathcal{A}, s, \tau, m$)
  i ← nil   // instruction pointer for body(m)
  π ← ⟨⟩   // plan produced from body(m)
  loop
    if τ is a goal and $s \models \tau$ then return π (*ii*)
    if i is the last step of m then
      if τ is a goal and $s \not\models \tau$ then return failure (*iii*)
      return π
    i ← nextstep(m, i)
    case type($m[i]$)
      assignment: update s according to $m[i]$
      command:
        a ← the descriptive model of $m[i]$ in A
        if $s \models$ pre(a) then
          s ← $\gamma(s, a)$; π ← $\pi.a$
        else return failure
      task or goal:
        π' ← SeRPE($\mathcal{M}, \mathcal{A}, s, m[i]$)
        if π' = failure then return failure
        s ← $\gamma(s, \pi')$; π ← $\pi.\pi'$

---

where Σ is the planning domain (S, A, γ), A is the set of actions corresponding to each command, and S is the set of states constructed with a generative approach from s and γ. In the modification proposed above for line (i), find-plan could be one of the planning algorithms in Chapter 2, with modifications to make it return control to SeRPE if it sees a goal for which there is an applicable method (see the discussion of this in Section 3.5.2).

Refinement trees. SeRPE can be modified so that when invoked on a task τ, instead of returning a plan π it returns a *refinement tree*. This is a tree in which the root node contains the task or goal τ, the intermediate nodes contain the methods chosen by SeRPE and the subtasks produced by those methods, and the terminal nodes contain the actions in π.

    Such a modification will be useful for integrating SeRPE with RAE (see Section 3.4), and the modification is relatively straightforward: in each of SeRPE's recursive calls, it would add to the tree a node containing the task or action that SeRPE chose at this point in its search.

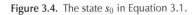

Figure 3.4. The state s_0 in Equation 3.1.

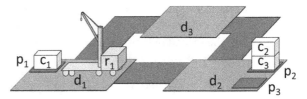

In the rest of this chapter, we refer to the input of RAE as a planning problem $P = (\mathcal{M}, \mathcal{A}, s, \tau)$, where $\mathcal{M}$ is a set of methods, $\mathcal{A}$ is a set of action templates, s is a state, and τ is a task.

Example 3.8. Figure 3.4 shows a state in a planning domain similar to the one in Example 2.12 except that there is only one robot. Consider the tasks of uncovering a container and putting it into a specified pile. Following are methods to accomplish those tasks in some (but not all) cases. The variables in these methods have the following ranges: $c \in Containers$; $r \in Robots$; $d, d' \in Docks$; $p, p' \in Piles$. There are three kinds of tasks:

- put-in-pile(c, p') is the task of putting container c into pile p' if it is not already there. There are two methods for this task. One is for the case where c is already in p', and it does nothing. The other uses a robot to take c, move (if it is not already there) to the dock where p' is located, and put c on p'. Here they are:

m1-put-in-pile(c, p')
   task: put-in-pile(c, p')
   pre: pile$(c) = p'$
  body: // empty

m2-put-in-pile(r, c, p, d, p', d')
   task: put-in-pile(c, p')
   pre: pile$(c) = p \wedge$ at$(p, d) \wedge$ at(p', d')
         $\wedge\ p \neq p' \wedge$ cargo$(r) =$ nil
  body: if loc$(r) \neq d$ then navigate(r, d)
       uncover(c)
       load$(r, c, pos(c), p, d)$
       if loc$(r) \neq d'$ then navigate(r, d')
       unload$(r, c, top(p'), p', d')$

- uncover(c) is the task of ensuring that c is at the top of a pile p. There are two methods for this task: one for the case where c is already at the top of p, and another that uses a robot r to move containers from p to another pile p' until c is at the top of p. In the latter case, r must be empty, and r and p' must have the same location as p.

m1-uncover(c)
   task: uncover(c)
   pre: top(pile$(c)) = c$
  body: // empty

m2-uncover(r, c, p, p', d)
   task: uncover(c)
   pre: pile$(c) = p \wedge$ top$(p) \neq c$
        $\wedge$ at$(p, d) \wedge$ at$(p', d) \wedge p \neq p'$
        $\wedge$ loc$(r) = d \wedge$ cargo$(r) =$ nil
  body: while top$(p) \neq c$ do
       $c' \leftarrow$ top(p)
       load$(r, c', pos(c'), p, d)$
       unload$(r, c', top(p'), p', d)$

- navigate(r, d') is the task of moving r along some undetermined route that ends at dock d'. In an actual application, such a task would probably be handled by calling a specialized route-planning algorithm, but in this simple example, we can use the following three methods. The first is for the case in which r is already at d, and it does nothing. The second one moves r to d' if $\text{loc}(r)$ is adjacent to d'. The third one moves to an adjacent dock other than d'.

m1-navigate(r, d')
    task: navigate(r, d')
    pre: $\text{loc}(r) = d'$
    body: // *empty*

m2-navigate(r, d')
    task: navigate(r, d')
    pre: $\text{loc}(r) \neq d' \wedge$
        adjacent($\text{loc}(r), d'$)
    body: move($r, \text{loc}(r), d'$)

m3-navigate(r, d, d')
    task: navigate(r, d')
    pre: $\text{loc}(r) \neq d' \wedge d \neq d'$
        $\wedge$ adjacent($\text{loc}(r), d$)
    body: move($r, \text{loc}(r), d$)
          navigate(r, d')

Now consider the planning problem $P = (\mathcal{M}, \mathcal{A}, s_0, \text{put-in-pile}(c_1, p_2))$, where $\mathcal{M}$ contains the six methods defined above, $\mathcal{A}$ contains the four actions defined in Example 2.12, and s_0 is the following state, which is shown in Figure 3.4:

$$s_0 = \{\text{cargo}(r_1) = \text{nil}, \quad \text{loc}(r_1) = d_1, \tag{3.1}$$
$$\text{occupied}(d_1) = T, \text{occupied}(d_2) = F, \text{occupied}(d_3) = F,$$
$$\text{pile}(c_1) = p_1, \quad\quad \text{pile}(c_2) = p_2, \quad\quad \text{pile}(c_3) = p_2,$$
$$\text{pos}(c_1) = \text{nil}, \quad\quad \text{pos}(c_2) = c_3, \quad\quad \text{pos}(c_3) = \text{nil},$$
$$\text{top}(p_1) = c_1, \quad\quad\; \text{top}(p_2) = c_2, \quad\quad \text{top}(p_3) = \text{nil}\}.$$

Assuming we modify SeRPE to include cycle-checking (see Section 2.2), there are two possible refinement trees for P. The two trees, which are shown in Figure 3.5, are produced by two applicable method instances for the task navigate(r_1, d_2). They correspond to two different routes that r_1 can take from d_1 to d_2: either go directly to d_2, or go there via d_3.

Figure 3.5 shows the refinement trees for both choices. These trees correspond to the following solution plans:

$$\pi_1 = \langle \text{load}(r_1, c_1, c_2, p_1, d_1), \text{move}(r_1, d_1, d_2), \text{unload}(r_1, c_1, c_3, p_2, d_2) \rangle;$$

$$\pi_2 = \langle \text{load}(r_1, c_1, c_2, p_1, d_1), \text{move}(r_1, d_1, d_3), \text{move}(r_1, d_3, d_2),$$

$$\text{unload}(r_1, c_1, c_3, p_2, d_2) \rangle. \qquad\qquad\qquad \square$$

Discussion. For simplicity of presentation, we wrote the SeRPE pseudocode to choose a method m nondeterministically from the set of candidate methods. An implementation of SeRPE would make this choice using search techniques like those in Section 2.2, modified to search over methods as well as actions. In such an implementation, the search algorithm's efficiency depends on what the refinement methods are like (writing the body of a refinement method is basically a programming task) and what kinds of search heuristics are used.

When RAE has a single task to accomplish, RAE's refinement of that task proceeds in a depth-first, left-to-right fashion, since that is the order in which RAE will need to

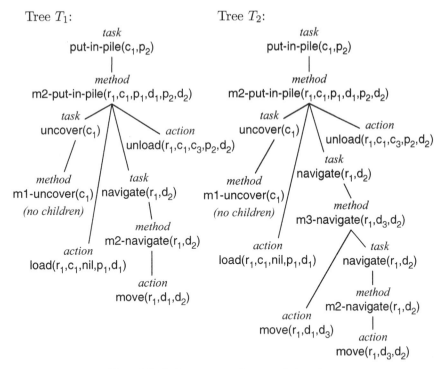

Figure 3.5. Refinement trees for two solution plans.

execute the actions. Because SeRPE works by simulating RAE's execution, it explores its search space in the same depth-first, left-to-right fashion.

In some application domains, it would be desirable to have a planning engine that can explore the nodes of the search space in a different order. For example, to take an airplane trip from the United States to Europe, one needs to get to the airport before taking a flight, but to *plan* the trip, one usually wants to examine alternative flight itineraries before planning how to get to the airport. Something like this can be accomplished by giving the planner a different set of refinement methods than the ones used by the actor, but that makes it difficult to ensure consistency between the deliberation done by the planner and the deliberation done by the actor. An alternative approach is to combine task refinement with plan-space planning (see Section 3.5.2) or to use input/output automata that allow for interactions between different tasks (see Chapter 5).

3.3.2 Interleaved Plans

In Section 3.3.1, one of the restrictions was that none of the methods in $\mathcal{M}$ could contain the "concurrent" programming construct described in Section 3.2.4. The main reason for this restriction is the difficulty of reasoning about what will happen when several primitive commands are running concurrently, which requires a temporal-planning model that we will not introduce until Chapter 4. However, it can be useful to loosen

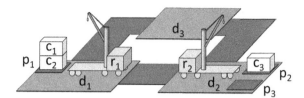

Figure 3.6. The initial state s_0 from Example 2.5.

the restriction by allowing multiple tasks to be interleaved provided that at most one primitive command will be executed at a time. Here is a motivating example:

Example 3.9. Let s_0 be as shown in Figure 3.6. Suppose we want to move c_1 to p_2 and move c_3 to p_1, using the following two plans:

$$\pi_3 = \langle \text{load}(r_1, c_1, c_2, p_1, d_1), \text{move}(r_1, d_1, d_2), \text{unload}(r_1, c_1, p_3, \text{nil}, d_2) \rangle,$$

$$\pi_4 = \langle \text{load}(r_2, c_3, \text{nil}, p_2, d_2), \text{move}(r_2, d_2, d_3), \text{move}(r_2, d_3, d_1),$$

$$\text{unload}(r_2, c_3, c_2, p_1, d_1) \rangle.$$

If we tried to use either π_3 or π_4 alone, some of the actions would fail. Only one robot can occupy a loading dock at a time, so neither robot can move to the other dock unless the other robot first leaves that dock. We can accomplish this by interleaving π_3 and π_4 to produce a plan such as this:

$$\pi_5 = \langle \text{load}(r_1, c_1, c_2, p_1, d_1), \text{load}(r_2, c_3, \text{nil}, p_2, d_2),$$

$$\text{move}(r_2, d_2, d_3), \text{move}(r_1, d_1, d_2), \text{move}(r_2, d_3, d_1),$$

$$\text{unload}(r_1, c_1, p_3, \text{nil}, d_2) \rangle, \text{unload}(r_2, c_3, c_2, p_1, d_1) \rangle. \qquad \square$$

To provide a way of specifying that a plan such as π_5 is a permissible solution, we will allow the body of a method to include steps of the form

$$\{\text{interleave: } p_1, \ldots, p_n\},$$

where each p_i is a sequence of steps $\langle v_{i,1}, \ldots, v_{i,j} \rangle$ for some j. This operator has the same semantics as the "concurrent" operator in Section 3.2.4, except that only one command can be performed at a time.

Example 3.10. Continuing with Example 3.9, suppose that $\mathcal{M}$ includes the following additional method, where $c, c' \in$ *Containers* and $p, p' \in$ *Piles*:

$$\text{put-interleaved}(c, p, c', p')$$
$$\text{task: put-both}(c, p, c', p')$$
$$\text{pre: } none$$
$$\text{body: } \{\text{interleave:}$$
$$\langle \text{put-in-pile}(c, p) \rangle,$$
$$\langle \text{put-in-pile}(c', p') \rangle\}$$

Then from the task put-both(c_1, p_2, c_3, p_1), we can get the refinement tree in Figure 3.7, which corresponds to π_5. $\qquad \square$

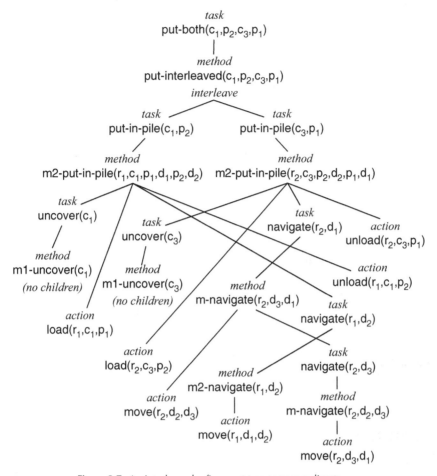

Figure 3.7. An interleaved refinement tree corresponding to π_5.

Algorithm 3.5, the IRT (Interleaved Refinement Tree) algorithm, generates refinement trees like the one in Figure 3.7, in planning domains where the bodies of the methods may include "interleave" statements. The IRT pseudocode requires the planning domain to have no goals, that is, no tasks of the form achieve(g). These could be added, but we omit them for simplicity of presentation. IRT's refinement trees contain five kinds of nodes:

- A *task node* and an *action node* contain a task or action, respectively.
- A *method node* or *program node* is labeled with a pair (p, i), where p is a method or a program, and i is a program counter.
- An *interleaving node* represents a statement of the form {interleave: $p_1, \ldots, p_k$}. It is an empty node whose children include program nodes $v_1, \ldots, v_k$.

Generally there may be many different possible orders in which to expand the nodes below each interleaving node. IRT handles this by repeatedly making nondeterministic choices from a list called *Pending* that includes all nodes IRT has not yet finished expanding.

Algorithm 3.5 IRT, a refinement-planning algorithm that can do interleaving. Interleaving nodes are handled by the IRT-progress subroutine, Algorithm 3.6.

IRT(D, s, τ)
    $\pi \leftarrow \langle\rangle$
    $\rho \leftarrow$ a new task node; data(ρ) $\leftarrow \tau$
    Pending $\leftarrow \{\rho\}$
    while *Pending* $\neq \varnothing$ do
        nondeterministically choose a node $\mu \in$ *Pending*
                that has no children in *Pending*   (*i*)
        case type(μ)
            task:
                $\tau \leftarrow$ data(μ)
                remove μ from *Pending*
                $M \leftarrow$ Instances($\mathcal{M}(\tau), s$)
                if $M = \varnothing$ then return failure
                nondeterministically choose $m \in M$
                $\nu \leftarrow$ a new method node; data(ν) $\leftarrow (m, 0)$
                make ν a child of μ // this will be μ's only child
                insert ν into *Pending*
            action:
                $a \leftarrow$ data(μ)
                remove μ from *Pending*
                if a is not applicable in s then return failure
                $s \leftarrow \gamma(s, a)$; $\pi \leftarrow \pi.a$
            program or method:
                $\upsilon \leftarrow$ IRT-progress(D, μ, s, *Pending*)
                if $\upsilon =$ failure then return failure
    return (π, ρ)

Implementation considerations. The practical considerations for implementing IRT are similar to the ones for implementing SeRPE. However, the efficiency consideration is especially critical in IRT. The nondeterministic choice in (*i*) makes IRT consider all feasible orderings of the nodes in *Pending*. To implement IRT, it would be necessary to implement this as a deterministic search. Because the number of feasible orderings can be exponentially large, this is not practical unless the algorithm has a way (e.g., some sort of heuristic guidance) to find a satisfactory ordering without too much backtracking.

Simulating concurrency. IRT's "interleave" operator can be used, in a limited way, to do predictive simulations of concurrent tasks in RAE, by making some changes to the domain representation. Recall that each action a is a descriptive model of a command to the execution platform. For simplicity of presentation, let us assume that a's preconditions need to be true when the command starts executing, and a's effects occur when the command finishes executing. Instead of modeling the command with a single action a, let us use a task named do-a, the body of which contains two actions start-a and

---

Algorithm 3.6 Subroutine of IRT to simulate the next step in a method.

IRT-progress($D, \mu, s, Pending$)
  $(p, i) \leftarrow$ data(μ)
  if i is the last step of m then
    remove μ from *Pending*
    return
  else if $p[i]$ is a task then
    $v \leftarrow$ a new task node; data(v) $\leftarrow p[i]$
    append v to μ's list of children
    insert v into *Pending*
  else if $p[i]$ is a primitive command then do
    $v \leftarrow$ a new action node; data(v) $\leftarrow a_{p[i]}$
    append v to μ's list of children
    insert v into *Pending*
  else
    // $p[i]$ has the form {interleave: $p_1, \ldots, p_k$}
    $v \leftarrow$ a new interleaving node
    append v to μ's list of children
    for $i = 1, \ldots, k$ do
      $v_i \leftarrow$ a new program node; data(v) $\leftarrow (p_i, 0)$
      insert v_i into v's set of children
      insert v_i into *Pending*

---

end-a that represent the command's starting and ending points.[6] If a's preconditions and effects are p and e, then the method and the two actions are as shown in Figure 3.8.

In the body of each method, let us replace all occurrences of the action a with the task do-a, and replace all occurrences of "concurrent" with "interleave". Thus, {concurrent: $a_1, a_2, \ldots, a_n$} will become

$$\{\text{interleave: do-}a_1, \ldots, \text{do-}a_n\}. \tag{3.2}$$

In Figure 3.8, the state variable running-a prevents multiple overlapping occurrences of the same action. If we want to allow multiple overlapping occurrences for some reason, then IRT will need to be modified so that each time it refines an instance of do-a, it uses a different state variable in start-a and end-a.

Limitations. The biggest difficulty with this way of simulating concurrency is that IRT will impose a specific linear order on the starting points and ending points of the actions in Equation 3.2. Without knowing something about the amount of time each action will take, there is no way to know whether the ordering chosen by IRT is a realistic one; and even if it is realistic, it will not provide sufficient flexibility to deal with situations in

---

[6] More generally, one may need to represent preconditions and effects that occur at several points during a command's execution. In this case, we would need to include one or more additional actions during$_1$-a, during$_2$-a, $\ldots$, so that there is an action at each point where a precondition or effect occurs.

m-do-a
  task: do-a
  pre: // no preconditions
  body: start-a, end-a

start-a
  pre: p, running-a = F
  eff: running-a ← T

end-a
  pre: running-a = T
  eff: e, running-a ← F

Figure 3.8. Translation of a command a into one refinement method and two actions.

which the duration of an action may vary and is not controllable. If we extract a partial order from the linear order (which can be done reasoning about which actions establish the preconditions of other actions) and modify the actions to include time stamps, it will alleviate the problem but not fully solve it. Chapter 4 presents a more comprehensive way to reason about time.

3.4 ACTING AND REFINEMENT PLANNING

We now consider how to integrate refinement planning with acting. Section 3.4.1 shows how to modify the procedures in Section 2.6 to use an online version of SeRPE; and Section 3.4.2 describes REAP, a modified version of RAE that incorporates a SeRPE-like refinement planner.

3.4.1 Planning and Acting at Different Levels

At the start of Section 3.3, our stated motivation for SeRPE was to provide guidance for RAE by simulating its possible execution paths. However, another possibility is to use SeRPE and RAE at different levels of an actor's hierarchy. The actor could use a SeRPE-like planning procedure to generate plans consisting of abstract actions and a RAE-like acting procedure to refine the abstract actions into lower-level commands, for example, as shown in the planning and acting levels of Figure 1.2.

To illustrate some ways to accomplish this, Algorithms 3.7, 3.8, and 3.9 are straightforward modifications of the algorithms in Section 2.6.1. In them, SeRPE-Lookahead is a version of SeRPE that has been modified to incorporate online-planning techniques such as receding-horizon planning or sampling (see Section 2.6.2), and Perform is a procedure for performing a by using a RAE-like procedure to refine the action a into commands for the actor's execution platform.

Algorithm 3.7 Replanning before every action.

Refine-Lookahead($\mathcal{M}, \mathcal{A}, \tau$)
    while (s ← abstraction of observed state ξ) $\not\models \tau$ do (i)
        π ← SeRPE-Lookahead($\mathcal{M}, \mathcal{A}, s, \tau$)
        if π = failure then return failure
        a ← pop-first-action(π)); Perform(a)

Algorithm 3.8 Replanning only when necessary.

Refine-Lazy-Lookahead($\mathcal{M}, \mathcal{A}, \tau$)
    $s \leftarrow$ abstraction of observed state ξ
    while $s \not\models \tau$ do
        $\pi \leftarrow$ SeRPE-Lookahead($\mathcal{M}, \mathcal{A}, s, \tau$)
        if $\pi =$ failure then return failure
        while $\pi \neq \langle\rangle$ and $s \not\models \tau$ and Simulate(Σ, s, τ, π) $\neq$ failure do
            $a \leftarrow$ pop-first-action(π)); Perform(a)
            $s \leftarrow$ abstraction of observed state ξ

Simulate is the same kind of plan simulator as in Section 2.6.1, except that the third argument is a task τ rather than a goal g, and it is only when $\tau =$ achieve(g) that Simulate will check whether π achieves g.

Example 3.11. Consider an actor that uses Refine-Lookahead. Suppose that in line (i) of Refine-Lookahead, the state-abstraction function is the identity function, that is, it always assigns $s \leftarrow \xi$.

Suppose the actor begins with the state s_0 shown in Figure 3.4 and the task $\tau =$ put-in-pile(c_1, p_2). In the first iteration of the while loop, suppose SeRPE-Lookahead returns

$$\pi_1 = \langle \text{load}(r_1, c_1, c_2, p_1, d_1), \text{move}(r_1, d_1, d_2), \text{unload}(r_1, c_1, c_3, p_2, d_2) \rangle.$$

Then Refine-Lookahead pops load(r_1, c_1, p_1) from π_1 and calls Perform(load(r_1, c_1, p_1)). If no execution errors or other unanticipated events occur, then the observed state and its abstraction are $s_1 = \gamma(s_0, \text{load}(r_1, c_1, c_2, p_1, d_1))$.

In the second iteration of the while loop, if SeRPE-Lookahead's nondeterministic choices are consistent with the ones it made the previous time, then it returns

$$\pi_2 = \langle \text{move}(r_1, d_1, d_2), \text{unload}(r_1, c_1, c_3, p_2, d_2) \rangle,$$

Algorithm 3.9 Replanning concurrently with acting.

Refine-Concurrent-Lookahead($\mathcal{M}, \mathcal{A}, \tau$)
    $\pi \leftarrow \langle\rangle$; $s \leftarrow$ abstraction of observed state ξ
    thread 1:   // threads 1 and 2 run concurrently
      loop
        $\pi \leftarrow$ SeRPE-Lookahead($\mathcal{M}, \mathcal{A}, s, \tau$)
    thread 2:
      loop
        if $s \models \tau$ then return success
        else if $\pi =$ failure then return failure
        else if $\pi \neq \langle\rangle$ and Simulate(Σ, s, τ, π) $\neq$ failure then
            $a \leftarrow$ pop-first-action(π)); Perform(a)
            $s \leftarrow$ abstraction of observed state ξ

---

so Refine-Lookahead pops and performs $move(r_1, d_1, d_2)$. If no execution errors or other unanticipated events occur, then the observed state and its abstraction are $s_2 = \gamma(s_1, move(r_1, d_1, d_2))$.

In the third iteration, if SeRPE-Lookahead's nondeterministic choices are consistent with its previous ones, then it returns

$$\pi_3 = \langle unload(r_1, c_1, c_3, p_2, d_2) \rangle,$$

so Refine-Lazy-Lookahead pops and performs $unload(r_1, c_1, c_3, p_2, d_2)$. If no execution errors or other unanticipated events occur, then the observed state and its abstraction are $s_3 = \gamma(s_2, unload(r_1, c_1, c_3, p_2, d_2))$.

In the fourth loop iteration, $s_3 \models g$, so Refine-Lazy-Lookahead exits.

Instead of Refine-Lookahead, suppose the actor uses Refine-Lazy-Lookahead or Refine-Lazy-Lookahead, with the same abstraction function and the same version of SeRPE-Lookahead as before. If no execution errors or unanticipated events occur, then the actor will perform the same actions as before, in the same order.   □

Limitations. Because Algorithms 3.7–3.9 are analogous to the procedures in Section 2.6.1, they have several of the same trade-offs discussed in that section. Moreover, as illustrated in the following example, additional problems can occur if the author of the domain model does not specify refinement methods for all of the possible states in which SeRPE-Lookahead might be invoked.

Example 3.12. Suppose a programmer writes a method m to accomplish a task τ. This method is applicable in a state s_0 and it produces a sequence of commands $\langle a_1, a_2, a_3 \rangle$. Suppose the programmer believes s_0 is the only state in which the actor will ever be given τ as an external task, and thus the programmer does not write any methods to accomplish τ in any other state. Suppose the actor starts in a state ξ_0 whose abstraction is s_0 and uses Refine-Lookahead:

- Refine-Lookahead calls SeRPE-Lookahead$(\mathcal{M}, \mathcal{A}, s_0, \tau)$, and SeRPE-Lookahead uses m to produce a plan π.
- The actor removes the first action from π and performs it, producing a state ξ_1 whose abstraction is s_1. Then Refine-Lookahead calls SeRPE-Lookahead$(\mathcal{M}, \mathcal{A}, s_1, \tau)$. Because m is inapplicable in s_1, SeRPE-Lookahead returns failure, even though the remaining actions in π are still capable of accomplishing τ.

A similar problem will occur if the actor uses Refine-Concurrent-Lookahead. If Refine-Lookahead returns a complete solution plan, the problem will not occur if the actor uses Refine-Lazy-Lookahead, which will continue to perform actions in π as long as Simulate predicts that π will execute correctly. But the problem will occur in Refine-Lazy-Lookahead if SeRPE-Lookahead returns a partial solution plan (e.g., if Refine-Lookahead does a receding-horizon search).   □

A more robust (although more complicated) approach is to integrate SeRPE-like refinement planning with RAE-like refinement acting at all levels of the actor's hierarchy. The next section describes a way to do that.

Algorithm 3.10 Main procedure of REAP, a modified version of RAE that calls a planner to choose method instances.

REAP-main($\mathcal{M}, \mathcal{A}$)
  Agenda ← ∅
  loop
    until the input stream of external tasks and events is empty do
      read τ in the input stream
      Candidates ← Instances($\mathcal{M}, \tau, \xi$)
      if *Candidates* = ∅ then output("failed to address" τ)
      s ← abstraction of observed state ξ
      T ← Refinement-tree(*Candidates*, $\mathcal{M}, \mathcal{A}, s, \tau$)   (*i*)
      if T = failure then
        output("failed to address" τ)   (*ii*)
      else do
        m ← the method instance at the top of T (*iii*)
        Agenda ← *Agenda* ∪ {⟨(τ, m, nil, ∅, T)⟩}
    for each *stack* ∈ *Agenda* do
    REAP-progress($\mathcal{M}, A$, *stack*)
    if *stack* = ∅ then *Agenda* ← *Agenda* \ {*stack*}

3.4.2 Integrated Acting and Planning

This section describes REAP (Refinement Engine for Acting and Planning). Most of the REAP pseudocode (algorithms 3.10, 3.11, and 3.12) is quite similar to RAE in Section 3.2, except that REAP uses a planner (Refinement-tree in the pseudocode) to help it choose methods in *Candidates*. Refinement-tree is an online SeRPE-like planner similar to SeRPE-Lookahead in Section 3.4.1, but modified to use *Candidates* rather than $\mathcal{M}$ as the methods for the task τ and to return a refinement tree instead of a plan.

We introduced the notion of refinement trees briefly in Section 3.3.1 and gave two examples in Figure 3.5. In more detail, if T is the refinement tree for a task τ, then T has a root node t that is labeled with τ, and t has one child u that is labeled with the method instance m that the planner chose for τ. Let $\tau_1, \ldots, \tau_k$ be the subtasks and actions in the planner's simulation of body(m), in the order that they were created. Then μ has children $t_1, \ldots, t_k$ defined as follows. For each τ_i that is a task, t_i is the root node of the refinement tree for τ_i; and for each τ_i that is an action, t_i is a leaf node that is labeled with τ_i.

REAP-main calls Refinement-tree on a planning problem in which the only methods available for the current state are the ones in *Candidates*. If the planner returns a refinement tree T for a task τ, then the method at the top of T is the one that the planner recommends using for τ, so REAP-main chooses this method in line (*iii*).

In line (*ii*), REAP-main stops trying to accomplish τ if Refinement-tree returns failure. However, REAP-main can be modified to incorporate various fallback options. Depending on the planning domain and the developer's objectives, a modified version of REAP-main could call Refinement-tree with a set $\mathcal{M}'$ of fallback methods that it would

---

Algorithm 3.11 REAP's procedure for progressing a refinement stack.

REAP-progress($\mathcal{M}, \mathcal{A}, stack$)
  $(\tau, m, i, tried, T) \leftarrow$ top($stack$)
  if $i \neq$ nil and $m[i]$ is a command then
    case status($m[i]$)
      running: return
      failure: REAP-retry($\mathcal{M}, \mathcal{A}, stack$); return
      done:
        $T' \leftarrow$ the unexecuted part of T
        if Simulate(ξ, T') = failure then   *(i)*
          REAP-retry($\mathcal{M}, \mathcal{A}, stack$); return
        else continue
  if i is the last step of m then
    pop($stack$)   // remove $(\tau, m, i, tried, T)$
  else
    $i \leftarrow$ nextstep(m, i)
    case type($m[i]$)
      assignment: update ξ according to $m[i]$; return
      command: trigger command $m[i]$; return
      task or goal: continue
    $\tau' \leftarrow m[i]$
    $Candidates \leftarrow$ Instances($\mathcal{M}, \tau', \xi$)
    if $Candidates = \varnothing$ then
      REAP-retry($\mathcal{M}, \mathcal{A}, stack$); return
    $s \leftarrow$ abstraction of observed state ξ
    $T' \leftarrow$ Refinement-tree($Candidates, \mathcal{M}, \mathcal{A}, s, \tau$)   *(ii)*
    if $T' =$ failure then REAP-retry($\mathcal{M}, A, stack$)
    else do
      $m' \leftarrow$ the topmost method in T' *(iii)*
      $stack \leftarrow$ push($(\tau', m', nil, \varnothing, T'), stack$)

---

not otherwise use, postpone accomplishment of τ until the environment changes in a way that makes τ feasible, or modify τ (see "goal reasoning" in Section 1.3.4) to make it easier to accomplish.

In lines *(ii)–(iii)* of REAP-progress, the same approach is used to choose a method m' for the task τ'. Because τ' is a subgoal of the task τ in REAP-main, this can be viewed as a kind of subgoaling (see Section 2.6.2). The same approach is used again in lines *(i)–(ii)* of REAP-retry.

Simulation. In line *(i)* of REAP-progress, Simulate is a plan simulator like the one in Section 3.4.1, but with two significant differences. First, its argument is a refinement tree T, and it simulates the plan contained in T's leaf nodes. Second, REAP-progress calls it many times on many different refinement trees.

Algorithm 3.12 REAP's version of RAE's Retry subroutine.

REAP-retry($\mathcal{M}, \mathcal{A}, stack$)
  $(\tau, m, i, tried, T) \leftarrow$ pop($stack$)
  $tried \leftarrow tried \cup \{m\}$
  $Candidates \leftarrow$ Instances($\mathcal{M}, \tau, \xi$) \ $tried$
  if $Candidates = \varnothing$ then output("failed to address" τ)
  $s \leftarrow$ abstraction of observed state ξ
  $T' \leftarrow$ Refinement-tree($Candidates, \mathcal{M}, \mathcal{A}, s, \tau$)   (i)
  if $T' \neq$ failure then
    $m' \leftarrow$ the topmost method in T' (ii)
    push($(\tau, m', nil, tried, T'), stack$)
  else
    if $stack \neq \varnothing$ then REAP-retry($\mathcal{M}, \mathcal{A}, stack$)
    else do
      output("failed to accomplish" τ)
      $Agenda \leftarrow Agenda$ \ $stack$

Every time REAP-progress refines a stack element, it calls Refinement-tree in line (ii). Hence each stack element $(\tau, m, tried, T)$ contains a refinement tree that is a subtree of the refinement tree in the stack element below it. To obtain a prediction of whether the rest of body(m) will execute correctly, REAP-progress calls Simulate(ξ, T) in line (i). If the simulation predicts a failure, then REAP-progress calls REAP-retry.

Example 3.13. Let us repeat Example 3.11 using REAP. As before, we will suppose that no execution errors or unforeseen events occur.

In REAP-main's first loop iteration, it reads $\tau =$ put-in-pile(c_1, p_2) and calls Refinement-tree. Suppose Refinement-tree returns the refinement tree T_1 in Figure 3.5. The topmost method in T is $m =$ carry-to-pile($r_1, c_1, p_1, d_1, c_3, p_2, d_2$), and REAP-main puts $stack_1 = \langle (\tau, m, nil, \varnothing, T) \rangle$ into $Agenda$. Assuming that nothing else arrives in the input stream, REAP-main calls REAP-progress repeatedly on $stack_1$ until τ has been accomplished, as follows:

- In the first call to REAP-progress, the top element of the stack is $(\tau, m, nil, \varnothing, T)$. After the call to nextstep, this is replaced by $(\tau, m, i, \varnothing, T)$, with i pointing to $\tau_1 =$ uncover(c_1). REAP-progress calls Refinement-tree, which returns a tree T_1 that is a copy of T's leftmost branch. The topmost method in T_1 is $m_1 =$ m-uncover(c_1), and REAP-progress pushes $(\tau_1, m_1, nil, \varnothing, T_1)$ onto $stack_1$.
- In the second call to REAP-progress, the top element of $stack_1$ is $(\tau_1, m_1, nil, \varnothing, T_1)$. Because c_1 is already uncovered, the method produces no actions or subtasks, and REAP-progress removes $(\tau_1, m_1, nil, \varnothing, T_1)$ from $stack_1$.
- In the third call to REAP-progress, i points at uncover(c_1) until nextstep is called. Afterward, i points at the action load(r_1, c_1, p_1), which REAP-progress sends as a command to the execution platform. In the fourth call to REAP-progress, let us suppose that the command is still running. Then REAP-progress just returns.

- In the fifth call to REAP-progress, suppose the command has finished. Then Simulate returns success, and the call to nextstep makes i point to $\tau_2 = \text{navigate}(r_1, d_2)$. REAP-progress calls Refinement-tree, which returns a tree T_2 that is a copy of T's third branch. The topmost method in T_2 is $m_2 = \text{m2-navigate}(r_1, d_1, d_2)$, and REAP-progress pushes $(\tau_2, m_2, \text{nil}, \varnothing, T_2)$ onto $stack_1$.

- In the sixth call to REAP-progress, the top element of the stack is $(\tau_2, m_2, \text{nil}, \varnothing, T_2)$. After the call to nextstep, this is replaced by $(\tau_2, m_2, i, \varnothing, T_2)$, with i pointing to the action $\text{move}(r_1, d_1, d_2)$. REAP-progress sends it as a command to the execution platform. In the seventh and eighth calls to REAP-progress, suppose the command is still running. Then REAP-progress returns.

- In the ninth call to REAP-progress, suppose the command has finished. Then Simulate returns success, and i is the last step of m, so REAP-progress removes $(\tau_2, m_2, i, \varnothing, T_2)$ from $stack_1$.

- In the tenth call to REAP-progess, the top element of the stack is $(\tau_1, m_1, i, \varnothing, T_1)$, and i points at $\tau_2 = \text{navigate}(r_1, d_2)$. After the call to nextstep, i points at the action $\text{unload}(r_1, c_1, c_3, p_2, d_2)$. REAP-progress sends it as a command to the execution platform. In the eleventh call to REAP-progress, suppose the command is still running. Then REAP-progress returns.

- In the twelfth call to REAP-progress, suppose the command has finished. Then Simulate returns success, and i is the last step of m, so REAP-progress removes $(\tau_1, m_1, i, \varnothing, T_1)$ from $stack_1$. $\square$

At this point, Agenda is empty, so REAP-main continues to iterate its main loop without any further calls to REAP-progess unless something new arrives in the input stream.

Comparison with RAE. In our examples, often only one method instance was applicable in a given state. In such cases, RAE would have chosen the same method instance as REAP, without needing to call a planner. Thus it may not be immediately evident to the reader why REAP's planner is useful. It is useful in two ways:

- In situations where multiple method instances are applicable, planning can be useful to explore the alternatives and suggest which method instance to use. For example, in Example 3.13, REAP had to choose whether to go directly from d_1 to d_2, or to go from d_1 to d_3 and then to d_2. Here, the planner was useful for telling it what route to choose.

- By using the planner to look ahead, REAP sometimes can detect cases when future failure is inevitable, so that it can abandon the current course of action and try something else. This may enable it to accomplish a task in cases where RAE would just continue until the failure occurred.

3.5 DISCUSSION AND HISTORICAL REMARKS

3.5.1 Refinement Acting

Early planning and acting systems relied on a uniform set of action primitives, that is, planned actions were assument to be directly executable without refinement. This is exemplified in Planex by Fikes [196], one of the first acting systems, which was coupled with the STRIPS planner. Planex assumes correct and complete state updates after each action execution, from which it detects failures but also opportunities for pursuing a plan. It relies on *triangle tables* to monitor the progress of a plan with respect to the goal.

The lack of robustness of this and similar systems was addressed by various approaches for specifying operational models of actions and techniques for context-dependent refinement into lower level commands. Among these, procedure-based systems are quite popular. RAP (Reactive Action Package), proposed by Firby [199], is an early example. Each package is in charge of satisfying a particular goal, corresponding to a planned action. Deliberation chooses the appropriate package according to the current context.

PRS (Procedural Reasoning System), by Ingrand et al. [293], is a widely used procedure-based action refinement and monitoring system. As in RAP, one writes procedures to achieve goals or react to particular events and observations. The system commits to goals and tries alternative procedures when needed. It allows for concurrent procedure execution and multithreading. Some planning capabilities were added to PRS by Despouys and Ingrand [152] to anticipate execution paths leading to failure by simulating the execution of procedures and exploring different branches.

TCA by Simmons [539] and TDL by Simmons and Apfelbaum [541] extend the capabilities of procedure-based systems with a wide range of synchronization constructs between commands and temporal constraints management. These and other timeline-oriented acting systems, such as RMPL of Ingham et al. [292] are further discussed in Section 4.6.

XFRM by Beetz and McDermott [49] uses transformation rules to modify hand written conditional plans expressed in a representation called Reactive Plan Language [48]. It searches in plan space to improve its refinements, using simulation and probabilities of possible outcomes. It replaces the currently executed plan on the fly if it finds another one more adapted to the current situation. Beetz [47] extended this approach with more elaborate reactive controllers.

Other procedure-based approaches have been proposed, such as IPEM by Ambros-Ingerson and Steel [18], EXEC by Muscettola et al. [441], or CPEF by Myers [442]. Concurrency and synchronization issues, which often arise at the command level, have been addressed by a few Petri nets – based systems. For example, Wang et al. [595] model with Petri nets the proper order of the execution of commands and their required coordination. The model can be used in simulation for verification and performance testing. Similar approaches have been pursued by Barbier et al. [36] and Ziparo et al. [629] to specify an acting system whose properties can be validated with reachability and deadlock analysis.

Finite State Automata have also been used as acting models, in which an abstract action is represented as an FSA whose transitions are labelled with sensory-motor signals and commands. For example, FSA have been used jointly with IxTeT by Chatilla et al. [115]. Verma et al. [583] illustrate in PLEXIL a representation in which the user specifies nodes as computational abstractions. A node can monitor events, execute commands, or assign values to variables. It may refer hierarchically to a list of lower level nodes. Execution is controlled by constraints (start, end), guards (invariant), and conditions.

SMACH, the ROS execution system of Bohren et al. [79], also implements an automata-based approach. The user writes a set of hierarchical state machines. Each state corresponds to the execution of a particular command. The interface with ROS actions, services, and topics is very natural, but the semantics of constructs available in SMACH is limited for reasoning on goals and states. Let us also mention the approach of Pistore et al. [486], based on the Business Process Execution Language (BPEL, of Andrews et al. [22]), which proposes to plan and compose asynchronous software services represented as state transition systems. The approach produces a controller that takes into account uncertainty and the interleaving of the execution of different processes. It is extended by Bucchiarone et al. [101] to deal at run-time with a hierarchical representation that includes abstract actions; Pistor et al. [485] address the problem of automated synthesis and run-time monitoring of processes. This work is further discussed in Chapter 5.

Unlike the procedure-based approaches, automata and Petri net approaches allow for formal analysis, such as reachability and dead locks checking, which can be critical for the specification and the verification of acting models. A few systems try to overcome the engineering bottleneck of hand specification of procedures or automata by relying on logic inference mechanisms for extending high-level specifications. Examples are the Temporal Action Logic approach of Doherty et al. [158] for monitoring but not action refinement and the situation calculus approach. The latter is exemplified in GOLEX by Hähnel et al. [251], an execution system for the GOLOG planner. In GOLOG and GOLEX, the user specifies respectively planning and acting knowledge in the situation calculus representation. GOLEX provides Prolog hand-programmed "exec" clauses that explicitly define the sequence of commands a platform has to execute. It also provides monitoring primitives to check the effects of executed actions. GOLEX executes the plan produced by GOLOG, but even if the two systems rely on the same logic programming representation, they remain completely separated, limiting the interleaving of planning and acting. The PLATAS system of Claßen et al. [124] relies on GOLOG with a mapping between the PDDL langage and the Situation Calculus. The READYLOG language of Ferrein and Lakemeyer [194], a derivative of GOLOG, combines planning with programming. It relies on a decision-theoretic planner used by the acting component when a problem needs to be solved. The acting component monitors and perceives the environment through passive sensing, and acts or plans accordingly.

Finally, there are several systems that rely on probabilistic approaches, possibly with sampling techniques, which are discussed in Section 6.8.

3.5.2 Refinement Planning

HTN planning. Hierarchical Task Network (HTN) planning uses *HTN methods*, which are like refinement methods except that instead of being a program to execute, the body of a method is a partially or totally ordered set of tasks and actions, along with constraints that the state variables need to satisfy over various parts of the partial ordering.

The first HTN planning systems, which were developed in the mid-1970s [520, 561], used *plan-space HTN planning*, that is, they combined HTN task refinement with plan-space search [307]. Theoretical models for plan-space HTN planning began to be developed in the early 1990s [615, 309], culminating in a formal semantics [180], a provably correct planning algorithm [181], and analysis showing that HTN planning has greater expressive power than classical planning [179]. Work was also done on making plan-space HTN planning more efficient using planning-graph techniques [397, 396].

Most current HTN planning algorithms use a forward-search procedure such as the one in SeRPE (Algorithm 3.4). For example, the SHOP algorithm [446] can be rewritten as a special case of SeRPE, and a slightly modified version[7] of the SHOP2 algorithm [448] can be rewritten as a special case of IRT (Algorithm 3.5), using HTN methods that include "interleave" operators. The approach of Biundo and Schattenberg [72] integrates HTN with plan space planning; it has been extended with efficient heuristics using task decomposition and landmarks [177, 52]. Other extensions to HTN planning have been proposed, for example, to temporal planning [110] (see Chapter 4) and planning with preferences [553].

A recent formal model of HTN search spaces [10] has shown that because they have a more complex structure than classical search spaces, there is a wider variety of possible ways to search them, including some possibilities for which no planning algorithms have yet been written. The model suggests it may be feasible to develop domain-independent HTN planning heuristics using a relaxation of one of these search spaces, but such heuristics have not yet been developed.

HTN methods can be useful for encoding "standard operating procedures" for accomplishing tasks in various application domains [603]. Some examples include scheduling [604], logistics and crisis management [133, 562, 72], spacecraft planning and scheduling [1, 183], equipment configuration [6], manufacturing process planning [550], evacuation planning [438], computer games [551, 113], and robotics [430, 431].

Combining refinement planning and classical planning. When a classical planner is trying to achieve a goal g, it may examine any sequence of actions that it thinks will lead toward g. When a refinement planner is trying to accomplish a task, it will examine only those action sequences that can be produced using the available refinement methods. Thus if we use refinement planning to plan for a task of the form achieve(g), this can be considered a way of constraining the search for g.

On one hand, constraining the search in this manner can convey a substantial efficiency advantage [445]. On the other hand, Example 3.12 demonstrates that unless the planner is given a comprehensive set of methods that cover all of the possible tasks to accomplish, and all of the possible situations in which they might need to be accomplished, planning can fail in situations in which one would want it to succeed.

---

[7] The modification is to remove SHOP2's requirement that a method m's preconditions must be evaluated in the same state as the preconditions of the first action in the decomposition tree below m. Enforcing such a requirement is not feasible in dynamic environments, and IRT and RAE do not attempt to do so.

Consequently, several researchers have investigated ways to combine the advantages of both refinement planning and classical planning by using refinement methods when they are applicable and classical planning when no refinement methods are available.

One approach involves running a classical planner and an HTN planner as two separate subroutines, with the refinement planner passing control to the classical planner whenever it encounters a task for which no methods have been defined, and the classical planner passing control to the refinement planner whenever it encounters an "action" that matches the head of an HTN method [220].

Another approach achieves the same kind of effect by compiling a set of HTN methods (subject to certain restrictions because HTN planning has greater expressivity than classical planning) into a set of classical "actions" whose names, preconditions, and effects encode the steps involved in applying the methods, and using these actions in a classical planner [8].

A third approach [533] uses an HTN-like formalism in which there are goals rather than tasks, and the body of a method is a sequence of goals and actions. If the planner encounters a goal for which there is an applicable method then it uses the method. Otherwise it invokes a landmark-based forward search. During each episode of landmark generation, the planner treats the landmarks as intermediate goals, reverting to refinement planning whenever it encounters a landmark for which there is an applicable method.

3.5.3 Translating Among Multiple Domain Models

Throughout this chapter, we assumed that all of the refinements took place in the same state space, but in applications in which refinements are done at multiple levels of abstraction (e.g., see Figure 1.2), different state and action representations may be needed at different levels of abstraction.

In principle, the algorithms and procedures in this chapter can be generalized to accommodate this, using techniques somewhat like the ones used in abstraction heuristics (see Section 2.7.9). However, such a generalization will require formal definitions of the relationships among tasks, states and actions at different levels, translation algorithms based on these definitions, and planning and acting algorithms that can accommodate these translations. A comprehensive approach for this problem has yet to be developed.

3.6 EXERCISES

3.1. Modify the m-search method of Example 3.2 by assuming it uses a planning function, plan-path, which computes an optimized sequence of locations with content that is not yet known; the search proceeds according to this sequence.

3.2. Complete the methods of Example 3.2 by considering that move-to is not a command but a task addressed by a method that calls a motion planner, which returns a trajectory, then controls the motion of the robot along that trajectory.

3.3. Complete the methods of Example 3.2 by considering that perceive is not a command but a task that requires calling a perception planner that returns a sequence of observation poses. Define two methods: (i) for a complete survey of a location where perceive goes through the entire sequence of observation poses and (ii) for a focus perception that stops when the searched object is detected.

3.4. Analyze how the methods in Exercises 3.1, 3.2, and 3.3 embed planning capabilities in refinement methods at the acting level. Relate this to Figure 1.2 and the discussion in Section 1.2.2.

3.5. Combine the two scenarios of Examples 3.2 and 3.3: while the robot is searching for a container, it has to react to an emergency. What needs to be done to ensure that the robot returns to its search when the task address-emergency finishes (see Section 3.2.4)?

3.6. In Example 3.4, in the body of m-opendoor, why is the first word "while" rather than "if"?

3.7. Complete the methods of Example 3.4 for refining the tasks unlatch(r, d) and throw-wide(r, d) when the door turns to the right, when the door opens away from the robot, and when the door slides.

3.8. Complete the methods of Example 3.4 with appropriate steps to survey the grasping status of whatever the robot is grasping and to turn the handle in the opposite direction before ungrasping it.

3.9. Extend Example 3.4 for a robot with two arms: the robot uses its left (or right) arm if the door turns or slides to the left (or right, respectively). Add a method to move an object from one of the robot's hands to the other that can be used if the hand holding the object is needed for the opening the door.

3.10. Extend Example 3.4 for the case in which the door might be locked with an RFID lock system and the robot's RFID chip is attached to its left arm.

3.11. Redefine the pseudocode of Rae, Progress, and Retry to implement the extensions discussed in Section 3.2.4 for controlling the progress of a task.

3.12. Implement and test the fetch task of Example 3.2 in OpenPRS (https://git.openrobots .org/projects/openprs/wiki). Integrate the results of Exercise 3.1 in your implementation; use for plan-path a simple Dijkstra graph-search algorithm. Is it possible to extend your OpenPRS implementation to handle the requirements stated in Exercise 3.5?

3.13. In Example 3.8, rewrite the two methods for put-in-pile(c, p') as a single method. What are the benefits and drawbacks of having them as one method rather than two?

3.14. For the task uncover(c) in Example 3.8, write a method or set of methods for the case where there are containers on c but no other pile at the same dock.

3.15. Professor Prune says that the m-navigate method in Example 3.8 can cause excessive backtracking. Is he correct? Explain why or why not, and if he is correct, then write a better method or set of methods.

3.16. Following is a domain-specific acting algorithm to find near-optimal solutions for blocks world problems (see Exercise 2.10), where "optimal" means the smallest possible number of actions. In it, s_0 is an initial state in which holding = nil, and g is a set of loc atoms (e.g., as in Figure 2.18). Here are some definitions of terms used in the algorithm:

- For each block b, if g contains an atom of the form $\text{loc}(b) = c$, then $goal(b) = c$. If there is no such atom, then $goal(b) = $ nil.
- A block b is *unfinished* if $s_0(\text{loc}(b)) \neq goal(b)$ and $goal(b) \neq$ nil or if $s_0(\text{loc}(b))$ is an unfinished block. Otherwise b is *finished*.
- A block b is *clear* if $\text{top}(b) = $ nil.

Here is the acting algorithm:

Stack-blocks(s_0, g)
    while there is at least one unfinished block do
      if there is an unfinished clear block b such that
           $goal(b) = $ table or $goal(b)$ is a finished clear block
      then
        move b to $goal(b)$
      else
        choose a clear unfinished block b
        move b to table

  (a) What sequence of actions will this algorithm produce for the planning problem in Exercise 2.10(b)?

  (b) Write a set of refinement methods that encode this algorithm. You may assume that there is already a function *finished*(b) that returns true if b is finished and false otherwise.

3.17. Suppose we try to use SeRPE on the problem in Example 3.6. Draw as much of the refinement tree as you can. What problem prevents you from drawing the entire refinement tree? Suggest a way to resolve the problem.

3.18. Rewrite the pseudocode for SeRPE, replacing the nondeterministic choice with depth-first backtracking.

3.19. In Example 3.11, suppose that every time r_1 starts down the road from d_1 to d_2, it hits a bump that knocks c_1 off of r_1 and back onto p_1.

  (a) What sequence of commands will ARP-lazy, ARP-interleaved, and ARP-asynchronous execute?

  (b) What sequence of commands will REAP execute?

3.20. In Exercise 3.16, suppose that when the robot hand tries to pick up a block, sometimes it will drop the block onto the table.

  (a) What sequence of commands will ARP-lazy, ARP-interleaved, and ARP-asynchronous execute?

  (b) What sequence of commands will REAP execute? What kind of modification could you make to REAP to make it keep trying until it succeeds?

3.21. Redo Example 3.11 using a refinement planner that does a receding-horizon search. More specifically, the planner is a modified version of SeRPE that generates the first two actions of every refinement plan (hence it looks at all partial plans of two steps or less), and it returns the partial plan that (according to some kind of heuristic evaluation) is closest to accomplishing the task or goal. You can assume that the heuristic evaluation always gives accurate results.

CHAPTER 4

Deliberation with Temporal Models

This chapter is about planning and acting approaches in which time is explicit in the descriptive and operational models of actions, as well as in the models of the expected evolution of the world. It describes several algorithms and computation methods for handling durative and concurrent activities with respect to a predicted dynamics.

The first section addresses the need of making time explicit in the deliberation of an actor. A knowledge representation for modeling actions with temporal variables is presented in Section 4.2. It relies on an extension of the refinement methods introduced earlier, which are seen here as *chronicles*, that is, collections of assertions and tasks with explicit temporal constraints. A planning algorithm with temporal refinement methods is developed in Section 4.3. The basic techniques for managing temporal constraints and the controllability of temporal plans are then presented in Section 4.4. Acting problems with temporal domain models are discussed, considering different types of operational models, in Section 4.5. The chapter concludes with a discussion and historical remarks, followed by exercises.

4.1 INTRODUCTION

To perform an action, different kinds of resources may need to be borrowed (e.g., space, tools) or consumed (e.g., energy). Time is a resource required by every action, but it differs from other types of resources. It flows independently from whether any actions are being performed, and it can be shared ad infinitum by independent actors as long as their actions do not interfere with each other.

In previous chapters, we left time implicit in our models: an action produced an instantaneous transition from one state to the next. However, deliberative acting often requires explicit temporal models of actions. Rather than just specifying an action's pre-conditions and effects, temporal models must specify what things an action requires and what events it will cause at various points during the action's performance. For example, moving a robot r_1 from a loading dock d_1 to a loading dock d_2 does not require d_2's availability at the outset but does require it shortly before r_1 reaches d_2.

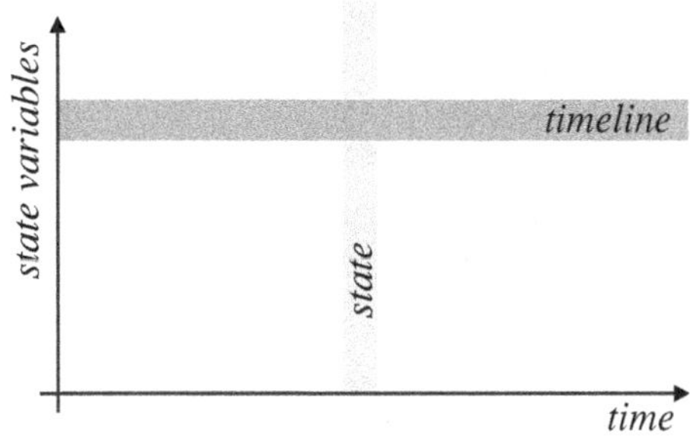

Figure 4.1. State-oriented versus time-oriented views.

Actions may, and sometimes must, overlap, even if their conditions and effects are not independent. As one example, r_1 may move from d_1 to d_2 while r_2 is moving from d_2 to d_1. As another, opening a door that has a knob and a spring latch that controls the knob requires two tightly synchronized actions: *(i)* pushing and maintaining the latch while *(ii)* turning the knob. Modeling such concurrency requires an explicit representation of time.

Goals are sometimes constrained with absolute deadlines. Events may be expected to occur at future time periods, for example, the arrival of scheduled ships at a harbor. Actions may have to be located in time with respect to expected events or deadlines. Time can be required *qualitatively*, to handle synchronization between actions and with events, and *quantitatively*, to model the duration of actions with respect to various parameters.

In summary, the main motivations for making time explicit in planning and acting are the following:

- modeling the duration of actions;
- modeling the effects, conditions, and resources borrowed or consumed by an action at various moments along its duration, including delayed effects;
- handling the concurrency of actions that have interacting and joint effects;
- handling goals with relative or absolute temporal constraints;
- planning and acting with respect to exogenous events that are expected to occur at some future time; and
- planning with actions that maintain a value while being executed, as opposed to just changing that value (e.g., tracking a moving target or keeping a spring latch in some position).

An explicit representation of time for the purpose of acting and planning can be either:

- "State-oriented": one keeps the notion of global states of the world, as we have done so far, and one includes time explicitly in the model of the transitions between states (e.g., as in timed automata and various forms of temporal logics). The dynamics of the world are modeled as a collection of global snapshots, each of which gives a complete description of the domain at some time point.
- "Time-oriented": one represents the dynamics of the world as a collection of partial functions of time, describing local evolutions of state variables. Instead of a state, the building block here is a *timeline* (horizontal slice in Figure 4.1) that focuses on one

state variable and models its evolution in time. Time-oriented approaches use either instants or intervals as temporal primitives, with qualitative and/or quantitative relations.

We use the time-oriented approach in this chapter; a comparison to the state-oriented approach is briefly discussed in Section 4.6.

4.2 TEMPORAL REPRESENTATION

This section describes timelines, chronicles, and temporal refinement methods for modeling and reasoning about actions.

4.2.1 Assertions and Timelines

We rely on a quantitative discrete model of time described by a collection of temporal variables, e.g., $t, t', t_1, t_2, \ldots$; each variable designates a time point. An *interval* is a pair $[t, t']$ such that $t < t'$; its duration is $t' - t > 0$. We also use open intervals, for example, $[t, t')$, in the usual sense. For simplicity, we assume that temporal variables range over the set of integers.[1]

These temporal variables will not be instantiated at planning time into precise values. They will be constrained with respect to other temporal variables or constants; we will have to keep the constraints consistent. The value of a temporal variable will be set by the execution platform when an action is performed, that is, when the commands executing that action are triggered or when their effects are observed. In other words, a temporal variable remains constrained but uninstantiated as long as it refers to the future; it receives as its value the *current time* when the fact that this variable qualifies takes place, either controlled or observed by the actor. After that point, the variable refers to the past.

Temporal constraints are specified with the usual arithmetic operators ($<, \leq, =$, etc.) between temporal variables and integer constants, for example, $t < t'$ says that t is before t'; $d \leq t' - t \leq d'$ constrains the duration of the interval $[t, t']$ between the two bounds d and d'.

In the time-oriented view, each state variable x is a function of time; hence the notation $x(t)$ refers to the value of that variable at time t. The knowledge about the evolution of a state variable as a function of time is represented with temporal assertions.

Definition 4.1. A *temporal assertion* on a state variable x is either a persistence or a change:

- A *persistence*, denoted $[t_1, t_2]x = v$, specifies that $x(t) = v$ for every t in the interval $t_1 \leq t \leq t_2$.
- A *change*, denoted $[t_1, t_2]x:(v_1, v_2)$, specifies that the value of x changes over the interval $[t_1, t_2]$ from $x(t_1) = v_1$ to $x(t_2) = v_2$, with $v_1 \neq v_2$.   □

---

[1] This assumption avoids some minor issues regarding closed versus open intervals.

Figure 4.2. A timeline for the state variable loc(r1) (the position of the points on the two axis are qualitative; the rough ride lines do not represent necessarily linear changes).

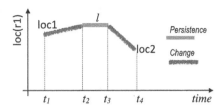

As a shorthand, $[t]x = v$ stands for $[t, t+1)x=v$ and $[t]x : (v, v')$ stands for $[t, t+1]x:(v, v')$; the former gives the value of x at a single time point and the latter expresses a transition from v to v' over two consecutive time points. In general, and assertion $[t, t']x:(v, v')$ does not model how the change takes place within the interval $[t, t']$; it can be gradual over possibly intermediate values or instantaneous at any moment in $[t, t']$. However, if $t' = t + 1$, then the value of x changes discretely from v at time t to v' at time $t + 1$.

For example, the assertion $[t_1, t_2]$loc(r1):(loc2,loc3) says that r1's location changes from loc2 to loc3. The precise moments of this change and intermediate values of loc(r1) are not stated by this assertion. Their values will be established by the command that performs the change from loc2 to loc3.

Temporal assertions are parameterized, for example, $[t_1, t_2]$loc(r):(l, loc1) states that some robot r moves from a location l to loc1. The values of r and l will be fixed at some planning or acting stage; the values of t_1 and t_2 are instantiated only at acting time.

Definition 4.2. A *timeline* is a pair $(\mathcal{T}, \mathcal{C})$ where $\mathcal{T}$ is a conjunction of temporal assertions on a state variable, possibly parameterized with object variables, and $\mathcal{C}$ is a conjunction of constraints on the temporal variables and the object variables of the assertions in $\mathcal{T}$.   □

$\mathcal{T}$ and $\mathcal{C}$ are denoted as sets of assertions and constraints. Constraints on temporal variables are unary and binary inequalities and equalities. Constraints on object variables are with respect to rigid relations, for example, connected(l,loc1), or binding constraints, as in the following example.

Example 4.3. The whereabouts of the robot r1, as depicted in Figure 4.2, can be expressed with the following timeline:

$$(\{[t_1, t_2]\text{loc(r1)}:(\text{loc1}, l), \ [t_2, t_3]\text{loc(r1)}=l, \ [t_3, t_4]\text{loc(r1)}:(l, \text{loc2})\},$$

$$\{t_1 < t_2 < t_3 < t_4, l \neq \text{loc1}, l \neq \text{loc2}\})$$

In this timeline, $\mathcal{T}$ has three assertions: one persistence and two changes; $\mathcal{C}$ has temporal and object constraints. The constraints are in this particular case entailed from the three intervals and two change assertions in $\mathcal{T}$. Instances of the timeline are substitutions of possible values in these assertions for the five variables $l, t_1, \ldots, t_4$.

Note that this timeline does not say what happens between t_1 and t_2; all we know is that r1 leaves loc1 at or after t_1, and it arrives at l at or before t_2. To say that these two changes happen exactly at t_1 and t_2, we can add the following assertions in the timeline: $[t_1, t_1 + 1]$ loc(r1):(loc1,route), and $[t_2 - 1, t_2]$ loc(r1):(route, l), where route is some intermediate location. These assertions say that $[t_1]\text{loc}(r1)=\text{loc}1$, $[t_1 + 1]\text{loc}(r1)=\text{route}$, $[t_2 - 1]\text{loc}(r1)=\text{route}$, and $[t_2]\text{loc}(r1) = l$.   □

Temporal assertions in a timeline $(\mathcal{T}, \mathcal{C})$ are expressed with temporal and object variables that can be instantiated within their respective domains with the usual unification mechanisms. Not every instance of a timeline makes sense as a possible evolution of the corresponding state variable.

Definition 4.4. An instance of $(\mathcal{T}, \mathcal{C})$ is *consistent* if it satisfies all the constraints in $\mathcal{C}$ and does not specify two different values for a state variable at the same time. A timeline $(\mathcal{T}, \mathcal{C})$ is *consistent* if its set of consistent instances is not empty.   □

A pair of temporal assertions is *possibly conflicting* (conflicting, for short) if it can have inconsistent instances; otherwise, it is nonconflicting. Because change assertions abstract away the precise times at which the changes occur, we consider that two assertions $[t_1, t_2]x:(v_1, v_2)$ and $[t_1', t_2']x:(v_1', v_2')$ are conflicting if they overlap in time, unless the overlap is only at their endpoints (i.e., $v_2 = v_1'$ and $t_2 = t_1'$, or $v_2' = v_1$ and $t_2' = t_1$) or if they are strictly identical.

A *separation constraint* for a pair of conflicting assertions is a conjunction of constraints on object and temporal variables that exclude inconsistent instances. The set of separation constraints of a conflicting pair of assertions contains all possible conjunctions that exclude inconsistent instances.

Example 4.5. The two persistence assertions $\{[t_1, t_2] \text{loc}(r)=\text{loc}1, [t_3, t_4] \text{loc}(r1)=l\}$ are conflicting, because they can have inconsistent instances. For example, if $r = r1, l \neq \text{loc}1$ and either $t_1 \leq t_3 \leq t_2$ or $t_1 \leq t_4 \leq t_2$, then the robot r1 would have to be at loc1 and at $l \neq \text{loc}1$ simultaneously.

The assertions $\{[t_1, t_2]\text{loc}(r1) = \text{loc}1, [t_2, t_3]\text{loc}(r1) : (\text{loc}1, \text{loc}2)\}$ is nonconflicting: they have no inconsistent instances.

The pair $\{[t_1, t_2]\text{loc}(r1) = \text{loc}1, [t_3, t_4]\text{loc}(r1) : (l, l')\}$ is conflicting. A separation constraint is: $(t_2 = t_3, l = \text{loc}1)$.

The set of separation constraints for that pair is: $\{(t_2 < t_3), (t_4 < t_1), (t_2 = t_3, l = \text{loc}1), (t_4 = t_1, l' = \text{loc}1)\}$.   □

A set of assertions is conflicting if any pair of the set is. A separation constraint for a set of conflicting assertions is a consistent conjunction of constraints that makes every pair of the set nonconflicting. Note that a set of assertions may have separation constraints for every pair while there is no consistent conjunction of separation constraints for the entire set.

Example 4.6. Consider the set of assertions $\{[t_1, t_2]\text{loc}(r1):(\text{loc}1, \text{loc}2), [t_2, t_3]\text{loc}(r1)=l, [t_3, t_4]\text{loc}(r1):(\text{loc}3, \text{loc}4)\}$. The constraint $l = \text{loc}2$ is a separation for the first two assertions, while the constraint $l = \text{loc}3$ is required for the last two assertion.   □

Note that the consistency of a timeline $(\mathcal{T}, \mathcal{C})$ is a stronger notion than just satisfying the constraints in $\mathcal{C}$. It also requires the assertions in $\mathcal{T}$ to have a nonconflicting instance that meets $\mathcal{C}$. A timeline is inconsistent if in particular there are no separation constraints, or none that is consistent with $\mathcal{C}$. A convenient case is when $\mathcal{C}$ includes the separation constraints needed by $\mathcal{T}$. For such a case, satisfying the constraints in $\mathcal{C}$ guarantees the consistency of the timeline. This is the notion of secure timelines.

Definition 4.7. A timeline $(\mathcal{T}, \mathcal{C})$ is *secure* iff it is consistent and every instance that meets the constraints in $\mathcal{C}$ is consistent. □

In secure timeline $(\mathcal{T}, \mathcal{C})$, no instance that meets $\mathcal{C}$ specifies different values for the same state variable at the same time. In other words, every pair of assertions in $\mathcal{T}$ is either nonconflicting or has a separation constraint entailed from $\mathcal{C}$. A consistent timeline may possibly be augmented with separation constraints to make it secure.

Example 4.8. The timeline $(\{[t_1, t_2]\mathsf{loc}(\mathsf{r1})=\mathsf{loc1}, [t_3, t_4]\ \mathsf{loc}(\mathsf{r1}){:}(\mathsf{loc1},\ \mathsf{loc2})\}, \{t_2 < t_3\})$ is secure; its assertions are nonconflicting. The timeline $(\{[t_1, t_2]\ \mathsf{loc}(r)=\mathsf{loc1},$ $[t_3, t_4]\mathsf{loc}(\mathsf{r1})=l\}, \{t_1 < t_2, t_3 < t_4\})$ is consistent but not secure; when augmented with either $(r \neq \mathsf{r1})$ or $(t_2 < t_3)$ it becomes secure. □

Another important notion is that of the *causal support* of an assertion in a timeline. Timelines are used to reason about the dynamic evolution of a state variable. An actor's reasoning about a timeline requires every element in this evolution to be either given by its observation or prior knowledge (e.g., for the initial state) or explained by some reason due the actor's own actions or to the dynamics of the environment. For example, looking at the timeline in Figure 4.2, the locations of the robot in l, then in $\mathsf{loc2}$, are explained by the two change assertions in that timeline. However, nothing explains how the robot got to $\mathsf{loc1}$; we have to state an assertion saying that it was there initially or brought there by a move action.

Definition 4.9. An assertion $[t, t']x=v$ or $[t, t']x{:}(v, v')$ in a timeline is *causally supported* if the timeline contains another assertion $[t'', t]x=v$ or $[t'', t]x{:}(v'', v)$ that asserts the value v at time t. □

Note that by definition of the intervals $[t'', t]$ and $[t, t']$ we have $t'' < t < t'$. Hence this definition excludes circular support, that is, assertion α cannot support assertion β while β supports α, regardless of whether this support is direct or by transitivity via some other assertions.

Example 4.10. In Example 4.3 assertion $[t_2, t_3]\mathsf{loc}(\mathsf{r1})=l$ is supported by $[t_1, t_2]\mathsf{loc}(\mathsf{r1}){:}(\mathsf{loc1}, l)$. Similarly, assertion $[t_3, t_4]\mathsf{loc}(\mathsf{r1}){:}(l, \mathsf{loc2})$ is supported by $[t_2, t_3]\mathsf{loc}(\mathsf{r1})=l$. However, the first assertion in that timeline is unsupported: nothing asserts $[t_1]\ \mathsf{loc}(\mathsf{r1})=\mathsf{loc1}$. □

It may be possible to support an assertion in a timeline by adding constraints on object and temporal variables. For example, $[t_1, t_2]\mathsf{loc}(\mathsf{r1}){:}(\mathsf{loc1},\mathsf{loc2})$ can be supported by $[t, t']\mathsf{loc}(r)=l$ if the following constraints are added to the timeline: $(t' = t_1, r = \mathsf{r1}, l = \mathsf{loc1})$. Another way of supporting an assertion is by adding a persistence condition. For example, in the timeline $(\{[t_1, t_2]\mathsf{loc}(\mathsf{r1}){:}(\mathsf{loc1},\mathsf{loc2}), [t_3, t_4]\mathsf{loc}(\mathsf{r1}){:}$ $\mathsf{loc2},\mathsf{loc3})\}, \{t_1 < t_2 < t_3 < t_4\})$, the second assertion can be supported by adding the following persistence: $[t_2, t_3]\ \mathsf{loc}(\mathsf{r1})=\mathsf{loc2}$. Adding a change assertion can also be used to support assertions. As we'll see in Section 4.3.3, adding a new action to a plan results in new assertions that can provide the required support.

It is convenient to extend to sets of timelines the previous notation and definitions. If $\mathcal{T}$ is a set of temporal assertions on several state variables and $\mathcal{C}$ are constraints, then the pair $(\mathcal{T}, \mathcal{C})$ corresponds to a set of timelines $\{(\mathcal{T}_1, \mathcal{C}_1), \dots, (\mathcal{T}_k, \mathcal{C}_k)\}$. $(\mathcal{T}, \mathcal{C})$ is consistent or secure if each of its timelines is. While reasoning about actions and their effects, an actor will perform the following operations on a set of timelines $(\mathcal{T}, \mathcal{C})$:

- add constraints to $\mathcal{C}$, to secure a timeline or support its assertions; for example, for the first timeline in Example 4.8, the constraint $t_2 = t_3$ makes the assertion $[t_3, t_4]$loc(r1):(loc1, loc2) supported.
- add assertions to $\mathcal{T}$, for example, for the timeline in Figure 4.2 to take into account additional motions of the robot.
- instantiate some of the variables, which may possibly split a timeline of the set with respect to different state variables, for example, assertions related to loc(r) and loc(r') refer to the same state variable, but that timeline will be split if r is instantiated as r1 and r' as r2.

4.2.2 Actions

We model an action as a collection of timelines. More precisely, a primitive action template, or a primitive for short, is a triple $(head, \mathcal{T}, \mathcal{C})$, where $head$ is the name and arguments of the primitive, and $(\mathcal{T}, \mathcal{C})$ is a set of timelines. The reader may view this representation as an extension of the action templates of Chapter 2 with explicit time, expressing conditions and effects at different moments during the time span of an action.

Example 4.11. Suppose several robots are moving in a connected network of roads connected to some loading docks. Fixed in each dock are one crane and several piles where containers are stacked. A dock can contain at most one robot at a time. Robots and cranes can carry at most one container at a time. Waypoints in roads guide the robot navigation.

The objects in this domains are of the following types: $r \in Robots$, $k \in Cranes$, $c \in Containers$, $p \in Piles$, $d \in Docks$, $w \in Waypoints$.

The invariant structure of the domain is given by three rigid relations:

$$attached \subseteq (Cranes \cup Piles) \times Docks$$

$$adjacent \subseteq Docks \times Waypoints$$

$$connected \subseteq Waypoints \times Waypoints$$

The domain is described with the following state variables:

$$loc(r) \in Docks \cup Waypoints \qquad \text{for } r \in Robots$$

$$freight(r) \in Containers \cup \{empty\} \qquad \text{for } r \in Robots$$

$$grip(k) \in Containers \cup \{empty\} \qquad \text{for } k \in Cranes$$

$$pos(c) \in Robots \cup Cranes \cup Piles \qquad \text{for } c \in Containers$$

$$\text{stacked-on}(c) \in \textit{Containers} \cup \{\text{empty}\} \qquad \text{for } c \in \textit{Containers}$$

$$\text{top}(p) \in \textit{Containers} \cup \{\text{empty}\} \qquad \text{for } p \in \textit{Piles}$$

$$\text{occupant}(d) \in \textit{Robots} \cup \{\text{empty}\} \qquad \text{for } d \in \textit{Docks}.$$

The constant empty means that a robot, a crane, a pile, or a dock is empty, or that a container is not stacked on any other container.

The task in this example is to bring containers from their current position to a destination pile. It is specified with primitives, tasks, and methods (to which we come back in the next section). The primitives are the following:

leave(r, d, w) : robot r leaves dock d to an adjacent waypoint w,

enter(r, d, w) : r enters d from an adjacent wyapoint w,

navigate(r, w, w') : r navigates from waypoint w to a connected one w',

stack(k, c, p) : crane k holding container c stacks it on top of pile p,

unstack(k, c, p) : crane k unstacks a container c from the top of pile p,

put(k, c, r) : crane k holding a container c and puts it onto r,

take(k, c, r) : crane k takes container c from robot r.

A descriptive model of leave is specified by the following template:

leave(r, d, w)
 assertions: $[t_s, t_e]$loc(r):(d, w)
       $[t_s, t_e]$occupant(d):(r, empty)
 constraints: $t_e \leq t_s + \delta_1$
       adjacent(d, w)

This expression says that the leave action changes the location of r from dock d to the adjacent waypoint w, with a delay smaller than δ_1 after the action starts at t_s; the dock d is empty when the action ends at t_e.

Similarly, enter is defined by the following action template:

enter(r, d, w)
 assertions: $[t_s, t_e]$loc(r):(w, d)
       $[t_s, t_e]$occupant(d):(empty, r)
 constraints: $t_e \leq t_s + \delta_2$
       adjacent(d, w)

The take primitive is specified as follows:

take(k, c, r)
 assertions: $[t_s, t_e]$pos(c):(r, k)
       $[t_s, t_e]$grip(k):(empty, c)
       $[t_s, t_e]$freight(r):(c, empty)
       $[t_s, t_e]$loc(r)=d
 constraints: attached(k, d), attached(p, d)

The assertions in this primitive say that a container c loaded on r at t_s is taken by crane k at t_e; r remains in the same dock as k.

Similar specifications are required for the primitives $\text{put}(k, c, r)$, to put a container on r, $\text{stack}(k, c, p)$, to put the container c held by k on top of pile p, $\text{unstack}(k, c, p)$, to take with k the top container c of pile p, and $\text{navigate}(r, w, w')$ to navigate between connected waypoints (see Exercise 4.1).

Note that actions leave, enter, take, and so on, are said to be primitive at the planning level, but they will be refined at the acting level. We'll see in Example 4.25 how to further refine them into executable commands.   □

As illustrated in Example 4.11, primitives are specified as assertions and constraints on temporal variables and object variables. By convention, t_s and t_e denote the starting point and ending point of each primitive. The temporal variables of an action template are not in its list of parameters because we are going to handle them differently from the object variables. The planner will instantiate object variables, but it will only constrain the temporal variables with respect to other time points. Their instantiation into constants is performed at acting time, from the triggering of controllable time points and the observation of the uncontrollable points (see Section 4.4.3).

Note that this representation does not use two separate fields for preconditions and effects. A change assertion in a primitive, such as $[t_s, t]\text{grip}(k){:}(\text{empty}, c)$, expresses both the precondition that k should be empty at t_s and the effect that k holds c at t. Furthermore, the temporal assertions in a primitive refer to several instants, not necessarily ordered, within the time span of an action.

Temporal and object variables in a primitive are free variables. To make sure that different instances of a primitive, say take, refer to different variables t_s, t_e, k, r, c, we rely on the usual variable renaming, which is further detailed later in the chapter.

4.2.3 Methods and Tasks

We define a task as in the previous chapter, that is, a label naming an activity to be performed by refining it into a collection of subtasks and primitives. A task has temporal qualifications, written as follows:

$$[t, t']task.$$

The preceding expression means that *task* takes place over an interval contained within $[t, t']$, that is, it starts at or after t, and finishes at or before t'. Note that $[t, t']task$ has different semantics than a persistence condition on a state variable. It just says *task* should happen within $[t, t']$ and does not require *task* to persist throughout the entire interval.

A task is refined into subtasks and primitives using refinement methods. A temporal refinement method is a tuple (*head, task, refinement, $\mathcal{T}, \mathcal{C}$*), where *head* is the name and arguments of the methods, *task* gives the task to which the method applies, *refinement* is the set of temporally qualified subtasks and primitives in which it refines *task*, $\mathcal{T}$ are assertions and $\mathcal{C}$ constraints on temporal and object variables. A temporal refinement method does not need a separate precondition field, as in the methods of previous

Figure 4.3. Assertions, actions, and subtasks of a refinement method for the bring task (arrows represent precedence constraints).

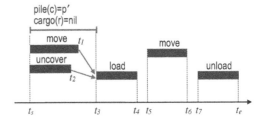

chapter. This is because temporal assertions may express conditions as well as effects in a flexible way and at different moments. Temporal refinement methods are illustrated in Example 4.12.

Example 4.12. Let us further develop the domain in Example 4.11 by specifying a few tasks as temporal refinement methods. The task of bringing containers to destination piles can be broken into the following tasks: bring, move, uncover, load, and unload. Some of the methods for performing these tasks are the following:

> m-bring(r, c, p, p', d, d')
>> task: bring(r, c, p) # r brings container c to pile p
>> refinement: $[t_s, t_1]$move(r, d')
>>> $[t_s, t_2]$uncover(c, p')
>>> $[t_3, t_4]$load(k', r, c, p')
>>> $[t_5, t_6]$move(r, d)
>>> $[t_7, t_e]$unload(k, r, c, p)
>> assertions: $[t_s, t_3]$pile$(c)=p'$
>>> $[t_s, t_3]$freight$(r)=$empty
>> constraints: attached(p', d'), attached$(p, d), d \neq d'$
>>> attached(k', d'), attached(k, d)
>>> $t_1 \leq t_3, t_2 \leq t_3, t_4 \leq t_5, t_6 \leq t_7$

This method refines the bring task into five subtasks to move the robot to d' then to d, to uncover container c to have it at the top of pile p', to load the robot in d' and unload in d in the destination pile p. As depicted in Figure 4.3, the first move and uncover are concurrent (t_2 and t_3 are unordered). When both tasks finish, the remaining tasks are sequential. Container c remains in its original pile, and robot r remains empty until the load task starts.

> m-move1(r, d, d', w, w')
>> task: move(r, d) #moves a robot r to a dock d
>> refinement: $[t_s, t_1]$leave(r, d', w')
>>> $[t_2, t_3]$navigate(w', w)
>>> $[t_4, t_e]$enter(r, d, w)
>> assertions: $[t_s, t_s + 1]$loc$(r)=d'$
>> constraints: adjacent(d, w), adjacent$(d', w'), d \neq d'$
>>> connected(w, w')
>>> $t_1 \leq t_2, t_3 \leq t_4$

This method refines the move to a destination dock d into three successive steps: leave the starting dock d' to an adjacent waypoint w', navigate to a connected waypoint w adjacent to the destination and enter the destination d, which is required to be empty only when the robot gets there. The move task requires additional methods to address cases in which the robot starts from a road or when it is already there (see Exercise 4.2).

m-uncover(c, p, k, d, p')
     task: uncover(c, p)   #un-pile p until its top is c
  refinement: $[t_s, t_1]$unstack(k, c', p)
       $[t_2, t_3]$stack(k, c', p')
       $[t_4, t_e]$uncover(c, p)
   assertions: $[t_s, t_s + 1]$pile(c)=p
       $[t_s, t_s + 1]$top(p)=c'
       $[t_s, t_s + 1]$grip(k)=empty
  constraints: attached(k, d), attached(p, d)
       attached(p', d), $p \neq p', c' \neq c$
       $t_1 \leq t_2, t_3 \leq t_4$

This method refines the uncover task into unstacking the container at the top of pile p and moving it to a nearby pile p' and then invoking uncover again recursively if the top of p is not c. Another method should handle the case where c is at the top of p.

Finally, the task load can be refined into unstack and put primitives; task unload is similarly refined into take and stack (see Exercise 4.2).   □

As in primitives, assertions in methods specify conditions as well as effects at any moment during the duration of the task. Note that the specific conditions of subtasks and primitives of a task τ should be expressed in their respective definitions, instead of being in the specification of the methods handling task τ. Redundancy between conditions in methods of tasks and conditions in subtasks and primitives is not desirable. For example, the primitive enter has the assertion $[t_s, t_e]$occupant(d):(empty, r); the same assertion (with different variables that will be unified with t_s, t_e, d and r) may appear in the method m-move1, but it is not needed. Redundancy, as well as incomplete specifications, are sources of errors.

Planning and acting procedures will view tasks as labeled networks with associated constraints. For example, a task bring in Example 4.12 can be the root of a network whose first successor with method m-bring is a task move, which in turn leads with m-move1 to the primitive leave. A leaf in a task network is a primitive. An inner node is a task, which, at some point in the planning and/or acting process, is either:

- *refined*: it is associated with a method; it has successors labeled by subtasks and primitives as specified in the method with the associated constraints; or
- *nonrefined*: its refinement with an applicable method is pending.

This refinement mechanism takes place within a data structure called a chronicle.

4.2.4 Chronicles

A *chronicle* is a collection of temporally qualified tasks, primitives, and assertions with associated constraints. It is used, among other things, to give the initial specifications of a planning problem, including the following:

(i)   the tasks to be performed;
(ii) the current and future known facts that will take place independently of the planned activities; and
(iii) the assertions to be achieved; these are constraints on future states of the world that planning has to meet.

Because the elements in (ii) are also expressed as temporal assertions, we refer to them as a priori *supported* assertions to distinguish them from assertions in (iii), which require support from the planned activities. More formally:

Definition 4.13. A chronicle is a tuple $(\mathcal{A}, \mathcal{S}_T, \mathcal{T}, \mathcal{C})$ where $\mathcal{A}$ is a set of temporally qualified primitives and tasks, $\mathcal{S}_T$ is a set of a priori supported assertions, $\mathcal{T}$ is a set of assertions, and $\mathcal{C}$ is a conjunction of constraints on the temporal and object variables in $\mathcal{A}, \mathcal{S}_T$, and $\mathcal{T}$. □

Example 4.14. Let us augment the domain of Example 4.12 by specifying that a pile p can be on a ship and that a crane k on a dock d can unstack containers from that pile p only when the corresponding ship is docked at d (see Exercise 4.2).

Consider the case in which this domain has two robots r1 and r2, initially in dock1 and dock2, respectively. A ship ship1 is expected to be docked at dock3 at a future interval of time; it has a pile, pile-ship1, the top element of which is a container c1. The problem is to bring container c1 to dock4 using any robot and to have the two robots back at their initial locations at the end. This problem is expressed with the following chronicle:

ϕ_0 :
  tasks: $[t, t']$bring(r, c1, dock4)
  supported: $[t_s]$loc(r1)=dock1
         $[t_s]$loc(r2)=dock2
         $[t_s + 10, t_s + \delta]$docked(ship1)=dock3
         $[t_s]$top(pile-ship1)=c1
         $[t_s]$pos(c1)=pallet
  assertions: $[t_e]$loc(r1) = dock1
         $[t_e]$loc(r2) = dock2
  constraints: $t_s < t < t' < t_e, 20 \leq \delta \leq 30, t_s = 0$

By convention, t_s and t_e denote the starting and end points of a chronicle. Here t_s has an absolute value (origin of the clock). □

Chronicles will also be used to express partial plans that will be progressively transformed by the planner into complete solution plans.

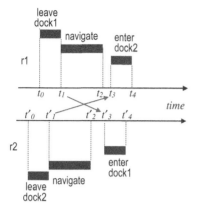

Figure 4.4. Temporally qualified actions of two robots, r1 and r2 (arrows express the precedence constraints $t_1' < t_3$ and $t_1 < t_3'$).

Example 4.15. Consider two robots r1 and r2 in the domain of Example 4.12 performing concurrent actions where each robot moves from its dock to the other robot's dock as depicted in Figure 4.4. The following chronicle (where $\mathcal{S}_T$ and $\mathcal{T}$ are not detailed) expresses this set of coordinated actions:

$$\phi:$$

tasks: $[t_0, t_1]$leave(r1,dock1,w1)
$[t_1, t_2]$navigate(r1,w1,w2)
$[t_3, t_4]$enter(r1,dock2,w2)
$[t_0', t_1']$leave(r2,dock2,w2)
$[t_1', t_2']$navigate(r2,w2,w1)
$[t_3', t_4']$enter(r2,dock1,w1) }

supported: $\mathcal{S}_T$
assertions: $\mathcal{T}$
constraints: $t_1' < t_3, t_1 < t_3', t_s < t_0, t_s < t_0', t_4 < t_e, t_4' < t_e$
adjacent(dock1,w1), adjacent(dock2,w2), connected(w1,w2)

This chronicle says that r1 leaves dock1 before r2 enters dock1 ($t_1 < t_3'$); similarly, r2 leaves dock2 before r1 gets there ($t_1' < t_3$). Each action navigate starts when the corresponding leave finishes (t_1 and t_1'). However, an enter may have to wait until after the navigate finishes (t_2 to t_3) and the way is free. □

The set $\mathcal{T}$ of assertions in a chronicle $\phi = (\mathcal{A}, \mathcal{S}_T, \mathcal{T}, \mathcal{C})$ contains all the assertions of the primitives already in $\mathcal{A}$, for example, leave and enter in Example 4.15. When a task $\tau \in \mathcal{A}$ is refined with a method m, τ is replaced in $\mathcal{A}$ by the subtasks and primitives specified in m, and $\mathcal{T}$ and $\mathcal{C}$ are augmented with the assertions and constraints of m and those of its primitives.

When a task is refined, the free variables in methods and primitives are renamed and possibly instantiated. For example, enter is specified in Example 4.11 with the free variables r, d, w, t_s, t_e. In the first instance of enter in the chronicle of Example 4.15, these variables are respectively bound to r1, dock2, w2, t_3, and t_4. In the second instance of enter, they are bounded to r2, dock1, w1, t_3', and t_4'. The general mechanism for every instance of a primitive or a method is to rename the free variables in its template to new names then to constrain and/or instantiate these renamed variables when needed.

Furthermore, when refining a task and augmenting the assertions and contraints of a chronicle, as specified by a method, we need to make sure that $(\mathcal{T}, \mathcal{C})$ remains secure. Separation constraints will be added to $\mathcal{C}$ to handle conflicting assertions. The consistency of the resulting constraints will be checked. This is detailed in Section 4.4.

Finally, all the assertions of a chronicle must be supported through the mechanisms presented next.

4.3 PLANNING WITH TEMPORAL REFINEMENT METHODS

A temporal planning domain Σ is defined by giving the sets of objects, rigid relations and state variables of the domain, and by specifying the primitives and methods for the tasks of the domain.

A planning problem is defined as a pair (Σ, ϕ_0), where Σ is a temporal planning domain and $\phi_0 = (\mathcal{A}, \mathcal{S}_T, \mathcal{T}, \mathcal{C})$ is an initial chronicle. This chronicle gives the tasks to perform, the goals to achieve, and the supported assertions stating the initial and future states of the world that are expected to occur independently of the activities to be planned for. The pair $(\mathcal{T}, \mathcal{C})$ in ϕ_0 is required to be secure. Note that the planning problem ϕ_0 is defined in terms of tasks as well as goals. Hence planning will proceed by refinement of tasks as well as by generative search for goals.

Partial plans are also expressed as chronicles. A chronicle ϕ defines a solution plan when all its tasks have been refined and all its assertions are supported. At that point, ϕ contains all the primitives initially in ϕ_0 plus those produced by the recursive refinement of the tasks in ϕ_0, according to methods in Σ, and those possibly needed to support the assertions in ϕ_0 or required by the task refinements. It also contains the assertions and constraints in ϕ_0 plus those of the primitives in ϕ and the methods used in the task refinements, together with their constraints and possible separation constraints. More formally:

Definition 4.16. A chronicle ϕ is a valid solution plan of the temporal planning problem (Σ, ϕ_0) iff the following conditions hold:

(i) ϕ does not contain nonrefined tasks;
(ii) all assertions in ϕ are causally supported, either by supported assertions initially in ϕ_0 or by assertions from methods and primitives in the plan; and
(iii) the chronicle ϕ is secure. □

Condition (i) says that all tasks in ϕ_0 have been refined recursively down into primitives; this is similar to what we saw in Section 3.3.1. Condition (ii) extends to temporal domains the notion of causal link seen in Section 2.5. Condition (iii) is a requirement to make sure that the solution chronicle cannot have inconsistent instances. This is because a solution plan has in general noninstantiated temporal and object variables, which are instantiated at execution time (see Sections 4.4.3 and 4.5).

Algorithm 4.1 A chronicle temporal planner.

TemPlan(ϕ, Σ)
   Flaws ← set of flaws of ϕ
   if *Flaws*=∅ then return ϕ
   arbitrarily select $f \in$ *Flaws*   *(i)*
   Resolvers ← set of resolvers of f *(ii)*
   if *Resolvers*=∅ then return failure
   nondeterministically choose $\rho \in$ *Resolvers*   *(iii)*
   ϕ ← Transform(ϕ, ρ)   *(iv)*
   Templan(ϕ, Σ)

4.3.1 Temporal Planning Algorithm

A temporal planning algorithm proceeds by transforming the initial chronicle ϕ_0 with refinement methods and the addition of primitives and separation constraints until the preceding three conditions are met. Let ϕ be the current chronicle in that transformation process; ϕ may contain three types of *flaws* with respect to the requirements of a valid plan in Definition 4.16:

- ϕ has nonrefined tasks: violates condition *(i)*;
- ϕ has nonsupported assertions: violates condition *(ii)*; and
- ϕ has conflicting assertions: violates condition *(iii)*.

Because ϕ is obtained by transforming ϕ_0, when ϕ does not contain nonrefined tasks, then all tasks of ϕ_0 have been refined into actions, that is, planning primitives.

A flaw of one of the three preceding types is addressed by finding its *resolvers*, that is, ways of solving that flaw. The planning algorithm chooses a resolver nondeterministically and transforms the current chronicle accordingly. This is repeated until either the current chronicle is without flaws, that is, it is a valid solution, or a flaw has no resolver, in which case the algorithm must backtrack to previous choices. Algorithm 4.1, TemPlan, is a recursive algorithm to do this.

In the preceding pseudocode, step *(i)* is a heuristic choice of the order in which the resolvers of a given flaw are searched. This choice affects the performance but not the completeness of the algorithm. Step *(iii)* is a backtracking point in a deterministic implementation of TemPlan: all resolvers for a flaw may need to be tried to ensure completeness.

The main technical issues in this temporal planning algorithm are the following:

- How to find the flaws in ϕ and their resolvers and how to transform ϕ with a resolver ρ, that is, the Transform subroutine in Templan. This is discussed for the different types of flaws in Sections 4.3.2−4.3.4.
- How to organize and explore the search space efficiently. This is discussed in Section 4.3.5.
- How to check and maintain the consistency of the constraints in ϕ. This is discussed in Section 4.4.

4.3.2 Resolving Nonrefined Tasks

An nonrefined task is easy to detect in the current ϕ. A resolver for a flaw of that type is an applicable instance of a temporal refinement method for the task. An instance is obtained by renaming all variables in the method and instantiating some of these variables with the task parameters and with the variables and constraints of the current chronicle ϕ.

An instance m of a method is applicable to a chronicle ϕ when its task matches a task in ϕ and all the constraints of m are consistent with those of ϕ. Transforming $\phi = (\mathcal{A}, \mathcal{S}_T, \mathcal{T}, \mathcal{C})$ with such a resolver m consists of the following transformations of ϕ:

- replacing in $\mathcal{A}$ the task by the subtasks and actions of m,
- adding the assertions of m and those of the primitives in m either to $\mathcal{S}_T$ if these assertions are causally supported or to $\mathcal{T}$, and
- adding to $\mathcal{C}$ the constraints of m and those of its actions.

Note that an applicable instance of a method m may have assertions that are not causally supported by ϕ. For instance, in Example 4.12, the method m-bring is applicable for refining a task bring(r, c, p) if m-bring has an instance such that the constraints (attached(p', d'), attached(p, d), $d \neq d'$, $t_2 \leq t_1$, $t_3 \leq t_1$) are consistent with those of current ϕ, given the current binding constraints of these variables. However, the assertion $[t_s, t_1]$freight(r)=empty in that method may or may not be already supported by another assertion in ϕ. If it is not, then refining a task in ϕ with m-bring adds a nonsupported assertion in the current chronicle.

4.3.3 Resolving Nonsupported Assertions

Nonsupported assertions in $\phi = (\mathcal{A}, \mathcal{S}_T, \mathcal{T}, \mathcal{C})$ are those initially in ϕ_0 plus those from the refinement of tasks and the insertion of primitives. As discussed in Section 4.2.1, the three ways to support an assertion $\alpha \in \mathcal{T}$ and move it to $\mathcal{S}_T$ are the following:

- add in $\mathcal{C}$ constraints on object and temporal variables,
- add in $\mathcal{S}_T$ a persistence assertion, and
- add in $\mathcal{A}$ a task or primitive that brings an assertion supporting α.

For the last type of resolver, a supporting assertion for α may come from either a primitive or a method for a task. Supporting α by inserting the body of a method in ϕ is equivalent to refining a task. Supporting it with a primitive introduces primitives in the plan, which may not result from the refinement of tasks. The use of a primitive as a resolver for supporting an unsupported assertion is a generative search for a goal, similar to what we have seen in plan-space planning (Section 2.5). Let us assume at this point that all primitives in Σ can be freely used to augment a plan for supporting assertions, as well as through task refinement methods. We discuss this assumption in Section 4.3.7.

4.3.4 Resolving Conflicting Assertions

Flaws corresponding to conflicting assertions are more easily handled in an incremental way by maintaining ϕ as a secure chronicle and keeping track of what is needed for it to remain secure. The mechanisms here are a generalization of those used in Section 2.5 for handling threats in plan-space planning. There are, however, several substantial differences (see Exercise 4.6).

All assertions in ϕ_0 are required to be nonconflicting. Every transformation of ϕ by refinement, addition of persistence assertions or constraints, or addition of tasks or primitives requires detecting and marking as flaws potential conflicts between newly added assertions and those of current ϕ. Resolvers for a potential conflict are sets of separation constraints consistent with the constraints in the current ϕ, as discussed in Section 4.2.1. The corresponding transformation consists of adding the chosen separation constraints to those of ϕ. One way of keeping the current ϕ secure is to detect and solve potential conflicts at every transformation step. However, other flaw selection strategies can be applied.

4.3.5 Search Space

The search space of TemPlan is a directed acyclic graph in which search states are chronicles. An edge (ϕ, ϕ') in this graph is such that $\phi' = \text{Transform}(\phi, \rho)$, ρ being a resolver for some flaw in ϕ. The graph is acyclic because each edge augments the previous chronicle with additional constraints, primitives, and/or assertions and there is no removal transformation. In general, however, the search space is not finite: it can grow indefinitely by the addition of new primitives and tasks. It can be made finite by the specification of global constraints, such as the total duration of the plan.

Starting from ϕ_0, TemPlan explores a subtree of this complex search space. The problems for organizing and exploring this space are in many aspects similar to those of algorithm PSP in Section 2.5. Both follow the same approach of transforming a partial plan by finding flaws and repairing them. Their types of flaws are, however, different. Flaws corresponding to nonrefined tasks do no exist in PSP; they are inherent to the refinement methods used here. The nonsupported assertion flaws extend the open goal flaws of PSP to temporal domains. Similarly, conflicting assertions generalize what we referred to as threats in PSP.

Both Templan and PSP algorithms can be viewed as a dynamic constraint satisfaction approach where new constraints and variables are repeatedly added for solving the original problem. The approach of constraint satisfaction problems (CSP) is very general and allows taking into account not only time and variable binding constraints, as in TemPlan, but also resource constraints, which are quite often part of planning problems. The *Meta-CSP framework*, which expresses the disjunctions of possible resolvers for flaws as (meta) constraints, can help formalize the integration of several types of constraints related to time and resources and possibly help in their resolution (see discussion in Section 4.6.1).

Basic heuristics for TemPlan are similar to those of PSP. These are basically variants of the *variable-ordering* and *value-ordering* heuristics of CSP. A heuristic analogous to variable-ordering chooses a flaw f that has the smallest number of resolvers (step *(i)* of TemPlan). For a heuristic analogous to value ordering, the idea is to choose a resolver ρ that is the least constraining for the current chronicle ϕ. This notion is more difficult to assess; it leads to take into account differently resolvers that add constraints, assertions, or refinement methods from those that add new tasks or primitives. Adding new tasks and primitives augments the size of the problem at hand and requires the use of more elaborate heuristics.

Advanced heuristics rely on elaborate extensions of domain transition graphs, reachability graphs and some of the techniques presented in Section 2.3. They can be integrated within various search strategies such as iterative deepening or A*-based search. These considerations are essential for designing an efficient implementation of TemPlan. Possible options for heuristics and search strategies are briefly discussed in Section 4.6.2.

Algorithm TemPlan is sound when it is implemented with sound subroutines for finding flaws, resolvers and transforming chronicles. When a global constraint on the plan to find is set, such as the total duration of that plan or its maximum number of actions, then TemPlan is also complete, that is, at least one of its execution traces returns a solution plan, if there is one. These properties are conditioned on the soundness and completeness of the constraint handling procedures used in TemPlan, which are detailed in Section 4.4.

4.3.6 Illustration

Let us illustrate here some of the steps of TemPlan on a detailed example.

Example 4.17. Consider the problem depicted in Figure 4.5 for the domain of Example 4.11 where two robots, r1 and r2, are servicing four docks, d1 to d4, connected with

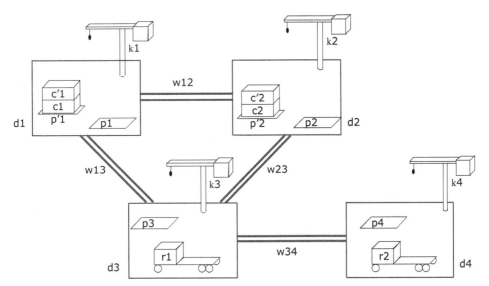

Figure 4.5. A planning problem involving two robots, r1 and r2, servicing four docks, d1 to d4; the task is to bring the containers c1 from pile p'1 to p3 and c2 from p'2 to p4.

four roads, as illustrated. Starting from the initial state shown in the figure, the task is to bring the containers c1 to pile p3 and c2 to p4. No constraint on the final location of the robots is stated. Hence the initial chronicle ϕ_0 has no unsupported assertion (see Exercise 4.3).

At the first recursion of TemPlan, there are two flaws in current ϕ: the nonrefined tasks bring(r, c1, p3) and bring(r', c2, p4). Suppose the method m-bring is used to refine the first one into move, uncover, load, move, and unload. At this point, c, p, p', d, d', k, and k' are instantiated, respectively, to c1, p3, p'1, d3, d1, k1 and k3, r is constrained to be in {r1, r2}; and the time points are constrained as depicted in Figure 4.3.

At the following recursion, there are six nonrefined tasks in ϕ. Assume m-bring is similarly used to refine bring(r', c2, p4). Now the resulting chronicle contains ten nonrefined tasks (two uncovers, loads and unloads, and four moves) as well as conflicting assertions related to the loc(r) and loc(r') assertions in the four load and unload tasks. Separation constraints are either $r \neq r'$ or precedence constraints such that the tasks are run sequentially.

If the former separation is chosen, a final solution plan would be, for example, to have r1 navigate to d2 while r2 navigates to d1. At the same time, k1 uncovers c1 while k2 uncovers c2. Two synchronizations then take place: before load(k2,r1,c2,p'2) and, concurrently, before load(k1,r2,c1,p'1) (as in Figure 4.3). These two concurrent actions are then followed by move(r1,d4) concurrently with move(r2,d3), and finally with the two unload actions. The details of the remaining steps through reaching a solution are covered in Exercise 4.4.

If we assume more realistically that navigation between waypoints is constrained by the traversal of docks, and that no dock can contain more than one robot at a time, then additional synchronizations will be required for the motion of the two robots (see Exercise 4.5).   □

4.3.7 Free Versus Task-Dependent Primitives

This section discusses some of the issues for integrating in TemPlan a task-oriented approach with refinement methods to a goal-oriented approach with a generative search mechanism. Indeed, the initial chronicle $\phi_0 = (\mathcal{A}, \mathcal{S}_T, \mathcal{T}, \mathcal{C})$ specifies (in $\mathcal{A}$) the tasks to perform as well as (in $\mathcal{T}$) the goals to achieve in the form of temporal assertions. However, the flexibility of the representation and the search space can limit the computational performance of the algorithm when the domain has few methods to depend on and relies significantly on generative search.

There is another issue regarding the use of primitives to support assertions that relates to the specification style of a domain. A primitive a is specified in our representation as a collection of assertions and constraints; it is also a temporally qualified component of one or several methods. A method m may contain other assertions and primitives that are needed as a context for performing a. Hence a may or may not be freely usable in a plan, independently of a method m that refines a task into several primitives, including a.

These considerations motivate a distinction between *free* and *task-dependent* primitives. A primitive is free if it can be used alone for supporting assertions. A primitive is task-dependent if it can be used only as part of a refinement method in generative planning. Such a property is a matter of design and specification style of the planning domain.

Example 4.18. The designer of the domain in Example 4.24 may consider that the primitives unload, load, stack, and unstack are free. These actions can be performed whenever their specified conditions are met; they can be inserted in a plan when their assertions are needed to support nonsupported assertions. However, the primitives leave and enter can be specified as being task-dependent; they should necessarily appear as the result of a decomposition of a move task. In other words, the designer does not foresee any reason to perform an action such as leave or enter except within tasks that require leaving or entering a place.   □

The use of a task-dependent primitive branches over the choice of which task to use if the same action appears in the decomposition of several tasks. It introduces a nonrefined task flaw, which branches over several methods for its decomposition.

Note that if all primitives in a domain are free, then the refinement in Templan is limited to the tasks in the initial chronicle. However, if all primitives are task-dependent, then refinement will be needed for every nonsupported assertion that cannot be supported by constraints and persistence assertions.

4.4 CONSTRAINT MANAGEMENT IN TEMPORAL PLANNING

At each recursion of TemPlan, we have to find resolvers for current flaws and transform the current chronicle ϕ by refinement and insertion of assertions, constraints, primitives, and tasks. Each transformation must keep the set C of constraints in ϕ consistent; it must detect conflict in the set of assertions in ϕ and find separation constraints consistent with C. The two steps *(ii)* and *(iv)* of TemPlan (Algorithm 4.1) require checking the consistency of the constraints in C.

Definition 4.2 introduces two types of constraints in C: temporal constraints and object constraints. Let us assume that these two types of constraints are *decoupled*, that is, there is no constraint that restricts the value of a time point as a function of object variables or vice versa. For example, we introduced constant parameters δ_i in Example 4.11; there would be a coupling if these delays where not constant but functions of which robot r is doing the leave or which crane the unload actions. With this simplifying assumption, C is consistent iff its object constraints and its temporal constraints are consistent. Constraint checking relies on two independent constraint managers for the two types of constraints. Let us discuss them in the next sections.

4.4.1 Consistency of Object Constraints

A temporal planner has to check and maintain the consistency of unary and binary constraints on object variables that come from binding and separation constraints and from rigid relations. This corresponds to maintaining a general CSP over finite domains, the consistency checking of which is an NP-complete problem. Restrictions on the representation that may give a tractable CSP are not practical; even inequality constraints, such as $x \neq y$ in a separation constraint, make consistency checking NP-complete.

Filtering techniques, such as incremental arc or path consistency, are not complete, but they are efficient and offer a reasonable trade-off for testing the consistency of object constraint networks. Indeed, if TemPlan progresses with an inconsistent set of object constraints, it will later detect that some variables do not have consistent instantiations; it will have to backtrack. Incomplete consistency checking in each search node does not reduce the completeness of the algorithm; it just prunes fewer nodes in its search tree. Hence, there is trade-off between (i) an early detection of all inconsistencies with a complete but costly consistency checking at each node of the search and (ii) using incremental constraint filtering techniques and performing a complete variable instantiation checking only at the end of TemPlan search, which may require further backtracking.

A good principle for balancing this trade-off is to perform low-complexity procedures at each search node and to keep more complex ones as part of the search strategy. In that sense, filtering techniques efficiently remove many inconsistencies and reduce the search space at a low cost. They may be used jointly with complete algorithms, such as forward-checking at regular stages of the search. Such a complete consistency check has to be performed on the free variables remaining in the final plan. Other trade-offs, such as choosing flaws that lead to instantiate object variables, are also relevant for reducing the complexity of maintaining variable binding constraints.

4.4.2 Consistency of Temporal Constraints

Simple Temporal Networks (STN) provide a convenient framework for handling temporal constraints. An STN is a pair $(\mathcal{V}, \mathcal{E})$, where $\mathcal{V}$ is a set of temporal variables $\mathcal{V} = \{t_1, t_2, \dots, t_n\}$, and $\mathcal{E}$ is a set of binary constraints of the form:

$$a_{ij} \leq t_j - t_i \leq b_{ij}, \text{ denoted } r_{ij} = [a_{ij}, b_{ij}], \text{ where } a_{ij} \text{ and } b_{ij} \text{ are integers.}$$

Note that r_{ij} entails $r_{j,i} = [-b_{ij}, -a_{ij}]$. To represent unary constraints (i.e., constraints on one variable rather than two), let us introduce an additional temporal variable t_0 with a fixed value $t_0 = 0$. Then $r_{0j} = [a, b]$ represents the constraint $a \leq t_j \leq b$.

A solution to an STN $(\mathcal{V}, \mathcal{E})$ gives an integer value to each variable in $\mathcal{V}$. The STN is *consistent* if it has a solution that meets all the constraints in $\mathcal{E}$. It is *minimal* if every value in each interval r_{ij} belongs to a solution.

TemPlan proceeds by transforming a chronicle $\phi = (\mathcal{A}, \mathcal{S}_T, \mathcal{T}, \mathcal{C})$ such as to meet the conditions of a solution plan. These transformations add in $\mathcal{C}$ constraints of methods for refining tasks, constraints for supporting assertions, and separation constraints for conflicting assertions. Each transformation should keep $\mathcal{C}$ consistent. The set of temporal constraints in $\mathcal{C}$ is an STN $(\mathcal{V}, \mathcal{E})$, which evolves by the addition of new variables and constraints while staying consistent. TemPlan requires checking incrementally that an STN remains consistent when more variables and constraints are added to it. This is more easily done when the network it is also maintained minimal, as explained next.

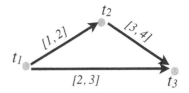

Figure 4.6. A simple temporal network.

Two operations are essential for checking the consistency of $\mathcal{E}$:

- *composition*: $r_{ik} \bullet r_{kj} = [a_{ik} + a_{kj}, b_{ik} + b_{kj}]$, which corresponds to the transitive sum of the two constraints from i to j through k: $a_{ik} \le t_k - t_i \le b_{ik}$ and $a_{kj} \le t_j - t_k \le b_{kj}$;
- *intersection*: $r_{ij} \cap r'_{ij} = [\max\{a_{ij}, a'_{ij}\}, \min\{b_{ij}, b'_{ij}\}]$ which is the conjunction two constraints on (t_i, t_j): $a_{ij} \le t_j - t_i \le b_{ij}$ and $a'_{ij} \le t_j - t_i \le b'_{ij}$.

Three constraints, r_{ik}, r_{kj}, and r_{ij}, are consistent when $r_{ij} \cap (r_{ik} \bullet r_{kj}) \ne \emptyset$.

Example 4.19. Consider the network in Figure 4.6 where vertices are time points and edges are labeled with temporal constraints: $r_{12} = [1, 2]$, $r_{2,3} = [3, 4]$ and $r_{13} = [2, 3]$. r_{12} and $r_{2,3}$ entail by transitivity $r'_{13} = r_{12} \bullet r_{23} = [4, 6]$. But r'_{13} is not compatible with r_{13}: the upper bound of r_{13} is 3, smaller than the lower bound of r'_{13}, which is 4. That is $r_{13} \cap r'_{13} = \emptyset$. There is no pair of variables t_1, t_3 that can satisfy both r_{13} and r'_{13}: this network is inconsistent. □

The path-consistency algorithm PC (Algorithm 4.2) tests all triples of variables in $\mathcal{V}$ with a *transitive update* operation: $r_{ij} \leftarrow r_{ij} \cap (r_{ik} \bullet r_{kj})$. If a pair (t_i, t_j) is not constrained, then we take $r_{ij} = (-\infty, +\infty)$; in that sense, an STN corresponds implicitly to a complete graph.

PC is complete and returns the minimal network. Its complexity is $O(n^3)$. It is easily transformed into an incremental version. Assume that the current network $(\mathcal{V}, \mathcal{E})$ is consistent and minimal; a new constraint r'_{ij} is inconsistent with $(\mathcal{V}, \mathcal{E})$ if and only if $r_{ij} \cap r'_{ij} = \emptyset$. Furthermore, when $r_{ij} \subseteq r'_{ij}$, the new constraint does not change the minimal network $(\mathcal{V}, \mathcal{E})$. Otherwise r_{ij} is updated as $r_{ij} \cap r'_{ij}$ and propagated over all constraints r_{ik} and r_{kj} with the transitive update operation; any change is subsequently propagated. Incremental path consistency is in $O(1)$ for consistency checking and in $O(n^2)$ for updating a minimal network.

Example 4.20. Let us give the network in Figure 4.7 as input to PC (Algorithm 4.2). The first iteration of PC for $k = 1$ with $2 \le i < j \le 5$ does not change the constraints $r_{23}, r_{24}, r_{25}, r_{34}, r_{35}$; it updates r_{25} as follows: $r_{25} \leftarrow r_{25} \cap [r_{21} \bullet r_{15}] = (-\infty, +\infty) \cap [-2, -1] \bullet [6, 7] = [4, 6]$. The remaining iterations confirm that this network is consistent and minimal (see Exercise 4.8) □

Algorithm 4.2 Path consistency algorithm for simple constraint networks.

PC$(\mathcal{V}, \mathcal{E})$
    for $k = 1, \dots, n$ do
        for each pair i, j such that $1 \le i < j \le n, i \ne k$, and $j \ne k$ do
            $r_{ij} \leftarrow r_{ij} \cap [r_{ik} \bullet r_{kj}]$
            if $r_{ij} = \emptyset$ then return *inconsistent*

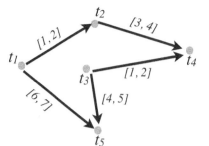

Figure 4.7. A consistent STN.

Another approach for maintaining the consistency of STNs is the Floyd-Warshall all-pairs minimal distance algorithm. Here, a network $(\mathcal{V}, \mathcal{E})$ is transformed into a distance graph, the vertices of which are again the time points in $\mathcal{V}$. Each constraint $r_{ij} = [a_{ij}, b_{ij}]$ of the network defines two edges in the graph: (i) an edge from t_i to t_j labeled with a distance b_{ij} and (ii) an edge from t_j to t_i labeled with a distance $-a_{ij}$. The original network is consistent if and only if there is no negative cycle in this distance graph. The Floyd-Warshall algorithm checks the consistency and computes the minimal distances between all pairs of vertices in the graph in $O(n^3)$ time. An incremental version of this algorithm has been devised for planning.

The Bellman-Ford algorithm computes the single source distances in the distance graph. It can also be used for consistency checking with a complexity in $O(n \times m)$, where n is the number of vertices and m the number of edges of the distance graph. The graph is kept sparse ($m < n^2$), but the algorithm does not maintain a minimal network. There is also an incremental version of this algorithm.

4.4.3 Controllability of Temporal Constraints

TemPlan returns a valid chronicle that meets the conditions of Definition 4.16. Temporal variables in ϕ are generally not instantiated but related with a set of consistent constraints. Let t_s and t_e be the time points referring to the start and end of an action a in that plan. At acting time, a will be triggered according to the constraints on t_s. The precise triggering moment of a is under the control of the actor. However, the moment at which the action terminates and the other intermediate instants while the action is taking place are generally not under its control. These time points are observable, that is, the execution platform will report when the action terminates and when the intermediate time points in its model are reached, but these are not controllable. Let us discuss here the controllability issue at the planning level, that is, what must be done at planning time to take into account that some temporal variables of the plan are not controllable.

For an action a in $[t_s, t_e]$, a constraint on its controllable starting point is such that: $l \leq t_s - t \leq u$, where t is an observable time point, either controllable or not. This requirement on t_s can be met by choosing freely the starting point in the range $[l, u]$ after observing t. If required for meeting other constraints, this interval can be *squeezed* into any other nonempty interval $[l', u'] \subseteq [l, u]$. However, a constraint on the end point of action a such as $l \leq t_e - t_s \leq u$, has a different meaning; it says that the duration of the interval $[t_s, t_e]$ is a random number in the range $[l, u]$. This duration will be *observed* once

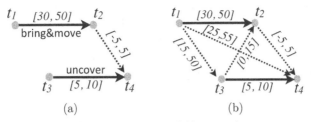

Figure 4.8. An uncontrollable network.

a terminates; we assume that it will range in the uncertainty interval $[l, u]$. The actor has no freedom for the choice of t_e. This constraint cannot be squeezed. Consequently, the transitive update operation $r_{ij} \leftarrow r_{ij} \cap (r_{ik} \bullet r_{kj})$ for checking and maintaining the consistency of a network, which squeezes intervals, is not applicable to action durations.

These considerations are not specific to action durations. They hold for any contingent time point and constraint. They apply in particular to expected events that can be specified in the initial chronicle (as in Example 4.14). We view the time distance between an absolute reference point and the expected event as a contingent duration similar to that of an action.

Example 4.21. Consider the robot of Example 4.12 that has to achieve a task, denoted bring&move, that will take it to dock1. Concurrently, the crane at dock1 has to uncover a container that will be loaded on the robot. The duration of bring&move from t_1 to t_2 is specified in the model of the task to be in $[30, 50]$ time units; task uncover from t_2 to t_3 takes 5 to 10 time units. Further, the initial chronicle requires the two tasks to be synchronized such that neither one lags after the other by more than 5 time units, that is, $-5 \leq t_4 - t_2 \leq 5$. This is depicted in Figure 4.8(a) (where the tasks are depicted as plain arrows and the synchronization constraints as dashed arrows).

A direct application of PC to the network in Figure 4.8(a) shows that this network is consistent; it returns the minimal network in Figure 4.8(b) (see Exercise 4.10). Let us assume that this network is used by an actor who only controls the triggering of the two tasks, t_1 and t_3. It is clear that t_1 should precede t_3 because $[t_1, t_3] \subseteq [15, 50]$. Suppose the first task is triggered at time $t_1 = 0$. When should the second task be triggered such to meet the synchronization constraint between t_2 and t_4?

Let d and d' be the respective durations of the two tasks. The synchronization constraint says: $-5 \leq t_4 - t_2 \leq 5$, that is $-5 \leq t_3 + d' - d \leq 5$. The choice of t_3 should satisfy the constraints: $d - d' - 5 \leq t_3$ and $t_3 \leq d - d' + 5$ for all values of d and d' in their respective intervals. Clearly this is not feasible (e.g., taking $d = 50$, $d' = 5$ for the lower bound and $d = 30$, $d' = 10$ for the upper bound gives $40 \leq t_3$ and $t_3 \leq 25$).

How do we explain this inconsistency in a network that is said to be consistent and minimal (meaning that every value in the allowed constraints is part of a solution)? The reason is simple: the consistency and minimality of an STN assumes full control over *every* variable, which is not the case here. The reader can easily check that there is no problem in meeting all the constraints if one can freely choose d and d' in their intervals, for example, $d = 30$, $d' = 10$ leaves $t_3 \in [15, 25]$.

The actor does not control the end points of actions but it can *observe* them. It may devise a *conditional* strategy on the basis of what it observes. For example, it may start uncover at most 40 units after t_1 or earlier if bring&move finishes before. In this particular example, such a strategy does not work, but if the actor can observe an intermediate time point between t_1 and t_2, this may make his synchronization problem controllable, as explained next. ☐

The issues raised in the previous example are addressed through the notion of *Simple Temporal constraint Networks with Uncertainty* (STNU). An STNU is like an STN except that its time points and constraints are partitioned into controllable ones and contingent ones.

Definition 4.22. An STNU is a tuple $(\mathcal{V}, \tilde{\mathcal{V}}, \mathcal{E}, \tilde{\mathcal{E}})$ where $\mathcal{V}$ and $\tilde{\mathcal{V}}$ are disjoint sets of time points, and $\mathcal{E}$ and $\tilde{\mathcal{E}}$ are disjoint sets of binary constraints on time points. $\mathcal{V}$ and $\mathcal{E}$ are said to be *controllable*; $\tilde{\mathcal{V}}$ and $\tilde{\mathcal{E}}$ are said to be *contingent*. If $[l, u]$ is a contingent constraint in $\tilde{\mathcal{E}}$ on the time points $[t_s, t_e]$, then $0 < l < u < \infty$ and t_e is a contingent point in $\tilde{\mathcal{V}}$. ☐

The intuition is that elements in $\tilde{\mathcal{V}}$ denote the *ending* time points of actions, while contingent constraints in $\tilde{\mathcal{E}}$ model the positive nonnull durations of actions, predicted with uncertainty. If $[t_s, t_e] \subseteq [l, u]$ is a contingent constraint, then the actual duration $t_e - t_s$ can be viewed as a *random* variable whose value will be observed within $[l, u]$, once the corresponding action terminates. The actor *controls* t_s: it assigns a value to it. However, it only *observes* t_e, knowing in advance that it will be within the bounds set for the contingent constraint on $t_e - t_s$. A meaningful STNU cannot have a contingent variable t_e, which is the end point of two contingent constraints.

The controllability issue is to make sure (at planning time) that there *exist* values for the controllable variables such as for *any* observed value of the contingent variables the constraints are met. One can view controllable variables as being existentially quantified, while contingent ones are universally quantified. However, the actor does not need to commit to values for all its controllable variables before starting to act. It can choose a value for a controllable variable only when needed at acting time. It can make this choice as a function of the observed values of *past* contingent variables.

Definition 4.23. A *dynamic execution strategy* for an STNU $(\mathcal{V}, \tilde{\mathcal{V}}, \mathcal{E}, \tilde{\mathcal{E}})$ is a procedure for assigning values to controllable variables $t \in \mathcal{V}$ while acting, in some order consistent with $\mathcal{E}$, such that all the constraints in $\mathcal{E}$ related to t are met, and given that the values of all contingent variables in $\tilde{\mathcal{V}}$ preceding t are known and fit the constraints in $\tilde{\mathcal{E}}$. An STNU is *dynamically controllable* if there exists a dynamic execution strategy for it. ☐

Example 4.24. As discussed at the end of Example 4.21, the STNU in Figure 4.8(a) is not dynamically controllable. Now consider a modification of this network in which task bring&move is broken down into two tasks: bring from t_1 to t then move from t' to t_2 (Figure 4.9). The total duration $[t_1, t_2]$ remains in $[30, 50]$.

A dynamic execution strategy for this STNU can be the following: assign t_1, observe t, assign t' at any moment after t in $[0, 5]$ then assign t_3 10 units after t'. It is easy to check

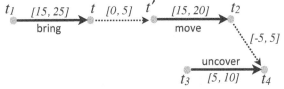

Figure 4.9. A dynamically controllable STNU.

that, whatever the durations of the three tasks are, within the bounds of the contingent constraints, the constraint $[-5, +5]$ on their end points t_2 and t_4 will be met. $\square$

These considerations lead to an additional requirement for TemPlan: to synthesize a plan whose underlying STNU is dynamically controllable. TemPlan has to test not only the consistency of the current temporal network but also its dynamic controllability. It turns out that dynamic controllability checking is feasible on the basis of an extension of the consistency-checking algorithm. This extension is technically involved, but fortunately it does not change the computational complexity of the algorithm.

A first step would be to consider an STNU just like an ordinary STN on which PC is run: if the transitive update operation $(r_{ij} \leftarrow r_{ij} \cap (r_{ik} \bullet r_{kj}))$ reduces any contingent constraint, then the network is not dynamically controllable. A network in which all the contingent constraints are minimal (in the PC sense) is said to be *pseudo-controllable*, a necessary but not a sufficient condition of dynamic controllability.

Dynamic controllability can be analyzed with three constraints between two controllable points and a contingent one, as depicted in Figure 4.10. This network is assumed to be consistent and minimal. It may or may not be dynamically controllable: depending on the values of the parameters and the eventual observation of t_e, there are cases in which it is possible to choose t while meeting constraints. To do so, further reductions on the controllable constraints can be needed. These reductions would have to be propagated to other time points that may possibly be related to t_s, t_e, and t.

The position of t with respect to t_e fits into three main cases:

(i) $v < 0$: t follows necessarily t_e; the observation of t_e allows the choice of t while meeting the constraint $[u, v]$.

(ii) $u \geq 0$: t is before or simultaneous with t_e. t has to be chosen before observing t_e in an interval that meets all the constraints regardless of the value of t_e, if such an interval exists. The constraint on $[t, t_e]$ requires $t_e - v \leq t \leq t_e - u$. At the latest t_e is such that $t_e = t_s + b$; at the earliest $t_e = t_s + a$. Hence $t_s + b - v \leq t \leq t_s + a - u$. If this inequality can be met, then the choice of t in $[b - v, u - a]$ after t_s meets all the constraints. Constraint $[p, q]$ has to be reduced to $[b - v, a - u]$. Note that $[b - v, a - u] \subseteq [p, q]$ because the

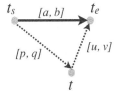

Figure 4.10. Basic constraints for dynamic controllability.

Table 4.1. Constraint propagation rules for dynamic controllability, where $a' = a - u, b' = b - v$, double arrows are contingent constraints, and $\langle t, \alpha \rangle$ are wait constraints

Conditions	Propagated constraint
$t_s \overset{[a,b]}{\Longrightarrow} t_e$, $t \xrightarrow{[u,v]} t_e$, $u \geq 0$	$t_s \xrightarrow{[b',a']} t$
$t_s \overset{[a,b]}{\Longrightarrow} t_e$, $t \xrightarrow{[u,v]} t_e$, $u < 0$, $v \geq 0$	$t_s \xrightarrow{\langle t_e, b' \rangle} t$
$t_s \overset{[a,b]}{\Longrightarrow} t_e$, $t_s \xrightarrow{\langle t_e, u \rangle} t$	$t_s \xrightarrow{[min\{a,u\}, \infty]} t$
$t_s \xrightarrow{\langle t_e, b \rangle} t$, $t' \xrightarrow{[u,v]} t$	$t_s \xrightarrow{\langle t_e, b' \rangle} t'$
$t_s \xrightarrow{\langle t_e, b \rangle} t$, $t' \overset{[u,v]}{\Longrightarrow} t$, $t_e \neq t$	$t_s \xrightarrow{\langle t_e, b-u \rangle} t'$

network is minimal. However, $[b - v, a - u]$ can be empty, in which case the network is not dynamically controllable (see Exercises 4.11 and 4.12).

(iii) $u < 0$ and $v \geq 0$: t may either precede or follow t_e. A dynamic execution strategy should *wait* for t_e until some point, and depending on whether t_e has occurred or not at that point, different choices for t will be taken. A reasoning identical to case *(ii)* shows that t cannot be earlier than $t \geq t_s + b - v$, if t_e does not occur before. The waiting point is $t_s + b - v$. If $a < b - v$ then either $[t_s, t_e]$ occurs in $[a, b - v]$: the wait will make t follow t_e, and we are back to case *(i)*, or $[t_s, t_e]$ occurs in $[b - v, b]$: t is before t_e which is case *(ii)*. If $a \geq b - v$ then t_e cannot occur before the wait expires.

The preceding analysis gives the constraints to be reduced to meet dynamic controllability (e.g., $[p, q]$ reduced to $[b - v, a - u]$ in case *(ii)*). It also exhibits a ternary *wait* relation: t should wait until either t_e or $t_s + b - v$. The trick is to consider this *wait* as a particular binary relation on the pair $[t_s, t]$: the corresponding edge in the network is labeled with a constraint denoted $\langle t_e, b - v \rangle$. Specific propagation rules for handling jointly these *wait* constraints and the normal ones in a network need to be devised.

These propagation rules are given in Table 4.1. A row in this table is similar to the propagated contraint $(r_{ik} \bullet r_{kj})$ from i to j through k that we used in PC. The left column gives the conditions under which a propagation rule applies, and the right column states the constraint to be added to the network according to that rule. Double arrows represent contingent constraints, and angle brackets are wait constraints. The first and second rules implement, respectively, the cases *(ii)* and *(iii)*. The third rule adds a lower bound constraint to a *wait*, which follows directly from the above argument. The last two rules correspond to transitive propagations of a *wait*.

It can be shown that a modified path consistency algorithm relying on these rules is correct: a network is dynamically controllable if and only if it is accepted by the algorithm. Furthermore, the reduced controllable constraints obtained in the final network give a dynamic execution strategy. The transposition of the *wait* constraints as a distance graph allows the incremental testing of dynamic controllability with a an algorithm in $O(n^3)$ inspired from Bellman-Ford.

Synthesis of dynamically controllable plans. From the preceding discussion, it is clear that the conditions in Definition 4.16 are not sufficient. We need to add a fourth requirement that the temporal constraints in chronicle ϕ define a dynamically controllable STNU. This requirement has to be taken into account in TemPlan as follows: dynamic controllability is checked whenever a resolver adds to current ϕ a contingent constraints; that resolver is rejected if the resulting STNU is not dynamically controllable.

This strategy can, however, be demanding of computational resources. Indeed, the complexity growth of dynamic controllability checking is polynomial, but the constant factor is high. A possible compromise is to maintain solely the pseudo-controllability of ϕ. The standard PC algorithm already tests that a network is pseudo-controllable (no contingent constraint should be reduced during propagation), a necessary condition for dynamic controllability. Hence consistency checking allows to filter out incrementally resolvers that make the STNU not pseudo-controllable. Dynamic controllability is checked before terminating with a complete solution or at a few regular stages. The risk of excessive backtracking, as for any incremental filtering strategy, has to be assessed empirically.

4.5 ACTING WITH TEMPORAL MODELS

As seen in Chapter 3, acting deliberately may or may not rely on an a priori synthesized plan. For critical applications with well-modeled domains and limited variability, an actor first synthesizes a plan, then follows it as much as possible by refining the plan steps into low-level commands and revising the plan when needed. In less predictable and more variable environments, it may be preferable to act by choosing opportunistically among available methods relying, when feasible, on lookahead mechanisms. These general considerations apply to temporal domains, with specific issues for handling time constraints. This section presents successively the following

- techniques for acting by refining the primitives in a temporal plan with atemporal methods,
- techniques for acting without a temporal plan but with temporal refinement methods, and
- open issues where acting and planning with temporal methods are mixed.

4.5.1 Acting with Atemporal Refinement Methods

The motivations here are those discussed in previous chapters and summarized in the Figures 1.1(b) and 3.1: the actor plans, refines the planned actions into commands and revises its plan when needed. It queries TemPlan for producing a plan for the tasks it has to achieve; TemPlan receives as input the appropriate initial chronicle with the current state and the predicted exogenous events. It returns a chronicle ϕ that meets the conditions of Definition 4.16.

Actions in the solution plan ϕ are primitives for TemPlan, for example, leave, enter, stack, unstack, etc. (as in Example 4.11). However, these primitives are compound tasks at the acting level, to be refined into commands with appropriate refinement methods. This acting refinement goes one level down in the representation hierarchy. We consider here primitive refinements using the atemporal methods of Chapter 3.

Example 4.25. In Example 4.11, we defined several primitives such as leave or unstack. Here are two methods to decompose them into commands:

m-leave(r, d, w, e)
   task: leave(r, d, w)
    pre: loc(r)=d, adjacent(d, w), exit(e, d, w)
  body: until empty(e) wait(1)
      goto(r, e)

The method m-leave waits until the exit e from dock d toward waypoint w is empty, then it moves the robot to that exit. The method m-unstack locates the grasping position for container c on top of a pile p, moves the crane to that position, grasps it, ensures the grasp (e.g., closes latches) to guarantee a firm grasp, raises the container slowly above the pile, then moves away to the neutral position of that crane.

m-unstack(k, c, p)
   task: unstack(k, c, p)
    pre: pos(c)=p, top(p)=c, grip(k)=empty
       attached(k, d), attached(p, d)
  body: locate-grasp-position(k, c, p)
      move-to-grasp-position(k, c, p)
      grasp(k, c, p)
      until firm-grasp(k, c, p) ensure-grasp(k, c, p)
      lift-vertically(k, c, p)
      move-to-neutral-position(k, c, p)

It is interesting to compare these methods with the descriptive models of the same primitives in Example 4.11. Here effects are not predicted; they will be observed from the execution of commands. However, the operational models given in these methods detail the commands needed to perform the action, including conditionals and loops.   □

The acting refinement methods in this subsection are not temporal. In other words, our model for refining an action into commands does not break down its temporal qualifications from planning level to finer temporal requirements at the execution level. As illustrated in the preceding example, the temporal qualification $[t_s, t_e]$ of an action a in ϕ is not detailed into smaller durations for the commands in which a is refined.

An important motivation for combining temporal planning with atemporal action refinement is the uncertainty in the duration of a, represented through the interval $[t_s, t_e]$. It certainly makes sense to reason about contingent constraints at the abstract level of actions, but at the lower level of commands, one may take into account a global constraint without refining it into bounds that can be even more uncertain and difficult to model in a meaningful way. For example, it may be useful to account for the time needed to open a door, which can be assessed from statistics. However, breaking this duration into how long it takes to reach for the handle and how long to turn the handle introduces more noise in operational models. There is also a computational complexity issue for reasoning at a finer temporal granularity level that is clarified next.

Acting with atemporal methods allows us to rely on the techniques seen in Chapter 3 for refining a task into commands achieving it. We'll use an extended version of the reactive engine RAE and call it eRAE. Even without temporal refinement at the acting level, there is still a need for temporal reasoning in eRAE: we require a *dispatching* function to trigger actions and controllable events at the right moments. Dispatching takes into account past occurrences and the current time; these are propagated into the temporal network to keep it dynamically controllable.

Given a dynamically controllable STNU $(\mathcal{V}, \tilde{\mathcal{V}}, \mathcal{E}, \tilde{\mathcal{E}})$, dispatching has to trigger elements of $\mathcal{V}$ at the right moment, given the observation of elements of $\tilde{\mathcal{V}}$ and given the progress of current time, denoted *now*. Values of observed and triggered time points are propagated in the network. The network remains dynamically controllable as long as there are no violations of contingent constraints, for example, the observed durations of actions fit within their stated bounds. A violation of a contingent constraint can be due to a delay exceeding the modeled upper bound or to a failure of the action. It can lead to a failure of the plan.

Recall that acting triggers only commands, not the effects specified the action models. These effects have to be observed, as in RAE. There can be several intermediate time points in the network maintained by TemPlan that are not the beginnings and ends of actions, for example, point t in the definition of leave or unstack in Example 4.11. At the acting level, we consider them as contingent points. Constraints issued through propagation from these intermediate points are essential for the dynamic controllability of the network. However, unless there is a wait constraint for such an intermediate point, it does not concern the dispatching algorithm. It can be removed from the network used for dispatching.

Example 4.26. Assume that RAE is acting according to the plan in Figure 4.4: it has to perform the three actions leave(r1,dock1), navigate(r1,w1,w2), enter(r1,dock2) and the symmetrical three actions for r2. The two leave actions are triggered concurrently in any order. As soon as an exit is free, the robot gets to the corresponding way and immediatly starts its navigation. When a navigation finishes, the enter action is triggered only when the other robot has left its original position.   □

A temporal network is *grounded* when at least one of its temporal variable receives an absolute value with respect to current time. Before starting the execution, the STNU may or may not be grounded, but as soon as the execution of a plan starts, the network is necessarily grounded. In a grounded network, every time point t is bounded within an absolute interval $[l_t, u_t]$ with respect to current time. As time goes by, some time points in the network have occurred (i.e., triggered by the actor for controllable points or observed for contingent ones), and others remain in the future. Dispatching is concerned with the latter and more precisely with enabled time points.

Definition 4.27. A controllable time point $t \in [l_t, u_t]$ that remains in the future is *alive* if the current time *now* $\in [l_t, u_t]$. t is *enabled* if *(i)* t is alive, *(ii)* for every precedence constraints $t' < t$, t' has occurred, and *(iii)* for every wait constraint $\langle t_e, \alpha \rangle$, either t_e has occurred or α has expired. $\qquad\qquad\qquad\qquad\qquad\qquad\qquad\qquad\qquad\qquad\qquad$ □

Recall that in a wait constraint $\langle t_e, \alpha \rangle$, α is defined with respect to a controllable time point t_s; α has expired when t_s has occurred and $t_s + \alpha \leq now$ (see Section 4.4.3).

Algorithm 4.3, the Dispatch algorithm, allows the actor to control when to start each action. It triggers repeatedly enabled points whose upper bound is *now*: these cannot wait any longer. It has the flexibility to trigger any other enabled point; the arbitrary choice in step *(i)* of Dispatch can be made with respect to domain specific considerations. It then propagates in the network the value of triggered points. Because the network is dynamically controllable, this propagation is guaranteed to succeed and keep the network dynamically controllable as long as contingent constraints are not violated. Initialization consists of deciding when to start the plan if the network is not already grounded, or assigning a value (or absolute bounds) to at least one enabled time point.

Algorithm 4.3 A dispatching function for eRAE.

Dispatch($\mathcal{V}, \tilde{\mathcal{V}}, \mathcal{E}, \tilde{\mathcal{E}}$)
    initialize the network
    while there are elements in $\mathcal{V}$ that have not occurred do
        update *now*
        update contingent points in $\tilde{\mathcal{V}}$ that have been observed
        enabled ← set of enabled time points
        for every $t \in enabled$ such that $now = u_t$ trigger t
        arbitrarily choose other points in *enabled* and trigger them   *(i)*
        propagate in the network the values of triggered points

---

The propagation step is the most costly one in Dispatch: its complexity is in $O(n^3)$ where n is the number of remaining future points in the network. Ideally, this propagation should be fast enough to allow iterations and updates of *now* that are consistent with the temporal granularity of the plan. As discussed earlier about the motivation for atemporal refinement, this complexity is lower when temporal refinement does not break down primitives at the finer command level.

Example 4.28. Let us extend Example 4.26 by requiring robot r1 to bring a container c1 in dock d2 to some destination. TemPlan synthesizes a plan ϕ, part of which is shown in Figure 4.11. To keep the figure readable, the value of the constraints and parameters are omitted; the end point of an action starting at t_i is implicitly named t_i'. Note that some of the object variables are instantiated, but some are not (e.g., c'); temporal variables in ϕ are not instantiated.

The initial step in Dispatch triggers t_1. When t_1' is observed, t_2 is enabled and triggered, which make t_3 and t_4 enabled. t_3 will be triggered enough in advance to free dock d2 allowing r1 to get in (at t_5). Similarly for the subtask of uncovering container c, which is triggered at t_4. When t_2' and t_3' are observed, t_5 become enabled and triggered. t_7 will become enabled after observing t_5' and t_6'. The rest of the plan follows linearly. $\qquad$ □

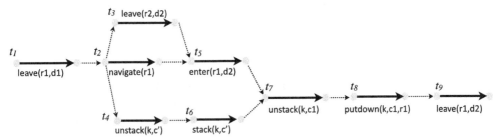

Figure 4.11. Part of a temporal plan given to eRAE for execution.

The Dispatch algorithm is easily integrated into eRAE. Triggering the starting point of an action a means putting a new task in the input stream of RAE (Algorithm 3.1), that is, starting a new stack for progressing on the refinement of a. The upper bound on the duration of a is taken as a deadline for terminating this stack. Progress, and eventually Retrace, will pursue refinements in this stack until the action succeeds or fails, or until the deadline is reached, which is another failure condition. The proximity of the deadline can be used as a heuristics for prioritizing the most urgent tasks in RAE.

Failures are addressed as plan repairs. For a deadline failure, the repair can take two forms:

- stopping the delayed action and seeking alternate ways for achieving the plan from the current state, as for other types of failure, or
- finishing the delayed action despite the delay and repairing the remaining part of the plan.

The latter option is preferable when the violated contingent constraint can be resolved at the STNU propagation level. For example, if navigate(r1) in Figure 4.11 takes slightly longer than the maximum duration specified, the entire plan will still be feasible with a delay, which is possibly acceptable. However, if this navigation is taking longer than expected because robot r1 broke down, a better option is to seek another robot to perform the task. These considerations must be integrated in the actor's monitoring function (Section 7.2).

Plan repair in case of a failure has to be performed with respect to the current state, and to remaining predicted events and tasks whose achievement is still in the future. The repair can be local or global. In the latter case, a full replanning is performed. A local repair can benefit from the plan-space planning approach of TemPlan as follows. The failed action is removed from the remaining chronicle ϕ together with all the assertions coming from that action template. This removal introduces flaws in ϕ with respect to which TemPlan is recursively called. This can lead to other flaws (including for the refinement of the task that lead the failure); it may or may not succeed in finding a repair and may require a full replanning. Monitoring should help assess the failure and decide whether to try a local repair.

In summary, this section illustrated how actions in a temporal plan can be handled with an extended version of the acting engine RAE through a dispatch function. Atemporal refinement methods are used to map, in a context-dependent way, each action a into commands whose execution achieves a.

4.5.2 Acting with Temporal Refinement Methods

Refinement methods can be used for both planning and acting (Chapter 3). Temporal refinement methods can also be used for both functions. We demonstrated their use for planning (Section 4.3). Let us discuss here temporal refinement for acting.

There are cases in which the actor does not have to plan for the task at hand. This can happen because that plan is trivially given in the task model, descriptive models of actions are unreliable, or the environment is too dynamic and acting with possible errors is not critical. In these cases it may still be meaningful to reason about time at the acting level, even without a temporal plan. This is evidently the case when acting has to be synchronized with future predicted event, for example, take the next bus and leave it at the train station stop.

The idea is to extend the refinement acting engine illustrated in Figure 3.1 with a library of temporal refinement methods. Let us call TemRAE the corresponding engine. The methods used by this engine have two characteristics (Section 4.2.3):

- their body is not a sequence of tasks, commands, assignments, and control steps, as in RAE, but a chronicle with a collection of temporally qualified tasks, assertions, and constraints, and
- they do not have a precondition field; they are conditioned on their temporal assertions.

In RAE the evaluation of a conditional expression is with respect to the current observed state ξ. In TemRAE, we need to extend ξ with temporal qualifications to provide causal support to temporal assertions in chronicles (Definition 4.9).

Extending ξ with temporal qualification may require, in general, maintaining the past timelines for every state variable as well as the predicted future timelines for exogenous variables about which the actor has predictions. To keep things simple, let us assume that the qualifications in temporal methods with respect to the past do not extend beyond when each state variable acquired its current value (this assumption is akin to the Markovian property, which is introduced in Section 6.1). With this assumption, our interest in the past is satisfied by keeping track for each state the variable x of a pair $(t, x{=}v)$, meaning that the value of variable is $x = v$ since time t. In other words, the following assertion holds in ξ:

$$[t, now]x{=}v, \text{ where } now \text{ it the value of current time.}$$

ξ also contains predictions about exogenous future events, as seen in the initial chronicle in temporal planning. In this sense, ξ is a particular chronicle which maintains the current present and the exogenous future.

TemRAE works in a similar way to RAE. It reads its input stream for a task to perform. For each such a task τ, it finds $\mathcal{M}(\tau)$, the set of methods whose task is τ. It chooses a method m in $\mathcal{M}(\tau)$ that is applicable for current ξ; it refines τ according to the subtasks specified in m. There are, however, differences in how methods are evaluated as applicable and in how refinements proceed.

Definition 4.29. An instance in a method $m \in \mathcal{M}(\tau)$ is applicable for the current chronicle ξ if and only if:

- every assertion in m is causally supported by ξ and
- the constraints in m are consistent with ξ and there are no conflicting assertions. $\square$

The second condition guarantees that the application of this instance of m to ξ (in the sense seen in Section 4.3.2) gives a secure chronicle. The first condition represents a strong requirement. Assertions in m such as $[t, t']x=v$ or $[t, t']x:(v, v')$, where $t \leq t_s \leq t'$ and t_s is the starting point of m, needs naturally to be supported before any command issued from the refinement of m can begin. Moreover, according to this definition, assertions in m about the future have also to be supported by predictions in ξ, for m to be applicable to ξ. In other words, assertions that are required to be supported by the effects of actions, other than those in m or issued from the refinement of its subtasks, are not allowed by TempRAE. This is because the acting engine is not inserting additional actions to satisfy the requirements of a method.

It is interesting to compare the previous definition to Definition 4.16 of a valid solution plan. Their difference is with respect to nonrefined tasks, forbidden in a solution plan but allowed here, because TemRAE refines a task τ with the subtasks in a method m. Let us illustrate how this can be done through an example.

Example 4.30. Consider the domain specified in Example 4.11. Assume that TempRAE is given a set of methods to handle the tasks bring, move, and uncover of Example 4.12, in addition to methods for leave, enter, navigate, unload, load, stack, and unstack, as illustrated in the previous section.

The task is to bring a container c1, which is *now* in pile p1 in dock d1, to a pile p2 in d2. There is *now* an empty robot r1 in d3. An instance of the method m-bring is applicable to this task with c=c1, p=p2, p'=p1, d=d2, d'=d1, r=r1; t_s can be instantiated to *now*: TemRAE triggers the tasks move(r1,d1) and uncover(c1). Because of the constraints $t_2 \leq t_1$ and $t_3 \leq t_1$, the three other tasks have to wait until both move and uncover finish.

The method m-move1 is applicable to move(r1,d1). The action leave will be triggered; when it is observed that it has finished, navigate then enter will be successively triggered.

Concurrently with this process, TempRAE addresses the uncover task: method m-uncover is applicable; it will lead to triggering a succession of unstack and stack actions until d1 is at the top of pile p1.

The termination of the last actions issued from the refinement of move(r1,d1) and uncover(c1) will set respectively time points t_2 and t_3 of m-bring, allowing the method to pursue on the remaining subtasks load, move and unload. $\square$

As illustrated in the previous example, TemRAE requires an elaborate bookkeeping mechanism, in particular for monitoring observed changes, as reported in ξ, with respect to expected time points, before progressing in its refinements. We are not providing a detailed pseudocode specification of TempRAE, but let us discuss briefly its main principles and limitations.

TempRAE selects a method m applicable for a task τ; it refines τ into a collection of temporally qualified subtasks. Progressing in this refinement requires a synchronization according to the temporal specifications in m. This synchronization is based on a simplified dispatching algorithm that triggers enabled controllable time points and waits for expected contingent ones. TempRAE can implement a Retry procedure for trying alternative methods if the chosen one fails (similar to the atemporal case in Algorithm 3.3): a Retry is possible as long as upper bounds on a task and its refinements have not been violated.

The limitations of TempRAE are due to its lack of lookahead. As underlined from Definition 4.29, temporal refinement acting cannot cope with the requirement of a future change that is not brought by the subtasks of a method and their refinements. Furthermore, the STNU corresponding to the entire refinement tree of a task τ is not guaranteed to be dynamically controllable. This STNU is discovered progressively as tasks and actions are achieved and effects and events are observed. Precedence constraints with respect to contingent events or absolute time (e.g., bringing a container before the scheduled departure of a ship) may lead to deadline failures. In this approach, it is the responsibility of the designer to specify methods that refine into dynamically controllable networks. Techniques presented in Section 4.4.3 can be used to verify this requirement.

4.5.3 Acting and Planning with Temporal Refinement Methods

As clear from the previous discussion, a temporally constrained domain cannot to be always addressed with reactive refinement. TempRAE requires enough lookahead for the choice of its methods and the dynamic controllability of the temporal network.

One approach is to plan for the task at hand with TemPlan then act with TempRAE on the basis of the methods and the dynamically controllable STNU found at the planning stage. Here, TempRAE does not need to test the applicability of its methods with the restrictive definition 4.29. This testing is done at planning time by adding, when and where needed, actions in the plan to support every assertions in the predicted future. TempRAE has to monitor that the current ξ is the one expected at planning time. TempRAE has also to synchronize the subtasks and actions in the plan with a Dispatch algorithm according to the constraints in the dynamically controllable STNU.

The preceding approach is not substantially different from what we developed in Section 4.5.1 with atemporal refinement for acting. However, there can be a significant difference if the actor is able to control the level at which refinement planning is pursued in a context-dependent way. The idea is to allow TemPlan to decide not refine a subtask. This can be done if TempPlan can evaluate the likely effects and temporal bounds of that subtask and assess that they are sufficient to stop planning and start acting on a partial plan that contains unrefined tasks. These can be refined at acting time by planning concurrently with acting on some other predecessor subtasks, or even when an unrefined task is dispatched.

The implementation of this idea requires further research, in particular for defining the likely effects and bounds of a subtask and assessing whether a partial plan is acceptable and can be used to start acting with. Approaches in that direction are discussed in the next section.

4.6 DISCUSSION AND HISTORICAL REMARKS

4.6.1 Temporal Representation and Reasoning

Temporal models are widely used in artificial intelligence well beyond planning. Numerous works are devoted to knowledge representations and reasoning techniques for handling time, in particular, for dealing with change, events, actions, and causality; see, for example, Allen [11], McDermott [414], Shoham [536], Shoahm and McDermott [534], Sandewall [523], and the handbook of Fisher et al. [200].

Most of the work cited above relies on a state-oriented view based on various temporal logics. The timeline approach developed in this chapter decomposes a reasoning task into a specialized solver – say, a planner – and a temporal reasoner that maintains, through queries and updates, a consistent network of temporal references. In addition to planning, this approach is used in other applications, such as temporal databases [99], monitoring [500], diagnosis [98, 374], multimedia document management [187, 5], video interpretation [591], and process supervision [162, 163].

Temporal networks can use as primitives either time points or intervals; they can manage either qualitative or quantitative constraints. A synthetic introduction to temporal networks can be found in Ghallab et al. [230, chap. 13] and the recent book of Barták et al. [44].

Qualitative approaches to temporal reasoning were introduced by Allen [13] with a specific algebra over intervals and a path consistency filtering algorithm. Vilain and Kautz [588] introduced the point algebra and showed that the consistency checking problem is NP-complete. Several tractable subclasses of the interval or the time point algebra have been proposed, for example, by Vilain et al. [589], Meiri [419], Nebel and Burckert [449], and Drakengren and Jonsson [164]. Other authors, such as Ligozat [385], Golumbic and Shamir [242], and Jonsson et al. [302], studied representations integrating time points and intervals and their tractable subclasses.

Quantitative approaches to handling time relied initially on linear equations and linear programming techniques, e.g., in Malik and Binford [400]. Temporal constraint satisfaction problems and their tractable subclass of Simple Temporal Networks, used in this chapter, were introduced by Dechter et al. [147]. Several improvements have been proposed, e.g. for the incremental management of STNs, by Cesta and Oddi [111] or Planken [487]. Various extensions to STNs have been studied, such as preferences in Khatib et al. [328] or specific constraints in Koubarakis [354].

The controllability issue and STNUs were introduced by Vidal and Ghallab [587]. Different levels of strong, weak and dynamic controllability were analyzed in Vidal and Fargier [586]. Algorithms for the strong and weak controllability cases were respectively proposed by Cimatti et al. [119] and Cimatti et al. [118]. State space planning with strong controllability is studied by Cimatti et al. [120]. A polynomial algorithm for dynamic controllability was proposed by Morris et al. [433] and improved in Morris and

Muscettola [434]. Incremental dynamic controllability has been introduced by Stedl and Williams [557]; the algorithm of cubic complexity is due to Nilsson et al. [458, 459].

Constraints in planning can play an important role. Naturally authors have sought ways to efficiently structure them, in particular with meta-CSPs. A meta-CSP is a CSP above lower level CSPs. Its meta-variables are the lower level constraints; their values are alternative ways to combine consistently these constraints. For example, with disjunctive temporal constraints the values correspond to possible disjuncts. The approach has been used in different CSP settings, such as for example the management of preferences in temporal reasoning by Moffitt and Pollack [428], Moffitt [427] or Barták et al. [44]. It has been applied to temporal planning by several authors, e.g., Gerevini et al. [222], Rodriguez-Moreno et al. [515] and Gregory et al. [245]. It appears to be particularly appealing for handling temporal and other constraints on different kind of resources, as illustrated by Mansouri and Pecora [401].

4.6.2 Temporal Planning

There is a long and rich history of research in temporal planning. Numerous temporal planners have been proposed, starting from early HTN planners such as Deviser by Vere [581], SIPE by Wilkins [604], FORBIN by Dean et al. [141] or O-PLAN by Currie and Tate [133]; these planners integrate various temporal extensions to HTN representations and algorithms.

The state-oriented view in temporal planning extends the classical model of instantaneous precondition-effect transitions with *durative actions*. The basic model considers a start point and a duration. It requires preconditions to hold at the start and effects at the end of an action; this is illustrated in TGP by Smith and Weld [547] or in TP4 by Haslum and Geffner [262]. Extensions of this model with conditions that prevail over the duration of the action, (as in the model of Sandewall and Rönnquist [524]) have been proposed, e.g., in the SAPA planner of Do and Kambhampati [154], or in the domain description language specifications PDDL2.1 of Fox and Long [204]. Several planners rely on the latter representation, among which HS by Haslum and Geffner [262], TPSYS by Garrido [214] or CRICKEY by Coles et al. [127].

A few planners using the durative action model adopt the plan-space approach, notably Zeno of Penberthy and Weld [471] which relies on linear programming techniques, or VHPOP of Younes and Simmons [623] which uses STN algorithms. Some planners pursue the HTN approach, as the earlier planners mentioned above, or more recently SHOP2 by Nau et al. [448] or Siadex by Castillo et al. [109].

Most durative actions temporal planners rely on state-based search techniques. A few are based on temporal logic approaches. Among these are TALplanner by Doherty and Kvarnstrom [156, 366], a model-checking based planner by Edelkamp [169], and a SAT-based planner by Huang et al. [289]. Significant effort has been invested in generalizing classical state-space planning heuristics to the durative action case. The action compression technique, which basically abstract the durative transition to an instantaneous one for the purpose of computing a heuristic, is quite popular, for example in the work of Gerevini and Schubert [224] or Eyerich et al. [185]. Various temporal extensions of the relaxed planning graph technique (Section 2.3.2), as in Metric RPG of Hoffmann

[277], have been proposed, e.g., Haslum and Geffner [262], Long and Fox [395], Coles et al. [127], Haslum [258]. Sampling over a duration interval with action compression has also been investigated by Kiesel and Ruml [330].

A few durative action planners can handle hybrid discrete-continuous change. Some planners address continuous effects through repeated discretization, e.g., UPMurphy of Penna et al. [473]. Linear programming techniques, when the continuous dynamics is assumed to be linear, have been used since ZENO [471] by several planners. A recent and quite elaborate example is COLIN of Coles et al. [128]. The Kongming planner of Li and Williams [381] relies on domain specific dynamic models.

The durative action model led to the design of quite performant planners. But it usually has a weak notion of concurrency that basically requires independence between concurrent actions. Interfering effects, as discussed in Example 4.15, can be addressed by a few of the above mentioned planners, e.g., notably COLIN [128]. Alternatively, interfering effects can be addressed with the time-oriented view.

Planning along the time-oriented view was introduced by Allen and Koomen [16] in a planner based on the interval algebra and plan-space search Allen [14, 12]. The Time-Map Manager of Dean and McDermott [145] led to the development of a few planners [141, 75] and several original ideas related to temporal databases and temporal planning operators.

Planning with chronicles was introduced in IxTeT by Ghallab et al. [227][228]. The IxTeT kernel is an efficient manager of time point constraints of Ghallab and Mounir-Alaoui [229]. IxTeT handles concurrent interfering actions, exogenous events and goals situated in time. It uses distance-based heuristics of Garcia and Laborie [212] integrated to abstraction techniques in plan-space planning. Its performance and scalability were improved by several other timeline oriented planners using similar representations. These are notably: ParcPlan of El-Kholy and Richard [176] and Liatsos and Richard [383] ASPEN of Rabideau et al. [501], PS of Jónsson et al. [301], IDEA of Muscettola et al. [439], EUROPA of Frank and Jónsson [206], APSI of Fratini et al. [208], and T-REX of Py, Rajan et al. [498, 503, 504]. Elaborate heuristics, generalizing the reachability and dependency graphs of state-space planning, have been designed for these representations, e.g., by Bernardini and Smith [58]. A few of the mentioned planners have been deployed in demanding applications, e.g., for controlling autonomous space systems and underwater vehicles.

An interesting development has been brought by the Action Notation Modeling Language (ANML) proposed by Smith et al. [545]. ANML is a representation that combines HTN decomposition methods with the expressivity of the timeline representation, as developed in the temporal refinement methods of this chapter. FAPE by Dvorak et al. [165] is a first planning and acting system based on ANML.

Refinement methods reduce the search complexity by providing domain-specific knowledge, but they do not palliate the need of good heuristics. Some temporal logic based planners, like TALplan, rely on control rules. Most of the state-based temporal planners referred to earlier exploit successfully the techniques of Section 2.3. The use of classical planning heuristics has even been an important motivation for the state-oriented view of temporal planning. These techniques have been extended to plan-space planning (e.g., in RePop [454] and VHPOP [623]) and further developed for timeline based planners. There is notably the mutual exclusion technique of Bernardini and Smith [55] and their dependency graph approach [58]. Dependency graphs record relationship between possible activities in a domain. They are based on activity transition graphs [56, 57], which are a direct extension of the domain transition graphs of state variables [267]. These techniques have been successfully demonstrated on the EUROPA2 planner.

Finally, let us mention that temporal planning has naturally been associated with resources handling capabilities. Several of the planners mentioned above integrate planning and scheduling functions, in particular with constraint-based techniques, which where introduced early in IxTeT by Laborie and Ghallab [370]. Algorithmic issues for the integration of resource scheduling and optimization in planning attracted numerous contributions such as Smith et al. [546], Cesta et al. [112], Laborie [369], Verfaillie et al. [582]. A global overview of scheduling and resource handling in planning is proposed by Baptiste et al. [35].

4.6.3 Acting with Temporal Models

Several of the acting representations and systems discussed in Section 3.5.1, based on procedures, rules, automata, Petri-nets or CSPs, integrates directly or have been extended with temporal primitives and techniques for handling explicit time. The PRS system of Ingrand et al. [293] or the RPL language of McDermott [415] offer some mechanisms for handling real-time "watchdogs" and delay primitives. More elaborate synchronization constructs have been developed by Simmons [540] in TCA and TDL [541].

A few of the temporal planners discussed earlier have been integrated to an actual planning and acting system. This is in particular the case for timeline oriented planners along an approach akin to that of Section 4.5.1. For example, Cypress of Wilkins and Myers [605] is the combination of SIPE for planning and PRS for acting. DS1/RAX of Muscettola et al. [441] implements a procedure-based acting technique combined with the PS planner. Casper of Knight et al. [332] is a temporal constraint-based executor for the ASPEN planner. IxTeT-Exec of Lemai-Chenevier and Ingrand [375] integrates IxTeT and PRS with plan repair and action refinement mechanisms. T-REX of Rajan and Py [503] follows a distributed approach over a set of "reactors" sharing timelines. It has been used mostly with the EUROPA planner. The *dispatchability property* studied in Muscettola et al. [440] and [432] requires simplifying the STNs resulting from the above planners in order to rely on local propagation at acting time. This technique provides some improvements in the dispatching algorithm but does not handle dynamic controllability.

The Reactive Model-based Programming Language (RMPL) of Ingham et al. [292] follows an approach more akin to that of Section 4.5.2. RMPL programs are transformed into the Temporal Plan Networks (TPN) representation of Williams and Abramson [606]. TPN extends STN with symbolic constraints and decision nodes. Planning with a TPN is finding a path in the explicit network that meets the constraints. Conrad et al. [129] introduce choices in the acting component of RMPL. TPNs with error recovery, temporal flexibility, and conditional context dependent execution are considered in Effinger et al. [175]. There, tasks have random variable durations with probability distributions. A particle-sampling dynamic execution algorithm finds an execution guaranteed to succeed with a given probability. Santana and Williams [526] studied probabilistic TPNs with the notions of weak and strong consistency, and proposed techniques to check these properties. TPNUs of Levine and Williams [380] add the notion of uncertainty for contingent decisions taken by the environment and other agents. The acting system adapts the execution to observations and predictions based on the plan. It has been illustrated with a service robot which observes and assists a human.

4.7 EXERCISES

4.1. Specify the primitives stack, unstack and navigate of Example 4.11. For the latter, assume that navigation between connected waypoints is unconstrained.

4.2. Augment the domain of Example 4.12 by considering that a pile p can be attached to a ship and that a crane k on a dock d can unstack containers from a pile p only when the corresponding ship is docked at d.

4.3. Specify the initial chronicle ϕ_0 for the problem of Example 4.17 and Figure 4.5.

4.4. In Example 4.17, develop the steps of TemPlan until reaching a solution to the planning problem.

4.5. For the domain in Example 4.12, redefine navigate as a task which refines into the traversal of roads and the crossing to docks. The navigation between two roads adjacent to a dock d requires crossing d which should not be occupied during the crossing interval. For example, in Figure 4.5 the navigation from d4 to d1 requires the traversal of d3 which should be empty when the robot gets there. Analyze the conflicting assertions that result from this modification in the first few steps of TemPlan for Example 4.17 and find resolvers for the corresponding flaws.

4.6. Analyse the commonalities and differences between the notion of threats in Section 2.5 and that of conflicting assertions. Notice that the former relate actions while the latter are with respect to assertions. Since a threat is a menace to a causal link, can there be conflicting assertions without a causal support? If the answer is affirmative, give an example.

4.7. In Example 4.17, implement the modification introduced in Exercise 4.3: consider that piles p'1 and p'2 are not fixed in their respective docks but attached to two ships that will be docked respectively to d1 and d2 at two future intervals of time $[t_1, t_1 + \delta_1]$ and $[t_2, t_2 + \delta_2]$. How is modified the solution found in Exercise 4.4 when these two intervals do not overlap. What happens when $[t_1, t_1 + \delta_1]$ and $[t_2, t_2 + \delta_2]$ are overlapping?

4.8. Run algorithm PC on the networks in Figure 4.7. Show that it adds the constraints $r_{1,3} = [1, 3], r_{24} = [1, 2]$ and $r_{45} = [2, 3]$.

4.9. Specify and implement an incremental version of the PC algorithm; use it to analyze how the network in Figure 4.7 evolves when are added to it successively $t_6, r_{36} = [5, 8], r_{56} = [2, 5]$ then $t_7, r_{47} = [3, 6], r_{67} = [1, 7]$.

4.10. Run algorithm PC on the networks in Figures 4.8 and 4.9 and compute all the implicit constraints entailed from those in the networks; show that both networks are minimal.

4.11. Prove that the minimal network in Figure 4.10 is such that $[b - v, a - u] \subseteq [p, q]$.

4.12. Consider the minimal network in Figure 4.10 for the case where $u \geq 0$ and $[b - v, a - u] = \varnothing$. Prove that this network is not dynamically controllable.

4.13. Consider the temporal network associated to the solution of Exercise 4.4: under what condition is it dynamically controllable?

4.14. For all the primitives in Example 4.11, define atemporal acting refinement methods similar to the two given in Example 4.25.

4.15. Run algorithm Dispatch for the solution plan found in Exercise 4.4 assuming that robot r1 is much faster than r2.

CHAPTER 5   Deliberation with Nondeterministic Models

In this chapter we drop the unrealistic assumption of determinism, that is, the assumption that each action performed in one state leads deterministically to one state. This apparently simple extension introduces uncertainty in the model of the domain and requires new approaches to planning and acting. Deliberation must take into account that actions can lead to a set of states; plans are no longer sequences of actions, but conditional plans; solutions may have different strengths. Deliberative acting with nondeterministic models allows us to take into account uncertainty when actions are performed.

The main motivations for planning and acting with nondeterministic models are in Section 5.1. The planning problem is formalized in Section 5.2. In the subsequent three sections we present some different approaches to planning with nondeterministic models: And/Or graph search (Section 5.3), symbolic model checking (Section 5.4), and determinization techniques (Section 5.5). In Section 5.6, we present techniques that interleave planning and acting. In Section 5.7, we present planning techniques with refinement methods and nondeterministic models, and in Section 5.8 we show techniques for deliberative acting with input/output automata. Comparisons among different approaches and main references are given in the discussion and historical remarks in Section 5.9. The chapter ends with a few exercises.

5.1 INTRODUCTION AND MOTIVATION

Recall that in deterministic models, the prediction of the effects of an action is deterministic: only one state is predicted as the result of performing an action in a state (see Chapter 2, Section 2.1.1, assumption in item 3). Nondeterministic models predict alternative options: an action when applied in a state may result in one among several possible states. Formally, $\gamma(s, a)$ returns a set of states rather than a single state. The extension allowed by nondeterministic models is important because it allows for modeling the uncertainty of the real world.

In some cases, using a deterministic or a nondeterministic model is a design choice. For instance, in the real world, the execution of an action may either succeed or fail.

Despite this, in many cases, it still makes sense to model just the so-called nominal case (in which failure does not occur), monitor execution, detect failure when it occurs, and recover, for example, by replanning or by re-acting with some failure-recovery mechanism. In these cases, deterministic models can still be a convenient choice. Indeed, despite the fact that nondeterministic models may have some advantages, because they allow us to model the world more accurately and to plan for recovery mechanisms at design time, they have clear disadvantages, because taking into account all the different possible outcomes may become much more complicated, both conceptually and computationally.

In other cases, modeling the world with nondeterminism is instead a must. Indeed, in certain environments there is no nominal case. And sometimes we need to consider different possible action outcomes during both planning and acting, independently of the fact that no model is perfect and the world is seldom completely predicable. For instance, there is no nominal case in the throw of a dice or in the toss of a coin or in a sensing action of a robot. There is no nominal case in the method for an online payment if the choice is left to the user (cash, credit card, or bank transfer). There is no nominal case in the confirmation given to a Web service by the user. And if we need to generate a software service that works, we need to consider equally all possibilities.

Notice that, of course, even nondeterministic models are not perfect models of the world. Even if we model the six outcomes of the throw of a dice, the tossed dice might run off the playing board, and end up under the table. Similarly, a coin may land on its edge, and the operating system of the hosting of a Web service can break. In all these cases, however, nondeterministic models are definitely more realistic, and often not avoidable, independently of the fact that everything can always happen in the world and no perfect model exists.

Planning and acting with nondeterministic models is a different and much more challenging task than the deterministic case:

- The search space is no longer represented as a graph. It becomes an And/Or graph (see Appendix A) in which each And-branch corresponds to applying an action that may lead from one state to many possible states, and each Or-branch corresponds to choosing which action to apply in a state. We can choose the action, but we cannot choose which outcome it will produce.
- Plans cannot be restricted to sequences of actions.[1] In the nondeterministic case, we need to generate conditional plans, that is, plans with conditional control structures that sense the actual action outcome among the many possible ones, and act accordingly to the information gathered at execution time.
- The definition of solution plan is not trivial because solutions of different strength can be devised. For instance, a plan may either guarantee the achievement of a goal or just have some chances of success, or it may guarantee the achievement of the goal according to some assumptions.

As a consequence, in the case of nondeterministic domains the problem of devising practical algorithms that can deal effectively with the search space is much harder than

---

[1] Conformant planning generates sequences of plans in nondeterministic domains. It is, however, a restricted and specific case.

in the deterministic case. Planning algorithms need to analyze not only single paths to find one that leads to the goal, but all the execution paths of a plan. Keeping track of the different possible branches of execution typically induces large search spaces.

Online planning and acting is one of the most effective techniques for dealing with large state spaces. In Chapter 2, we presented the idea of interleaving planning and acting to deal with large models. This motivation for online planning and acting is even stronger in the case of nondeterministic models. Interleaving acting with planning can be used to determine which of the nondeterministic outcomes has actually taken place.

Last but not least, nondeterministic domains are key models for deliberative acting (see the discussion in Section 1.2.3 and Section 2.6). They are a proper and natural way to represent operational models that describe how to perform an action because operational models have to take into account possibly different evolutions of the execution of commands. Planning in nondeterministic domains can thus be a powerful deliberation mechanism.

5.2 THE PLANNING PROBLEM

Planning with nondeterministic models relaxes the assumption that $\gamma(s, a)$ returns a single state. Then for every state s and action a, either $\gamma(s, a) = \varnothing$ (i.e., the action is not applicable) or $\gamma(s, a)$ is the set of states that may result from the application of a to the state s, i.e., $\gamma : S \times A \to 2^S$.

Following the notation introduced in Chapter 2, Section 2.1.3, an operator can be represented with multiple effects:

$$act(z_1, z_2, \ldots, z_k)$$
$$\text{pre: } p_1, \ldots, p_m$$
$$\text{eff1: } e_{11}, \ldots$$
$$\ldots$$
$$\text{effn: } e_{1n}, \ldots$$

5.2.1 Planning Domains

A nondeterministic planning domain can be described in terms of a finite set of states S, a finite set of actions A, and a transition function $\gamma(s, a)$ that maps each state s and action a into a set of states:

Definition 5.1. (Planning Domain) A *nondeterministic planning domain* Σ is the tuple (S, A, γ), where S is the finite set of states, A is the finite set of actions, and $\gamma : S \times A \to 2^S$ is the state transition function. $\qquad\square$

An action $a \in A$ is applicable in state $s \in S$ if and only if $\gamma(s, a) \neq \varnothing$. Applicable$(s)$ is the set of actions applicable to state s:

$$\text{Applicable}(s) = \{a \in A \mid \gamma(s, a) \neq \varnothing\}$$

Example 5.2. In Figure 5.1, we show a simple example of nondeterministic planning domain, inspired by the management facility for a harbor, where an item (e.g., a container, a car) is unloaded from the ship, stored in some storage area, possibly moved to transit areas while waiting to be parked, and delivered to gates where it is loaded

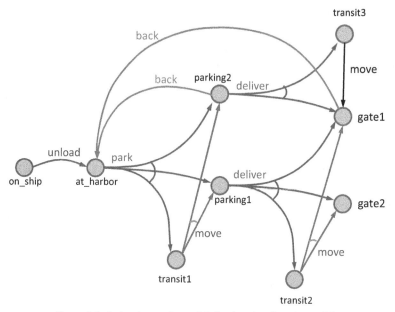

Figure 5.1. A simple nondeterministic planning domain model.

on trucks. In this simple example, we have just one state variable, pos(item), which can range over nine values: on_ship, at_harbor, parking1, parking2, transit1, transit2, transit3, gate1, and gate2. For simplicity we label each state in Figure 5.1 only with the value of the variable pos(item).

In this example, we have just five actions. Two of them are deterministic, unload and back, and three are nondeterministic, park, move, and deliver. Action unload unloads the item from the ship to the harbor, its preconditions are pos(item) = on_ship, and its effects pos(item) ← at_harbor. Action back moves the item back from any position in the harbor to the position pos(item) = at_harbor. To keep the figure simple, in Figure 5.1 we show only two instances of actions back from the state where pos(item) = parking2 and the state where pos(item) = gate1, but a back arrow should be drawn from each state where the position is parking1, parking2, transit1, transit2, transit3, gate1, and gate2.

A possible description of action park is the following, where eff1, eff2, and eff3 are the three possible effects of the action:

park
    pre: pos(item) = at_harbor
    eff1: pos(item) ← parking2
    eff2: pos(item) ← parking1
    eff3: pos(item) ← transit1

The actions park, move, and deliver are nondeterministic. In the case of action park, we represent with nondetermism the fact that the storage areas parking1 and parking2 may be unavailable for storing items, for example, because they may be closed or full. Whether an area is available or not cannot be predicted, because there are other actors parking and delivering items, for example, from different ships. However, we assume that it is always possible either to park the item in one of the two parking areas or to move it to transit area transit1. The item waits in transit1 until one of the two parking areas are available, and it can be stored by the action move. Also in the case of move, we use nondeterminism to represent the fact that we do not know a priori which one of the two areas may become available.[2] From the two parking areas, it is possible to deliver the container and load them on trucks or to a transit area, from which it is necessary to move the container into either one of the two parking areas. The deliver action moves containers from parking1 to one of the two gates where trucks are loaded or to a transit area from which it is necessary to move the container again to load trucks in one of the two gates.[3] The same action from parking2 may lead to gate1 or to another transit area. □

5.2.2 Plans as Policies

A plan for a nondeterministic domain can be represented as a policy, that is, a partial[4] function π that maps states into actions. Intuitively, if $\pi(s) = a$, it means that we should perform action a in state s.

Definition 5.3. (Policy) Let $\Sigma = (S, A, \gamma)$ be a planning domain. Let $S' \subseteq S$. A *policy* π for a planning domain Σ is a function $\pi : S' \to A$ such that, for every $s \in S', \pi(s) \in Applicable(s)$. It follows that $\text{Dom}(\pi) = S'$. □

Example 5.4. Consider the domain of Example 5.2 shown in Figure 5.1. The following are policies for this planning domain:

$$\pi_1 : \pi_1(\text{pos(item)=on\_ship}) = \text{unload}$$
$$\pi_1(\text{pos(item)=at\_harbor}) = \text{park}$$
$$\pi_1(\text{pos(item)=parking1}) = \text{deliver}$$
$$\pi_2 : \pi_2(\text{pos(item)=on\_ship}) = \text{unload}$$
$$\pi_2(\text{pos(item)=at\_harbor}) = \text{park}$$
$$\pi_2(\text{pos(item)=parking1}) = \text{deliver}$$
$$\pi_2(\text{pos(item)=parking2}) = \text{back}$$
$$\pi_2(\text{pos(item)=transit1}) = \text{move}$$
$$\pi_2(\text{pos(item)=transit2}) = \text{move}$$
$$\pi_2(\text{pos(item)=gate1}) = \text{back}$$
$$\pi_3 : \pi_3(\text{pos(item)=on\_ship}) = \text{unload}$$
$$\pi_3(\text{pos(item)=at\_harbor}) = \text{park}$$
$$\pi_3(\text{pos(item)=parking1}) = \text{deliver}$$
$$\pi_3(\text{pos(item)=parking2}) = \text{deliver}$$
$$\pi_3(\text{pos(item)=transit1}) = \text{move}$$
$$\pi_3(\text{pos(item)=transit2}) = \text{move}$$
$$\pi_3(\text{pos(item)=transit3}) = \text{move}$$

□

[2] In general, if an action's outcome depends on something that is unknown to the actor, then it is sometimes useful for the actor to think of the possible outcomes as nondeterministic. As an analogy, we think of random number generators as having nondeterministic outcomes, even though many of these generators are deterministic.
[3] Notice that deliver action has two possible effects in one instance and three in another. This is allowed because the degree of nondeterminism can depend on the state at which an action is performed.
[4] That is, there may be states for which it is undefined.

Algorithm 5.1 Procedure for performing the actions of a policy.

PerformPolicy(π)
   $s \leftarrow$ observe the current state
   while $s \in \mathrm{Dom}(\pi)$ do
     perform action $\pi(s)$
     $s \leftarrow$ observe the current state

A procedure that performs the actions of a policy consists of observing the current state s, performing the corresponding action $\pi(s)$, and repeating these two steps until the state is no longer in the domain of π (See Algorthm 5.1).

A remark is in order. A policy is a convenient way to represent plans in nondeterministic domain models. An alternative is to represent plans with decision trees or with conditional statements. The expressiveness of policies and the one of decision trees are incomparable. On one hand, policies allow for infinite iterations of the application of actions, which are not allowed by finite decision trees. On the other hand, decision trees allow for performing different actions in the same state depending on at which point we are in the tree, whereas policies always perform the same action in a state. We should also remember that we restrict to the case of memoryless policies. We call our policies *memoryless policies*. A policy with memory is a mapping from a history of states to an action. Policies with memory allow for performing different actions in the same state, depending on the states visited so far.

5.2.3 Planning Problems and Solutions

In deterministic domains, a plan is a sequence of actions that, when performed from an initial state induces a sequence of states, one for each action in the plan. A solution to a planning problem in a deterministic domain is a plan that induces a sequence of states such that the last state is in the set of goal states. The states reachable from a state s by a sequence of applicable actions $a_1, a_2, \ldots$ can be defined easily by composing the transition function: $\{s\} \cup \gamma(s, a_1) \cup \gamma(\gamma(s, a_1), a_2) \cup \ldots$.

To define a solution to a planning problem in nondeterministic domains, we need to do something similar, that is to define which states are reached by a policy π in a planning domain $\Sigma = (S, A, \gamma)$. However, we have to take into account that, in a nondeterministic planning domain, $\gamma(s, a)$ returns a set of states, and therefore a plan can result in many possible different paths, that is, sequences of states that are reached by the policy.

We start by introducing the notion of *the set of states reachable from state s by a policy π*:

$\widehat{\gamma}(s, \pi)$ denotes the transitive closure of $\gamma(s, \pi(s))$, that is, the set that includes s and all its successors states reachable by π

To check whether a policy reaches some goals, we are interested in the final states that are reached by the policy π from state s, that is in what we call the *leaves* of a policy

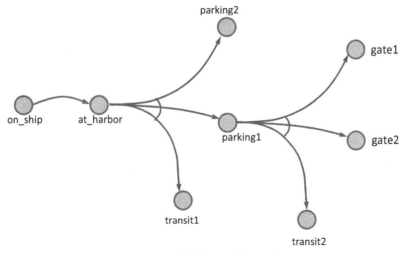

Figure 5.2. Reachability graph for policy π_1.

π from state s:

$$leaves(s, \pi) = \{s' \mid s' \in \widehat{\gamma}(s, \pi) \text{ and } s' \notin \mathrm{Dom}(\pi)\}$$

Notice that $leaves(s, \pi)$ can be empty, that is, there may be no leaves. This is the case of policies that cycle on the same set of states. If π is the empty plan, then $leaves(s, \pi) = \{s\}$. We define the reachability graph that connects the reachable states from state s through a policy π:

$$Graph(s, \pi) = \{\widehat{\gamma}(s, \pi), (s', s'') \mid s' \in \widehat{\gamma}(s, \pi) \text{ and } s'' \in \gamma(s', \pi(s'))\}$$

We call $\widehat{\Gamma}(s)$ the *set of states reachable from a state s*.

Example 5.5. Let π_1, π_2, and π_3 be as in Example 5.4. Their leaves from state pos(item)=on_ship are:[5]

$$leaves(\text{pos(item)=on\_ship}, \pi_1) = \{\text{pos(item)=parking2},$$
$$\text{pos(item)=transit1},$$
$$\text{pos(item)=gate1},$$
$$\text{pos(item)=gate2},$$
$$\text{pos(item)=transit2}\}$$
$$leaves(\text{pos(item)=on\_ship}, \pi_2) = \{\text{pos(item)=gate2}\}$$
$$leaves(\text{pos(item)=on\_ship}, \pi_3) = \{\text{pos(item)=gate1}, \text{pos(item)=gate2}\}$$

Figures 5.2, 5.3, and 5.4 show the reachability graphs of π_1, π_2, and π_3 from the state where pos(item)=on_ship. Notice also that all states are reachable from state where pos(item)=on_ship. □

Given these preliminary definitions, we can now introduce formally the notion of a planning problem and solution in a nondeterministic domain.

---

[5] In this case, the value on_ship of the state variable pos(item) identifies a single state.

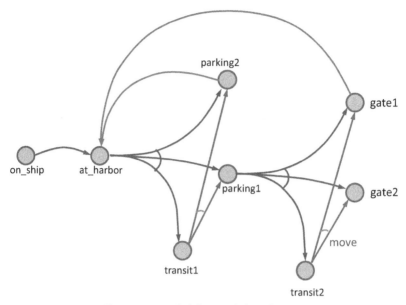

Figure 5.3. Reachability graph for policy π_2.

Definition 5.6. (Planning Problem) Let $\Sigma = (S, A, \gamma)$ be a planning domain. A *planning problem P* for Σ is a tuple $P = (\Sigma, s_0, S_g)$, where $s_0 \in S$ is the initial state and $S_g \subseteq S$ is the set of goal states.   □

Notice that we have a single initial state s_0 rather than a set of initial states $S_0 \subseteq S$. A set of initial states represents partially specified initial conditions, or in other words uncertainty about the initial state. However, restricting to a single initial state is not

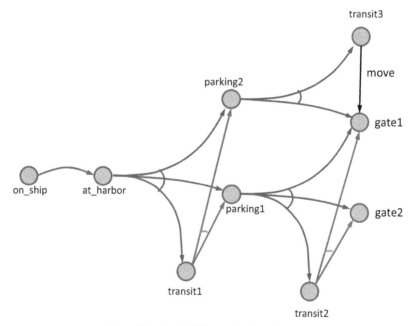

Figure 5.4. Reachability graph for policy π_3.

a limitation because a domain with a set of initial states S_0 is equivalent to a domain where we have a single initial state $s_0 \notin S$ and an additional action $a_o \notin A$ such that $\gamma(s_0, a_0) = S_0$.

We can now define different kinds of solutions to a planning problem.

Definition 5.7. (Solution) Let $P = (\Sigma, s_0, S_g)$ be a planning problem for a domain $\Sigma = (S, A, \gamma)$. Let π be a policy for Σ. Then π is a *solution* if and only if $leaves(s_0, \pi) \cap S_g \neq \varnothing$ □

Solutions are policies that *may* lead to a goal. They can achieve the goal in different ways, with different levels of guarantee, and with different strengths. The requirement we impose on a policy to be a solution is that at least one state of its leaves is a goal state. We are interested in safe solutions.

Definition 5.8. (Safe Solution) Let $P = (\Sigma, s_0, S_g)$ be a planning problem for a domain $\Sigma = (S, A, \gamma)$. Let π be a solution for Σ. Then π is a *safe solution* if and only if $\forall s \in \widehat{\gamma}(s_0, \pi)(leaves(s, \pi) \cap S_g \neq \varnothing)$ □

Safe solutions are policies in which the goal is reachable from the initial state. Notice that, in general, they are not policies in which the goal is reachable from any state of the domain of the policy $(\mathrm{Dom}(\pi))$ because we may have a state in $\mathrm{Dom}(\pi)$ that is not the initial state and from which we do not reach the goal.

Definition 5.9. (Unsafe Solution) Let $P = (\Sigma, s_0, S_g)$ be a planning problem for a domain $\Sigma = (S, A, \gamma)$. Let π be a solution for Σ. Then π is an *unsafe solution* if it is not safe. □

Unsafe solutions either have a leaf that is not in the set of goal states or there exists a reachable state from which it is not possible to reach a leaf state. It is easy to prove that π is an unsafe solution if and only if $\exists s \in leaves(s_0, \pi) \mid s \notin S_g \vee \exists s \in \widehat{\gamma}(s_0, \pi) \mid leaves(s, \pi) = \varnothing$.

Intuitively, unsafe solutions may achieve the goal but are not guaranteed to do so. If an agent tries to perform the actions dictated by the policy, the agent may end up at a nongoal state or end up in a "bad cycle" where it is not possible to go out and reach the goal.

It is important to distinguish between two kinds of safe solutions, cyclic and acyclic. Acyclic solutions are safe solutions whose reachability graph is acyclic; all other safe solutions are cyclic.

Definition 5.10. (Cyclic Safe Solution) Let $P = (\Sigma, s_0, S_g)$ be a planning problem for a domain $\Sigma = (S, A, \gamma)$. Let π be a solution for Σ. Then π is a *cyclic safe solution* if and only if $leaves(s_0, \pi) \subseteq S_g \wedge (\forall s \in \widehat{\gamma}(s_0, \pi))(leaves(s, \pi) \cap S_g \neq \varnothing) \wedge Graph(s_0, \pi)$ is cyclic □

Cyclic Safe Solutions are safe solutions with cycles.

Definition 5.11. (Acyclic Safe Solution) Let $P = (\Sigma, s_0, S_g)$ be a planning problem for a domain $\Sigma = (S, A, \gamma)$. Let π be a solution for Σ. Then π is an *acyclic safe solution* if and only if $leaves(s_0, \pi) \subseteq S_g \wedge Graph(s_0, \pi)$ is acyclic. □

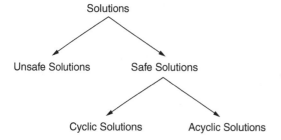

Figure 5.5. Different kinds of solutions: a class diagram.

Acyclic Safe Solutions are safe solutions that are guaranteed to terminate and to achieve the goal despite nondeterminism. They are guaranteed to reach the goal in a bounded number of steps, and the bound is the length of the longest path in $Graph(s_0, \pi)$. This amounts to saying that all the leaves are goal states and there are no cycles in the reachability graph.

Figure 5.5 depicts in a class diagram the different forms of solutions. *Unsafe Solutions* are not of interest because they do not guarantee to achieve the goal. However, as we will see in Section 5.5, planning for (possibly unsafe) solutions can be used by planning algorithms to guide the search for Safe Solutions. In general, we are interested in safe (cyclic and acyclic) solutions because they provide (with different strengths) some assurance to achieve the goal despite nondeterminism. *Acyclic Safe Solutions* are the best because they can really ensure that we get to the goal. *Cyclic Safe Solutions* provide a weaker degree of assurance to achieve the goal: assuming that sooner or later execution will get out of possibly infinite loops, they are guaranteed to achieve the goal. They guarantee that there is always a possibility to terminate the loop. However, for some applications, this may be not enough.

Example 5.12. Consider the three policies π_1, π_2, and π_3 in Example 5.4. Consider the planning problem P with domain Σ the nondeterministic domain described in Example 5.2, initial state s_0 where pos(item)=on_ship, and goal states $S_g =$ {pos(item)=gate1, pos(item)=gate2}.

All three policies are solutions for the planning problem P; indeed there exists at least one leaf state that is in the set of goal states. Policy π_1 is an unsafe solution because there are leaves that do not belong to S_g from which it is impossible to reach the goal: such leaves are the states where pos(item)=parking2, or pos(item)=transit1, or pos(item)=transit2.

Policies π_2 and π_3 are safe solutions. Policy π_2 is a safe cyclic solution since from each state in its graph it is possible to reach a state in the goal (pos(item)=gate2). Policy π_3 is a safe acyclic solution because it is guaranteed to reach one of the two gates, pos(item)=gate1 or pos(item)=gate2, without the danger of getting trapped in cycles.

Notice that for the planning problem P' on the same domain, the same initial state, but with goal $S_g = $ {pos(item)=gate2}, a safe acyclic solution does not exist, and the safest solution we can find is the safe cyclic solution π_2.   □

A remark is in order. We require that solutions have some leaf states. In this way, we do not consider policies that lead to the goal and then loop inside the set of goal states. One may argue that such policies might be considered as solutions. However, notice

Table 5.1. Solutions: different terminologies in the literature.

Our terminology	Nondeterminism	Probabilistic
solutions	*weak solutions*	–
unsafe solutions	–	*improper solutions*
safe solutions	*strong cyclic solutions*	*proper solutions*
cyclic safe solutions	–	–
acyclic safe solutions	*strong solutions*	–

that for any solution of this kind, there exists a solution according to our definition. It is indeed enough to eliminate the states in the policy that lead to the loop inside the set of goal states.

In the following, we specify the relations among different kinds of solutions.

$$\textit{unsafe solutions} \cup \textit{safe solutions} = \textit{solutions}$$
$$\textit{cyclic safe solutions} \cup \textit{acyclic safe solutions} = \textit{safe solutions}$$
$$\textit{unsafe solutions} \cap \textit{safe solutions} = \varnothing$$
$$\textit{cyclic safe solutions} \cap \textit{acyclic safe solutions} = \varnothing$$

Notice that our terminology here and in Chapter 6 are identical, but different from the usual terminology in the literature, in which our *solutions* and *safe solutions* are called *weak solutions* and *strong cyclic solutions*, respectively. In the literature, every strong solution is also a weak solutions, which can be confusing. In most of the literature on probabilistic planning, our *safe* and *unsafe* solutions are called *proper* and *improper*, and there is no notion that makes a distinction between *cyclic safe solutions* and *acyclic safe solutions*, despite the different strength they provide. We will not also differentiate cyclic and a cyclic safe solutions in probabilistic planning in Chapter 6, despite their differences (see discussion in Section 6.7.5). Table 5.1 summarizes the corresponding terminology used in planning with nondeterminism and in probabilistic planning literature.

5.3 AND/OR GRAPH SEARCH

A nondeterministic planning domain can be represented as an And/Or graph (see Appendix A), in which each Or-branch corresponds to a choice among the applicable actions, and each And-branch corresponds to the action's possible outcomes. In this section, we present algorithms that search And/Or graphs to find solutions.

5.3.1 Planning by Forward-Search

We first present a simple algorithm that finds a solution by searching the And/Or graph forward from the initial state. Find-Solution (see Algorithm 5.2) is guaranteed to find a solution if it exists. The solution may be either safe or unsafe. It is a simple modification of forward state-space search algorithms for deterministic planning domains (see Chapter 2). The main point related to nondeterminism is in the "progression" line (see line (i)), where we nondeterministically search for all possible states generated by $\gamma(s, a)$.

Algorithm 5.2 Planning for solutions by forward-search.

Find-Solution (Σ, s_0, S_g)
    $\pi \leftarrow \varnothing$; $s \leftarrow s_0$; *Visited* $\leftarrow \{s_0\}$
    loop
        if $s \in S_g$ then return π
        $A' \leftarrow$ Applicable(s)
        if $A' = \varnothing$ then return failure
        nondeterministically choose $a \in A'$
        nondeterministically choose $s' \in \gamma(s, a)$ (i)
        if $s' \in$ *Visited* then return failure
        $\pi(s) \leftarrow a$; *Visited* $\leftarrow$ *Visited* $\cup \{s'\}$; $s \leftarrow s'$

Find-Solution simply searches the And/Or graph to find a path that reaches the goal, without keeping track of which states are generated by which action. In this way, Find-Solution ignores the real complexity of nondeterminism in the domain. It deals with the And-nodes as if they were Or-nodes, that is, as if it could choose which outcome would be produced by each action.

Recall that the nondeterministic choices "nondeterministically choose $a \in A'$" and "nondeterministically choose $s' \in \gamma(s, a)$" correspond to an abstraction for ignoring the precise order in which the algorithm tries actions a among all the applicable actions to state s and alternative states s' among the states resulting from performing a in s.

Example 5.13. Consider the planning problem described in Example 5.2. Let the initial state s_0 be pos(item)=on_ship, and let the set of goal states S_g be {pos(item)=gate1, pos(item)=gate2}. Find-Solution proceeds forward from the initial state on_ship. It finds initially only one applicable action, that is, unload. It then expands it into at_harbor, one of the possible nondeterministic choices is $s' =$ parking1, which gets then expanded to gate2; π_1 (see Example 5.4) is generated in one of the possible nondeterministic execution traces.   □

Algorithm 5.3 is a simple algorithm that finds safe solutions. The algorithm performs a forward search and terminates when all the states in *Frontier* are goal states.

Algorithm 5.3 Planning for safe solutions by forward-search.

Find-Safe-Solution (Σ, s_0, S_g)
    $\pi \leftarrow \varnothing$
    Frontier $\leftarrow \{s_0\}$
    for every $s \in$ *Frontier* $\setminus S_g$ do
        Frontier $\leftarrow$ *Frontier* $\setminus \{s\}$
        if Applicable$(s) = \varnothing$ then return failure
        nondeterministically choose $a \in$ Applicable(s)
        $\pi \leftarrow \pi \cup (s, a)$
        Frontier $\leftarrow$ *Frontier* $\cup (\gamma(s, a) \setminus \text{Dom}(\pi))$
        if has-unsafe-loops$(\pi, a, Frontier)$ then return failure
    return π

Algorithm 5.4 Planning for safe acyclic solutions by forward-search.

Find-Acyclic-Solution (Σ, s_0, S_g)
  $\pi \leftarrow \varnothing$
  Frontier $\leftarrow \{s_0\}$
  for every $s \in$ *Frontier* $\setminus S_g$ do
    Frontier $\leftarrow$ *Frontier* $\setminus \{s\}$
    if Applicable$(s) = \varnothing$ then return failure
    nondeterministically choose $a \in$ Applicable(s)
    $\pi \leftarrow \pi \cup (s, a)$
    Frontier $\leftarrow$ *Frontier* $\cup (\gamma(s, a) \setminus \text{Dom}(\pi))$
    if has-loops$(\pi, a, \text{Frontier})$ then return failure
  return π

Find-Safe-Solution fails if the last action introduces a "bad loop," that is, a state from which no state in *Frontier* is reachable. The routine has-unsafe-loops checks whether a "bad loop" is introduced. A "bad loop" is introduced when the set of states resulting from performing action a, which are not in the domain of π, will never lead to the frontier:

$$\text{has-unsafe-loops}(\pi, a, \text{Frontier}) \text{ if}$$
$$\exists s \in (\gamma(s, a) \cap \text{Dom}(\pi)) \text{ such that } \hat{\gamma}(s, \pi) \cap \text{Frontier} = \varnothing.$$

Algorithm 5.4 is a simple algorithm that finds safe acyclic solutions. The algorithm is the same as Find-Safe-Solution, but in the failure condition. It fails if the last action introduces a loop, that is, a state from which the state itself is reachable by performing the plan:

$$\text{has-loops}(\pi, a, \text{Frontier}) \text{ iff}$$
$$\exists s \in (\gamma(s, a) \cap \text{Dom}(\pi)) \text{ such that } s \in \hat{\gamma}(s, \pi)$$

Example 5.14. Consider the planning problem P with domain Σ the nondeterministic domain described in Example 5.2, initial state pos(item)=on_ship, and set of goal states S_g as {pos(item)=gate1, pos(item)=gate2}. Find-Acyclic-Solution starts from the initial state on_ship, for every state s in the frontier expands the frontier by performing $\gamma(s, a)$. A successful trace of execution evolves as follows[6]:

$$\text{Step}_0 : \text{on\_ship}$$
$$\text{Step}_1 : \text{at\_harbor}$$
$$\text{Step}_2 : \text{parking2, parking1, transit1}$$
$$\text{Step}_3 : \text{transit3, gate1, gate2, transit2}$$
$$\text{Step}_4 : \text{gate1, gate2}$$ □

5.3.2 Planning by MinMax Search

This section introduces a technique that is based on a cost model of actions. Recall cost models defined in Chapter 2. We assign a cost to each action that is performed in a

---

[6] For simplicity, in the following we use on_ship and gate1, as names of states rather than a state variable notation.

Algorithm 5.5 Planning for safe acyclic solutions by MinMax Search.

Find-Acyclic-Solution-by-MinMax (Σ, S_0, S_g)
  return Compute-worst-case-for-action$(S_0, S_g, \infty, \varnothing)$

Compute-worst-case-for-action$(S, S_g, \beta, \text{ancestors})$
  $c' \leftarrow -\infty$
  $\pi' \leftarrow \varnothing$
  // if S is nonempty, this loop will be executed at least once:
  for every $s \in S$
    if $s \in$ ancestors then
      return (π', ∞)
    $(\pi, c) \leftarrow$ Choose-best-action$(s, S_g, \beta, \text{ancestors} \cup \{s\})$
    $\pi' \leftarrow \pi \cup \pi'$
    $c' \leftarrow \max(c', c)$
    if $c' \geq \beta$ then
      break
  return (π', c')

---

state, $cost(s, a)$. Weighting actions with cost can be useful in some application domains, where, for instance, actions consume resources or are more or less difficult or expensive to perform.

Algorithm 5.5 uses costs to identify which may be the best direction to take. It starts from the initial state and selects actions with minimal costs among the ones that are applicable. We are interested in finding a solution with the minimum accumulated cost, that is, the minimum of the costs of each action that is selected in the search. Because the domain model is nondeterministic and $\gamma(s, a)$ results in different states, we want to minimize the *worst-case* accumulated cost, that is, the maximum accumulated cost of each of the possible states in $\gamma(s, a)$. This is given by the following recursive formula:

$$c(s) = \begin{cases} 0 & \text{if } s \text{ is a goal,} \\ \min_{a \in \text{Applicable}(s)} (\text{cost}(a) + \max_{s' \in \gamma(s,a)} c(s')) & \text{otherwise.} \end{cases}$$

For this reason, the algorithm is said to perform a "MinMax search." While performing the search, the costs of actions that are used to expand the next states are accumulated, and the algorithm checks whether the accumulated cost becomes too high with respect to alternative selections of different actions. In this way, the accumulated cost is used to find an upper bound in the forward iteration.

Find-Acyclic-Solution-by-MinMax (Algorithm 5.5) finds safe acyclic solutions for nondeterministic planning problems in domains that may have cycles. It returns a pair (π, c), where π is a safe acyclic solution that is *worst-case optimal*, that is, the maximum cost of executing π is as low as possible, and c is the maximum cost of executing π.

Algorithm 5.6 The policy with minimal cost over actions.

Choose-best-action(s, S_g, β, ancestors)
  if $s \in S_g$ then
    return $(\varnothing, 0)$
  else if Applicable(s) $= \varnothing$ then
    return $(\varnothing, \infty)$
  else do
    $c = \infty$
    // this loop will always be executed at least once:
    for every $a \in$ Applicable(s) do
      $(\pi', c') \leftarrow$ Compute-worst-case-for-action($\gamma(s, a), S_g, \beta$, ancestors)
      if $c > c' + cost(s, a)$ then do
        $c \leftarrow c' + cost(s, a)$
        $\pi(s) \leftarrow a$
      $\beta \leftarrow min(\beta, c)$
    return (π, c)

Find-Acyclic-Solution-by-MinMax implements a depth-first search by minimizing the maximum sum of the costs of actions along the search. It alternates recursively between calls to Choose-best-action (Algorithm 5.6) and Compute-worst-case-for-action. The former calls the latter on the set of states $\gamma(s, a)$ resulting from the application of actions a that are applicable to the current state s, where Compute-worst-case-for-action returns the policy π' and its corresponding cost c'. Visited states are accumulated in the "ancestors" variable. Choose-best-action then updates the cost of π with the cost of the action ($c = c' + cost(s, a)$), and updates the policy with the selected action in the current state ($\pi = \pi' \cup (s, a)$). In the Choose-best-action procedure, β keeps track of the minimum cost of alternative policies computed at each iteration, which is compared with the maximum cost computed over paths in π by Compute-worst-case-for-action (see the instruction $c' = max(c', c)$). If the current children's maximum cost c' is greater than or equal to the current minimum cost β, then the policy π' gets discarded and control gets back to Choose-best-action which chooses a different action.

Indeed, while we are considering each state $s' \in \gamma(s, a)$, the worst-case cost of a policy that includes an action a is greater than the maximum cost at each s' visited so far. We know that elsewhere in the And/Or graph there exists a policy whose worst-case cost is less than β. If the worst-case cost of a policy that includes a is greater or equal to β, then we can discard a.

Find-Acyclic-Solution-by-MinMax's memory requirement is linear in the length of the longest path from s_0 to a goal state, and its running time is linear in the number of paths from s_0 to a goal state.

Find-Acyclic-Solution-by-MinMax ignores the possibility of multiple paths to the same state. If it comes to a state s again along a different path, it does exactly the same search below s that it did before. One could use memoization techniques to store these values rather than recomputing them, which would produce better running time but would require exponentially more memory. See Exercise 5.9.

5.4 SYMBOLIC MODEL CHECKING TECHNIQUES

The conceptually simple extension led by nondeterminism causes a practical difficulty. Because one action can lead to a set of states rather than a single state, planning algorithms that search for safe (cyclic and acyclic) solutions need to analyze all the states that may result from an action. Planning based on symbolic model checking attempts to overcome the difficulties of planning in nondeterministic domains by working on a symbolic representation of sets of states and actions. The underlying idea is based on the following ingredients:

- Algorithms search the state space by working on sets of states, rather than single states, and on transitions from sets of states through sets of actions, rather than working separately on each of the individual transition.
- Sets of states, as well as sets of transitions, are represented as propositional formulas, and search through the state space is performed by logical transformations over propositional formulas
- Specific data structures, Binary Decision Diagrams (BDDs), are used for the compact representation and effective manipulation of propositional formulas

Example 5.15. In this example, we give a first intuition on how a symbolic representation of sets of states can be advantageous. Consider the planning problem P with the nondeterministic domain Σ described in Example 5.2, the initial state s_0 is the state labeled in Figure 5.1 as on_ship, and goal states $S_g = \{\text{gate1}, \text{gate2}\}$. The states of this simple planning domain can be described by a single state variable indicating the position of the item, for example, a container. The state variable pos(item) can assume values on_ship, at_harbor, parking1, parking2, transit1, transit2, transit3, gate1 and gate2.

Now let's suppose that at each position, the item can be either on the ground or on a vehicle for transportation. We would have a second variable loaded, the value of which is either on_ground or on_vehicle.

Let's also suppose that we have a variable that indicates whether a container is empty, full, or with some items inside. The domain gets to 54 states.

Now, if we want to represent the set of states in which the container is ready to be loaded onto a truck, this set can be compactly represented by the formula pos(item) = gate1 $\lor$ pos(item) = gate2. This is a symbolic, compact representation of a set of states. Now suppose that further 10 state variables are part of the domain representation. There may be many states in which the container is ready to be loaded onto a truck, while their representation is the same as before: pos(item) = gate1 $\lor$ pos(item) = gate2.

BDDs provide a way to implement the symbolic representation just introduced. A BDD is a directed acyclic graph (DAG). The terminal nodes are either "truth" or "falsity" (alternatively indicated with 0 and 1, respectively). The corresponding BDDis in Figure 5.6.   □

In the rest of this section, we describe the algorithms for planning via symbolic model checking both as operation on sets of states and as the corresponding symbolic transformations on formulas.

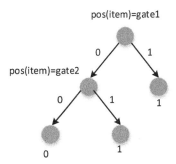

Figure 5.6. BDD for pos(item) = gate1 ∨ pos(item) = gate2.

5.4.1 Symbolic Representation of Sets of States

A state variable representation, where each variable x_i can have a value $v_{ij} \in \text{Range}(x_i)$, can be mapped to an equivalent representation based on propositional variables. We can represent a state by means of assignments to propositional variables rather than assignments to state variables: For each state variable x_i and for each value $v_{ij} \in \text{Range}(x_i)$, we have a binary variable that is true if $x_i = v_{ij}$, and $x_i = v_{ik}$ is false for each $k \neq j$.

In symbolic model checking, a state is represented by means of propositional variables (i.e., state variables that have value either true (T) or false (F)) that hold in that state. We write $P(s)$ a formula of propositional variables whose unique satisfying assignment of truth values corresponds to s. Let $\boldsymbol{x}$ be a vector of distinct propositional variables.

This representation naturally extends to any *set of states* $Q \subseteq S$. We associate a set of states with the disjunction of the formulas representing each of the states.

$$P(Q) = \bigvee_{s \in Q} P(s).$$

The satisfying assignments of $P(Q)$ are the assignments representing the states of Q.

Example 5.16. In Example 5.2, consider the case in which the item (e.g., a car) that needs to be moved to a parking area may get damaged. Moreover, the parking area can be either open or closed, and the area can be either full or have a slot where the item can be stored. We can represent the set of states of this domain with three propositional variables in $\boldsymbol{x}$:

$$x_1 : \text{status(car)} = \text{damaged}$$
$$x_2 : \text{areaavailability} = \text{open}$$
$$x_3 : \text{areacapacity} = \text{full}$$

The set of states S of the domain has eight states. The single state s_1 in which the item is not damaged, the storage area is open, and there is a slot available for storage can be represented by the assignment of truth values to the three proposition variables

$$x_1 \leftarrow F$$
$$x_2 \leftarrow T$$
$$x_3 \leftarrow F$$

or analogously by the truth of the formula

$$P(s_1) = \neg x_1 \wedge x_2 \wedge \neg x_3.$$

The four states in which the car is undamaged is represented by the single variable assignment

$$x_1 \leftarrow \mathsf{F}$$

or analogously by the truth of the formula

$$P(Q) = \neg x_1. \qquad \qquad \square$$

The main effectiveness of the symbolic representation is that the cardinality of the represented set is not directly related to the size of the formula. As a further advantage, the symbolic representation can provide an easy way to ignore irrelevant information. For instance, in the previous example, notice that the formula $\neg x_1$, because it does not say anything about the truth of x_2 and x_3, represents four states, where the item is not damaged in all of them. The whole state space S (eight states) can thus be represented with the propositional formula that is always true, T, while the empty set can be represented by falsity, F. These simple examples give an intuitive idea of one of the main characteristics of a symbolic representation of states: the size of the propositional formula is not directly related to the cardinality of the set of states it represents. If we have one billion propositional variables to represent 2^{10^9} states, with a proposition of length one, for example, x, where x is one of the propositional variables of $\boldsymbol{x}$, we can represent all the states where x is true.

For these reasons, a symbolic representation can have a dramatic improvement over an explicit state representation which enumerates the states of a state transition system.

Another advantage of the symbolic representation is the natural encoding of set-theoretic transformations (e.g., union, intersection, complementation) with propositional connectives over propositional formulas, as follows:

$$P(Q_1 \cup Q_2) = P(Q_1) \vee P(Q_2)$$
$$P(Q_1 \cap Q_2) = P(Q_1) \wedge P(Q_2)$$
$$P(S - Q) \quad = \quad P(S) \wedge \neg P(Q)$$

5.4.2 Symbolic Representation of Actions and Transitions

We can use a vector of propositional variables, say $\boldsymbol{y}$, to name actions. Naming actions with a binary string of $\boldsymbol{y}$ bits will allow us to use BDDs at the implementation level in the next sections. If we have n actions, we can use $\lceil \log n \rceil$ propositional variables in $\boldsymbol{y}$. For instance, in the previous example, we can use variables y_1 and y_2 in $\boldsymbol{y}$ to name actions park, move, and deliver. We can use for instance the following encoding:

$$P(\mathsf{park}) = \neg y_1 \wedge \neg y_2 \quad P(\mathsf{move}) = y_1 \wedge \neg y_2 \quad P(\mathsf{deliver}) = \neg y_1 \wedge y_2.$$

Now we represent symbolically the transition function $\gamma(s)$. We will call the states in $\gamma(s)$ the *next states*. To represent next states, we need a further vector of propositional variables, say, $\boldsymbol{x}'$, of the same dimension of $\boldsymbol{x}$. Each variable $x' \in \boldsymbol{x}'$ is called a *next-state variable*. We need it because we need to represent the relation between the old and the new variables. Similarly to $P(s)$ and $P(Q)$, $P'(s)$ and $P'(Q)$ are the formulas representing state s and the set of states Q using the next state variables in $\boldsymbol{x}'$. A transition is therefore an assignment to variables in $\boldsymbol{x}, \boldsymbol{y}$, and $\boldsymbol{x}'$

Example 5.17. Consider Example 5.16 and Example 5.2. Suppose the item to be moved is a car. The unloading operation may damage the car, and the parking area may be closed and full,[7] We have therefore some level of nondeterminism. Let x_4 and x_5 be the propositional variable for pos(car)=on_ship and pos(car)=at_harbour The transition pos(car)=at_harbour $\in \gamma$(pos(car)=on_ship, unload) can be symbolically represented as[8]

$$x_4 \wedge (\neg y_1 \wedge \neg y_2) \wedge x_5'$$

which means that in the next state the car is at the harbor and may or may not be damaged. □

We define now the transition relation R corresponding to the transition function γ (this will be convenient for the definition of the symbolic representation of transition relations):

$$\forall s \in S, \forall a \in A, \forall s' \in S \, (R(s, a, s') \iff s' \in \gamma(s, a)).$$

In the rest of this section, we adopt the following notation[9]:

- Given a set of states Q, $Q(\boldsymbol{x})$ is the propositional formula representing the set of states Q in the propositional variables $\boldsymbol{x}$ and
- $R(\boldsymbol{x}, \boldsymbol{y}, \boldsymbol{x}')$ is the propositional formula in the propositional variables $\boldsymbol{x}, \boldsymbol{y}$, and $\boldsymbol{x}'$ representing the transition relation.

We also adopt a QBF-like notation, the logic of Quantified Boolean Formulas, a definitional extension of propositional logic in which propositional variables can be universally and existentially quantified. According to this notation, we have, for instance:

- $\exists x Q(\boldsymbol{x})$ stands for $Q(\boldsymbol{x})[x \leftarrow \mathsf{T}] \vee Q(\boldsymbol{x})[x \leftarrow \mathsf{F}]$, where $[x \leftarrow \mathsf{T}]$ stands for the substitution of x with T in the formula;
- $\forall x Q(\boldsymbol{x})$ stands for $Q(\boldsymbol{x})[x \leftarrow \mathsf{T}] \wedge Q(\boldsymbol{x})[x \leftarrow \mathsf{F}]$.

Let us show how operations on sets of states and actions can be represented symbolically. Consider the set of all states s' such that from every state in Q, s' is a possible outcome of every action. The result is the set of states containing any next state s' that for any state s in Q and for any action a in A satisfies the relation $R(s, a, s')$:[10]

$$\{s' \in S \mid \forall s \in Q \text{ and } \forall a \in A. \, R(s, a, s')\}.$$

---

[7] This nondeterminism models the fact that we do not know at planning time whether the parking area will be available.

[8] Here we omit the formalization of the invariant that states what does not change.

[9] Recall that a set of states is represented by a formula in state variables in **x**.

[10] The formula is equivalent to $\bigcup_{s \in A, a \in A} \gamma(s, a)$.

Such set can be represented symbolically with the following formula, which can be represented directly as a BDD:

$$(\exists xy(R(x, y, x') \wedge Q(x)))[x' \leftarrow x].$$

In this formula, the "and" operation symbolically simulates the effect of the application of any applicable action in A to any state in Q. The explicit enumeration of all the possible states and all the possible applications of actions would exponentially blow up, but symbolically we can compute all of them in a single step.

Policies, or functions that given a state return an action to be applied to the state, are relations between states and actions and can therefore be represented symbolically as propositional formulas in the variables x and y. In the following, we write such a formula as $\pi(x, y)$.

We are now ready to describe the planning algorithms based on symbolic model checking. In the subsequent sections, we consider an extension of the definition of planning problem where we allow for a set of initial states rather than a single initial state because this does not complicate the definitions of our planning algorithms.

5.4.3 Planning for Safe Solutions

In Find-Safe-Solution-by-ModelChecking, Algorithm 5.7, univpol is the so-called "universal policy," that is, the set of all state-action pairs (s, a) such that a is applicable in s. Notice that starting from the universal policy may appear unfeasible in practice because the set of all state action pairs can be very large. We should not forget, however, that very large sets of states can be represented symbolically in a compact way. Indeed, the symbolic representation of the universal policy is:

$$\text{univpol} = \exists x' R(x, y, x'),$$

which also represents the applicability relation of actions in states.

Algorithm 5.7 Planning for safe solutions by symbolic model checking.

Find-Safe-Solution-by-ModelChecking(Σ, s_0, S_g)
    univpol $\leftarrow \{(s, a) \mid s \in S$ and $a \in$ Applicable$(s) \}$
    $\pi \leftarrow$ SafePlan(univpol, S_g)
    if $s_0 \in (S_g \cup \text{Dom}(\pi))$ then return π
    else return(failure)

SafePlan(π_0, S_g)
    $\pi \leftarrow \varnothing$
    $\pi' \leftarrow \pi_0$
    while $\pi \neq \pi'$ do
        $\pi \leftarrow \pi'$
        $\pi' \leftarrow \pi' \setminus \{(s, a) \in \pi' \mid \gamma(s, a) \nsubseteq (S_g \cup \text{Dom}(\pi'))\}$ (i)
        $\pi' \leftarrow$ PruneUnconnected(π', S_g)   (ii)
    return RemoveNonProgress(π', S_g)   (iii)

Algorithm 5.8 PruneUnconnected: Removing unconnected states.

PruneUnconnected(π,S_g)

    Oldπ ← fail

    Newπ ← ∅

    while Oldπ ≠ Newπ do

        Oldπ ← Newπ

        Newπ ← π ∩ $preimgpol$(S_g ∪ Dom(Newπ))

    return Newπ

Find-Safe-Solution-by-ModelChecking calls the SafePlan routine that refines the universal policy by iteratively eliminating pairs of states and corresponding actions. This is done in two steps. First, line (i) removes from π' every state-action pair (s, a) for which $\gamma(s, a)$ includes a nongoal state s' that has no applicable action in π'. Next, line (ii) removes from π' every state-action pair (s, a) for which π' contains no path from s to the goal. This second step is performed by the routine PruneUnconnected, Algorithm 5.8. PruneUnconnected repeatedly applies the intersection between the current policy π and the *"preimage"* policy, that is, *preimgpol* applied to the domain of the current policy and the goal states. The preimage policy, given a set of states $Q \subseteq S$, returns the policy that has at least one out-coming state to the given set of states:

$$preimgpol(Q) = \{(s, a) \mid \gamma(s, a) \cap Q \neq \varnothing\}.$$

$preimgpol(Q)$ is represented symbolically as a formula in the current state variables x and the action variables y:

$$preimgpol(Q) = \exists x'(R(x, y, x') \wedge Q(x')).$$

The pruning of outgoing and unconnected states is repeatedly performed by the while loop in SafePlan until a fixed point is reached. Then in line (iii), SafePlan removes states and corresponding actions in the policy that do not lead toward the goal. This is done by calling the RemoveNonProgress routine (see Algorithm 5.9) that repeatedly performs the pruning in two steps. First, the preimage policy preπ that leads to the domain of the policy or to the goal state in computed ("preimage policy" step). Then the states and actions that lead to the same domain of the preimage policy or to the goal are pruned away by the PruneStates routine (let $Q \subseteq S$):

$$PruneStates(\pi, Q) = \{(s, a) \in \pi \mid s \notin Q\}.$$

The routine PruneStates that eliminates the states and actions that lead to the same domain of a policy is computed symbolically as follows:

$$PruneStates(\pi, Q) = \pi(x, y) \wedge \neg Q(x).$$

SafePlan thus returns the policy π that has been obtained from the universal policy by removing outgoing, unconnected and nonprogressing actions. Find-Safe-Solution-by-ModelChecking finally tests whether the set of states in the returned policy union with

---

Algorithm 5.9 RemoveNonProgress: Removing states/actions that do not lead toward the goal.

RemoveNonProgress(π , S_g)
   Oldπ ← fail
   Newπ ← $\varnothing$
   while Old$\pi \neq$ Newπ do
      preπ ← $\pi \cap preimgpol(S_g \cup \text{Dom(New}\pi))$
      Oldπ ← Newπ
      Newπ ← PruneStates(preπ, $S_g \cup \text{Dom(New}\pi))$
   return Newπ

---

the goal states contains all the initial states. If this is the case, π is a safe solution; otherwise no safe solution exists.

Example 5.18. Let us consider the planning problem on the domain described in Example 5.2, initial state s_0 where pos(car)=on_ship, and goal states $S_g = \{$pos(car)=gate2$\}$. The "elimination" phase of the algorithm does not remove any policy from the universal policy. Indeed, the goal state is reachable from any state in the domain, and therefore there are no outgoing actions. As a consequence, function RemoveNonProgress receives in input the universal policy and refines it, taking only those actions that may lead to a progress versus the goal. The sequence π_i of policies built by function RemoveNonProgress is as follows (in the following we indicate with parking1 the state where pos(car)=parking1, etc.):

    Step 0 : $\varnothing$
    Step 1 : π_1(parking1) = deliver; π_1(transit2) = move
    Step 2 : π_2(parking1) = deliver; π_2(transit2) = move; π_2(at_harbor) = park;
          π_2(transit1) = move
    Step 3 : π_3(parking1) = deliver; π_3(transit2) = move; π_3(at_harbor) = park;
          π_3(transit1) = move; π_3(parking2) = back; π_3(transit3) = back;
          π_3(gate1) = back; π_3(on_ship) = unload
    Step 4 : π_3 □

A remark is in order. Algorithm 5.7 can find either safe cyclic or safe acyclic solutions. It can be modified such that it looks for a safe acyclic solution, and only if there is no such solution does it search for a safe cyclic solution (see Exercise 5.11).

5.4.4 Planning for Safe Acyclic Solutions

Find-Acyclic-Solution-by-ModelChecking (Algorithm 5.10) performs a backward breadth-first search from the goal toward the initial states. It returns a safe acyclic solution plan π if it exists, otherwise it returns failure. The policy π is constructed iteratively by the while loop. At each iteration step, the set of states S for which a safe acyclic policy

---

Algorithm 5.10 Planning for safe acyclic solutions by symbolic model checking.

Find-Acyclic-Solution-by-ModelChecking(Σ, S_0, S_g)

$\quad \pi_0 \leftarrow$ failure

$\quad \pi \leftarrow \emptyset$

$\quad$ while ($\pi_0 \neq \pi$ and $S_0 \not\subseteq (S_g \cup \text{Dom}(\pi))$) do

$\quad\quad$ strongpre$\pi \leftarrow$ *strongpreimgpol*($S_g \cup \text{Dom}(\pi)$)

$\quad\quad \pi_0 \leftarrow \pi$

$\quad\quad \pi \leftarrow \pi \cup$ PruneStates(strongpre$\pi, S_g \cup \text{Dom}(\pi)$)

$\quad$ if ($S_0 \subseteq (S_g \cup \text{Dom}(\pi))$)

$\quad\quad$ then return π

$\quad\quad$ else return failure

---

has already been found is given in input to the routine *strongpreimgpol*, which returns a policy that contains the set of pairs (s, a) such that a is applicable in s and such that a leads to states which are all in $Q \subseteq S$:

$$strongpreimgpol(Q) = \{(s, a) \mid a \in \text{Applicable}(s) \text{ and } \gamma(s, a) \subseteq Q\}.$$

The routine *strongpreimgpol*, which returns a policy that contains the set of pairs (s, a) such that a is applicable in s and such that a leads to states which are all in $Q \subseteq S$:

$$strongpreimgpol(Q) = \forall x'(R(x, y, x') \rightarrow Q(x')) \wedge \exists x' R(x, y, x'),$$

which states that any next state must be in Q and the action represented by y must be applicable, $\exists x' R(x, y, x')$. Notice that both *preimgpol*(Q) and *strongpreimgpol*(Q) are computed in one step. Moreover, policies resulting from such computation may represent an extremely large set of pairs of state actions.

The routine PruneStates that eliminates the states and actions that lead to the same domain of a policy,

$$\text{PruneStates}(\pi, Q) = \{(s, a) \in \pi \mid s \notin Q\}$$

can be represented symbolically very simply by the formula

$$\pi(x, y) \wedge \neg Q(x)).$$

PruneStates removes from strongpreπ the pairs (s, a) such that a solution is already known. This step is what allows to find the worst-case optimal solution.

Example 5.19. Let us consider the planning problem on the domain described in Example 5.2, initial set of states $S_0 = \{\text{on\_ship}\}$, and goal states $S_g = \{\text{gate1}, \text{gate2}\}$. The sequence π_i of policies built by algorithm Find-Acyclic-Solution-by-ModelChecking is as follows:

$\pi_0 : \varnothing$

$\pi_1 : \pi_1(\text{transit3}) = \text{move}; \pi_1(\text{transit2}) = \text{move}$

$\pi_2 : \pi_2(\text{transit3}) = \text{move}; \pi_2(\text{transit2}) = \text{move};$
$\quad\quad \pi_2(\text{parking1}) = \text{deliver}; \pi_2(\text{parking2}) = \text{deliver}$

$\pi_3 : \pi_3(\text{transit3}) = \text{move}; \pi_3(\text{transit2}) = \text{move};$
$\quad\quad \pi_3(\text{parking1}) = \text{deliver}; \pi_3(\text{parking2}) = \text{deliver};$
$\quad\quad \pi_3(\text{transit1}) = \text{move}$

$\pi_4 : \pi_4(\text{transit3}) = \text{move}; \pi_4(\text{transit2}) = \text{move};$
$\quad\quad \pi_4(\text{parking1}) = \text{deliver}; \pi_4(\text{parking2}) = \text{deliver};$
$\quad\quad \pi_4(\text{transit1}) = \text{move}; \pi_4(\text{at\_harbor}) = \text{park}$

$\pi_5 : \pi_5(\text{transit3}) = \text{move}; \pi_5(\text{transit2}) = \text{move};$
$\quad\quad \pi_5(\text{parking1}) = \text{deliver}; \pi_5(\text{parking2}) = \text{deliver};$
$\quad\quad \pi_5(\text{transit1}) = \text{move}; \pi_5(\text{at\_harbor}) = \text{park};$
$\quad\quad \pi_5(\text{on\_ship}) = \text{unload}$

$\pi_6 : \pi_5$

Notice that at the fifth iteration, PruneStates removes from π_5 all the state-action pairs that move the container back (action back) from states such that a solution is already known. For instance, $\pi_5(\text{parking2}) = \text{back}, \pi_5(\text{gate1}) = \text{back}$, and so on.   □

5.4.5 BDD-based Representation

In the previous section, we showed how the basic building blocks of the planning algorithm can be represented through operations on propositional formulas. In this section, we show how specific data structures, Binary Decision Diagrams (BDDs), can be used for the compact representation and effective manipulation of propositional formulas.

A BDD is a directed acyclic graph (DAG). The terminal nodes are either *True* or *False* (alternatively indicated with 0 and 1, respectively). Each nonterminal node is associated with a boolean variable and with two BDDs, which are called the left and right branches. Figure 5.7 *(a)* shows a BDD for the formula $(a_1 \leftrightarrow b_1) \wedge (a_2 \leftrightarrow b_2) \wedge (a_3 \leftrightarrow b_3)$.

Given a BDD, the value corresponding to a given truth assignment to the variables is determined by traversing the graph from the root to the leaves, following each branch indicated by the value assigned to the variables. A path from the root to a leaf can visit nodes associated with a subset of all the variables of the BDD. The reached leaf node is labeled with the resulting truth value. If v is a BDD, its size $|v|$ is the number of its nodes.[11] If n is a node, we will use $var(n)$ to denote the variable indexing node n. BDDs are a canonical representation of boolean formulas if

- there is a total order $<$ over the set of variables used to label nodes, such that for any node n and correspondent nonterminal child m, their variables must be ordered, $var(n) < var(m)$, and
- the BDD contains no subgraphs that are isomorphic to the BDD itself.

---

[11] Notice that the size can be exponential in the number of variables. In the worst case, BDDs can be very large. We do not search through the nodes of a BDD, however, but rather represent compactly (possibly very large) sets of states and work on such a representation of sets of states.

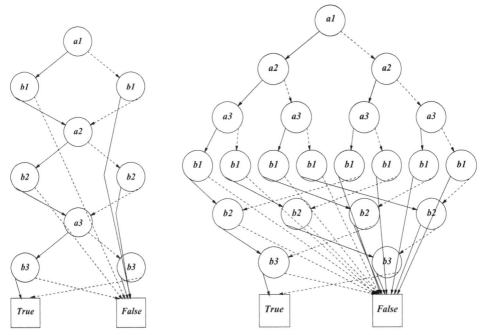

Figure 5.7. Two BDDs for the formula $(a_1 \leftrightarrow b_1) \wedge (a_2 \leftrightarrow b_2) \wedge (a_3 \leftrightarrow b_3)$.

The choice of variable ordering may have a dramatic impact on the dimension of a BDD. For example, Figure 5.7 depicts two BDDs for the same formula $(a_1 \leftrightarrow b_1) \wedge (a_2 \leftrightarrow b_2) \wedge (a_3 \leftrightarrow b_3)$ obtained with different variable orderings.[12]

BDDs can be used to compute the results of applying the usual boolean operators. Given a BDD that represents a formula, it is possible to transform it to obtain the BDD representing the negation of the formula. Given two BDDs representing two formulas, it is possible to combine them to obtain the BDD representing the conjunction or the disjunction of the two formulas. Substitution and quantification on boolean formulas can also be performed as BDD transformations.

5.5 DETERMINIZATION TECHNIQUES

Recent works address the problem of planning in nondeterministic domains by *determinizing the planning domain*. Intuitively the idea is to consider one of the possible many outcomes of a nondeterministic action at a time, using an efficient classical planning technique to find a plan that works in the deterministic case. Then different nondeterministic outcomes of an action are considered and a new plan for that state is computed, and finally the results are joined in a contingent plan that considers all the possible outcomes of actions. Of course, it may be that when a partial plan is extended

---

[12] A state variable representation can lead to a variable ordering in which closely related propositions are grouped together, which is critical to good performance of BDD exploration.

Algorithm 5.11 Guided planning for safe solutions.

Guided-Find-Safe-Solution (Σ,s_0,S_g)
  if $s_0 \in S_g$ then return($\varnothing$)
  if $Applicable(s_0) = \varnothing$ then return(failure)
  $\pi \leftarrow \varnothing$
  loop
    $Q \leftarrow leaves(s_0, \pi) \setminus S_g$
    if $Q = \varnothing$ then do
      $\pi \leftarrow \pi \setminus \{(s, a) \in \pi \mid s \notin \widehat{\gamma}(s_0, \pi)\}$
      return(π)
    select arbitrarily $s \in Q$
    $\pi' \leftarrow$ Find-Solution(Σ, s, S_g)
    if $\pi' \neq$ failure then do
      $\pi \leftarrow \pi \cup \{(s, a) \in \pi' \mid s \notin \mathrm{Dom}(\pi)\}$
    else for every s' and a such that $s \in \gamma(s', a)$ do
      $\pi \leftarrow \pi \setminus \{(s', a)\}$
      make a not applicable in s'

---

to consider new outcomes, no solution is possible, and the algorithm must find an alternative solution with different actions.

5.5.1 Guided Planning for Safe Solutions

Before getting into the details, we show a basic idea underlying determinization techniques. Safe solutions can be found by starting to look for (possibly unsafe) solutions, that is plans that may achieve the goal but may also be trapped in states where no action can be executed or in cycles where there is no possibility of termination. The idea here is that finding possibly unsafe solutions is much easier than finding safe solutions. Compare indeed the algorithm for finding solutions Find-Solution and the one for finding safe solutions Find-Safe-Solution in Section 5.3. While Find-Solution does not distinguish between And branches and Or branches, Find-Safe-Solution needs to check that there are no unsafe loops, and this is done with the has-unsafe-loops routine.

Algorithm 5.11 is based on this idea, that is, finding safe solutions by starting from possibly unsafe solutions that are found by Find-Solution.

Guided-Find-Safe-Solution takes in input a nondeterministic domain Σ with initial state s_0 and goal states S_g. If a safe solution exists, it returns the safe solution π.

The algorithm checks first whether there are no applicable actions in s_0. If this is the case, it returns failure.

In the loop, Q is the set of all nongoal leaf states reached by π from the initial state. If there are no nongoal leaf states, then π is a safe solution. When we have the solution, we get rid of the part of π whose states are not reachable from any of the initial state (we say we "clean" the policy).

If there are instead nongoal leaf states reached by π, then we have to go on with the loop. We select arbitrarily one of the nongoal leaf states, say, s, and find a (possibly unsafe) solution from initial state s with the routine Find-Solution, see Algorithm 5.2.

If Find-Solution does not return failure, then π' is a (possibly unsafe) solution, and therefore we add to the current policy π all the pairs (s, a) of the (possibly unsafe) solution π' that do not have already a state s in π.

If a (possibly unsafe) solution does not exists (the else part of the conditional) this means we are trapped in a loop or a dead end without any possibility of getting out. According to Definition 5.9, then, this is not a safe solution. We therefore get rid from π of all the pairs (s', a) that lead to dead-end state s, and remember this makes action a not applicable in s'.[13] In this way, at the next loop iteration, we will not have the possibility to become stuck in the dead end.

5.5.2 Planning for Safe Solutions by Determinization

The idea underlying the Guided-Find-Safe-Solution algorithm is to use possibly-unsafe solutions to find safe solutions. Find-Solution returns a path to the goal by considering only one of the many possible outcomes of an action. Looking for just one action outcome and finding paths inspires the idea of determinization. If we replace each action a leading from state s to n states $s_1, \ldots, s_n$ with n deterministic actions $a_1, \ldots, a_n$, each one leading to a single state $s_1, \ldots, s_n$, we obtain a deterministic domain, and we can use classical efficient planners to find solutions in the nonderministic domain as sequences of actions in the deterministic domain. We will then only have to transform a sequential plan into a corresponding policy to extend it to consider multiple action outcomes. According to this idea, we define a determinization of a nondeterministic domain.[14]

Algorithm 5.12 is an algorithm that exploits domain determinization and replaces Find-Solution in Guided-Find-Safe-Solution with search in a deterministic domain. Here we use the simple forward search algorithm Forward-search presented in Chapter 2, but we could use a more sophisticated classical planner, as long as it is complete (i.e., it finds a solution if it exists). This algorithm is similar to the first algorithm for planning by determinization proposed in literature.

Find-Safe-Solution-by-Determinization is like Guided-Find-Safe-Solution but the following five steps:

1. **The determinization step:** We add a determinization step. The function mk-deterministic returns a determinization of a nondeterministic planning domain.

2. **The classical planner step:** We apply Forward-search on the deterministic domain Σ_d rather than using Find-Solution on the nondeterministic domain Σ. In general, we could apply any (efficient) classical planner.

---

[13] This operation can be done in different ways and depends on which kind of representation we use for the domain. This operation may not be efficient depending on the implementation of Σ.

[14] The operation of transforming each nondeterministic action into a set of deterministic actions is complicated by the fact that we have to take into account that in different states the same action can lead to a set of different states. Therefore, if the set of states has exponential size with respect to the number of state variables, then this operation would generate exponentially many actions.

Algorithm 5.12 Planning for safe solutions by determinization.

Find-Safe-Solution-by-Determinization (Σ, s_0, S_g)
  if $s_0 \in S_g$ then return$(\varnothing)$
  if $Applicable(s_0) = \varnothing$ then return(failure)
  $\pi \leftarrow \varnothing$
  $\Sigma_d \leftarrow$ mk-deterministic(Σ)
  loop

    $Q \leftarrow leaves(s_0, \pi) \setminus S_g$
    if $Q = \varnothing$ then do
      $\pi \leftarrow \pi \setminus \{(s, a) \in \pi \mid s \notin \widehat{\gamma}(s_0, \pi)\}$
      return(π)
    select $s \in Q$
    $p' \leftarrow$ Forward-search (Σ_d, s, S_g)
    if $p' \neq fail$ then do
      $\pi' \leftarrow$ Plan2policy(p', s)
      $\pi \leftarrow \pi \cup \{(s, a) \in \pi' \mid s \notin \text{Dom}(\pi)\}$
    else for every s' and a such that $s \in \gamma(s', a)$ do
      $\pi \leftarrow \pi \setminus \{(s', a)\}$
      make the actions in the determinization of a
      not applicable in s'

Algorithm 5.13 Transformation of a sequential plan into a corresponding policy.

Plan2policy$(p = \langle a_1, \ldots, a_n \rangle, s)$
  $\pi \leftarrow \varnothing$
  loop for i from 1 to n do
    $\pi \leftarrow \pi \cup (s, \text{det2nondet}(a_i))$
    $s \leftarrow \gamma_d(s, a_i)$
  return π

---

3. **The plan2policy transformation step:** We transform the sequential plan p' found by Forward-search into a policy (see routine Plan2policy, Algorithm 5.13), where $\gamma_d(s, a)$ is the γ of Σ_d obtained by the determinization of Σ. The routine det2nondet returns the original nondeterministic action corresponding to its determinization a_i.

4. **The action elimination step:** We modify the deterministic domain Σ_d rather than the nondeterministic domain Σ.

5.6 ONLINE APPROACHES

In Chapter 1 (see Section 1.3.3), we introduced the idea of interleaving planning and acting. Interleaving is required because planning models are just approximations, and

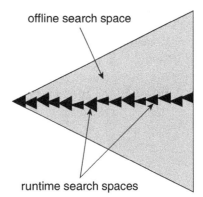

offline search space

Figure 5.8. Offline versus run-time search spaces: intuitions.

runtime search spaces

sensing is required to adapt to a changing environment. Another motivation is the ability to deal with realistic large domains. Dealing with large state spaces is even more difficult in the case of nondeterministic domains. The idea is that while offline planners have to find a large policy exploring a huge state space, if we interleave acting and planning, we significantly reduce the search space. We need indeed to find a partial policy, for example, the next few "good" actions, perform all or some of them, and repeat these two interleaved planning and acting steps from the state that has been actually reached. This is the great advantage of interleaving acting and planning: we know exactly which of the many possible states has been actually reached, and the uncertainty as well as the search space is significantly reduced.

Intuitively, the difference in search space between planning offline and interleaving planning and acting is shown in Figure 5.8. In the case of purely offline planning, uncertainty in the actual next state (and therefore the number of states to search for) increases exponentially from the initial state (the left vertex of the triangle) to the set of possible final states (the right part of the triangle): the search space is depicted as the large triangle. In planning and acting, we plan just for a few next steps, then we act and know exactly in which state the application of actions results. We repeat the interleaving of planning and acting until we reach a goal state. The search space is reduced to the sequence of small triangles depicted in Figure 5.8.

Notice that there is a difference between the search space depicted in Figure 5.8 and the ones depicted in Figures 1.3 and 1.4 because here we have uncertainty in the outcome of each action, and the basis of each small triangle represents all the possioble outcomes of an action rather than the different outcomes of the search for each different action in a deterministic domain.

The selection of "good" actions (i.e., actions that tend to lead to the goal) can be done with estimations of distances from and reachability conditions to the goal, like in heuristic search, and by learning step by step after each application better estimates of the distance.

A critical issue is the possibility of getting trapped in dead ends. In *safely explorable domains* (see also Chapter 6), that is, domains where execution cannot get trapped in situations where there is no longer a path to the goal, it is possible to devise methods that are complete, that guarantee to reach the goal if there exists a solution, and that

---

Algorithm 5.14 Interleaving planning and execution by lookahead.

Lookahead-Partial-Plan(Σ, s_0, S_g)

    $s \leftarrow s_0$

    while $s \notin S_g$ and Applicable(s) $\neq \varnothing$ do

        $\pi \leftarrow$ Lookahead(s, θ)   (*i*)

        if $\pi = \varnothing$ then return failure

        else do

            perform partial plan π (*ii*)

            $s \leftarrow$ observe current state

---

guarantee the termination of the planning/acting loop if no solution exists. However, not all domains are safely explorable, and not all actions are reversible. A navigation robot can be trapped in a hole where no navigation operation is possible anymore; a bank transaction is critical and cannot be easily undone. Even worse, the actor may not easily recognize that it is trapped in a dead end, for example, a navigation robot can enter an area where it is possible to navigate but impossible to get out of that area. Despite these problems, planning and acting methods remain a viable solution to problems that cannot be solved purely offline.

In this section, we present some basic techniques that can be used to interleave planning and execution.

5.6.1 Lookahead

The idea underlying lookahead methods is to generate a partial plan to interleave planning and acting. The Lookahead-Partial-Plan procedure, Algorithm 5.14, interleaves partial planning in line (*i*) with acting in line (*ii*). At each loop, Lookahead searches for a partial plan rooted at s. It returns a partial plan as a policy π that is partially defined, at least in s. A context-dependent vector of parameters θ restricts in some way the search for a solution. Working with a progressively generated policy, defined when and where it is needed, allows us to deal with large domain models that cannot be represented a priori and with complexity and partial domain knowledge. This approach combines naturally with a *generative definition* of Σ. A full specification of a domain is not necessary to a partial exploration, as discussed in more detail in Chapter 6.

There are different ways in which the generated plan can be partial and different ways for interleaving planning and acting. Indeed, the procedure Lookahead-Partial-Plan is parametric along two dimensions:

The *first parametric dimension* is in the call to the lookahead planning step, that is, Lookahead(s, θ). The parameter θ determines the way in which the generated plan π is partial. For instance, it can be partial because *the lookahead is bounded*, that is, the forward search is performed for a bounded number of steps without reaching the goal. In the simplest case, Lookahead(s, θ) can look ahead just one step, choose an action a (in this case $\pi = a$), and at the next step perform action a. This is the extreme case of interleaving in which the actor is as reactive as possible. In general, however,

Lookahead(s, θ) can look ahead for $n \geq 1$ steps.[15] The greater n is, the more informed is the choice on the partial plan to execute; the drawback is that the cost of the lookahead increases. In the extreme case in which the lookahead reaches the goal from the initial state s_0, if performing the found plan succeeds, then there is no actual interleaving.

Rather than specifying the bound as a number of steps to search, θ can specify other kinds of bounds for the plan generation phase, for example, some real-time interruption mechanism corresponding to the planning deadline and the need to switch to acting.

However, there are other ways in which the generated plan is partial. For instance, Lookahead can consider some of the outcomes of a nondeterministic action, that is, only some of its possible outcomes of a nondeterministic action, and in this way the lookahead procedure can reach the goal. Even if the goal is reached, the plan is still partial because it is not guaranteed that the execution will actually go through the considered outcomes of the actions because they are not complete. In the extreme case, Lookahead can consider just one of the possible outcomes of an action: look for a possibly unsafe solution to the goal or, in other words, pretend that the domain model is deterministic. In this case, the lookahead procedure is not bounded, but the plan is still partial. The policy π in this case can be reduced to a sequential plan.

It is of course possible to combine the two types of partiality – bounded lookahead and partial number of outcomes – in any arbitrary way.

The *second parametric dimension* is in the application of the partial plan that has been generated, that is, in the execution of the partial plan π. Independently of the lookahead, we can still execute π in a partial way. Suppose, for instance, that we have generated a branching plan of depth n; we can decide to perform $m \leq n$ steps.

Two approaches to the design of a Lookahead procedure are presented next:

- lookahead by determinization and
- lookahead with a bounded number of steps.

The former approach does not bound the search to a limited number of steps but searches for a (possibly unsafe) solution to the goal. At execution time, it checks whether the reached state corresponds to the one predicted by the (possibly unsafe) solution. The latter approach bounds the search to a limited number of steps (in the simplest case, just one step), selects an action according to some heuristics, memorizes the results, and performs a value update to learn a better heuristics in possible future searches.

5.6.2 Lookahead by Determinization

Lookahead can be realized by determinizing the domain. FS-Replan (Algorithm 5.15) illustrates a *determinization* relaxation introduced in Section 5.5.2. The idea is to generate a path π_d from the current state to a goal for for all outcomes of the determinized domain Σ_d using a deterministic planner – in this case Forward-search, but it could be any efficient deterministic planner, as in the case of the offline determinization (Algorithm 5.12). The actor acts using π_d until reaching a state s that is not in the domain of π_d.

---

[15] In nondeterministic domains, lookahead for n steps means to generate a branching tree.

Algorithm 5.15 Online determinization planning and acting algorithm.

FS-Replan (Σ, s, S_g)
   $\pi_d \leftarrow \varnothing$
   while $s \notin S_g$ and Applicable$(s) \neq \varnothing$ do
      if π_d undefined for s then do
         $\pi_d \leftarrow$ Plan2policy(Forward-search $(\Sigma_d, s, S_g), s)$
         if $\pi_d = $ failure then return failure
      perform action $\pi_d(s)$
      $s \leftarrow$ observe resulting state

At that point, a new deterministic plan starting at s is generated. If the planning domain is safely explorable and because Forward-search is a complete deterministic planner, then FS-Replan will lead to a goal. If the domain has dead ends, then FS-Replan is not guaranteed to reach the goal.

Notice the relation between FS-Replan and Lookahead-Partial-Plan. In the case FS-Replan the parameter θ of Lookahead-Partial-Plan is realized by the condition checking whether π_d is undefined for the current state s. FS-Replan does not look ahead for only some steps, but until the goal is reached according to a simplified (i.e., determinized) model of the domain.

5.6.3 Lookahead with a Bounded Number of Steps

Algorithm MinMax Learning Real Time A* (Min-Max LRTA*, Algorithm 5.16) searches the state space forward from the initial state s_0 until in line (i), the *termination checking* step, the search reaches the goal or a state that has no applicable actions. In line (ii), the *action selection* step, the algorithm looks for the best worst-case action. This is the action a that produces the smallest maximum value for $h(s')$, where $h(s')$ is the estimated distance from s' to the goal. In line (iii), the *value update* step, the algorithm improves the estimate $h(s)$ using the h-values of s's children. This step is useful if we perform multiple runs of the planning and acting routine and we learn from each run. The *acting step* applies the action, and the *state change step* updates the current state with the worst-case next state.

Algorithm 5.16 MinMax Learning Real Time A*.

Min-Max LRTA* (Σ, s_0, S_g)
   $s \leftarrow s_0$
   while $s \notin S_g$ and Applicable$(s) \neq \varnothing$ do (i)
      $a \leftarrow \text{argmin}_{a \in \text{Applicable}(s)} \max_{s' \in \gamma(s,a)} h(s')$ (ii)
      $h(s) \leftarrow \max\{h(s), 1 + \max_{s' \in \gamma(s,a)} h(s')\}$ (iii)
      perform action a
      $s \leftarrow$ the current state

Min-Max LRTA* is guaranteed to terminate and to generate a solution only in safely explorable domains. Notice that the termination condition Applicable$(s) \neq \varnothing$ can check only whether we are in a direct dead end. To check whether we might end up in a indirect dead end, we would need to explore all of the states that are reachable s.

Min-Max LRTA* can be easily extended to deal with domains that include costs of actions. We need only replace the formula in the value update step with this: $\max\{h(s), c(s,a) + \max_{s' \in \gamma(s,a)} h(s')\}$.

To choose the action a, the algorithm does a lookahead of one step. It is possible to extend it to look ahead n steps by generating a partial search tree by searching forward from the current state s. Then we can update the values in the local search space by assigning at each state the minmax (i.e., smallest worst-case) distance under the assumptions that such values do not overestimate the correct minimax distance to the goal.

5.7 REFINEMENT METHODS WITH NONDETERMINISTIC MODELS

In Chapter 3, we introduced a formalism for operational models based on *refinement methods*. A method specifies how to accomplish a task (an abstract activity of some kind) by refining it into other activities that are less abstract. These activities may include other tasks that will need further refinement. We devised the SeRPE and IRT algorithms to do refinement planning and choose among different possible refinements in a deterministic model. We extended the formalism to include goals, which can be further refined with different refinement methods.

In this section, we use nondeterministic models in refinement methods. This allows us to model commands and tasks with nondeterministic outcomes, and to search for safe cyclic or acyclic solutions. We consider tasks that are specified with programs. Tasks can be iteratively refined in subtasks and goals through programs that contain the usual control constructs, like constructs for sequences of steps, conditionals, loops, and so on. Planning algorithms that use deterministic models, such as SeRPE and IRT, can simply simulate the execution through such control structures and replace commands with the corresponding γ, which leads from one state to a single state. Planning algorithms that use nondeterministic models must instead take into account that programs might be executed in different states. A simple simulation starting from one state does not allow us to know exactly in which state the program will be executed. This makes the planning algorithms much more complicated.

In the following subsections, we first recall the formalism for tasks and adapt it to nondeterministic models (Section 5.7.1). We then define *context-dependent plans* (Section 5.7.2). They are more expressive than policies because they can take into account the context in which a step of the plan is executed, and the context can depend of the steps that have been executed so far. In the subsequent two subsections, we provide a planning algorithm to generate context dependent plans that achieve tasks. We do this in two steps. First, we generate automatically search *automata* from given tasks (Section 5.7.3). Search automata are used to guide the search for context-dependent plans.

Second, we define the planning algorithm that exploits the generated planning automata (Section 5.7.4).

5.7.1 Tasks in Refinement Methods

We start from a slightly revised version of the formalism defined in Chapter 3, Section 3.1.2. A refinement method is a *task* with a *body*.[16] The *body* is a program that refines the task into a sequence of subtasks, commands, and goals. The program contains usual control structures, like sequences, conditionals, and loops, over tasks, goals, and commands.

In Section 3.1.2 we defined the following kinds of tasks:

- A *reachability goal* g, that is, a partial state variable assignment $x_i = v_i, \ldots, x_k = v_k$, for each $x_i, \ldots, x_k \in X$, and each $v_i \in \mathrm{Range}(x_i), \ldots, v_k \in \mathrm{Range}(x_k)$. To distinguish between safe cyclic and safe acyclic solutions (see Definition 5.10 and Definition 5.11, respectively), we now have two kinds of reachability goals:
  - *achieve-cyclic(g)*
  - *achieve-acyclic(g)*
- A command *cmd*. We model each command in a nondeterministic domain $\Sigma = (A, S, \gamma)$, where γ is nondeterministic: $\gamma : S \times A \rightarrow 2^S$.
- A *sequence of tasks*: $t_1; t_2$, where t_1 and t_2 are tasks.
- A *conditional task*: *if p then t_1 else t_2*, where t_1 and t_2 are tasks and p is partial variable assignment.
- An *iterative task*: *while p do t*, where t is a task and p is partial variable assignment.
- A *test*: *test p*, where p is partial variable assignment.

We also will define another kind of task that is specifically useful when we plan in nondeterministic domains:

- A *failure-handling task*:
  if t_1 fails then t_2, where t_1 and t_2 are tasks.

The failure-handling task *if t_1 fails then t_2* is the basic construct for handling failure. It expresses a preference to achieve t_1 if possible, and to try to achieve t_2 only if t_1 is impossible.

5.7.2 Context-Dependent Plans

Policies as defined so far are *stationary or memoryless policies*, that is, they always perform the same action in the same state, independently of the actions that have been previously performed and the states that have been previously visited. Policies are not enough to represent plans that can satisfy tasks with programs in the body a refinement methods. Plans should take into account previously-executed steps. Consider for instance a sequence of tasks $t_1; t_2$, where both t_1 and t_2 are reachability goals, for example, $t_1 = achieve\ acyclic\ g_1$ and $t_2 = achieve\ acyclic\ g_2$. In this case, we might need to

---

[16] Here we do not have a separate precondition field but use conditional tasks.

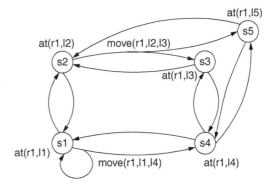

Figure 5.9. An example of nondeterministic planning domain.

perform different actions (and execute the different corresponding commands) in the same state depending on whether the actor is trying to achieve the first goal in the first task g_1 or the second task g_2. As a simple example, consider the case in which a robot has to move to a given location and has to come back afterward. Similar examples can be given for the constructs for conditional and iterative tasks, as well for failure-handling and recovery constructs.

One could address this issue by extending the representation of a state to include all relevant data, for example, the history of states visited so far. This might work in theory, but its implementation is not practical. We take a different approach by introducing the notion of *context*. A context specifies which subtask the actor is in the process of satisfying. For instance, in the previous example, where we have the task $t_1; t_2$, then the actor is in a context while trying to satisfy task t_1, and in a different context while trying to satisfy task t_2. In this way, actions to be performed can depend not only on the current state of the domain but also on the "internal state" of the actor, on its "intention" to satisfy one subtask or another. To represent this kind of plans, we introduce the notion of *context-dependent plan*.

Definition 5.20. (context-dependent plans) A context-dependent plan π for a domain $\Sigma = (S, A, \gamma)$ is a structure $(C, c_0, act, ctxt)$, where:

- C is a set of contexts, representing the internal state of the actor
- c_0 is the initial context,
- $act : S \times C \rightharpoonup A$ is the action function, and
- $cxtx : S \times C \times S \rightharpoonup C$ is the context function. ☐

If we are in a state s and in a context c, then $act(s, c)$ returns the action to be performed by the plan, while $ctxt(s, c, s')$ associates to each reached state s' a new context. The pair $(s, c) \in S \times C$ defines the state of the context-dependent plan.

Example 5.21. In Figure 5.9, we have a nondeterministic planning domain for a navigation robot. Each state s_i corresponds to a location of the robot in a building. Some of the actions for moving the robot are nondeterministic. Let us suppose that the robot is initally in state s_1, and the task is *achieve-acyclic*(s_2); *achieve-cyclic*(s_4).

state	context	action	next state	next context
s1	c1	move(r1,l1,l2)	s2	c2
s1	c2	move(r1,l1,l4)	s1	c1
s1	c2	move(r1,l1,l4)	s4	c1
s2	c2	move(r1,l2,l1)	s1	c2
s4	c1	move(r1,l4,l1)	s1	c1

Figure 5.10. A context-dependent plan.

There is no policy on the set of states $S = \{s_1, s_2, s_3, s_4\}$ that can achieve such task. The context-dependent plan in Figure 5.10 achieves instead the task (we write the context-dependent plan in a tabular form to make it easier to read).   □

An important remark is in order. One may think that it is enough to define policies on the domain of pairs state contexts $S \times C$ rather than on the set of states S, and reuse all the algorithms and approach defined so far. Notice however, that we need to know which are the possible contexts in C, and this can be done in practice only with a generative approach that, given a task, constructs the contexts corresponding to the subtasks. This will be explained in Section 5.7.3.

We need to define now when a context-dependent plan achieves a task. In the following, we provide just an intuitive idea.

- When t is *achieve-cyclic*(g) or *achieve-acyclic*(g), then π satisfies t if and only if π is equivalent to a safe cyclic solution or a safe acyclic solution for g, respectively.
- When t is a command *cmd*, then π achieves t in state (s, c) if and only if there exists an action a corresponding to *cmd* that is applicable in state (s, c). Otherwise, it fails.
- When t is a sequence t_1; t_2, then π achieves t if and only if π achieves first t_1 and, if t_1 is achieved , then π achieves t_2. If π achieves t_1 and then it does not achieve t_2, then π fails. If π does not achieve t_1, then π fails.
- When t is *if p then t_1 else t_2*, then π needs to satisfy t_1 if p holds in (s, c), and it needs to satisfy t_2 if p does not hold in (s, c).
- When t is *while p do t_1*, then π must satisfy cyclically t_1 while p holds. Moreover, π should guarantee the termination of the loop.
- When t is *test p*, then π must lead to a state (s, c) where p holds.
- When t is *if t_1 fails then t_2*, then π must satisfy t_1. In the case it fails (i.e., there is no possibility to satisfy t_1), then is must satisfy t_2.

5.7.3 Search Automata

In this subsection, we define a mapping from tasks to a class of automata, called *Search Automata*. In the subsequent subsection (see Section 5.7.4), we show how search automata can be used to guide the search for context-dependent plans.

The states of each search automaton correspond to the contexts of the plan under construction, according to Definition 5.20. Given a task, we generate the contexts that we need in the context-dependent plan. It is a generative approach, which allows us determine the set of contexts C. The transitions from a state (context) to other states (contexts) of each search automaton define constraints on the states that have to be searched for by the planning algorithm.

Definition 5.22. (Search Automata) Let S be the set of states of the planning domain. A search automaton is a tuple (C, c_0, T, RB) where:

- C is the set of states of the search automaton.[17]
- $c_0 \in C$ is the initial state of the search automaton.
- $T(c) = (t_1, \ldots, t_m)$ is the list of transition for state $c \in C$. Each transition t_i is either
  - *normal*, in which case $t_i \in 2^S \times (C \times \{always, some\})^*$
  - *immediate*, in which case $t_i \in 2^S \times (C \cup \{succ, fail\})$.
- $RB = \{rb_1, \ldots, rb_n\}$, with $rb_i \subseteq C$ is the set of red blocks states where the execution cannot stay forever. $\qquad \square$

A list of transitions $T(c)$ is associated to each state c. Each transition determines the behavior that should be satisfied if we move from c to $T(c)$. The order of the list represents the preference among these transitions. It is important to have such order among transitions because it will allow us to distinguish between "main" tasks that we need to achieve from recovery tasks we need to achieve only if the main task cannot be achieved.

The transitions of a search automaton are either *normal* or *immediate*. The former transitions correspond to performing an action in the plan. The latter ones describe updates in the search state, which do not correspond to performing an action.[18]

The *normal transitions* are defined by a condition on the states of the planning domain and by a list of target search states. Each target search state is marked either by always or some. Let p be a partial state assignment. State s satisfies a normal transition $(p, ((c'_1, k'_1), \ldots, (c'_n, k'_n)))$, with $k'_i \in \{always, some\}$, if it satisfies condition p, and if there is some action a from s such that:

- all the next states reachable from s when performing action a are compatible with some of the target search states, and
- for each target search state marked some, there is a compatible next state.

When a target search state is marked with some, it means that there should be always at least one next state that satisfies a condition. It is used in the case of safe cyclic solutions, in which we have to guarantee that from each state we should reach a given goal.

The *immediate transitions* are defined by both a condition and by a target search state. A state satisfies an immediate transition (p, c') if it satisfies condition p and if it is compatible with the target state c'. Special target search states *succ* and *fail* are used to represent success and failure: all states are compatible with success, while no state is compatible with failure.

---

[17] We intentionally call the set of states of the search automaton C, like the set of contexts of the context-dependent plans in Definition 5.20. Indeed the states of the search automaton correspond to the contexts of the plan that is generated by the algorithm described in Section 5.7.4.

[18] Immediate transitions resemble ϵ-transitions of classical automata theory. An ϵ-transition allows an automaton to change its state spontaneously, that is without consuming an input symbol [286].

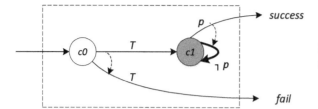

Figure 5.11. Search automaton for safe acyclic solutions.

The *red blocks* of a search automaton represent sets of search states where the execution cannot stay forever. Typically, a red block consists of the set of search states in which the execution is trying to achieve a given condition, as in the case of a reachability goal. If an execution persists inside such a set of search states, then the condition is never reached, which is not acceptable for a reachability goal. In the search automaton, a red block is used to represent the fact that any valid execution should eventually leave these search states.

We now describe the search automata that are automatically constructed from tasks. Rather than providing the formal definition of the search automata, we represent them using a graphical notation. We start with the search automaton for a reachability goal p, that is, a safe solution as defined in Section 5.2.3. We have to distinguish the case of cyclic from acyclic solutions (see Definitions 5.10 and 5.11, respectively).

Let us start with acyclic solutions (see Figure 5.11). The search automaton has two search states: c_0 (the initial state) and c_1. There are two transitions leaving state c_1. The first one, guarded by condition p, is a success transition that corresponds to the cases where p holds in the current domain state. The second transition, guarded by condition $\neg p$, represents the case in which p does not hold in the current state, and therefore, to achieve goal p in a safe acyclic way, we have to ensure that the goal can be achieved from all the next states. We recall that this is the condition for the plannig algorithm that will be devised in the next section (Section 5.7.4). We remark that the second transition is a normal transition because it requires performing an action in the plan; the first transition, instead, is immediate. In the diagrams, we distinguish the two kinds of transitions by using thin arrows for the immediate ones and thick arrows for the normal ones. A domain state is compatible with state c_1 only if it satisfies in a safe acyclic way goal p, that is, if condition p holds in the current state (first transition from c_1) or if the goal will be reachable in all the next states (second transition from c_1).

According to the semantics of safe acyclic solutions, it is not possible for the search to stay in state c_1 forever, as this corresponds to the case in which condition p is never reached. That is, set $\{c_1\}$ is a red block of the search automaton. In the diagrams, states that are in a red block are marked in grey. State c_0 takes into account that it is not always possible to ensure that condition p will be eventually reached and that if this is not the case, then p cannot be satisfied in a safe acyclic way, and therefore the search fails. The precedence order among the two transitions from state c_0, represented by the small circular dotted arrow between them, guarantees that the transition leading to a failure is followed only if it is not possible to satisfy the constraints of state c_1.

We provide now the search automaton for safe cyclic solutions (see Figure 5.12). The difference with respect to the search automaton for safe acyclic solutions is in the

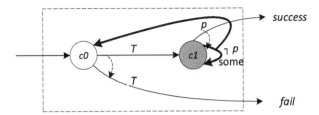

Figure 5.12. Search automaton for safe cyclic solutions.

transition from c_1 guarded by condition $\neg p$. In this case we do not require that the goal holds from all the next states, but only from some of them. Therefore, the transition has two possible targets, namely states c_1 (corresponding to the next states were we expect to achieve the safe cyclic solution for p) and c_0 (for the other next states). The semantics of safe cyclic solutions requires that there should be always at least one next state that satisfies the definition of safe cyclic solution for goal p; that is, target c_1 of the transition is marked by some in the search automaton. This "nonemptiness" requirement is represented in the diagram with the mark some on the arrow leading back to c_1. The preferred transition from state c_0 is the one that leads to c_1. This ensures that the algorithm will try to find a safe cyclic solution whenever possible.

Figure 5.13 shows the simple search automaton for the primitive action $a \in A$ corresponding to a command. The transition from the state c_1 guarantees that a domain state is acceptable only if the next state is achieved by performing action a, that is, only if the next state is reachable by performing action a.

The search automaton for the sequence $t_1; t_2$ is shown in Figure 5.14. The initial state of the compound automaton coincides with the initial state of automaton A_{t_1} for t_1, and the transitions that leave A_{t_1} with success are redirected to the initial state of A_{t_2}, the automaton for t_2. The search automaton for the conditional task *if p then t_1 else t_2* is in Figure 5.15. The context c_0 immediately moves the acting to the initial context of one of the search automata for the tasks t_1 or t_2 according to the current domain state, that is whether the property p holds in the current domain state or not.

The search automaton for the while loop *while p do t_1* is in Figure 5.16. The context c_0 has two immediate transitions guarded by the conditions p and $\neg p$. The former leads to the initial context of the automaton for t_1, that is, the body of the cycle, and the latter leads to the success of the compound automaton. The successful transitions of the automaton for t_1 return back to context c_0, but the failure transition for t_1 falsifies the compound automaton. The context c_0 is marked as a red block. It guarantees that the loop is finite.

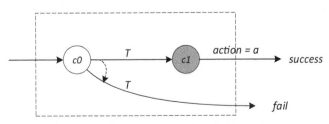

Figure 5.13. Search automaton for primitive actions.

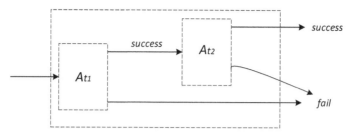

Figure 5.14. Search automaton for the sequence $t_1; t_2$.

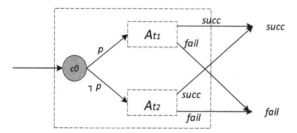

Figure 5.15. Search automaton for conditional task *if p then t_1 else t_2*.

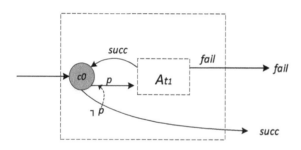

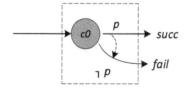

Figure 5.16. Search automaton for loop task *while p do t_1*.

Figure 5.17. Search automaton for test point *test p*.

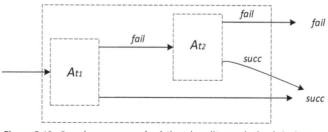

Figure 5.18. Search automaton for failure-handling task *if t_1 fails then t_2*.

Figure 5.17 shows the simple search automaton for *test p*. All transitions are immediate, because action performing is not required. The automaton only checks that the current domain state satisfies formula p.

Figure 5.18 shows the search automaton for the failure-handling construct *if t_1 fails then t_2*. The search automaton is defined similarly to that for sequences t_1; t_2. The difference is that in this case, the transitions that leave A_{t_1} (the search automaton for t_1) with failure are redirected to the initial state of A_{t_2}.

5.7.4 Planning Based on Search Automata

As stated in the previous section, the search automata that we have generated in the previous section are used to guide the search of the planning algorithm that we present in this section. The algorithm is guaranteed to find solution plans if a solution exists. It terminates with failure otherwise. The algorithm works on sets of states. For this reason, it is specially suited for symbolic model checking techniques (see Section 5.4).

Algorithm 5.17 is the main procedure for generating plan π. It takes in input a non-deterministic planning domain Σ, a set of initial states S_0, and a task t as defined in Section 5.7.1. It works in three main steps. In the first step, build_automaton constructs the search automaton as defined in Section 5.7.3. The states in the resulting *automaton* are the contexts of the generated context-dependent plan π that is being built (see Definition 5.20), and the transitions represent the possible evolutions of the contexts. In the second step, compute_associated_states explores the planning domain and associates a set of states of the planning domain to each state in the search automaton. Intuitively, these are the states for which a plan exists from the given context. In the third step, synthesize-plan constructs a plan by exploiting the information on the states associated to the context.

Once the search automaton is built by the function build_automaton, the planning algorithm proceeds by associating to each context in the search automaton a set of states in the planning domain. The association is built by compute_associated_states, see Algorithm 5.18. The algorithm starts with an optimistic association, which assigns all the states in the planning domain (S is the set in $\Sigma = (S, A, \gamma)$) to each context (line (*i*)). The algorithm computes the so-called *Green-Block* of contexts (see line (*ii*)), which is the set of contexts that are not contained in any red block (see Section 5.7.3 and Definition 5.22). We need indeed to distinguish contexts in the green block from those in red blocks because the search should eventually leave a context in a red block, whereas this is not required for contexts in the green block.

Algorithm 5.17 Planning based on search automata.

Plan-with-search-automata(Σ, S_0, t)
   automaton ← build_automaton(Σ, S_0, t)
   AssociatedStates = compute_associated_states$(\Sigma, S_0, t, automaton)$
   π = synthesize-plan$(automaton, AssociatedStates)$
   return π

Algorithm 5.18 Associating states to contexts.

---

compute_associated_states($\Sigma, S_0, t, automaton$)
    foreach $c \in automaton.C$ do $assoc(c) \leftarrow S$ (i)
    Green-Block $\leftarrow \{c \in C$ such that $\forall rb_i \in RB \ c \notin rb_i\}$ (ii)
    Blocks $\leftarrow \{Green\text{-}Block\} \cup RB$
    while $\exists b \in Blocks$ such that a fixed point is not reached do (iii)
        if $b \in RB$ then for each $c \in b$ do $assoc(c) \leftarrow \varnothing$ (iv)
        while $\exists c \in b$ such that c needs update do   (v)
           $assoc(c) \leftarrow$ update-ctxt($automaton, assoc, c$)   (vi)
    return $assoc$

The association is then iteratively refined. At any iteration of the loop (lines (iii)–(vi)), a block of context is chosen, and the corresponding associations are updated. Those states are removed from the association, from which the algorithm discovers that the tasks in the context are not satisfiable. The algorithm terminates when a fixed point is reached, that is, whenever no further refinement of the association is possible: in this case, the while condition at line (iii) evaluates to false for each $b \in Blocks$ and the guard of the while loop fails.

The chosen block of contexts may be either one of the red blocks or the green block. In case the green block is chosen, the refinement step must guarantee that all the states associated to the contexts are "safe," that is, that they never lead to contexts where the goal can no longer be achieved. This refinement (lines (v)–(vi)) is obtained by choosing a context in the green block and by "refreshing" the corresponding set of states (function update-ctxt). Once a fixed point is reached and all the refresh steps on the contexts in b do not change the association (i.e., no context in b needs updates), the loop at lines (v)–(vi) is left, and another block is chosen.

In the case of red blocks, the refinement needs to guarantee not only that the states in the association are "safe" but also that the goal is eventually resolved, that is, that the contexts in the red block are eventually left. To this purpose, the sets of states associated to the red block contexts are initially emptied (line (iv)). Then, iteratively, one of the red-block contexts is chosen, and its association is updated (lines (v))–(vi)). In this way, a least fixed point is computed for the states associated to the red block.

The core step of compute_associated_states is function update-ctxt. It takes in input the search automaton (C, c_0, T, RB), the current association of states $assoc$, that is, a function $assoc : C \rightarrow 2^S$ and a context $c \in C$, and returns the new set of states in S to be associated to context c. It is defined as follows:

    update-ctxt($automaton, assoc, c$) =
    $\{s \in S \mid \exists trans \in T(c)$ such that $s \in$ trans-assoc($automaton, trans, assoc$)$\}$.

According to this definition, a state s is compatible with a search state c if it satisfies the conditions of some transition t from that search state. If $trans = (p, c')$ is an immediate transition, then:

    trans-assoc($automaton, trans, assoc$) = $\{s \in S \mid s \models p$ and $s \in assoc(c')\}$, where we assume that $assoc(fail) = \varnothing$ and $assoc(succ) = S$. That is, in the case of an immediate transition, we require that s satisfies property p and that it is compatible with the new search state c' according to the current association $assoc$.

If $trans = (p, ((c_1', k_1'), \ldots, (c_n', k_n')))$ is a normal transition, then:

$$\text{trans-assoc}(automaton, trans, assoc) =$$
$$\{s \in S \mid s \models p \text{ and } \exists a \in \text{Applicable}(s) \text{ such that}$$
$$(s, a) \in \text{gen-preimage}((assoc(c_1'), k_1'), \ldots, (assoc(c_n'), k_n'))\}$$

where:

$$\text{gen-preimage}((S_1, k_1), \ldots, (S_n, k_n)) =$$
$$\{(s, a) \mid \exists S_1' \subseteq S_1 \ldots S_k' \subseteq S_k \text{ such that}$$
$$\gamma(s, a) = S_1' \cup \ldots \cup S_k' \text{ and}$$
$$S_i' \cap S_j' = \varnothing \text{ if } i \neq j \text{ and } S_i' \neq \varnothing \text{ if } k_i = \text{some}\}$$

Also in the case of normal transitions, trans-assoc requires that s satisfies property p. Moreover, it requires that there is some action a such that the next states $\gamma(s, a)$ satisfy the following conditions:

- all the next states are compatible with some of the target search states, according to association $assoc$; and
- some next state is compatible with each target search state marked as some.

These two conditions are enforced by requiring that the state-action pair (s, a) appears in the generalized preimage of the sets of states $assoc(c_i')$ associated by $assoc$ to the target search states c_i'.

It is now possible to explain in detail more the iterative refinement at lines (iii)–(vi) in Algorithm 5.18. Recall that in the iterative refinement loop, the following conditions are enforced:

- **(C1)** a domain state s is associated to a search state c only if s can satisfy the condition described by some transition of c and
- **(C2)** actions from a given state s cannot be performed if they stay forever inside a red block.

In each step of the iterative refinement, either a search state in the green block is selected and the corresponding set of domain states is refined according to **(C1)**; or a red block is selected and all the sets of domain states associated to its search states are refined according to **(C2)**. The refinement algorithm terminates when no further refinement step is possible, that is, when a fixed point is reached.

Function update-ctxt($automaton, assoc, c$) is used in the refinement steps corresponding to **(C1)** as well as in the refinement steps corresponding to **(C2)**. In the former case, the refinement step simply updates $assoc(c)$ to the value of update-ctxt($automaton, assoc, c$). In the latter case, the refinement should guarantee that any valid execution eventually leaves the search states in the selected red block rb_i. To this purpose, the empty set of domain states is initially associated to the search states in the red block; then, iteratively, one of the search states $c \in rb_i$ is chosen, and its association $assoc(c)$ is updated to update-ctxt($automaton, assoc, c$). These updates terminate

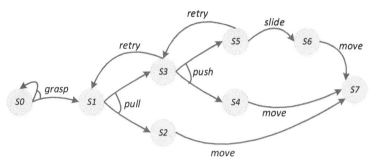

Figure 5.19. Nondeterministic model for an open-door method.

when a fixed point is reached, that is, when $assoc(c) =$ update-ctxt($automaton, assoc, c$) for each $c \in rb_i$. In this way, a least fixed point is computed, which guarantees that a domain state is associated to a search state in the red block only if there is a plan from that domain state that leaves the red block in a finite number of actions.

Finally, extract_plan extracts a plan by using the information about the associated domain states to each search state. Indeed, once a stable association $assoc$ from search states to sets of domain states is built for a search automaton, a plan can be easily obtained. The contexts for the plan correspond to the states of the search automaton. The information necessary to define functions act and $ctxt$ is implicitly computed during the execution of the refinement steps. Indeed, function trans-assoc defines the possible actions $a = act(s, c)$ to be performed in the state-context pair (s, c), namely the actions that satisfy the constraints of one of the normal transitions of the search automaton. Moreover, function gen-preimage defines the next acting context $ctxt(s, c, s')$ for any possible next state $s' \in \gamma(s, a)$.

5.8 ACTING WITH INPUT/OUTPUT AUTOMATA

In this section we introduce a different kind of nondeterministic model to represent refinements at the acting level. It is based on the notion of input/output automata and allows us to model refinements with a distributed approach.

Example 5.23. Consider Example 3.4 of opening a door. For simplicity, here we consider the case in which the door is not locked. The robot does not know whether the door can be opened by pulling, pushing, or sliding the door. Moreover, we assume the robot has no reliable way to detect in advance how the door should be opened. The open-door action is refined in a single refinement method, the model of which is partly shown in Figure 5.19. For the sake of simplicity, the acting states are simply labeled instead of giving a full definition of their state variables as in Example 3.4. In states s_2, s_4, and s_6 the door has been opened by pushing, pulling, and sliding it, respectively. When in s_1, if the robot tries to pull the door but the door is still closed, we then go to state s_3. When in s_3, if the robot tries to push the door but the door is still closed, we then go to state s_5. We assume that if we are in state s_6, the door can be opened by sliding it. In this simple

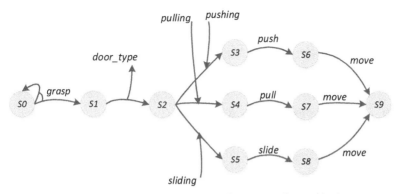

Figure 5.20. Input/output automaton for an open-door method.

example, we assume that after a failing attempt to open the door the robot can retry, possibly with different parameters for the commands, such as increased forces. □

5.8.1 Input/Output Automata

In Example 5.23, we suppose we have a robot that is not able to recognize (e.g., by artificial vision capabilities) the way to open the door. The robot therefore tries to open the door by pulling, then by pushing, and finally by sliding the door. Suppose now that, rather than equipping the robot with such capability, doors are able to interact with the robot, for example, by answering to its requests and informing about the way in which they can be opened.[19] In some way, we "distribute the intelligence" in the environment. The task for the robot becomes much simpler, and it can be described in the next example.

Example 5.24. In Figure 5.20, the robot gets the door's type, for example, by sending a request to the door, which replies with information about the way the door can be opened. Notice that differently from the model in Figure 5.19 for Example 5.23, now we have three different kinds of transitions in the nondeterministic model: commands (grasp, pull, push, slide, and move), inputs that are received by the robot (pulling, pushing, and sliding), and outputs that are sent by the robot (door_type). □

As introduced informally in Example 5.24, the idea is to specify bodies of methods as *input/output automata*, the main feature of which is to model components that interact with each other through inputs and outputs. This is the main representational shift with respect to the usual acting/sensing representation. Input/output automata allow for modeling distributed systems where each automaton is a component that interacts with other components through inputs and outputs. They make it possible to simplify the design process by abstracting away the details of their internal representation.

Formally, input/output automata are very similar to state transition systems described in Chapter 2 and planning domains described in this chapter, with the

---

[19] Automated doors are widely used, but there can be situations in which using a RFID stick is preferable to changing the door.

following differences. Input/output automata can evolve to new states by receiving *inputs* from other automata and sending *outputs* to other automata. Moreover, they can evolve with *internal transitions* without sending outputs and receiving inputs. Internal transitions represent *commands* that are sent to the execution platform,[20] as they have been introduced in the definition of RAE methods in Chapter 3.

Definition 5.25. (Input/Output Automaton) An input/output automaton is $A = (S, S^0, I, O, C, \gamma)$, where

- S is a finite set of states;
- $S^0 \subseteq S$ is the set of possible initial states in which the automaton can start;
- I is the set of inputs, O is the set of outputs, and C is a set of commands, with I, O, and C disjoint sets; and
- $\gamma : S \times (I \cup O \cup C) \to 2^S$ is the nondeterministic[21] state transition function. $\qquad \square$

The distinction between inputs and outputs is a main characteristic of input/output automata. The intended meaning is that outputs are under the full control of the automaton, that is, the automaton can decide when and which output to send. In contrast inputs are not under its control. If and when they are received, which input is received from other automata cannot be determined by the automaton receiving inputs. An automaton can wait for the reception of an input, but whether it will receive it, and when it will receive it is not under its control.

The automaton can determine when to perform an internal transition, that is, to execute a command. However, notice that such transition can end up in different states. This allows us to model the execution of commands that are sent to the execution platform without knowing a priori the result of execution.

In simple cases like the one in Figure 5.20, the input/output automaton can be reduced to a simple nondeterministic state transition system, simply by replacing the sequences of outputs and inputs with a nondeterministic action, for example, get-doorkind that leads to three possible states. In this case, we can apply any of the techniques described in the previous sections, either off line or on line (e.g., determinization, symbolic model checking, lookahead), to generate a policy or a context-dependent plan π that acts with deliberation.

The different possible evolutions of an input/output automaton can be represented by its set of possible *runs*.

Definition 5.26. (Run of input/output automaton) A *run* of an input/output automaton $A = (S, S^0, I, O, C, \gamma)$ is a sequence $s_0, a_0, s_1, a_1, \ldots$ such that $s_0 \in S^0$, $a_i \in I \cup O \cup C$, and $s_{i+1} \in \gamma(s_i, a_i)$. $\qquad \square$

A run may be either finite or infinite.

---

[20] In most automata formalizations, the symbol τ is used to denote internal transitions, which are called τ-transitions. In our representation, internal transitions are triggered by commands.

[21] Commands can be modeled with nondeterministic actions (see e.g., the sense(door) command in Figure 5.21). One way to "move" the nondeterminism outside of the automaton is to send an output to another automaton and wait for different kinds of inputs. However, this does not eliminate the need to reason about nondeterminism because the automaton does not know a priori which input it will receive.

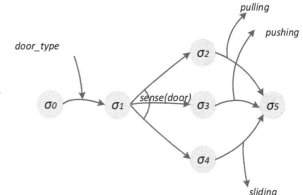

Figure 5.21. Input/output (I/O) automaton to control the robot I/O automaton.

5.8.2 Control Automata

An input/output automaton can behave in different ways depending on the inputs it receives. For instance, the automaton in Figure 5.20 opens the door either by pushing, pulling, or sliding the door, on the basis of the input it receives. Some other system can get the information on how the door can be opened, for example, a different module of the robot with sensing capabilities, or a software that can access a centralized database with information about the doors in the building, or, in a truly distributed environment, a door equipped with the ability to interact with the robot. Such information must be sent as an input to the input/output automaton of the robot.

The idea therefore is to have *a controller* or *control automaton*, that is, an automaton that interacts with input/output automata by reading their outputs and sending them inputs in order to control them to reach some desired states.[22] A control automaton A_c for an input/output automaton A is an input/output automaton whose inputs are the outputs of A and whose outputs are the inputs of A. Indeed, A_c controls A by interacting with A, i.e., by receiving in inputs the outputs of A and sending outputs that are inputs of A.

Definition 5.27. (Control Automaton) Let $A = (S, S^0, I, O, C, \gamma)$ be an input/output automaton. A control automaton for A is an input/output automaton $A_c = (S_c, S_c^0, O, I, C_c, \gamma_c)$. □

Notice that in the definition the inputs I and the outputs O are exchanged in the two automata A and A_c.

Example 5.28. Figure 5.21 shows a control automaton for the I/O automaton in Figure 5.20. Notice that the inputs and outputs of the automaton in Figure 5.21 are the outputs and inputs of the automaton in Figure 5.20, respectively. The control automaton receives a request about the door type (input door_type), determines the door type with the command sense(door), and sends the proper input to the controlled automaton.

---

[22] We cannot control an input/output automaton with a policy because a policy cannot interact with the automaton.

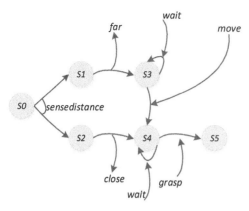

Figure 5.22. Input/output automaton for approaching a door.

The information acquisition about the door type can be done in different ways. The nondeterministic command sense(door) can activate a module of an "intelligent" door that replies to requests by the method of the robot, or sense(door) can be a request to a centralized database that may have a priori the information about the door, or sense(door) might activate a module of the robot that has some perception capabilities.   □

5.8.3 Automated Synthesis of Control Automata

We can specify the control automata by hand by means of a proper programming language. Controllers can be designed and implemented manually offline once for all. It is interesting, however, to generate control automata automatically, either offline (at design time) or at run-time. Indeed, such automated synthesis, when feasible, can provide important advantages. In realistic cases, the manual specification of controllers can be difficult, time-consuming, and error prone. Moreover, in most highly dynamic domains, it is difficult if not impossible to predict all possible cases and implement a fixed controller that can deal with all of them. Synthesis of controllers at run-time can provide a way to act with deliberation taking into account the current situation and context.

In the rest of this section, we formalize the problem of generating a control automaton that interacts with an input/output automaton A and satisfies some desired goal, representing the objective the controller has to reach. We will see that this problem can be solved by planning in nondeterministic domains.

The synthesis problem has two inputs: the automaton A to be controlled and a goal to be achieved. Indeed the control automaton, independently of whether it is defined manually or synthesized automatically, is always thought with a goal in mind. For instance, the automaton in Example 5.28 has been defined with the requirement in mind to open the door in the right way. In the automaton in Figure 5.20, it means to end up in state s_9. Notice that such automaton just represents the nominal case. If it receives a wrong input, for example, to pull a door that should be pushed, then the move command will fail. Consider the following example.

Example 5.29. In Figure 5.22, a method of the robot checks whether it is close enough to the door (command sensedistance) and sends outputs accordingly. If it is far, it can receive the input either to wait or to move (state s3). Let us suppose the goal is to make the automaton reach state s5. It is clear that a control automaton that receives the input far from the automaton in Figure 5.22 and sends output wait does not satisfies the goal, while the one that sends the sequence of outputs move and then grasp does.

Notice that we may have a control automaton that never makes the controlled automaton reach state s5, or that do it only in one of the two cases in which the robot is close or far, or that do it in both cases. All of this resembles the idea of unsafe and safe (cyclic and acyclic) solutions.   □

The synthesis problem is therefore the problem of generating a control automaton A_c that interacts with an input/output automaton A to satisfy some goal g. In this section, we restrict to reachability goals.[23] We define now the automaton describing the behaviors of A when controlled by a control automaton A_c, that is, the controlled system $A_c \triangleright A$.

Definition 5.30. (Controlled System) Let $A = (S, S^0, I, O, C, \gamma)$ be an input/output automaton. Let $A_c = (S_c, S_c^0, , O, I, C_c, \gamma_c)$ be a control automaton for A. Let $s, s' \in S$, $s_c, s_c' \in S_c, c \in C$, and $c_c \in C_c$. The controlled system $A_c \triangleright A$, describing the behavior of A when controlled by A_c, is defined as: $A_c \triangleright A = (S_c \times S, S_c^0 \times S^0, I, O, C, \gamma_\triangleright)$, where:

- $\langle s_c', s \rangle \in \gamma_\triangleright(\langle s_c, s \rangle, c_c)$ if $s_c' \in \gamma_c(s_c, c_c)$,
- $\langle s_c, s' \rangle \in \gamma_\triangleright(\langle s_c, s \rangle, c)$ if $s' \in \gamma(s, c)$,
- for any $i \in I$ from A_c to A,
  $\langle s_c', s' \rangle \in \gamma_\triangleright(\langle s_c, s \rangle, i)$ if $s_c' \in \gamma_c(s_c, i)$ and $s' \in \gamma(s, i)$, and
- for any $o \in O$ from A to A_c,
  $\langle s_c', s' \rangle \in \gamma_\triangleright(\langle s_c, s \rangle, o)$ if $s_c' \in \gamma_c(s_c, o)$ and $s' \in \gamma(s, o)$.   □

The set of states of the controlled system are obtained by the Cartesian product of the states of A and those of A_c. In Definition 5.30, the first two items specify that the states of the controlled system evolve according to the internal evolutions due to the execution of both commands of A_c (first item) and of commands of A (second item). The third and fourth items regard the evolutions that depend on inputs and outputs. In this case, the state of the controlled system $\langle s_c, s \rangle$ evolves by taking into account the evolutions of both A and A_c.

A remark is in order. We need to rule out controllers that can get trapped in deadlocks. In other words, we need to rule out the case in which an automaton sends outputs that the other automaton is not able to receive. If an automaton sends an output, then the other automaton must be able to consume it, either immediately or after executing internal commands that lead to a state where the input is consumed. In other words, an automaton A in a state s must be able to receive as one of its inputs $i \in I$ the output $o' \in O'$ of another automaton A', or for all the possible executions of commands $c \in C$ of automaton A, there exists a successor of s where o' can be received as an input i.

Given this notion, we define intuitively the notion of a **deadlock-free controller** for a controlled input/output automaton. It is a control automaton such that all of its

---

[23] Along the lines described in Chapter 2, goal g is a partial variable assignment to state variables $x_i = v_i, \dots, x_k = v_k$, for each $x_i, \dots, x_k \in X$, with each of them having values in their range: $v_i \in \text{Range}(x_i), \dots, v_k \in \text{Range}(x_k)$.

outputs can be received by the controlled automaton, and vice versa, all the outputs of the controlled automaton can be received by the controller.[24]

Informally, the synthesis problem is the problem of generating a control automaton A_c such that the controlled system $A_c \rhd A$ satisfies a goal g, that is, we have to synthesize A_c that interacts with A by making A reach some desired state. In other words, a control automaton A_c is a solution for a goal g if its every run of the controlled system $A_c \rhd A$ ends up in a state where g holds.

Definition 5.31. (Satisfiability). Let g be a partial state variable assignment $x_i = v_i, \ldots, x_k = v_k$, for each $x_i, \ldots, x_k \in X$, and each $v_i \in \text{Range}(x_i), \ldots, v_k \in \text{Range}(x_k)$. Let A be an input/output automaton. A satisfies g, denoted with $A \models g$, if

- there exists no infinite run[25] of A and
- every final state s of A satisfies g. □

We can now define when a control automaton is a solution for an input/output automaton with respect to a goal, that is, when it controls the automaton satisfying our desired requirement.

Definition 5.32. (Solution Control Automaton). A control automaton A_c is a solution for the goal g and an input/output automaton A, if the controlled system $A_c \rhd A \models g$ and A_c is a deadlock-free controller for A. □

5.8.4 Synthesis of Control Automata by Planning

In the following, we discuss informally how the problem of the automated synthesis of a controller can be solved by planning with nondeterministic domain models.

Consider the automaton in Figure 5.22. We want to generate a controller with the goal that the controlled automaton reaches state s5. In order to map the synthesis problem to a planning problem we must consider the fact that A models a domain that may be only partially observable by A_c. That is, at execution time, A_c generally has no way to find out what A's current state is.[26] For instance, if A is the input/output automaton in Figure 5.22, a controller A_c that interacts with A has no access to the values of A's internal variables and can only deduce their values from the messages it receives. A_c cannot know whether the command sensedistance in Figure 5.22 has been executed or not, that is, whether the automaton is still in state s_0 (the state before executing the command) or in one of the two states after the command has been executed, that is, s_1 or s_2. This uncertainty disappears only when one of the two outputs (far or close) is sent by the controlled automaton A and received by the controller A_c.

---

[24] See Exercise 5.12.
[25] See Definition 5.26 for the definition of run of an automaton
[26] There might be applications in which the controller A_c might have access to the state of the controlled automaton A. However, in general, the advantage of a representation based on input/output automata is to hide or abstract away the details of the internal operations.

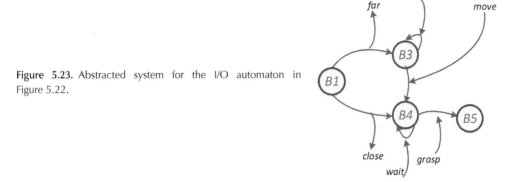

Figure 5.23. Abstracted system for the I/O automaton in Figure 5.22.

We take into account this uncertainty by considering evolutions of the controlled system $A_c \triangleright A$ in terms of sets of states rather than states, each of them containing all the states where the controlled system could be. We have therefore to deal with sets of states rather than single states. This is a way to deal with partial observability while still making use of algorithms that work in fully observable domains (see the discussion and historical remark section of this chapter, Section 5.9).

The initial set of states is updated whenever A performs an observable input or output transition. If $B \subseteq S$ is the current set of states and an action $io \in I \cup O$ is observed, then the new set $B' = evolve(B, io)$ is defined as follows: $s \in evolve(B, io)$ if and only if, there is some state s' reachable from B by performing a sequence of commands, such that $s \in \gamma(s', io)$. That is, in defining $evolve(B, io)$, we first consider every evolution of states in B by the commands in C, and then, from every state reachable in this way, their evolution caused by io.

Under the assumption that the execution of commands terminate, that is, that commands cannot be trapped in loops, we can define an *Abstracted System* whose states are sets of states of the automaton and whose evolutions are over sets of states.

Definition 5.33. (Abstracted System) Let $A = (S, S^0, I, O, C, \gamma)$ be an automaton. The corresponding abstracted system is $\Sigma_B = (S_B, S_B^0, I, O, \gamma_B)$, where:

- S_B are the sets of states of A reachable from the set of possible initial states S^0,
- $S_B^0 = \{S^0\}$, and
- if $evolve(B, a) = B' \neq \varnothing$ for some $a \in I \cup O$, then $B' \in \gamma_B(B, a)$.   □

An abstracted system is an input/output automaton with a single initial state and no commands. To define a synthesis problem in terms of a planning problem in nondeterministic domains, we need to transform an automaton $A = (S, S^0, I, O, C, \gamma)$ into a nondeterministic domain D. To do this transformation, we first transform the automaton into its corresponding abstracted system. This is necessary to handle partial observability and apply the plan generation algorithms we have defined in this chapter for fully observable nondeterministic domain models.

Example 5.34. In Figure 5.23, we show the abstracted system for the controlled automaton in Figure 5.22. States $s_0, s_1,$ and s_2 generate the set of states $B_1 = \{s_0, s_1, s_2\}$ because

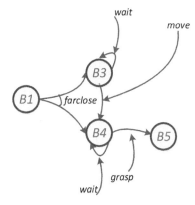

Figure 5.24. Nondeterministic planning domain for the I/O automaton in Figure 5.22.

there is no way for the controller to distinguish them until it receives either input far or input close by the controlled automaton. We have $B_3 = \{s_3\}$, $B_4 = \{s_4\}$, and $B_5 = \{s_5\}$.   □

Given the generated abstracted system, output actions of the controlled automaton are those that cause nondeterminism. We therefore move output actions from transitions into the states of the domain and replace output transitions with nondeterministic internal transitions.

Example 5.35. In Figure 5.24, we show the nondeterministic planning domain for the automaton in Figure 5.23. We have moved the output far in state B_3 and the output close in state B_4, and transformed the two (deterministic) output transitions into one nondeterministic internal transition. Now we have a nondeterministic planning domain as defined in Section 5.2: $\Sigma = (S, A, \gamma)$, with states $S = \{B_1, B_3, B_4, B_5\}$, and actions $A = \{\text{farclose, wait, move, grasp}\}$, where farclose is nondeterministic. The policy

$$\pi(B_1) = \text{farclose}$$
$$\pi(B_3) = \text{move}$$
$$\pi(B_4) = \text{grasp}$$

is a safe acyclic solution for the planning problem $P = (\Sigma, B_1, B_5)$, where B_1 is the initial state and B_5 is the goal state. From π we can easily construct the control automaton A_c that controls A in Figure 5.22 and satisfies the reachability goal s_5.   □

The synthesis problem can thus be solved by generating a nondeterministic domain and by planning for a safe, possibly acyclic, solution (see Definitions 5.8 and 5.11), that is, by generating a policy π that is guaranteed to reach the goal independently of the outcomes of nondeterministic actions that are due to commands and output actions of automata A.

This means that we can automate the synthesis by using algorithms that we have illustrated in this chapter for planning with nondeterministic domain models and that can find safe (acyclic) solutions, for example, planning with And/Or search (see Section 5.3) planning by symbolic model checking (see Section 5.4), and planning by determinization (see Section 5.5).

5.8.5 Acting by Interacting with Multiple Automata

In the previous section, we did not exploit the real advantage of the distributed and asynchronous nature of input/output automata. Indeed, Example 5.24 may include two input/output automata, one for the method of the robot and one for the door. The two automata interact by sending/receiving inputs/outputs, and this interaction must be controlled at the acting level. The main characteristic of a model based on input/output automata is that a complex model can be obtained as the "composition" of much simpler components, thus providing the following advantages:

- the ability to simplify the design process, starting from simple components whose composition defines a model of a complex system;
- the ability to model distributed domains naturally, that is, domains where we have different components with their own behaviors;
- the ability to model naturally dynamic environments when different components join or leave the environment;
- the composition of different components can be localized, that is, each component can get composed only with the components that it needs to interact with, thus simplifying significantly the design task; and
- for each component, we can specify how other components need to interact with the component itself, abstracting away the details of their internal operations.

We continue with our example of opening a door, but we reduce the tasks that can be performed by the robot while we enrich the autonomy capabilities of the doors. Consider indeed two active devices that interact with the environment, a navigation robot able to move but without any manipulation capabilities, and an active door, which is able to open and close itself on request. This scenario is presented in Example 5.36

Example 5.36. In Figure 5.25, the door and the robot are modeled as two input/output automata. The door receives a request to open (the input I-open). It then activates its engines to open (the command cmd-open). The command may either succeed or fail, and the door sends outputs accordingly (O-succes-open or O-fail-open). If the command succeeds, then the door waits for two possible inputs, one indicating that the door can be closed (because, e.g., the robot passed successfully), that is, the input I-done, or that there is a problem and the door should stop with failure, that is, I-cancel. The robot has a similar input/output automaton: it waits for an input to move (I-move), then it moves (cmd-move). If the operation succeeds, then it waits for an input stating either that everything is fine (I-done) and it can stop (cmd-stop) or that a failure from the environment occurred (I-cancel).   □

Notice that with this model, the robot and any other actor in the environment do not even need to know whether the door is a sliding door or a door that can be opened by pulling/pushing, because this is hidden in the command cmd-open of the door input/output automaton. This abstraction mechanism is one of the advantages of a model based on multiple input/output automata.

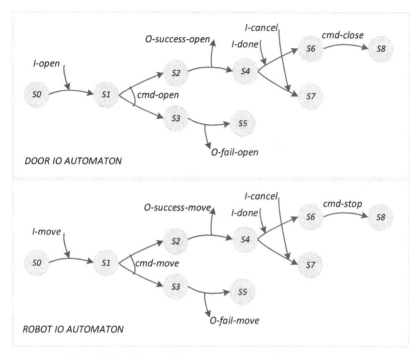

Figure 5.25. Robot and door interacting input/output automata.

Synthesis of Controllers of Multiple Automata

Given a model with two or more input/output automata, we generalize the idea presented for controlling a single automaton, that is, synthesize a controller, represented by a plan π (see Definition 5.20) that interacts with the different input/output automata and satisfies some goal. Consider the following example.

Example 5.37. Figure 5.26 shows an input/output automaton representing a controller that makes the robot and the door interact in a proper way. It requests that the door open; if it succeeds, it then requests the robot to move and, only if the moving operation has also succeeded, it asks the door and the robot to finish their job, that is, the robot should stop and the door should close.   □

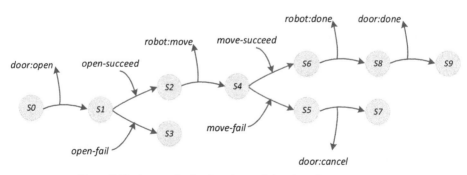

Figure 5.26. A controller for the robot and door input/output automata.

In the rest of this section, we formalize the problem of generating a controller represented by a plan π that interacts with a set of input/output automata $A_1, \ldots, A_n$ and satisfies some desired goal. The problem has two inputs:

- A finite set of automata $A_1, \ldots, A_n$. This set can be dynamic and determined at runtime, for example, as a representation of the current methods for the actions to be performed.
- A requirement g that is defined as a partial state variable assignment in the acting state space of each automaton A_i: $x_i = v_i, \ldots, x_k = v_k$, for each $x_i, \ldots, x_k \in X$, and each $v_i \in$ Range$(x_i), \ldots, v_k \in$ Range(x_k). The requirement can be either given at design time, or it can be generated at run-time (see Section 7.2)

Informally, we want to generate a controller A_c that interacts with $A_1, \ldots, A_n$ in such a way to make the automata $A_1, \ldots, A_n$ to reach some states where the requirement g is satisfied. We introduce first the product of the automata $A_1, \ldots, A_n$:

$$A_{\|} = A_1 \| \ldots \| A_n$$

Such product is a representation of all the possible evolutions of automata $A_1, \ldots, A_n$, without any control by A_c.

We formally define the product of two automata A_1 and A_2, which models the fact that the two automata may evolve independently. In the following definition, we assume that the two automata do not send messages to each other, that is, the inputs of A_1 cannot be outputs of A_2 and vice versa. This is a reasonable assumption in our case, where we suppose that each available automaton $A_1, \ldots, A_n$ interacts only with the controller A_c that we have to generate. The assumption can, however, be dropped by modifying in a suitable way the definition of product.

Definition 5.38. (Product of Input/Output Automata) Let $A_1 = (S_1, S_1^0, I_1, O_1, C_1, \gamma_1)$ and $A_2 = (S_2, S_2^0, I_2, O_2, C_2, \gamma_2)$ be two automata with $(I_1 \cup O_1 \cup C_1) \cap (I_1 \cup O_1 \cup C_1) = \varnothing$. The product of A_1 and A_2 is $A_1 \| A_2 = (S, S_0, I_1 \cup I_2, O_1 \cup O_2, C_1 \cup C_2, \gamma)$, where:

- $S = S_1 \times S_2$,
- $S_0 = S_1^0 \times S_2^0$,
- $\langle s_1', s_2 \rangle \in \gamma(\langle s_1, s_2 \rangle, a)$ if $\gamma_1(s_1, a) = s_1'$, and
- $\langle s_1, s_2' \rangle \in \gamma(\langle s_1, s_2 \rangle, a)$ if $\gamma_2(s_2, a) = s_2'$. 						□

The automaton $A_{\|} = A_1 \| \ldots \| A_n$ represents all the possible ways in which automata $A_1, \ldots, A_n$ can evolve without any control. We can therefore define the automaton describing the behaviors of $A_{\|}$ when controlled by a controller A_c that interacts with $A_1, \ldots, A_n$, that is, the controlled system $A_c \triangleright A_{\|}$, simply by recasting the definition of controlled system (see Definition 5.30) by replacing the single automaton A with $A_{\|}$. We can therefore apply all the considerations, definitions, and algorithms that we have discussed for the case of a single automaton.

5.9 DISCUSSION AND HISTORICAL REMARKS

5.9.1 Comparison among Different Approaches

The main advantage of determinization techniques with respect to other approaches is the possibility of exploiting fast algorithms for finding solutions that are not guaranteed to achieve the goal but just may lead to the goal, that is, unsafe solutions. Indeed, finding an unsafe solution in Σ can be done by finding a sequential plan in Σ_d. Then the sequence of actions can be easily transformed into a policy. Fast classical planners can then be used to find efficiently a solution which is unsafe for the nondeterministic model. Determinization techniques tend to work effectively when nondeterminism is limited and localized, whereas their performances can decrease when nondeterminism is high (many possible different outcomes of several actions) and in the case nondeterminism cannot be easily reconducted to exceptions of the nominal case. For these reasons, several techniques have been proposed to improve the performances when there is a high level of nondeterminism, from conjunctive abstraction (a technique to compress states in a similar way to symbolic model checking), to techniques that exploit state relevance (see Section 5.9.2). With such improvements, determinization techniques have been proven to be competitive with, and in certain cases to outperform, both techniques based on And/Or search and techniques based on symbolic model checking. Finally, determinization techniques have focused until now on safe cyclic planning, and extensions to safe acyclic planning should be investigated.

The basic idea underlying symbolic model checking techniques is to work on sets. Routines for symbolic model checking work on sets of states and on transitions from sets of states through sets of actions, rather than on single states and single state transitions. Also policies are computed and managed as sets of state action pairs.

The symbolic model checking approach is indeed advantageous when we have a high degree of nondeterminism, that is, the set of initial states is large and several actions have many possibly different outcomes. Indeed, in these cases, dealing with a large set of initial states or a large set of outcomes of an action may have even a simpler and more compact symbolic representation than a small set. The symbolic approach may instead be outperformed by other techniques, for example, determinization techniques, when the degree of uncertainty is lower, for example, in the initial state or in the action outcomes.

Online approaches are effective techniques to deal with large state spaces and highly dynamic environments. In non–safely explorable domains, both Min-Max LRTA* and FS-Replan can be trapped in (indirect) dead ends and are not guaranteed to terminate. The work in Bertoli et al. [63] describes how to generate a partial plan and interleave planning and acting in partially observable nondeterministic domains by symbolic model checking: even though it is in general impossible to guarantee that a goal state will be reached, such approach guarantees that the planning/acting loop always terminates: either the goal is reached or it is recognized that a state has been reached from which there is no chance to find a safe acyclic solution, and the loop terminates.

5.9.2 Historical Remarks

Nondeterministic domain models are considered unavoidable in several areas, such as computer-aided verification, model checking, theory of controllers, and games theory. All work in these areas uses nondeterministic models.

For planning in nondeterministic domains, some important characteristics of the domain include:

- The degree of observability: null observability (which is called *conformant planning*) and either full or partial observability (the case of contingent or conditional planning), and
- The kind of goals: reachability goals and (temporally) extended goals.

Various techniques have been devised to deal with these domain characteristics. The idea of planning in nondeterministic domains was first addressed in the 1980s. The first attempts to deal with nondeterminism were based on some pioneering work on conditional planning by Warren [596], Peot and Smith [474], Pryor and Collins [496]. This work was based on extensions to plan-space planning by extending classical planning operators (see Section 2.7.1) to have operators to have several mutually exclusive sets of outcomes.

More recently, techniques that were originally devised for classical planning in deterministic domains have been extended to deal with nondeterministic domains. Planning graph techniques [74] have been extended to deal with conformant planning [548] and some limited form of partial observability [600]. Planning as satisfiability [322] has been extended to deal with nondeterministic domains in [108, 107, 193, 234].

Different approaches have addressed the problem of planning with deterministic models in a theorem proving setting; for example, techniques based on situation calculus [198] and the Golog Language [378, 417] have been devised for the conformant planning problem. Planning based on quantified Boolean formulas (QBF) (see Section 5.4.2) has addressed the problem of conformant planning and contingent planning under partial observability [511, 514, 513]. According to this approach, a bounded planning problem, i.e., a planning problem where the search is restricted to plans of maximum length n, is reformulated as a QBF formula. QBF formulas are not encoded with BDDs as in Section 5.4, instead a QBF solver is used to generate a plan. This approach can tackle several different conditional planning problems. In QBF planning, like in the planning as satisfiability, it is impossible to determine the nonexistence of a solution plan.

The idea of planning by using explicit state model checking techniques has been around since the work by Kabanza [304] and SimPlan, a planner that addresses the problem of planning under full observability for temporally extended goals expressed in (an extension of) Linear Temporal Logic (LTL) [178]. The idea of planning as model checking was first introduced in [117, 236]. Planning for safe acyclic solutions was first proposed in [123], and planning for safe cyclic solutions was first proposed in [122] and then revised in [136]. A full formal account and an extensive experimental evaluation of the symbolic model checking approach has been presented in [121].

The framework has been extended to deal with partial observability [61] and with extended goals [484, 482, 135]. [531] extended the approach to deal with preferences. All the results described in the works cited have been implemented in the Model Based Planner (MBP) [59].

There have been various proposals along this line. The work by Jensen and Veloso [297] exploits the idea of planning via symbolic model checking as a starting point for the work on the UMOP planner. Jensen and Veloso extended the framework to deal with contingent events in their proposal for adversarial planning [299]. They also provided a novel algorithm for strong (safe acyclic) and strong cyclic (safe cyclic) planning which performs heuristic based guided OBDD-based search for nondeterministic domains [298]. Kissmann et al. [331] proposed a symbolic planner based on BDDs for safe cyclic and acyclic solutions. The planner is based on a translation of the nondeterministic planning problem into a two-player game, where actions can be selected by the planner and by the environment. The Yoyo planner [362, 363] does hierarchical planning in nondeterministic domains by combining an HTN-based mechanism for constraining the search and a Binary Decision Diagram (BDD) representation for reasoning about sets of states and state transitions.

BDDs have also been exploited in classical planners (see [570] for one of the first reports about BDD-based planners for classical planning in deterministic domains). Among them, MIPS encodes PDDL planning problems into BDDs, see [170, 171] and showed remarkable results in the AIPS'00 planning competition for deterministic planning domains as well as in the ICAPS'14 planning competition [173]. More recently, techniques based on BDDs have proved very competitive for classical planning, see, for example, [168, 172]. For a recent survey, see [174]. The performance of planners that make use of BDDs may depend heavily on the choice of variable ordering (see Section 5.4.5). A state-variable representation can be of help in the choice of the variable ordering, mainly for two reasons: it can reduce the number of variables required in the BDD encoding and can lead to a variable ordering where closely related propositions are grouped together, which is critical to good performance of BDD exploration.

Other approaches are related to model checking techniques. Bacchus and Kabanza [28] use explicit-state model checking to embed control strategies expressed in LTL in TLPlan. The work of Robert Goldman and David Musliner [240, 239, 241] presents a method where model checking with timed automata is used to verify that generated plans meet timing constraints.

Recent work on planning for cyclic safe solutions in fully observable nondeterministic domains (FOND) has focused on determinization techniques. This approach was first proposed in [364] with the NDP planner. A complete formal account and extensive experimental evaluation is presented in [9]. The new planner NDP2 finds cyclic safe solutions (strong-cyclic solutions) by using a classical planner (FF). NDP2 makes use of a procedure that rewrites the original planning problem to an abstract planning problem, thus improving performances. NDP2 is compared with the MBP planner. The work in [9] shows how the performances of the two planners depend on the amount of nondeterminism in the planning domain, how the NPD2 can use effectively its abstraction mechanisms, and whether the domain contains dead ends.

A lot of interesting work has been proposed along the lines of NDP. The work in [405] proposes a planner based on the And/Or search algorithm LAO* and the pattern database heuristics to guide LAO* toward goal states. In [209], the FIP planner builds on the idea of NDP and shows how such technique can solve all of the problems presented in the international planning competition in 2008. Furthermore, FIP improves its performance by avoiding reexploration of states that have been already encountered during the search (this idea is called *state reuse*). The work in [436], implemented in the PRP planner, devises a technique to focus on relevant aspects of states for generating safe cyclic solutions. Such technique manages to improve significantly the performance of the planner. Another study [435] extends the work to conditional effects.

In [506, 139], the synthesis of controllers from a set of components is accomplished by planning for safe acyclic solutions through model checking techniques. The work in [507] combines symbolic model-checking techniques and forward heuristic search.

Bonet and Geffner [81, 82, 85] have introduced the idea of planning in belief space (i.e., the space of sets of states) using heuristic forward search. Brafman and Hoffman [96] address the conformant planning problem by using SAT to reason about the effects of an action sequence and heuristic search based on FF relaxation techniques [280]. They extend the technique to deal with contingent planning in [279]. Partially observable contingent planning is further addressed in [399], a work that interleaves conformant planning with sensing actions and uses a landmark-based heuristic for selecting the next sensing action, together with a projection method that uses classical planning to solve the intermediate conformant planning problems. Another work [89] studies the complexity of belief tracking for planning with sensing both in the case of deterministic actions and uncertainty in the initial state as well as in the case of nondeterminstic actions.

A notable work on interleaving planning and execution in nondeterministic domains is presented in [344, 343, 342]. These authors propose different techniques based on real-time heuristic search. Such algorithms are based on distance heuristics in the search space. Koenig [342] proposes the MinMax Learning Real Time A* presented in this chapter (see Algorithm 5.16): the learning mechanism can be amortized over several planning runs. On one hand, these techniques allow for dealing with large planning domains that cannot be addressed by offline algorithms. On the other hand, they work on the assumption of "safely explorable" domains, that is, domains that do not contain dead ends.

Algorithm FS-Replan can be the basis for extensions in probabilistic planning that take into account probability distributions, see Chapter 6, algorithm RFF. Vice versa, some algorithms devised for probabilistic planning can be used in nondeterministic domains without taking into account the probabilistic distribution. This is the case of algorithms based on sparse sampling lookahead (see Chapter 6, algorithm SLATE).

The work in [63] proposes a different technique based on symbolic model checking for partially observable domains, which guarantees termination in non-safely-explorable domains, still not guaranteeing to reach the goal in the unlucky case a dead end is reached. The FS-Replan Algorithm presented in this chapter is based on the FF-Replan algorithm presented in [619].

The work in [532] focuses on fully observable domains and shows a technique that is able to interleave planning and execution in a very general and efficient way by using symbolic model checking techniques and by expressing goals that contain procedural statements (executable actions and plans) and declarative goals (formulas over state variables).

The techniques presented in this chapter for planning with input/output automata are based on the work on planning with asynchronous processes, which have has been first proposed in [486] and then formalized and extensively evaluated in [64]. Such techniques have been extended to deal with service oriented applications [101], and the related work on adaptation inspired by a Harbor Operation Management (HOM) facility for the sea port of Bremen, Germany, originally presented in [76, 101]. Techniques for planning in nondeterministic domain models have been used to interleave reasoning about processes and ontology reasoning [483].

The technique for the synthesis of controllers presented in this chapter shares some ideas with work on the automata-based synthesis of controllers (see, e.g., [488, 489, 490, 576, 324, 358, 359, 575]).

In Section 5.8.4 we dealt with the problem of planning under partial observability by encoding in different states the different possible values of variables that cannot be observed. Work in planning under partial observability has been done in the framework of planning via symbolic model checking [62, 63, 60], real-time heuristic search [342, 344], and heuristic search [399].

5.10 EXERCISES

5.1. Can all (memoryless) policies be written as contingent plans, that is, plans with conditional tests? Vice versa? Explain the answer with some examples.

5.2. Consider Figure 5.27.
   (a) Give an example of an unsafe solution π_1, a cyclic safe solution π_2 and an acyclic safe solution π_3 to the problem of moving from s1 to s5, if one exists. Draw their reachability graphs, circling the leaves.
   (b) Suppose the initial state was s2 instead of s1. Are π_1, π_2, and π_3 solutions? If so, what kinds?

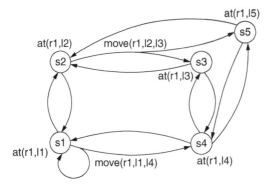

Figure 5.27. A nondeterministic state-transition system.

5.3. Prove that a policy π is an unsafe solution iff $\exists s \in leaves(s_0, \pi) \mid s \notin S_g \vee \exists s \in \hat{\gamma}(s_0, \pi) \mid leaves(s, \pi) = \varnothing$

5.4. Consider Definition 5.10 and Definition 5.11. Write definitions of safe cyclic and acyclic solutions that reach the goal and then continue looping inside the set of goal states, and definitions of solutions that traverse infinitely often the set of goal states. More formally, write definitions of safe cyclic and acyclic solutions π such that PerformPolicy(π) (see the acting procedure in Algorithm 5.1) reaches the goal and then loops forever with the condition that PerformPolicy(π) is guaranteed to loop inside the set of goal states. Write the same definition but with the condition that PerformPolicy(π) is guaranteed to traverse the set of goal states infinitely many often.

5.5. Provide a definition of a "worst-case optimal" safe acyclic solution, that is a solution that results in a path with the minimal longest distance from the goal. Rewrite algorithms for finding safe acyclic solutions (see Algorithm 5.4) by replacing the nondeterministic choice and guaranteeing that the solution is worst-case optimal.

5.6. Write a deterministic algorithm for Find-Safe-Solution and Find-Acyclic-Solution, see Algorithm 5.3 and Algorithm 5.4.

5.7. Figure 5.28 is a domain model for a washing problem. To make the domain nondeterministic, suppose we assume that sometimes the `start` action may either succeed or fail. If it fails, it will not change the state. The `run` and `finish` actions are guaranteed to succeed. Also, say that the set of goal states S_g are all the states where {`clean(clothes)=T, clean(dishes)=T`} are satisfied.
  (a) Draw the state-transition system. (**Hint:** It can be rather large. To make it easier to draw rather than name the states, and use abbreviated names for actions.)
  (b) Trace the execution of Find-Solution on this problem by drawing the And/Or search tree. The nondeterministic choices are left to the reader.
  (c) Do the same for Find-Safe-Solution.
  (d) Suppose A and A_d, respectively, represent the set of actions in the nondeterministic model and the determinized model respectively. Compute $|A|$ and $|A_d|$.
  (e) Write down a plan π_d from the initial state to a goal state using the determinized model.
  (f) Let us suppose that π_d is returned by the first call to Forward-Search in FS-Replan. Furthermore, suppose that the second `start` action in π_d fails during execution.[27] Explain what FS-Replan does at this point.

5.8. Prove that an acyclic safe solution π to the problem $P = (\Sigma, s_0, S_g)$ satisfies the condition
$$(\forall s \in \hat{\gamma}(s_0, \pi)(leaves(s, \pi) \cap S_g \neq \varnothing)) \iff leaves(s_0, \pi) \subseteq S_g.$$

5.9. Notice that Find-Acyclic-Solution-by-MinMax ignores the possibility of multiple paths to the same state. If it comes to a state s again along a different path, it does exactly the same search below s that it did before. Modify Find-Acyclic-Solution-by-MinMax such that it avoids reperforming the same search in already visited states by storing remembering the already visited states and storing the obtained solutions.

---

[27] There should be two `start` actions, one each for dishwasher and clothes washer. Assume that the second one fails.

Objects: $B = Items \cup Machines \cup Booleans \cup Statuses \cup Availability$
     $Items = \{$dishes, clothes$\}$,
     $Machines = \{$dw,cw$\}$ (i.e., dishwasher and clothes washer),
     $Booleans = \{$T,F$\}$,
     $Statuses = \{$ready,filling,running$\}$,
     $Availability = \{$free,inuse$\}$

State variables (where $i \in Items$ and $m \in Machines$):
     clean(i) $\in Booleans$, status(m) $\in Statuses$, water $\in Availability$

Initial state and goal:
     $s_0 = \{$clean(dishes)=F, clean(clothes)=F, loc(dishes)=dw, loc(clothes)=cw,
         status(dw)=ready, status(cw)=ready, water=free$\}$
     $g = \{$clean(dishes)=T, clean(clothes)=T$\}$

Action templates (where $i \in Items$ and $m \in Machines$):
     start(m)   run(m)
         Pre: status(m)=ready, water=free   Pre: status(m)=filling
         Eff: status(m)=filling, water=inuse   Eff: status(m)=running, water=free
                                          finish(m,i)
                                          Pre: status(m)=running, loc(i)=m
                                          Eff: status(m)=ready, clean(i)=T

Figure 5.28. A planning domain in which there are two devices that use water: a washing machine and a dishwasher. Because of water pressure problems, only one device can use water at a time.

5.10. Determinization techniques rely on a transformation of nondeterministic actions into a sets of deterministic actions. Write a definition of a procedure to transform a nondeterministic domain into a deterministic one. Notice that this operation is complicated by the fact that we have to take into account that in different states, the same action can lead to a set of different states. Therefore, if the set of states has exponential size with respect to the number of state variables, then this operation would generate exponentially many actions.

5.11. The algorithm for planning for safe solutions by symbolic model checking presented in this chapter (see Algorithm 5.7) can find either safe cyclic or safe acyclic solutions. Modify the algorithm such that it finds a safe acyclic solution and only if one does not exist does it search for a safe cyclic solution.

5.12. Consider the definition of controlled system: Definition 5.30. A control automaton A_c may be not adequate to control an automaton $A_{\|}$. Indeed, we need to guarantee that, whenever A_c sends an output, $A_{\|}$ is able to receive it as an input, and vice versa. A controller that satisfies such condition is called a deadlock-free controller. Provide a formal definition of a deadlock-free controller. Suggestion: see the paper [486] where automata are defined without commands but with τ-actions.

CHAPTER 6 Deliberation with Probabilistic Models

In this chapter, we explore various approaches for using probabilistic models to handle the uncertainty and nondeterminism in planning and acting problems. These approaches are mostly based on dynamic programming optimization methods for Markov decision processes. We explain the basic principles and develop heuristic search algorithms for stochastic shortest-path problems. We also propose several sampling algorithms for online probabilistic planning and discuss how to augment with probabilistic models refinement methods for acting. The chapter also discusses the critical issue of specifying a domain with probabilistic models.

Our motivations for using probabilistic models, and our main assumptions, are briefly introduced next. Section 6.2 defines stochastic shortest-path problems and basic approaches for solving them. Different heuristic search algorithms for these problems are presented and analyzed in Section 6.3. Online probabilistic planning approaches are covered in Section 6.4. Refinement methods for acting with probabilistic models are presented in Section 6.5. Sections 6.6 and 6.7 are devoted to factored representations and domain modeling issues with probabilistic models, respectively. The main references are given in the discussion and historical remarks Section 6.8. The chapter ends with exercises.

6.1 INTRODUCTION

Some of the motivations for deliberation with probabilistic models are similar to those introduced in Chapter 5 for addressing nondeterminism: the future is never entirely predictable, models are necessarily incomplete, and, even in predictable environments, complete deterministic models are often too complex and costly to develop. In addition, probabilistic planning considers that the possible outcomes of an action are not equally likely. Sometimes, one is able to estimate the likelihood of each outcome, relying for example on statistics of past observations. Probabilistic planning addresses those cases in which it is desirable to seek plans optimized with respect to the estimated likelihood of the effects of their actions.

The usual formal model of probabilistic planning is that of *Markov decision processes* (MDPs). An MDP is a nondeterministic state-transition system together with a probability distribution and a cost distribution. The probability distribution defines how likely it is to get to a state s' when an action a is performed in a state s.

A probabilistic state-transition system is said to be *Markovian* if the probability distribution of the next state depends only on the current state and not on the sequence of states that preceded it. Moreover, the system is said to be *stationary* when the probability distributions remain invariant over time. Markovian and stationary properties are not intrinsic features of the world but are properties of its model. It is possible to take into account dependence on the past within a Markovian description by defining a "state" that includes the current configuration of the world, as well as some information about how the system has reached that configuration. For example, if the past two values of a state variable x_t are significant for characterizing future states, one extends the description of the "current" state with two additional state variables x_{t-1} and x_{t-2}. One may also add ad hoc state variables to handle dependence on time within a stationary model.

We restrict ourselves to stationary Markovian systems. We focus this chapter on *stochastic shortest path* problems (SSPs). SSPs generalize the familiar shortest path problems in graphs to probabilistic And/Or graphs. SSPs are quite natural for expressing probabilistic planning problems. They are also more general than MDP models.

6.2 STOCHASTIC SHORTEST PATH PROBLEMS

This section introduces the main definitions, concepts and techniques needed for addressing probabilistic planning and acting problems.

6.2.1 Main Definitions

Definition 6.1. A *probabilistic planning domain* is a tuple $\Sigma = (S, A, \gamma, \Pr, \text{cost})$ where:

- S and A are finite sets of states and actions, respectively;
- $\gamma : S \times A \to 2^S$ is the state transition function; it corresponds to the following stationary Markovian probability distribution;
- $\Pr(s'|s, a)$ is the probability of reaching $s' \in \gamma(s, a)$ when action a takes place in s; it is such that $\Pr(s'|s, a) \neq 0$ if and only if $s' \in \gamma(s, a)$; and
- $\text{cost} : S \times A \to \mathbb{R}^+$ is a cost function: $\text{cost}(s, a)$ is the cost of a in s.   □

We follow the notation introduced in Section 5.2.3:[1]

- A *policy* is a function $\pi : S' \to A$, with $S' \subseteq S$, such that for every $s \in S'$, $\pi(s) \in$ Applicable(s). Thus Dom$(\pi) = S'$.
- $\widehat{\gamma}(s, \pi)$ is the set composed of s and all its descendants reachable by π, that is, the transitive closure of γ with π.

---

[1] To remain consistent with Chapter 5, we depart slightly from the classical definitions and notations of the MDP planning literature; differences are discussed in Section 6.8.

- *Graph*(s, π) is the graph induced by π whose nodes are the set of states $\widehat{\gamma}(s, \pi)$. It is a cyclic graph rooted at s.
- *leaves*(s, π) is the set of *tip* states in this graph, i.e., states in $\widehat{\gamma}(s, \pi)$ that are not in the domain of π, and hence have no successors with π.

Definition 6.2. An SSP problem for the planning domain Σ is a triple (Σ, s_0, S_g), where $s_0 \in S$ is the initial state and $S_g \subseteq S$ is a set of goal states. $\qquad \square$

Definition 6.3. A *solution* to the SSP problem (Σ, s_0, S_g) is a policy $\pi : S' \to A$ such that $s_0 \in S'$ and *leaves*$(s_0, \pi) \cap S_g \neq \varnothing$. The solution is said to be *closed* if and only if every state reachable from s_0 by π is either in the domain of π, is a goal or has no applicable actions, that is, $\forall s \in \widehat{\gamma}(s_0, \pi), (s \in \text{Dom}(\pi)) \vee (s \in S_g) \vee \text{Applicable}(s) = \varnothing$. $\qquad \square$

In other words, a closed solution π must provide applicable actions, if there are any, to s_0 and to its all descendants reachable by π, and have at least one path in *Graph*(s_0, π) that reaches a goal state. Note that π is a *partial* function, not necessarily defined everywhere in S ($\text{Dom}(\pi) \subseteq S$). We are chiefly interested in *closed partial policies*, which are defined over the entire $\widehat{\gamma}(s_0, \pi)$, except at goal states and states that have no applicable action. As usual in planning, goals are considered to be *terminal* states requiring no further action.

Example 6.4. Here is a simple example, inspired from casino coin machines called *one-armed bandits*. This domain has three state variables x, y, and z, ranging over the set $\{a, b, c\}$. The domain has nine states: $\{x = a, y = a, z = a\} \ldots \{x = c, y = c, z = c\}$, which are abbreviated as $S = \{(aaa), (aab), \ldots, (ccc)\}$. There are three actions: pull left, pull right, and pull both arms simultaneously, denoted respectively Left, Right, and Both. If the three state variables are distinct, then the three actions are applicable. If $x \neq y = z$, only Left is applicable. If $x = y \neq z$, only Right is applicable. If $x = z \neq y$, only Both is applicable. Finally, when the three variables are equal no action is applicable. Here is a possible specification of Left (each outcome is prefixed by its corresponding probability):

Left:
pre: $(x \neq y)$
eff: $(\frac{1}{3})$: $\qquad \{x \leftarrow a\}$
$\qquad (\frac{1}{3})$: $\qquad \{x \leftarrow b\}$
$\qquad (\frac{1}{3})$: $\qquad \{x \leftarrow c\}$

Similarly, when applicable, Right randomly changes z; Both randomly changes y. We assume these changes to be uniformly distributed. Figure 6.1 gives part of the state space of this domain corresponding to the problem of going from $s_0 = (abc)$ to a goal state in $S_g = \{(bbb), (ccc)\}$. Note that every action in this domain may possibly leave the state unchanged, that is, $\forall s, a, s \in \gamma(s, a)$. Note also that the state space of this domain is not fully connected: once two variables are made equal, there is no action to change them. Consequently, states (acb), (bac), (bca), (cab) and (cba) are not reachable from (abc).

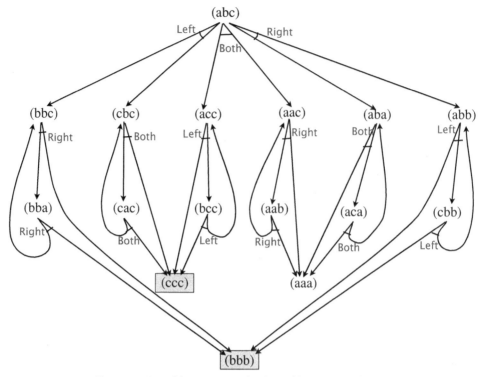

Figure 6.1. Part of the state space for the problem in Example 6.4.

A solution to the problem in Figure 6.2 is, for instance,

$$\pi(abc) = \text{Left}, \pi(bbc) = \pi(bba) = \text{Right}, \pi(cbc) = \pi(cac) = \text{Both}.$$

Here, π is defined over $\text{Dom}(\pi) = \{s_0, (bbc), (cbc), (bba), (cac)\}$ and $\hat{\gamma}(s_0, \pi) = \text{Dom}(\pi) \cup S_g$. Figure 6.2 gives the $Graph(s_0, \pi)$ for that solution. □

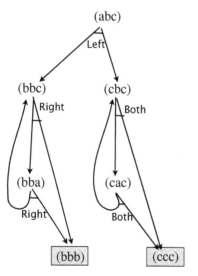

Figure 6.2. A safe solution for Example 6.4 and its $Graph(s_0, \pi)$.

6.2.2 Safe and Unsafe Policies

Let π be a solution to the problem (Σ, s_0, S_g). For the rest of this chapter we require all solutions to be closed. Algorithm 6.1 is a simple procedure for acting with a policy π, by performing in each state s the action given by $\pi(s)$ until reaching a goal or a state that has no applicable action.[2]

Algorithm 6.1 A simple procedure to run a policy.

Run-Policy(Σ, s_0, S_g, π)

$\quad s \leftarrow s_0$
$\quad$ while $s \notin S_g$ and Applicable$(s) \neq \varnothing$ do
$\quad\quad$ perform action $\pi(s)$
$\quad\quad s \leftarrow$ observe resulting state

Let $\sigma = \langle s_0, s_1, \dots, s_h \rangle$ be a sequence of states followed by this procedure in some run of policy π that reaches a goal, that is, $s_h \in S_g$. σ is called a history; it is a path in $Graph(s_0, \pi)$ from s_0 to S_g. For a given π there can be an exponential number of such histories. The cost of σ is the total sum of the cost of actions along the history σ, that is: $\text{cost}(\sigma) = \sum_{i=0}^{h-1} \text{cost}(s_i, \pi(s_i))$. The probability of following the history σ is $\Pr(\sigma) = \prod_{i=0}^{h-1} \Pr(s_{i+1}|s_i, \pi(s_i))$. Note that σ may not be a simple path: it may contain loops, that is, $s_j = s_i$ for some $j > i$. But because actions are nondeterministic, a loop does not necessarily prevent the procedure from eventually reaching a goal: the action $\pi(s_i)$ that led to an already visited state may get out of the loop when executed again at step j. However, a solution policy may also get trapped forever in a loop, or it may reach a nongoal leaf. Hence Run-Policy may not terminate and reach a goal. Planning algorithms for SSPs will preferably seek solutions that offer some guarantee of reaching a goal.

Example 6.5. For the policy in Figure 6.2, the history $\sigma = \langle s_0, (cbc), (cac), (cbc), (cbc), (ccc) \rangle$ reaches eventually a goal despite visiting the same state three times. $\quad\square$

Let $\Pr^l(S_g|s, \pi)$ be the probability of reaching a goal from a state s by following policy π for up to l steps: $\Pr^l(S_g|s, \pi) = \sum_\sigma \Pr(\sigma)$, over all $\sigma \in \{\langle s, s_1, \dots, s_h \rangle \mid s_{i+1} \in \gamma(s_i, \pi(s_i)), s_h \in S_g, h \leq l\}$. Let $\Pr(S_g|s, \pi) = \lim_{l \to \infty} \Pr^l(S_g|s, \pi)$. With this notation, it follows that:

- if π is a solution to the problem (Σ, s_0, S_g) then $\Pr(S_g|s_0, \pi) > 0$; and
- a goal is reachable from a state s with policy π if and only if $\Pr(S_g|s, \pi) > 0$.

Definition 6.6. A solution π to the SSP problem (Σ, s_0, S_g) is said to be *safe* if and only if $\Pr(S_g|s_0, \pi) = 1$. If $0 < \Pr(S_g|s_0, \pi) < 1$ then policy π is an *unsafe* solution.[3] $\quad\square$

A policy π is safe if and only if $\forall s \in \widehat{\gamma}(s_0, \pi)$ there is a path from s to a goal. With a safe policy, procedure Run-Policy(Σ, s_0, S_g, π) always reaches a goal.[4] However, the

---

[2] Section 6.5 further details how to "perform action $\pi(s)$" in probabilistic models.
[3] The literature often refers to safe and unsafe solutions as proper and improper solutions. Here we keep the terminology introduced in Chapter 5.
[4] In this chapter, "always" is synonymous to a probability of occurrence equal to one.

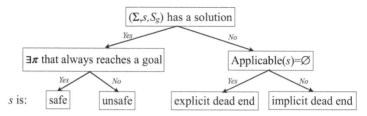

Figure 6.3. Partition of the set of states with respect to solutions.

number of steps needed to reach the goal is not bounded a priori. Such a bound would require a *safe acyclic* policy (see Section 6.7.5). With an unsafe policy, Run-Policy may or may not terminate; if it does terminate, it may reach either a goal or a state with no applicable action.

It is useful to extend the concept of safe solutions from policies to states:

Definition 6.7. A state s is *safe* if and only if $\exists \pi$ such that $\Pr(S_g|s, \pi) = 1$; s is *unsafe* if and only if $\forall \pi \; 0 < \Pr(S_g|s, \pi) < 1$; s is a *dead end* if and only if $\forall \pi \; \Pr(S_g|s, \pi) = 0$. An SSP problem (Σ, s_0, S_g) is said to be safe when s_0 is safe.   □

A state s is safe if and only if there exists a policy π such that for every $s' \in \widehat{\gamma}(s, \pi)$ there is a path from s' to a goal. Note that policy π is a safe solution of (Σ, s_0, S_g) if and only if $\forall s \in \widehat{\gamma}(s_0, \pi)$ s is safe. Conversely, s is unsafe if and only if it has a dead-end descendant for every policy: $\forall \pi \; \exists s' \in \widehat{\gamma}(s, \pi)$ s' is a dead end. If a state s is a dead end, then there is no solution to the problem (Σ, s, S_g).

A state that has no applicable action is a dead end, but so is a state from which every policy is trapped forever in a loop or leads only to other dead ends. The former are called *explicit dead ends*; the latter are *implicit dead ends*.

Example 6.8. In Figure 6.1, the state (aaa) is an explicit dead end, the states (aac), (aab), (aba), and (aca) are implicit dead ends, the states (bbb) and (ccc) are goals, and all of the other states are safe. Any policy starting in the safe state s_0 with either action Both or Right is unsafe because it leads to dead ends. The policy given in Figure 6.2 is safe.   □

Explicit dead ends are easy to detect: in such a state, Run-Policy(Σ, s_0, S_g, π) finds that Applicable$(s) = \varnothing$ and terminates unsuccessfully. Implicit dead ends create difficulties for many algorithms, as we discuss later. Figure 6.3 summarizes the four types of states with respect to goal reachability.

A domain has no dead end if and only if every state in S is safe. A domain has no reachable dead end if and only if every state reachable from s_0 by any policy is safe. These desirable cases are difficult to detect in advance. A problem has a safe solution when the domain dead ends are *avoidable*: there is a π such that $\widehat{\gamma}(s_0, \pi)$ avoids dead ends. Example 6.5 illustrates a domain where dead ends are avoidable. Planning algorithms will seek to avoid dead ends, searching for safe solutions. If the domain has at least one *unavoidable* dead end reachable from s_0, then s_0 is unsafe. In that case, one may accept an unsafe solution whose probability of reaching a goal is maximal. The trade-off between cost and probability of reaching the goal is discussed in Section 6.7.3.

In summary, an SSP problem (Σ, s_0, S_g) can be such that *(i)* it has a solution, possibly unsafe; *(ii)* it has a safe solution, its possible dead ends are avoidable; *(iii)* it has no reachable dead end; or *(iv)* it has no dead end. These four cases are in increasing order of restriction. We'll start by assuming to be in the most restricted case and relax it afterwards.

6.2.3 Optimality Principle of Dynamic Programming

As mentioned in the introduction, probabilistic planning is generally an optimization process. Planning algorithms search for a plan that is optimal with respect to some optimization criteria for the probability and cost parameters of the problem. Let us discuss the usual optimization criteria and the building blocks of this optimization process. Throughout this section, we restrict ourselves to *SSP problems without dead ends*.

Let $V^\pi : \mathrm{Dom}(\pi) \to \mathrm{R}^+$ be a *value function* giving the expected sum of the cost of the actions obtained by following a safe policy π (which necessarily exists given our assumption) from a state s to a goal:

$$V^\pi(s) = E[\sum_i \mathrm{cost}(s_i, \pi(s_i))] \tag{6.1}$$

where the expected value is over all histories $\sigma \in \{\langle s, s_1 \ldots, s_h\rangle \mid s_{i+1} \in \gamma(s_i, \pi(s_i)), s_h \in S_g\}$.

$V^\pi(s)$ is the expected cost for running the procedure Run-Policy(Σ, s, S_g, π) from s until termination. It is the total cost of following a history σ from s to S_g, averaged over all such histories in $Graph(s, \pi)$:

$$V^\pi(s) = \sum_\sigma \mathrm{Pr}(\sigma)\,\mathrm{cost}(\sigma), \tag{6.2}$$

where $\mathrm{cost}(\sigma) = \sum_i \mathrm{cost}(s_i, \pi(s_i))$ and $\mathrm{Pr}(\sigma) = \prod_i \mathrm{Pr}(s_{i+1}|s_i, \pi(s_i))$.

The number of steps needed to reach a goal with a safe solution is not bounded a priori. Consequently, the expected sum in Equation 6.1 is over an unbounded number of terms. However, because π is safe, the probability of reaching a goal is 1, hence $V^\pi(s)$ is necessarily finite. Note that when π is unsafe the expected sum of action costs until reaching a goal is not well defined: on a history σ on which Run-Policy(Σ, s, S_g, π) does not terminate, the sum in Equation 6.2 grows to infinity.

It is possible to prove that $V^\pi(s)$ is given by the following recursive equation (see Exercise 6.2):

$$V^\pi(s) = \begin{cases} 0 & \text{if } s \in S_g, \\ \mathrm{cost}(s, \pi(s)) + \sum_{s' \in \gamma(s,\pi(s))} \mathrm{Pr}(s'|s, \pi(s))V^\pi(s') & \text{otherwise} \end{cases} \tag{6.3}$$

The value function V^π plays a critical role in solving SSPs: it makes it possible to rank policies according to their expected total cost, to use optimization techniques for seeking a safe optimal policy, and, as we will see later, to heuristically focus the search on a part of the search space.

A policy π' *dominates* a policy π if and only if $V^{\pi'}(s) \le V^\pi(s)$ for every state for which both π and π' are defined. An *optimal policy* is a policy π^* that dominates all other policies. It has a minimal expected cost over all possible policies:

$V^*(s) = \min_\pi V^\pi(s)$. Under our assumption of probabilistic planning in a domain without dead ends, π^* exists and is unique.

The *optimality principle* extends Equation 6.3 to compute V^*:

$$V^*(s) = \begin{cases} 0 & \text{if } s \in S_g \\ \min_a\{\text{cost}(s, a) + \sum_{s' \in \gamma(s,a)} \Pr(s'|s, a)V^*(s')\} & \text{otherwise} \end{cases} \quad (6.4)$$

The optimal policy π^* is easily derived from V^*:

$$\pi^*(s) = \text{argmin}_a\{\text{cost}(s, a) + \sum_{s' \in \gamma(s,a)} \Pr(s'|s, a)V^*(s')\} \quad (6.5)$$

Let π be an arbitrary safe solution, and V^π be as defined in Equation 6.3. Let us define:

$$Q^\pi(s, a) = \text{cost}(s, a) + \sum_{s' \in \gamma(s,a)} \Pr(s'|s, a)V^\pi(s') \quad (6.6)$$

$Q^\pi(s, a)$ is called the *cost-to-go*: it is the sum of the immediate cost of a in s plus the following expected cost of the successors in $\gamma(s, a)$, as estimated by V^π.

Given a policy π, we can compute the corresponding V^π from which we define a *greedy policy* π', which chooses in each state the action that minimizes the cost to-go, as estimated by V^π:

$$\pi'(s) = \text{argmin}_a\{Q^\pi(s, a)\} \quad (6.7)$$

In case of ties in the preceding minimum relation, we assume that π' keeps the value of π, that is, when $\min_a\{Q^\pi(s, a)\} = V^\pi(s)$ then $\pi'(s) = \pi(s)$.

Proposition 6.9. *When π is a safe solution, then policy π' from Equation 6.7 is safe and dominates π, that is: $\forall s \ V^{\pi'}(s) \leq V^\pi(s)$. Further, if π is not optimal, then there is at least one state s for which $V^{\pi'}(s) < V^\pi(s)$.*

Starting with an initial safe policy, we can repeatedly apply Proposition 6.9 to keep improving from one policy to the next. This process converges because there is a finite number of distinct policies and each iteration brings a strict improvement in at least one state, unless already optimal. This is implemented in the Policy Iteration algorithm, detailed next.

6.2.4 Policy Iteration

Policy Iteration (PI, Algorithm 6.2), starts with an initial policy π_0, for example, $\pi_0(s) = \text{argmin}_a\{\text{cost}(s, a)\}$. It iterates over improvements of the current policy. At each iteration, it computes the value function $V^\pi(s)$ for the current π in every state s (step *(i)*). It then improves π with the greedy policy for the newly found V^π (step *(ii)*). Possible ties in argmin are broken by giving preference to the current π. The algorithm stops when reaching a fixed point where π remains unchanged over two iterations.

There are two ways of computing V^π for current π. The direct method is to solve Equation 6.3 considered over the entire S as a system of n linear equations, where $n = |S|$, the n unknown variables being the values of $V^\pi(s)$. There is a solution to this n linear

---

Algorithm 6.2 Policy Iteration algorithm.

$PI(\Sigma, \pi_0)$

   $\pi \leftarrow \pi_0$

   loop until reaching a fixed point

      compute $\{V^\pi(s) \mid s \in S\}$ (i)

      for every $s \in S \setminus S_g$ do

         $\pi(s) \leftarrow \operatorname{argmin}_a\{\text{cost}(s, a) + \sum_{s' \in \gamma(s,a)} \Pr(s'|s, a)V^\pi(s')\}$ (ii)

---

equations if and only if the current π is safe. The value function V^π for the current π can be computed using classical linear calculs methods, such as Gaussian elimination.

The second method for finding V^π is iterative. It consist in computing the following series of value functions:

$$V_i(s) = \text{cost}(s, \pi(s)) + \sum_{s' \in \gamma(s,\pi(s))} \Pr(s'|s, \pi(s))V_{i-1}(s'). \tag{6.8}$$

It can be shown that, for any initial V_0, if π is safe, then this series converges asymptotically to a fixed point equal to V^π. In practice, one stops when $\max_s |V_i(s) - V_{i-1}(s)|$ is small enough; V_i is then taken as an estimate of V^π (more about this in the next section).

Algorithm PI, when initialized with a safe policy, strictly improves in each iteration the current policy over the previous one, until reaching π^*. In a domain that has no dead ends, there exists a safe π_0; all successive policies are also safe and monotonically decreasing for the dominance relation order. In other words, if the successive policies defined by PI are $\pi_0, \pi_1, \ldots, \pi_k, \ldots, \pi^*$ then $\forall s\ V^*(s) \leq \cdots \leq V^{\pi_k}(s) \leq \cdots \leq V^{\pi_1}(s) \leq V^{\pi_0}(s)$. Because there is a finite number of distinct policies, algorithm PI with a safe π_0 converges to an optimal policy in a finite number of iterations.

The requirement that π_0 is safe is easily met for domains without dead ends. However, this strong assumption is difficult to meet in practice. It makes PI difficult to generalize to domains with dead ends. Algorithm Value Iteration, detailed next, also makes this assumption, but it can be generalized with heuristic search techniques to handle dead ends; it is often more efficient in practice than PI.

6.2.5 Value Iteration

Earlier, we defined Q^π and the greedy policy π' with respect to the value function V^π of a policy π. However, the same equations 6.6 and 6.7 can be applied to any value function $V : S \to \mathbb{R}^+$. This gives a cost-to-go $Q^V(s, a) = \text{cost}(s, a) + \sum_{s' \in \gamma(s,a)} \Pr(s'|s, a)V(s')$ and a greedy policy for V, $\pi(s) = \operatorname{argmin}_a\{Q^V(s, a)\}$.[5] From V, a new value function can be computed with the following equation:

$$V'(s) = \min_a\{\text{cost}(s, a) + \sum_{s' \in \gamma(s,a)} \Pr(s'|s, a)V(s')\}. \tag{6.9}$$

---

[5] The greedy policy for V is sometimes denoted π^V. In the remainder of this chapter, we simply denote π the greedy policy for the current V, unless otherwise specified.

Algorithm 6.3 Synchronous Value Iteration algorithm. V_0 is implemented as a function, computed once in every state; V, V' and π are lookup tables.

$VI(\Sigma, V_0)$
  $V \leftarrow V_0$
  loop until until reaching a fixed point
    for every $s \in S \setminus S_g$ do
      $V'(s) \leftarrow \min_a\{cost(s, a) + \sum_{s' \in \gamma(s,a)} \Pr(s'|s, a)V(s')\}$
      $V \leftarrow V'$
    $\pi(s) \leftarrow \operatorname{argmin}_a\{cost(s, a) + \sum_{s' \in \gamma(s,a)} \Pr(s'|s, a)V(s')\}$

V' is the minimum cost-to-go in s when the value of the successors is estimated by V. Dynamic programming consists in applying Equation 6.9 repeatedly, using V' as an estimate for computing another cost-to-go $Q^{V'}$ and another value function $\min_a\{Q^{V'}(s, a)\}$. This is implemented in the algorithm Value Iteration (Algorithm 6.3).

VI starts with an arbitrary heuristic function V_0, which estimates the expected cost of reaching a goal from s. An easily computed heuristic is, for example, $V_0(s) = 0$ when $s \in S_g$, and $V_0(s) = \min_a\{cost(s, a)\}$ otherwise. The algorithm iterates over improvements of the current value function by performing repeated updates using Equation 6.9. An update at an iteration propagates to $V'(s)$ changes in $V(s')$ from the previous iteration for the successors $s' \in \gamma(s, a)$. This is pursued until a fixed point is reached. A fixed point is a full iteration over S where $V'(s)$ remains identical to $V(s)$ for all s. The returned solution π is the greedy policy for the final V.

Algorithm 6.3 is the *synchronous* version of Value Iteration. It implements a stage-by-stage sequence of updates where the updates at an iteration are based on values of V from the previous iteration.

An alternative is the *asynchronous* Value Iteration (Algorithm 6.4). There, $V(s)$ stands for the current value function for s at some stage of the algorithm. It is initialized as V_0 then repeatedly updated. An update of $V(s)$ takes into account values of successors of s and may affect the ancestors of s within that same iteration over S. In the pseudocode, a local update step in s is performed by the Bellman-Update procedure (Algorithm 6.5), which iterates over $a \in$ Applicable(s) to compute $Q(s, a)$ and its minimum as $V(s)$. Several algorithms in this chapter use Bellman-Update. Throughout this chapter, we assume that ties in $\operatorname{argmin}_a\{Q(s, a)\}$, if any, are broken in favor of the previous value of $\pi(s)$ and in a systematic way (e.g., lexical order of action names).

Algorithm 6.4 Asynchronous Value Iteration algorithm.

$VI(\Sigma, V_0)$
  $V \leftarrow V_0$
  loop until reaching a fixed point
    for every $s \in S \setminus S_g$ do
      Bellman-Update(s)

Algorithm 6.5 The Bellman update procedure computes $V(s)$ as in Equation 6.9, and $\pi(s)$ as the greedy policy for V. Q can be implemented as a local data structure, π and V as internal data structures of algorithms using this procedure.

Bellman-Update(s)
   for every $a \in$ Applicable(s) do
      $Q(s, a) \leftarrow \text{cost}(s, a) + \sum_{s' \in \gamma(s,a)} \Pr(s'|s, a)V(s')$
      $V(s) \leftarrow \min_a\{Q(s, a)\}$
      $\pi(s) \leftarrow \text{argmin}_a\{Q(s, a)\}$

At any point of Value Iteration, either synchronous or asynchronous, an update of a state makes its ancestors no longer meeting the equation $V(s) = \min_a\{\text{cost}(s, a) + \sum_{s' \in \gamma(s,a)} \Pr(s'|s, a)V(s')\}$. A change in $V(s')$, for any successor s' of s (including when s is its own successor), requires an update of s. This is pursued until a fixed point is reached.

The termination condition of the outer loop of VI checks that such a fixed point has been reached, that is, a full iteration over S without a change in V. At the fixed point, every state s meets Equation 6.3, that is: $\forall s\ V(s) = V^\pi(s)$ for current $\pi(s)$.

In previous section, we emphasized that because there is a finite number of policies, it make sense to stop PI when the fixed point is reached. Here, there is an infinite number of value functions; the precise fixed point is an asymptotic limit. Hence, VI stops when a fixed point is *approximately* reached, within some acceptable margin of error. This can be assessed by the amount of change in the value of $V(s)$ during its update in Bellman-Update. This amplitude of change is called the *residual* of a state:

Definition 6.10. The *residual* of a state s with respect to V is
$residual(s) = |V(s) - \min_a\{\text{cost}(s, a) + \sum_{s' \in \gamma(s,a)} \Pr(s'|s, a)V(s')\}|$. The global *residual* over S is $residual = \max_{s \in S}\{residual(s)\}$.   □

At each iteration of VI, $residual(s)$ is computed before each update with respect to the values of V at the previous iteration. The *termination condition* of VI with a margin of error set to a small parameter $\eta > 0$ is: $residual \le \eta$. Note, however, that with such a termination condition, the value of $V(s)$ at the last iteration is not identical to $V^\pi(s)$ for current $\pi(s)$, as illustrated next.

Example 6.11. Consider the very simple domain in Figure 6.4. Σ has three states, s_0, s_1, and the goal g, and two actions a and b. Action a leads in one step to g with probability p; it loops back on s_0 with probability $1 - p$. Action b is deterministic.

Figure 6.4. A very simple domain.

Assume $cost(a) = 10$, $cost(b) = 100$ and $p = .2$. Σ has two solutions, denoted π_a and π_b. Their values are:

$$V^{\pi_a}(s_0) = cost(a) \sum_{i=0,\infty}(1-p)^i = \frac{cost(a)}{p} = 50 \text{ and}$$
$$V^{\pi_b}(s_0) = 2 \times cost(b) = 200. \text{ Hence } \pi^* = \pi_a.$$

Let us run VI (say, the synchronous version) on this simple domain assuming $V_0(s) = 0$ in every state. After the first iteration $V_1(s_0) = 10$ and $V_1(s_1) = 100$. In the following iterations, $V_i(s_0) = 10 + .8 \times V_{i-1}(s_0)$, and $V_i(s_1)$ remains unchanged. The successive values of V in s_0 are: 18, 24.4, 29.52, 33.62, 36.89, 39.51, 41.61, 43.29, 44.63, 45.71, 46.56, and so on, which converges asymptotically to 50.

With $\eta = 10^{-4}$, VI stops after 53 iterations with solution π_a and $V(s_0) = 49.9996$. With $\eta = 10^{-3}$, 10^{-2}, and 10^{-1}, termination is reached after 43, 32, and 22 iterations, respectively. With a larger value of η, say, $\eta = 5$, termination is reached after just 5 iterations with $V(s_0) = 33.62$ (at this point: $residual(s_0) = 33.62 - 29.52 < \eta$). Note that at termination $V(s_0) \neq V^{\pi_a}(s_0)$ for the found solution π_a. We'll see next how to bound the difference $V^{\pi}(s_0) - V(s_0)$.   □

Properties of Bellman updates. The iterative dynamic programming updates corresponding to Equation 6.9 have several interesting properties, which are conveniently stated with the following notation. Let (BV) be a value function corresponding to a Bellman update of V over S, that is, $\forall s\ (BV)(s) = \min_a\{Q^V(s, a)\}$. Successive updates are denoted as: $(B^kV) = (B(B^{k-1}V))$, with $(B^0V) = V$.

Proposition 6.12. *For any two value functions V_1 and V_2 such that $\forall s\ V_1(s) \leq V_2(s)$, we have: $\forall s\ (B^kV_1)(s) \leq (B^kV_2)(s)$ for $k = 1, 2, \ldots$.*

In particular, if a function V_0 is such that $V_0(s) \leq (BV_0)(s)$, then a series of Bellman updates is *monotonically non decreasing*, in other words:
$\forall s\ V_0(s) \leq (BV_0)(s) \leq \cdots \leq (B^kV_0)(s) \leq (B^{k+1}V_0)(s) \leq \cdots$.

Proposition 6.13. *In a domain without dead end, the series of Bellman updates starting at any value function V_0 converges asymptoticaly to the optimal cost function V^*, that is, $\forall s\ \lim_{k\to\infty}(B^kV_0)(s) = V^*(s)$.*

Convergence and complexity of VI. For an SSP problem without dead ends and for any value function V_0, VI terminates. Each inner loop iteration runs in time $O(|A| \times |S|)$ (assuming $|\gamma(s, a)|$ to be upper bounded by some constant), and the number of iterations required to reach the termination condition $residual \leq \eta$ is finite and can be bounded under some appropriate assumptions.

Proposition 6.14. *For an SSP problem without dead ends, VI reaches the termination condition $residual \leq \eta$ in a finite number of iterations.*

Regardless of the value function V_0, VI converges *asymptotically* to the optimum:

Proposition 6.15. *At termination of VI with residual $\leq \eta$ in an SSP problem without dead ends, the value V is such that $\forall s \in S\ \lim_{\eta\to 0} V(s) = V^*(s)$.*

More precisely, it is possible to prove that at termination with V and π (the greedy policy for V), the following bound holds:

$$\forall s \ |V(s) - V^*(s)| \leq \eta \times \max\{\Phi^*(s), \Phi^\pi(s)\} \tag{6.10}$$

where $\Phi^*(s)$ and $\Phi^\pi(s)$ are the expected number of steps to reach a goal from s by following π^* and π respectively. However, this bound is difficult to compute in the general case.

More interesting properties can be established when VI uses a heuristic function V_0 that is admissible or monotone.

Definition 6.16. V_0 is an *admissible* heuristic function if and only if $\forall s \ V_0(s) \leq V^*(s)$. V_0 is a *monotone* heuristic function if and only if $\forall s \ V_0(s) \leq \min_a\{Q(s, a)\}$. $\square$

Proposition 6.17. *If V_0 is an admissible heuristic function, then at any iteration of VI, the value function V remains admissible. At termination with residual $\leq \eta$, the found value V and policy π meet the following bounds: $\forall s \ V(s) \leq V^*(s) \leq V(s) + \eta \times \Phi^\pi(s)$ and $V(s) \leq V^\pi(s) \leq V(s) + \eta \times \Phi^\pi(s)$.*

Given π, $\Phi^\pi(s_0)$, the expected number of steps to reach a goal from s_0 following π is computed by solving the n linear equations:

$$\Phi^\pi(s) = \begin{cases} 0 & \text{if } s \in g \\ 1 + \sum_{s' \in \gamma(s, \pi(s))} \Pr(s'|s, \pi(s)) \Phi^\pi(s') & \text{otherwise} \end{cases} \tag{6.11}$$

Note the similarity between the two Equations 6.3 and 6.11: the expected number of steps to a goal is simply V^π with unit costs. Note also that the bound $\eta \times \Phi^\pi(s_0)$ can be arbitrarily large.

VI does not guarantee a solution whose difference with the optimum is bounded in advance. This difference is bounded a posteriori. The bounds in Proposition 6.17 entail $0 \leq V^\pi(s) - V^*(s) \leq V^\pi(s) - V(s) \leq \eta \times \Phi^\pi(s)$. However, a guaranteed approximation procedure is easily defined using VI with an admissible heuristic. Such a procedure is illustrated in Algorithm 6.6.

Procedure GAP with an admissible heuristic returns a solution π guaranteed to be within ϵ of the optimum, that is, $V^\pi(s_0) - V^*(s_0) \leq \epsilon$. It repeatedly runs VI (with V from the previous iteration) using decreasing value of η until the desired bound ϵ is reached. GAP underlines the distinct role of η, the margin of error for the fixed point, and ϵ the upper bound of the difference to the optimum.

Algorithm 6.6 A guaranteed approximation procedure for VI.

$\text{GAP}(V_0, \epsilon)$
 $V \leftarrow V_0$; initialize $\eta > 0$ arbitrarily
 loop
  run $\text{VI}(\Sigma, V)$
  compute $\Phi^\pi(s_0)$ for the found solution π
  if $\eta \times \Phi^\pi(s_0) \leq \epsilon$ then return
  else $\eta \leftarrow \min\{\epsilon/\Phi^\pi(s_0), \eta/2\}$

Example 6.18. Going back to the simple domain in Example 6.11, assume we want a solution no further than $\epsilon = .1$ from the optimum. Starting with $\eta = 5$, VI finds the solution π_a after 5 iterations. Equation 6.11 for solution π_a gives $\Phi^{\pi_a}(s_0) = 5$. VI is called again with the previous V and $\eta = .02$; it stops after 23 iterations with the same solution and $V(s_0) = 49.938$. This solution is within at most .1 of π^*. Note that $V(s_0)$ is also guaranteed to be within .1 of $V^{\pi_a}(s_0)$.   □

At termination of VI, $V^\pi(s_0)$ for the found solution π is unknown. It is bounded with: $V(s_0) \le V^\pi(s_0) \le V(s_0) + \eta \times \Phi^\pi(s_0)$. It is possible to compute V^π, as explained in Section 6.2.4, either by solving Equation 6.3 as a system of n linear equations, or by repeated updates as in Equation 6.8 until the residual is less than an accepted margin.

Finally, when the heuristic function is both admissible and monotone, then the number of iterations needed to reach termination is easily bounded. Indeed, when V_0 is monotone, then $V_0 \le (BV_0)$ by definition, hence the remark following Proposition 6.12 applies. $V(s)$ cannot decrease throughout Bellman updates, and it remains monotone. Each iteration of VI increases the value of $V(s)$ for some s by at least η, and does not decrease V for any state. This entails the following bound on the number of iterations:

Proposition 6.19. *The number of iterations needed by VI to reach the termination condition residual $\le \eta$ with an admissible and monotone heuristic is bounded by $1/\eta \sum_s [V^*(s) - V_0(s)]$.*

In summary, VI performs a bounded number of iterations, each of polynomial complexity in $|S|$. VI looks as a quite efficient and scalable planning algorithm. Unfortunately, the state space in planning is exponential in the size of the input data: $|S|$ in the order of m^k, where k is the number of ground state variables and m is the size of their range. Practical considerations are further discussed in Section 6.7.6.

Example 6.20. Consider a robot servicing an environment that has six locations $l_0, l_1, \ldots, l_5$, which are connected as defined by the undirected graph of Figure 6.5.

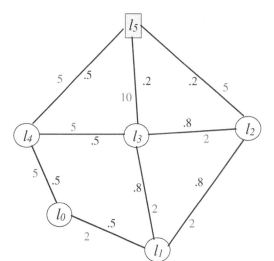

Figure 6.5. Connectivity graph of a simple environment.

Table 6.1. $V(l)$ after the first three and last three iterations of VI on the domain of Figure 6.5

iteration	l_0	l_1	l_2	l_3	l_4
1	2.00	2.00	2.00	3.60	5.00
2	4.00	4.00	5.28	5.92	7.50
3	6.00	7.00	7.79	8.78	8.75
10	19.52	21.86	21.16	19.76	9.99
11	19.75	22.18	21.93	19.88	10.00
12	19.87	22.34	22.29	19.94	10.00

Traversing an edge has a cost and a nondeterministic outcome: the tentative traversal of a temporarily busy road has no effect. For example, when in location l_0 the robot takes the action move(l_0, l_1); with a probability .5 the action brings the robot to l_1, but if the road is busy the robot remains in l_0; in both cases the action costs 2. Edges are labeled by their traversal cost and probability of success.

In a realistic application, the robot would know (e.g., from sensors in the environment) when an edge is busy and for how long. Let us assume that the robot knows about a busy edge only when trying to traverse it; a trial gives no information about the possible outcome of the next trial. Finding an optimal policy for traversing between two locations can be modeled as a simple SSP that has as many states as locations. A state for a location l has as many actions as outgoing edges from l; each action has two possible outcomes: reaching the adjacent edge or staying in l.

Let us run Value Iteration on this simple domain for going from l_0 to l_5. With $V_0 = 0$ and $\eta = .5$, VI terminates after 12 iterations (see Table 6.1 which gives $V(l)$ for the first three and last three iterations). It finds the following policy: $\pi(l_0) = $ move(l_0, l_4), $\pi(l_4) = $ move(l_4, l_5), $\pi(l_1) = $ move(l_0, l_4), $\pi(l_2) = $ move(l_0, l_4), $\pi(l_3) = $ move(l_0, l_4). π corresponds to the path $\langle l_0, l_4, l_5 \rangle$. Its cost is $V^\pi(l_0) = 20$, which is easily computed from $V^\pi(l_4) = 5/.5$ and $V^\pi(l_0) = (5 + .5 \times V^\pi(l_4))/.5$. Note that at termination $V(l_0) = 19.87 \neq V^\pi(l_0)$. The residual after iteration 12 is $22.29 - 21.93 = .36 < \eta$.

Let us change the cost of the edge (l_0, l_4) to 10. The cost of the previous policy is now 30; it is no longer optimal. VI terminates (with the same η) after 13 iterations with a policy corresponding to the path $\langle l_0, l_1, l_3, l_5 \rangle$; its cost is 26.5. □

VI versus PI. The reader has noticed the formal similarities between VI and PI: the two algorithms rely on repeated updates until reaching a fixed point. Their differences are worth being underlined:

- PI approaches V^* from *above*, while VI approaches the optimum from *below*. Hence the importance of starting with an admissible heuristic for the latter. PI does not require a heuristic but a safe initial π_0. However, heuristics, when available, can bring a significant efficiency gain.
- PI computes V^π for the current and final solution π, while VI relies on an approximate V of the value V^π of the greedy policy π.
- PI reaches exactly its fixed point while a margin of error has to be set for VI, allowing for the flexibility illustrated in procedure GAP.

Note, however, that when PI relies on the iterative method of Equation 6.8 for computing V^π, the two algorithms can be quite close.

Extensions of VI. Algorithm VI allows for several improvements and optimizations, such as ordering S according to a dynamic priority scheme or partitioning S into acyclic components. The latter point is motivated by the fact that VI can be made to converge with just one outer loop iteration on acyclic And/Or graphs.

A variant of VI, called *Backward Value Iteration*, focuses VI by performing updates in reverse order, starting from the set of goal states, and updating only along the current greedy policy (instead of a Bellman update over all applicable actions). A symmetrical variant, *Forward Value Iteration*, performs the outer loop iteration on subsets of S, starting from s_0 and its immediate successors, then their successors, and so on.

More generally, asynchronous VI does not need to update all states at each iteration. It can be specified as follows: pick up a state s and update it. As long as the pick up is fair, that is, no state is left indefinitely non updated, the algorithm converges to the optimum. This opens the way to an important extension of VI for domains that have safe solutions but also dead ends. For that, two main issues need to be tackled:

- do not require termination with a fixed point for *every* state in S because this is needed only for the safe states in $\widehat{\gamma}(s_0, \pi)$ and because there may not be a fixed point for unsafe states; and
- make sure that the values $V(s)$ for unsafe states keep growing strictly to drive the search toward safe policies.

These issues are developed next with heuristic search algorithms.

6.3 HEURISTIC SEARCH ALGORITHMS

Heuristic search algorithms exploit the guidance of an initial value function V_0 to focus an SSP planning problem on a small part of the search space. Before getting in the specifics of a few algorithms, let us explain their commonalities on the basis of the following search schema.

6.3.1 A General Heuristic Search Schema

The main idea of heuristic search algorithms is to explore a focused part of the search space and to perform Bellman updates within this focused part, instead of over the entire S. This explored part of the search space starts with $\{s_0\}$ and is incrementally expanded. Let the *Envelope* be the set of states that have been generated at some point by a search algorithm. The *Envelope* is partitioned into:

(i) goal states, for which $V(s) = 0$,
(ii) *fringe* states, whose successors are still unknown; for a fringe state $\pi(s)$ is not yet defined and $V(s) = V_0(s)$,
(iii) *interior* states, whose successors are already in the *Envelope*.

Expanding a fringe state s means finding its successors and defining $Q(s, a) = \text{cost}(s, a) + \sum_{s' \in \gamma(s,a)} \Pr(s'|s, a)V(s')$, $V(s) = \min_a\{Q(s, a)\}$, and the greedy policy for current V, which is $\pi(s) = \text{argmin}_a\{Q(s,a)\}$. Updating an interior state s means performing a Bellman update on s. When a descendant s' of s gets expanded or updated, $V(s')$ changes, which makes $V(s)$ no longer equal to $\text{min}_a\{Q(s,a)\}$ and requires updating s.

Let us define the useful notions of *open* and *solved* states with respect to η, a given margin of error.

Definition 6.21. A state $s \in Envelope$ is *open* when s is either a fringe or an interior state such that $residual(s) = |V(s) - \text{min}_a\{Q(s,a)\}| > \eta$. □

Definition 6.22. A state $s \in Envelope$ is *solved* when the current $\widehat{\gamma}(s,\pi)$ has no open state; in other words, s is solved when $\forall s' \in \widehat{\gamma}(s,\pi)$ either $s' \in S_g$ or $residual(s') \leq \eta$. □

Recall that $\widehat{\gamma}(s,\pi)$ includes s and the states in the *Envelope* reachable from s by current π. It defines $Graph(s,\pi)$, the *current solution graph* starting from s. Throughout Section 6.3, π is the greedy policy for current V; it changes after an update. Hence $\widehat{\gamma}(s,\pi)$ and $Graph(s,\pi)$ are defined dynamically.

Most heuristic search algorithms use the preceding notions and are based on different instantiations of a general schema called Find&Revise (Algorithm 6.7), which repeatedly performs a *Find* step followed by a *Revise* step.

Algorithm 6.7 Find&Revise schema. The specifics of the *Find* and the *Revise* steps depend on the particular algorithm instantiating this schema.

Find&Revise(Σ, s_0, S_g, V_0)
   until s_0 is solved do
      choose an *open* state s in $\widehat{\gamma}(s_0,\pi)$ *(i) Find*
      expand or update s *(ii) Revise*

The *Find* step is a traversal of the current $\widehat{\gamma}(s_0,\pi)$ for finding and choosing an open state s. This *Find* step has to be *systematic*: no state in $\widehat{\gamma}(s_0,\pi)$ should be left open forever without being chosen for revision.

The *Revise* step updates an interior state whose *residual* $> \eta$ or expands a fringe state. Revising a state can change current π and hence $\widehat{\gamma}(s_0,\pi)$. At any point, either a state s is open, or s has an open descendant (whose revision will later make s open), or s is solved. In the latter case, $\widehat{\gamma}(s,\pi)$ does not change anymore.

Find&Revise iterates until s_0 is solved, that is, there is no open state in $\widehat{\gamma}(s_0,\pi)$. With an admissible heuristic function, Find&Revise converges to a solution which is asymptotically optimal with respect to η. More precisely, if the SSP problem has no dead ends, and if V_0 is an admissible heuristic, then Find&Revise with a systematic *Find* step has the following properties, inherited from VI:

- the algorithm terminates with a safe solution,
- $V(s)$ remains admissible for all states in the *Envelope*,
- the returned solution is asymptotically optimal with respect to η; its difference with V^* is bounded by: $V^*(s_0) - V(s_0) \leq \eta \times \Phi^\pi(s_0)$, where Φ^π is given by Equation 6.11, and
- if V_0 is admissible and monotone then the number of iterations is bounded by $1/\eta \sum_s[V^*(s) - V_0(s)]$.

Dealing with dead ends. As discussed earlier, Dynamic Programing algorithms are limited to domains without dead ends, whereas heuristic search algorithms can overcome this limitation. First, only reachable dead ends can be of concern to an algorithm focused on the part of the state space reachable from s_0. Further, it is possible to show that all the preceding properties of Find&Revise still hold for domains with safe solutions that have reachable dead ends, implicit or explicit, as long as for every dead-end s, $V(s)$ grows indefinitely over successive updates. Let us explain why this is the case:

- Assume that V grows indefinitely for dead ends, then $\forall s$ unsafe and $\forall \pi$, $V^\pi(s)$ also grows indefinitely; this is entailed from Definition 6.7 because an unsafe state has at least a dead end descendant for any policy and because all costs are strictly positive.
- With a systematic *Find*, successive Bellman updates will make at some point: $V(s') < V(s'')$ for two sibling states where s' is safe and s'' unsafe. Consequently, if s is safe, the minimization $\min_a\{Q(s, a)\}$ will rule out unsafe policies.
- Finally, Find&Revise does not iterate over the entire state space but only over the current $\widehat{\gamma}(s_0, \pi)$. Because we are assuming s_0 to be safe, $\widehat{\gamma}(s_0, \pi)$ will contain at some point only safe states over which the convergence to a goal is granted.

Consider a domain with a safe solution that has implicit dead ends but no explicit dead end, that is, $\forall s$ Applicable$(s) \neq \varnothing$. There, a dead end is a state from which every action leads to an infinite loop never reaching a goal. In such a domain, Equation 6.1 ensures that $V(s)$ will grow indefinitely when s is a dead end. Indeed, $V(s)$ is the expected sum of strictly positive costs over sequences of successors of s that grow to infinite length without reaching a goal.

For a domain with explicit dead ends, such as Example 6.4, our previous definition makes V possibly undefined at unsafe states. We can extend the definition by adding a third clause in Equation 6.3, stating simply: $V(s) = \infty$ if Applicable$(s) = \varnothing$. Alternatively, we can keep all the definitions as introduced so far and extend the specification of a domain with a dummy action, $a_{deadend}$, applicable only in states that have no other applicable action; $a_{deadend}$ is such as $\gamma(s, a_{deadend}) = \{s\}$ and cost$(s, a_{deadend}) = $ constant> 0. This straightforward trick brings us back to the case of solely implicit dead ends: $V(s)$ grows unbounded when s is a dead end.

Note that these considerations about dead ends do not apply to algorithm VI, which iterates over the entire set S, hence cannot converge with unsafe states because there is no fixed point for implicit dead ends (reachable or not). Heuristic search algorithms implementing a Find&Revise schema can find a near-optimal partial policy by focusing on $\widehat{\gamma}(s_0, \pi)$, which contains only safe states when s_0 is safe.

Find&Revise opens a number of design choices for the instantiation of the *Find* and the *Revise* steps and for other practical implementation issues regarding the possible memorization of the envelope and other needed data structure. Find&Revise can be instantiated in different ways, for example:

- with a best-first search, as in algorithms AO*, LAO* and their extensions (Section 6.3.2);
- with a depth-first and iterative deepening search, as in HDP, LDFS, and their extensions (Sections 6.3.3 and 6.3.4); and
- with a stochastic simulation search, as in RTDP, LRTDP, and their extensions (Section 6.4.3).

These algorithms inherit the preceding properties Find&Revise. They have additional characteristics, adapted to different application features. In the remainder of this chapter, we present some of them, assuming to have SSP problems where s_0 is safe and V_0 is admissible.

6.3.2 Best-First Search

In deterministic planning, best-first search is illustrated with the A* algorithm for finding optimal paths in graphs. In SSPs, best-first search relies on a generalization of A* for finding optimal graphs in And/Or graphs. This generalization corresponds to two algorithms: AO* and LAO*. AO* is limited to acyclic And/Or graphs, while LAO* handles cyclic search spaces. Both algorithms iterate over two steps, which will be detailed shortly:

(i) traverse $\widehat{\gamma}(s_0, \pi)$, the current best solution graph, starting at s_0; find a fringe state $s \in \widehat{\gamma}(s_0, \pi)$; expand s; and

(ii) update the search space starting from s.

The main difference between the two algorithms is in step *(ii)*. When the search space is acyclic, AO* is able to update the search space in a bottom-up stage-by-stage process focused on the current best policy. When the search space and the solution graph can be cyclic, LAO* has to combine best first search with a Dynamic Programming update.

Algorithm 6.8 AO*, best-first search algorithm for acyclic domains. Replacing step *(ii)* by a call to LAO-Update(s) gives LAO*.

AO* (Σ, s_0, g, V_0)
  Envelope $\leftarrow \{s_0\}$
  while $\widehat{\gamma}(s_0, \pi)$ has fringe states do
    traverse $\widehat{\gamma}(s_0, \pi)$ and select a fringe state $s \in \widehat{\gamma}(s_0, \pi)$ *(i)*
    for all $a \in$ Applicable(s) and $s' \in \gamma(s, a)$ do
      if s' is not already in *Envelope* then do
        add s' to *Envelope*
        $V(s') \leftarrow V_0(s')$
    AO-Update(s)   *(ii)*

Starting at s_0, each iteration of AO* (Algorithm 6.8) extracts the current best solution graph by doing a forward traversal along current π. In each branch, the traversal stops when it reaches a goal or a fringe state. The selection of which fringe state to expand is arbitrary. This choice does not change the convergence properties of the algorithm but may affect its efficiency. The expansion of a state s changes generally $V(s)$. This requires updating s and all its ancestors in the envelope

AO-Update (Algorithm 6.9) implements this update in a bottom-up stage-by-stage procedure, from the current state s up to s_0. The set of states that need to be updated consists of all ancestors of s from which s is reachable along current π. Note that this set is not strictly included in current $\widehat{\gamma}(s_0, \pi)$. It is generated incrementally as the set Z of predecessors of s along current π. Bellman update is applied to each state in Z whose

---

Algorithm 6.9 Bottom-up update for AO*.

AO-Update(s)
  $Z \leftarrow \{s\}$
  while $Z \neq \varnothing$ do
    select $s \in Z$ such that $Z \cap \widehat{\gamma}(s, \pi) = \{s\}$
    remove s from Z
    Bellman-Update(s)
    $Z \leftarrow Z \cup \{s' \in Envelope \mid s \in \gamma(s', \pi(s'))\}$

---

descendants along current π are not in Z. Because the search space is acyclic, this implies that the update of a state takes into account all its known updated descendants, and has to be performed just once. The update of s redefines $\pi(s)$ and $V(s)$. The predecessors of s along π are added to Z.

A few additional steps are needed in this pseudocode for handling dead ends. The dummy action $a_{deadend}$, discussed earlier, introduces cycles; this is not what we want here. In the acyclic case, the only dead ends are explicit, that is, states not in S_g with no applicable action. This is directly detected when such a state is selected as a fringe for expansion; that state is labeled a dead end. In AO-Update, for a state s that has a dead-end successor in $\gamma(s, \pi(s))$, the action corresponding to $\pi(s)$ is removed from Applicable(s); if s has no other applicable action then s is in turn labeled a dead end, otherwise Bellman-Update(s) is performed, which redefines $\pi(s)$.

AO* on an acyclic search space terminates with a solution. When V_0 is admissible, $V(s)$ remains admissible; at termination the found solution π is optimal and $V(s_0)$ is its cost. We finally note that an efficient implementation of AO* may require a few incremental bookkeeping and simplifications. One consists in changing Z after the update of s only if $V(s)$ has changed. Another is to label solved states to avoid revisiting them. Because the space is acyclic, a state s is solved if it is either a goal or if all the successors of s in $\gamma(s, \pi(s))$ after an update are solved.

Example 6.23. Consider the domain in Figure 6.6, which has 17 states, s_0 to s_{16} and three actions a, b, and c. Connectors are labeled by the action name and cost; we assume uniform probability distributions. Let us take $V_0(s) = \min_a\{cost(s, a)\}$ and $S_g = \{s_{12}, s_{15}, s_{16}\}$.

AO* terminates after 10 iterations, which are summarized in Table 6.2. In the first iteration, $V(s_0) = \min\{5 + \frac{2+4}{2}, 19 + 15, 12 + \frac{5+9}{2}\} = 8$. In the second iteration, $V(s_1) = \min\{7.5, 24.5, 7\}$; the update changes $V(s_0)$, but not $\pi(s_0)$. Similarly after s_2 is expanded. When s_6 is expanded, the update changes $\pi(s_2)$, $\pi(s_1)$, and $\pi(s_0)$. The latter changes again successively after s_3, s_4, and s_9 are expanded $\pi(s_0) = c$. $\pi(s_2)$ changes after s_{11} then s_{13} are expanded. After the last iteration, the update $\pi(s_0) = \pi(s_1) = \pi(s_2) = \pi(s_5) = \pi(s_{11}) = a$ and $\pi(s_4) = b$; the corresponding solution graph has no fringe state; its cost is $V(s_0) = 26.25$.

Only 10 states in this domain are expanded: the interior states s_7, s_8, s_{10}, and s_{14} are not expanded. The algorithm performs in total 31 Bellman updates. In comparison,

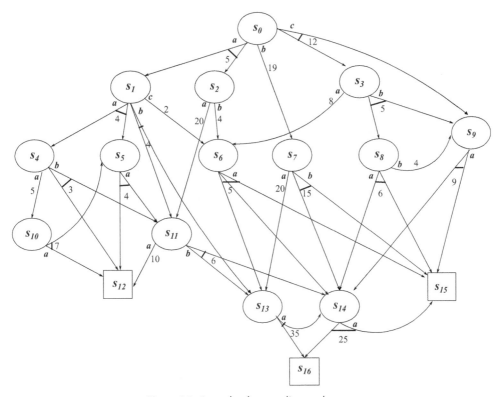

Figure 6.6. Example of an acyclic search space.

Value Iteration terminates after five iterations corresponding to 5×17 calls to Bellman-Update. With a more informed heuristic, the search would have been more focused (see Section 6.3.5 and Section 6.3.5). □

Let us now discuss best first search for a cyclic search space, for which updates cannot be based on a bottom-up stage-by-stage procedure. LAO* handle this general case. It corresponds to Algorithm 6.8 where step *(ii)* is replaced by a call to LAO-Update(s).

Table 6.2. Iterations of AO* on the domain of Figure 6.6: expanded state, sequence of updated states, value, and policy in s_0 after the update.

s	$V(s)$	$\pi(s)$	Updated states	$\pi(s_2)$	$\pi(s_1)$	$\pi(s_0)$	$V(s_0)$
s_0	8	a				a	8
s_1	7	c	s_0		c	a	10.5
s_2	9	b	s_0	b	c	a	13
s_6	25	a	s_2, s_1, s_0	a	a	c	19
s_3	11.5	b	s_0	a	a	a	21.75
s_4	6	b	s_1, s_0	a	a	c	22.25
s_9	21.5	a	s_3, s_0	a	a	a	22.5
s_5	7	a	s_1, s_0	a	a	a	23.5
s_{11}	10	a	s_4, s_5, s_2, s_1, s_0	b	a	a	25.75
s_{13}	47.5	a	s_6, s_2, s_1, s_0	a	a	a	26.25

Algorithm 6.10 A "VI-like" update for LAO*

LAO-Update(s)
  $Z \leftarrow \{s\} \cup \{s' \in Envelope \mid s \in \widehat{\gamma}(s', \pi)\}$
  iterate until *termination condition*
    $\forall s \in Z$ do
      Bellman-Update(s)

The latter (Algorithm 6.10) performs a VI-like series of repeated updates that are limited to the states on which the expansion of s may have an effect. This is the set Z of s and all its ancestors along current π. Again, Z is not limited to $\widehat{\gamma}(s_0, \pi)$.

LAO-Update is akin to an asyncronous VI focused by current π. However, an update may change current π, which may introduce new fringe states. Consequently, the *termination condition* of LAO-Update is the following: either an update introduces new fringe states in $\widehat{\gamma}(s_0, \pi)$ or the *residual* $\leq \eta$ over all updated states.

The preceding pseudo-code terminates with a solution but no guarantee of its optimality. However, if the heuristic V_0 is admissible, then the bounds of Proposition 6.17 apply. A procedure such as GAP (Algorithm 6.6) can be used to find a solution with a guaranteed approximation.

Explicit dead ends can be handled with the dummy action $a_{deadend}$ and the management of loops. If the current π is unsafe then the updates will necessarily change that current policy, as discussed in the previous section. When there is no dead end, it is possible to implement LAO-Update using a Policy Iteration procedure, but this was not found as efficient as the VI-like procedure presented here.

LAO* is an instance of the Find&Revise schema (see Exercise 6.10). On an SSP problem with a safe solution and an admissible heuristic V_0, LAO* is guaranteed to terminate and to return a safe and asymptotically optimal solution.

The main heuristic function for driving LAO* is V_0 (see Section 6.3.5). Several additional heuristics have been proposed for selecting a fringe state in current $\widehat{\gamma}(s_0, \pi)$ to be expanded. Examples include choosing the fringe state whose estimated probability of being reached from s_0 is the highest, or the one with the lowest $V(s)$. These secondary heuristics do not change the efficiency of LAO* significantly. A strategy of *delayed updates* and *multiple expansions* was found to be more effective. The idea here is to expand in each iteration several fringe states in $\widehat{\gamma}(s_0, \pi)$ before calling LAO-Update on the union of their predecessors in $\widehat{\gamma}(s_0, \pi)$. Indeed, an expansion is a much simpler step than an update by LAO-Update. It is beneficial to perform updates less frequently and on more expanded solution graphs.

A variant of LAO* (Algorithm 6.11) takes this idea to the extreme. It expands all fringe states and updates all states met in a post-order traversal of current $\widehat{\gamma}(s_0, \pi)$ (the traversal marks states already visited to avoid getting into a loop). It then calls VI on $\widehat{\gamma}(s_0, \pi)$ with the termination condition discussed earlier. The while loop is pursued unless VI terminates with *residual* $\leq \eta$. Again, a procedure like GAP is needed to provided a guaranteed approximation.

Like AO*, LAO* can be improved by labeling solved states. This is illustrated next with depth-first search.

Algorithm 6.11 ILAO*, a variant of LAO* best-first search algorithm for cyclic domains.

ILAO* (Σ, s_0, g, V_0)
  $Envelope \leftarrow \{s_0\}$
  while $\widehat{\gamma}(s_0, \pi)$ has fringe states do
    for each s visited in a depth-first post-order traversal of $\widehat{\gamma}(s_0, \pi)$ do
      unless s has already been visited in this traversal do
        if s is a fringe then expand s
        Bellman-Update(s)
    perform VI on $\widehat{\gamma}(s_0, \pi)$ until termination condition

---

6.3.3 Depth-First Search

A direct instance of the Find&Revise schema is given by the HDP algorithm (for Heuristic Dynamic Programming). HDP performs the *Find* step by a depth-first traversal of the current solution graph $\widehat{\gamma}(s_0, \pi)$ until finding an open state, which is then revised. Furthermore, HDP uses this depth-first traversal for finding and labeling solved states: if s is solved, the entire graph $\widehat{\gamma}(s, \pi)$ is solved and does not need to be searched anymore.

The identification of solved states relies on the notion of *strongly connected components* of a graph. HDP uses an adapted version of Tarjan's algorithm for detecting these components (see Appendix B and Algorithm B.1). The graph of interest here is $\widehat{\gamma}(s_0, \pi)$. Let C be a strongly connected component of this graph. Let us define a component C as being *solved* when every state $s \in C$ is solved.

Proposition 6.24. *A strongly connected component C of the current graph $\widehat{\gamma}(s_0, \pi)$ is solved if and only if C has no open state and every other component C' reachable from a state in C is solved.*

Proof. The proof follows from the fact that the strongly connected components of a graph define a partition of its vertices into a DAG (see Appendix B). If C meets the conditions of the proposition, then $\forall s \in C$ $\widehat{\gamma}(s, \pi)$ has no open state, hence s is solved. □

HDP (Algorithm 6.12) is indirectly recursive through a call to Solved-SCC, a slightly modified version of Tarjan's algorithm. HDP labels goal states and stops at any solved state. It updates an open state, or it calls Solved-SCC on a state s whose *residual* $\leq \eta$ to check whether this state and its descendant in the current solution graph are solved and to label them. Note that the disjunction produces a recursive call only when its first

---

Algorithm 6.12 A heuristic depth-first search algorithm for SSPs.

HDP(s)
  if $s \in S_g$ then label s solved
  if s is solved then return false
  else if ($residual(s) > \eta) \vee$ Solved-SCC(s, false) then do
    Bellman-Update(s)
    return true

Algorithm 6.13 Procedure for labeling strongly connected components.

Solved-SCC(s, *updated*)
  index(s) ←low(s) ← i
  $i \leftarrow i + 1$
  push(s,*stack*)
  for all $s' \in \gamma(s, \pi(s))$ do
    if index(s') is undefined than do
      updated ← HDP(s') ∨ *updated*   *(i)*
      low(s) ← min{low(s), low(s')}
    else if s' is in *stack* then low(s) ← min{low(s), low(s')}
  if ($\neg$ *updated*) ∧ (index(s)=low(s)) then do   *(ii)*
    repeat
      $s' \leftarrow$ pop(*stack*)
      label s' solved
    until $s' = s$
  return *updated*

---

clause is false. HDP and Solved-SCC returns a binary value that is true if and only if s or one of its descendants has been updated.

Procedure Solved-SCC (Algorithm 6.13) finds strongly connected components and labels them as solved if they meet the conditions of Proposition 6.24. It is very close to Tarjan's algorithm. It has a second argument that stands for a binary flag, true when s or one of its descendant has been updated. Its differences with the original algorithm are the following. In step *(i)* the recursion is through calls to HDP, while maintaining the *updated* flag. In step *(ii)*, the test for a strongly connected component is performed only if no update took place below s. When the conjunction holds, then s and all states below s in the depth-first traversal tree make a strongly connected component C and are not open. Further, all strongly connected components reachable from these states have already been labeled as solved. Hence, states in C are solved (see details in Appendix B).

Procedure HDP is repeatedly called on s_0 until it returns false, that is, until s_0 is solved. Appropriate reinitialization of the data structures needed by Tarjan algorithm ($i \leftarrow 0$, *stack* $\leftarrow \varnothing$ and index undefined for states in the *Envelope*) have to be performed before each call to HDP(s_0). Finally, for the sake of simplicity, this pseudocode does not differentiate a fringe state from other open states: expansion of fringe states (over all its successors for all applicable actions) is simply performed in HDP as an update step.

HDP inherits of the properties of Find&Revise: with an admissible heuristic V_0, it converges asymptotically with η to the optimal solution; when V_0 is also monotone, its complexity is bounded by $1/\eta \sum_s [V^*(s) - V_0(s)]$.

6.3.4 Iterative Deepening Search

While best first search for SSPs relied on a generalization of A* to And/Or graphs, iterative deepening search relies on an extension of the IDA* algorithm.

Algorithm 6.14 Algorithm LDFS$_a$.

LDFS$_a(s)$
  if $s \in S_g$ then label s solved
  if s is solved return true
  $updated \leftarrow$ true
  iterate over $a \in$ Applicable(s) and while $(updated)$ *(i)*
    if $|V(s) - [\text{cost}(s, a) + \sum_{s' \in \gamma(s,a)} \Pr(s'|s, a)V(s')]| \leq \eta$ then do   *(ii)*
      $updated \leftarrow$ false
      for each $s' \in \gamma(s, a)$ do   *(iii)*
        $updated \leftarrow$ LDFS$_a(s') \vee updated$
  if $updated$ then Bellman-Update(s)
  else do
    $\pi(s) \leftarrow a$
    label s solved
  return $updated$

IDA*(Iterative Deepening A*) proceeds by repeated depth-first, heuristically guided explorations of a deterministic search space. Each iteration goes deeper than the previous one and, possibly, improves the heuristic estimates. Iterations are pursued until finding an optimal path. The extension of IDA* to And/Or graphs is called LDFS; it also performs repeated depth-first traversals where each traversal defines a graph instead of a path.

We first present a simpler version of LDFS called LDFS$_a$ (Algorithm 6.14), which handles only acyclic SSPs. LDFS$_a$ does a recursive depth-first traversal of the current $\widehat{\gamma}(s_0, \pi)$. A traversal expands fringe states, updates open states, and labels as *solved* states that do not, and will not in the future, require updating. LDFS$_a(s_0)$ is called repeatedly until it returns s_0 as solved.

In an acyclic SSP, a state s is solved when either it is a goal or when its *residual*$(s) \leq \eta$ and all its successors in $\gamma(s, \pi)$ are solved. This is expressed in line *(ii)* for the current action a of iteration *(i)*.

Iteration *(i)* skips actions that do not meet the preceding inequality. It proceeds recursively on successor states for an action a that meets this inequality. If these recursions returns false for all the successors in $\gamma(s, a)$, then *updated*=false at the end of the inner loop *(iii)*; iteration *(i)* stops and s is labeled as solved. If no action in s meets inequality *(ii)* or if the recursion returns true on some descendant, then s is updated. This update is propagated back in the sequence of recursive calls through the returned value of *updated*. This leads to updating the predecessors of s, improving their values $V(s)$.

Due to the test on the *updated* flag, *(i)* does not run over all applicable actions; hence LDFS$_a$ performs *partial* expansions of fringe states. However, when a state is updated, all its applicable actions have been tried in *(i)*. Furthermore, the updates are also back-propagated partially, only within the current solution graph. Finally, states labeled as solved will not be explored in future traversals.

LDFS extends LDFS$_a$ to SSPs with cyclic safe solutions. This is done by handling cycles in a depth-first traversal, as seen in HDP. Cycles are tested along each depth-first traversal by checking that no state is visited twice. Recognizing solved states for cyclic solutions is performed by integrating to LDFS a book keeping mechanism similar to the Solved-SCC procedure presented in the previous section. This integration is, however, less direct than with HDP.

Let us outline how LDFS compares to HDP. A recursion in HDP proceeds along a *single* action, which is $\pi(s)$, the current best one. LDFS examines *all* $a \in$ Applicable(s) until it finds an action a that meets the condition *(ii)* of Algorithm 6.14, and such that there is no $s' \in \gamma(s, a)$, which is updated in a recursive call. At this point, *updated*=false: iteration *(i)* stops. If no such action exists, then *residual*$(s) > \eta$ and both procedures LDFS and HDP perform a normal Bellman-update. Partial empirical tests show that LDFS is generally, but not systematically, faster than HDP.

LDFS is an instance of the Find&Revise schema. It inherits its convergence and complexity properties, including the bound on the number of trials when used with an admissible and monotone heuristic.

6.3.5 Heuristics and Search Control

As for all search problems, heuristics play a critical role in scaling up probabilistic planning algorithms. Domain-specific heuristics and control knowledge draw from a priori information that is not explicit in the formal representation of the domain. For example, in a stochastic navigation problem where traversal properties of the map are uncertain (e.g., as in the Canadian Traveller Problem [457]), the usual Euclidian distance can provide a lower bound of the cost from a state to the goal. Domain-specific heuristics can be very informative, but it can be difficult to acquire them from domain experts, estimate their parameters, and prove their properties. Domain-independent heuristics do not require additional knowledge specification but are often less informative. A good strategy is to combine both, relying more and more on domain-specific heuristics when they can be acquired and tuned. Let us discuss here a few domain-independent heuristics and how to make use of a priori control knowledge.

Heuristics. A straightforward simplification of Equation 6.4 gives:

$$V_0(s) = \begin{cases} 0 & \text{if } s \in g \\ \min_a\{\text{cost}(s, a)\} & \text{otherwise} \end{cases}$$

V_0 is admissible and monotone. When |Applicable(s)| and $|\gamma(s, a)|$ are small, one may perform a Bellman update in s and use the following function V_1 instead of V_0:

$$V_1(s) = \begin{cases} 0 & \text{if } s \in g \\ \min_a\{\text{cost}(s, a) + \sum_{s' \in \gamma(s,a)} \Pr(s'|s, a)V_0(s')\} & \text{otherwise} \end{cases}$$

V_1 is admissible and monotone. So is the simpler variant heuristic

$$V_1'(s) = \min_a\{\text{cost}(s, a) + \min_{s' \in \gamma(s,a)} V_0(s')\}$$

for nongoal states, because $\min_{s' \in \gamma(s,a)} V_0(s') \leq \sum_{s' \in \gamma(s,a)} \Pr(s'|s, a)V_0(s')$.

More informed heuristics rely on a relaxation of the search space. A widely used relaxation is the so-called *determinization*, which transforms each probabilistic action into a few deterministic ones (as seen in Section 5.5).

We can map a nondeterministic domain $\Sigma = (S, A, \gamma)$ into a deterministic one $\Sigma_d = (S, A_d, \gamma_d)$ with the following property: $\forall s \in S, a \in A, s' \in \gamma(s, a), \exists a' \in A_d$ with $s' = \gamma_d(s, a')$ and $\text{cost}(s, a') = \text{cost}(s, a)$. In other words, Σ_d contains a deterministic action for each nondeterministic outcome of an action in Σ. This is the *all-outcomes* determinization, as opposed to the *most-probable outcomes* determinization. In the latter, A_d contains deterministic actions only for states $s' \in \gamma(s, a)$ such that $\Pr(s'|s, a)$ is above some threshold. For SSPs in factorized representation, it is straightforward to obtain Σ_d from Σ.

Let $h^*(s)$ be the cost of an optimal path from s to a goal in the all-outcomes determinization Σ_d, with $h^*(s) = \infty$ when s is a dead end, implicit or explicit. It is simple to prove that h^* is an admissible and monotone heuristic for Σ. But h^* can be computationally expensive, in particular for detecting implicit dead ends. Fortunately, heuristics for Σ_d are also useful for Σ.

Proposition 6.25. *Every admissible heuristic for Σ_d is admissible for Σ.*

Proof. Let $\sigma = \langle s, s_1, \ldots, s_g \rangle$ be an optimal path in Σ_d from s to a goal; its cost is $h^*(s)$. Clearly σ is also a possible sequence of state in Σ from s to a goal with a non null probability. No other such a history has a strictly lower cost than $h^*(s)$. Hence, $h^*(s)$ is a lower bound on $V^*(s)$, the expected optimal cost over all such histories. Let $h(s)$ be any admissible heuristics for Σ_d: $h(s) \leq h^*(s) \leq V^*(s)$. $\square$

Hence, the techniques discussed in Section 2.3 for defining admissible heuristics, such as $h^{\max}$, are applicable in probabilistic domains. Further, informative but nonadmissible heuristics in deterministic domains, such as h^{add}, have also been found informative in probabilistic domains when transposed from Σ_d to Σ.

Control knowledge in probabilistic planning. The idea here is to express a domain specific knowledge, which allows to focus the search in each state s on a subset of applicable actions in s. Let us denote this subset: $\text{Focus}(s, \mathcal{K}) \subseteq \text{Applicable}(s)$, where $\mathcal{K}$ is the control knowledge applicable in s. Convenient approaches allow to compute $\mathcal{K}$ incrementally, for example, with a function Progress such that $\mathcal{K}' \leftarrow \text{Progress}(s, a, \mathcal{K})$. In control formula methods, $\mathcal{K}$ is a set of control formula, $\text{Focus}(s, \mathcal{K})$ are the applicable actions that meet these formula, and Progress allows to compute the Focus for a successor of s and a. In HTN, $\mathcal{K}$ is the current task network, $\text{Focus}(s, \mathcal{K})$ are first primitive actions in totally ordered decompositions of $\mathcal{K}$, and $\text{Progress}(s, a, \mathcal{K})$ is the next step in the decomposition of $\mathcal{K}$. A forward search deterministic planning algorithm embeds one of these approaches to focus the possible choices of the next action, hence reducing its branching factor.

Two ingredients are needed to transpose these approaches to probabilistic planning: *(i)* a forward-search algorithm and *(ii)* a representation and techniques for computing $\text{Focus}(s, \mathcal{K})$ and $\text{Progress}(s, a, \mathcal{K})$ for nondeterministic actions. The latter can be obtained from Σ_d, the determinized version of a domain. Regarding the former, we already mentioned a Forward Value Iteration variant of VI; most instances of the Find&Revise schema, including best-first and depth-first, perform a forward search. These control methods can even be applied to online and anytime lookahead algorithms discussed in the next section. They can be very powerful in speeding up a search, but they evidently reduce its convergence (e.g., to safe and optimal solution) with respect to the actions that remain in the Focus subset.

6.4 ONLINE PROBABILISTIC APPROACHES

In probabilistic domains, as in many other cases, the methodology of finding a complete plan then acting according to that plan is often not feasible nor desirable. It is not feasible for complexity reasons in large domains, that is, a few dozens ground state variables. Even with good heuristics, algorithms seen in Section 6.3 cannot always address large domains, unless the designer is able to carefully engineer and decompose the domain. Even memorizing a safe policy as a table lookup in a large domain is by itself challenging to current techniques (that is, decision diagrams and symbolic representations). However, a large policy contains necessarily many states that have a very low a priori probability of being reached, for example, lower than the probability of unexpected events not modeled in Σ. These highly improbable states may not justify being searched, unless they are highly critical. They can be further explored if they are reached or become likely to be reached while acting.

Furthermore, even when heuristic planning techniques do scale up, acting is usually time constrained. A trade-off between the quality of a solution and its computing time is often desirable, for example, there is no need to improve the quality of an approximate solution if the cost of finding this improvement exceeds its benefits. Such a trade-off can be achieved with an online anytime algorithm that computes a rough solution quickly and improves it when given more time.

Finally, the domain model is seldom precise and complete enough to allow for reliable long-term plans. Shorter lookaheads with progressive reassessments of the context are often more robust. This is often implemented in a receding horizon scheme, which consists in planning for h steps toward the goal, performing one or a few actions according to the found plan, then replanning further.

This section presents a few techniques that perform online lookaheads and permit to interleave planning and acting in probabilistic domains. These techniques are based on a general schema, discussed next.

6.4.1 Lookahead Methods

Lookahead methods allow an actor to progressively elaborate its deliberation while acting, using a procedure such as Run-Lookahead, Algorithm 6.15. Instead of using an a priori defined policy, this procedure calls a bounded lookahead planning step. Procedure Lookahead searches for a partial plan rooted at s. It computes partially π, at least in s, and returns the corresponding action. A context-dependent vector of parameters θ gives bounds for the lookahead search. For example, θ may specify the depth

---

Algorithm 6.15 Acting with the guidance of lookahead search.

Run-Lookahead(Σ, s_0, S_g)

    $s \leftarrow s_0$
    while $s \notin S_g$ and Applicable$(s) \neq \varnothing$ do
      $a \leftarrow$ Lookahead(s, θ)
      if $a =$ failure then return failure
      else do
        perform action a
        $s \leftarrow$ observe resulting state

---

of the lookahead, its maximum processing time, or a real-time interruption mechanism corresponding to an acting deadline. The simple pseudo-code below can be extended when Lookahead fails by retrying with another θ.

Generative model. The comparison of Run-Lookahead with Run-Policy (Algorithm 6.1) shows that their sole difference is in the substitution of $\pi(s)$ in the latter by a call to Lookahead in the former. Both require in general further refinement to apply an action (see Section 6.5). Working with a progressively generated policy, defined when and where it is needed, makes it possible to address the concerns mentioned earlier of interleaving planning and acting, while dealing with complexity and partial domain knowledge.

Further, a full definition of $\gamma(s, a)$ for all $a \in$ Applicable(s) is not necessary to a partial exploration. Several partial exploration techniques rely on *sampling* methods. They search only one or a few random outcomes in $\gamma(s, a)$ over a few actions in Applicable(s).

Definition 6.26. A *generative sampling model* of a domain $\Sigma = (S, A, \gamma, \Pr, \text{cost})$ is a stochastic function, denoted Sample: $S \times A \rightarrow S$, where Sample(s, a) is a state s' randomly drawn in $\gamma(s, a)$ according to the distribution $\Pr(s'|s, a)$. □

In addition to s', Sample may also return the cost of the transition from s to s'. A planning algorithm interfaced with such a Sample function does not need a priori estimates of the probability and cost distributions of a domain Σ. A domain simulator is generally the way to implement the function Sample.

Approaches and properties of Lookahead. One possible option is to memorize the search space explored progressively: each call to Lookahead relies on knowledge acquired from previous calls; its outcome augments this knowledge. As an alternative to this *memory-based* approach, a *memoryless* strategy would start with a fresh look at the domain in each call to Lookahead. The choice between the two options depends on how stationary the domain is, how often an actor may reuse its past knowledge, how easy it is to maintain this knowledge, and how this can help improve the behavior.

The advantages of partial lookahead come naturally with a drawback, which is the lack of a guarantee on the optimality and safety of the solution. Indeed, it is not possible in general to choose $\pi(s)$ with a bounded lookahead while being sure that it is optimal, and, if the domain has dead ends, that there is no dead-end descendant in $\widehat{\gamma}(s, \pi)$.

Finding whether a state s is unsafe may require in the worst case a full exploration of the search space starting at s. In the bounded lookahead approach, optimality and safety are replaced by a requirement of bounds on the distance to the optimum and on the probability of reaching the goal. In the memory-based approaches, one may also seek asymptotic convergence to safe and/or optimal solutions.

Three approaches to the design of a Lookahead procedure are presented next:

- domain determinization and replanning with deterministic search,
- stochastic simulation, and
- sparse sampling and Monte Carlo planning techniques.

The last two approaches are interfaced with a generative sampling model of Σ using a Sample function: they do not need a priori specification of probability and cost distributions. The third one is also memoryless; it is typically used in a receding horizon scheme. However, many algorithms implementing these approaches can be used for offline planning as well as in the online interleaved planning and acting framework presented here: their control parameters allow for a continuum from the computation of a greedy policy computed at each state to a full exploration and definition of $\pi(s_0)$.

6.4.2 Lookahead with Deterministic Search

In Section 5.6.2, we introduced FS-Replan, a lookahead algorithm using repeated deterministic planning. The approach simply generates a path π_d from the current state to a goal for the all-outcomes determinized domain using some deterministic planner, then it acts using π_d until reaching a state s that is not in the domain of π_d. At that point FF-Replan generates a new deterministic plan starting at s.

This approach can also be applied to probabilistic domains. Note, however, that FS-Replan does not cope adequately with dead ends: even if the deterministic planner is complete and finds a path to the goal when there is one, executing that path may lead along a nondeterministic branch to an unsafe state.

RFF (Algorithm 6.16) relies, as FS-Replan does, on a deterministic planner, called Det-Plan, to find in Σ_d an acyclic path from a state to a goal. Procedure Det-Plan returns such a path as a policy. RFF improves over FS-Replan by memorizing previously generated deterministic paths and extending them for states that have a high reachability probability. RFF can be used as an offline planner as well as an online Lookahead procedure, possibly with additional control parameters.

RRF initializes the policy π with the pairs (state, action) corresponding to a deterministic plan from s_0 to a goal, then it extends π. It looks for a fringe state along a nondeterministic branch of that policy, that is, a state s reachable from s_0 with current π

Algorithm 6.16 A determinization planning algorithm.

$\text{RFF}(\Sigma, s_0, S_g, \theta)$
  $\pi \leftarrow \text{Det-Plan}(\Sigma_d, s_0, S_g)$
  while $\exists s \in \widehat{\gamma}(s_0, \pi)$ such that
      $s \notin S_g \wedge \pi(s)$ is undefined $\wedge \Pr(s|s_0, \pi) \geq \theta$ then do
      $\pi \leftarrow \pi \cup \text{Det-Plan}(\Sigma_d, s, S_g \cup \text{Targets}(\pi, s))$

---

that is not a goal and for which π is undefined. If the probability of reaching s is above some threshold θ, RFF extends π with another deterministic path from s to a goal or to another state already in the domain of π. The set of additional goals given to Det-Plan, denoted Targets(π, s), can be the already computed Dom(π) or any subset of it. If the entire Dom(π) is too large, the overhead of using it in Det-Plan can be larger than the benefit of reusing paths already planned in π. A trade-off reduces Targets(π, s) to k states already in the domain of π. These can be taken randomly in Dom(π) or chosen according to some easily computed criterion.

Computing Pr$(s|s_0, \pi)$ can be time-consuming (a search and a sum over all paths from s_0 to s with π). This probability can be estimated by sampling. A number of paths starting at s_0 following π are sampled; this allows the estimation of the frequency of reaching nongoal states that are not in the domain of π. RFF terminates when this frequency is lower than θ.

Algorithm 6.16 requires (as FS-Replan does) a domain without reachable dead ends. However, RFF can be extended to domains with avoidable dead ends, that is, where s_0 is safe. This is achieved by introducing a backtrack point in a state s which is either an explicit deadend or for which Det-Plan fails. That state is marked as unsafe; a new search starting from its predecessor s' is attempted to change $\pi(s')$ and avoid the previously failed action.

RFF algorithm does not attempt to find an optimal or near optimal solution. However, the offline version of RFF finds a *probabilistically safe* solution, in the sense that the probability of reaching a state not in the domain of π, either safe or unsafe, is upper bounded by θ.

6.4.3 Stochastic Simulation Techniques

The techniques in this section use a generative sampling model of the domain Σ through a function Sample. The idea is to run simulated walks from s_0 to a goal along best current actions by sampling one outcome for each action. Algorithms implementing this idea are inspired from LRTA* [350]. They can be implemented as offline planners as well as online Lookahead procedures.

One such algorithm, called RTDP, runs a series of simulated trials starting at s_0. A trial performs a Bellman update on the current state, then it proceeds to a randomly selected successor state along the current action $\pi(s)$, that is, from s to some random $s' \in \gamma(s, \pi(s))$. A trial finishes when reaching a goal. The series of trials is pursued until either the residual condition is met, which reveals near convergence, as in Find&Revise, or the amount of time for planning is over. At that point, the best action in s_0 is returned. With these assumptions RTDP is an anytime algorithm.

If a goal is reachable from *every* state in the search space and if the heuristic V_0 is admissible then every trial reaches a goal in a finite number of steps and improves the values of the visited states over the previous values. Hence, RTDP converges asymptotically to V^* but not in a bounded number of trials. Note that these assumptions are stronger than the existence of a safe policy.

Algorithm 6.17, LRTDP (for *Labeled RTDP*), improves over RTDP by explicitly checking and labeling solved states. LRTDP avoids visiting solved states twice. It calls LTRDP-Trial(s_0) repeatedly until planning time is over or s_0 is solved. A trial is a

---

Algorithm 6.17 Algorithm LRTDP.

LRTDP(Σ, s_0, g, V_0)
   until s_0 is solved or planning time is over do
      LRTDP-Trial(s_0)

LRTDP-Trial(s)
   visited ← empty stack
   while s is unsolved do
      push($s, visited$)
      Bellman-Update(s)
      $s ←$ Sample($s, \pi(s)$)
   $s ←$pop(*visited*)
   while Check-Solved(s) is true and *visited* is not empty do
      $s ←$pop(*visited*)

---

simulated walk along current best actions, which stops when reaching a solved state. A state s visited along a trial is pushed in a stack *visited*; when needed, it is expanded and Bellman updated. The trial is pursued on a randomly generated successor of s: the procedure Sample(s, a) returns a state in $\gamma(s, \pi(s))$ randomly drawn according to the distribution $\Pr(s'|s, \pi(s))$.

The states visited along a trial are checked in LIFO order using the procedure Check-Solved (Algorithm 6.18) to label them as solved or to update them. Check-Solved(s) searches through $\hat{\gamma}(s, \pi)$ looking for a state whose residual is greater than

---

Algorithm 6.18 Procedure to check and label solve states for LRTDP.

Check-Solved(s)
   flag ← true
   open ← *closed* ← empty stack
   if s is unsolved then push($s, open$)
   while *open* is not empty do
      $s ←$ pop(*open*)
      push($s, closed$)
      if $|V(s) - Q(s, \pi(s))| > \eta$ then *flag* ← false
      else for all $s' \in \gamma(s, \pi(s))$ do
         if s' is unsolved and $s' \notin open \cup closed$
            then push($s', open$)
   if *flag*= true then do
      for all $s' \in closed$ label s' as solved   (i)
   else do
      while *closed* is not empty do
         $s ←$ pop(*closed*)
         Bellman-Update(s)
   return *flag*

---

the error margin η. If it does not find such a state ($flag = $ true), then there is no open state in $\widehat{\gamma}(s, \pi)$. In that case, it labels as solved s and its descendants in $\widehat{\gamma}(s, \pi)$ (kept in the *closed* list). Otherwise, there are open states in $\widehat{\gamma}(s, \pi)$. The procedure does not explore further down the successors of an open state (the residual of which is larger than η), but it continues on its siblings.

When all the descendants of s whose residual is less or equal to η have been examined (in that case $open = \varnothing$), the procedure tests the resulting $flag$. If s is not yet solved (i.e., $flag = $ false), a Bellman update is performed on all states collected in *closed*. Cycles in the *Envelope* are taken care of (with the test $s' \notin open \cup closed$): the search is not pursued down on successor states that have already been met. The complexity of Check-Solved(s) is linear in the size of the *Envelope*, which may be exponential in the size of the problem description.

Note that by definition, goal states are solved; hence the test "s is unsolved" in the two preceding procedures checks the explicit labeling performed by Check-Solved (*labeling step*) as well as the goal condition.

If a goal is reachable from every state and V_0 is admissible, then LRTDP-Trial always terminates in a finite number of steps. Furthermore, if the heuristic V_0 is admissible and monotone, then the successive values of V with Bellmann updates are nondecreasing. Under these assumptions, each call to Check-Solved(s) either labels s as solved or increases the value of some of its successors by at least η while decreasing the value of none. This leads to the same complexity bound as VI:

Proposition 6.27. *LRTDP with an admissible and monotone heuristic on a problem where a goal is reachable from every state converges in a number of trials bounded by* $1/\eta \sum_s [V^*(s) - V_0(s)]$

This bound is mainly of theoretical interest. Of more practical value is the anytime property of LRTDP: the algorithm produces a good solution that it can improve if given more time or in successive calls in Run-Lookahead. Because Sample returns states according to their probability distribution, the algorithm converges on (i.e., solves) frequent states faster than on less probable ones. As an offline planner (i.e., repeated trials until s_0 is solved), its practical performances are comparable to those of the other heuristic algorithms presented earlier.

6.4.4 Sparse Sampling and Monte Carlo Search

This section also relies on a generative sampling model of the domain Σ through a function Sample. The stochastic simulation approach of the previous section can be extended and used in many ways, in particular with the bounded walks and sampling strategies discussed here.

Let π_0 be an arbitrary policy that is used at initialization, for example, $\pi_0(s)$ is the greedy policy, locally computed when needed, $\pi_0(s) = \text{argmin}_a Q^{V_0}(s, a)$ for some heuristic V_0. If the actor has no time for planning, then $\pi_0(s)$ is the default action. If it can afford some lookahead, then an easy way of improving π_0 in s is the following.

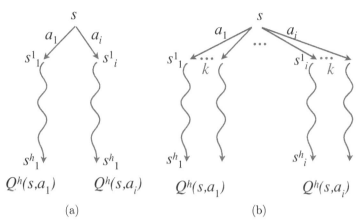

Figure 6.7. (a) Single Monte Carlo rollout; (b) Multiple rollout.

Monte Carlo Rollout. Let us use the Sample procedure to simulate a bounded walk of h steps whose first step is an action a and the remaining $h-1$ steps follow the initial policy π_0. Let $\sigma_{\pi_0}^h(s, a) = \langle s, s_1, s_2, \ldots, s_h \rangle$ be the sequence of states visited during this walk, with $s_1 \in \gamma(s, a)$ and $s_{i+1} \in \gamma(s_i, \pi_0(s_i))$. This history $\sigma_{\pi_0}^h(s, a)$ is called a *rollout* for a in s with π_0. The sum of the costs of this rollout is:

$$Q_{\pi_0}^h(s, a) = \text{cost}(s, a) + V_0(s_h) + \sum_{i=1}^{h-1} \text{cost}(s_i, \pi_0(s_i)), \text{ over } s_i \text{ in } \sigma_{\pi_0}^h(s, a).$$

Let us perform a rollout for every action applicable in s, as depicted in Figure 6.7(a), and let us define a new policy:

$$\pi(s) = \text{argmin}_a Q_{\pi_0}^h(s, a).$$

The simple argument used for Proposition 6.9 applies here: policy π dominates the base policy π_0.

The *multiple rollout* approach performs k similar simulated walks of h steps for each action a applicable in s (see Figure 6.7(b)). It then averages their costs to assess $Q_{\pi_0}^h(s, a)$. This approach is *probabilistically approximately correct*, that is, it provides a probabilistically safe solution (not guaranteed to be safe) whose distance to the optimum is bounded. It requires a number of calls to Sample equal to $|\text{Applicable}(s)| \times k \times h$.

Sparse Sampling. The sparse sampling technique performs bounded multiple rollouts in s and in each of its descendants reached by these rollouts. It is illustrated by the procedure SLATE (Algorithm 6.19).

SLATE builds recursively a tree in which nodes are states; arcs correspond to transitions to successor states, which are randomly sampled. Two parameters h and k bound the tree, respectively in depth and sampling width (see Figure 6.8). At depth h, a leaf of the tree gets as a value a heuristic estimate given by V_0. In an interior state s and for each action a applicable in s, k successors are randomly sampled. The average of their estimated values is used to compute recursively the cost-to-go $Q(a, s)$. The minimum over all actions in Applicable(s) gives $\pi(s)$ and $V(s)$, as in Bellman-Update.

Algorithm 6.19 Sampling lookahead Tree to Estimate.

SLATE(s, h, k)
  if $h = 0$ then return $V_0(s)$
  if $s \in S_g$ then return 0
  for each $a \in$ Applicable(s) do
    samples $\leftarrow \varnothing$
    repeat k times
      samples $\leftarrow$ *samples* $\cup$ Sample(Σ, s, a)
    $Q(s, a) \leftarrow$ cost$(s, a) + \frac{1}{k} \sum_{s' \in samples}$ SLATE$(s', h - 1, k)$
  $\pi(s) \leftarrow \text{argmin}_a\{Q(s, a)\}$
  return $Q(s, \pi(s))$

Assuming that a goal is reachable from every state, SLATE has the following properties:

- It defines a near-optimal policy: the difference $|V(s) - V^*(s)|$ can be bounded as a function of h and k.
- It runs in a worst-case complexity independent of $|S|$, in $O((\alpha k)^h)$, where $\alpha = \max |\text{Applicable}(s)|$.
- As a Monte Carlo rollout, it does not require probability distribution parameters: calls to Sample(Σ, s, a) return states in $\gamma(s, a)$ distributed according the $\Pr(s'|s, a)$, which allows to estimate $Q(s, a)$.

Note the differences between SLATE and the multiple rollouts approach: the latter is polynomial in h, but its approximation is probabilistic. SLATE provides a guaranteed approximation, but it is exponential in h. More precisely, SLATE returns a solution whose distance to the optimal policy is upper bounded $|V(s) - V^*(s)| < \epsilon$; it runs in $O(\epsilon^{log\epsilon})$.

A few improvements can be brought to this procedure. One may reduce the sampling rate with the depth of the state: the deeper is a state, the less influence it has on the cost-to-go of the root. Further, *samples* can implemented as a set with counters on its elements such as to perform a single recursive call on a successor s' of s that is sampled more than once. Note that the sampling width k can be chosen independently of $|\gamma(s, a)|$. However, when $k > |\gamma(s, a)|$, further simplifications can be introduced, in

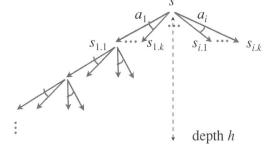

Figure 6.8. Sparse sampling tree of procedure SLATE.

particular for deterministic actions. Finally, it is easy to refine SLATE into an anytime algorithm: an iterative deepening scheme with caching increases the horizon h until acting time (see Exercise 6.16).

UCT and Monte Carlo Tree Search. SLATE has an important limitation: it has no sampling strategy. All actions in Applicable(s) are looped through and explored in the same way. A sampling strategy would allow to further explore a promising action and would prune out rapidly inferior options, but no action should be left untried. A sampling strategy seeks a trade-off between the number of times an action a has been sampled in s and the value $Q(s, a)$. This trade-off is used to guarantee with high probability an approximate solution while minimizing the search.

UCT, Algorithm 6.20, is a Monte Carlo Tree Search technique that builds up such a sampling strategy. Like SLATE, UCT expands, to a bounded depth, a tree rooted at the current node. However, it develops this tree in a nonuniform way. At an interior node of the tree in a state s, it selects a *trial* action $\tilde{a}$ with the strategy described subsequently. It samples a successor s' of s along $\tilde{a}$. It estimates the value of s', and it uses this estimate to update $Q(s, \tilde{a})$; it also updates the predecessors of s up to the root node, by averaging over all previously sampled successors in $\gamma(s, \tilde{a})$, as is done in SLATE. The estimate of s' is done by a recursive call to UCT on s' with the cumulative cost of the rollout below s'.

UCT is called repeatedly on a current state s until planning time terminates. When this happens, the solution policy in s is given, as in other algorithms, by $\pi(s) = \text{argmin}_a Q(s, a)$. This process is repeated on the state observed after performing the action $\pi(s)$. UCT can be stopped anytime.

Algorithm 6.20 A recursive UCT procedure.

UCT(s, h)
  if $s \in S_g$ then return 0
  if $h = 0$ then return $V_0(s)$
  if $s \notin Envelope$ then do
    add s to *Envelope*
    $n(s) \leftarrow 0$
    for all $a \in$ Applicable(s) do
      $Q(s, a) \leftarrow 0; n(s, a) \leftarrow 0$
  Untried $\leftarrow \{a \in$ Applicable(s) $\mid n(s, a) = 0\}$
  if *Untried* $\neq \varnothing$ then $\tilde{a} \leftarrow$ Choose(*Untried*)
  else $\tilde{a} \leftarrow \text{argmin}_{a \in \text{Applicable}(s)} \{Q(s, a) - C \times [\log(n(s))/n(s, a)]^{\frac{1}{2}}\}$
  $s' \leftarrow$ Sample($\Sigma, s, \tilde{a}$)
  cost-rollout $\leftarrow$ cost($s, \tilde{a}$) + UCT($s', h - 1$)
  $Q(s, \tilde{a}) \leftarrow [n(s, \tilde{a}) \times Q(s, \tilde{a}) + \textit{cost-rollout}]/(1 + n(s, \tilde{a}))$
  $n(s) \leftarrow n(s) + 1$
  $n(s, \tilde{a}) \leftarrow n(s, \tilde{a}) + 1$
  return *cost-rollout*

The strategy for selecting trial actions is a trade-off between actions that need further exploration and actions that appear as promising. A trial action $\tilde{a}$ in a state s is selected as follows:

- If there is an action that has not been tried in s, then Choose(*Untried*) chooses $\tilde{a}$ as any such action,
- If all actions have been tried in s, then the trial action is given by
  $\tilde{a} \leftarrow \text{argmin}_a\{Q(s, a) - C \times [\log(n(s))/n(s, a)]^{1/2}\}$, where $n(s, a)$ is the number of time a has been sampled in s, $n(s)$ is the total number of samples in that state, and $C > 0$ is a constant.

The constant C fixes the relative weight of *exploration* of less sampled actions (when C is high) to *exploitation* of promising actions (C low). Its empirical tuning significantly affects the performance of UCT.

It was shown that the preceding selection strategy minimizes the number of times a suboptimal action is sampled. UCT can also be proved to converge asymptotically to the optimal solution.

All approaches described in this Section 6.4.4 can be implemented as memoryless procedures (in the sense discussed in Section 6.4.1). They are typically used in a receding horizon Run-Lookahead schema. This simplifies the implementation of the planner, in particular when the lookahead bounds are not uniform and have to be adapted to the context. This has another important advantage that we have not discussed up to now: the capability to generate nonstationary policies, possibly stochastic. Indeed, an actor may find it desirable to apply a different action on its second visit to s than on its first. For finite horizon problems in particular, nonstationary policies can be shown to outperform stationary ones.

6.5 ACTING WITH PROBABILISTIC MODELS

The considerations discussed earlier (Sections 3.4, 4.5 and 5.7) apply also to probabilistic domains. In some applications, it is possible to act deliberately using procedures Run-Policy or Run-Lookahead by relying on a synthesized policy generated offline or with the online techniques we just saw. However, in most cases, the step "perform action a" in these procedures is not a primitive command; it requires further context dependent deliberation and refinement. In other applications, there is no planning per se (the plan is given, or planning impossible); all the deliberation is at the acting level, possibly with probabilistic models.

6.5.1 Using Deterministic Methods to Refine Policy Steps

Here we assume that the actor has a policy (a priori defined, or synthesized offline or online) and that the actor's refinement models are deterministic at the acting level. This makes sense when planning has to consider various probabilistic contingencies and events, but acting in each given context is based on the specifics of that context, as observed at acting time, and on deterministic models.

Acting in this case can rely on the techniques developed in Chapter 3. Deterministic refinement methods can be expressed, as seen earlier, and used by an engine such as RAE to refine each action $\pi(s)$ into the commands appropriate for the current context. The lookahead for the choice of refinement methods is also deterministic and based on a procedure such as SeRPE.

A few extensions to deterministic methods for acting can be desirable when combined with probabilistic models for planning. Among these, in particular, are the following:

- Acting according to the equivalent of a stochastic policy when needed. For example, when a refined action $\pi(s)$ is performed and leads back to the state s, this action may be performed again with a different refinement. It may even make sense to switch in s to some action other than $\pi(s)$.
- Specifying in methods ways to monitor the transition from s to a state in $\gamma(s, \pi(s))$: because γ is not deterministic, it may not be obvious to decide when current action $\pi(s)$ has terminated and which state in $\gamma(s, \pi(s))$ is its outcome.

Note, however, that the preceding features in deterministic refinement methods can be desirable for acting even when planning does not use probabilistic models.

6.5.2 Acting with Probabilistic Methods

Here we consider the more interesting case in which acting relies on probabilistic models. As underlined earlier, sensing-actuation loops and retrials are common at the acting level (see Example 3.4). The refinement methods introduced earlier embed mechanisms for expressing rich control structures to adapt acting to the diversity of the environment. Probabilistic models can be even more convenient for addressing this need, in particular when coupled with learning techniques to acquire the models.

It is natural to combine refinement methods with probabilistic models. We defined a refinement method as a triple $m = (role, precondition, body)$. Here, we specify the body of a method as an SSP problem for a probabilistic model $\Sigma = (S, A, \gamma, \Pr, cost)$, where A is the set of commands for that specific methods and S is the acting state space. Refining an action with a probabilistic method m reduces to two problems:

(i) finding a policy π rooted at the current acting state ξ and
(ii) running π with procedures Run-Policy or Run-Lookahead.

Clearly *(i)* is a planning problem to which the techniques seen earlier in this chapter are applicable. Here, S is the acting space, and A is the command space. For problem *(ii)*, the step "perform action $\pi(s)$" in Run-Policy or Run-Lookahead is replaced by "trigger command $\pi(s)$," which is directly executable by the execution platform.

If the probability and cost distributions can be acquired offline and are stable, and if the computational time remains compatible with acting constraints, planning algorithms of Section 6.3 can be used to compute an optimal or near optimal policy. However, these conditions will not often be met. The online lookahead techniques of Section 6.4 are usually more adapted to acting with probabilistic models. This is particularly the case when a generative sampling model can be designed. Sampling techniques of the previous section, when combined with informed heuristics V_0, are able to drive efficiently lookahead techniques. A Sample stochastic function basically allows one to run, to a controlled depth, several simulations for choosing the next best command to pursue the refinement of an action.

Example 6.28. Consider Example 3.4 of opening a door. We can specify the corresponding action with a single refinement method, the model of which is partly pictured in Figure 6.9. For the sake of simplicity, the acting states are simply labeled instead of a full definition of their state variables, as described in Example 3.4. For example, s_2 correspond to the case in which a door is closed; in s_3 it is cracked; locked and blocked are two failure cases, while open is the goal state. Furthermore, the figure does not give all applicable actions in a state, for example, there are several grasps in s_2 and s_3 (left or right hand, on "T" shaped or spherical handle) and several turns in s_4. Parameter values are also not shown.   □

Recall that an acting engine not only has to refine actions into commands but also to react to events. Probabilistic models and techniques are also relevant when the role of a method is an event instead of a task. Probabilistic methods can be convenient for specifying reactions to unexpected events.

A natural extension of sampling techniques to guide a refinement acting engine is in reinforcement learning approaches (see Section 7.3). These have been found more useful and feasible at the low level of acting in focused situations then at the level of learning abstract complex tasks. They can be adapted for learning acting refinement methods.

6.6 REPRESENTATIONS OF PROBABILISTIC MODELS

The modeling stage of a domain is always critical, in particular with probabilistic models. It requires good representations. The extreme case is a "flat" representation of an SSP using a single state variable s, whose range is S. Such a representation requires the explicit definition of the entire state space, a requirement that is rarely feasible. Structured representations are exponentially more compact. They allow for the implicit definition of the ingredients of a domain through a collection of objects, parametrized state

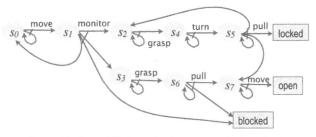

Figure 6.9. Probabilistic model for an open-door method.

variables, and operators, together with a dense specification of probability and cost distributions, policies, and value function.

6.6.1 Probabilistic Precondition-Effect Operators

Probabilistic precondition-effect operators are a direct extension of deterministic precondition-effect operators where the set $\gamma(s, a)$ and the distribution $\Pr(s'|s, a)$ are explicitly given as possible effects of planning operators, the instances of which are ground actions. Let us illustrate this representation through a few instances of a domain with increasingly more elaborate examples.

Example 6.29. Consider a simple service robot domain, called PAM_p, with one robot rbt and four locations {pier1, pier2, exit1, exit2}. At each location, there are containers of different types. The robot can move between locations; it can take a container from a location and put it in a location. The motion is deterministic, and the four locations are pairwise adjacent. Actions take and put are constrained by the activity in the corresponding location: if it is busy, these actions fail to achieve their intended effect and do nothing. A location becomes or ceases to be busy randomly with probability p. We model this as an exogenous event, switch(l), that switches the busy attribute of location l. We assume at this stage to have a full knowledge of the state of the world. This simple domain is modeled with the following state variables:

- loc(r) ∈ {pier1, pier2, exit1, exit2}: location of robot r;
- ctrs(l, τ) ∈ {0, 1, ..., k}: number of containers in location l of some type τ; we assume τ ∈ {red,blue};
- load(r) ∈ {red, blue, empty}: type of the container on robot r if any; and
- busy(l) ∈ Boolen.

A typical problem in PAM_p is to move red containers from any of the piers to exit1 and blue ones to exit2.   □

Even a domain as simple as PAM_p can have a huge state space (up to $4 \times 8^{k+1} \times 3 \times 4^2$, that is, 1.6×10^{12} for $k = 10$), forbidding an explicit enumeration or a drawing such as Figure 6.1. An adequate specification of the actions in the previous example has to take into account their effects as well as the effects of concurrent exogenous events. Indeed, recall that nondeterminism accounts for the possible outcomes of an action a when the world is static, but also for events that may happen in the world while a is taking place and have an impact on the effects of a. Hence, $\gamma(s, a)$ represents the set of possible states corresponding to the joint effects of a and concurrent exogenous events. When the $|\gamma(s, a)|$ are not too loarge, probabilistic precondition-effect operators, illustrated next, can be a convenient representation.

Example 6.30. In PAM_p the deterministic effect of action move has to be combined with the effects of events switch(l) in any of the four locations. These random events are assumed to be independent. Hence in total $|\gamma(s, \text{move})| = 2^4$. Action move can be written as follow:

$$\text{move}(r : Robots; l, m, l_1, l_2, l_3, l_4 : Locations)$$
$$\text{pre}: \quad \text{loc}(r) = l, l_1 \neq l_2 \neq l_3 \neq l_4$$
$$\text{eff}: p_0 : \text{loc}(r) \leftarrow m$$
$$p_1 : \text{loc}(r) \leftarrow m, \text{busy}(l_1) \leftarrow \neg\text{busy}(l_1)$$
$$p_2 : \text{loc}(r) \leftarrow m, \text{busy}(l_1) \leftarrow \neg\text{busy}(l_1), \text{busy}(l_2) \leftarrow \neg\text{busy}(l_2)$$
$$p_3 : \text{loc}(r) \leftarrow m, \text{busy}(l_1) \leftarrow \neg\text{busy}(l_1), \text{busy}(l_2) \leftarrow \neg\text{busy}(l_2),$$
$$\text{busy}(l_3) \leftarrow \neg\text{busy}(l_3)$$
$$p_4 : \text{loc}(r) \leftarrow m, \text{busy}(l_1) \leftarrow \neg\text{busy}(l_1), \text{busy}(l_2) \leftarrow \neg\text{busy}(l_2),$$
$$\text{busy}(l_3) \leftarrow \neg\text{busy}(l_3), \text{busy}(l_4) \leftarrow \neg\text{busy}(l_4)$$

p_0 is the probability that no switch event occurs, p_1 that one event occurs in one location, p_2 corresponds to two events, and so on, that is, $p_0 = (1 - p)^4$, $p_1 = p \times (1 - p)^3$, $p_2 = p^2 \times (1 - p)^2$, $p_3 = p^3 \times (1 - p)$, and $p_4 = p^4$. Note that there are four possible instances with probability p_1, six instances with p_2 and four instances to p_3, giving: $p_0 + 4 \times p_1 + 6 \times p_2 + 4 \times p_3 + p_4 = 1$.

The take action is similarly specified: when the robot location l is not busy and contains at least one container of the requested type c, then take may either lead to a state where l is busy with no other effect, or it may achieve its effects of a container of type τ being loaded and $\text{ctrs}(l,c)$ being reduced by one. For each of these two cases, additional switch events may occur in any of the three other locations. This is similar for action Put (see Exercises 6.17 and 6.18). □

To summarize, the probabilistic precondition-effect operators have preconditions and effects, as the deterministic operators, but they have as many alternative sets of effects as possible outcomes. Each alternative effect field is specified with a probability value, which can be a function of the operator's parameters.

6.6.2 Dynamic Bayesian Networks

Parameterized probabilistic precondition-effect operators can be quite expressive, but they require going through all the alternative joint effects of an action and possible exogenous events and computing their probability. In many cases, it is not easy to factor out a large $\gamma(s, a)$ into a few alternative effects, as illustrated earlier. This representation quickly meets its limits.

Example 6.31. PAM_q is a more realistic version of the PAM_p domain. It takes into account the arrival of containers of different types in one of the two piers and their departure from one of the two exit locations, but it ignores the ship unloading and truck loading operations. The arrival and departure of containers and their types are considered as exogenous events. Locations have a maximum capacity of K containers of each type, K being a constant parameter. When an exit location reaches its maximum capacity for some type then the robot cannot put additional containers of that type. When a pier is full, no arrival event of the corresponding type is possible. In addition to the move,

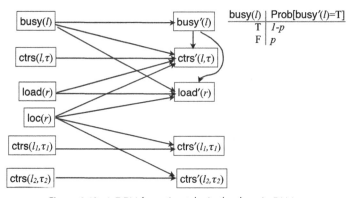

Figure 6.10. A DBN for action take in the domain PAM_q.

take, and put actions and the switch event seen earlier, we now have two additional
events:

- arrival(l): at each state transition, if a pier l is not full and the robot is not at l then one
  container may arrive at l with probability q; further, 60% of arrivals in pier1 are red
  containers, and 80% are blue in pier2;
- departure(l): if the robot is not at an exit location l and there are containers there, then
  there is a probability q' that a container may depart from l; only red containers depart
  from exit1 and only blue ones depart from exit2.

A typical task for the robot in domain PAM_q is to move all red containers to exit1 and
all blue ones to exit2.   □

With only three exogenous events as in PAM_q, the joint effects of actions and events
become complex: the size and intricacy of $\gamma(s, a)$ reaches a point where the specification of precondition-effect operators is not easy (see Exercise 6.19). Bayesian networks
is the appropriate representation for expressing conditional distributions on random
variables. It offers powerful techniques for reasoning on these distributions. A Bayesian
network is a convenient way for specifying a joint probability function for a collection
of random variables. It is a DAG where nodes are the random variables associated to a
priori or conditional probability distributions. An edge between two random variables
x and y expresses a conditional probability dependance of y with respect to x. Dynamic
Bayesian networks (DBNs) extend the static representation to handle different stages
in time of the same variables. They are particularly convenient in our case for expressing probabilistic state transitions from s to $\gamma(s, a)$, with a focus on the state variables
relevant for the action a and the events that may take place concurrently with a. This is
illustrated in the following example.

Example 6.32. Figure 6.10 represents the DBN characterizing action take in the PAM_q
domain. It shows the state variables that condition or are affected by take and the events
switch, arrival and departure. If x is a state variable of state s, we denote x' that same
state variable in $s' \in \gamma(s, a)$. Here, we extend slightly the ground representation with
parameterized random variables, for example, busy(l) is a Boolean random variable

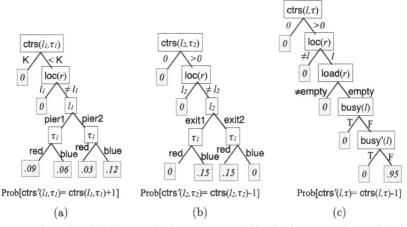

Figure 6.11. Conditional probability trees for the ctrs state variables for the action take combined with the possible events switch, arrival, and departure: (a) accounts for the arrival of a container at a pier location, (b) for a departure at an exit location, and (c) for a container being taken by the robot.

true when location l is busy. Note that variable $loc(r)$ conditions take but is not affected by the action and events: it appears only in the left side of the DBN.

A DBN specifies *conditional probability tables* that give the distribution over the values of a variable as a function of the values of its predecessors. Figure 6.10 illustrates such a table for the simple case of variable $busy(l)$ that has a single predecessor. Note that p in this table varies in general with l.   ☐

When a variable in a DBN has m ground predecessors that range over k values, the conditional probability table is of size k^m. This can quickly become a bottleneck for the specification of a DBN. Fortunately, in well-structured domains, conditional probably tables can be given in a factorized form as decision trees. These decision trees are also convenient for expressing constraints between instances of the parametrized state variables in the network.

Example 6.33. Figure 6.11 gives the conditional probabilities for the ctrs variables in the DBN of Figure 6.10. The leaves of each tree give the probability that the number of containers of some type at some location increases or decreases by one container (the probability that this number remains unchanged is the complement to 1). To simplify the picture, we take $p = .05$ and $q = q' = .15$. Tree (a) accounts for the possible arrival of a container of some type at a pier location: if the location is full ($ctrs(l_1, \tau_1) = K$) or if the robot is in that location ($loc(r) = l_1$), then no container arrival is possible, otherwise there is a probability of $.15 \times .6$ for the arrival of a red container at pier1, and so forth. Similarly, tree (b) accounts for the departure of a container at an exit location. Tree (c) gives the proper effect of action take: the probability that ctrs changes is conditioned by the five ancestor variables of that node in the DBN.   ☐

In Example 6.31, the interactions between exogenous events and actions are quite simple: events are independent and have almost no interference with the robot actions. In applications with more complex probabilistic interferences between the effects of

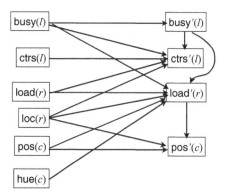

Figure 6.12. DBN for action take in domain PAM$_o$.

actions and possible events, the DBN representation is especially needed. It is also convenient for the modeling of sensing actions, where sensor models must be used to relate sensed features to values of state variables.

Example 6.34. Consider PAM$_o$, a variant of the previous domain where the robot does not have full knowledge of the state of the world. It still knows the exact number of containers in each location, but it does not know their types. However, it has a perceive action: when the robot is sensing a container c, perceive(c) gives the value of an observable feature, denoted hue(c), which is conditionally dependent on the container's type. To model this domain, we keep the state variables loc(r), load(r), and busy(l) as earlier; ctrs(l) is now the total number of containers in l. We further introduce the following variables:

- type(c) ∈ {red, blue}: type of container c,
- pos(c) ∈ {pier1, pier2, exit1, exit2, rbt}: location of container c, and
- hue(c) ∈ {a, b, c, d, unknown}: the observed feature of c.

Action perceive(c) can be modeled as requiring the robot to be at the same location as c and hue(c) to be unknown; its effect is to change the value of hue(c) to a, b, c, or d. Furthermore, the sensor model gives a conditional probability table of type(c) given hue(c) (Figure 6.13(a)). Action take(r, l, c) is now conditioned by two additional variables pos(c), which should be identical to loc(r), and hue(c) that should be not unknown. Figure 6.12 gives a DBN for that action. A conditional probability tree for Prob[load'(r)=red] is in Figure 6.13(b). It takes into account the probability of the location becoming busy (.95), as well as the probability of looking at a red container when its observed feature has some value. Prob[load'(r)=blue] is the complement to one of the numbers in the last four leaves; it is equal to zero in the other leaves where Prob[load'(r)=empty]=1.   □

The previous example illustrates two important representation issues:

- An observed feature informs probabilistically about the value of a nonobservable variable. A nonobservable variable (type(c) in the example) is replaced by a state variable that can be observed (here hue(c)) and to which the probabilistic planning and acting models and techniques apply normally.
- The effects of a sensing action can be required (e.g., the precondition that hue(c) ≠ unknown) and planned for, as with any other state transformation action.

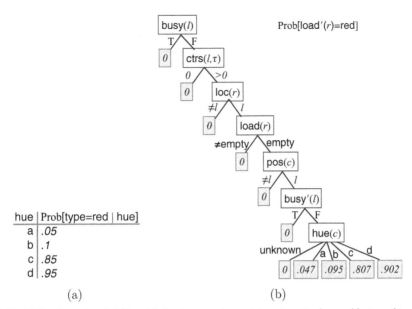

Figure 6.13. (a) Conditional probability table for the type of a container given its observed feature; (b) condition probability trees for load′(r)=red.

6.7 DOMAIN MODELING AND PRACTICAL ISSUES

Factored representations, such as those of the previous section, augment the expressiveness but do not reduce the difficulties of modeling a probabilistic domain. Numerous design choices remain open. Some of them require alternative models or extensions to the SSP model discussed so far.

This section briefly surveys some of the issues involved in designing and structuring probabilistic domains with the SSP and alternative models. It discusses some practical considerations for solving them with the techniques previously introduced.

6.7.1 Sources of Nondeterminism

The sources of nondeterminism that one chooses to model in Σ are a critical issue. The usual consideration of nominal effects versus erroneous effects of an action might not be the most relevant in practice. For example, the classical benchmark of navigating in a grid or a topological model of an environment where a move action can lead to other nodes than the intended ones is often unrealistic: it does not take into account the necessary recursive refinement of each action into lower level steps until reaching closed-loop controlled motion and localization. Further, very rare events, such as component failures leading to nonmodeled effects, have to be dealt with using specific approaches such as diagnosis and recovery.

Most important sources of nondeterminism are observation actions and exogenous events. Observations related to a particular state variable x can be modeled as actions applicable in some states and associated with a priori and conditional distributions over possible values of x (e.g., Prob[type|hue] in Example 6.34). Observation actions that inform on x change the distribution of its values. Conditional distributions of state variables given observations can be obtained from probabilistic models of sensors.

Exogenous events and the proper dynamics of the environment are often difficult to model deterministically as predictable events. When their possible effects interfere weakly with those of deliberate actions, events can also be modeled as probability distributions over possible effects. For example, when a container arrives while the robot is going somewhere, this may change the rest of its plan, but it does not always interfere with its navigation. A closed road might affect the navigation. It is possible to model events as random variables whose values affect the outcome of an action. The DBN representation of actions can handle that directly (see Example 6.31). Conditional expressions have to be added to the probabilistic precondition-effect representation to take into account a posteriori probabilities given the observed events.

6.7.2 Sparse Probabilistic Domains

In some applications, nondeterminism is naturally limited to parts of the domain. This is the case, for example, when most of the environment is known but a few areas are partially unknown, or when only observation and information-gathering actions are nondeterministic, while all other actions have a unique predictable outcomes. In these cases, it is worthwhile to combine deterministic models with probabilistic ones.

A possible approach for planning with deterministic and nondeterministic actions can be the following. Assume that while planning from a current state s to a goal, the algorithm finds at some point a sequence $\langle (s, a_1), (s_2, a_2), \ldots, (s_{k-1}, a_{k-1}), (s_k, a) \rangle$ such that actions a_1 through a_{k-1} are deterministic, but a is nondeterministic. It is possible to compress this sequence to a single nondeterministic step (s, a), the cost of which is the sum of cost of the k steps and the outcome $\gamma(s, a)$ of which is the outcome of the last step. This idea can be implemented as sketched in Algorithm 6.21. Its advantage is to focus the costly processing on a small part of the search space.

The notion of sparse probabilistic domains can be extended further to cases in which $|\gamma(s, a)| < k$ and Applicable$(s) < m$ for some small constants k and m. Sampling techniques such as the SLATE procedure (Algorithm 6.19) are particularly useful in these cases.

Algorithm 6.21 Compression framework for sparse probabilistic domains.

Incremental-compression-and-search(Σ, s_0, S_g)
    while there is an unsolved state s in current $\widehat{\gamma}(s_0, \pi)$
        search for an optimal path from s to a goal
            until a nondeterministic action a
        compress this path to a single nondeterministic step $\pi(s) \leftarrow a$
        revise with Bellman-Update

6.7.3 Goals and Objectives

Models of probabilistic domains other than the SSP model discussed so far can be more adapted to a given application. Let us briefly discuss few of them.

Process-oriented problems. In this class of problems, there is no goal. The objective of the actor is to optimize its behavior over an infinite horizon. This is meaningful for applications related to the control of a process, for example, a robot in charge of keeping an office space clean and tidy or a system maintaining a power supply unit in best functioning condition. A solution for a process-oriented problem is an optimal policy that runs "forever," that is, as long as this policy does not prescribe an emergency stop action or does not reach a failure state.

Process-oriented problems are often addressed by considering the criteria of the expected sum of *amortized* cost over an infinite horizon: Equation 6.1 is changed into $V^{\pi}(s_0) = E[\sum_{i=0}^{\infty} \delta^i \times \text{cost}(s_i, \pi(s_i))]$ where $0 < \delta < 1$. Mathematically, the amortization factor is needed for the convergence of this sum. However, it is less obvious to justify and pickup a value for δ from the specifics of an application. The literature often refers to a comparison with financial applications in which costs are amortized over some horizon. But this rather shallow metaphor does not give a convincing rational for amortized cost beyond the convenience of summing over an infinite horizon. Often, the average cost per step is a more relevant criteria.

Dynamic programming techniques (Section 6.2) work well for process-oriented problems when the state space remains of a size small enough to be enumerated. For larger problems, one has either to use online receding horizon techniques (section Section 6.4) or to decompose and hierarchize the problem into smaller tractable subproblems, as discussed in the next section.

Goal-oriented problems. This is the class of problems studied in this chapter where goals are given explicitly. One may address these problems using either a satisficing approach or an optimizing approach with different criteria than the one considered so far.

A possible satisficing approach can be obtained as a particular case of optimizing with unit costs: one minimizes the expected distance to the goal, which usually leads to good heuristics for finding it.

Instead of the expected sum of the cost of actions leading to a goal, an alternative objective function is the average cost per step. More interesting is the criterion that maximizes the probability of reaching a goal, a very meaningful concern in practice. With such a criterion, further discussed subsequently, one does not need to assume before hand the existence of a safe policy because one optimizes over the entire set of policies.

Finally, let us mention that goal-oriented problems are sometime specified with a set of possible initial states. This case can be handled by adding a conventional s_0 with a single applicable action leading to any of the real initial states of the problem.

Other optimization criteria. In addition to action costs, one can be interested in taking into account *rewards* for reaching particular states. In the simplest case in which rewards replaces costs, one switches from a minimization problem to a maximization problem. The more general case is equivalent to considering the cost as a function $f(s, a, s')$ of three arguments: the origin state s, the action in s, and the destination state s'. A straightforward approximation consists in taking $\text{cost}(s, a) = \sum_{s' \in \gamma(s,a)} \Pr(s'|s, a) f(s, a, s')$.

The main issue with a general cost model is to accept cost ranging over $\mathbb{R}$, instead of $\mathbb{R}^+$, as assumed so far. SSP problems with costs over $\mathbb{R}$ are often addressed with an additional assumption: $V(s)$ is infinite for every unsafe state s. As seen earlier, this property is granted with strictly positive costs, but it is difficult to grant it when designing a domain with real costs. One has to check that every cycle not containing a goal has positive cost. The Find&Revise schema and other heuristic search algorithms have to be extended to properly handle dead ends involving loops with negative or null costs. This was done for the Generalized SSP (GSSP) model Kolobov et al. [348]. For process-oriented problems, dynamic programming works with amortized cost over $\mathbb{R}$, again for domains of manageable size.

Maximizing the probability of reaching a goal. In many applications, one is more concerned about the probability of reaching a goal than about the expected cost of a policy. This is particularly the case when s_0 is unsafe.

One way of addressing this criteria is to take a reward maximization approach in which every transition (s, a) has a reward of 0 except transitions leading to a goal, which have a reward of 1. In such a model, the expected value of a policy π is exactly the probability $\Pr(S_g|s_0, \pi)$ of reaching a goal from s_0 by following π. Dynamic programming techniques can be used to find a policy π^* maximizing this criteria. The Find&Revise extension for the GSSP model, referred to earlier, can handle this criteria without iterating over the entire state space. The *Stochastic safest and shortest path* problems (S^3P) [565] go further by considering a dual optimization criterion: among policies that have a maximal probability of reaching a goal, find one whose expected cost to the goal is minimal (only goal-reaching paths are taken into account in this expected cost).

In some applications, a low-cost solution with an acceptable probability of reaching the goal can be preferred to a high cost and high probability policy. Approaches may either look for acceptable trade-offs or optimize over all policies above some probability threshold.

6.7.4 Domain Decomposition and Hierarchization

The expressiveness of factored representations for probabilistic problems allows for a dense specification of a domain that corresponds to a huge state space, often not directly tractable with available techniques. Ideally, a domain may exhibit enough structure to permit it to be reduced to tractable subdomains. Modeling a domain using factored representation can be helpful in exhibiting the structure of the problem. Two related principles for exploiting the structure of a domain are *abstraction* and *decomposition*. Let us some approaches.

Abstraction methods. Abstraction consists in defining a partition of S into clusters. A cluster is a subset of states that are close enough to be considered indistinguishable with respect to some characteristics, such as to be processed jointly as a single abstract state, for example, they may be attributed the same value of $V(s)$ or $\pi(s)$. The original problem is solved with respect to abstract states that are these clusters, the solution of which is then possibly refined within each abstract state. Abstraction is the complement of refinement.

A popular form of abstraction is based on focusing a cluster on some relevant state variables and ignoring the other variables, considered less relevant. The conditional probability trees in Section 6.6.2 illustrate the idea: the state variables that are not part of any tree are nonrelevant. Often the irrelevant variables at one stage can be important at some other stage of the problem: the abstraction is not uniform. Furthermore, one may have to resort to approximation to find enough structure in a problem: variables that affect slightly the decision-making process (e.g., $V(s)$) are abstracted away.

Another abstraction approach extends model minimization techniques for computing minimal models of finite-state machines.[6] One starts with an a priori partition of S into clusters, for example, subset of states having (approximately) the same V_0. A cluster is split when its states have different probability transitions to states in the same or other clusters. When all clusters are homogenous with respect to state transitions, then the problem consisting of these clusters, considered as abstract states, is equivalent to the original problem. The effort in model reduction is paid off by solving a smaller problem. This is particularly, the case when the clusters and the value function are represented in a factored form, as state variable formulas (see the references and discussion in Section 6.8.6).

Symbolic algorithms (as in Section 5.4) develop this idea further with the use of algebraic decision diagrams (ADD). An ADD generalizes a decision tree to a rooted acyclic graph whose nodes are state variables, branches are possible values of the corresponding variables, and leaves are sets of states. An ADD represents a function whose values label its leaves. For example, an ADD can encode the function $V(s)$ in which all the states corresponding to a leaf have the same value. Similarly, one can represent $\Pr(s'|s, a)$ and $\mathrm{cost}(s, a)$ as ADDs. When the structure of the problem can be mapped into compressed ADDs – a condition not easily satisfied – then fast operations on ADDs allow to perform efficiently Belmann updates on the entire S, or on the relevant part of it. Symbolic VI and Symbolic LAO* make use of ADDs, together with approximation techniques, to efficiently solve well-structured problems.

Decomposition methods. The idea is to decompose the original problem into independent or loosely coupled subproblems that are solved independently. Their solutions are recomposed together to get the solution of the global problem. For example, serial decomposition addresses the original task as a sequence of subtasks whose solutions will be sequentially run.

The notion of *closed subsets* of states is convenient for decomposing a domain. $C \subseteq S$ is closed if there is no transition from a state in C to a state outside of C. It is a maximal closed subset, if it does not have a proper subset that is also closed. For

---

[6] For any given finite state machine M, there is a machine M', minimal in the number of states, which is equivalent to M, that is, recognizes the same language.

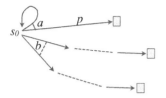

Figure 6.14. A simple domain for comparing features of probabilistic and nondeterministic models.

process-oriented problems, an optimal policy can be constructed independently for each maximal closed subset without bothering with the rest of the domain. A maximal closed subset C can be viewed as an independent subprocess. Once reached, the system stays in this subprocess forever. C can be collapsed to a single absorbing state, at which point, other closed subsets can be found.

The *kernel decomposition* method implements this idea with more flexibility. The set S is decomposed into blocks, with possible transitions between blocks through a few states for each block. These states permitting block transitions are called the kernel of the domain. Starting with some initial V_0 for the kernel states, optimal policies are computed independently for each block, allowing one to update the values of the kernel and iterate until updates are negligible.

Finally, let us mention that abstraction and decomposition are also used for computing heuristics and control knowledge to guide or focus a global search. There is a large overlap between abstraction or decomposition methods and the techniques discussed in Section 6.3.5.

6.7.5 Probabilistic Versus Nondeterministic Approaches

We studied in Chapters 5 and 6 two types of nondeterministic models, with and without probabilities. These models have several similarities but also differences. Let us discuss which of the two approaches to choose when faced with a practical problem where nondeterminism requires modeling and can be expressed explicitly.

An obvious remark is that probabilistic models without costs and probability parameters correspond to nondeterministic models. These parameters enrich the description of a domain and allow for choosing a solution according to some optimization criterion. However, estimating costs and probabilities adds a significant burden to the modeling step. There are domains in which modeling transitions with costs and probabilities is difficult in practice, for example, when not enough statistical data are available. Probabilistic approaches may also lead a modeler to hide qualitative preferences and constraints through arbitrary quantitative measures.

But there is more to it than just adding or removing parameters from one model to get the other, as illustrated in the following example.

Example 6.35. Consider the simplistic domain in Figure 6.14 that has two policies π_a and π_b. $\pi_a(s_0) = a$; a leads to a goal with probability p in one step, or it loops back on s_0. π_b starts with action b which has a few possible outcomes, all of them lead to a goal after several steps without loops, that is, $Graph(s_0, \pi_b)$ is acyclic, all its leaves are goal states and its paths to goals are of length $\leq k$. Both π_a and π_b are safe policies; π_a is cyclic, whereas π_b is acyclic. The value of π_a is $V_a = cost(a) \sum_{i=0,\infty}(1-p)^i = \frac{cost(a)}{p}$. The value V_b of π_b is the weighted sum of the cost of the paths of $Graph(s_0, \pi_b)$. $\square$

In this example, the probabilistic approach compares V_a to V_b and chooses the policy with the minimum expected cost. If $cost(a)/p < V_b$, then π_a is preferred to π_b, because π_b is a more expensive solution in average. However, π_b is preferable in the *worst case* because it guarantees reaching a goal in a bounded number of steps.

The nondeterministic approach does not handle probabilities and expected costs, but it distinguishes qualitatively acyclic from cyclic solutions. There are applications in which an acyclic solution like π_b is clearly preferable whatever the values of the parameters are. This is particularly the case when these parameters are unknown or difficult to estimate. This is also the case for safety critical applications in which the worst case is more meaningful than average cost.

Finally, nondeterministic approaches may potentially scale up better than probabilistic ones, because the former allow for a higher level of factorization, for example, with an efficient use of symbolic representations.

To summarize, probabilistic approaches require parameters but are able to make fine choices on the basis of average case considerations; they allow choosing among unsafe solutions when optimizing the probability to reach a goal. Nondeterministic approaches do not need parameters and their costly estimation step, they select solutions according to a qualitative criteria, and they may scale up better.

6.7.6 Practical Considerations

Several considerations have to be taken into account for using the algorithms presented in this chapter and their variants, among which:

- the size of S,
- the possible existence of dead ends,
- the accuracy of the probability and cost parameters,
- the amortization trade-off between the use of an approximate solution and the computational cost of its improvement, and
- the degree of nondeterminism of the domain.

The parameters of a model are always estimated with some margin of error. There is no need to seek an exact optimal solution with respect to imprecise parameters. An approximate solution whose degree of optimality matches the accuracy of the cost and probability parameters is sufficient.

The amortization trade-off takes into account how many times a suboptimal solution will be used for acting. It compares the corresponding loss in the cost of actions to the cost of further refining a suboptimal solution. For example, in a receding horizon approach in which π is used just once and recomputed at every stage, a suboptimal solution is often sufficient, whereas for a process-oriented problem, the same policy is used for a long time and may require careful optimization.

The degree of nondeterminism can be appreciated by the size of $|\gamma(s, a)|$ and how overlapping are the sets $\gamma(s, a)$, over applicable actions in s. In *sparse* probabilistic planning problems, $\gamma(s, a)$ is a small set. Possibly, most actions are deterministic but of a few that have a couple of nondeterministic outcomes, as discussed in Section 6.7.2. Other algorithms such as Busoniu et al. [103] are adapted to sparse probabilistic problems.

When S is of a small enough size to be entirely explicited and maintained in the memory of the planning computer (typically on the order of few mega states), then VI is an easily implemented and practical algorithm. For reasonably small values of η (in the order of 10^{-3}), often VI converges in a few dozen iterations and is more efficient than PI. Depending on the amortization trade-off, the user may not even bother to compute Φ^π and rely on a heuristic value of the error parameter η. There are even cases in which VI may be used online, for example, on a receding horizon schema: for $|S|$ in the order of few thousands states, the running time of VI is on the order of a few milliseconds. This may happen in small domains and in well-engineered state spaces.

Most planning problems do not allow for an explicit enumeration of their entire state space. Realistically, a few dozen parametrized state variables, that is, a few hundred ground state variables, may be needed for modeling a realistic domain. The corresponding state space is on the order of d^k, where k is the number of ground state variables and d is the size of their domain. In many practical cases k is so large (that is, a few hundred) that iterating over S is not feasible. Options in such a case are to use focused search algorithms that explore a small part of the search space as seen in Section 6.3, to refine the model, to decompose the planning problem into feasible subproblems, and to use domain configurable control knowledge to reduce sharply the branching factor of a problem and allow for a significant scaling up, as discussed in Section 6.3.5.

6.8 DISCUSSION AND HISTORICAL REMARKS

6.8.1 Foundations

Sequential decision making under uncertainty benefits from a long line of work in mathematics, starting with Andrei Markov in the 19th century, who initiated the theory of stochastic processes, now called Markov processes. The field developed extensively in the early 1960s with contributions from control theory, operations research, and computer science. *Dynamic Programming* by Bellman [50] opened the way to numerous developments, detailed into influential monographs, for example, Derman [151], Bertsekas [65], Puterman [497] and Bertsekas and Tsitsiklis [66].

Many of the early developments were focused on process-oriented problems (Section 6.7.3). Goal-oriented problems were also defined quite early: the analysis of Bertsekas and Tsitsiklis [67], who coined the name SSP, traces back their origin to Eaton and Zadeh [166]. However, their development is in many aspects more recent and remains active within the artificial intelligence and planning communities, as illustrated with numerous articles and books, for example, Buffet and Sigaud [102], Mausam and Kolobov [407].

6.8.2 SSP Models

The Markov Decision Process (MDP) class of problems grew up into a profusion of extended models and special cases, notably SSP and POMDP.[7] We focused this chapter on the SSP model for two reasons: *(i)* it is a simple and quite natural model for goal-oriented probabilistic planning problems, and *(ii)* it is more general than the MDP model. Regarding the latter point, Bertsekas [65] demonstrates that the SSP model includes as special cases the discounted infinite horizon as well as the finite horizon MDP models. The propositions in Section 6.2 are also demonstrated in this book.

SSPs are defined in the literature with a few variations related to how the so-called *connectivity assumption* and the *positive cycle assumption* are expressed. The first is defined either by assuming that every state is safe or that s_0 is safe. This amounts to requiring either that there is no dead end in the domain or that existing dead ends are avoidable with a safe policy starting at s_0. The second assumption is equivalent to requiring that every cycle not containing the goal has positive costs. These two assumptions should preferably be expressed as conditions that are easily testable at the specification stage of the domain. For example, demanding that every unsafe policy has infinite cost is less restrictive than constraining all costs to be positive, but it is also less easy to verify.

A more general approach is to allow for real costs and use algorithms able to check and avoid dead ends, as in the amortized-cost approach of Teichteil-Königsbuch et al. [568] or in the GSSP model of Kolobov et al. [348]. This model accounts for maximizing the probability of reaching the goal, which is an important criterion, also addressed by other means in Puterman [497] and Teichteil-Königsbuch et al. [567]. The approaches of Kolobov et al. [347] and Teichteil-Königsbuch [565] for the S^3P model go one step further with a dual optimization criterion combining a search for a minimal cost policy among policies with the maximum probability of reaching a goal.

6.8.3 Partially Observable Models

The model of Partially Observable Markov Decision Process (POMDP) provides an important generalization regarding the epistemic condition of an actor, that is, what it knows about the state it is in. The SSP and MDP models assume that after each state transition the actor knows which state s it has reached; it then proceeds with the action $\pi(s)$ appropriate for s. The POMDP model considers that the actor does not know its current state, but it knows about the value of some observation variable o. It also has a probability distribution $\Pr(o|s, a)$ of observing o after running action a in s. This gives it a probability distribution of possible states it might be in, called the current *actor's belief*: $b(s|a, o)$. It has been demonstrated by Åström [25] that the last observation o does not summarize the past execution, but the last belief does. Hence, a POMDP planning problem can be addressed as an MDP problem in the belief space. One starts with an initial belief b_0 (distribution for initial states) and computes a policy that gives for every belief point b an action $\pi(b)$, ideally leading to the goal.

---

[7] Plus many other models, for example, SMDP, MOMDP, CoMDP, MMDP, SIMDP, MDPIP, HMDP, HDMDP, GSSP, S^3P, DSSP, POSB-MDP, NEG-MDP, MAXPROB-MDP MDP-IP, TiMDP, CPTP, Dec-MDP, Dec-SIMDP, Dec-POMDP, MPOMDP, POIPSG, and COM-MTDP.

Several approaches generalizing Dynamic Programming or Heuristic Search methods to POMDPs have been proposed, for example, Kaelbling et al. [305] and Smith and Simmons [552]. Policy search methods for parametrized POMDPs policies are studied in Ng and Jordan [453]. Approximate methods that focus Bellman updates on a few belief points (called *point-based methods*) are surveyed in Shani et al. [530]; they are compared to an extension of RTDP in Bonet and Geffner [87]. Online algorithms for POMDPs are surveyed in Ross et al. [516]. A Monto Carlo sampling approach is proposed by Silver and Veness [538]. Several interesting POMDP applications have been developed, for example, in robotics by Pineau et al. [480], Foka and Trahanias [201], and Guez and Pineau [250]. However, the POMDP developer faces several difficulties, among which:

- Tremendous complexity: a discretized belief point corresponds to a subset of states; hence the belief space is in $O(2^{|S|})$. Because $|S|$ is already exponential in the number of state variables, sophisticated algorithms and heuristics do not scale up very far. Significant modeling effort is required for decomposing a domain into small loosely coupled problems amenable to a solution. For example, the approach of Pineau et al. [480], even though it is applied to a small state space (less than 600 states), requires a clever hierarchization technique to achieve a solution.
- A strong assumption (not always highlighted in the POMDP literature): a policy from beliefs to actions requires the action $\pi(b)$ to be applicable in *every* state s compatible with a belief b. It is not always the case that the intersection of Applicable(s) for every s compatible with b is meaningful. Sometimes, one would like to be able to choose an action that is feasible in a subset of $\pi(b)$ on the basis of states likelihood, for example, as in the assumption-based planning for partially observable nondeterministic domains of Albore and Bertoli [7].
- The partial observability model of POMDP is quite restrictive and often unrealistic. It should be called the *invisible state MDP* model because it does not consider any part of s as being observable. An actor that distinguishes between invisible and observable state variables and dynamically decomposes the latter into visible and hidden variables (as discussed in Section 1.3.2) should handle them differently in its deliberation, in particular to reduce the uncertainty about the states it will face during its planed course of action. Such a partial observability approach is pursued for example with the MOMDP models of Ong et al. [463] and Araya-Lopez et al. [23], which consider that the set of states is the Cartesian product of a set of visible states and a set of hidden ones.
- Finally, observability issues require a specific handling of observation actions. One does not observe at every step all observable variables. One observes only what is relevant for the current stage of the task at hand; irrelevant unknown variables are ignored. Further, it is not a single observation step; it can be a succession of observations until reducing the uncertainty to a level consistent with what's at stake. These observation actions have a cost and need to be planned for. This is for example illustrated in the HiPPo systems of Sridharan et al. [555] for a robotics manipulation task.

6.8.4 Other Extended MDP Models

So far, we referred to probabilistic models with timeless state transitions. Many applications require explicit time, durations, concurrency, and synchronization concepts. A simple MDP extension adds time in the state representation, for example, time as an additional state variable. In this direct extension, timeless MDP techniques can be used to handle actions with deterministic durations and goals with deadlines, but this model cannot handle concurrent actions. The Semi-Markov Decision Process (SMDP) model of Howard [288] and Forestier and Varaiya [202] extends this simple temporal MDP model with probabilistic integer durations. The Time-dependent MDP (TiMDP) model of Boyan and Littman [95] considers distribution of continuous relative or absolute time durations. Concurrent MDPs of Mausam and Weld [410] extend the timeless MDP model to handle concurrent steps of unit duration, where each transition is a subset of actions. The Generalized SMDP model of Younes and Simmons [624] combines semi-Markov models with concurrency and asynchronous events. Algorithms for these models have been proposed by several authors, notably Mausam and Weld [408], Little et al. [388], and Mausam and Weld [409]. It is interesting to note that SMDPs provide a foundation to reinforcement learning approaches of Parr and Russell [465], Andre and Russell [21], Marthi et al. [404], and Fernández and Veloso [192].

Another important extension is related to *continuous* and *hybrid* state space and action space. The hybrid state space combines discrete and continuous state variables (see Section 7.4). The latter have been addressed with severable discretization techniques such as adaptive approximation by Munos and Moore [437], piecewise constant or linear approximation by Feng et al. [188], and parametric function approximation by Liu and Koenig [390] and Kveton et al. [368]. Linear Programming approaches for hybrid state spaces have been proposed by several authors, for example, Guestrin et al. [248]. Heuristic search techniques have been extended to hybrid cases, for example, the HAO* algorithm of Meuleau et al. [420].

Finally, there are several extensions of the stationary and deterministic policy models on which we focused this chapter. A *stochastic* policy maps states into probability distributions over actions. A *nonstationary* policy evolve with time, that is, it is a mapping of state and time into either actions when it is deterministic, or into probability distributions over actions when the policy is both stochastic and nonstationary. In some cases, such as in finite horizon problems, a nonstationary policy can be better than a stationary one, for example, $\pi(s)$ is not the same action when visiting s the first time then on the nth visit. However, extending the state representation (with variables representing the context) is often easier than handling general nonstationary stochastic models, for which fewer algorithms and computational results are known (e.g., [527]).

6.8.5 Algorithms and Heuristics

The Dynamic Programming foundations and main algorithms go back to the early work already cited of Bellman, Bertsekas, Putermann, and Tsitsiklis. More recent studies disclosed additional properties of the VI algorithm, for example, Bonet [80] for complexity results with positive costs and lower bound heuristics and Hansen [253] for suboptimality bounds. Several extension and improved VI algorithms have been proposed, for example, with a prioritized control in Andre et al. [20], with a focus mechanism in Ferguson and Stentz [191], McMahan and Gordon [418], and Wingate and Seppi [609] or with a backward order of updates from goals back along a greedy policy in Dai and Hansen [134].

Policy Search methods (not the be confused with Policy Iteration algorithm) deal with parametrized policies π_θ and perform a local search in the parameter space of θ (e.g., gradient descent). The survey of Deisenroth et al. [148] covers in particular their use for continuous space domains and reinforcement learning problems.

Hansen and Zilberstein [254] developed the LAO* algorithm as an extension of AO* of Nilsson [460]. The Find&Revise schema was proposed by Bonet and Geffner [83], who also developed several instantiation of this schema into heuristic search algorithms such as HDP [83], LRTDP [84], and LDFS [86]. A few other heuristic algorithms are presented in their recent textbook [217, chap. 6 & 7]. RTDP has been introduced by Barto et al. [46]. The domain-configurable control technique presented in Section 6.3.5 was developed by Kuter and Nau [361].

The FF-Replan planner has been developed by Yoon et al. [619] in the context of the International Planning Competition. A critical analysis of its replanning technique appears in Little and Thiébaux [389] together with a characterization of "probabilistically interesting problems." These problems have dead ends and safe solutions. To take the latter into account, Yoon et al. [620] proposed an online receding horizon planner, called FF-Hindsight, which relies on estimates through averaging and sampling over possible determinizations with a fixed lookahead. The RFF algorithm has been proposed by Teichteil-Königsbuch et al. [566]; it has been generalized to hybrid MDPs with continuous state variables [564].

The SLATE procedure is due to Kearns et al. [325]. UCT was proposed by Kocsis and Szepesvári [339]. An AO* version of it is described in Bonet and Geffner [88]. UCT is based on Monte Carlo Tree Search techniques that were developed with success for games such as Go by Gelly and Silver [219]. UCT was implemented into a few MDP planners such as PROST by Keller and Eyerich [327]. An extension of UCT addressing POMDPs is studied by Silver and Veness [538].

Several authors have exploited determinization techniques in probabilistic planning, for example, Boutilier et al. [92] for pruning unnecessary Bellman update, Karabaev and Skvortsova [313] for performing Graphplan like reachabilitiy analysis, Bonet and Geffner [85] for computing heuristics for the mGPT planner, and Teichteil-Königsbuch et al. [568] also for computing heuristics. Proposition 6.25 is demonstrated in the latter reference.

For many planners, implicit dead ends can lead to inefficiency or even to nontermination (e.g., as in RTDP and LRTDP). Dead ends can be detected, but unreliably, through heuristics. They are more safely avoided through the unbounded growth of the value function V, as in Find&Revise instances and other variants, for example, Kolobov and Weld [349] and Teichteil-Königsbuch et al. [568], but this can be quite expensive. Kolobov et al. [346] propose an explanation-based learning technique to acquire clauses that soundly characterize dead ends. These clauses are easily detected when states are represented as conjunction of literals. They are found through a bottom-up greedy search and further tested to avoid false positives. This technique can be usefully integrated into the generalized Find&Revise schema proposed for the GSSP model of Kolobov et al. [348].

6.8.6 Factored and Hierarchical MDPs

The survey of Boutilier et al. [93] presents a comprehensive overview of factored representations in probabilistic planning and analysis of their respective merits and problems. The probabilistic operators representation is a direct extension of the deterministic and nondeterministic operators; it is used in particular in the PPDDL language of Younes and Littman [621]. Bayesian Networks are extensively covered in the textbook of Koller and Friedman [345]. Their use for representing actions has been introduced in Dean and Kanazawa [143]. The RDDL language of Sanner [525] is a compact representation integrating DBNs and influence diagrams. Dynamic programming techniques for factored MDPs are studied by Boutilier et al. [94]. Guestrin et al. [249] developed elaborate approximation techniques for MDPs represented with DBNs. Their use of approximate value function represented as a linear combination of basis functions on a small subset of the domain variables demonstrates impressive scalability.

Symbolic techniques with binary and algebraic decision diagrams have also been used in probabilistic planning, for example, Hoey et al. [275] developed a symbolic VI algorithm in the SPUDD planner, Feng et al. [190] used these techniques in an RDTP algorithm, Feng and Hansen [189] proposed a symbolic LAO*, and Mausam et al. [406] extended the nondeterministic MBP planner to MDPs.

Several algorithms have been proposed to take advantage of the structure of a probabilistic planning problem. This is the case, for example, for hierarchical MDPs of the HiAO* algorithm of Meuleau and Brafman [421]. Different methods can be used to hierarchize a domain, for example, the methods of Givan et al. [237]. The model minimization techniques have been studied in Dean et al. [142]. A kernel decomposition approach has been developed in Dean and Lin [144]. Hauskrecht et al. [263] propose approximate solutions to large MDPs with macro actions, that is, local policies defined in particular regions of the state space. The approach of Barry et al. [42] and their DetH* algorithm [43] clusters a state space into aggregates of closely connected states, then it uses a combination of determinization at the higher level and VI at the lower level of a hierarchical MDP.

Sparse probabilistic domains have been studied in particular by Busoniu et al. [103] and Likhachev et al. [386]. The path compression technique of Algorithm 6.21 is detailed in the latter reference.

6.9 EXERCISES

6.1. In the domain of Example 6.4, consider a policy π such that $\pi(s_0) = $ Both. Is π a safe policy when s_0 is either (acb), (bca) or (cba)? Is it safe when s_0 is (bac) or (cab)?

6.2. Prove that the recursive Equation 6.3 follows from the definition of $V^\pi(s)$ in Equation 6.1.

6.3. Prove that a policy π^* that meets Equation 6.5 is optimal.

6.4. Consider the domain Σ in Example 6.4.
   (a) Extend Σ with a fourth action denoted All, which is applicable only in the state (aaa) and flips randomly the three variables at once. Does the corresponding state

space have dead ends ? If not, run algorithm VI on this example, assuming uniform cost and probability distributions.

(b) Extend Σ by having the three state variables range over $\{1, 2, \ldots, m\}$, such that actions Left, Right, and Both are as defined initially; action All is applicable only to a state of the form (i, i, i) where i is even; it flips randomly the three variables. Assume $s_0 = (1, 2, 3)$ and goals are of the form (i, i, i) where i is odd. Run VI on this extended example and analyze its performance with respect to m.

6.5. Run algorithm PI on the problem of Figure 6.15 starting from the following policy: $\pi_0(s_1) = \pi_0(s_2) = a, \pi_0(s_3) = b, \pi_0(s_4) = c$.
  (a) Compute $V^{\pi_0}(s)$ for the four nongoal states.
  (b) What is the greedy policy of V^{π_0}?
  (c) Iterate on the above two steps until reaching a fixed point.

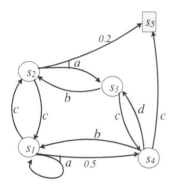

Figure 6.15. An SSP problem with five states and four actions a, b, c, and d; only action a is nondeterministic, with the probabilities shown in the figure; the cost of a and b is 1, the cost of c and d is 100; the initial state is s_1; the goal is s_5.

6.6. Run VI on the problem of Figure 6.15 with $\eta = .5$ and the following heuristics:
  (a) $V_0(s) = 0$ in every state.
  (b) $V_0(s_1) = V_0(s_2) = 1$ and $V_0(s) = 100$ for the two other states.

6.7. In the problem of Figure 6.15, add a self loop as a nondeterministic effect for actions b, c, and d; that is, add s in $\gamma(s, a)$ for these three actions wherever applicable. Assume that the corresponding distributions are uniform. Solve the two previous exercises on this modified problem.

6.8. Run AO* on the domain of Figure 6.6 with the heuristics V_1 of Section 6.3.5.

6.9. Modify the domain of Figure 6.6 by making the state s_{12} an explicit dead end instead of a goal; run AO* with the heuristics V_0 and V_1 of Section 6.3.5.

6.10. Prove that algorithm LAO* is an instance of the Find&Revise schema.

6.11. Modify the domain of Figure 6.6 by changing $\gamma(s_9, a) = \{s_3, s_8\}$ and making the state s_{15} an explicit dead instead of a goal. Run LAO* and ILAO* on this problem and compare their computation steps.

6.12. Run FF-Replan on the problem of Figure 6.15, using a Forward–Search algorithm that always returns the least-cost path to a goal state. What is the probability that FF-Replan will reach the goal?

6.13. Run RFF on the problem of Figure 6.15 with $\theta = 0.7$. Suppose the Det–Plan subroutine calls the same Forward–Search algorithm as in the previous exercise and turns the plan into a policy. What is π after one iteration of the "while" loop?

6.14. Prove that algorithm FF-Replan (Section 6.4.2) is complete when using a complete Det-Plan deterministic planner.

6.15. Run Algorithm 6.21 on the problem of Figure 6.15; compare with the computations of RFF on the same problem.

6.16. Specify the SLATE procedure (Algorithm 6.19) as an anytime algorithm implementing an incremental backup at each increase of the depth h. Implement and test on a few domains.

6.17. Write the probabilistic precondition-effect operators for the take and put actions of the domain PAM_p (Example 6.30). How many ground actions are there is this domain?

6.18. Implement and run algorithm VI for a few problem instances of the domain PAM_p. Up to how many containers does your implementation scale up?

6.19. For the domain in Example 6.31, analyze the interactions among the arrival, departure, and switch events with the action take and put. Compute the sets $\gamma(s, \text{take})$ and $\gamma(s, \text{put})$ for different states s.

6.20. Analyze a generalized PAM_q domain where the arrival and departure of containers can take place even in the robot location. Define conditional probability trees for the variable ctrs.

CHAPTER 7

Other Deliberation Functions

As discussed in Section 1.3, there is more to deliberation than planning and acting. This point is particularly clear in robotics, as shown in the survey by Ingrand and Ghallab [294].[1] Here, we briefly cover a few deliberation functions, other than planning and acting, that may be needed by an actor. We discuss in Section 7.1 deliberation on sensing tasks: how to model them and control them to recognize the state of the world and detect objects, events, and activities in the environment that are relevant to the actor, for and while performing its own actions. Section 7.2 is about monitoring and goal reasoning, that is, detecting and interpreting discrepancies between predictions and observations, anticipating what needs be monitored, controlling monitoring actions, and assessing the relevance of commitments and goals from observed evolutions, failures, and opportunities. Learning and model acquisition techniques in planning and acting are surveyed in Section 7.3; we cover in particular reinforcement learning and learning from demonstration approaches.

This chapter surveys also approaches for handling hybrid models that have continuous and discrete components (Section 7.4), which are needed in domains where part of the dynamics is naturally expressed with continuous differential equations. We finally devote Section 7.5 to representations for expressing ontologies, which can be essential for modeling a domain; we discuss their use in planning and acting.

7.1 PERCEIVING

Deliberation is mostly needed for an actor facing a diversity of situations in an open environment. Such an actor generally has partial knowledge about the initial state of world and its possible evolution. It needs to be able to perceive what is relevant for its activity and to deliberate about its perception, while acting and perceiving.

---

[1] The material of some sections in this chapter is based on that survey.

Reasoning on perception leads to several problems, among which for example those of:

- Reliability: how reliable are sensing and information gathering actions? What verification and confirmation steps are needed to confirm that the sensed value of a state variable is correct? How to assess the distribution of values if uncertainty is explicitly modeled?
- Observability: how to acquire information about non observable state variables from the observable ones? How to balance costly observations with approximate estimates?
- Persistence: How long can one assume that a state variable keeps its previous value as long as new observations do no contradict it?

Furthermore, there are numerous additional sensing problems for a physical actor that has to reason on and determine how to handle its sensors (how and where to use a sensor, how to process and qualify given data), as well as to perform information-gathering actions through communication with and query of information sources. Handling sensors changes perception reasoning problems considerably.

The details of these problems are beyond the scope of this short overview section. In the following sections, we mention a few approaches to *(i)* planning and acting with information gathering actions, *(ii)* planning sensing actions, *(iii)* anchoring and signal-to-symbol matching problems, and *(iv)* recognizing plans and situations.

7.1.1 Planning and Acting with Information Gathering

As already discussed, the *closed-world assumption* (i.e., the assumption that facts not explicitly stated are false)[2] is too restrictive. A deliberative actor lives in an *open world*. It has to handle partially specified instances of a domain (e.g., as seen with timelines) and extend its knowledge when needed. In particular, it needs the following capabilities:

- Plan with respect to domain objects and properties that are unknown when planning starts but that can be discovered at acting time through planned information-gathering actions. New facts resulting from these actions will be used to further refine the rest of the plan.
- Query databases for facts the actor needs specifically to address a given planning problem and query knowledge bases for additional models of its environment that are relevant to the task at hand.

Planning with information gathering is studied by several authors using conditional planning approaches, as in the PKS system of Petrick and Bacchus [476]. The continual planning approach of Brenner and Nebel [97] in MAPL postpones part of the planning process. It introduces information-gathering actions that will later allow development of the missing parts of the plan. The planner uses assertions that abstract actions to be refined after information gathering. The approach is well adapted to dynamic environments where planning for subgoals that depend on yet unknown states

---

[2] Alternatively, facts not entailed from explicit statements are assumed to be false.

can be delayed until the required information is available through properly planned information-gathering actions.

Acquiring additional data and models at planning time is inspired from *semantic Web* functionalities. For example, the ObjectEval system of Samadi et al. [521] acquires from the Web statistics about possible locations of objects of different classes. It uses them in a utility function for finding and delivering objects in an office environment. Other approaches use Description Logic (DL), a fragment of first-order logic, to handle statements about objects, properties, relations, and their instances with inference algorithms for querying large stores of data and models over the Web [27]. Most implementations rely on OWL, the standard Web Ontology Language. OWL handles an open-world representation where facts can be *true, false*, or *unknown*. This point is further developed in Section 7.5.3.

7.1.2 Planning to Perceive

An information-gathering action may not be a directly executable command. It may require using sensor models to decide where to put a sensor, how to use it, and how to best acquire the needed information. Planning to perceive is concerned with integrating the selection of viewpoints and sensor modalities to the other activities of an actor. It is very important in robotics. It relies on extensive work on the sensor placement problem, which is usually addressed as a search for the next best viewpoint for solving specific sensing tasks, such as modeling an environment or recognizing an object. An illustration is given in the approach of Laporte and Arbel [372].

The integrated sensor placement and task planning problem is sometimes addressed with POMDPs, for example, by Pineau et al. [481] and Prentice and Roy [495]. The HiPPo system of Sridharan et al. [555] offers a good illustration of sensor placement for the recognition of objects on a table, as typically required in a manipulation task. A hierarchical POMDP technique is used to have a computationally tractable problem, although limited in perception tasks and domain size (a few regions of interest).

An alternative and more scalable approach for synthesizing an observation plan within a navigation task is proposed in Velez et al. [578]. This work seeks to detect and map objects of interest while reaching a destination. It uses a Bayesian approach that correlates measurements from subsequent observations to improve object detection; detours are weighed against motion cost to produce robust observation plans using a receding horizon sampling scheme. The approach was tested in an indoor environment for recognizing doors and windows.

7.1.3 Symbol Anchoring

Deliberation reasons about objects in the environment through their symbolic attributes and through relations linking these symbols. Observing handles perceptual data and signals. It is essential that the abstract description of the former and the data of the latter agree when referring to the same reality. *Anchoring* is the problem of creating and maintaining over time a correspondence between symbols and sensor data that refer to the same *physical object*. It can be seen as a particular case of the *symbol grounding* problem, which deals with broad categories, for example, any "door," as opposed to, say, door-2.

Coradeschi and Saffiotti [130] propose achieving anchoring by establishing and keeping a link called an *anchor* between the perceptual system and the symbol system, together with a signature that estimates some of the attributes of the object it refers to. The anchor is based on a model that relates relations and attributes to perceptual features and their values.

Establishing an anchor corresponds to a pattern recognition problem, where the challenge is to handle the uncertainty of sensor data and the ambiguity of models, a challenge dealt with, for example, by maintaining multiple hypotheses. Karlsson et al. [315], for example, handle ambiguous anchors with a conditional planner, called PTL, exploring a space of belief states, representing the incomplete and uncertain knowledge due to partial matching between symbolic properties and observed perceptual features. The approach distinguishes between definite symbolic descriptions, which are matched with a single object, and indefinite descriptions. Actions have causal effects that change object properties. Observations can change the partition of a belief state into several new hypotheses.

Anchoring raises additional problems, such as which anchors to establish, and when and how. Anchors are needed in principle for all objects relevant to the actor's activity. Often, these objects cannot be defined extensionally (by specifying a list of objects). They must be defined by their properties in a context-dependent way. Object recognition is required not only to label specifically queried objects but also to create new anchors relevant to the task.

Tracking anchors is another issue, taking into account object properties that persist across time or evolve in a predictable way. Predictions are needed to check that new observations are consistent with the anchor and that the updated anchor still satisfies the object's properties. Finally reacquiring an anchor when an object is reobserved after some time is a mixture of finding and tracking; if the object moves, it can be quite complex to account consistently for its behavior.

The DyKnow system of Heintz et al. [265] illustrates several of the preceding capabilities. It offers a comprehensive perception reasoning architecture integrating different sources of information, with hybrid symbolic and numeric data at different levels of abstraction, with bottom-up and top-down processing, managing uncertainty, and reasoning on explicit models of its content. It has been integrated with the planning, acting, and monitoring system of Doherty et al. [158] and demonstrated for the control of UAV rescue and traffic surveillance missions. In the latter, a typical anchoring task consists of recognizing a particular vehicle, tracking its motion despite occlusions, and reestablishing the anchor when the vehicle reappears (e.g., after a period in a tunnel).

7.1.4 Event and Situation Recognition

The dynamics of the environment is an essential source of information for an actor, as we just saw in the anchor tracking and reacquiring problems. It needs to be interpreted: what an observed sequence of changes means, what can be predicted next from past evolutions. These issues are essential for interacting with other actors, to understand their intensions and behavior, for example, for tutoring a robot to perform complex tasks (Argall et al. [24]) or in surveillance applications (Hongeng et al. [284]; Fusier et al. [210]).

The survey of Krüger et al. [355] covers an extensive list of contributions to action and plan recognition. These deal with *(i)* human action recognition, *(ii)* general activity recognition, and *(iii)* plan recognition. The former two types of processing provide input to the latter. Most surveyed approaches rely on signal processing and plan recognition techniques. The former use filtering approaches, Markov Chains, and Hidden Markov Models (HMM, e.g., Rabiner and Juang [502]). They have been successfully applied to movement tracking and gesture recognition by Wu and Huang [612] and Moeslund et al. [426]. The latter rely on the deterministic planning approaches of Kautz and Allen [320], Ramirez and Geffner [505], or the probabilistic approach of Geib and Goldman [218], as well as the parsing techniques of Pynadath and Wellman [499].

Most plan recognition approaches assume as input a sequence of symbolic actions. This assumption is hard to meet in practice. Usually actions are sensed through their effects on the environment. The recognition of actions from their effects depends strongly on the plan level. Decomposing the problem into recognizing actions then recognizing plans from these actions is fragile. More robust approaches have to start from the observation of changes.

Chronicle recognition techniques can be relevant to this problem. As defined in Chapter 4, a chronicle is a model for a collection of possible scenarios. It describes classes of events, persistence assertions, nonoccurrence assertions, and temporal constraints. A ground instance of a chronicle can be formalized as a nondeterministic timed automata. Beyond planning operators, chronicles can be used to describe situations and plans and recognize their occurrences from observations. The approach proposed by Ghallab [226] and Dousson et al. [162] is able to monitor a stream of observed events and recognize, on the fly, instances of modeled chronicles that match this stream. The recognition is efficiently performed by maintaining incrementally a tree of hypotheses for each partially recognized chronicle instance. These trees are updated or pruned as new events are observed or time advances. It has been demonstrated in robotics surveillance tasks. Recent development by Dousson and Le Maigat [163] have introduced hierarchization and the focus on rare events

The chronicle approach offers an interesting link between planning and observing. The SAM system of Pecora et al. [468] is a good illustration of such a link in the development of a system providing assistance to an elderly person. It uses a chronicle-like representation (timelines with interval algebra) offering online recognition, planning, and execution with multiple hypotheses tracking over weeks.

7.2 MONITORING AND GOAL REASONING

We argued in Chapter 1 that acting deliberately requires predicting continually what may come next. In open, variable, and dynamic environments, an actor should not be confident that its predictions are always going to occur. Performing actions in a blind open-loop manner would be brittle and lead frequently to failure. A deliberative actor needs a closed-loop feedback, allowing it to correct its actions when there is a discrepancy between its predictions and its observations. This is the role of monitoring.

More precisely, monitoring is in charge of *(i)* detecting discrepancies between predictions and observations, *(ii)* diagnosing their possible causes, and *(iii)* taking first recovery actions.

Monitoring has a broad scope, ranging from monitoring the low-level execution platform to the high-level reasoning on the appropriate goals for pursuing the actor's objectives and mission. Indeed, discrepancies between predictions and observations can be caused by platform errors and failures, for example, malfunctioning sensors or actuators and buggy commands. They can also be produced by unexpected events and environment contingencies that make the chosen refinement of current action or the chosen plan inappropriate. Finally, the actor has to keep its goals in perspective and monitor that they remain not only feasible but also relevant. In the remainder of this section, we discuss successively these three levels of monitoring.

7.2.1 Platform Monitoring

A physical actor has necessarily to monitor its platform and adapt its actions to the functioning status of its sensory-motor capabilities.[3] Low-level monitoring may be needed even when the execution platform is solely computational. One may argue that this monitoring is a platform dependent issue, which is not a component of deliberate acting. This is in part true. However, we already saw that deliberation has to rely on models of the actor's platform, including when the platform evolves. Further, deliberation techniques can be very relevant for performing platform monitoring functions. Let us briefly survey a few approaches.

The techniques for monitoring physical sensory-motor platforms often rely on signal filtering and parameter identification methods for fault detection and identification, and statistical and pattern recognition methods for diagnosis (see the survey of Pettersson [477]). More of interest to deliberation are the model-based diagnosis techniques. These usually take as input a triple *(System description, Components, Observation)* where the first term is a model of the platform, the second a finite list of its components, the third is an assertion inconsistent with the model expressing the observed fault. The diagnosis task is to find a minimum subset of components whose possible failure explains the observation. The recent framework of Baier et al. [32] formulates a model-based diagnosis problem as a planning problem with information gathering and reasoning on change.

Model-based techniques are well illustrated in a comprehensive monitoring, diagnosis, and recovery system called Livingstone for an earth observation spacecraft developed by Muscettola et al. [441] and Bernard et al. [53]. Livingstone relies on the approach of *qualitative model-based diagnosis* of Williams and Nayak [607]. The spacecraft is modeled as a collection of components, for example, a thrust valve. Each component is described by a graph whose nodes correspond to normal functioning states or to failure states of that component, for example, a valve closed, open or stuck. Edges

---

[3] This level of monitoring is sometime referred to as fault detection, identification, and recovery (FDIR).

are either nominal transition *commands* or exogenous transition *failures*. The latter are labeled by transition probabilities; the former are associated with transition costs and preconditions of the commands. A node is associated with a set of finite domain constraints describing the component's properties in that state, for example, when the valve is closed, *inflow* = 0 and *outflow* = 0. The dynamics of each component is constrained such that, at any time, exactly one nominal transition is enabled but zero or more failure transitions are possible. Models of all components are compositionally assembled into a system where concurrent transitions compatible with the constraints and preconditions may take place. The entire model is compiled into a temporal propositional logic formula, which is queried through a specific solver (with a truth-maintenance and a conflict-directed best-first search). Two query modes are used: *(i) diagnosis*, which finds the most likely transitions consistent with the observation, and *(ii) recovery*, which finds the least cost commands that restore the system into a nominal state. This monitoring system is well integrated with the spacecraft acting system. It computes a focused sequence of recovery commands that meets additional constraints specified by the acting system.

Livingstone and other similar model-based diagnosis systems are focused on the monitoring on the execution platform itself.[4] Monitoring the actor's interactions with a dynamic environment (e.g., in searching for an object and bringing it to a user) requires other techniques, which are discussed next.

7.2.2 Action and Plan Monitoring

Monitoring the causal structure of a plan. The synthesis of a plan provides a collection of actions, organized as a sequence, a partial order, a chronicle, or a policy. It also provides an important information for monitoring the progress of the plan, which is the causal structure of the plan. Basically, this causal structure says which effects of an action a are predicted to support which preconditions of an action a', constrained to come after a.

We have already discussed the causal structure of a plan in previous chapters, through the notion of causal links in a partial plan (Definition 2.30 in Section 2.5) or the notion of causally supported assertions in a timeline (Definition 4.9 in Section 4.2). Let us briefly discuss its use for monitoring in the simple case of sequential plans.

Let $\pi = \langle a_1, \ldots, a_i, \ldots, a_k \rangle$ be a sequential plan to be monitored for achieving a goal g. Let us use the regression of a goal through an action (see Equation 2.14) to define the sequence of intermediate goals associated with π as:

$$\mathcal{G} = \langle g_0, g_1, \ldots, g_i, \ldots, g_{k+1} \rangle, \text{ with}$$

$$g_i = \gamma^{-1}(g_{i+1}, a_i) \text{ for } 1 \leq i \leq k, \ g_{k+1} = g, \text{ and } g_0 = \varnothing.$$

In other words, action a_k can be performed in a state s and achieves g only if s supports g_k. Similarly, the subsequence $\langle a_{k-1}, a_k \rangle$ can be performed in a state s' and

---

[4] They can be qualified as *proprioceptive monitoring* approaches.

Algorithm 7.1 A simple monitoring of the progression of a plan

---

Progress-Plan$(\pi, \mathcal{G})$
  loop
    $\xi \leftarrow$ observed current state
    $i \leftarrow \max_j\{0 \le j \le k+1 \mid \xi$ supports $g_j\}$
    if $i = k+1$ then return success
    if $i = 0$ then return failure
    else perform action a_i

---

achieves g only if s' supports g_{k-1}. The entire plan π is applicable and achieves g only in a state that supports g_1.

$\mathcal{G}$ is easily defined from π and can be used to monitor the progress of π with the simple procedure in Algorithm 7.1. This procedure searches $\mathcal{G}$ in reverse order, looking for the first g_i, which is supported by current state. It then performs action a_i. The goal is achieved when the current state supports $g_{k+1} = g$. If the only supported intermediate goal is $g_0 = \varnothing$ (trivially supported by every state), then the plan π has failed.

Note that the procedure Progress-Plan does not follow π sequentially. It "jumps" to the action closest to the goal that allow to progress toward g. It may also go back and repeat several times previously performed actions until their required effects for following intermediate goals are observed.

Example 7.1. Consider a service robot for which a planner produces the following sequential plan: $\pi = \langle$move(door), open(door), move(table), pickup(tray), move(sink), putdown(tray, sink), pickup(medic), move(chest), putdown(medic,chest)$\rangle$. π says to move to door and open it because the robot cannot open it while holding the tray. When starting this plan the robot may observe that, despite its initial model of the environment, the door is already open. Progress-Plan would skip the first two actions and proceed with the move(table). Later on, after picking up the medic if the robot observes that it gripper is empty, it would repeat the pickup action. □

The intermediate goals in the sequence $\mathcal{G}$ are not independent. They can be organized such as to reduce the computational effort for finding the largest i such that ξ support g_i. The corresponding data structure is a tabular representation of a causal graph called a *triangle table*. It has been proposed together with the preceding procedure by Fikes [196] in Planex, an early monitoring and execution system associated with the Strips planner.

Progress-Plan alone is limited and remains at an abstract and simple level of monitoring. It has to be augmented with the monitoring of the commands refining the actions in π, with diagnosis of possible problems (i.e., why the state observed after performing a_i does not support g_{i+1}) and the control of repeated actions on the basis of this diagnosis (e.g., when does it make sense to repeat a pickup action).

Monitoring the invariants of a plan. An invariant of a state transition system is a condition that holds in every state of the system. For a planning problem (Σ, s_0, g), an invariant characterizes the set of reachable states of the problem. A state that violates the invariant cannot be reached from s_0 with the actions described in Σ. In other words, if φ is an invariant of (Σ, s_0, g), then for any plan π and any state $s \in \widehat{\gamma}(s_0, \pi)$, s supports φ. Going back to Example 7.1, if the robot has no action to lock or unlock the door, and if the door is initially unlocked, then door-status(door)=unlocked is an invariant of this domain. Note that the world *invariant* qualifies here a particular model of the world, not the world itself; monitoring violation of the invariant allows to detect discrepancies with respect to that model.

Invariants of a planning problem can be synthesized automatically, as shown for example by Kelleher and Cohn [326] or Rintanen [512]. Several authors have used invariants to speed up planning algorithms (e.g., Fox and Long [203]). However, at the acting level, we know that the assumption of a static environment does not hold: there can be other state transitions than those due to the actor's actions. For example, the door of Example 7.1 may become locked, this violating a plan that requires opening that door. The actor has to monitor that the current state supports the invariants relevant to its plan.

However, the invariants of a planning problem are often not sufficient for the purpose of monitoring. Many of the invariants entailed from (Σ, s_0, g) express syntactical dependencies between the variables of the problem, for example, a locked door is necessarily closed; it cannot be open.[5] Often, an actor has to monitor specific conditions that express the appropriate context in which its activity can be performed. For example, the robot has to monitor the status of its battery: if the charge level is below a threshold, than at most τ units of time are available in normal functioning before plugging at a recharge station. Such conditions cannot be deduced from the specification of (Σ, s_0, g); they have to be expressed specifically as monitoring rules.

A simple approach, proposed by Fraser et al. [207], considers an *extended planning problem* as a tuple $(\Sigma, s_0, g, \varphi)$, where φ is a condition, expressed formally in the same way as the preconditions of actions. Condition φ is a requirement for planning: π is a solution to the problem if every state $s \in \widehat{\gamma}(s_0, \pi)$ supports φ. It is also a requirement for acting: the actor has to monitor at acting time that every state observed while performing a plan π supports φ. A violation of this condition, due to any exogenous event or malfunction, means a failure of the plan. It allows quite early detection of infeasible goals or actions, even if the following actions in the plan appear to be applicable and produce their expected effects.

Several authors have developed elaborate versions of the foregoing idea with monitoring rules, in some logical or temporal formalism, associated to sensing and recovery actions together with efficient incremental evaluation algorithms at acting time. For example, the approach of Fichtner et al. [195] relies on the fluent calculus of Sandewall [523] with actions described by *normal* and *abnormal* preconditions. The former are the usual preconditions; the latter are assumed away by the planner as default; they are used as a possible explanation of a failure. For example, delivery of an object to a person may fail with abnormal preconditions of the object being lost or the person not being traceable. Abnormal effects are similarly specified. Discrepancies between

---

[5] The use of multivalued state variables reduces these dependencies compared with the use of predicates, but it does not eliminate them.

expectations and observations are handled by a prioritized nonmonotonic default logic and entail that default assumptions no longer hold. These explanations are ranked using relative likelihood, when available. The system is able to handle incomplete world models and observation updates received while acting or on demand from the monitoring system through specific sensory actions.

Ben Lamine and Kabanza [51] propose an interesting variant where Linear Temporal Logic formulas are used to express goals as well as correctness statements and execution progress conditions. A trace of the execution, observed and predicted at planning time is incrementally checked for satisfied and violated LTL formulas. For that, a *delayed formula progression* technique evaluates at each state the set of pending formulas; it returns the set of formulas that has to be satisfied by any remaining trace. The same technique is used both for planning (with additional precondition-effect operators and some search mechanism) and for monitoring.

The approach of Bouguerra et al. [91] uses domain knowledge expressed in description logic to derive expectations of the effects of actions in a plan to be monitored during execution. A first-order query language allows online matching of these expectations against observations. The parameters of action refer to world objects that have derived properties. These properties are checked to be either consistent or inconsistent with observations. Their consistency may be undetermined, triggering observation actions. An interesting extension handles flexible monitoring with probabilistic models, akin to Bayesian belief update. It relies on probabilistic plans with nondeterministic actions as well as on probabilistic sensing models.

Finally, let us mention the comprehensive approach of Doherty et al. [158], which relies on a *Temporal Action Logics* formalism of Kvarnström and Doherty [366] for specifying operators and domain knowledge. Formal specifications of global constraints and dependencies, together with planning operators and control rules, are used by the planner to control and prune the search. *Monitoring formulas* are generated from the descriptive models of planning operators (preconditions, effects, and temporal constraints) and from the complete synthesized plan, for example, constraints on the persistence of causal links. This automated synthesis of monitoring formulas is not systematic but selective, on the basis of hand-programmed conditions of what needs to be monitored and what does not. Additional monitoring formulas are also specified by the designer in the same expressive temporal logic formalism. For example, a UAV (the application domain of Doherty et al. [158]) should have its winch retracted when its speed is above a given threshold; it can exceed its continuous maximum power by a factor of η for up to τ units of time if this is followed by normal power usage for a period of at least τ'. The system produces plans with concurrent and durative actions together with conditions to be monitored during execution. These conditions are evaluated online using formula progression techniques. When actions do not achieve their desired results, or when some other conditions fail, recovery via a plan repair phase is triggered.

Monitoring integrated with operational models of actions. The previous examples of monitoring rules for a UAV express conditions on the normal functioning of the execution platform and its environment; they allow the detection of deviations from the required specifications. Such a detection is naturally integrated to operational models of actions with the refinement methods introduced earlier. Furthermore, detections of a malfunction or a deviation may trigger events to which are associated refinement methods for taking first corrective actions specific to the context.

Most of the acting systems discussed in Section 3.5.1, such as PRS, RAP, or TCA, have been used for action refinement and reaction to events as well as for monitoring. Most implementations using these systems integrate specific methods or part of such methods to handle monitoring functions.

Refinement methods introduced in Chapter 3 are adequate for expressing monitoring activities; RAE procedure can be used for triggering observation and commands required for monitoring.

7.2.3 Goal Reasoning

A deliberative actor has to keep its goals in perspective to make sure that they remain feasible and relevant to its long-term objectives or mission; when needed, it has to synthesize alternate goals. Goal reasoning is a monitoring function at the highest level; it continuously checks for unexpected events that may interfere with current goals.

Goal reasoning has been deployed in a few experiments. Let us mention briefly a few of them. The Mission Manager in the DS1 spacecraft experiment of Muscettola et al. [441] and Bernard et al. [53] offers some goal reasoning capabilities. It analyses the progress of the mission and determines which goals should be satisfied for the next planning window (one to two weeks). The selected goals are passed to the planner, together with constraints that need to be satisfied at waypoints identified by the Mission Manager (e.g., the amount of energy left in the batteries should be above a threshold at the end of the planning phase).

There is an analogous manager in the CPEF system of Myers [442], used in the simulation of operational deployments; this manager provides appropriate goals to the planner and controls the generation of plans. For a similar class of applications, the ARTUE system of Molineaux et al. [429] detects discrepancies when executing a plan; it generates an explanation, possibly produces a new goal, and manages possible conflict between goals currently under consideration. It uses decision theory techniques to decide which goal to choose. The approach proposes an original explanation system, which uses Assumption-based Truth Maintenance techniques to find the possible explanation of the observed facts. In Powell et al. [494], the authors extend ARTUE with a facility for teaching the system new goal selection rules.

Another example is the Plan Management Agent of Pollack and Horty [492] for handling personal calendars and workflow systems. This system addresses the following functions:

- Commitment management: commits to a plan already produced and avoids new plans that conflict with the existing ones.
- Alternative assessment: decides which of the possible alternative goals and plans should be kept or discarded.
- Plan control: decides when and how to generate a plan.

- Coordination with other agents: takes into account others' commitments and the cost of decisions involving their plans.

That system relies on temporal and causal reasoning; it is able to plan with partial commitments that can be further refined later.

Finally let us mention a class of approaches, called *Goal Driven Autonomy* (GDA) for reasoning about possibly conflicting goals and synthesizing new ones. These approaches are surveyed by Hawes [264] and Vattam et al. [577]. The former surveys a number of architectures supporting goal reasoning in intelligent systems. The latter reviews more than 80 contributions on various techniques for goal monitoring, goal formulation, and goal management, organized within a comprehensive goal reasoning analysis framework.

7.3 LEARNING AND MODEL ACQUISITION

Recall that methods for automated planning and acting rely on two types of action models: operational and descriptive. The acquisition of these models, as for any other kind of models to be used automatically, is a challenging bottleneck. Machine learning techniques, especially statistical techniques, have progressed significantly. Some of these techniques are relevant for the acquisition of planning and acting models, in particular learning operational models of actions. Indeed, operational models are at a lower level, more detailed, and often more domain-specific than descriptive models. They are more difficult to specify by hand.

Consequently, this section is mostly devoted to learning operational models for acting. We briefly introduce and survey methods for reinforcement learning (Section 7.3.1) and learning from demonstration (Section 7.3.2). A short discussion of approaches for learning descriptive models and domain specific heuristics for planning concludes the section.

7.3.1 Reinforcement Learning

Reinforcement learning methods aim at improving the performance of an actor by direct interaction with the world. They are based on statistics of trials and errors on past experiences. The actor learns how to perform a task by maximizing the long-term perceived benefit of its actions. There is no teacher providing examples of good behaviors in certain situations or advice about how to choose actions. The only feedback given to the actor at each step is a scalar: the reward associated with the action it has performed. As long as the actor has not tried all feasible actions in all encountered situations, it will not be sure that it uses the best ones. Reinforcement learning has to solve the compromise of *exploration* versus *exploitation*: the actor must make the most of what it already knows to maximize the benefit of its actions for the task at hand; to find the best actions, it must explore options it does not know enough about.

To introduce our notations, consider the elementary case in which a single action $a \in \{a_1, \ldots, a_n\}$ is sufficient to perform the task at hand. Let $r_i(a) > 0$ be the reward received after running action a at the ith time. We can estimate the quality $Q(a)$ of action a that has been executed k_a times by its average reward:

$$Q(a) = \begin{cases} q_0 & \text{if } k_a = 0, \\ \frac{1}{k_a} \sum_{i=1}^{k_a} r_i(a) & \text{othersise.} \end{cases} \tag{7.1}$$

An equivalent formulation maintains Q by incremental updates:

$$Q(a) \leftarrow Q(a) + \alpha[r_{k_a}(a) - Q(a)], \text{ with } \alpha = \frac{1}{k_a}. \tag{7.2}$$

When $k_a \rightarrow \infty$ for all a, the choice of the action that maximizes the reward is given by $\text{argmax}_a\{Q(a)\}$. However, as long as the exploration of alternatives has not been sufficient, the actor must try actions other than the estimated best one, according to various heuristics. We can define a function $\text{Select}_a\{Q(a)\}$ that favors the current best action and allows for exploring alternatives by various methods such as:

- choose action $\text{argmax}_a\{Q(a)\}$ with probability $(1 - \epsilon)$ and a randomly drawn action other $\text{argmax}_a\{Q(a)\}$ with probability ϵ, where ϵ is decreasing with experience; and
- choose an action according to a probabilistic sampling distribution, for example, with Boltzmann sampling, according to a probability distribution given by $e^{\frac{Q(a)}{\tau}}$, where τ is decreasing with experience.

When the environment is stationary, the update of $Q(a)$ in Equation 7.2 after performing action a becomes increasingly weak with big k_a. If the environment is not stationary, we can keep $\alpha < 1$ constant. Note also that the initialization value q_0 fosters exploration if q_0 is high with respect to other rewards. For example, if $q_0 = r_{max}$, the maximum reward, never-tried actions will be systemically preferred.

With these basic notions, let us now consider the interesting case where the task at hand requires a sequence of several actions, each interfering with the following ones, influencing the overall success and the sum of rewards. The framework generally used is that of Markov decision processes, as seen in Chapter 6. The actor seeks to learn an optimal policy that maximizes the expected sum of rewards.

One approach is to learn the MDP model and then to apply the planning techniques seen earlier (with rewards instead of costs, and maximization instead of minimization) to find the optimal policy and then use it. Learning a model means collecting enough statistics through an exploratory phase to estimate the probability distributions $\text{Pr}(s'|s, a)$ and the rewards $r(s, a)$. This direct approach requires a costly exploratory phase to acquire the model. It is often better to start performing the task at hand, given what is known, while continuing to learn, that is, combine the two phases of acquiring a model and finding the best action for the current model.

The Q-learning algorithm, Algorithm 7.2, meets this objective while avoiding the need to build the MDP model explicitly. Using the notations introduced in the previous chapter, Equation 6.6 can be reformulated as:

$$Q(s, a) = r(s, a) + \sum_{s' \in \gamma(s,a)} P(s'|s, a) \max_{a'}\{Q(s', a')\}.$$

Algorithm 7.2 Q-learning, a reinforcement learning algorithm.

Q-learning
  loop
    $a \leftarrow \text{Select}_a\{Q(s, a)\}$
    apply action a
    observe resulting reward $r(s, a)$ and next state s'
    $Q(s, a) \leftarrow Q(s, a) + \alpha[r(s, a) + \max_{a'}\{Q(s', a')\} - Q(s, a)]$ (i)
    $s \leftarrow s'$
  until termination condition

The basic idea of Q-learning is to perform an incremental update of $Q(s, a)$, similar to Equation 7.2. This update (ligne *(i)* in the algorithm) does not use the unknown probability parameters of the model, but the value of Q in a successor state s', as observed in current step of the trial.

Q-learning is called for each trial of the task at hand. The termination condition is the achievement of the task or a failure of the trial. Values of $Q(s, a)$ are initialized arbitrarily; they are global variables characterizing the task. The function $\text{Select}_a\{Q(s, a)\}$ favors $\text{argmax}_a\{Q(s, a)\}$ while allowing for the exploration of non maximal action with a frequency decreasing with experience. The parameter $\alpha \in [0, 1]$ is set empirically. When α is close to 1, Q follows the last observed values by weighting down previous experiences of a in s; when it is close to zero, previous experiences count more and Q does not change much; α can be set as decreasing with the number of instances (s, a) encountered.

It is possible to prove under reasonable assumptions the asymptotic convergence of Q-learning algorithm to optimal policies. In practice, however, this convergence is very slow in the number of trials. For physical actions, experiments are much more costly than the computational complexity. Simulated experiments can be a critical component in the implementation of a reinforcement learning approach.

There are several variants of the Q-learning algorithm. One of them, known as SARSA (for State, Action, Reward, State, Action), takes into account a sequence of two steps (s, a, s', a') before performing the update of the estimated quality of a in s by $Q(s, a) \leftarrow Q(s, a) + \alpha[R(s, a) + Q(s', a') - Q(s, a)]$. Other algorithms proceed by updating the value function $V(s)$ rather then the function $Q(s, a)$. Updates are performed over triplet (s, a, s') in a similar way: $V(s) \leftarrow V(s) + \alpha[r(s, a) + V(s') - V(s)]$. This algorithm, called TD(0), is generalized as the TD(λ) algorithm, which performs updates over all states, with a weighting depending on the frequency of meeting each state.

Another approach, illustrated by the DYNA algorithm, combines learning with planning. One maintains and updates estimates of the probability and reward parameters $\Pr(s'|s, a)$ and $r(s, a)$. At each step of a trial two updates are performed taking into account new estimates: a Q-learning update at current s and a, and a Value-Iteration type of update for other (state, action) pairs chosen randomly or according to some priority rule. Here, experience allows estimation of the model and the current policy.

The estimated model in turn allows for improvement of the policy. Each step is more computationally expensive than in Q-Learning, but the convergence occurs more rapidly in the number of trials.

The preceding approaches lack an important property in learning: the *capability to generalize*. When reaching a state s that has not been met before, an actor should be able to draw from its past experience with other states "similar" in some sense to s. The extension of Q-learning to continuous state and action spaces allows naturally for such a property: when using a metric space, it is reasonable to assume that nearby states, according to the metric of the space, have close estimate values $V(s)$ or $Q(s, a)$, and hence, can benefit from similar actions.

The parametric version of Q-learning implements such an approach. Here S and A are represented as two vectors of continuous state and control variables. Let $\theta = (\theta_1, \ldots, \theta_n)$ be a vector of parameters. We assume that $Q(s, a)$ can be approximated parametrically as a function $Q_\theta(s, a)$ parametrized by θ. An a priori class of functions is taken, for example, linear functions of state and control variables. Learning amounts to estimating the parameters θ of this model. Q-Learning is as described earlier, except that the update *(i)* does not change values in a table but the parameters of $Q_\theta(s, a)$. The process generally involves minimizing the mean squared error of Q with respect to Q^*; the latter is estimated at each iteration by the last observed update. The gradient algorithm gives the following formulation:

$$\theta \leftarrow \theta + \alpha[r(s, a) + \max_{a'}\{Q_\theta(s', a')\} - Q_\theta(s, a)]\frac{\partial Q_\theta(s, a)}{\partial \theta}. \tag{7.3}$$

This expression replaces *(i)* in Q-learning for each parameter θ_i. A similar formulation can be obtained for the estimate of V_θ in variant of Q-learning.

The parametric version of reinforcement learning has been more successful than the discrete version. It has been used with success in robotics, in demonstrations such as stabilizing an inverse pendulum, and in playing darts and simple ball games [475].

One of the main problem of reinforcement learning (continuous or discrete) is in the definition rewards. Indeed, the previous algorithms indicates, rather improperly, "observe reward $r(s, a)$." Rewards are seldom observable, even when the states are. One must provide the means to estimate the rewards from what is observable. Sometimes a function $r(s, a)$ is easy to specify, for example, the deviation from equilibrium for a stabilization task, or the deviation from the target for a tracking task. But often this is difficult. For example, it is unclear what can be the rewards of primitive actions in the tasks of driving a car or cooking an elaborate recipe.

This difficulty leads to the *inverse reinforcement learning* problem [3]. It can be formulated as follows: given the optimal policy provided by a teacher in a few demonstrations, what is the corresponding reward function that generates this policy.

In the unrealistic ideal case of an explicit finite MDP where $\pi^*(s)$ is known everywhere, $Q(s, a)$ is easily expressed as a function of the unknown values of $r(s, a)$; we want $Q(s, a)$ to be maximal for $a = \pi^*(s)$. This formulation is under specified: it has infinite solutions that are of not much interest. It can be extended with an additional criterion, for example, maximize the expression: $\sum_s[Q(s, \pi^*(s)) - \max_{a \neq \pi^*(s)} Q(s, a)]$, that is, the distance to the next best action. The problem can be solved by linear programming.

The formulation makes sense in parametric approaches in which the teacher's demonstrations can be generalized. One defines rewards as a parametrized function $r_\theta(s, a)$ of state and control variables (e.g., a linear function) and seeks to estimate its parameters by requiring that it meets the teacher's actions in demonstrated states. This estimation problem is solved by a combination of quadratic programming (an additional criterion is also needed) and dynamic programming.

As the reader has certainly noticed, inverse reinforcement learning is akin to learning from demonstration, discussed next.

7.3.2 Learning from Demonstrations, Advices, and Partial Programs

As underlined earlier, the definition of reward functions necessary to reinforcement learning is far from obvious. Moreover, it is rare to have a fully observable Markov state space, as demanded in the MDP formulation. It is possible to make a state space Markovian, but this requires significant engineering and adds generally unobservable components. The complexity of learning and planning techniques in partially observable MDP is prohibitive. Moreover, the experimental complexity in number of trials is much more expensive than the computational complexity. Reinforcement learning requires a large number of experiments to converge. Finally, it is common that the task to learn cannot be treated as a simple sequence of pairs *(state, action)*; it requires a plan or a control structure, such as repeating subsequences of actions until a certain condition is reached. For these reasons, learning from demonstration is a good alternative when the actor can benefit from the demonstrations of a teacher.

In learning from demonstration, a teacher gives to the actor the appropriate actions in well-chosen settings. This allows the teacher to control the learning process and gradually focus learning on the most difficult part of the task. The learner generalizes from the teacher demonstrations and learns the required behavior, for example, as a policy in simple cases or as a mapping from sensory states to elaborate plans in the general case.

Learning from demonstration involves an important issue related to the form of the teacher's demonstrations. These may range from specifications in a formal representation or a programming language adapted to the learner, to actual actions of the teacher in the environment using the teacher's own sensory-motor capabilities that the learner observes through its proper platform.

Learning from specifications. The former case can be set in the MDP framework. In *passive imitation*, for example, the teacher provides its demonstrations as a set of sequences $\{\sigma_1, \ldots, \sigma_m\}$, each sequence $\sigma = \langle s_1, a_1, s_2, a_2, \ldots \rangle$ encodes an actual demonstration of the teacher performing an instance of the task to learn. The learner synthesizes a policy on the basis of these demonstrations and from additional interactions with the environment with cost and/or reward feedback. In *active imitation*, the learner is further able to query the teacher, when needed, about what to do in some state s, that is, what is the desirable value of $\pi(s)$. Each query has a cost that needs to be taken into account in the overall learning process. In a variant, called *advice taking*, the learner can query which of two sequences σ_i or σ_j the teacher recommends as the best. Here the learner has to synthesize (i.e., to plan) the most informative sequences for its learning process, given the cost of queries. Research in these issues is active (e.g., [608, 303]), but so far has been applied mostly in academic benchmarks such as those of the Reinforcement Learning Competition (e.g., balance a vertical pole or maintain equilibrium on a bicycle).[6]

The *partial programming* framework offers a powerful approach for learning from specifications. The formulation is more general than the preceding imitation approaches. It relies on Semi-Markov Decision Processes (SMDP, see Section 6.8.4) and hierarchical nondeterministic finite-state machines. The latter are specified by the teacher as partial programs, with the usual programming constructs augmented with open choice steps, where the best actions remain to be learned. These specifications constrain the class of policies that can be learned using an extended SMDP Q-learning technique. The partial programming framework can yield to a significant speed-up in the number of experiments with respect to unguided reinforcement learning, as demonstrated in benchmark problems (e.g., the "taxi" domain of [153] with navigation in a grid to mimic loading and unloading randomly distributed passengers to their destinations). Few partial programming languages and systems have been proposed (e.g., Alisp [21, 465] or A2BL [542]) and demonstrated in simulations and video games. The framework seems to be well adapted to the partial specification of acting methods, where operational models are further acquired through learning.

Learning from the teacher's own actions. When the demonstrations take place as actual actions of the teacher in the environment, using the teacher's own sensory-motor capabilities, complex additional issues arise. To learn, the actor must establish a double mapping:

- a sensory mapping to interpret the observed demonstrations of the teacher and
- an actuation mapping to transpose the demonstrated actions to its own capabilities.

This double mapping is difficult. It often limits learning from demonstration and requires the teacher to use some pedagogy, that is, to understand at a low level how the learner might be able to follow the teacher demonstrations and to map them into its capabilities. Imagine, for example, teaching a robot how to open various types of doors or how to cook an elaborate recipe. Teaching would be more successful if the demonstrations are limited to elementary grasping and manipulation actions close to those feasible by the robot (and avoid actions such as tasting that the robot cannot perform).

Most of the work on learning from a teacher's actions has tried to avoid the issues of understanding and transposing the demonstrations. For example in robotics, quite often the demonstrations take place, through various means, in the robot's sensory-motor space. This form of learning through *teleoperation*, where the teacher acts directly in the actuators and proprioceptive sensor spaces of the robot, is quite successful (see [537, 475] and the survey of [24]), including for quite complex tasks such as helicopter acrobatics [2, 125].

---

[6] http://rlcompetition.org

A more ambitious approach would take into account at a higher level the need to understand and transpose the teacher's demonstrations. Learning should aim at acquiring a mapping from particular sensory states to plans. These can be obtained by plan recognition methods (e.g., [218, 499, 505]). The learner than develops its own plans, taking into account its specific capabilities, to achieve the effects of the teacher's demonstrations. Developments along similar approaches are being investigated (e.g., [455, 518]). They cover potentially a more general class of behaviors that can be demonstrated by the teacher and acquired by the learner (e.g., iterative actions). They also allow for extended generalization since they lead to acquire basic principles and rely on the learner's planning capabilities. They are finally more natural and easier for the teacher, because the teacher's actions are interpreted in terms of their intended effects on the environment rather than in a sequence of their low-level commands.

7.3.3 Acquiring Descriptive Models and Heuristics

The acquisition of descriptive models of actions has naturally been addressed as a *knowledge engineering* issue. A few early planners developed into rich environments supporting the designer or the end user for producing and maintaining complex plans. Good examples of these environments are O-Plan2 [562] and SIPE-2 [602, 603]. There is today an active community that organizes regular workshops, called Knowledge Engineering for Planning and Scheduling (KEPS), and a competition (ICKEPS). It has developed knowledge engineering methods and tools supporting, for example, the specification of requirements (e.g., with UML-type approaches); the modeling and reuse of planning knowledge; the analysis, graphic representation, and verification of a domain; or the metrics analysis and interactive modification of synthesized plans. Two recent surveys of the field [574, 529] list about a dozen software environments for knowledge engineering in planning. Many of these environments are devoted to classical planning, relying on the PDDL language and its extensions (e.g., itSIMPLE [573] or VIZ [590]). A few tools have been proposed for planning with HTN approaches (e.g., GIPO [543] or JABBAH [243]) or timeline-oriented approaches (e.g., EUROPA [37] or KEEN [54]). Knowledge engineering for nondeterministic or probabilistic models or for the integration of operational models and acting methods remains to be developed.

Many machine learning techniques have been proposed in planning. The surveys of [628, 300] analyze a wide spectrum of approaches ranging from decision trees, inductive logic, and explanation-based learning, to classification methods, Bayesien learning, and neural nets. These techniques have been used to learn domain-specific heuristics [618, 614, 159], control knowledge and macro actions [452, 126, 116]. For example, the approach of de la Rosa and McIlraith [140] relies on inductive logic programming techniques to learn from training examples useful state variables and domain specific control rules in Linear Temporal Logic to guide a forward search state-space planner such as TLPlan [28]. Learning techniques have also been used to improve the quality of plans with respect to cost, success rate [398, 558], or user's preferences [17]. Learning planning operators and domain models from plan examples and solution traces has been addressed with logic-based techniques, for example, in classical planning [617, 594, 627] and HTN planning [626, 283]. Learning probabilistic planning operators with techniques complementary to those of Section 7.3.1 has also been investigated (e.g., [462, 466]).

7.4 HYBRID MODELS

In Section 1.2.3, we mentioned the need to consider discontinuities in the interaction of an actor with the environment (e.g., the different phases in a grasp action), as well the need for modeling continuous evolutions within each phase (e.g., the motion of a robot arm while turning a door handle). Discontinuous transitions between different phases can be modeled using discrete state variables, while continuous evolutions within each phase can be modeled with continuous variables. Models with both discrete and continuous variables are called hybrid models.

Consider, for instance, a bouncing ball, the dynamics of which can be modeled with two phases, falling down and jumping up, with a clear discontinuity in the speed of the ball. A walking robot is another example; its movement at each half step is a continuous evolution. A thermostat can be modeled with a simple hybrid model, which evolves between a heating and a cooling phase, and controls the continuous increasing/decreasing temperature of the environment. Similarly, an airplane controller can switch among different phases with different continuous behaviors and required controls (e.g., taxiing, taking off, landing, and cruising). In each phase, its dynamic can be represented with the continuous laws of flight dynamics. Most complex systems, like intelligent cruise control in cars, or aircraft autopilot systems can be properly modeled with hybrid models too.

In hybrid models, discrete state variables describe how a system switches from one phase to another, while continuous state variables describe the system dynamics within a given discrete phase. Discrete state variable evolutions can be modeled, for example, by finite state automata, while continuous variable evolutions can be modeled by differential equations. The switching between discrete phases is usually determined by some conditions on the value of continuous variables in the current phase.

In the rest of this section, we first provide a brief introduction to hybrid automata, that is, a way to formalize hybrid models (Section 7.4.1); we then introduce hybrid automata with inputs and outputs (Section 7.4.2), a representation that provides the ability to do planning and acting with hybrid models. We then review some current techniques for planning and acting with hybrid models: planning as model checking (Section 7.4.3) and flow tubes (Section 7.4.4). We conclude the section with a note about how planning and acting with hybrid models can be approximated by discretizing continuous variables (Section 7.4.5).

7.4.1 Hybrid Automata

In this section, we provide a brief introduction to hybrid automata, a kind of formal models for hybrid systems. A hybrid automaton is a formal model with both discrete and continuous variables. The definition that follows is partly taken and adapted from Henzinger [274].

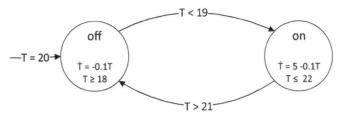

Figure 7.1. Hybrid automaton for a thermostat.

Definition 7.2. (Hybrid Automaton) A hybrid automaton is a tuple $H = (X, G, Init, Inv, Flow, Jump)$, where

- $X = \{x_1, \ldots, x_n\}$ is a finite set of continuous variables w.r.t. time, ranging over real values (each $x_i \in \mathrm{R}$). $\dot{X}$ is the set $\{\dot{x}_1, \ldots, \dot{x}_n\}$ where $\dot{x}_i$ stands for the first derivative of x_i w.r.t. time.
- G is a finite directed graph (V, E), called the Control Graph. Each $v_i \in V$ is called a *Control Mode*, each $e_{ij} = (v_i, v_j) \in E$ is called a *Control Switch*.
- $Init(v_i) \subseteq \mathrm{R}^n$ is a set of initial values of X for each control mode $v_i \in V$. It is a condition over the variables in X.
- $Inv(v_i) \subseteq \mathrm{R}^n$ is an invariant for each control mode $v_i \in V$. It is a condition over the variables in X.
- $Flow(v_i)$ represents the continuous change of variables in X for each control mode $v_i \in V$. It is a condition over the variables in X and $\dot{X}$.
- $Jump(e_{ij})$ represents the guard that triggers a control switch $e_{ij} = (v_i, v_j)$. It is a condition over X; when it is satisfied, it switches the control from mode v_i to mode v_j □

A control automaton H has a finite set of control modes V and can switch from one control mode to another one according to the control switches in E. The control graph $G = (V, E)$ is the discrete component of the control automaton H. In each control mode v_i, continuous change is modeled through the evolution of continuous variables in X. The invariant $Inv(v_i)$ states a condition over variables in X that is satisfied whenever H is in control mode v_i. $Flow(v_i)$ describes how continuous variables change while H is in control mode v_i. $Jump(e_{ij} = (v_i, v_j))$ is a condition over the continuous variables that determines when the control mode should switch from v_i to v_j.[7]

Example 7.3. A thermostat can be modeled with the hybrid automaton in Figure 7.1. It has a single variable T representing the temperature: $X = \{T\}$. The thermostat can be in two control modes, heater on or heater off. $G = \{V, E\}$, where $V = \{\text{on}, \text{off}\}$, $E = \{(\text{on}, \text{off}), (\text{off}, \text{on})\}$. We suppose that initially the heater is off and the temperature is 20 Celsius: $Init(\text{off}) \triangleq T = 20$. The heater remains off if the temperature is above 18 degrees Celsius: $Inv(\text{off}) \triangleq T \geq 18$. When the heater is off, the temperature falls according to the flow condition $Flow(\text{off}) \triangleq \dot{T} = -0.1T$. The heater may turn on as soon as the temperature falls below 19 degrees: $Jump((\text{off}, \text{on})) \triangleq T < 19$. Since $Inv(\text{off}) \triangleq T \geq 18$, at the latest the heater will go on when the temperature falls to 18 degrees. When the heater is on, the temperature rises according to $Flow(\text{on}) \triangleq \dot{T} = 5 - 0.1T$. The heater continues to heat while the temperature is below 22 degrees

---

[7] This interpretation of a guard is different from usual interpretations in planning [77].

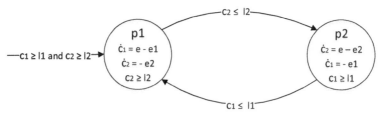

Figure 7.2. A charging station for two plants.

Celsius: $Inv(\text{on}) \triangleq T \leq 22$. It turns off when the temperature is higher than 21 degrees: $Jump((\text{on}, \text{off})) \triangleq T > 21$. □

The intended meaning of the *Jump* condition is that the switch takes place non-deterministically for any value that satisfies the control switch condition *Jump*. For instance, suppose that the variable x changes value in a control mode v_i by starting from a negative value and by increasing monotonically, and suppose that the control switch $Jump((v_i, v_j))$ is $x \geq 0$. The switch can happen when x has any positive value, and not necessarily when $x = 0$. However, we should notice that the actual condition for the switch is determined both by the control switch condition $Jump((v_i, vj))$ and by the inviariant condition $Inv(v_i)$. For instance, if $Inv(v_i)$ is $x \leq 1$, then the switch will take place nondeterministically when x satisfies the condition $0 \leq x < 1$, that is, at the latest when x rises to value 1. We can easily impose a deterministic switch, for instance, in our example, with $Jump((v_i, v_j)) = 0$, or with $Jump((v_i, v_j)) \geq 0$ and $Inv(v_i) < 0$.

Example 7.4. In this example, we consider an automatic battery charging station that has to charge two plants, depending on whether the level of the battery of each plant gets below two threshold values, l1 and l2 for the two plants p1 and p2, respectively. We suppose that the charging system charges at a constant rate e, for only one plant at a time; it can switch from one to the other instantaneously. We suppose that plant p1 and p2 consume energy with rate e1 and e2, respectively. The objective of the charging station is to keep the charge of each plant above the threshold values. The corresponding hybrid automaton is depicted in Figure 7.2.

The level of the each plant battery charges is described by two continuous variables: $X = \{c_1, c_2\}$, for each plant p1 and p2, respectively. The charging station can be on two control modes, charging one plant or the other. $G = \{V, E\}$, where $V = \{\text{p1}, \text{p2}\}$, $E = \{(\text{p1}, \text{p2}), (\text{p2}, \text{p1})\}$. We suppose that initially the station is charging plant p1, and both plants have charges above their threshold: $Init(\text{p1}) \triangleq c_1 \geq \text{l1}$ and $c_2 \geq \text{l2}$. While charging one of the two plants, the charge of the other one should be above the threshold: $Inv(\text{p1}) \triangleq c_2 \geq \text{l2}$ and $Inv(\text{p2}) \triangleq c_1 \geq \text{l1}$. While a plant is charged at rate e, its charge level increases linearly by e, but we have to take into account that it also consumes energy at its rate (the plant is supposed to work while it is charged). We also have to take into account that the other plant is consuming energy at its own rate: $Flow(\text{p1}) \triangleq \dot{c}_1 = e - \text{e1}$ and $\dot{c}_2 = -\text{e2}$, while $Flow(\text{p2}) \triangleq \dot{c}_2 = e - \text{e2}$ and $\dot{c}_1 = -\text{e1}$. The station switches from one mode to another when the opposite battery gets below its own threshold: $Jump((\text{p1}, \text{p2})) \triangleq c_2 \leq \text{l2}$ and $Jump((\text{p2}, \text{p1})) \triangleq c_1 \leq \text{l1}$. □

The behavior of the systems described in this section can be formalized as hybrid automata. As intuitively described in the previous examples, such behavior results in continuous change (flows) and discrete change (jumps). Hybrid automata are specifically suited for the verification of hybrid models. Different verification tasks have been studied, such as the reachability problem, that is, whether a set of states can be reached from an initial set of states, a basic task for the verification of safety and liveness requirements. In general, these verification tasks are undecidable. See Henzinger [274] for a formal account including complexity results about the verification of properties of hybrid automata.

7.4.2 Input/Output Hybrid Automata

To show how an actor can do planning and acting with hybrid models, we introduce *input/output (I/O) hybrid automata*, that is, hybrid automata where discrete and continuous variables are distinguished into input and output variables, and input variables are distinguished into controllable and uncontrollable variables.

To define I/O hybrid automata, let us first notice that the discrete component of an hybrid automaton can be described with discrete state variables. The set of control modes V (see Definition 7.2) can be represented with a set of discrete variables $Y = \{y_1, \ldots, y_m\}$ ranging over discrete values. Each complete assignment to variables $y_1, \ldots, y_m$ corresponds to a control mode $v_i \in V$. This is similar to a state variable representation of a set of states in Section 2.1.2.

Given the two sets X and Y of continuous and discrete variables, the definition of an I/O hybrid automaton extends Definition 7.2 by distinguishing (discrete and continuous) *input variables* from *output variables*: $X = X_{in} \cup X_{out}$ and $Y = Y_{in} \cup Y_{out}$, where $X_{in} \cap X_{out} = \varnothing$ and $Y_{in} \cap Y_{out} = \varnothing$.

Moreover, discrete and continuous input variables are distinguished into *controllable and uncontrollable variables*: $X_{in} = X_{in}^c \cup X_{in}^u$ and $Y_{in} = Y_{in}^c \cup Y_{in}^u$, where $X_{in}^c \cap X_{in}^u = \varnothing$ and $Y_{in}^c \cap Y_{in}^u = \varnothing$.

The idea is that a component of an actor can interact with a system modeled as an I/O hybrid automaton by determining the discrete/continuous controllable input variables of the system. The actor can perceive its status through the discrete/continuous output variables of the system. An actor can therefore assign values to the controllable inputs, although this is not possible for uncontrollable variables, the value of which is determined by the environment. Uncontrollable variables obey to dynamics that cannot typically be modeled. They can represent external forces, the result of exogenous events, actions of other agents, or noise in sensing the external environment.

In a conceptual model of an actor (see Figure 1.1), commands change the values of discrete and continuous controllable input variables, whereas percepts affect discrete and continuous output variables. The model can evolve through changes in both controllable and uncontrollable variables. The actor can be seen as a reactive systems that iteratively perceives the output variables in X_{out} and Y_{out} and reacts by determining the value of controllable input variables in X_{in}^c and Y_{in}^c.

An actor can plan for and perform actions that change the control mode of the hybrid automaton by assigning values to (some of) the variables in Y_{in}^c and in X_{in}^c. We might represent actions that change the values of discrete variables in Y_{in}^c with purely discrete models, like those presented in previous chapters. For instance, planning to determine the control mode of the hybrid system could be done with a planning domain $\Sigma = (S, A, \gamma)$, where states in S correspond to control modes in V represented with discrete variables in Y, and γ can be the transition function of deterministic models (Chapter 2), nondeterministic models (Chapter 5), or probabilistic models (Chapter 6).[8]

However, the actor has to take into account that the model allows for continuous variables X, like in the acting part of the hierarchical representation of Chapter 3. The actor needs also to determine which are the continuous variables in input to the system modeled with an hybrid automaton, that is, the variables in X_{in}^c. Moreover, the actor must deal with (discrete and continuous) uncontrollable variables, which may determine an uncontrollable switch of the control mode, that is, Y^u and X^u. The effects of uncontrollable discrete variables in Y^u can be modeled with nondeterministic domain models as in Chapter 5.

For all the reasons mentioned so far, planning and acting with hybrid models is much more complex than with purely discrete models.[9]

Example 7.5. Consider Example 7.4. The two control modes p1 and p2 can be represented by a discrete controllable input variable: $Y_{in}^c = \{p\}$, that can range over two values p1 and p2. Let us now modify the example: the charging station, rather than charging the plants at a constant rate e, can choose to charge plants at different rates between zero and a maximum rate emax. This can be modeled with a continuous controllable input variable x whose value is in R and in the interval (0, emax]: $\dot{X}_{in}^c = \{e\}$. Moreover, the two plants consume energy at a rate that depends on the load of tasks that they have to perform, and this load is not under the actor's control: we have therefore two continuous uncontrollable input variables e_1 and e_2: $X_{in}^u = \{e_1, e_2\}$. Finally, the current charge of the two plants can be perceived by the actor: $X_{out} = \{c_1, c_2\}$. The goal is to keep the charge of each plant above the two threshold values l1 for plant p1 and l2 for plant p2.   □

Let us now briefly introduce some techniques for planning and acting with hybrid models.

7.4.3 Planning as Model Checking

The idea is to use existing model checkers for hybrid automata (see, e.g., [274]) to do planning with hybrid models in the case of reachability goals. A goal in a hybrid model is defined as a condition on the continuous variables in X and as a subset of the set of control modes V (see Definition 7.2).

In hybrid model checking it is possible to represent a hybrid planning domain by encoding actions that have effects over discrete and continuous variables. For instance, we can have an additional state variable that represents the action that is performed

---

[8] If not all the variables in Y are observable in all situations, then we may need techniques that deal with partial observability; see Chapter 5.

[9] Even model checking is in general undecidable with hybrid models.

(see, e.g., [78]). Given a goal, we can define its complement, that is the set of control modes that are not in the set of control modes of the goal and the negation of the goal conditions on the continuous state variables in X. We can then search exhaustively (by model checking) whether the complement of the goal is satisfied. This amounts to verifying what in model checking literature is called a safety property, that is, verifying whether the complement of the goal is always satisfied. A safety property can be expressed in temporal logic, for example, LTL or CTL, extended with conditions over continuous variables, see Henzinger [274]. If the property is satisfied, then no plan that satisfies the original hybrid planning problem exists. If the property is not satisfied, it means that there is a plan. In this latter case, model checkers return an error trace called a counterexample, which in our case is a solution plan that reaches our original goal.

This approach reduces the planning problem to a verification problem. Two problems must, however, be taken into account. First, in general, reachability is not decidable with hybrid automata. Indeed, the number of possible values of continuous variables can be infinite, and the condition over continuous variables and their derivatives can be of any kind. There are classes of hybrid automata that are decidable. One of them is *rectangular hybrid automata* [274]. A hybrid automaton is rectangular if the flow conditions are independent of the control modes and the variables are pairwise independent.[10] In each control mode of a rectangular automaton, the first derivative of each variable is given a range of possible values, and that range does not change with control switches. With each control switch of a rectangular automaton, the value of each variable is either left unchanged, or changed nondeterministically to a new value within a given range of possibilities. The behaviors of the variables are decoupled because the ranges of possible values and derivative values for one variable cannot depend on the value or derivative value of another variable.

The second problem we have to take into account is the following. If we have nondeterminism in the switch mode, then the solution is not guaranteed to be a safe (cyclic or acyclic) solution, according to Definition 5.8. If we assume that all discrete and continuous transitions are deterministic, then the problem reduces to find a sequential plan.

One example along this direction is the work in Bogomolov et al. [78, 77], whose idea is to start from a language for describing planning domains with both discrete and continuous variables, to give semantics in terms of hybrid automata and then apply existing model checkers to find a solution. Bogomolov et al. [78, 77] start from the PDDL+ planning language [205]. PDDL+ allows for the definition of models with discrete and continuous variables. Continuous dynamics is modeled through processes and exogenous events, which model dynamics that are initiated by the environment.

In PDDL+, the discrete component of an hybrid system is described by a set of propositions, while the continuous component is modeled with a vector of real variables. Discrete transitions are described through preconditions and effects. Preconditions are conjunctions of propositions and numeric constraints over the continuous variables. Events are represented with preconditions that, when fired, trigger the event. Processes are active as long as their preconditions are true and describe the continuous change of continuous variables. PDDL+ allows for durative actions that have preconditions and

---

[10] This is a rather strong requirement.

effects as conjunctions on propositional variables as well as constraints on continuous variable; they have preconditions that should hold when the action starts, during its execution, and at the end of the action.

PDDL+ planning domains have therefore some similarities with hybrid automata. Bogomolov et al. [78, 77] exploit the close relationship of the PDDL+ semantics with hybrid automata. They provide a semantics of PDDL+ in terms of hybrid automata, even if PDDL+ assumptions raise some semantic issues. Among them, the PDDL+ "ϵ-separation assumption" states that no two actions are allowed to simultaneously occur if they update common variables (mutex actions). Plans have to meet the ϵ-separation condition, that is, interfering actions must be separated by at least a time interval of length ϵ. Indeed this problem is related to the PDDL2.1 model of temporal problems [204], whose model of durative actions does not allow for concurrency unless ϵ-separation is assumed.

A further difference between PDDL+ and hybrid automata is the semantics of events. A number of assumptions is made about events and processes, but the most relevant difference with hybrid automata is that events and processes start as soon as their preconditions become satisfied, while in hybrid automata transitions might happen at any time when the *Jump* condition is satisfied and the invariants are not satisfied (see Section 7.4.1).

In [78], a first translation from PDDL+ to hybrid automata is defined which does not take into account the different semantics of events. Since transitions are allowed to happen at any time when a condition is satisfied, then the model checker may not find a plan in the case in which a plan does exist with the restricted PDDL+ semantics, that is, with events that are triggered as soon as preconditions are true. For this reason, the approach is not complete, that is, it may not find a plan when a plan does exist. Such approach can instead be used to prove the non existence of a plan. The approach is complete when there are no events.

In Bogomolov et al. [77], the authors propose an exact translation of PDDL+ into hybrid automata that mimics the semantics of PDDL+ events. The translation guarantees that traces in the obtained hybrid automata correspond to sequential plans in the original planning domain in the case of linear hybrid automata and can handle hybrid automata with affine dynamics with an over-approximation that can be made arbitrarily precise.

7.4.4 Flow Tubes

Flow tubes represent a set of trajectories of continuous variables with common characteristics that connect two regions. The underlying idea is that a flow tube is a bounding envelope of different possible evolutions of one or a few continuous variable that obey some constraints. Flow tubes can represent the preconditions and the effects of actions over continuous variables. They can be used to do planning with hybrid models. Let us illustrate the intuitive idea of flow tubes with a simple example.

Example 7.6. Figure 7.3 shows a simple flow tube for a continuous variable x that evolves over time t. The intended meaning of the flow tube is that if the value of variable x is in

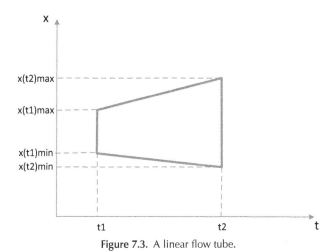

Figure 7.3. A linear flow tube.

$[x(t_1)_{min}, x(t_1)_{max}]$ at time t_1, then it is predicted that the value of x at time t_2 will be in $[x(t_2)_{min}, x(t_2)_{max}]$, and that x between these two time points will remain in the drawn trapezium.

The interval of initial possible values $[x(t_1)_{min}, x(t_1)_{max}]$ of x is called the initial region, and interval $[x(t_2)_{min}, x(t_2)_{max}]$ is the final region. The flow tube depicted in Figure 7.3 connects the initial region $[x(t_1)_{min}, x(t_1)_{max}]$ to the final region $[x(t_2)_{min}, x(t_2)_{max}]$.

The idea is that an action a can modify the continuous variable x according to the law described by the flow tube. We can express preconditions of action a with regions of continuous variables (interval of values of x in our example) where the action is applicable, and postconditions with the resulting final region in a given duration (e.g., after the interval $t_2 - t_1$ in our example).

Figure 7.3 shows a simple linear flow tube that can be represented with a linear equation in the variables x and $\dot{x}$, assuming that $\dot{x}$ is constant.

$$x(t_2)_{min} = x(t_1)_{min} + \dot{x}(t_2 - t_1)$$
$$x(t_2)_{max} = x(t_1)_{max} + \dot{x}(t_2 - t_1)$$

Conditions *Init*, *Inv*, and *Flow* of hybrid automata (Definition 7.2) could be used to represent flow tubes. For instance, let us suppose that in a node v_i variable x can evolve as described by the flow tube in Figure 7.3. We have that $Init(v_i)$ is a condition that contraints the values of x between $x(t_1)_{min}$ and $x(t_1)_{max}$; $Flow(v_i)$ and $Inv(v_i)$ should represent the bundle of lines from any x with value between $x(t_1)_{min}$ and $x(t_1)_{max}$ to a point between $x(t_2)_{min}$ and $x(t_2)_{max}$. $Flow(v_i)$ and $Inv(v_i)$ should constrain the bundle to remain in the flow tube envelop.   □

Flow tubes can be more complex than the one shown in Figure 7.3, like that in the next example.

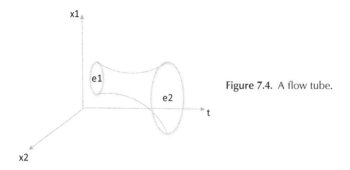

Figure 7.4. A flow tube.

Example 7.7. Figure 7.4 shows a flow tube of two variables x_1 and x_2, which evolve over time t. The intended meaning of the flow tube is that if the value of variables x_1 and x_2 at time t_1 is in ellipse e_1, then it is predicted that the value of x_1 and x_2 at time t_2 will be in ellipse e_2, and that x_1 and x_2 between these two time points will remain in the drawn envelope.   □

The most notable example of planning with hybrid models based on flow tube is the work in [381]. The idea is based on the notion of hybrid planning graph: a planning graph [74] is used to represent the effects of actions over discrete variables, while flow tubes are used to represent the effects over continuous variables. Hybrid planning graphs are encoded as an extension of mixed integer programming (linear/nonlinear), which represents discrete elements with logic prositions.

The planning domain is described through a set of hybrid actions, each of which has preconditions, effects, continuous evolution dynamics, and a duration. Preconditions can be continuous or discrete. A continuous precondition is a conjunction of (in)equalities over state variables, and a discrete precondition is a conjunction of propositions. Effects are both discrete facts, represented by a conjunction of propositions, and the continuous effect of the action.

Conceptually, the difference with respect to planning in discrete state transition system is that instead of looking for a path in a graph, planning searches for a path through connected flow tubes (see Figure 7.5). Flow tubes are connected by finding an intersection between the final region of a flow tube (the effects of an actions over continuous variables) and the preconditions of a subsequent action (represented as well as a region of the flow tube). Connection conditions guarantee that all valid plans are included in

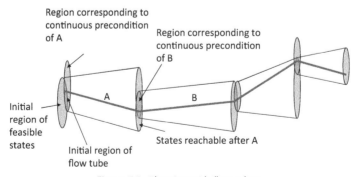

Figure 7.5. Planning with flow tubes.

the graph. However, the condition is not sound, meaning that not all plans in the graph are valid. A further step encodes the hybrid flow graph as a mixed integer program, which makes sure that the output plan is valid and optimal.

In the case of complex flow tubes that cannot be represented with linear equations, various approximation methods can be used. Hofmann and Williams [282] use a polyhedral approximation, which approximates the tubes as slices of polyhedra for each time step. Kurzhanskiy and Varaiya [360] use an ellipsoidal calculus for approximation that has proven highly efficient. The work of Li and Williams [381] makes use of and extends planning graphs with flow tubes. However, we believe the work is especially interesting because the ideas underlying flow tubes could be used in general with any state-space planner.

7.4.5 Discretization Techniques

Discretization techniques discretize the continuous variables of the hybrid model, and apply techniques suited to discrete models, like those described in the rest of this book. However, finding a suitable discretization is an important and critical issue: it can affect the plan generation speed, the precision of the solution and, sometimes even more critical, its correctness; that is, a plan that achieves a goal in the discretized model may not achieve a goal in the corresponding hybrid model.

A discretized problem is an approximation of the original problem, and it can of course induce errors. When continuous variables are discretized, while the system evolves, their real value can be different from what is foreseen. It is possible to prove that, given an error threshold, there always exists a discretization that allows to generate solution plans, which when mapped to the original hybrid model, have an approximation error below that threshold. It is possible to use a fixed discretization or to generate approximate solutions and then to perform a validation step to understand whether the approximate solution is acceptable and, in case it is not, to reiterate the process by refining the discretization. This process is similar to the guaranteed approximation procedure GAP for Value Iteration (Algorithm 6.6).

Löhr et al. [391] adopt a discretization approach. A temporal numeric planning task is defined with a set of state variables, which is partitioned into discrete and continuous state variables. The initial state is given by an assignment over all variables and the set of goal states is defined by a partial state assignment. Durative actions are represented with preconditions and effects over both continuous and discrete state variables. Preconditions and effects of durative actions specify conditions before, during, and after the action duration. An action is represented with a triple (C, E, δ), where C is a condition, E are the effects, and δ is the duration of a. A condition C is a triple of partial variable assignments over discrete variables, representing the start conditions before the action, the persistent conditions during the action, and the end conditions after action. E is a tuple with start effects and end effects, δ represents the duration of the action. The start and the end effects are finite sets of conditional effects (c, e). The effects condition c is again a triple of start, persistent, and end conditions, and e is an effect that assigns a value to a continuous variable. This approach handles time with the durative action model of PDDL2.1 [205] (see the discussion in Section 4.6).

For solving the generated planning tasks, the approach described in Löhr et al. [391] makes use of the Temporal Fast Downward planner (TFD) [186]. While in Löhr et al.'s 2006 work [391] the assumption is that the estimated state is the actual state, their later work [392] extends the approach to uncertain state information thus providing the ability to deal with noisy sensors and imperfect actuators.

The work of Della Penna et al. [149] proposes an iterative discretization approach based on explicit-state model checking techniques for the generation of universal plans. The idea is to start with a coarse discretization, and refine the discretization until the discretized solution is valid against the hybrid model according to a desired error threshold. The planner, UPMurphy, asks the user for the definition of a discretization granularity. It then creates the discretized model and performs a breadth-first reachability analysis. The idea is to use a model checker to perform an exhaustive search for a sequence of states leading to a goal state and collect all the sequences instead of the first one. This approach allows UPMurphy to generate universal plans. To apply explicit model checking on a finite number of states, UPMurphy fixes a finite temporal horizon that requires each plan to reach the goal in at most a given number of actions.

The approach can lead to a state explosion in the case a coarse discretization is required.

7.5 ONTOLOGIES FOR PLANNING AND ACTING

Research in automated planning and research in ontologies and related semantic representations have been pursued along distinct and separated research agenda. Despite this, there are several important intersections and connections among them.

Ontologies can be used to describe the elements of a planning domain, that is, relations among objects of a planning domain, but also relations among actions, tasks, plans, and goals. Planning algorithms can be integrated to and extended with techniques for reasoning about ontologies. Description Logic (DL) is a well studied family of approaches devised for such reasoning.

In the rest of this section, we first provide a brief and informal introduction to ontologies and DL (Section 7.5.1). We then discuss their relations and possible usage for planning and acting (Section 7.5.2). We finally conclude with a discussion on the need for research in semantic mapping in hierarchical representations for planning and acting (Section 7.5.4).

7.5.1 Ontologies and Description Logic

An ontology is informally defined as "an explicit specification of a conceptualization" [247], where a "conceptualization" is a definition of concepts, their relationships and properties. This definition is used as an abstract model of some aspects of the world. Concepts are typically classes, individuals (i.e., members of a class), attributes (e.g., properties of classes and members of classes), and relationships (e.g., relations among class members). The definitions of concepts provide a semantics description, that is, information about their meaning, including constraints they must obey. Ontologies are an "explicit specification" in the sense that the model should be specified in some formal unambiguous language, making it processable in an automated way by a computer. An ontology consists of:

- A set C of concepts (or class) and a set R of binary relations.
- A hierarchy H in which concepts and relations are hierarchically related by a subsumption relation $\sqsubseteq$ (a partial ordering): if c_1 and c_2 are concepts, then $c_1 \sqsubseteq c_2$ means that c_1 is a subclass of c_2. Similarly for relations: $r_1 \sqsubseteq r_2$ means that relation r_1 is a subclass of relation r_2. Members of a subclass inherit the properties of their parent class.
- A set A of ontology axioms that describe and provide constraints over concepts and relations.

For instance, in Example 2.3, we have robots that are subclasses of vehicles, containers that are subclasses of objects that can be transported, and so on.

Description Logic (DL) [27] is a family of formal knowledge representation languages suited for representing ontologies and for reasoning about them. The DL family languages differ in expressivity and computational complexity of the reasoning algorithms for each language. In general, a DL language can express definitions of classes and relations (see also [232] for a brief introduction to DL). Class definitions can include disjunction and negation as well as constraints on the relations to other classes. A relation between a class (its domain) and another class (its range) can be constrained in cardinality and type. A class can be defined as a subclass of another class. Similarly, relations can also be given definitions and therefore have subclasses as well. Class partitions can be defined by specifying a set of subclasses that represent the partitions and can be exhaustive if all instances of the class belong to some partition and disjoint if there is no overlap in the subclasses. A class can be denoted as a primitive class and not given a definition, and in that case, their subclasses and instances must be explicitly indicated.

Description logic reasoning systems use these definitions to automatically organize class descriptions in a taxonomic hierarchy and automatically classify instances into classes whose definitions are satisfied by the features of the instance. Specifically, description logic reasoners provide the following main mechanisms:

- class subsumption, where a class c_1 subsumes another class c_2 if its definition includes a superset of the instances included in c_2;
- instance recognition, where an instance belongs to a class if the instance's features (roles and role values) satisfy the definition of the class;
- consistency checking, that is, mechanisms to detect inconsistent definitions; and
- inheritance inference, that is, the automated inheritances of properties by members of subclasses.

7.5.2 Ontologies and Planning

A first obvious use of ontologies for planning is for the description of objects in the planning domain. A planning domain model describes how actions change the state of the world, and this is done through state variables that change values. Each state variable represents a specific object of the domain and has an intended semantics. In the examples of this book, we refer to objects such as robots, rooms, doors, containers, and cars. A representation of a planning domain should take into account relations (e.g., hierarchical relations) among different classes of objects, and their instances. For instance, it is clear in Example 3.4 that *sliding door*, *pushing door*, and *pulling door* are subclasses of the class *door*. This use of ontologies is a way to represent rigid relations (see Section 2.1.2). Ontologies can represent such relations among (classes of) objects of the domain, on which reasoning (e.g., with DL) can be an important component for solving planning problems.

Reasoning can be performed using ontologies that describe the objects of the planning domain, but also ontologies about actions, tasks, plans, and goals. For instance, DL subsumption mechanism can be used to automatically infer class-subclass subsumption relations as well as classify instances into classes based on their definitions. DL descriptions of domain objects, actions, plans, and goals, as well as DL reasoning capabilities can be exploited during plan generation, plan recognition, or plan evaluation. As clearly described in the survey paper by Gil [232], some of the reasoning capabilities of DL have been investigated within the Knowledge Representation and Reasoning community, but they have not been incorporated within state of the art planning algorithms. In Gil's work [232], four main uses of description logic are advocated, namely ontologies about:

- **objects**, to reason about different types objects in the domain;
- **actions**, to reason about action types at different levels of abstraction;
- **plans**, to reason about plan subsumption; and
- **goals**, to reason about relations among different goals.

7.5.3 Planning and Acting Based on Description Logic

There has actually been work using ontologies and DL in planning, starting from De Giacomo et al. [137], which exploits the correspondence between dynamic logic and description logic to represent actions, including sensing actions. Moreover, planning and ontologies have been used in several approaches to composition of semantic Web services, most of them based on the Web Ontology Language (OWL), and OWL-S (OWL for Services), which is a language for implementing the DL formalism (see, e.g., [544, 365, 417, 554]). The basic idea of all these approaches is to use planning over domains that are described with ontology-based languages. A different approach is proposed in [483], where the idea is instead to keep separate and to use different formalisms for the description of actions and the ontological descriptions of objects, and to link them through semantic annotations. This approach provides the ability to exploit simple reasoning mechanisms at the ontological level, integrated with effective reasoning mechanisms for planning for Web services.

DL and other knowledge representation techniques have also been integrated with planning techniques and applied to the field of robotics (see, e.g., [138]), including the work based in GOLOG [379, 377]. A recent approach along this line is proposed by Hartanto and Hertzberg [257], where the planning domain as well as HTN planning concepts are represented in DL. Resoning in DL is then used to generate concise versions of each individual planning problem for the HTN planner, where irrelevant aspects are filtered away. On the basis of this idea, the work in Awaad et al. [26] deals in some way with the problem of planning and acting by adapting plans to changes in the environment. This work is a preliminary proposal toward the objective to build actors that can recover from failures both during planning and execution by finding alternative objects to be used in their plans to achieve their goals and by taking advantage of opportunities that can arise at run-time. This is done by using the concept of "functional affordance," which describes in DL what an object is used for. The notion of "conceptual space" is used to measure the similarity among different objects that, through the description of their affordances, can be used in place of unavailable objects during both planning and acting. For instance, in case a plan fails because of a missing object, the actor can reason (possibly at run-time) about possible substitutes and thus recover from failure. State variable types are modeled as classes in an ontology, and OWL-based reasoning mechanisms can be used to infer affordance properties on the hierarchical classes of objects. For instance, in our Example 3.4, the class "sliding door" would inherit every affordance property by the superclass "door," for example, the property that it is used for moving from one room to another one. In Awaad et al. [26], the authors also propose learning new functional affordances of objects through experience.

The Open Robot Ontology (ORO) system of Lemaignan et al. [376] had a broader motivation than improving the performance of a planner; it aimed at extending the robot's knowledge base. ORO is built with the same OWL representation and reasoner as the previous systems. It offers queries and updates of a knowledge base about the environment.

The RoboEarth and KnowRob projects of Waibel et al. [592] and Tenorth and Beetz [569] aim at allowing actors having different platforms to share and reuse knowledge over the network for the purpose of performing new tasks. An OWL open source library stores shared models of objects, environments (e.g., maps and object locations), and descriptive models of actions together with their relations and properties in a general ontology. Each actor is able to query and update this database and adapt its models.

7.5.4 Semantic Mapping for Hierarchical Representations

Ontology reasoning, and in general reasoning about the semantics of different objects, actions, tasks, and goals, is an important topic of research for planning and acting. In the hierarchical representation described in Chapter 3, intuitively, tasks are refined from one level to a lower more detailed level. Such representation is based on the idea that at different levels we have different and possibly heterogeneous representations of objects (through possibly different kinds of state variables), actions, and tasks. Therefore the semantics of objects, actions, and tasks should be given considering the relations between different levels, that is, a mapping of state variables, actions, and tasks from one level to another one.

State variables and actions at one level should be mapped to state variables and actions at a different level. In most cases, the mapping from a level to a lower more

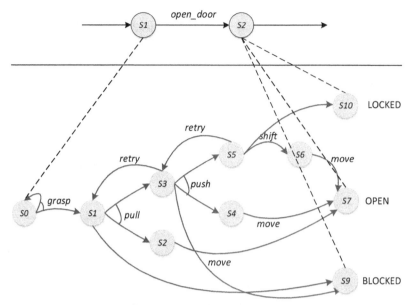

Figure 7.6. Open door: state variables and actions semantic mapping.

detailed level is a one-to-many mapping. Consider the case of state variables. A value of a state variable corresponds to possibly many different values of a state variable at a lower, more detailed level. For example, the position of a robot defined by the state variable pos(r) ranges over a set of locations such as room1, corridor, and room2. It is mapped at the path planning level to coordinates (x, y, θ) in local reference frames of room1, corridor, and room2. On the other way around, the mapping from the value of a state variable to a higher level should be many to one, and therefore a value at the lower level should correspond to just one value at the higher level. Therefore the "mapping down" of values from higher levels to lower levels is a *nondeterministic mapping*, because it can result in many possible different values, while the "mapping up" is *deterministic*.

In the examples just mentioned, we have a state variable with some values that are mapped down to a state variable with more possible values. Further, at a lower level we may need more state variables. For example, we may need to add at a lower level a variable about the configuration of the robot gripper. In this case, not only do we have a one-to-many mapping over values of variables, but we may have variables at a lower level that do not have a mapping up at a higher level.

Similar considerations arise for the mapping of actions from one level to another. In Example 3.4, action open-door is refined to several different actions at a lower level, and such actions can be combined in different ways: move-close, grasp, turn, and so on. Even in this case, the "mapping down" is nondeterministic, while the mapping up is deterministic. These ideas are depicted in Figure 7.6 as an example related to open door.

Finally, we should recall that, even if the hypothesis that mapping down is nondeterministic and mapping up is deterministic is reasonable in several cases, this may not be always true. At a higher level, we can consider parameters that are not considered at a lower level. As a simple example, consider the case in which at the level of the topological map we may add information about dangerous, or crowded rooms, where the robot should avoid to pass through. Some of the variables at the higher levels do not need to be mapped at the lower.

CHAPTER 8   Concluding Remarks

In this book, we have studied computational reasoning principles and mechanisms to support choosing and performing actions. Here are some observations about the current status of work on those topics.

Extensive work has been done on automated planning, ranging from classical planning techniques to extended approaches dealing with temporal, hierarchical, nondeterministic, and probabilistic models. The field has progressed tremendously, and a strong community of scientists is continually producing new results, technology, and tools.

Issues related to acting have also attracted much attention, and the state of the art is broad and rich, but it is quite fragmented. The relationships among different approaches have not yet been studied in depth, and a unifying and formal account of acting is not available in the same way as it is in the field of automated planning.

Furthermore, the problems of how to generate plans and how to perform synthesized actions have been mainly studied separately, and a better understanding is needed of the relationships between planning and acting. One of the usual assumptions in research on planning is that actions are directly executable, and this assumption is used even in the work on interleaving online planning and execution. In most cases, however, acting cannot be reduced to the direct execution of atomic commands that have been chosen by a planner. Significant deliberation is needed for an actor to perform what is planned.

In this book, we have addressed the state of the art from a unifying perspective. We have presented techniques for doing planning with deterministic, hierarchical, temporal, nondeterministic, and probabilistic models, and have discussed approaches for reacting to events and refining actions into executable commands. In doing this, we have distinguished between two kinds of models:

- *Descriptive models* of actions specify the actor's "know what." They describe which state or set of possible states may result from performing an action. They are used by the actor to reason about which actions may achieve its objectives.
- *Operational models* of actions specify the actor's "know how." They describe how to perform an action, that is, what commands to execute in the current context and how to organize them to achieve the action's intended effects. The actor relies on operational models to perform the actions that it has decided to perform.

310

While planning techniques use descriptive models, deliberation for acting needs operational models. These models go beyond the descriptive preconditions-and-effects representation; they organize action refinement within rich control structures. We have proposed refinement methods as a first step toward the integration of planning and acting to act effectively in the real world.

Significant research is needed regarding this integration. First, deliberation may use different planning techniques, including a flexible mix of general purpose and domain-dependent techniques. Second, deliberative acting may be done in different yet well-integrated state and actions spaces. Relations and mappings among such heterogeneous representations should be addressed systematically. Third, although we distinguished in each chapter between the part dedicated to planning and the one dedicated to acting, and between descriptive models and operational models, realistic applications most often need a flexible mix of planning and acting.

Finally, other deliberation functions – monitoring, reasoning about goals, reasoning about sensing and information-gathering actions, learning and acquiring deliberation models while acting, reasoning with semantics and ontology based representations, reasoning with hybrid models – are only briefly covered in the last chapter. They should be tightly integrated with planning and acting techniques.

The take-home message from this book is twofold. Extensive work has been done on planning and acting. The work on their integration is promising and strongly motivated, but still fragmented. This book has attempted to cover a relevant part of it in a unified view. Many research problems in automated deliberation remain open. We hope the reader will find this book helpful for addressing them.

Search Algorithms

This appendix provides background information about several of the search algorithms used in this book. These are nondeterministic state-space search (Section A.1) and And/Or search (Section A.2).

A.1 NONDETERMINISTIC STATE-SPACE SEARCH

Many of the planning algorithms in this book have been presented as nondeterministic search algorithms and can be described as instances of Algorithm A.1, Nondeterministic-Search. In most implementations of these algorithms, line (*iii*) corresponds to trying several members of R sequentially in a trial-and-error fashion. The "nondeterministically choose" command is an abstraction that lets us ignore the precise order in which those values are tried. This enables us to discuss properties that are shared by a wide variety of algorithms that search the same space of partial solutions, even though those algorithms may visit different nodes of that space in different orders.

There are several theoretical models of nondeterministic choice that are more-or-less equivalent mathematically [213, 464, 131]. The one that is most relevant for our purposes is the nondeterministic Turing machine model, which works roughly as follows.

Let $\psi(P)$ be a process produced by calling Nondeterministic-Search on a search problem P. Whenever this process reaches line (iii), it replaces $\psi(P)$ with $|R|$ copies of $\psi(P)$ running in parallel: one copy for each $r \in R$. Each process corresponds to a different execution trace of $\psi(P)$, and each execution trace follows one of the paths in $\psi(P)$'s search tree (see Figure A.1). Each execution trace that terminates will either return failure or return a purported answer to P.

Two desirable properties for a search algorithm ψ are *soundness* and *completeness*, which are defined as follows:

- ψ is *sound* over a set of search problems $\mathbf{P}$ if for every $P \in \mathbf{P}$ and every execution trace of $\psi(P)$, if the trace terminates and returns a value $\pi \neq$ failure, then π is a solution for P. This will happen if the solution test in line (i) is sound.

313

Algorithm A.1 Equivalent iterative and recursive versions of a generic nondeterministic search algorithm. The arguments include the search problem P and (in the recursive version) a partial solution π, the initial value of which should be the empty plan.

Nondeterministic-Search(P)   // iterative version
   $\pi \leftarrow$ an initial partial solution for P
   while π is not a solution for P do (i)
      $R \leftarrow \{$candidate refinements of $\pi\}$ (ii)
      if $R = \varnothing$ then return failure
      nondeterministically choose $r \in R$ (iii)
      $\pi \leftarrow$ refine(π, r)
   return π

Nondeterministic-Search(P, π)   // recursive version
   if π is a solution for P then return π (i)
   $R \leftarrow \{$candidate refinements of $\pi\}$ (ii)
   if $R = \varnothing$ then return failure
   nondeterministically choose $r \in R$ (iii)
   $\pi \leftarrow$ refine(π, r)
   return Nondeterministic-Search(P, π)

- ψ is *complete* over **P** if for every $P \in$ **P**, if P is solvable then at least one execution trace of $\psi(P)$ will return a solution for P. This will happen if each set of candidate refinements in line (ii) are complete, that is, if it includes all of the possible refinements for π.

In deterministic implementations of nondeterministic search, the nondeterministic choice is replaced with a way to decide which nodes of the search tree to visit, and in what order. The simplest case is depth-first backtracking, which we can get from the recursive version of Nondeterministic-Search by making a nearly trivial modification: change the nondeterministic choice to a loop over the elements of R. For this reason,

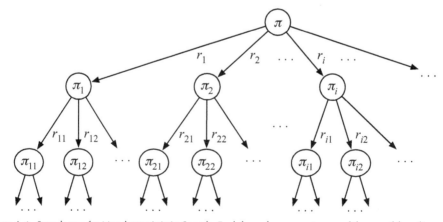

Figure A.1. Search tree for Nondeterministic-Search. Each branch represents one of the possible refinements.

Algorithm A.2 A deterministic counterpart to Nondeterministic-Search. Depending on how π is selected in line (i), the algorithm can do a depth-first search, breadth-first search, or best-first search.

Deterministic-Search(P)
  $\pi \leftarrow$ initial partial solution
  $\Pi \leftarrow \{\pi\}$
  while $\Pi \neq \varnothing$ do
    select $\pi \in \Pi$ (i)
    remove π from Π
    if π is a solution for P then return π
    $R \leftarrow$ {candidate refinements for π}
    for every $r \in R$ do
      $\pi \leftarrow$ refine(π, r)
      add π' to Π
  return failure

the nondeterministic choice points in nondeterministic search algorithms are sometimes called *backtracking points*.

Deterministic-Search, Algorithm A.2, is a general deterministic search algorithm. Depending on the *node-selection strategy*, that is, the technique for selecting π in line (i), we can get a depth-first search, breadth-first search, or a best-first search. Furthermore, by making some modifications to the pseudocode, we can get a greedy search, A* search, branch-and-bound search, or iterative-deepening search (see Chapter 2 for some examples).

Earlier we said that Nondeterministic-Search is sound and complete if its solution test is sound and its sets of candidate refinements are complete (i.e., each set includes all of the possible refinements). Under the same conditions, Deterministic-Search is sound, but whether it is complete depends on the node-selection strategy. For example, with breadth-first node selection it will be complete, but not with depth-first node selection unless the search space is finite. Although completeness is a desirable property, other considerations can often be more important: for example, the memory requirement usually is exponentially larger for a breadth-first search than for a depth-first search.

A.2 AND/OR SEARCH

In addition to choosing among alternative refinements, some search algorithms involve decomposing a problem P into a set of subproblems $P_1, \ldots, P_n$ whose solutions will provide a solution for P. Such algorithms can be described as instances of a nondeterministic And-Or-Search algorithm, Algorithm A.3. The search space for this algorithm is an And/Or tree such as that in Figure A.2.

We will not include a deterministic version of And-Or-Search here because the details are somewhat complicated and generally depend on the nature of the problem

---

Algorithm A.3 A generic nondeterministic And/Or search algorithm.

And-Or-Search(P)
  return Or-Branch(P)

Or-Branch(P)
  $R \leftarrow$ {candidate refinements for P}
  if $R = \varnothing$ then return failure
  nondeterministically choose $r \in R$ *(i)*
  $\pi \leftarrow$ refine(P, r)
  return And-Branch(P, π)

And-Branch(P, π)
  if π is a solution for P then return π
  $\{P_1, \ldots, P_n\} \leftarrow$ {unsolved subproblems in π}
  for every $P_i \in \{P_1, \ldots, P_n\}$ do   *(ii)*
    $\pi_i \leftarrow$ Or-Branch(P_i)
    if $\pi_i =$ failure then return failure
  if $\pi_1, \ldots, \pi_n$ are not compatible then return failure
  incorporate $\pi_1, \ldots, \pi_n$ into π
  return π

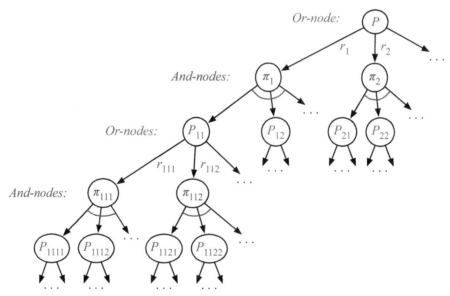

Figure A.2. And/Or search tree. Or-nodes correspond to calls to Or-Branch in Figure A.2, and the edges below each or-node correspond to members of R. And-nodes correspond to calls to And-Branch, and the edges below each and-node correspond to subproblems of π.

domain. One of the complications arises from the fact that unlike line (i) of And-Or-Search, line (ii) is not a backtracking point. The subproblems $P_1, \ldots, P_n$ must all be solved to solve P, and not every combination of solutions will be compatible. For example, if P_1 and P_2 are "find a container c and bring it to location l" and "put all of the books at location l into c," a solution to P_1 is useful for solving P_2 only if the container c is large enough to contain all of the books.

Strongly Connected Components of a Graph

Let $G = (V, E)$ be a directed graph. A strongly connected component of G is a subset C of V such that every vertex of C is reachable from every other vertex of C. The relation $\sim$ on vertices can be defined as follows: $v \sim v'$ iff either $v = v'$ or v is reachable from v' and v' is reachable from v. It is an equivalence relation on V. It partitions V into equivalence classes, each being a strongly connected component of G. Furthermore, the set of strongly connected components of G is a directed acyclic graph that has an edge from C to C' when there is a vertex in C' reachable from a vertex in C.

The Tarjan algorithm [560] finds in a single depth-first traversal of G its strongly connected components. Each vertex is visited just once. Hence the traversal organizes G as a spanning forest. Some subtrees of this forest are the strongly connected components of G. During the traversal, the algorithm associates two integers to each new vertex v it meets:

- index(v): the order in which v is met in the traversal, and
- low(v) = min{index(v')|v' reachable from v}

It is shown that index(v)=low(v) iff v and all its successors in a traversal subtree are a strongly connected component of G.

This is implemented in Algorithm B.1 as a recursive procedure with a stack mechanism. At the end of a recursion on a vertex v, if the condition index(v)=low(v) holds, then v and all the vertices above v in the stack (i.e., those below v in the depth-first traversal tree) constitute a strongly connected component of G.

With the appropriate initialization ($i \leftarrow 0$, $stack \leftarrow \varnothing$ and index undefined everywhere), Tarjan(v) is called once for every $v \in V$ such that index(v) is undefined. The algorithm run in $0(|V| + |E|)$. It finds all the strongly connected components of G in the reverse order of the topological sort of the DAG formed by the components, that is, if (C, C') is an edge of this DAG, then C' will be found before C.

Algorithm B.1 Tarjan's algorithm for finding strongly connected components of a graph.

Tarjan(v)
  index(v) $\leftarrow$low(v) $\leftarrow i$
  $i \leftarrow i+1$
  push(v,*stack*)
  for all v' adjacent to v do
    if index(v') is undefined than do
      Tarjan(v')
      low(v) $\leftarrow$ min{low(v), low(v'}
    else if v' is in *stack* then low(v) $\leftarrow$ min{low(v), low(v')}
  if index(v)=low(v) then do
    start a new component $C \leftarrow \varnothing$
    repeat
      $w \leftarrow$ pop(*stack*) ; $C \leftarrow C \cup \{w\}$
    until $w = v$

Bibliography

[1] Aarup, M., Arentoft, M. M., Parrod, Y., Stader, J., and Stokes, I. (1994). OPTIMUM-AIV: A knowledge-based planning and scheduling system for spacecraft AIV. In *Intelligent Scheduling*, pp. 451–469. Morgan Kaufmann.

[2] Abbeel, P., Coates, A., and Ng, A. (2010). Autonomous helicopter aerobatics through apprenticeship learning. *Intl. J. Robotics Research*, 29(13):1608–1639.

[3] Abbeel, P. and Ng, A. Y. (2010). Inverse reinforcement learning. In Sammut, C. and Webb, G. I., editors, *Encyclopedia of Machine Learning*, pp. 554–558. Springer.

[4] Abdul-Razaq, T. and Potts, C. (1988). Dynamic programming state-space relaxation for single-machine scheduling. *J. Operational Research Soc.*, pp. 141–152.

[5] Adali, S., Console, L., Sapino, M. L., Schenone, M., and Terenziani, P. (2000). Representing and reasoning with temporal constraints in multimedia presentations. In *Intl. Symp. on Temporal Representation and Reasoning (TIME)*, pp. 3–12.

[6] Agosta, J. M. (1995). Formulation and implementation of an equipment configuration problem with the SIPE-2 generative planner. In *AAAI-95 Spring Symp. on Integrated Planning Applications*, pp. 1–10.

[7] Albore, A. and Bertoli, P. (2004). Generating safe assumption-based plans for partially observable, nondeterministic domains. In *Proc. AAAI*, pp. 495–500.

[8] Alford, R., Kuter, U., and Nau, D. S. (2009). Translating HTNs to PDDL: A small amount of domain knowledge can go a long way. In *Proc. IJCAI*.

[9] Alford, R., Kuter, U., Nau, D. S., and Goldman, R. P. (2014a). Plan aggregation for strong cyclic planning in nondeterministic domains. *Artificial Intelligence*, 216:206–232.

[10] Alford, R., Shivashankar, V., Kuter, U., and Nau, D. S. (2014b). On the feasibility of planning graph style heuristics for HTN planning. In *Proc. ICAPS*.

[11] Allen, J. (1984). Towards a general theory of action and time. *Artificial Intelligence*, 23:123–154.

[12] Allen, J. (1991a). Temporal reasoning and planning. In Allen, J., Kautz, H., Pelavin, R., and Tenenberg, J., editors, *Reasoning about Plans*, pp. 1–68. Morgan Kaufmann.

[13] Allen, J. F. (1983). Maintaining knowledge about temporal intervals. *Communications ACM*, 21(11):832–843.

[14] Allen, J. F. (1991b). Planning as temporal reasoning. In *Proc. Intl. Conf. on Principles of Knowledge Representation and Reasoning (KR)*.

[15] Allen, J. F., Hendler, J., and Tate, A., editors (1990). *Readings in Planning*. Morgan Kaufmann.

[16]   Allen, J. F. and Koomen, J. A. (1983). Planning using a temporal world model. In *Proc. IJCAI*.

[17]   Ambite, J. L., Knoblock, C. A., and Minton, S. (2000). Learning plan rewriting rules. In *Proc. ICAPS*.

[18]   Ambros-Ingerson, J. A. and Steel, S. (1988). Integrating planning, execution and monitoring. In *Proc. AAAI*, pp. 21–26.

[19]   Anderson, J. R., Bothell, D., Byrne, M. D., Douglass, S., Lebiere, C., and Qin, Y. (2004). An integrated theory of the mind. *Psychological Review*, 111(4):1036–1060.

[20]   Andre, D., Friedman, N., and Parr, R. (1997). Generalized prioritized sweeping. In *Adv. in Neural Information Processing Syst. (Proc. NIPS)*.

[21]   Andre, D. and Russell, S. J. (2002). State abstraction for programmable reinforcement learning agents. In *Proc. AAAI*.

[22]   Andrews, T., Curbera, F., Dolakia, H., Goland, J., Klein, J., Leymann, F., Liu, K., Roller, D., Smith, D., Thatte, S., Trickovic, I., and Weeravarana, S. (2003). Business Process Execution Language for Web Services. http://msdn.microsoft.com/en-us/library/ee251594(v=bts.10).aspx.

[23]   Araya-Lopez, M., Thomas, V., Buffet, O., and Charpillet, F. (2010). A closer look at MOMDPs. In *IEEE Intl. Conf. on Tools with AI (ICTAI)*, pp. 197–204.

[24]   Argall, B. D., Chernova, S., veloso, M. M., and Browning, B. (2009). A survey of robot learning from demonstration. *Robotics and Autonomous Systems*, 57(5):469–483.

[25]   Åström, K. J. (1965). Optimal control of Markov decision processes with incomplete state estimation. *J. Math. Analysis and Applications*, 10:174–205.

[26]   Awaad, I., Kraetzschmar, G. K., and Hertzberg, J. (2014). Finding ways to get the job done: An affordance-based approach. In *Proc. ICAPS*.

[27]   Baader, F., Calvanese, D., McGuinness, D., Nardi, D., and Patel-Schneider, P., editors (2003). *The Description Logic Handbook: Theory, Implementation and Applications*. Cambridge Univ. Press.

[28]   Bacchus, F. and Kabanza, F. (2000). Using temporal logics to express search control knowledge for planning. *Artificial Intelligence*, 116(1–2):123–191.

[29]   Bäckström, C. (1991). Planning in polynomial time: The SAS-PUB class. *Computational Intelligence*, 7:181–197.

[30]   Bäckström, C. and Nebel, B. (1993). Complexity results for SAS+ planning. In *Proc. IJCAI*.

[31]   Bäckström, C. and Nebel, B. (1995). Complexity results for SAS+ planning. *Computational Intelligence*, 11(4):1–34.

[32]   Baier, J. A., Mombourquette, B., and McIlraith, S. (2014). Diagnostic problem solving: a planning perspective. In *Proc. Intl. Conf. on Principles of Knowledge Representation and Reasoning (KR)*, pp. 1–10.

[33]   Balas, E. (1968). A note on the branch-and-bound principle. *Operations Research*, 16:442–444.

[34]   Ball, M. and Holte, R. C. (2008). The compression power of symbolic pattern databases. In *Proc. ICAPS*, pp. 2–11.

[35]   Baptiste, P., Laborie, P., Le Pape, C., and Nuijten, W. (2006). Constraint-based scheduling and planning. In Rossi, F., Van Beek, P., and Walsh, T., editors, *Handbook of constraint programming*, chapter 22, pp. 759–798. Elsevier.

[36]   Barbier, M., Gabard, J.-F., Llareus, J. H., and Tessier, C. (2006). Implementation and flight testing of an onboard architecture for mission supervision. In *Intl. Unmanned Air Vehicle Syst. Conf.*

[37] Barreiro, J., Boyce, M., Frank, J., Iatauro, M., Kichkaylo, T., Morris, P., Smith, T., and Do, M. (2012). EUROPA: A platform for AI planning, scheduling, constraint programming, and optimization. In *Intl. Competition on Knowledge Engg. for Planning and Scheduling (ICKEPS)*.

[38] Barrett, A., Golden, K., Penberthy, J. S., and Weld, D. S. (1993). UCPOP user's manual (version 2.0). Technical Report TR-93-09-06, Univ. of Washington, Dept. of Computer Science and Engineering.

[39] Barrett, A. and Weld, D. S. (1993). Characterizing subgoal interactions for planning. In *Proc. IJCAI*, pp. 1388–1393.

[40] Barrett, A. and Weld, D. S. (1994). Partial order planning: Evaluating possible efficiency gains. *Artificial Intelligence*, 67(1):71–112.

[41] Barrett, C., Stump, A., and Tinelli, C. (2010). The SMT-LIB standard: Version 2.0. In Gupta, A. and Kroening, D., editors, *8th Intl. Wksp. on Satisfiability Modulo Theories*.

[42] Barry, J., Kaelbling, L. P., and Lozano-Perez, T. (2010). Hierarchical solution of large Markov decision processes. In *ICAPS Workshop*, pp. 1–8.

[43] Barry, J., Kaelbling, L. P., and Lozano-Perez, T. (2011). DetH*: Approximate hierarchical solution of large Markov decision processes. In *Proc. IJCAI*, pp. 1–8.

[44] Barták, R., Morris, R., and Venable, B. (2014). *An Introduction to Constraint-Based Temporal Reasoning*. Morgan&Claypool.

[45] Barták, R., Salido, M. A., and Rossi, F. (2010). Constraint satisfaction techniques in planning and scheduling. *J. Intelligent Manufacturing*, 21(1):5–15.

[46] Barto, A. G., Bradke, S. J., and Singh, S. P. (1995). Learning to act using real-time dynamic-programming. *Artificial Intelligence*, 72:81–138.

[47] Beetz, M. (1999). Structured reactive controllers: Controlling robots that perform everyday activity. In *Proc. Annual Conf. on Autonomous Agents*, pp. 228–235. ACM.

[48] Beetz, M. and McDermott, D. (1992). Declarative goals in reactive plans. In *Proc. AIPS*, p. 3.

[49] Beetz, M. and McDermott, D. (1994). Improving robot plans during their execution. In *Proc. AIPS*.

[50] Bellman, R. (1957). *Dynamic Programming*. Princeton Univ. Press.

[51] Ben Lamine, K. and Kabanza, F. (2002). Reasoning about robot actions: a model checking approach. In Beetz, M., Hertzberg, J., Ghallab, M., and Pollack, M. E., editors, *Advances in Plan-Based Control of Robotic Agents*, pp. 123–139. Springer.

[52] Bercher, P., Keen, S., and Biundo, S. (2014). Hybrid planning heuristics based on task decomposition graphs. *International Symposium on Combinatorial Search (SoCS)*, pp. 1–9.

[53] Bernard, D., Gamble, E., Rouquette, N., Smith, B., Tung, Y., Muscettola, N., Dorais, G., Kanefsky, B., Kurien, J. A., and Millar, W. (2000). Remote agent experiment DS1 technology validation report. Technical report, NASA.

[54] Bernardi, G., Cesta, A., Orlandini, A., and Finzi, A. (2013). A knowledge engineering environment for P&S with timelines. In *Proc. ICAPS*, pp. 16–23.

[55] Bernardini, S. and Smith, D. (2011). Finding mutual exclusion invariants in temporal planning domains. In *Intl. Wksp. on Planning and Scheduling for Space (IWPSS)*.

[56] Bernardini, S. and Smith, D. E. (2007). Developing domain-independent search control for Europa2. In *ICAPS Wksp. on Heuristics for Domain-Independent Planning*.

[57] Bernardini, S. and Smith, D. E. (2008). Automatically generated heuristic guidance for Europa2. In *Intl. Symp. on Artificial Intell., Robotics and Automation in Space (i-SAIRAS)*.

[58] Bernardini, S. and Smith, D. E. (2009). Towards search control via dependency graphs in Europa2. In *ICAPS Wksp. on Heuristics for Domain-Independent Planning.*

[59] Bertoli, P., Cimatti, A., Pistore, M., Roveri, M., and Traverso, P. (2001a). MBP: a model based planner. In *IJCAI Wksp. on Planning under Uncertainty and Incomplete Information,* pp. 93–97.

[60] Bertoli, P., Cimatti, A., Pistore, M., and Traverso, P. (2003). A framework for planning with extended goals under partial observability. In *Proc. ICAPS.*

[61] Bertoli, P., Cimatti, A., Roveri, M., and Traverso, P. (2001b). Planning in nondeterministic domains under partial observability via symbolic model checking. In *Proc. IJCAI,* pp. 473–478.

[62] Bertoli, P., Cimatti, A., Roveri, M., and Traverso, P. (2006). Strong planning under partial observability. *Artificial Intelligence,* 170(4):337–384.

[63] Bertoli, P., Cimatti, A., and Traverso, P. (2004). Interleaving execution and planning for nondeterministic, partially observable domains. In *Proc. ECAI,* pp. 657–661.

[64] Bertoli, P., Pistore, M., and Traverso, P. (2010). Automated composition of Web services via planning in asynchronous domains. *Artificial Intelligence,* 174(3-4):316–361.

[65] Bertsekas, D. (2001). *Dynamic Programming and Optimal Control.* Athena Scientific.

[66] Bertsekas, D. and Tsitsiklis, J. (1996). *Neuro-Dynamic Programming.* Athena Scientific.

[67] Bertsekas, D. P. and Tsitsiklis, J. N. (1991). An analysis of stochastics shortest path problems. *Mathematics of Operations Research,* 16(3):580–595.

[68] Betz, C. and Helmert, M. (2009). Planning with h^+ in theory and practice. In *Proc. Annual German Conf. on AI (KI),* volume 5803. Springer.

[69] Bhatia, A., Kavraki, L. E., and Vardi, M. Y. (2010). Sampling-based motion planning with temporal goals. In *IEEE Intl. Conf. on Robotics and Automation (ICRA),* pp. 2689–2696. IEEE.

[70] Bird, C. D. and Emery, N. J. (2009a). Insightful problem solving and creative tool modification by captive nontool-using rooks. *Proc. Natl. Acad. of Sci. (PNAS),* 106(25):10370–10375.

[71] Bird, C. D. and Emery, N. J. (2009b). Rooks use stones to raise the water level to reach a floating worm. *Current Biology,* 19(16):1410–1414.

[72] Biundo, S. and Schattenberg, B. (2001). From abstract crisis to concrete relief – A preliminary report on combining state abstraction and HTN planning. In *Proc. European Conf. on Planning (ECP),* pp. 157–168.

[73] Blum, A. and Langford, J. (1999). Probabilistic planning in the graphplan framework. In *Proc. European Conf. on Planning (ECP),* pp. 319–322. Springer.

[74] Blum, A. L. and Furst, M. L. (1997). Fast planning through planning graph analysis. *Artificial Intelligence,* 90(1–2):281–300.

[75] Boddy, M. and Dean, T. (1989). Solving time-dependent planning problems. In *Proc. IJCAI,* pp. 979–984.

[76] Boese, F. and Piotrowski., J. (2009). Autonomously controlled storage management in vehicle logistics applications of RFID and mobile computing systems. *Intl. J. RF Technologies: Research and Applications,* 1(1):57–76.

[77] Bogomolov, S., Magazzeni, D., Minopoli, S., and Wehrle, M. (2015). PDDL+ planning with hybrid automata: Foundations of translating must behavior. In *Proc. ICAPS,* pp. 42–46.

[78] Bogomolov, S., Magazzeni, D., Podelski, A., and Wehrle, M. (2014). Planning as model checking in hybrid domains. In *Proc. AAAI,* pp. 2228–2234.

[79] Bohren, J., Rusu, R. B., Jones, E. G., Marder-Eppstein, E., Pantofaru, C., Wise, M., Mösenlechner, L., Meeussen, W., and Holzer, S. (2011). Towards autonomous robotic butlers:

Lessons learned with the PR2. In *IEEE Intl. Conf. on Robotics and Automation (ICRA)*, pp. 5568–5575.

[80]   Bonet, B. (2007). On the speed of convergence of value iteration on stochastic shortest-path problems. *Mathematics of Operations Research*, 32(2):365–373.

[81]   Bonet, B. and Geffner, H. (2000). Planning with incomplete information as heuristic search in belief space. In *Proc. AIPS*, pp. 52–61.

[82]   Bonet, B. and Geffner, H. (2001). Planning as heuristic search. *Artificial Intelligence*, 129:5–33.

[83]   Bonet, B. and Geffner, H. (2003a). Faster heuristic search algorithms for planning with uncertainty and full feedback. In *Proc. IJCAI*.

[84]   Bonet, B. and Geffner, H. (2003b). Labeled RTDP: Improving the convergence of real-time dynamic programming. In *Proc. ICAPS*, pp. 12–21.

[85]   Bonet, B. and Geffner, H. (2005). mGPT: A probabilistic planner based on heuristic search. *J. Artificial Intelligence Research*, 24:933–944.

[86]   Bonet, B. and Geffner, H. (2006). Learning in depth-first search: A unified approach to heuristic search in deterministic, non-deterministic, probabilistic, and game tree settings. In *Proc. ICAPS*, pp. 142–151.

[87]   Bonet, B. and Geffner, H. (2009). Solving POMDPs: RTDP-Bel vs. point-based algorithms. In *Proc. IJCAI*, pp. 1641–1646.

[88]   Bonet, B. and Geffner, H. (2012). Action selection for MDPs: Anytime AO* versus UCT. In *Proc. AAAI*.

[89]   Bonet, B. and Geffner, H. (2014). Belief tracking for planning with sensing: Width, complexity and approximations. *J. Artificial Intelligence Research*, 50:923–970.

[90]   Bonet, B. and Helmert, M. (2010). Strengthening landmark heuristics via hitting sets. In *Proc. ECAI*, pp. 329–334.

[91]   Bouguerra, A., Karlsson, L., and Saffiotti, A. (2007). Semantic knowledge-based execution monitoring for mobile robots. In *IEEE Intl. Conf. on Robotics and Automation (ICRA)*, pp. 3693–3698. IEEE.

[92]   Boutilier, C., Brafman, R. I., and Geib, C. (1998). Structured reachability analysis for Markov decision processes. In *Proc. Conf. on Uncertainty in AI (UAI)*, pp. 24–32.

[93]   Boutilier, C., Dean, T., and Hanks, S. (1999). Decision-theoretic planning: Structural assumptions and computational leverage. *J. Artificial Intelligence Research*, 11:1–94.

[94]   Boutilier, C., Dearden, R., and Goldszmidt, M. (2000). Stochastic dynamic programming with factored representations. *Artificial Intelligence*, 121:49–107.

[95]   Boyan, J. A. and Littman, M. L. (2001). Exact solutions to time dependent MDPs. In *Adv. in Neural Information Processing Syst. (Proc. NIPS)*, pp. 1026–1032.

[96]   Brafman, R. and Hoffmann, J. (2004). Conformant planning via heuristic forward search: A new approach. In *Proc. ICAPS*.

[97]   Brenner, M. and Nebel, B. (2009). Continual planning and acting in dynamic multiagent environments. *J. Autonomous Agents and Multi-Agent Syst.*, 19(3):297–331.

[98]   Brusoni, V., Console, L., Terenziani, P., and Dupre, D. T. (1998). A spectrum of definitions for temporal model-based diagnosis. *Artificial Intelligence*, 102(1):39–79.

[99]   Brusoni, V., Console, L., Terenziani, P., and Pernici, B. (1999). Qualitative and quantitative temporal constraints and relational databases: Theory, architecture, and applications. *IEEE trans. on KDE*, 11(6):948–968.

[100]   Bucchiarone, A., Marconi, A., Pistore, M., and Raik, H. (2012). Dynamic adaptation of fragment-based and context-aware business processes. In *Intl. Conf. on Web Services*, pp. 33–41.

[101] Bucchiarone, A., Marconi, A., Pistore, M., Traverso, P., Bertoli, P., and Kazhamiakin, R. (2013). Domain objects for continuous context-aware adaptation of service-based systems. In *ICWS*, pp. 571–578.

[102] Buffet, O. and Sigaud, O., editors (2010). *Markov Decision Processes in Artificial Intelligence*. Wiley.

[103] Busoniu, L., Munos, R., De Schutter, B., and Babuska, R. (2011). Optimistic planning for sparsely stochastic systems. In *IEEE Symp. on Adaptive Dynamic Progr. and Reinforcement Learning*, pp. 48–55.

[104] Bylander, T. (1992). Complexity results for extended planning. In *Proc. AAAI*.

[105] Bylander, T. (1994). The computational complexity of propositional STRIPS planning. *Artificial Intelligence*, 69:165–204.

[106] Calvanese, D., Giacomo, G. D., and Vardi, M. Y. (2002). Reasoning about actions and planning in ltl action theories. In *Proc. Intl. Conf. on Principles of Knowledge Representation and Reasoning (KR)*, pp. 593–602. Morgan Kaufmann.

[107] Castellini, C., Giunchiglia, E., and Tacchella, A. (2001). Improvements to SAT-based conformant planning. In Cesta, A. and Borrajo, D., editors, *Proc. European Conf. on Planning (ECP)*.

[108] Castellini, C., Giunchiglia, E., and Tacchella, A. (2003). SAT-based planning in complex domains: Concurrency, constraints and nondeterminism. *Artificial Intellegence*, 147:85–118.

[109] Castillo, L., Fdez-Olivares, J., and Garcia-Pérez, O. (2006a). Efficiently handling temporal knowledge in an HTN planner. In *Proc. ICAPS*, pp. 1–10.

[110] Castillo, L., Fdez-Olivares, J., Garcıa-Pérez, O., and Palao, F. (2006b). Efficiently handling temporal knowledge in an HTN planner. In *Proc. ICAPS*, pp. 63–72.

[111] Cesta, A. and Oddi, A. (1996). Gaining efficiency and flexibility in the simple temporal problem. In *Intl. Symp. on Temporal Representation and Reasoning (TIME)*.

[112] Cesta, A., Oddi, A., and Smith, S. F. (2002). A constraint-based method for project scheduling with time windows. *J. Heuristics*, 8(1):109–136.

[113] Champandard, A., Verweij, T., and Straatman, R. (2009). The AI for Killzone 2's multiplayer bots. In *Game Developers Conf. (GDC)*.

[114] Chapman, D. (1987). Planning for conjunctive goals. *Artificial Intelligence*, 32:333–379.

[115] Chatilla, R., Alami, R., Degallaix, B., and Laruelle, H. (1992). Integrated planning and execution control of autonomous robot actions. In *IEEE Intl. Conf. on Robotics and Automation (ICRA)*, pp. 2689–2696.

[116] Chrpa, L. (2010). Combining learning techniques for classical planning: Macro-operators and entanglements. In *IEEE Intl. Conf. on Tools with AI (ICTAI)*, volume 2, pp. 79–86. IEEE.

[117] Cimatti, A., Giunchiglia, F., Pecchiari, P., Pietra, B., Profeta, J., Romano, D., Traverso, P., and Yu, B. (1997). A provably correct embedded verifier for the certification of safety critical software. In *Intl. Conf. on Computer Aided Verification (CAV)*, pp. 202–213.

[118] Cimatti, A., Micheli, A., and Roveri, M. (2012a). Solving temporal problems using SMT: Strong controllability. In *Proc. Int. Conf. Principles and Practice of Constraint Programming (CP)*.

[119] Cimatti, A., Micheli, A., and Roveri, M. (2012b). Solving temporal problems using SMT: Weak controllability. In *Proc. AAAI*.

[120] Cimatti, A., Micheli, A., and Roveri, M. (2015). Strong temporal planning with uncontrollable durations: A state-space approach. In *Proc. AAAI*, pp. 1–7.

[121] Cimatti, A., Pistore, M., Roveri, M., and Traverso, P. (2003). Weak, strong, and strong cyclic planning via symbolic model checking. *Artificial Intelligence*, 147(1–2):35–84.

[122] Cimatti, A., Roveri, M., and Traverso, P. (1998a). Automatic OBDD-based generation of universal plans in non-deterministic domains. In *Proc. AAAI*, pp. 875–881.

[123] Cimatti, A., Roveri, M., and Traverso, P. (1998b). Strong planning in non-deterministic domains via model checking. In *Proc. AIPS*, pp. 36–43.

[124] Claßen, J., Röger, G., Lakemeyer, G., and Nebel, B. (2012). Platas—integrating planning and the action language Golog. *KI-Künstliche Intelligenz*, 26(1):61–67.

[125] Coates, A., Abbeel, P., and Ng, A. (2009). Apprenticeship learning for helicopter control. *Communications ACM*, 52(7):97.

[126] Coles, A. and Smith, A. (2007). Marvin: a heuristic search planner with online macro-action learning. *J. Artificial Intelligence Research*, 28:119–156.

[127] Coles, A. I., Fox, M., Long, D., and Smith, A. J. (2008). Planning with problems requiring temporal coordination. In *Proc. AAAI*.

[128] Coles, A. J., Coles, A., Fox, M., and Long, D. (2012). COLIN: planning with continuous linear numeric change. *J. Artificial Intelligence Research*.

[129] Conrad, P., Shah, J., and Williams, B. C. (2009). Flexible execution of plans with choice. In *Proc. ICAPS*.

[130] Coradeschi, S. and Saffiotti, A. (2002). Perceptual anchoring: a key concept for plan execution in embedded systems. In Beetz, M., Hertzberg, J., Ghallab, M., and Pollack, M. E., editors, *Advances in Plan-Based Control of Robotic Agents*, pp. 89–105. Springer-Verlag.

[131] Cormen, T., Leirson, C., Rivest, R., and Stein, C. (2001). *Introduction to Algorithms*. MIT Press.

[132] Culberson, J. C. and Schaeffer, J. (1998). Pattern databases. *Computational Intelligence*, 14(3):318–334.

[133] Currie, K. and Tate, A. (1991). O-Plan: The open planning architecture. *Artificial Intelligence*, 52(1):49–86.

[134] Dai, P. and Hansen, E. A. (2007). Prioritizing Bellman backups without a priority queue. In *Proc. ICAPS*, pp. 113–119.

[135] Dal Lago, U., Pistore, M., and Traverso, P. (2002). Planning with a language for extended goals. In *Proc. AAAI*, pp. 447–454.

[136] Daniele, M., Traverso, P., and Vardi, M. (1999). Strong cyclic planning revisited. In *Proc. European Conf. on Planning (ECP)*, pp. 35–48.

[137] De Giacomo, G., Iocchi, L., Nardi, D., and Rosati, R. (1997). Description logic-based framework for planning with sensing actions. In *Intl. Wksp. on Description Logics*.

[138] De Giacomo, G., Iocchi, L., Nardi, D., and Rosati, R. (1999). A theory and implementation of cognitive mobile robots. *J. Logic and Computation*, 9(5):759–785.

[139] De Giacomo, G., Patrizi, F., and Sardiña, S. (2013). Automatic behavior composition synthesis. *Artificial Intelligence*, 196.

[140] de la Rosa, T. and McIlraith, S. (2011). Learning domain control knowledge for TLPlan and beyond. In *ICAPS Wksp. on Learning and Planning*.

[141] Dean, T., Firby, R., and Miller, D. (1988). Hierarchical planning involving deadlines, travel time and resources. *Computational Intelligence*, 6(1):381–398.

[142] Dean, T., Givan, R., and Leach, S. (1997). Model reduction techniques for computing approximately optimal solutions for Markov decision processes. In *Proc. Conf. on Uncertainty in AI (UAI)*, pp. 124–131.

[143] Dean, T. and Kanazawa, K. (1989). A model for reasoning about persistence and causation. *Computational Intelligence*, 5(3):142–150.

[144] Dean, T. and Lin, S.-H. (1995). Decomposition techniques for planning in stochastic domains. In *Proc. IJCAI*, pp. 1121–1127.

[145] Dean, T. and McDermott, D. (1987). Temporal data base management. *Artificial Intelligence*, 32(1):1–55.

[146] Dean, T. L. and Wellman, M. (1991). *Planning and Control*. Morgan Kaufmann.

[147] Dechter, R., Meiri, I., and Pearl, J. (1991). Temporal constraint networks. *Artificial Intelligence*, 49:61–95.

[148] Deisenroth, M. P., Neumann, G., and Peters, J. (2013). A survey on policy search for robotics. *Foundations and Trends in Robotics*, 2(1–2):1–142.

[149] Della Penna, G., Magazzeni, D., Mercorio, F., and Intrigila, B. (2009). UPMurphi: A tool for universal planning on PDDL+ problems. In *Proc. ICAPS*.

[150] Dennett, D. (1996). *Kinds of Minds*. Perseus.

[151] Derman, C. (1970). *Finite State Markovian Decision Processes*. Academic Press.

[152] Despouys, O. and Ingrand, F. (1999). Propice-Plan: Toward a unified framework for planning and execution. In *Proc. European Conf. on Planning (ECP)*.

[153] Dietterich, T. G. (2000). Hierarchical reinforcement learning with the maxq value function decomposition. *J. Artificial Intelligence Research*, 13:227–303.

[154] Do, M. B. and Kambhampati, S. (2001). Sapa: A domain independent heuristic metric temporal planner. In *Proc. European Conf. on Planning (ECP)*, pp. 109–121.

[155] Doherty, P. and Kvarnström, J. (1999). TALplanner: An empirical investigation of a temporal logic-based forward chaining planner. In *Intl. Symp. on Temporal Representation and Reasoning (TIME)*, pp. 47–54.

[156] Doherty, P. and Kvarnström, J. (2001). TALplanner: A temporal logic based planner. *AI Magazine*, 22(3):95–102.

[157] Doherty, P., Kvarnström, J., and Heintz, F. (2009a). A temporal logic-based planning and execution monitoring framework for unmanned aircraft systems. *J. Autonomous Agents and Multi-Agent Syst.*, 19(3):332–377.

[158] Doherty, P., Kvarnström, J., and Heintz, F. (2009b). A temporal logic-based planning and execution monitoring framework for unmanned aircraft systems. *J. Autonomous Agents and Multi-Agent Syst.*, 19(3):332–377.

[159] Domshlak, C., Karpas, E., and Markovitch, S. (2012). Online speedup learning for optimal planning. *J. Artificial Intelligence Research*.

[160] Doran, J. E. and Michie, D. (1966). Experiments with the graph traverser program. *Proceedings of the Royal Society of London A: Mathematical, Physical and Engineering Sciences*, 294(1437):235–259.

[161] Dorf, R. C. and Bishop, R. H. (2010). *Modern Control Systems*. Prentice Hall.

[162] Dousson, C., Gaborit, P., and Ghallab, M. (1993). Situation recognition: Representation and algorithms. In *Proc. IJCAI*, pp. 166–172.

[163] Dousson, C. and Le Maigat, P. (2007). Chronicle recognition improvement using temporal focusing and hierarchization. In *Proc. IJCAI*, pp. 324–329.

[164] Drakengren, T. and Jonsson, P. (1997). Eight maximal tractable subclasses of Allen's algebra with metric time. *J. Artificial Intelligence Research*, 7:25–45.

[165] Dvorak, F., Bit-Monnot, A., Ingrand, F., and Ghallab, M. (2014). A flexible ANML actor and planner in robotics. In Finzi, A. and Orlandini, A., editors, *ICAPS Wksp. on Planning and Robotics*, pp. 12–19.

[166] Eaton, J. H. and Zadeh, L. A. (1962). Optimal pursuit strategies in discrete state probabilistic systems. *Trans. ASME*, 84:23–29.

[167] Edelkamp, S. (2001). Planning with pattern databases. In *Proc. European Conf. on Planning (ECP)*.

[168] Edelkamp, S. (2002). Symbolic pattern databases in heuristic search planning. In *Proc. AIPS*, pp. 274–283.

[169] Edelkamp, S. (2003). Taming numbers and durations in the model checking integrated planning system. *J. Artificial Intelligence Research*, 20:195–238.

[170] Edelkamp, S. and Helmert, M. (1999). Exhibiting knowledge in planning problems to minimize state encoding length. In Biundo, S. and Fox, M., editors, *Proc. European Conf. on Planning (ECP)*, volume 1809 of *LNAI*, pp. 135–147. Springer.

[171] Edelkamp, S. and Helmert, M. (2000). On the implementation of MIPS. In *AIPS Wksp. on Model-Theoretic Approaches to Planning*, pp. 18–25.

[172] Edelkamp, S. and Kissmann, P. (2009). Optimal symbolic planning with action costs and preferences. In *Proc. IJCAI*, pp. 1690–1695.

[173] Edelkamp, S., Kissmann, P., and Rohte, M. (2014). Symbolic and explicit search hybrid through perfect hash functions – A case study in Connect Four. In *Proc. ICAPS*.

[174] Edelkamp, S., Kissmann, P., and Torralba, Á. (2015). BDDs strike back (in AI planning). In *Proc. AAAI*, pp. 4320–4321.

[175] Effinger, R., Williams, B., and Hofmann, A. (2010). Dynamic execution of temporally and spatially flexible reactive programs. In *AAAI Wksp. on Bridging the Gap between Task and Motion Planning*, pp. 1–8.

[176] El-Kholy, A. and Richard, B. (1996). Temporal and resource reasoning in planning: the ParcPlan approach. In *Proc. ECAI*, pp. 614–618.

[177] Elkawkagy, M., Bercher, P., Schattenberg, B., and Biundo, S. (2012). Improving hierarchical planning performance by the use of landmarks. *Proc. AAAI*.

[178] Emerson, E. A. (1990). Temporal and modal logic. In van Leeuwen, J., editor, *Handbook of Theoretical Computer Sci., Volume B: Formal Models and Semantics*, pp. 995–1072. Elsevier.

[179] Erol, K., Hendler, J., and Nau, D. S. (1994a). HTN planning: Complexity and expressivity. In *Proc. AAAI*.

[180] Erol, K., Hendler, J., and Nau, D. S. (1994b). Semantics for hierarchical task-network planning. Technical Report CS TR-3239, Univ. of Maryland.

[181] Erol, K., Hendler, J., and Nau, D. S. (1994c). UMCP: A sound and complete procedure for hierarchical task-network planning. In *Proc. AIPS*, pp. 249–254.

[182] Erol, K., Nau, D. S., and Subrahmanian, V. S. (1995). Complexity, decidability and undecidability results for domain-independent planning. *Artificial Intelligence*, 76(1–2):75–88.

[183] Estlin, T. A., Chien, S., and Wang, X. (1997). An argument for a hybrid HTN/operator-based approach to planning. In *Proc. European Conf. on Planning (ECP)*, pp. 184–196.

[184] Etzioni, O., Hanks, S., Weld, D. S., Draper, D., Lesh, N., and Williamson, M. (1992). An approach to planning with incomplete information. In *Proc. Intl. Conf. on Principles of Knowledge Representation and Reasoning (KR)*, pp. 115–125.

[185] Eyerich, P., Mattmuller, R., and Roger, G. (2009). Using the context-enhanced additive heuristic for temporal and numeric planning. In *Proc. ICAPS*.

[186] Eyerich, P., Mattmüller, R., and Röger, G. (2012). Using the context-enhanced additive heuristic for temporal and numeric planning. In Prassler, E., Zöllner, M., Bischoff, R., and Burgard, W., editors, *Towards Service Robots for Everyday Environments: Recent Advances in Designing Service Robots for Complex Tasks in Everyday Environments*, pp. 49–64. Springer.

[187] Fargier, H., Jourdan, M., Layaa, N., and Vidal, T. (1998). Using temporal constraint networks to manage temporal scenario of multimedia documents. In *ECAI Wksp. on Spatial and Temporal Reasoning*.

[188] Feng, Z., Dearden, R., Meuleau, N., and Washington, R. (2004). Dynamic programming for structured continuous Markov decision problems. In *Proc. AAAI*, pp. 154–161.

[189] Feng, Z. and Hansen, E. A. (2002). Symbolic heuristic search for factored Markov decision processes. In *Proc. AAAI*, pp. 455–460.

[190] Feng, Z., Hansen, E. A., and Zilberstein, S. (2002). Symbolic generalization for on-line planning. In *Proc. Conf. on Uncertainty in AI (UAI)*, pp. 209–216.

[191] Ferguson, D. I. and Stentz, A. (2004). Focussed propagation of MDPs for path planning. In *IEEE Intl. Conf. on Tools with AI (ICTAI)*, pp. 310–317.

[192] Fernández, F. and Veloso, M. M. (2006). Probabilistic policy reuse in a reinforcement learning agent. In *Proc. AAMAS*, pp. 720–727. ACM.

[193] Ferraris, P. and Giunchiglia, E. (2000). Planning as satisfiability in nondeterministic domains. In *Proc. AAAI*.

[194] Ferrein, A. and Lakemeyer, G. (2008). Logic-based robot control in highly dynamic domains. *Robotics and Autonomous Systems*, 56(11):980–991.

[195] Fichtner, M., Großmann, A., and Thielscher, M. (2003). Intelligent execution monitoring in dynamic environments. *Fundamenta Informaticae*, 57(2–4):371–392.

[196] Fikes, R. E. (1971). Monitored execution of robot plans produced by STRIPS. In *IFIP Congress*.

[197] Fikes, R. E. and Nilsson, N. J. (1971). STRIPS: A new approach to the application of theorem proving to problem solving. *Artificial Intelligence*, 2(3):189–208.

[198] Finzi, A., Pirri, F., and Reiter, R. (2000). Open world planning in the situation calculus. In *Proc. AAAI*, pp. 754–760.

[199] Firby, R. J. (1987). An investigation into reactive planning in complex domains. In *Proc. AAAI*, pp. 202–206. AAAI Press.

[200] Fisher, M., Gabbay, D. M., and Vila, L., editors (2005). *Handbook of Temporal Reasoning in Artificial Intelligence*. Elsevier.

[201] Foka, A. and Trahanias, P. (2007). Real-time hierarchical POMDPs for autonomous robot navigation. *Robotics and Autonomous Systems*, 55:561–571.

[202] Forestier, J. P. and Varaiya, P. (1978). Multilayer control of large Markov chains. *IEEE Trans. Automation and Control*, 23:298–304.

[203] Fox, M. and Long, D. (2000). Utilizing automatically inferred invariants in graph construction and search. In *Proc. ICAPS*, pp. 102–111.

[204] Fox, M. and Long, D. (2003). PDDL2.1: An extension to PDDL for expressing temporal planning domains. *J. Artificial Intelligence Research*, 20:61–124.

[205] Fox, M. and Long, D. (2006). Modelling mixed discrete-continuous domains for planning. *J. Artificial Intelligence Research*, 27:235–297.

[206] Frank, J. and Jónsson, A. K. (2003). Constraint-based attribute and interval planning. *Constraints*, 8(4).

[207] Fraser, G., Steinbauer, G., and Wotawa, F. (2004). Plan execution in dynamic environments. In *Proc. Intl. Cognitive Robotics Workshop*, pp. 208–217. Springer.

[208] Fratini, S., Cesta, A., De Benedictis, R., Orlandini, A., and Rasconi, R. (2011). APSI-based deliberation in goal oriented autonomous controllers. In *Symp. on Adv. in Space Technologies in Robotics and Automation (ASTRA)*.

[209] Fu, J., Ng, V., Bastani, F. B., and Yen, I.-L. (2011). Simple and fast strong cyclic planning for fully-observable nondeterministic planning problems. In *Proc. IJCAI*, pp. 1949–1954.

[210] Fusier, F., Valentin, V., Bremond, F., Thonnat, M., Borg, M., Thirde, D., and Ferryman, J. (2007). Video understanding for complex activity recognition. *Machine Vision and Applications*, 18(3–4):167–188.

[211] Garcia, C. E., Prett, D. M., and Morari, M. (1989). Model predictive control: theory and practice – a survey. *Automatica*, 25(3):335–348.

[212] Garcia, F. and Laborie, P. (1995). Hierarchisation of the search space in temporal planning. In *European Wksp. on Planning (EWSP)*, pp. 235–249.

[213] Garey, M. R. and Johnson, D. S. (1979). *Computers and Intractability: A Guide to the Theory of NP-Completeness*. W. H. Freeman.

[214] Garrido, A. (2002). A temporal plannnig system for level 3 durative actions of PDDL2.1. In *AIPS Wksp. on Planning for Temporal Domains*, pp. 56–66.

[215] Geffner, H. (2000). Functional Strips: A more flexible language for planning and problem solving. In Minker, J., editor, *Logic-Based Artificial Intelligence*, pp. 187–209. Kluwer.

[216] Geffner, H. (2003). PDDL 2.1: Representation vs. computation. *J. Artificial Intelligence Research*, 20:139–144.

[217] Geffner, H. and Bonet, B. (2013). *A Concise Introduction to Models and Methods for Automated Planning*. Morgan & Claypool.

[218] Geib, C. and Goldman, R. P. (2009). A probabilistic plan recognition algorithm based on plan tree grammars. *Artificial Intelligence*, 173:1101–1132.

[219] Gelly, S. and Silver, D. (2007). Combining online and offline knowledge in UCT. In *Proc. Intl. Conf. on Machine Learning (ICML)*, pp. 273–280.

[220] Gerevini, A., Kuter, U., Nau, D. S., Saetti, A., and Waisbrot, N. (2008). Combining domain-independent planning and HTN planning: The Duet planner. In *Proc. ECAI*, pp. 573–577.

[221] Gerevini, A., Saetti, A., and Serina, I. (2003). Planning through stochastic local search and temporal action graphs in LPG. *J. Artificial Intelligence Research*, 20:239–290.

[222] Gerevini, A., Saetti, A., and Serina, I. (2005). Integrating planning and temporal reasoning for domains with durations and time windows. In *Proc. IJCAI*, volume 19, pp. 1226–1232.

[223] Gerevini, A. and Schubert, L. (1996). Accelerating partial-order planners: Some techniques for effective search control and pruning. *J. Artificial Intelligence Research*, 5:95–137.

[224] Gerevini, A. and Schubert, L. (2000). Discovering state constraints in DISCOPLAN: Some new results. In *Proc. AAAI*.

[225] Gerevini, A. and Serina, I. (2002). LPG: A planner based on local search for planning graphs. In *Proc. AIPS*, pp. 968–973.

[226] Ghallab, M. (1996). On chronicles: Representation, on-line recognition and learning. In *Proc. Intl. Conf. on Principles of Knowledge Representation and Reasoning (KR)*, pp. 597–606.

[227] Ghallab, M., Alami, R., and Chatila, R. (1987). Dealing with time in planning and execution monitoring. In Bolles, R. and Roth, B., editors, *Intl. Symp. on Robotics Research (ISRR)*, pp. 431–443. MIT Press.

[228] Ghallab, M. and Laruelle, H. (1994). Representation and control in IxTeT, a temporal planner. In *Proc. AIPS*, pp. 61–67.

[229] Ghallab, M. and Mounir-Alaoui, A. (1989). Managing efficiently temporal relations through indexed spanning trees. In *Proc. IJCAI*, pp. 1297–1303.

[230] Ghallab, M., Nau, D. S., and Traverso, P. (2004). *Automated Planning: Theory and Practice*. Morgann Kaufmann.

[231] Ghallab, M., Nau, D., and Traverso, P. (2014). The actor's view of automated planning and acting: A position paper. *Artificial Intelligence*, 208:1–17.

[232] Gil, Y. (summer 2005). Description logics and planning. *AI Magazine*.

[233] Gischer, J. L. (1988). The equational theory of pomsets. *Theoretical Computer Science*, 61(2):199–224.

[234] Giunchiglia, E. (2000). Planning as satisfiability with expressive action languages: Concurrency, constraints and nondeterminism. In *Proc. Intl. Conf. on Principles of Knowledge Representation and Reasoning (KR)*, pp. 657–666.

[235] Giunchiglia, F. (1999). Using Abstrips abstractions – where do we stand? *AI Review*, 13(3):201–213.

[236] Giunchiglia, F. and Traverso, P. (1999). Planning as model checking. In *Proc. European Conf. on Planning (ECP)*, pp. 1–20.

[237] Givan, R., Dean, T., and Greig, M. (2003). Equivalence notions and model minimization in Markov decision processes. *Artificial Intelligence*, 142:163–223.

[238] Golden, K., Etzioni, O., and Weld, D. (1994). Omnipotence without omniscience: Efficient sensor management for planning. In *Proc. AAAI*, pp. 1048–154.

[239] Goldman, R., Pelican, M., and Musliner, D. (1999). Hard real-time mode logic synthesis for hybrid control: A CIRCA-based approach. In *Hybrid Systems and AI: Papers from the AAAI Spring Symp.* AAAI Technical Report SS-99-05.

[240] Goldman, R. P., Musliner, D. J., Krebsbach, K. D., and Boddy, M. S. (1997). Dynamic abstraction planning. In *Proc. AAAI*, pp. 680–686. AAAI Press.

[241] Goldman, R. P., Musliner, D. J., and Pelican, M. J. (2000). Using model checking to plan hard real-time controllers. In *AIPS Wksp. on Model-Theoretic Approaches to Planning*.

[242] Golumbic, M. and Shamir, R. (1993). Complexity and algorithms for reasoning about time: a graph-theoretic approach. *J. ACM*, 40(5):1108–1133.

[243] González-Ferrer, A., Fernández-Olivares, J., Castillo, L., et al. (2009). JABBAH: a java application framework for the translation between business process models and HTN. In *Proc. Intl. Competition on Knowledge Engineering for Planning and Scheduling (ICKEPS)*.

[244] Gopal, M. (1963). *Control Systems: Principles and Design*. McGraw-Hill.

[245] Gregory, P., Long, D., and Fox, M. (2007). A meta-CSP model for optimal planning. In *Abstraction, Reformulation, and Approximation*, pp. 200–214. Springer.

[246] Gregory, P., Long, D., Fox, M., and Beck, J. C. (2012). Planning modulo theories: Extending the planning paradigm. In *Proc. ICAPS*.

[247] Gruber, T. (2009). Ontology. In *Encyclopedia of Database Systems*, pp. 1963–1965. Springer.

[248] Guestrin, C., Hauskrecht, M., and Kveton, B. (2004). Solving factored MDPs with continuous and discrete variables. In *Proc. Conf. on Uncertainty in AI (UAI)*, pp. 235–242.

[249] Guestrin, C., Koller, D., Parr, R., and Venkataraman, S. (2003). Efficient solution algorithms for factored MDPs. *J. Artificial Intelligence Research*, 19:399–468.

[250] Guez, A. and Pineau, J. (2010). Multi-tasking SLAM. In *IEEE Intl. Conf. on Robotics and Automation (ICRA)*, pp. 377–384.

[251] Hähnel, D., Burgard, W., and Lakemeyer, G. (1998). GOLEX – bridging the gap between logic (GOLOG) and a real robot. In *Proc. Annual German Conf. on AI (KI)*, pp. 165–176. Springer.

[252] Hanks, S. and Firby, R. J. (1990). Issues and architectures for planning and execution. In *Proc. Wksp. on Innovative Approaches to Planning, Scheduling and Control*, pp. 59–70. Morgan Kaufmann.

[253] Hansen, E. A. (2011). Suboptimality bounds for stochastic shortest path problems. In *Proc. Conf. on Uncertainty in AI (UAI)*, pp. 301–310.

[254] Hansen, E. A. and Zilberstein, S. (2001). LAO*: A heuristic search algorithm that finds solutions with loops. *Artificial Intelligence*, 129(1):35–62.

[255] Hart, P. E., Nilsson, N. J., and Raphael, B. (1968). A formal basis for the heuristic determination of minimum cost paths. *IEEE Trans. Syst., Man, and Cybernetics*, pp. 1556–1562.

[256] Hart, P. E., Nilsson, N. J., and Raphael, B. (1972). Correction to a formal basis for the heuristic determination of minimum cost paths. *ACM SIGART Bulletin*, 37:28–29.

[257] Hartanto, R. and Hertzberg, J. (2008). Fusing DL reasoning with HTN planning. In *Proc. Annual German Conf. on AI (KI)*, pp. 62–69. Springer.

[258] Haslum, P. (2009). Admissible makespan estimates for PDDL2.1 temporal planning. In *ICAPS Wksp. on Heuristics for Domain-Independent Planning*.

[259] Haslum, P., Bonet, B., and Geffner, H. (2005). New admissible heuristics for domain-independent planning. In *Proc. AAAI*.

[260] Haslum, P., Botea, A., Helmert, M., Bonet, B., and Koenig, S. (2007). Domain-independent construction of pattern database heuristics for cost-optimal planning. In *Proc. AAAI*, volume 7, pp. 1007–1012.

[261] Haslum, P. and Geffner, H. (2000). Admissible heuristics for optimal planning. In *Proc. AIPS*, pp. 140–149.

[262] Haslum, P. and Geffner, H. (2001). Heuristic plannnig with time and resources. In *Proc. European Conf. on Planning (ECP)*, pp. 121–132.

[263] Hauskrecht, M., Meuleau, N., Kaelbling, L. P., Dean, T., and Boutilier, C. (1998). Hierarchical solution of Markov decision processes using macro-actions. In *Proc. Conf. on Uncertainty in AI (UAI)*, pp. 220–229.

[264] Hawes, N. (2011). A survey of motivation frameworks for intelligent systems. *Artificial Intelligence*, 175(5):1020–1036.

[265] Heintz, F., Kvarnström, J., and Doherty, P. (2010). Bridging the sense-reasoning gap: DyKnow – stream-based middleware for knowledge processing. *Advanced Engineering Informatics*, 24(1):14–26.

[266] Helmert, M. (2004). A planning heuristic based on causal graph analysis. In *Proc. ICAPS*.

[267] Helmert, M. (2006). The Fast Downward planning system. *J. Artificial Intelligence Research*, 26:191–246.

[268] Helmert, M. (2009). Concise finite-domain representations for PDDL planning tasks. *Artificial Intelligence*, 173(5):503–535.

[269] Helmert, M. and Domshlak, C. (2009). Landmarks, critical paths and abstractions: What's the difference anyway? In *Proc. ICAPS*, pp. 162–169.

[270] Helmert, M. and Geffner, H. (2008). Unifying the causal graph and additive heuristics. In *Proc. ICAPS*, pp. 140–147.

[271] Helmert, M., Haslum, P., and Hoffmann, J. (2007). Flexible abstraction heuristics for optimal sequential planning. In *Proc. ICAPS*, pp. 176–183.

[272] Helmert, M., Haslum, P., and Hoffmann, J. (2008). Explicit-state abstraction: A new method for generating heuristic functions. In *Proc. AAAI*, pp. 1547–1550.

[273] Helmert, M., Haslum, P., Hoffmann, J., and Nissim, R. (2014). Merge-and-shrink abstraction: A method for generating lower bounds in factored state spaces. *J. ACM*, 61(3):16.

[274] Henzinger, T. A. (1996). The theory of hybrid automata. In *IEEE Symp. on Logic in Computer Sci.*, pp. 278–292.

[275] Hoey, J., St-Aubin, R., Hu, A., and Boutilier, C. (1999). SPUDD: Stochastic planning using decision diagrams. In *Proc. Conf. on Uncertainty in AI (UAI)*, pp. 279–288.

[276] Hoffmann, J. (2001). FF: The Fast-Forward planning system. *AI Magazine*, 22(3):57–62.

[277] Hoffmann, J. (2003). The metric-FF planning system: Translating "ignoring delete lists" to numeric state variables. *J. Artificial Intelligence Research*, 20:291–341.

[278] Hoffmann, J. (2005). Where "ignoring delete lists" works: local search topology in planning benchmarks. *J. Artificial Intelligence Research*, pp. 685–758.

[279] Hoffmann, J. and Brafman, R. (2005). Contingent planning via heuristic forward search with implicit belief states. In *Proc. ICAPS*.

[280] Hoffmann, J. and Nebel, B. (2001). The FF planning system: Fast plan generation through heuristic search. *J. Artificial Intelligence Research*, 14:253–302.

[281] Hoffmann, J., Porteous, J., and Sebastia, L. (2004). Ordered landmarks in planning. *J. Artificial Intelligence Research*, 22:215–278.

[282] Hofmann, A. G. and Williams, B. C. (2010). Exploiting spatial and temporal flexibility for exploiting spatial and temporal flexibility for plan execution of hybrid, under-actuated systems. In *Cognitive Robotics*.

[283] Hogg, C., Kuter, U., and Muñoz-Avila, H. (2010). Learning methods to generate good plans: Integrating HTN learning and reinforcement learning. In *Proc. AAAI*.

[284] Hongeng, S., Nevatia, R., and Bremond, F. (2004). Video-based event recognition: activity representation and probabilistic recognition methods. *Computer Vision and Image Understanding*, 96(2):129–162.

[285] Hooker, J. N. (2006). Operations research methods in constraint programming. In Rossi, F., van Beek, P., and Walsh, T., editors, *Handbook of Constraint Programming*, pp. 527–570. Elsevier.

[286] Hopcroft, J. E., Motwani, R., and Ullman, J. D. (2006). *Introduction to Automata Theory, Languages, and Computation*. Addison-Wesley.

[287] Horowitz, S. S. E. and Rajasakaran, S. (1996). *Computer Algorithms*. W.H. Freeman.

[288] Howard, R. A. (1971). *Dynamic Probabilistic Systems*. Wiley.

[289] Huang, R., Chen, Y., and Zhang, W. (2009). An optimal temporally expressive planner: Initial results and application to P2P network optimization. In *Proc. ICAPS*.

[290] Ibaraki, T. (1976). Theoretical comparision of search strategies in branch and bound. *International Journal of Computer and Information Sciences*, 5:315 344.

[291] ICAPS (2015). ICAPS competitions. http://icaps-conference.org/index.php/Main/Competitions. [Accessed: 16 August 2015].

[292] Ingham, M. D., Ragno, R. J., and Williams, B. C. (2001). A reactive model-based programming language for robotic space explorers. In *Intl. Symp. on Artificial Intell., Robotics and Automation in Space (i-SAIRAS)*.

[293] Ingrand, F., Chatilla, R., Alami, R., and Robert, F. (1996). PRS: A high level supervision and control language for autonomous mobile robots. In *IEEE Intl. Conf. on Robotics and Automation (ICRA)*, pp. 43–49.

[294] Ingrand, F. and Ghallab, M. (2015). Deliberation for Autonomous Robots: A Survey. *Artificial Intelligence (In Press)*.

[295] Ivankovic, F., Haslum, P., Thiebaux, S., Shivashankar, V., and Nau, D. (2014). Optimal planning with global numerical state constraints. In *Proc. ICAPS*.

[296] Iwen, M. and Mali, A. D. (2002). Distributed graphplan. In *IEEE Intl. Conf. on Tools with AI (ICTAI)*, pp. 138–145. IEEE.

[297] Jensen, R. and Veloso, M. (2000). OBDD-based universal planning for synchronized agents in non-deterministic domains. *J. Artificial Intelligence Research*, 13:189–226.

[298] Jensen, R., Veloso, M., and Bryant, R. (2003). Guided symbolic universal planning. In *Proc. ICAPS*.

[299] Jensen, R. M., Veloso, M. M., and Bowling, M. H. (2001). OBDD-based optimistic and strong cyclic adversarial planning. In *Proc. European Conf. on Planning (ECP)*.

[300] Jiménez, S., de La Rosa, T., Fernández, S., Fernández, F., and Borrajo, D. (2012). A review of machine learning for automated planning. *The Knowledge Engg. Review*, 27(4):433–467.

[301] Jónsson, A. K., Morris, P. H., Muscettola, N., Rajan, K., and Smith, B. D. (2000). Planning in interplanetary space: Theory and practice. In *AIPS*, pp. 177–186.

[302] Jonsson, P., Drakengren, T., and Bäckström, C. (1999). Computational complexity of relating time points and intervals. *Artificial Intelligence*, 109:273–295.

[303] Judah, K., Fern, A. P., and Dietterich, T. G. (2012). Active imitation learning via reduction to IID active learning. In *Proc. Conf. on Uncertainty in AI (UAI)*, pp. 428–437.

[304] Kabanza, F., Barbeau, M., and St-Denis, R. (1997). Planning control rules for reactive agents. *Artificial Intelligence*, 95(1):67–113.

[305] Kaelbling, L. P., Littman, M. L., and Cassandra, A. (1998). Planning and acting in partially observable stochastic domains. *Artificial Intelligence*, 101:99–134.

[306] Kambhampati, S. (1993). On the utility of systematicity: Understanding the trade-offs between redundancy and commitment in partial-order planning. In *Proc. IJCAI*, pp. 1380–1385.

[307] Kambhampati, S. (1995). A comparative analysis of partial order planning and task reduction planning. *SIGART Bulletin*, 6(1).

[308] Kambhampati, S. (2003). Are we comparing Dana and Fahiem or SHOP and TLPlan? A critique of the knowledge-based planning track at ICP. http://rakaposhi.eas.asu.edu/kbplan.pdf.

[309] Kambhampati, S. and Hendler, J. A. (1992). A validation-structure-based theory of plan modification and reuse. *Artificial Intelligence*, 55:193–258.

[310] Kambhampati, S., Knoblock, C. A., and Yang, Q. (1995). Planning as refinement search: A unified framework for evaluating design tradeoffs in partial-order planning. *Artificial Intelligence*, 76(1–2):167–238.

[311] Kambhampati, S. and Nau, D. S. (1996). On the nature and role of modal truth criteria in planning. *Artificial Intelligence*, 82(2).

[312] Kambhampati, S. and Srivastava, B. (1995). Universal classical planner: An algorithm for unifying state-space and plan-space planning. In *Proc. European Conf. on Planning (ECP)*.

[313] Karabaev, E. and Skvortsova, O. (2005). A heuristic search algorithm for solving first-order MDPs. In *Proc. Conf. on Uncertainty in AI (UAI)*, pp. 292–299.

[314] Karaman, S. and Frazzoli, E. (2012). Sampling-based algorithms for optimal motion planning with deterministic μ-calculus specifications. In *American Control Conference (ACC)*, pp. 735–742. IEEE.

[315] Karlsson, L., Bouguerra, A., Broxvall, M., Coradeschi, S., and Saffiotti, A. (2008). To secure an anchor – A recovery planning approach to ambiguity in perceptual anchoring. *AI Communincations*, 21(1):1–14.

[316] Karpas, E. and Domshlak, C. (2009). Cost-optimal planning with landmarks. In *Proc. IJCAI*, pp. 1728–1733.

[317] Karpas, E., Wang, D., Williams, B. C., and Haslum, P. (2015). Temporal landmarks: What must happen, and when. In *Proc. ICAPS*.

[318] Katz, M. and Domshlak, C. (2008). Optimal additive composition of abstraction-based admissible heuristics. In *Proc. ICAPS*, pp. 174–181.

[319] Katz, M. and Domshlak, C. (2009). Structural-pattern databases. In *Proc. ICAPS*.

[320] Kautz, H. and Allen, J. (1986). Generalized plan recognition. In *Proc. AAAI*, pp. 32–37.

[321] Kautz, H., McAllester, D., and Selman, B. (1996). Encoding plans in propositional logic. In *Proc. Intl. Conf. on Principles of Knowledge Representation and Reasoning (KR)*, pp. 374–384.

[322] Kautz, H. and Selman, B. (1992). Planning as satisfiability. In *Proc. ECAI*.

[323] Kautz, H. and Selman, B. (1996). Pushing the envelope: Planning, propositional logic, and stochastic search. In *Proc. AAAI*, pp. 1194–1201.

[324] Kautz, H. A., Thomas, W., and Vardi, M. Y., editors (2006). *Synthesis and Planning*, Dagstuhl Seminar Proceedings.

[325] Kearns, M., Mansour, Y., and Ng, A. (2002). A sparse sampling algorithm for near-optimal planning in large Markov decision processes. *Machine Learning*, 49:193–208.

[326] Kelleher, G. and Cohn, A. G. (1992). Automatically synthesising domain constraints from operator descriptions. In *Proc. ECAI*, pp. 653–655.

[327] Keller, T. and Eyerich, P. (2012). PROST: Probabilistic planning based on UCT. *Proc. ICAPS*, pp. 119–127.

[328] Khatib, L., Morris, P., Morris, R., and Rossi, F. (2001). Temporal constraint reasoning with preferences. In *Proc. IJCAI*.

[329] Khatib, S. and Siciliano, B. (2007). *Handbook of Robotics*. Springer.

[330] Kiesel, S. and Ruml, W. (2014). Planning under temporal uncertainty using hindsight optimization. In *ICAPS Wksp. on Planning and Robotics*, pp. 1–11.

[331] Kissmann, P. and Edelkamp, S. (2009). Solving fully-observable non-deterministic planning problems via translation into a general game. In *Proc. Annual German Conf. on AI (KI)*, pp. 1–8. Springer.

[332] Knight, R., Rabideau, G., Chien, S., Engelhardt, B., and Sherwood, R. (2001). Casper: space exploration through continuous planning. *IEEE Intelligent Systems*, 16(5):70–75.

[333] Knoblock, C. (1992). An analysis of ABSTRIPS. In *Proc. AIPS*.

[334] Knoblock, C. A. (1994). Automatically generating abstractions for planning. *Artificial Intelligence*, 68(2):243–302.

[335] Knoblock, C. A., Tenenberg, J. D., and Yang, Q. (1991). Characterizing abstraction hierarchies for planning. In *Proc. AAAI*, pp. 692–698.

[336] Knoblock, C. A. and Yang, Q. (1994). Evaluating the trade-offs in partial-order planning algorithms. In *AAAI Wksp. on Comparative Analysis of AI Planning Systems*.

[337] Knoblock, C. A. and Yang, Q. (1995). Relating the performance of partial-order planning algorithms to domain features. *SIGART Bulletin*, 6(1).

[338] Knuth, D. E. and Moore, R. W. (1975). An analysis of alpha-beta pruning. *Artificial Intelligence*, 6:293–326.

[339] Kocsis, L. and Szepesvári, C. (2006). Bandit based Monte-Carlo planning. In *Proc. European Conf. on Machine Learning (ECML)*, volume 4212 of *LNAI*, pp. 1–12. Springer.

[340] Koehler, J. (1998). Planning under resource constraints. In *Proc. ECAI*, pp. 489–493.

[341] Koehler, J. (1999). Handling of conditional effects and negative goals in IPP. Technical Report 128, Albert-Ludwigs-Universität Freiburg.

[342] Koenig, S. (2001). Minimax real-time heuristic search. *Artificial Intelligence*, 129(1–2):165–197.

[343] Koenig, S. and Simmons, R. (1998). Solving robot navigation problems with initial pose uncertainty using real-time heuristic search. In *Proc. AIPS*.

[344] Koenig, S. and Simmons, R. G. (1995). Real-time search in non-deterministic domains. In *Proc. IJCAI*, pp. 1660–1669.

[345] Koller, D. and Friedman, N. (2009). *Probabilistic Graphical Models: Principles and Techniques*. MIT Press.

[346] Kolobov, A., Mausam, and Weld, D. (2010). SixthSense: Fast and reliable recognition of dead ends in MDPs. In *Proc. AAAI*.

[347] Kolobov, A., Mausam, and Weld, D. (2012). Stochastic shortest path MDPs with dead ends. *Proc. ICAPS Workshop HSDIP*.

[348] Kolobov, A., Mausam, Weld, D., and Geffner, H. (2011). Heuristic search for generalized stochastic shortest path MDPs. In *Proc. ICAPS*.

[349] Kolobov, A. and Weld, D. (2009). ReTrASE: integrating paradigms for approximate probabilistic planning. In *Proc. IJCAI*.

[350] Korf, R. (1990). Real-time heuristic search. *Artificial Intelligence*, 42(2–3):189–211.

[351] Korf, R. E. (1985). Depth-first iterative-deepening: an optimal admissible tree search. *Artificial Intelligence*, 27:97–109.

[352] Korf, R. E. (1987). Planning as search: A quantitative approach. *Artificial Intelligence*, 33:65–88.

[353] Korf, R. E. (1993). Linear-space best-first search. *Artificial Intelligence*, 62(1):41–78.

[354] Koubarakis, M. (1997). From local to global consistency in temporal constraint networks. *Theoretical Computer Science*, 173(1):89–112.

[355] Krüger, V., Kragic, D., Ude, A., and Geib, C. (2007). The meaning of action: a review on action recognition and mapping. *Advanced Robotics*, 21(13):1473–1501.

[356] Kumar, V. and Kanal, L. (1983a). The composite decision process: A unifying formulation for heuristic search, dynamic programming and branch and bound procedures. In *Proc. AAAI*, pp. 220–224.

[357] Kumar, V. and Kanal, L. (1983b). A general branch and bound formulation for understanding and synthesizing and/or tree search procedures. *Artificial Intelligence*, pp. 179–198.

[358] Kupferman, O., Madhusudan, P., Thiagarajan, P. S., and Vardi, M. Y. (2000). Open systems in reactive environments: Control and synthesis. In *Proc. Intl. Conf. on Concurrency Theory (CONCUR)*, pp. 92–107.

[359] Kupferman, O. and Vardi, M. Y. (2001). Synthesizing distributed systems. In *IEEE Symp. on Logic in Computer Sci.*, pp. 389–398.

[360] Kurzhanskiy, A. A. and Varaiya, P. (2007). Ellipsoidal techniques for reachability analysis of discrete-time linear systems. *IEEE Trans. Automat. Contr.*, 52(1):26–38.

[361] Kuter, U. and Nau, D. (2005). Using domain-configurable search control for probabilistic planning. In *Proc. AAAI*, pp. 1169–1174.

[362] Kuter, U., Nau, D. S., Pistore, M., and Traverso, P. (2005). A hierarchical task-network planner based on symbolic model checking. In *Proc. ICAPS*, pp. 300–309.

[363] Kuter, U., Nau, D. S., Pistore, M., and Traverso, P. (2009). Task decomposition on abstract states, for planning under nondeterminism. *Artificial Intelligence*, 173:669–695.

[364] Kuter, U., Nau, D. S., Reisner, E., and Goldman, R. (2008). Using classical planners to solve nondeterministic planning problems. In *Proc. ICAPS*, pp. 190–197.

[365] Kuter, U., Sirin, E., Nau, D. S., Parsia, B., and Hendler, J. (2004). Information gathering during planning for web service composition. In McIlraith, S. A., Plexousakis, D., and van Harmelen, F., editors, *Proc. Intl. Semantic Web Conf. (ISWC)*, volume 3298 of *LNCS*, pp. 335–349. Springer.

[366] Kvarnström, J. and Doherty, P. (2001). TALplanner: A temporal logic based forward chaining planner. *Annals of Mathematics and Artificial Intelligence*, 30:119–169.

[367] Kvarnström, J., Doherty, P., and Haslum, P. (2000). Extending TALplanner with concurrency and resources. In *Proc. European Conf. on Planning (ECP)*.

[368] Kveton, B., Hauskrecht, M., and Guestrin, C. (2006). Solving factored MDPs with hybrid state and action variables. *J. Artificial Intelligence Research*, 27:153–201.

[369] Laborie, P. (2003). Algorithms for propagating resource constraints in ai planning and scheduling: Existing approaches and new results. *Artificial Intelligence*, 143(2):151–188.

[370] Laborie, P. and Ghallab, M. (1995). Planning with sharable resource constraints. In *Proc. IJCAI*, pp. 1643–1649.

[371] Laird, J., Rosenbloom, P., and Newell, A. (2012). *Universal Subgoaling and Chunking: The Automatic Generation and Learning of Goal Hierarchies*, volume 11. Springer Science & Business Media.

[372] Laporte, C. and Arbel, T. (2006). Efficient discriminant viewpoint selection for active Bayesian recognition. *Intl. J. Robotics Research*, 68(3):267–287.

[373] Lawler, E. L. and Wood, D. E. (1966). Branch-and-bound methods: A survey. *Operations Research*, 14(4):699–719.

[374] Le Guillou, X., Cordier, M.-O., Robin, S., Rozé, L., et al. (2008). Chronicles for on-line diagnosis of distributed systems. In *Proc. ECAI*, volume 8, pp. 194–198.

[375] Lemai-Chenevier, S. and Ingrand, F. (2004). Interleaving temporal planning and execution in robotics domains. In *Proc. AAAI*.

[376] Lemaignan, S., Espinoza, R. R., Mösenlechner, L., Alami, R., and Beetz, M. (2010). ORO, a knowledge management platform for cognitive architectures in robotics. In *IEEE/RSJ Intl. Conf. on Intelligent Robots and Syst. (IROS)*.

[377] Lesperance, Y., H. J., Lin, L. F., Marcus, D., Reiter, R., and Scherl, R. (1994). A logical approach to high-level robot programming – a progress report. In *AAAI Fall Symp. on Control of the Physical World by Intelligent Agents*. AAAI Technical Report FS-94-03.

[378] Levesque, H., Reiter, R., Lespérance, Y., Lin, F., and Scherl, R. (1997a). GOLOG: A logic programming language for dynamic domains. *J. Logic Programming*, 31:59–84.

[379] Levesque, H. J., Reiter, R., Lesperance, Y., Lin, F., and Scherl, R. (1997b). GOLOG: a logic programming language for dynamic domains. *J. Logic Progr.*, 31:59–83.

[380] Levine, S. J. and Williams, B. C. (2014). Concurrent plan recognition and execution for human-robot teams. In *Proc. ICAPS*.

[381] Li, H. X. and Williams, B. C. (2008). Generative planning for hybrid systems based on flow tubes. In *Proc. ICAPS*, pp. 206–213.

[382] Liaskos, S., McIlraith, S. A., Sohrabi, S., and Mylopoulos, J. (2010). Integrating preferences into goal models for requirements engineering. In *Intl. Requirements Engg. Conf.*, pp. 135–144.

[383] Liatsos, V. and Richard, B. (1999). Scalability in planning. In Biundo, S. and Fox, M., editors, *Proc. European Conf. on Planning (ECP)*, volume 1809 of *LNAI*, pp. 49–61. Springer.

[384] Lifschitz, V. (1987). On the semantics of STRIPS. In Georgeff, M. P. and Lansky, A. L., editors, *Reasoning about Actions and Plans: Proc. 1986 Wksp.*, pp. 1–9. Morgan Kaufmann. Reprinted in [15], pp. 523–530.

[385] Ligozat, G. (1991). On generalized interval calculi. In *Proc. AAAI*, pp. 234–240.

[386] Likhachev, M., Gordon, G. J., and Thrun, S. (2004). Planning for Markov decision processes with sparse stochasticity. In *Adv. in Neural Information Processing Syst. (Proc. NIPS)*, volume 17.

[387] Lin, S. (1965). Computer solutions of the traveling salesman problem. *Bell System Technical Journal*, 44(10):2245–2269.

[388] Little, I., Aberdeen, D., and Thiébaux, S. (2005). Prottle: A probabilistic temporal planner. In *Proc. AAAI*, pp. 1181–1186.

[389] Little, I. and Thiébaux, S. (2007). Probabilistic planning vs. replanning. In *ICAPS Wksp. on the Intl. Planning Competition*.

[390] Liu, Y. and Koenig, S. (2006). Functional value iteration for decision-theoretic planning with general utility functions. In *Proc. AAAI*.

[391] Löhr, J., Eyerich, P., Keller, T., and Nebel, B. (2012). A planning based framework for controlling hybrid systems. In *Proc. ICAPS*.

[392] Löhr, J., Eyerich, P., Winkler, S., and Nebel, B. (2013). Domain predictive control under uncertain numerical state information. In *Proc. ICAPS*.

[393] Long, D. and Fox, M. (1999). Efficient implementation of the plan graph in STAN. *J. Artificial Intelligence Research*, 10(1–2):87–115.

[394] Long, D. and Fox, M. (2003a). The 3rd international planning competition: Results and analysis. *J. Artificial Intelligence Research*, 20:1–59.

[395] Long, D. and Fox, M. (2003b). Exploiting a graphplan framework in temporal planning. In *Proc. ICAPS*, pp. 52–61.

[396] Lotem, A. and Nau, D. S. (2000). New advances in GraphHTN: Identifying independent subproblems in large HTN domains. In *Proc. AIPS*, pp. 206–215.

[397] Lotem, A., Nau, D. S., and Hendler, J. (1999). Using planning graphs for solving HTN problems. In *Proc. AAAI*, pp. 534–540.

[398] Magnenat, S., Chappelier, J. C., and Mondada, F. (2012). Integration of online learning into HTN planning for robotic tasks. In *AAAI Spring Symposium*.

[399] Maliah, S., Brafman, R., Karpas, E., and Shani, G. (2014). Partially observable online contingent planning using landmark heuristics. In *Proc. ICAPS*.

[400] Malik, J. and Binford, T. (1983). Reasoning in time and space. In *Proc. IJCAI*, pp. 343–345.

[401] Mansouri, M. and Pecora, F. (2016). Robot waiters: A case for hybrid reasoning with different types of knowledge. *J. Experimental & Theoretical Artificial Intelligence*.

[402] Marthi, B., Russell, S., and Wolfe, J. (2007). Angelic semantics for high-level actions. In *Proc. ICAPS*.

[403] Marthi, B., Russell, S., and Wolfe, J. (2008). Angelic hierarchical planning: Optimal and online algorithms. In *Proc. ICAPS*, pp. 222–231.

[404] Marthi, B. M., Russell, S. J., Latham, D., and Guestrin, C. (2005). Concurrent hierarchical reinforcement learning. In *Proc. AAAI*, p. 1652.

[405] Mattmüller, R., Ortlieb, M., Helmert, M., and Bercher, P. (2010). Pattern database heuristics for fully observable nondeterministic planning. In *Proc. ICAPS*, pp. 105–112.

[406] Mausam, Bertoli, P., and Weld, D. (2007). A hybridized planner for stochastic domains. In *Proc. IJCAI*, pp. 1972–1978.

[407] Mausam and Kolobov, A. (2012). *Planning with Markov Decision Processes: An AI Perspective*. Morgan & Claypool.

[408] Mausam and Weld, D. (2005). Concurrent probabilistic temporal planning. In *Proc. ICAPS*.

[409] Mausam and Weld, D. (2006). Probabilistic temporal planning with uncertain durations. In *Proc. AAAI*, pp. 880–887.

[410] Mausam and Weld, D. (2008). Planning with durative actions in stochastic domains. *J. Artificial Intelligence Research*, 31(1):33–82.

[411] McAllester, D. and Rosenblitt, D. (1991). Systematic nonlinear planning. In *Proc. AAAI*, pp. 634–639.

[412] McCarthy, J. (1990). *Formalizing Common Sense: Papers by John McCarthy*. Ablex Publishing.

[413] McCarthy, J. and Hayes, P. J. (1969). Some philosophical problems from the standpoint of artificial intelligence. In Meltzer, B. and Michie, D., editors, *Machine Intelligence 4*, pp. 463–502. Edinburgh Univ. Press. Reprinted in [412].

[414] McDermott, D. (1982). A temporal logic for reasoning about processes and plans. *Cognitive Science*, 6:101–155.

[415] McDermott, D. (1991). A reactive plan language. Technical Report YALEU/CSD/RR 864, Yale Univ.

[416] McDermott, D. M. (2000). The 1998 AI planning systems competition. *AI Magazine*, 21(2):35.

[417] McIlraith, S. A. and Son, T. C. (2002). Adapting GOLOG for composition of semantic web services. In *Proc. Intl. Conf. on Principles of Knowledge Representation and Reasoning (KR)*, pp. 482–496.

[418] McMahan, H. B. and Gordon, G. J. (2005). Fast exact planning in Markov decision processes. In *Proc. ICAPS*, pp. 151–160.

[419] Meiri, I. (1990). Faster Constraint satisfaction algorithms for temporal reasoning. Tech. report R-151, UC Los Angeles.

[420] Meuleau, N., Benazera, E., Brafman, R. I., and Hansen, E. A. (2009). A heuristic search approach to planning with continuous resources in stochastic domains. *J. Artificial Intelligence Research*, 34(1):27.

[421] Meuleau, N. and Brafman, R. I. (2007). Hierarchical heuristic forward search in stochastic domains. In *Proc. IJCAI*, pp. 2542–2549.

[422] Miguel, I., Jarvis, P., and Shen, Q. (2000). Flexible graphplan. In *Proc. ECAI*, pp. 506–510.

[423] Minton, S., Bresina, J., and Drummond, M. (1991). Commitment strategies in planning: A comparative analysis. In *Proc. IJCAI*, pp. 259–265.

[424] Minton, S., Drummond, M., Bresina, J., and Philips, A. (1992). Total order vs. partial order planning: Factors influencing performance. In *Proc. Intl. Conf. on Principles of Knowledge Representation and Reasoning (KR)*, pp. 83–92.

[425] Mitten, L. G. (1970). Branch and bound methods: General formulations and properties. *Operations Research*, 18:23–34.

[426] Moeslund, T. B., Hilton, A., and Krüger, V. (2006). A survey of advances in vision-based human motion capture and analysis. *Computer Vision and Image Understanding*, 104(2–3):90–126.

[427] Moffitt, M. D. (2011). On the modelling and optimization of preferences in constraint-based temporal reasoning. *Artificial Intelligence*, 175(7):1390–1409.

[428] Moffitt, M. D. and Pollack, M. E. (2005). Partial constraint satisfaction of disjunctive temporal problems. In *Proc. Intl. Florida AI Research Soc. Conf. (FLAIRS)*, pp. 715–720.

[429] Molineaux, M., Klenk, M., and Aha, D. (2010). Goal-driven autonomy in a Navy strategy simulation. In *Proc. AAAI*, pp. 1548–1554.

[430] Morisset, B. and Ghallab, M. (2002a). Learning how to combine sensory-motor modalities for a robust behavior. In Beetz, M., Hertzberg, J., Ghallab, M., and Pollack, M., editors, *Advances in Plan-based Control of Robotics Agents*, volume 2466 of *LNAI*, pp. 157–178. Springer.

[431] Morisset, B. and Ghallab, M. (2002b). Synthesis of supervision policies for robust sensory-motor behaviors. In *Intl. Conf. on Intell. and Autonomous Syst. (IAS)*, pp. 236–243.

[432] Morris, P. (2014). Dynamic controllability and dispatchability relationships. In *Integration of AI and OR*, pp. 464–479.

[433] Morris, P., Muscettola, N., and Vidal, T. (2001). Dynamic control of plans with temporal uncertainty. In *Proc. IJCAI*, pp. 494–502.

[434] Morris, P. H. and Muscettola, N. (2005). Temporal dynamic controllability revisited. In *Proc. AAAI*, pp. 1193–1198.

[435] Muise, C., McIlraith, S. A., and Belle, V. (2014). Non-deterministic planning with conditional effects. In *Proc. ICAPS*.

[436] Muise, C. J., McIlraith, S. A., and Beck, J. C. (2012). Improved non-deterministic planning by exploiting state relevance. In *Proc. ICAPS*.

[437] Munos, R. and Moore, A. W. (2002). Variable resolution discretization in optimal control. *Machine Learning*, 49:291–323.

[438] Muñoz-Avila, H., Aha, D. W., Nau, D. S., Weber, R., Breslow, L., and Yaman, F. (2001). SiN: Integrating case-based reasoning with task decomposition. In *Proc. IJCAI*.

[439] Muscettola, N., Dorais, G., Fry, C., Levinson, R., and Plaunt, C. (2002). IDEA: Planning at the core of autonomous reactive agents. In *Intl. Wksp. on Planning and Scheduling for Space (IWPSS)*.

[440] Muscettola, N., Morris, P. H., and Tsamardinos, I. (1998a). Reformulating temporal plans for efficient execution. In *Principles of Knowledge Representation and Reasoning*, pp. 444–452.

[441] Muscettola, N., Nayak, P. P., Pell, B., and Williams, B. C. (1998b). Remote Agent: To boldly go where no AI system has gone before. *Artificial Intelligence*, 103:5–47.

[442] Myers, K. L. (1999). CPEF: A continuous planning and execution framework. *AI Magazine*, 20(4):63–69.

[443] Nareyek, A., Freuder, E. C., Fourer, R., Giunchiglia, E., Goldman, R. P., Kautz, H., Rintanen, J., and Tate, A. (2005). Constraints and AI planning. *IEEE Intelligent Systems*, 20(2):62–72.

[444] Nau, D. S., Au, T.-C., Ilghami, O., Kuter, U., Muñoz-Avila, H., Murdock, J. W., Wu, D., and Yaman, F. (2005). Applications of SHOP and SHOP2. *IEEE Intelligent Systems*, 20(2):34–41.

[445] Nau, D. S., Au, T.-C., Ilghami, O., Kuter, U., Murdock, J. W., Wu, D., and Yaman, F. (2003). SHOP2: An HTN planning system. *J. Artificial Intelligence Research*, 20:379–404.

[446] Nau, D. S., Cao, Y., Lotem, A., and Muñoz-Avila, H. (1999). SHOP: Simple hierarchical ordered planner. In *Proc. IJCAI*, pp. 968–973.

[447] Nau, D. S., Kumar, V., and Kanal, L. N. (1984). General branch and bound, and its relation to A* and AO*. *Artificial Intelligence*, 23(1):29–58.

[448] Nau, D. S., Muñoz-Avila, H., Cao, Y., Lotem, A., and Mitchell, S. (2001). Total-order planning with partially ordered subtasks. In *Proc. IJCAI*.

[449] Nebel, B. and Burckert, H. (1995). Reasoning about temporal relations: a maximal tractable subclass of Allen's interval algebra. *J. ACM*, 42(1):43–66.

[450] Newell, A. and Ernst, G. (1965). The search for generality. In *Proc. IFIP Congress*, volume 65, pp. 17–24.

[451] Newell, A. and Simon, H. A. (1963). GPS, a program that simulates human thought. In Feigenbaum, E. A. and Feldman, J. A., editors, *Computers and Thought*. McGraw-Hill.

[452] Newton, M. A. H., Levine, J., Fox, M., and Long, D. (2007). Learning macro-actions for arbitrary planners and domains. In *Proc. ICAPS*.

[453] Ng, A. and Jordan, M. (2000). PEGASUS: a policy search method for large MDPs and POMDPs. In *Proc. Conf. on Uncertainty in AI (UAI)*, pp. 406–415.

[454] Nguyen, N. and Kambhampati, S. (2001). Reviving partial order planning. In *Proc. IJCAI*.

[455] Nicolescu, M. N. and Mataric, M. J. (2003). Natural methods for robot task learning: instructive demonstrations, generalization and practice. In *Proc. AAMAS*, pp. 241–248.

[456] Nieuwenhuis, R., Oliveras, A., and Tinelli, C. (2006). Solving SAT and SAT modulo theories: From an abstract Davis-Putnam-Logemann-Loveland procedure to DPLL (T). *J. ACM*, 53(6):937–977.

[457] Nikolova, E. and Karger, D. R. (2008). Route planning under uncertainty: The Canadian traveller problem. In *Proc. AAAI*, pp. 969–974.

[458] Nilsson, M., Kvarnström, J., and Doherty, P. (2014a). EfficientIDC: A faster incremental dynamic controllability algorithm. In *Proc. ICAPS*.

[459] Nilsson, M., Kvarnström, J., and Doherty, P. (2014b). Incremental dynamic controllability in cubic worst-case time. In *Intl. Symp. on Temporal Representation and Reasoning*.

[460] Nilsson, N. (1980). *Principles of Artificial Intelligence*. Morgan Kaufmann.

[461] Oaksford, M. and Chater, N. (2007). *Bayesian rationality the probabilistic approach to human reasoning*. Oxford Univ. Press.

[462] Oates, T. and Cohen, P. R. (1996). Learning planning operators with conditional and proba-bilistic effects. In *Proc. AAAI Spring Symposium on Planning with Incomplete Information for Robot Problems*, pp. 86–94.

[463] Ong, S. C. W., Png, S. W., Hsu, D., and Lee, W. S. (2010). Planning under uncertainty for robotic tasks with mixed observability. *Intl. J. Robotics Research*, 29(8):1053–1068.

[464] Papadimitriou, C. (1994). *Computational Complexity*. Addison Wesley.

[465] Parr, R. and Russell, S. J. (1998). Reinforcement learning with hierarchies of machines. In *Adv. in Neural Information Processing Syst. (Proc. NIPS)*, pp. 1043–1049.

[466] Pasula, H., Zettlemoyer, L. S., and Kaelbling, L. P. (2004). Learning probabilistic relational planning rules. In *Proc. ICAPS*, pp. 73–82.

[467] Pearl, J. (1984). *Heuristics: Intelligent Search Strategies for Computer Problem Solving*. Addison-Wesley.

[468] Pecora, F., Cirillo, M., Dell'Osa, F., Ullberg, J., and Saffiotti, A. (2012). A constraint-based approach for proactive, context-aware human support. *J. Ambient Intell. and Smart Envi-ronments*, 4(4):347–367.

[469] Pednault, E. (1988). Synthesizing plans that contain actions with context-dependent effects. *Computational Intelligence*, 4:356–372.

[470] Pednault, E. P. (1989). ADL: Exploring the middle ground between STRIPS and the situa-tion calculus. In *Proc. Intl. Conf. on Principles of Knowledge Representation and Reasoning (KR)*, pp. 324–332.

[471] Penberthy, J. and Weld, D. S. (1994). Temporal planning with continuous change. In *Proc. AAAI*, pp. 1010–1015.

[472] Penberthy, J. S. and Weld, D. (1992). UCPOP: A sound, complete, partial order planner for ADL. In *Proc. Intl. Conf. on Principles of Knowledge Representation and Reasoning (KR)*.

[473] Penna, G. D., Intrigila, B., Magazzeni, D., and Mercorio, F. (2009). Upmurphi: a tool for universal planning on PDDL+ problems. In *Proc. ICAPS*, pp. 19–23.

[474] Peot, M. and Smith, D. (1992). Conditional nonlinear planning. In *Proc. AIPS*, pp. 189–197.

[475] Peters, J. and Ng, A. Y. (2009). Special issue on robot learning. *Autonomous Robots*, 27(1–2).

[476] Petrick, R. and Bacchus, F. (2004). Extending the knowledge-based approach to planning with incomplete information and sensing. In *Proc. ICAPS*, pp. 2–11.

[477] Pettersson, O. (2005). Execution monitoring in robotics: A survey. *Robotics and Autonomous Systems*, 53(2):73–88.

[478] Piaget, J. (1951). *The Psychology of Intelligence*. Routledge.

[479] Piaget, J. (2001). *Studies in Reflecting Abstraction*. Psychology Press.

[480] Pineau, J., Gordon, G. J., and Thrun, S. (2002). Policy-contingent abstraction for robust robot control. In *Proc. Conf. on Uncertainty in AI (UAI)*, pp. 477–484.

[481] Pineau, J., Montemerlo, M., Pollack, M. E., Roy, N., and Thrun, S. (2003). Towards robotic assistants in nursing homes: Challenges and results. *Robotics and Autonomous Systems*, 42(3–4):271–281.

[482] Pistore, M., Bettin, R., and Traverso, P. (2001). Symbolic techniques for planning with extended goals in non-deterministic domains. In *Proc. European Conf. on Planning (ECP)*, LNAI. Springer.

[483] Pistore, M., Spalazzi, L., and Traverso, P. (2006). A minimalist approach to semantic anno-tations for web processes compositions. In *Euro. SemanticWebConf. (ESWC)*, pp. 620–634.

[484] Pistore, M. and Traverso, P. (2001). Planning as model checking for extended goals in non-deterministic domains. In *Proc. IJCAI*, pp. 479–484. Morgan Kaufmann.

[485] Pistore, M. and Traverso, P. (2007). Assumption-based composition and monitoring of web services. In *Test and Analysis of Web Services*, pp. 307–335. Springer.

[486] Pistore, M., Traverso, P., and Bertoli, P. (2005). Automated composition of web services by planning in asynchronous domains. In *Proc. ICAPS*, pp. 2–11.

[487] Planken, L. R. (2008). Incrementally solving the STP by enforcing partial path consistency. In *Proc. Wksp. of the UK Planning and Scheduling Special Interest Group (PlanSIG)*, pp. 87–94.

[488] Pnueli, A. and Rosner, R. (1989a). On the synthesis of a reactive module. In *Proc. ACM Conf. on Principles of Programming Languages*, pp. 179–190.

[489] Pnueli, A. and Rosner, R. (1989b). On the synthesis of an asynchronous reactive module. In *Proc. Intl. Colloq. Automata, Langs. and Program. (ICALP)*, pp. 652–671.

[490] Pnueli, A. and Rosner, R. (1990). Distributed reactive systems are hard to synthesize. In *31st Annual Symposium on Foundations of Computer Science*, pp. 746–757.

[491] Pohl, I. (1970). Heuristic search viewed as path finding in a graph. *Artificial Intelligence*, 1(3):193–204.

[492] Pollack, M. E. and Horty, J. F. (1999). There's more to life than making plans: Plan management in dynamic, multiagent environments. *AI Magazine*, 20(4):1–14.

[493] Porteous, J., Sebastia, L., and Hoffmann, J. (2001). On the extraction, ordering, and usage of landmarks in planning. In *Proc. European Conf. on Planning (ECP)*.

[494] Powell, J., Molineaux, M., and Aha, D. (2011). Active and interactive discovery of goal selection knowledge. In *FLAIRS*.

[495] Prentice, S. and Roy, N. (2009). The belief roadmap: Efficient planning in belief space by factoring the covariance. *IJRR*, 28(11–12):1448–1465.

[496] Pryor, L. and Collins, G. (1996). Planning for contingency: A decision based approach. *J. Artificial Intelligence Research*, 4:81–120.

[497] Puterman, M. L. (1994). *Markov Decision Processes: Discrete Stochastic Dynamic Programming*. Wiley.

[498] Py, F., Rajan, K., and McGann, C. (2010). A systematic agent framework for situated autonomous systems. In *Proc. AAMAS*, pp. 583–590.

[499] Pynadath, D. V. and Wellman, M. P. (2000). Probabilistic state-dependent grammars for plan recognition. In *Proc. Conf. on Uncertainty in AI (UAI)*, pp. 507–514.

[500] Quiniou, R., Cordier, M.-O., Carrault, G., and Wang, F. (2001). Application of ILP to cardiac arrhythmia characterization for chronicle recognition. In *Inductive Logic Programming*, pp. 220–227. Springer.

[501] Rabideau, G., Knight, R., Chien, S., Fukunaga, A., and Govindjee, A. (1999). Iterative repair planning for spacecraft operations in the ASPEN system. In *Intl. Symp. on Artificial Intell., Robotics and Automation in Space (i-SAIRAS)*.

[502] Rabiner, L. and Juang, B. H. (1986). An introduction to hidden Markov models. *IEEE ASSP Mag.*, 3(1):4–16.

[503] Rajan, K. and Py, F. (2012). T-REX: Partitioned inference for AUV mission control. In Roberts, G. N. and Sutton, R., editors, *Further Advances in Unmanned Marine Vehicles*, pp. 171–199. The Institution of Engg. and Technology.

[504] Rajan, K., Py, F., and Barreiro, J. (2012). Towards deliberative control in marine robotics. In *Marine Robot Autonomy*, pp. 91–175. Springer.

[505] Ramirez, M. and Geffner, H. (2010). Probabilistic plan recognition using off-the-shelf classical planners. In *Proc. AAAI*, pp. 1121–1126.

[506] Ramírez, M., Yadav, N., and Sardiña, S. (2013). Behavior composition as fully observable non-deterministic planning. In *Proc. ICAPS*.

[507] Ramírez, M. and Sardina, S. (2014). Directed fixed-point regression-based planning for non-deterministic domains. In *Proc. ICAPS*.

[508] Reingold, E., Nievergelt, J., and Deo, N. (1977). *Combinatorial Optimization*. Prentice Hall.

[509] Richter, S., Helmert, M., and Westphal, M. (2008). Landmarks revisited. In *Proc. AAAI*, volume 8, pp. 975–982.

[510] Richter, S. and Westphal, M. (2010). The LAMA planner: Guiding cost-based anytime planning with landmarks. *J. Artificial Intelligence Research*, 39(1):127–177.

[511] Rintanen, J. (1999). Constructing conditional plans by a theorem-prover. *J. Artificial Intelligence Research*, 10:323–352.

[512] Rintanen, J. (2000). An iterative algorithm for synthesizing invariants. In *Proc. AAAI*, pp. 1–6.

[513] Rintanen, J. (2002). Backward plan construction for planning as search in belief space. In *Proc. AIPS*.

[514] Rintanen, J. (2005). Conditional planning in the discrete belief space. In *Proc. IJCAI*.

[515] Rodriguez-Moreno, M. D., Oddi, A., Borrajo, D., and Cesta, A. (2006). Ipss: A hybrid approach to planning and scheduling integration. *IEEE Trans. Knowledge and Data Engg. (TDKE)*, 18(12):1681–1695.

[516] Ross, S., Pineau, J., Paquet, S., and Chaib-Draa, B. (2008). Online planning algorithms for POMDPs. *J. Artificial Intelligence Research*, 32:663–704.

[517] Russell, S. and Norvig, P. (2009). *Artificial Intelligence: A Modern Approach*. Prentice-Hall.

[518] Rybski, P. E., Yoon, K., Stolarz, J., and Veloso, M. M. (2007). Interactive robot task training through dialog and demonstration. In *Conference on Human-Robot Interaction*, pp. 49–56.

[519] Sacerdoti, E. (1974). Planning in a hierarchy of abstraction spaces. *Artificial Intelligence*, 5:115–135.

[520] Sacerdoti, E. (1975). The nonlinear nature of plans. In *Proc. IJCAI*, pp. 206–214. Reprinted in [15], pp. 162–170.

[521] Samadi, M., Kollar, T., and Veloso, M. (2012). Using the Web to interactively learn to find objects. In *Proc. AAAI*, pp. 2074–2080.

[522] Samet, H. (2006). *Foundations of multidimensional and metric data structures*. Morgan Kauffmann.

[523] Sandewall, E. (1994). *Features and Fluents: The Representation of Knowledge about Dynamical Systems*. Oxford Univ. Press.

[524] Sandewall, E. and Rönnquist, R. (1986). A representation of action structures. In *Proc. AAAI*, pp. 89–97.

[525] Sanner, S. (2010). Relational dynamic influence diagram language (RDDL): Language description. Technical report, NICTA.

[526] Santana, P. H. R. Q. A. and Williams, B. C. (2014). Chance-constrained consistency for probabilistic temporal plan networks. In *Proc. ICAPS*.

[527] Scherrer, B. and Lesner, B. (2012). On the use of non-stationary policies for stationary infinite-horizon Markov decision processes. In *Adv. in Neural Information Processing Syst. (Proc. NIPS)*, pp. 1826–1834.

[528] Schultz, D. G. and Melsa, J. L. (1967). *State functions and linear control systems*. McGraw-Hill.

[529] Shah, M., Chrpa, L., Jimoh, F., Kitchin, D., McCluskey, T., Parkinson, S., and Vallati, M. (2013). Knowledge engineering tools in planning: State-of-the-art and future challenges. In *ICAPS Knowledge Engg. for Planning and Scheduling (KEPS)*, pp. 53–60.

[530] Shani, G., Pineau, J., and Kaplow, R. (2012). A survey of point-based POMDP solvers. *J. Autonomous Agents and Multi-Agent Syst.*, pp. 1–51.

[531] Shaparau, D., Pistore, M., and Traverso, P. (2006). Contingent planning with goal preferences. In *Proc. AAAI*, pp. 927–935.

[532] Shaparau, D., Pistore, M., and Traverso, P. (2008). Fusing procedural and declarative planning goals for nondeterministic domains. In *Proc. AAAI*, pp. 983–990.

[533] Shivashankar, V., Alford, R., Kuter, U., and Nau, D. (2013). The GoDeL planning system: A more perfect union of domain-independent and hierarchical planning. In *Proc. IJCAI*, pp. 2380–2386.

[534] Shoahm, Y. and McDermott, D. (1988). Problems in formal temporal reasoning. *Artificial Intelligence*, 36:49–61.

[535] Shoenfield, J. R. (1967). *Mathematical Logic*. Academic Press.

[536] Shoham, Y. (1987). Temporal logic in AI: semantical and ontological considerations. *Artificial Intelligence*, 33:89–104.

[537] Sigaud, O. and Peters, J. (2010). *From Motor Learning to Interaction Learning in Robots*, volume 264 of *Studies in Computational Intelligence*. Springer.

[538] Silver, D. and Veness, J. (2010). Monte-Carlo planning in large POMDPs. In *Adv. in Neural Information Processing Syst. (Proc. NIPS)*.

[539] Simmons, R. (1992). Concurrent planning and execution for autonomous robots. *IEEE Control Systems*, 12(1):46–50.

[540] Simmons, R. (1994). Structured control for autonomous robots. *IEEE Trans. Robotics and Automation*, 10(1):34–43.

[541] Simmons, R. and Apfelbaum, D. (1998). A task description language for robot control. In *IEEE/RSJ Intl. Conf. on Intelligent Robots and Syst. (IROS)*, pp. 1931–1937.

[542] Simpkins, C., Bhat, S., Isbell, Jr., C., and Mateas, M. (2008). Towards adaptive programming: integrating reinforcement learning into a programming language. In *Proc. ACM SIGPLAN Conf. on Object-Oriented Progr. Syst., Lang., and Applications (OOPSLA)*, pp. 603–614. ACM.

[543] Simpson, R. M., Kitchin, D. E., and McCluskey, T. (2007). Planning domain definition using GIPO. *The Knowledge Engineering Review*, 22(2):117–134.

[544] Sirin, E., Parsia, B., Wu, D., Hendler, J., and Nau, D. S. (2004). HTN planning for Web service composition using SHOP2. *J. Web Semant. (JWS)*, 1(4):377–396.

[545] Smith, D. E., Frank, J., and Cushing, W. (2008). The ANML language. *ICAPS Wksp. on Knowledge Engg. for Planning and Scheduling (KEPS)*.

[546] Smith, D. E., Frank, J., and Jónsson, A. K. (2000). Bridging the gap between planning and scheduling. *The Knowledge Engineering Review*, 15(1):47–83.

[547] Smith, D. E. and Weld, D. (1999a). Temporal planning with mutual exclusion reasoning. In *Proc. IJCAI*.

[548] Smith, D. E. and Weld, D. S. (1998). Conformant Graphplan. In *Proc. AAAI*, pp. 889–896.

[549] Smith, D. E. and Weld, D. S. (1999b). Temporal planning with mutual exclusion reasoning. In *Proc. IJCAI*, pp. 326–337.

[550] Smith, S. J. J., Hebbar, K., Nau, D. S., and Minis, I. (1997). Integrating electrical and mechanical design and process planning. In Mantyla, M., Finger, S., and Tomiyama, T., editors, *Knowledge Intensive CAD*, pp. 269–288. Chapman and Hall.

[551] Smith, S. J. J., Nau, D. S., and Throop, T. (1998). Computer bridge: A big win for AI planning. *AI Magazine*, 19(2):93–105.

[552] Smith, T. and Simmons, R. (2004). Heuristic search value iteration for POMDPs. In *Proc. Conf. on Uncertainty in AI (UAI)*.

[553] Sohrabi, S., Baier, J. A., and McIlraith, S. A. (2009). Htn planning with preferences. In *Proc. IJCAI*, pp. 1790–1797.

[554] Sohrabi, S. and McIlraith, S. A. (2010). Preference-based web service composition: A middle ground between execution and search. In *Proc. Intl. Semantic Web Conf. (ISWC)*, pp. 713–729. Springer.

[555] Sridharan, M., Wyatt, J. L., and Dearden, R. (2008). HiPPo: Hierarchical POMDPs for planning information processing and sensing actions on a robot. In *Proc. ICAPS*, pp. 346–354.

[556] Srivastava, B. (2000). Realplan: Decoupling causal and resource reasoning in planning. In *Proc. AAAI*, pp. 812–818.

[557] Stedl, J. and Williams, B. (2005). A fast incremental dynamic controllability algorithm. In *Proc. ICAPS Wksp. on Plan Execution*.

[558] Stulp, F. and Beetz, M. (2008). Refining the execution of abstract actions with learned action models. *J. Artificial Intelligence Research*, 32(1):487–523.

[559] Taha, H. A. (1975). *Integer Programming: Theory, Applications, and Computations*. Academic Press.

[560] Tarjan, R. E. (1972). Depth-first search and linear graph algorithms. *SIAM J. Computing*, 1(2):146–160.

[561] Tate, A. (1977). Generating project networks. In *Proc. IJCAI*, pp. 888–893.

[562] Tate, A., Drabble, B., and Kirby, R. (1994). *O-Plan2: An Architecture for Command, Planning and Control*. Morgan-Kaufmann.

[563] Téglás, E., Vul, E., Girotto, V., Gonzalez, M., Tenenbaum, J. B., and Bonatti, L. L. (2011). Pure reasoning in 12-month-old infants as probabilistic inference. *Science*, 332(6033):1054–1059.

[564] Teichteil-Königsbuch, F. (2012a). Fast incremental policy compilation from plans in hybrid probabilistic domains. In *Proc. ICAPS*.

[565] Teichteil-Königsbuch, F. (2012b). Stochastic safest and shortest path problems. In *Proc. AAAI*, pp. 1825–1831.

[566] Teichteil-Königsbuch, F., Infantes, G., and Kuter, U. (2008). RFF: A robust, FF-based MDP planning algorithm for generating policies with low probability of failure. In *Proc. ICAPS*.

[567] Teichteil-Königsbuch, F., Kuter, U., and Infantes, G. (2010). Incremental plan aggregation for generating policies in MDPs. In *Proc. AAMAS*, pp. 1231–1238.

[568] Teichteil-Königsbuch, F., Vidal, V., and Infantes, G. (2011). Extending classical planning heuristics to probabilistic planning with dead-ends. In *Proc. AAAI*, pp. 1–6.

[569] Tenorth, M. and Beetz, M. (2013). KnowRob: A knowledge processing infrastructure for cognition-enabled robots. *Intl. J. Robotics Research*, 32(5):566–590.

[570] Traverso, P., Veloso, M., and Giunchiglia, F., editors (2000). *AIPS Wksp. on Model-Theoretic Approaches to Planning*.

[571] van den Briel, M., Vossen, T., and Kambampati, S. (2005). Reviving integer programming approaches for AI planning: A branch-and-cut framework. In *Proc. ICAPS*, pp. 310–319.

[572] van den Briel, M., Vossen, T., and Kambhampati, S. (2008). Loosely coupled formulations for automated planning: An integer programming perspective. *J. Artificial Intelligence Research*, 31:217–257.

[573] Vaquero, T. S., Romero, V., Tonidandel, F., and Silva, J. R. (2007). itSIMPLE 2.0: An integrated tool for designing planning domains. In *Proc. ICAPS*, pp. 336–343.

[574] Vaquero, T. S., Silva, J. R., and Beck, J. C. (2011). A brief review of tools and methods for knowledge engineering for planning & scheduling. In *ICAPS Knowledge Engg. for Planning and Scheduling (KEPS)*, pp. 7–15.

[575] Vardi, M. Y. (1995). An automata-theoretic approach to fair realizability and synthesis. In *Proc. Intl. Conf. on Computer Aided Verification*, pp. 267–278.

[576] Vardi, M. Y. (2008). From verification to synthesis. In *Proc. Intl. Conf. on Verified Software: Theories, Tools, Experiments*.

[577] Vattam, S., Klenk, M., Molineaux, M., and Aha, D. W. (2013). Breadth of approaches to goal reasoning: A research survey. In *ACS Wksp. on Goal Reasoning*.

[578] Velez, J., Hemann, G., Huang, A., Posner, I., and Roy, N. (2011). Planning to perceive: Exploiting mobility for robust object detection. In *Proc. ICAPS*.

[579] Veloso, M. and Stone, P. (1995). FLECS: planning with a flexible commitment strategy. *J. Artificial Intelligence Research*, 3:25–52.

[580] Veloso, M. M. and Rizzo, P. (1998). Mapping planning actions and partially-ordered plans into execution knowledge. In *Wksp. on Integrating Planning, Scheduling and Execution in Dynamic and Uncertain Environments*, pp. 94–97.

[581] Vere, S. (1983). Planning in time: Windows and duration for activities and goals. *IEEE Trans. Pattern Analysis and Machine Intell.*, 5(3):246–264.

[582] Verfaillie, G., Pralet, C., and Michel, L. (2010). How to model planning and scheduling problems using timelines. *The Knowledge Engineering Review*, 25:319–336.

[583] Verma, V., Estlin, T., Jónsson, A. K., Pasareanu, C., Simmons, R., and Tso, K. (2005). Plan execution interchange language (PLEXIL) for executable plans and command sequences. In *Intl. Symp. on Artificial Intell., Robotics and Automation in Space (i-SAIRAS)*.

[584] Vernhes, S., Infantes, G., and Vidal, V. (2013). Problem splitting using heuristic search in landmark orderings. In *Proc. IJCAI*, pp. 2401–2407. AAAI Press.

[585] Verweij, T. (2007). A hierarchically-layered multiplayer bot system for a first-person shooter. Master's thesis, Vrije Universiteit of Amsterdam.

[586] Vidal, T. and Fargier, H. (1999). Handling contingency in temporal constraint networks: from consistency to controllabilities. *J. Experimental & Theoretical Artificial Intelligence*.

[587] Vidal, T. and Ghallab, M. (1996). Dealing with uncertain durations in temporal constraints networks dedicated to planning. In *ECAI*, pp. 48–52.

[588] Vilain, M. and Kautz, H. (1986). Constraint propagation algorithms for temporal reasoning. In *Proc. AAAI*, pp. 377–382.

[589] Vilain, M., Kautz, H., and van Beek, P. (1989). Constraint propagation algorithms for temporal reasoning: a revised report. In de Kleer, J. and Weld, D. S., editors, *Readings in Qualitative Reasoning about Physical Systems*. Morgan-Kaufmann.

[590] Vodrázka, J. and Chrpa, L. (2010). Visual design of planning domains. In *Wksp. on Knowledge Engg. for Planning and Scheduling (KEPS)*, pp. 68–69.

[591] Vu, V.-T., Bremond, F., and Thonnat, M. (2003). Automatic video interpretation: A novel algorithm for temporal scenario recognition. In *Proc. IJCAI*, pp. 1295–1300.

[592] Waibel, M., Beetz, M., Civera, J., D'Andrea, R., Elfring, J., Galvez-Lopez, D., Haussermann, K., Janssen, R., Montiel, J. M. M., Perzylo, A., Schiessle, B., Tenorth, M., Zweigle, O., and van de Molengraft, R. (2011). RoboEarth. *IEEE Robotics and Automation Magazine*, 18(2):69–82.

[593] Waldinger, R. (1977). Achieving several goals simultaneously. In *Machine Intelligence 8*, pp. 94–138. Halstead and Wiley. Reprinted in [15], pp. 118–139.

[594] Walsh, T. J. and Littman, M. L. (2008). Efficient learning of action schemas and Web-service descriptions. In *Proc. AAAI*.

[595] Wang, F. Y., Kyriakopoulos, K. J., Tsolkas, A., and Saridis, G. N. (1991). A Petri-net coordination model for an intelligent mobile robot. *IEEE Trans. Syst., Man, and Cybernetics*, 21(4):777–789.

[596] Warren, D. H. D. (1976). Generating conditional plans and programs. In *Proc. Summer Conf. on Artificial Intelligence and Simulation of Behaviour*.

[597] Weir, A. A. S., Chappell, J., and Kacelnik, A. (2002). Shaping of hooks in New Caledonian crows. *Science*, 297(5583):981.

[598] Weld, D. (1999). Recent advances in AI planning. *AI Magazine*, 20(2):93–122.

[599] Weld, D. S. (1994). An introduction to least commitment planning. *AI Magazine*, 15(4):27–61.

[600] Weld, D. S., Anderson, C. R., and Smith, D. E. (1998). Extending Graphplan to handle uncertainty and sensing actions. In *Proc. AAAI*, pp. 897–904.

[601] Weld, D. S. and Etzioni, O. (1994). The first law of robotics (a call to arms). In *Proc. AAAI*, pp. 1042–1047.

[602] Wilkins, D. (2000). Using the SIPE-2 planning system: A manual for version 6.1. Technical report, SRI International.

[603] Wilkins, D. and desJardins, M. (2001). A call for knowledge-based planning. *AI Magazine*, 22(1):99–115.

[604] Wilkins, D. E. (1988). *Practical Planning: Extending the Classical AI Planning Paradigm*. Morgan Kaufmann.

[605] Wilkins, D. E. and Myers, K. L. (1995). A common knowledge representation for plan generation and reactive execution. *J. Logic and Computation*, 5(6):731–761.

[606] Williams, B. C. and Abramson, M. (2001). Executing reactive, model-based programs through graph-based temporal planning. In *Proc. IJCAI*.

[607] Williams, B. C. and Nayak, P. P. (1996). A model-based approach to reactive self-configuring systems. In *Proc. AAAI*, pp. 971–978.

[608] Wilson, A., Fern, A. P., and Tadepalli, P. (2012). A bayesian approach for policy learning from trajectory preference queries. In *Adv. in Neural Information Processing Syst. (Proc. NIPS)*, pp. 1142–1150.

[609] Wingate, D. and Seppi, K. D. (2005). Prioritization methods for accelerating MDP solvers. *J. Machine Learning Research*, 6:851–881.

[610] Wittgenstein, L. (1999). *Philosophical Investigations*. Prentice Hall.

[611] Wongpiromsarn, T., Topcu, U., Ozay, N., Xu, H., and Murray, R. M. (2011). TuLiP: a software toolbox for receding horizon temporal logic planning. In *14th Intl. Conf. on Hybrid Syst.: Computation and Control*, pp. 313–314. ACM.

[612] Wu, Y. and Huang, T. S. (1999). Vision-based gesture recognition: A review. In Braffort, A., Gherbi, R., Gibet, S., Teil, D., and Richardson, J., editors, *Gesture-Based Communication in Human-Computer Interaction*, pp. 103–115. Springer.

[613] Xie, F., Müller, M., and Holte, R. (2015). Understanding and improving local exploration for gbfs. In *Proc. ICAPS*.

[614] Xu, Y., Fern, A., and Yoon, S. W. (2007). Discriminative learning of beam-search heuristics for planning. In *Proc. IJCAI*.

[615] Yang, Q. (1990). Formalizing planning knowledge for hierarchical planning. *Computational Intelligence*, 6(1):12–24.

[616] Yang, Q. (1997). *Intelligent Planning: A Decomposition and Abstraction Based Approach*. Springer.

[617] Yang, Q., Wu, K., and Jiang, Y. (2007). Learning action models from plan examples using weighted MAX-SAT. *Artificial Intelligence*, 171(2):107–143.

[618] Yoon, S., Fern, A., and Givan, R. (2006). Learning heuristic functions from relaxed plans. In *Proc. ICAPS*.

[619] Yoon, S., Fern, A. P., and Givan, R. (2007). FF-replan: A baseline for probabilistic planning. In *Proc. ICAPS*, pp. 352–359.

[620] Yoon, S., Fern, A. P., Givan, R., and Kambhampati, S. (2008). Probabilistic planning via determinization in hindsight. In *Proc. AAAI*.

[621] Younes, H. and Littman, M. (2004). PPDDL: The probabilistic planning domain definition language. Technical report, CMU.

[622]   Younes, H. and Simmons, R. (2002). On the role of ground actions in refinement planning. In *Proc. AIPS*, pp. 54–62.

[623]   Younes, H. and Simmons, R. (2003). VHPOP: Versatile heuristic partial order planner. *J. Artificial Intelligence Research*.

[624]   Younes, H. and Simmons, R. (2004). Solving generalized semi-Markov decision processes using continuous phase-type distributions. In *Proc. AAAI*, pp. 742–747.

[625]   Zhang, W. (1999). *State-space search: Algorithms, complexity, extensions, and applications*. Springer Science & Business Media.

[626]   Zhuo, H. H., Hu, D. H., Hogg, C., Yang, Q., and Muñoz-Avila, H. (2009). Learning HTN method preconditions and action models from partial observations. In *Proc. IJCAI*, pp. 1804–1810.

[627]   Zhuo, H. H., Yang, Q., Hu, D. H., and Li, L. (2010). Learning complex action models with quantifiers and logical implications. *Artificial Intelligence*, 174(18):1540–1569.

[628]   Zimmerman, T. and Kambhampati, S. (2003). Learning-assisted automated planning: Looking back, taking stock, going forward. *AI Magazine*, 24(2):73.

[629]   Ziparo, V. A., Iocchi, L., Lima, P. U., Nardi, D., and Palamara, P. F. (2011). Petri net plans. *J. Autonomous Agents and Multi-Agent Syst.*, 23(3):344–383.

Index